W9-BKK-499

Book Four
THE EARLY SCHOOL YEARS
(Ages 6 through 10)

Book Five
GROWING INTO ADOLESCENCE
(Ages 11 through 14)

Book Six
SELF-EVALUATION GUIDES
For Each Book

Parents' Magazine's

SELF-GUIDANCE PROGRAM TO SUCCESSFUL PARENTHOOD

Book One by Mary B. Hoover
WHAT MAKES A GOOD PARENT?

Book Two by Sara D. Gilbert
YOUR CHILD'S FIRST THREE YEARS

Book Three by Edith Neisser
GUIDING YOUR PRESCHOOLER

Book Four by Doris P. Mogol
THE EARLY SCHOOL YEARS

Book Five by Lynn Minton
GROWING INTO ADOLESCENCE

Book Six
SELF-EVALUATION GUIDES
For Each Book

MARY B. HOOVER
Editor-in-Chief

PUBLISHED BY PARENTS' MAGAZINE ENTERPRISES

Copyright © MCMLXXII by
Parents' Magazine Press
All rights reserved

International Standard Book Number 0-8193-0704-1

Printed in Canada by The Bryant Press Limited

ADVISORY BOARD

T. BERRY BRAZELTON, M.D.
Clinical Assistant Professor, Harvard Medical School; author: "INFANTS AND MOTHERS: Individual Differences in Development," etc.

SYLVIA BRODY, Ph.D.
Director, Child Development Research Project and Adjunct Professor of Psychology, Graduate Division of Psychology, City University of New York; co-author: "ANXIETY AND EGO FORMATION IN INFANCY," etc.

JOSEPH CHURCH, Ph.D.
Professor, City University of New York; co-author: "CHILDHOOD AND ADOLESCENCE: A Psychology of the Growing Person," etc.

ROBERT COLES, M.D.
Research Psychiatrist, Harvard University Medical Services; author: "CHILDREN OF CRISIS: A Study of Children and Fear," "ERIK H. ERIKSON: The Growth of His Work," etc.

SIDONIE M. GRUENBERG
Former Director, Child Study Association of America; author: "THE WONDERFUL STORY OF HOW YOU WERE BORN," etc.

JAMES L. HYMES, JR., Ed.D.
Specialist in Early Childhood Education; Consultant and Author: "THE CHILD UNDER SIX," "TEACHING THE CHILD UNDER SIX," etc.

ROY W. MENNINGER, M.D.
President, The Menninger Foundation

ISADORE ROSSMAN, M.D.
Medical Director, Department of Home Care and Extended Services, Montefiore Hospital; author, "TWO CHILDREN BY CHOICE: THE WHY AND HOW OF THE TWO CHILD FAMILY," etc.

LORNA J. SARREL, M.S.W.
Consultant in Sexual Problems, Yale University

PHILIP MARTIN SARREL, M.D.
Assistant Professor, Obstetrics & Gynecology, Yale University School of Medicine; Consultant, Yale University Health Service Sex Counseling

MOLLIE S. SMART, Ph.D.
Associate Professor of Child Development and Family Relations, University of Rhode Island; co-author: "IT'S A WISE PARENT," etc.

RUSSELL C. SMART, Ph.D.
Professor and Chairman, Child Development and Family Relations, University of Rhode Island; co-author with Mollie S. Smart of "READINGS IN CHILD DEVELOPMENT AND FAMILY RELATIONSHIPS," etc.

SPECIAL CONSULTANTS:

MRS. GENEVIEVE M. LANDAU
Editor of Parents' Magazine and mother of three.

MRS. MAJA BERNATH
Associate Editor of Parents' Magazine, Editor of Expecting and Baby Care, and mother of four.

INTRODUCING THE AUTHORS

Here are the authors—all parents themselves—who wrote The Self-Guidance Program to Successful Parenthood

MARY B. HOOVER, Author of Book One—

What Makes a Good Parent?

A Board Member of The Child Study Association of America, Mrs. Hoover has written many articles, including one which received a National Brotherhood Award from the National Conference of Christians and Jews in 1962. She is also Editor of *Guiding Your Child From 5 to 12,* and co-author of *You, Your Child, And Drugs.* Mrs. Hoover is the mother of three—a son and two daughters ranging in age from the teens to the twenties.

SARA D. GILBERT, Author of Book Two—

Your Child's First Three Years

Mrs. Gilbert has written extensively on social problems. Her article, *Hospitalization For False Beliefs,* in Liberty, won the 1969 Freedom Award of The Religious Liberty Association. She has also written for Good Housekeeping, MIT's Technology Review, The Washington Post's Potomac, The Legal Aid Society, and The Children's Book Council. Mrs. Gilbert is the mother of a young son.

EDITH G. NEISSER, Author of Book Three—

Guiding Your Preschooler

A Board Member of The Institute of Psychoanalysis, The Erikson Institute for Early Childhood Education, and The Jewish Children's Bureau, Mrs. Neisser is author of *Brothers and Sisters, The Eldest Child,* and *Mothers and Daughters,* widely read by parents and professionals who work with children. She has written many important pamphlets, and was formerly Child Guidance Editor of Childcraft. Mrs. Neisser is a grandmother and the mother of two married sons.

DORIS P. MOGAL, Author of Book Four—

The Early School Years

Mrs. Mogal has written for the Community Mental Health Journal, International Mental Health Research Newsletter, Independent School Bulletin, and the International Journal of Psychiatry and Psychosomatics. She is a member of the Yorkville (N.Y.C.) Committee on Drug Abuse, and serves on the Book Review Committee of The Child Study Association. Mrs. Mogal is the mother of a young son and an older son and daughter, both married.

LYNN MINTON, Author of Book Five—

Growing Into Adolescence

Mrs. Minton has written for McCall's, Redbook, Family Circle, Sepia, and Today's Living. Her article, *How To Bring Up Your Child Without Race Prejudice,* won the National Media Award Special Mention from The Family Service Society of America "in recognition of outstanding achievement in developing public understanding of the needs of families" (1969). Mrs. Minton is the mother of three children.

CONTENTS

Book One
WHAT MAKES A GOOD PARENT?
by Mary B. Hoover

Book Two
YOUR CHILD'S FIRST THREE YEARS
by Sara D. Gilbert

Book Three
GUIDING YOUR PRESCHOOLER
by Edith G. Neisser

Book Four
THE EARLY SCHOOL YEARS
by Doris P. Mogal

Book Five
GROWING INTO ADOLESCENCE
by Lynn Minton

Book Six
SELF-EVALUATION GUIDE
by Mary B. Hoover

PREFACE

Your reasons for wanting Parents' Magazine's SELF-GUIDANCE PROGRAM TO SUCCESSFUL PARENTHOOD in your home are most commendable. You obviously wish to do the best for your child. You want your youngster to have a happy and contented childhood. You are eager for your child to grow up into a worthy, well-adjusted, well-educated and responsible citizen of whom you can be proud.

The SELF-GUIDANCE PROGRAM TO SUCCESSFUL PARENTHOOD is divided into six "books", designed to help you become the kind of parents you most want to be—namely, *self-guiding* parents doing your best for your children and your family, and making *your own judgments* based on the best and most up-to-date counsel available.

Book One is devoted to *parenthood*... while books Two through Five are concerned with *childhood* at various specific stages—from infancy through adolescence and beyond. I suggest that you read Book One first, before you turn to any of the other volumes. This volume provides you with an overview of parenthood, focusing on the realities of parenthood today and giving you fresh insight into your child's motivations as well as your own as parents, so that you can intelligently face and solve problems in a manner best suited to *your own* goals and *your own* way of life.

So that you can chart your course and measure your progress in achieving your goals, Book Six offers five Self-Evaluation Guides—each relating to one of the five books of the Program. These Self-Evaluation Guides are an extremely important part of the Program, since only through honest, thorough and accurate appraisal of yourselves as parents can you develop the scope and vision needed to determine the direction and extent of your parental progress.

Throughout the SELF-GUIDANCE PROGRAM TO SUCCESSFUL PARENTHOOD, the authors share with you the latest knowledge about children and child rearing and family living. They do it with the humor, insight, and understanding that stem from their own experience as parents plus their skill as writers. Interesting information about the authors as parents and their professional backgrounds are briefly described for you on page vi.

The SELF-GUIDANCE PROGRAM TO SUCCESSFUL PARENTHOOD can be used for reading or reference in its entirety, or in part, as your children grow. It is meant to be used to help you establish a happier rapport between you and your children and a deeper, more harmonious understanding between husband and wife.

MARY B. HOOVER
Editor

BOOK ONE

What Makes A Good Parent?

By MARY B. HOOVER

Introduction

NOT LONG AGO a fourteen-year-old boy clumped into the living room of his home upon awakening and demanded, rubbing his eyes sleepily, "How's the avocado doing?" The plant seemed to have shot up several inches overnight, as such plants often do in the early months after the shoot pokes through. The boy's sleepy look changed to one of wonderment, mixed seconds later with concern. He ran a forefinger over the earth in the pot and headed for the kitchen. Returning with the watering can, he said, "They need a lot of water."

His mother, watching this procedure, was struck by the coincidence of the push to grow and the push to nurture growth: a seed sprouting breathtakingly; a boy sprouting equally so; and that boy touchingly bent on caring for the seed's issue. Was it a temporary matter of the boy's tending to identify with any similarly fast-developing organism? Or was it more than that: an expression of an urge we all have, male no less than female, to be nurturing where growing things are concerned?

Nobody knows, of course. In watching and helping our children grow, we often feel that we are being exposed, in microcosm, to the most profound and tantalizing mysteries of the universe. That today we can travel in space in no way diminishes the awe that the universe inspires in most of us. Likewise, all that is known today about psychology and how children develop in no way lessens our sense of the miraculous inherent in the growth of every human being.

Still, we have a body of knowledge about space travel that we use when undertaking it. We also have a body of knowledge pertinent to child-rearing that it makes equal sense to use when doing it. Interestingly, though the authors of the books in this program differ extensively in background, religious upbringing, and age, you will discover that they are curiously alike in their perceptions of what the job of being a parent is all about. This springs from a shared concern for focusing on the *general principles* that apply in spite of individual differences and regardless of circumstances.

This book is a kind of over-view of certain significant principles—and ambiguities—that enter into guiding children from infancy into adulthood and relating constructively to them all along the line. It is intended to help parents to think through their long-range goals, to examine themselves and their attitudes, and to approach the job of being a parent with a certain amount of psychological sophistication. It deals with areas where the "rub" is likely to be especially discomfiting or challenging, and it attempts to indicate to parents how to use their knowledge of themselves, their children, psychology, and child development so that everybody *grows* through, rather than just suffers through, such experiences.

In the succeeding books you will be

given a tour of life as it tends to be lived with children of a particular age; that is, the books are developmentally oriented (though, like this book, concerned with elucidating principles). Different as all children are, parents of children in a certain age range tend to find themselves rather often in the same boat—and so do the children. There is a discernible pattern in children's development, a more or less orderly progression from one stage to the next, no less in mastering intellectual and emotional tasks than in teething. Whether a baby cuts his first tooth at two weeks or at twelve months, we know where in the baby's mouth to look for it, and we also know that the others will appear in relatively predictable order—up and down, left and right, from the front of the jaw to the rear. Additionally, we are aware that babies tend to inform us, in their own way, that they are teething, just in case we can't figure it out from the appearance of their gums. And we know, too, that the child with four teeth at four months and the one with one at one year will eventually wind up with their full complement and nothing to show whether they were "early" or "late" teethers. So it goes with all aspects of development.

Familiarity with the master plan of development alerts us to what our child may be coping with along the way and thus supplements the cues he gives us as to what he needs from us to further his healthy growth. It helps us decide when he can use some nudging on, or some protecting, when to let go and when to dig in our heels, and all the rest.

Whatever the age of your child, you may find it useful from time to time to consult several books in this program simultaneously, in order to learn more about where you and your child are, where you have come from, and where you are headed. Also, a book may offer detailed information about a specific subject, such as vacation planning (*The Early School Years*), from which any parent (or nonparent) can glean useful leads. Flipping through the table of contents of the volume and consulting the index at the end is advisable whenever you have a problem or question.

In these and other ways, the program is meant to be used as a unit. Its goal at its inception was to provide a comprehensive resource for parents, covering the everyday challenges involved in rearing children at each stage of their growth and the emotional strengths that make for more creative marital and parent-child relationships and a more satisfying life in contemporary society. Obviously, the authors are alike in subscribing to the tenet that a man's (or woman's) reach should exceed his grasp.

Although, as the authors of the books in this program reiterate in their own words over and over again, there is no magic recipe for rearing children, there *are* ways of knowing what is going on in ourselves and in our children that can lead to healthier parent-child interaction, give the young the "watering" they require, and enable parents to grow as they nurture.

One more component of the program should be called to attention: Book 6 with the Self-Evaluation Guides that correspond to each book. Its purpose is to further the process of helping parents see themselves and their children more clearly. Husband and wife are to fill it in and discuss it together, as directed, *after* they have finished reading the book it relates to.

1
The Expert In Each Of Us

WE HAVE ALL been children, had parents. We have seen the world through a child's eyes, listened with a child's ears, reacted with a child's feelings. Before we become mothers or fathers, the shoe is on the other foot for a long time.

This vast reservoir of firsthand knowledge about childhood and child-rearing that each of us brings to the job of being a parent can be one of our most valuable assets. But we have to learn to tap it with discrimination, alert to all it can tell us about the way children tick and mature, yet knowing the pitfalls sometimes associated with generalizing from personal experience.

Some parents make better use of their built-in expertise than others. We will explore this, mainly through the medium of parents' own words, with the objective of identifying factors that make the difference.

The Value of Empathy

One of the most important strengths that we can gain from having been a child is the ability to empathize with children, to sense how the shoe may be pinching. Few other skills serve a parent (or teacher) so well. Empathy involves correctly perceiving the emotions or thoughts of other persons and identifying with them. When we empathize with people, we feel what they are feeling, "know what they are thinking." In a family, this makes for mutual respect, rapport, a spirit of helpfulness and cooperation.

Empathy not only smooths everyday parent-child relationships but also gives rise to those "inspired" ideas, those "instinctive" right reactions that often enable parents to resolve vexing problems. A father recalls:

> When our son went into second grade still unable to read, we were pretty uptight about it. Toward the middle of the year, his teacher suggested that I read aloud with him some primers she gave us and see if this might start him up. I did this several evenings in a row, until one night he said, "Daddy, I hate little words. I only like big words." It rang a bell with me. Since I'm a crossword puzzle fan, on the spur of the minute I said, "Okay, how'd you like to do today's crossword puzzle with me?" I thought he'd get bored quickly, but no. He even guessed a few words correctly. The next day I brought home a book of simple puzzles and we worked our way through them in a month or so. He may be the only kid in his class who learned to recognize "across" before "look" and "see," but by the end of the year he was reading well above grade level. He skipped the primers.

Flexibility Enters In

The point of the above incident is not that working crossword puzzles with children is a guaranteed way to teach them to read. As this father undoubtedly realizes, the number of nonreading seven-year-olds who are likely to stick around "helping" a father or a mother do the puzzle in the daily newspaper can probably be counted on one finger. Yet the father deserves credit for much more than astonishing good luck. His son's remark "rang a bell." Evidently it suggested to him that perhaps the way to help his child begin reading was to present the challenge in a more grown-up context, make it appear "harder." That's what the boy himself seemed to be asking for, and the father must have known, from personal experience or otherwise, that children are sometimes more responsive to "big" (adult) challenges than to "little" (childish) ones. The father empathized with his son at an important moment, coming up with what proved to be a very useful tactic. This is the message of the incident.

That crossword puzzles were, in this case, an appropriate challenge is probably due in large measure to the father's enthusiasm for them. Children enjoy sharing their parents' interests. Under different circumstances, "real" storybooks or the directions for putting together model ships might have been what worked. It should be noted that the father did not at first seize upon crossword puzzles as *the* solution to his son's problem. It was only after the boy showed surprising interest in staying with an activity that was over his head that the father saw the possibilities that simpler puzzles might offer. Operating in the father, along with empathy, are flexibility and sensitivity to the cues that a child gives.

Picking Up Cues

The mother of a three-year-old tells this story:

> A while back I was having a terrible time with Margie. She was in a stage of saying "no" to everything. It really got to me. I began having this awful urge to smack her down, show her who's boss once and for all. And I'm not like that. My husband would say, "It's just a phase. Don't let her get your goat." But I couldn't help it. One day I was struggling to get her bathed and she kept breaking loose from me and

climbing out of the tub, and I got furious and hit her really hard. She started yelling "No, no, no," and a weird thing happened. I remembered a time when I was little and screaming at my mother, "You can't make me." I don't remember what my mother was trying to make me do, but I could *feel* my determination never to give in, as if the whole thing were happening all over again. It stopped me cold. I hugged Margie and went into a spiel about how I didn't want to break her spirit. I'm sure she didn't understand, but something got through. She got back into the tub on her own. I can't say it's been all beer and skittles ever since, but there has been some kind of change in me. Her negativism doesn't infuriate me the way it used to do, and things seem a bit better.

Attitudes Can Change

Here, a mother's empathy is quite unexpectedly aroused during a highly charged encounter with her child. One minute she is threatened in her role as parent by her child's defiant behavior. She has a strong need to make her daughter acknowledge her as "boss." Then, suddenly, she remembers how being "bossed" feels to a child, and her attitude changes. She identifies with her daughter, which apparently makes it easier for her to gain the child's cooperation.

Regardless of whether the strong feelings that this young mother recalled, which changed her attitude, are the product of the incident in her childhood to which she ascribes them, or are the accumulated residue of many encounters that she has had with authority, she learned from them. She seems to have made a significant breakthrough in her relationship with her daughter, which ought to carry over into other relationships. She is starting to come to terms with her feelings about exercising authority, to see the problem as a matter of guiding and accepting guidance, rather than bossing and being bossed. Her statement, "I'm not like that," which for now has to be interpreted as "I don't want to be like that," may one day become literally true. Already she has used her memories of childhood to good advantage.

Using All We Know

In addition to giving us a capacity for empathy, our personal experience as a child leaves us with a great deal of specific information about how to cope with children in all kinds of situations. We should not underestimate its usefulness. Grandmother's knack for distracting us with an arresting question or suggestion when we were hell-bent on destruction is worthy of emulating. Some of her ideas may work the same magic with our children today that they formerly worked with us. In the back of our heads we carry around a treasure trove of knowledge about how to soothe, amuse, reassure a child, entertain him when he must be confined to bed, occupy him on a rainy day, help him learn new skills.

But the expert in each of us is not always to be trusted. We may misinterpret what various childhood experiences did for us—or to us. Our recollection of the past is spotty, at best. Time gets in its licks. Here or there we embroider, overlook or "forget" details that were extremely pertinent at the time. We may point the finger wrongly, or go to the other extreme and see events and people in a kindlier light than is psychologically defensible.

A very successful businessman, who grew up in a large, poverty-stricken farm family and worked his way through college, even sending money home all the time he was a student, says:

I've always felt I owe whatever success I've had to being able to work harder than most people and knowing the value of a nickel. My early life was no picnic, but the habits I learned then have put me where I am today. I wanted to teach my sons the same, for their own good. So they've earned their pocket money ever since they could push a lawnmower or wash a car. They've had paper routes, delivered groceries, the works. I thought it was all for the best, then my oldest was caught stealing from his last employer. The psychologist we've all been seeing since then put me onto something that never occurred to me. The way I grew up, everybody in the family had to work hard in order for us to survive. Believe me, I could always see how much my work was needed. That's certainly not true with my sons. I guess they're entitled to feel I'm stingy, though it hurts.

Blind Spots

This man, along with many other persons like him, mistakenly assumed that he succeeded in life *because* of his early deprivations, rather than in spite of them. His view of how children learn to value money and enjoy working is badly warped. (Both issues are dealt with at greater length in other books of this program.) He completely overlooked, until it was pointed out by his psychologist, what was undoubtedly one of the most important sources of the emotional strength that enabled him to overcome the handicap of grinding poverty: his feeling of being needed, of being able to contribute significantly to his family's welfare. In time, with the help that he is getting, he may be able to see why his sons need to feel needed, and find ways to give them this advantage.

All too often, parents tend to make virtues of the hardships that they survived as children, overlooking the positive factors in their experience that brought them through the hardships unscathed, or relatively unscathed. This may be why physical punishment is still viewed by some parents as "good for a child," rather than as one more example of children's capacity to weather parental imperfections as long as there is enough right in the picture.

Individual Differences

Another limit on the usefulness of our built-in expertise is the fact that it sometimes may not apply to our own children—or any other child. Often, the events from our past that we recall most vividly and accurately cannot teach us anything about anybody except ourself in a quite special environment at a particular moment in history. It is easy to overlook how different we all are, and what different worlds each of us lives in. It is especially easy to do this when we are members of the same family. All too frequently we fall into the same trap as Juan, who, when asked by his teacher what he had had for breakfast, responded, "Cream cheese and olives, like everybody else."

Always, we generalize from personal experience at our peril. The errors that this can lead us into may be, as in Juan's case, simply amusing and quickly discerned. One day, for example, discovering in an out-of-the-way drugstore a certain type of "penny candy" that we loved as a child, we stock up on it and return to our children expecting our find to elicit shouts of delight. What it elicits is more on the order of "You have to be kidding." On another occasion, we learn the hard way that the Disney nature movie we adored at ten is a flop with our son at that age. And so it goes.

Sometimes, however, the indiscriminate assumption that what was true of us when we were young will be true of our children produces results that are not amusing. Many a child whose parents adored summer camp has been packed off lovingly to spend an expensive, miserable two months wishing he were back home knocking about with his dog or a kid down the block. Many a lifelong antipathy to classical music and concert-going has been established by well-meaning parents who sincerely wanted their children to "have the advantages I had."

Of course, the reverse is also true. Just because we hated camp at eleven is no reason to turn a deaf ear to Peggy's request to be allowed to go. And our disenchantment with violin lessons when we were eight does not warrant arbitrarily turning down Johnny's plea for them. Johnny at eight may not be "too young." He may just have real talent.

The Meaning of Projection

On a more subtle level, this same mechanism can occasionally lead parents to seriously misconstrue their children's behavior. A mother who was shy and rather lonely during her adolescence has this to say about her relationship with her teen-age daughter:

> Soon after Elaine entered high school last year, I began to see a change in her. She seemed very tense and jumpy. She didn't talk much about the kids at school, and I figured she was having trouble making friends, especially boyfriends. As I had this problem at her age, I did all I could to reassure her, telling her about how I felt in high school, and later, and how people like us come into our own when we're older. Looking back, I realize she didn't open up much during these talks, but I thought we were as close as any other mother and daughter. I was shocked out of my mind when she got picked up on a drug charge recently. "Not Elaine," I kept saying to the officer. But it was true. Furthermore, all this time she's been going steady. That's how she started on drugs. Her boyfriend wanted her to keep him company. How could I have been so blind? I must seem terribly straight to her. I'm sorry about that, and I'm trying to treat her differently, but it's not easy. I'm worried crazy that she might get pregnant.

Examples of this sort represent a failure of empathy. Elaine's mother, and others who think that what held for them must hold for children, are *projecting* rather than empathizing. When we project, we arbitrarily assign to another person characteristics, motives, and feelings that are ours, not theirs, overlooking the clues that they give us to understanding them as they really are.

It would be a mistake to conclude that Elaine's mother missed the mark because she is different from her daughter. Actually, the two probably have much more in common than they realize. Neither seems especially outgoing or at ease with people. But that is really beside the point. We don't have to be like a person, or have lived our life in a way that parallels his, in order to empathize with him. It can help, of course, but it is far from essential. Our common humanity—the fact that we have all known rage, fear, sorrow, embarrassment, love, delight—makes empathy possible under the most unlikely circumstances. We can share laughter and tears with strangers. In a small shop in a foreign country where we do not speak the language, empathy gets our three-year-old whisked off in the nick of time to the proprietor's toilet.

Testing Our Expertise

So now we have two somewhat contradictory propositions. On the one hand, our experience as a child can help us in rearing children, give rise to empathy, brilliant problem-solving, breakthroughs in relationships, great ideas for things to do on a rainy day, and all that. On the other hand, we may sometimes be tempted by it into treating our children as if they were subject to the same wishes and pinches that we once were, which is not necessarily so. How do we make the most of our built-in expertise while avoiding the pitfalls that it may expose us to?

We can be alert to the chance that we might be projecting when we think we are empathizing. This possibility should certainly be checked out carefully when large issues—weightier matters than the choice of a casual treat or an afternoon's entertainment—are at stake.

For example, if Doug's fondness for a neighbor's dog makes his parents think of surprising him with a puppy on his birthday, they can check discreetly to discover whether the gift would indeed be as welcome as they suspect it might be. Is Doug ready for the responsibilities involved in caring for a dog? It may be that he enjoys playing with the neighbor's dog when he feels like it but doesn't really want one of his own for now. Or that if he is to be given a pet, he would choose hamsters. An offhand question or two asked at an opportune moment should bring out the information Doug's parents need to test their hunch thoroughly, without taking the edge off their planned surprise.

Granted, checking out our hunches is not always that easy. Elaine's mother faced a more demanding challenge. Communicating with adolescents can be tricky. They tend to resent anything that smacks of prying. Still, one feels that if Elaine's mother had not been so positive that she knew what her daughter was experiencing, if she had been less "blind" to her child's reactions, she would sooner or later have come closer to sensing the lay of the land. She would have given Elaine the opening that the girl apparenfly was looking for to confide in her mother and bring about meaningful communication.

We can be sensitive to the clues our children give us to what they are thinking and feeling. As the illustrations in this chapter suggest over and over, our child's behavior itself can provide us with one of our most reliable tests of the accuracy of our assumptions about him and the validity of our way of handling him in a given situation. From infancy on, he lets us know how well we are doing by him. When we make mistakes, as happens in the most empathic families, if we take our cues from our children, we tend to catch ourselves up quickly, before any great harm is done. A major goal all through this program is to help parents become better at perceiving and responding to all such cues.

We can be flexible. Of course, this enters into taking our cues from our children. Yet it is so important a quality that it deserves separate emphasis. Many psychiatrists and psychologists assert that flexibility is the key characteristic of the mentally healthy. (Others assign equal, or even greater, significance to the capacity for empathy.) We shall endeavor to help parents distinguish between being flexible and being wishy-washy or too tentative. We hope in various ways to encourage that combination of self-confidence and knowledgeability that enables parents to be decisive, yet able to shift gears, change course, roll with the punches, as circumstances warrant.

We can check our built-in expertise against authoritative source materials. If, for example, we feel strongly, on the basis of our memories of ourselves as a child, that occasional episodes of lying or stealing are normal in a six-year-old and no cause for parental alarm, it would still be wise to find out what the leading professional authorities have to say on the subject. When can a child be expected to outgrow such behavior and what are the best ways to help him do so? Is a friendly reminder really as effective as we remember its being?

It is a trifle inconvenient to whip off to the library every time you have questions of this sort, and do the research needed—wade through all the pertinent studies and case histories—in order to know what there is to know. Our goal is to present the latest information on child development and the principles of child-rearing in a way that will enable parents to inform themselves as easily and thoroughly as possible. Recognizing that young parents today are exposed to a steady barrage of advice about bringing up children, some of it conflicting, we always attempt to explain the "why" that lies behind any "how-to" offered here, so that you can make up your own mind about what to do.

We can work at acquiring a more mature perspective on our past. A young divorced mother, herself the child of divorced parents, tells this story about her relationship with her four-year-old daughter:

> I remember how after my parents were divorced I hated being left with a sitter night after night while my mother went out on dates. I was determined not to put Susie through that. So for months after my divorce I lived for my child. We were together almost constantly. The only time I had a date or did anything on my own was when she was visiting her father, or friends, or her grandparents. She's quite a kid, but I must admit I missed not having a normal social life. Finally, I weakened and accepted an invitation to go to a party with an old friend. I was sure Susie would be upset when I told her, but she wasn't. You should have seen her excite-

ment as she watched me get dressed up. She said, "I like to see you pretty." The next morning all she wanted to talk about was my party. I really think she enjoyed my going out as much as I did. It suddenly hit me that maybe I would have been even more unhappy after my parents' divorce if my mother had never dated. Who knows? I guess one extreme is as bad as the other.

Putting the past in proper perspective involves growth in understanding ourselves, a large and long-term task. As Susie's mother is discovering, there are seldom pat explanations for our feelings or behavior in a given situation. Nearly always, more is at work than is immediately apparent.

Aids to Growth in Self-understanding

Yet growth in self-understanding is possible. We can become more open to the multiplicity of factors that may affect the interaction between a person and his environment. Susie's mother now recognizes that she probably would have enjoyed, or at least accepted, her mother's dating if it hadn't been so frequent. She has discovered a useful concept: opposite extremes tend to be equally unsatisfactory. You will be introduced to many other psychological concepts that can help us make sense of our experience. In addition, parents will be encouraged all along, through firsthand accounts of experiences with children and other means, to examine themselves, to look for ways in which unrecognized attitudes or psychologically untenable opinions might be adversely affecting their children's behavior.

In passing, it should be noted that this kind of learning often comes through the arts. A novel, play, poem, painting, dance, music can give us insights into human nature and the human condition, stretch us. The "shock of recognition," or what the psychiatrist Fritz Perls has called the "Aha!" reaction, which marks psychological growth, is often part of the reward that we get from artistic experiences.

Of course, the furthering of growth in self-understanding is at the heart of all mental health education and all therapy. It is

important to recognize that we can get professional help with the job when we need it. Such help can be extremely useful, as has been discovered by the self-made businessman, mentioned earlier, who was having difficulties with his sons. However, one needs to be careful to seek help from qualified sources.

Professional Resources

There are a variety of professional persons and organizations equipped to help individuals and families understand themselves and their problems better: psychiatrists, psychoanalysts, psychologists, and social workers; trained and accredited counselors and therapists who work with specific problems, such as those involving learning or speech; mental health clinics, child guidance clinics, family service associations, and other public and private hospital-related, church-related, and university-related facilities that treat families and individuals and are often less expensive than private therapists. See the Bibliography for sources of more information about therapists, therapy, and how to go about getting such help.

It is a sign of strength to be able to seek out such aid when one reaches the limits of one's own resources for understanding and coping with what is happening to oneself or one's children. The need for professional help has always exceeded its availability. In recent years the burgeoning demand—swelled partly by persons who can function adequately enough but want more out of life, persons who feel they are overly inhibited—has led to the development of many shortcut approaches to self-understanding and self-realization: sensitivity training, encounter groups, marathons, touch groups, and the like. These approaches vary both in their potential for helping participants and their potential for harming the psychologically vulnerable who are unaware that they need professional therapy and not just to be "opened up."

The new movement has undoubtedly had a constructive effect on the overall practice of therapy. It has caused many traditionally trained therapists to adapt some of the new techniques to their purposes and to seek less time-consuming approaches to treatment.

However, the person interested in participating in any type of crash program aimed at heightening self-awareness and the ability to relate to others should be alert to the possible dangers involved. What are the credentials of the leader? What are the credentials of the sponsoring agency, if any? Are the participants carefully screened to eliminate persons with serious problems who might go to pieces during or after such an emotionally charged experience? Is there any professional follow-up; that is, are participants given the name of a trained person who can be reached quickly if one of them should feel especially depressed or disturbed after the experience?

Some people report that they benefited greatly from such experiences. Others report no gain. A few participants have become psychotic or committed suicide not too long after the experience, indicating that it may have triggered more awareness than they could handle without professional assistance. For the present, the crucial issue for would-be joiners seems to be the arrangements the program provides to cope with participants who may become emotionally upset during or after the experience. If you have doubts about joining, don't. Seek out more traditional resources for help.

Knowing Our Limits

You might say that the "expert" in each of us is limited by the degree to which we are emotionally healthy. Yet emotional health itself is relative, as is discussed in Chapter 4. Even the healthiest of us have our blind spots; and people with problems in some areas may have significant strengths in others. Our inborn expertise should never be sold short. The trick is to check it out, always, in the specific ways suggested here.

2 *The World We Live In*

WE DO NOT REAR our children in a vacuum. Our influence on them, as well as our ability to provide for and protect them, is decisively limited by the larger society in which we live, by the jobs, housing, schools, and health care available to us, the conditions in the neighborhoods where we reside, and the overall contemporary scene.

This is nothing new. What *is* new is the broad-scale discontent with society today that is evident among parents in all segments of our population, the white majority as well as minority groups, the well-to-do no less than the poor. Rarely, if ever, has society offered so little comfort and support to such a large proportion of its families. Rarely, if ever, have its values been so seriously questioned. Parents not only feel repelled or threatened by much that they see around them, but also share a sense of powerlessness, of being helpless victims of conditions over which they have no control.

Yet it is our world. There is no use in simply knocking it. Like every generation of parents before us, we have to meet the challenges of our times as constructively as we can. More than most, however, we need to try to understand our society as it is and how we can best involve ourselves in working for necessary changes.

Sources of Discontent

Not too long ago, those of us who did not have to worry about where our next meal was coming from viewed the threat of nuclear holocaust as the ultimate menace with which we and our children had to live.

Today we know that pollution may render the world uninhabitable.

Already some species of our native birds are becoming extinct; the accumulation of DDT in their bodies causes them to lay eggs with shells so fragile that they crack prematurely and no live young are hatched. As the environmentalists say, "Birds today. People tomorrow?"

Almost daily we learn of some new ecological disaster: another lake or stream or beach lost to pollution, another species of fish declared unsafe for human consumption, another suspected link between a variety of human illnesses and the contaminated air that we breathe or the contaminated earth in which we grow our crops. And every day the population of the United States swells by 6,000 persons. By the year 2000, if present growth patterns persist, our population will be double what it was in 1950, heralding the prospect of mounting pollution; increasingly crowded schools, highways, and public transportation systems; more "brown-outs"; longer lines at check-out counters; less speedy mail delivery—you name it.

Meanwhile, nuclear weapons continue to be stockpiled. As our supply of these and other implements of destruction mounts, some inevitably become outmoded. We are treated to the black comedy of government officials searching frantically for a safe way to bury, dump, or otherwise dispose of antiquated war matériel—nerve gas and the like—which, though obsolete, still has a destructive capacity at which the imagination boggles.

Often we feel that our leaders, on the community and the national level, are, like ourselves, helpless to control the institutions that exert such a pervasive influence over our lives. The local school system, no less than the military-industrial complex, frequently seems to function under a momentum of its own that renders it unresponsive even to the will of those in charge of it, much less the average citizen. Bureaucracy has got the better of us all, or so we often feel. It is easy to succumb to the belief that we are all simply numbers, being fed into computers and dealt with impersonally by the machinery of our technology, because precisely this does happen to many, possibly most, of us from time to time. Without doubt, our sense of self—of feeling that we have a voice, that we count for something—is increasingly being threatened, just as our physical person is increasingly in jeopardy when we walk the streets.

The Need to Become Involved

There is good reason to believe that we must, as never before, play an active role in the larger society. If our children are to inherit a livable environment, an aroused citizenry will have to effect changes in some areas very quickly. Time is running out. In regard to the ecological crisis, at least, we can no longer afford to "leave it to George," or "wait until the children are grown."

But what can or should we do? Granted, solving social problems is never simple. There are always conflicting interests to be reconciled. At a conference on technology, reported recently in *The New York Times,* space engineers in attendance were often asked, "If we can go to the moon, why can't we solve some of our pressing problems on earth?" The engineers continually countered that solutions to social ills are "not as neat and straightforward as developing a space-flight system."

Still, as the Chinese proverb has it, every long journey begins with a step. We must start where we can, perhaps in such limited ways as taking part in local programs to recycle bottles, aluminum containers, and paper, or joining a political club or a community group working for better schools or parks, better medical services, or improved relations with minority groups. In most communities today, if we look around carefully, we can find at least one organization striving to do a job that strikes us as "our thing." If not, we can start one.

Doing Our Homework

In the past, "volunteer" efforts to bring about social change have often foundered for lack of "professionalism." The volunteers did not inform themselves sufficiently well about the problem—education, recreation, housing, or whatever it happened to be—that they had banded together to tackle. They did not know enough about the situation to set appropriate goals and gain the community support needed to achieve them. Or, being inexperienced in community work, they gave in too quickly to cynicism or despair. Or being unsophisticated about the psychology of groups—the interpersonal tensions and conflicts that are likely to arise and the ways of handling them—they became so split by internal disagreements that they could not function.

Parents who wish to engage effectively in work of this sort need to do their homework. Some suggested reading about several current issues, community action techniques, and the dynamics of group functioning is included in the Bibliography.

Learning from the Young

Today we are beginning to see a new, more professional breed of volunteers—willing and able to educate themselves about the job they are undertaking, not easily discouraged or distracted, psychologically aware. To a considerable extent, young people deserve credit for the change. As was first indicated on a large scale during the presidential primaries of 1968, when the youth of today volunteer for a job, they can exhibit a capacity for thoroughness, organization, and mastering the necessary know-how that puts many a paid professional to shame. It has become an axiom among civic leaders that if you want to get a project moving, interest some young people in it.

The head of an organization set up in a small Southern city to combat air pollution said recently:

> We weren't getting anywhere until one of our members showed up at a meeting with his son, a high school senior, and two of the boy's friends. Within a few weeks the kids had come up with an impressive survey of industrial pollutants in our area, peak hours for pollution, weather conditions that might cause hazardous fallout, that sort of stuff. They suggested that we send out a daily release, "The Chemicals You Breathe Today," to our local newspaper. They assured us they could do the necessary analysis in the school laboratory under the supervision of one of the science teachers. Largely as a result of this, the Chamber of Commerce is showing an interest in our crusade. I'm afraid it will still be a while before we manage to get a satisfactory, enforceable Clean Air Code, but I'm in this fight to stay. I don't see how any of us could look our children in the eye otherwise.

Hidden Dividends

Implicit in this man's comment is a truth that all of us need to be aware of: though our efforts to change the world—or some small part of it—may not accomplish a great deal immediately, just being involved is good for us, as well as for our children.

A sound psychological case can be made for the importance of involvement to a person's emotional welfare, especially in today's world. In a society that is becoming increasingly depersonalized, our sense of identity is in danger of being eroded. It is easy to feel that we have no voice, that what we do does not matter. The next step is to feel that we do not matter as a person. This can result in pathological depression or in paranoid rage, as Albert Camus' novel *The Stranger* chillingly depicts. Working closely with others in enterprises designed to bring about needed changes in the world provides an antidote to the malaise that afflicted Camus' "hero." It restores our sense of mattering, our identity. This is why the experience is so often felt to be rewarding, even though the impact of our efforts on the larger society may seem to us to be limited. We all need what involvement does for us, perhaps more than we realize.

A mother who lives with her husband and children in an apartment in a large city reports:

> We decided a couple of years ago to organize the tenants in our building to bring pressure on the landlord to lock the front entrance and install a bell-buzzer intercom system. We held meetings in our apartment and negotiated with the landlord and worked at getting tenants to agree to reasonable rent increases to cover the cost. A whole frustrating year elapsed between our first tenants' meeting and the day when the new lock and the new intercom system were finally working. During that year, I often thought,

"Who needs it?" Then, after we achieved our goal, I began to appreciate all the other things we had accomplished in the process. The building is cleaner—we don't just leave everything to the super. We're like neighbors now, not intrusive but available when needed. I feel better about all those hours spent as tenants' representative than about any paid job I've ever had, and I think it's one of the best lessons our children have ever been exposed to—you know, nothing is easy, but cooperation does produce results, tangible and intangible, if you keep at it.

A psychiatrist says this:

> Originally, I went along with the recycling thing because of my son's feelings. Hands across the generation gap. Obviously, one family's trash is nothing. It's what the institutions do that counts, the hospitals, the restaurants, the manufacturers. I still say that's where the big battle has to be waged. But the first time we drove up to the receiving center with our two cartons of laboriously washed bottles and flattened cans, it came over me how important a symbolic act can be for the participants. All those beautiful people. If you're feeling down, I recommend a trip to your local recycling center.

Similarly, our children gain indirectly, as well as directly, from our efforts to make the world more livable for all its inhabitants. Our concern about getting better schools, for example, conveys to them, among other things, the message that education is important and reinforces their motivation to learn. Our work in a community project serving underprivileged youngsters says that we care about *all* children, and thus subtly reassures our own offspring that we value them as individuals, not as mere extensions of ourselves. Our involvement in community enterprises with people of other races and backgrounds takes the strangeness out of such differences; this makes the world seem less threatening to our children. So, too, does the fact that we *work* with the problems that they are exposed to by television and the conversation of their elders.

Other Challenges of the Times

But, while we are working for social change, we must live in the world as it is and help our children do so. Of course, every family, like every child, is different. The problems that will confront us as parents will vary according to where we live, our economic situation, family background, and personal life-style. Still, certain general conclusions can be drawn about living in today's world that will, to a greater or lesser degree, apply to us all.

We will need to accept rapid change, be open to new ideas and new solutions. Most sociologists and other observers of the social scene agree that the tempo of change today is more rapid than at any time in recorded history, including the period of the industrial revolution, and that we should expect the tempo to continue to quicken. This means that our experience with living, especially with technological living, will become outdated very rapidly. We will have to work increasingly hard at keeping up with the times.

A mother in her early thirties had a taste of this when she decided to replace the sewing machine that she had owned for about fifteen years:

> It was a real shock to my system. The new models they showed me were all so different from the machine I'm used to that I didn't see how I'd be able to thread one, much less run it. I felt so confused that I couldn't concentrate on what the saleswoman was showing me. I was ready to leave without buying anything when it struck me that I'm too young to start thinking that way. I was acting my grandmother's age. So I bought the simplest model, and I'm getting used to it gradually.

If you have recently replaced some of your old hi-fi equipment or investigated buying a "better" camera, you may sympathize with this young woman. In the same way, some of our ideas about children and growing up will tend to date faster. Young people who graduated from high school only five years ago report that already they feel rather strange with the current generation of high school

students, so much has changed since their day. This doesn't mean, of course, that our own experience will lose its relevance; it means only that we will have to be continually alert to the significance of changing customs and social mores.

Today, for example, the parents of children entering first grade must reckon with the fact that their youngsters need to be informed about the kinds of drug experimentation prevalent among the very young. Many parents are as troubled by this as their own parents were by the need to let their children know that at school they would be likely to hear sex talked about in language they had not encountered at home. Since the days of Socrates, at least, many parents have clung to the delusion that what they don't tell the young can't hurt them, whereas communicating honestly about ticklish subjects is the best hope that adults have of protecting the younger generation from destructive behavior and of influencing their choices. Parent-child communication is dealt with more fully in Chapter 7 of this book.

If we are to make any real progress in alleviating the grave social ills of today, such as the drug problem, poverty, discrimination, pollution, the widespread dissatisfaction with our schools, and the widespread disillusionment with our national priorities, we must be open to new ideas and approaches. In a period of rapid change such as ours, young people—whose nature it is to see the world freshly—can be helpful in the search for new solutions if ways can be found to further cooperation between them and their elders.

We cannot foresee what specific conditions we may have to cope with, as citizens and as parents, in the decades to come. But we can school ourselves to be aware of the changing scene, to remain flexible, and to maintain meaningful contact with the young in our rapidly changing world.

We will confront new relationships between men and women. One social change that will almost surely continue in the years ahead will be the shift, so much in evidence today, in society's attitudes toward women and in women's thinking about their own role. Predicting the future is always hazardous, but it appears fairly certain that, perhaps largely as a result of the population explosion and improved methods of birth control, child-bearing and child-rearing will cease to be viewed as woman's major function in life. Women may be expected to move steadily toward achieving equal status with men in access to professional education, employment opportunities, pay, politics, and many other areas.

Although many young women today express distaste or scorn for the "women's liberation" movement as such, it is interesting that nearly all will follow up their objections to the views and tactics of the more radical feminists with some such comment as, "Of course I believe in equal pay for equal work," or, "Certainly if a woman wants to go to medical school and has the qualifications, she should be judged on the same basis as male applicants," or, "I think it's ridiculous for a woman to be barred from a professional organization or a club just because she is a woman."

This heightened consciousness of their status seems to be shared by growing numbers of women in all strata of society. A mother in her forties reports that, in the course of doing research for an article about the educational experience of girls at the high school level, she changed from being rather opposed to the idea of women's liberation into being an outspoken advocate of women's rights. She says she had simply not been aware of, in her words, "the many subtle ways in which girls are brainwashed." Her husband, who shares her current views, remarks wryly, "But I could have told her." As more women—and men—come to feel similarly, the impact on society is bound to be far-reaching.

We will need to find new ways to recapture genuine community spirit. Ours is a mobile society. This lends a certain excitement to living, but we pay a price for it. Most of us in the course of our lives will call a number of places home, some so briefly that a decade later we would have difficulty finding our way back to them. Even if we stay put, our neighbors and our neighborhood change. Our relatives are more apt to be scattered at some distance from us than living nearby. Our children attend school with other children whose parents are, more often than not, strangers to us, and in going to and from school they are unlikely to encounter adults who have known and taken an interest in them since they were born.

There is less and less opportunity for most children to establish significant relationships with adults other than their parents. Likewise, parents tend to be more than ever left to their own devices in making important decisions about their children's upbringing, in dealing with emergencies, or just in coping with the daily exigencies of living. It used to be routine for neighborhoods to "look out for their own"—of all ages, but especially the young. Children were accustomed to being comforted, protected, advised, and admonished by a variety of familiar adults, which both contributed to their emotional security and broadened their horizons. It was a boon to parents, too, despite justifiable parental resentment against having neighbors meddle in their affairs. But this is now a rarity.

Today many young people in their late teens and early twenties are aware of the disadvantages of growing up in the kind of isolated "nuclear family" unit that is prevalent nowadays, in which children are dependent entirely on their parents for "parenting." These young people are experimenting with various ways to approximate the earlier "extended family." Their approaches range from communes to more casual cooperative arrangements for sharing child-care responsibilities and being neighborly. An excellent discussion of this trend can be found in *Parents and Their Older Children* by Margaret Albrecht.

The decentralization movement and the rise of tenants' groups and block associations in some urban areas may also contribute toward reviving a spirit of community. We cannot turn back the clock. Mobility, like technology, is here to stay. However, it must again become possible for neighbors to make common cause in various ways, and for neighborhoods to provide, even for those who settle in them only temporarily, the kind of expanded experience of "home" that they once offered.

We will have to face the possibility that our children may be more vulnerable than previous generations to pressures from their peers. As our children grow, they increasingly need to feel accepted in the world beyond home. Such acceptance is crucial to a child's concept of himself—his "identity." Much as he values his parents' good opinion of him, this alone is not sufficient reassurance that he is somebody. He seeks approval from others, especially his own age mates.

If a child's relationship with his parents is good, he tends, on the whole, to choose friends who share his family's values. Many other factors, however, will influence his choice of friends and his relationship with them at any given time. Though some youngsters seem to have a greater need than others to be accepted by their peers, and are therefore more vulnerable to pressures to "go along with the crowd," no child is totally immune to such pressures at every stage in his growing up. A quarrel with a best friend, difficulties with school work, reemergence of old rivalries with a brother or sister, any one of a myriad such stresses can intensify a youngster's need to be "in" with certain peers, or peer groups, and affect the lengths to which he is willing to go to achieve this reassurance.

In earlier times, youngsters usually gained considerable sense of status through "belonging" in a community where they and their family had lived for years. This contributed to their identity, reducing their need to win recognition in other ways and often easing the path to lasting friendships. The fact that such close community ties seldom exist today puts a premium, for many children, on the ability to relate to peers. Peer pressures may be harder to resist.

We will need to recognize that children are growing up faster these days. The average age of puberty, for both boys and girls, has been gradually lowering over the last few decades. Intellectually, too, youngsters tend to be ahead of where their parents were at the same age, judging by the change in scores on a variety of standardized tests. If you have looked recently at a teen-ager's school books and assignments, you probably don't need to be told this.

Improved nutrition has been credited by some authorities with bringing about earlier physical maturation, although nobody knows for sure why the age of puberty is falling or where it will stop. The information explosion and, especially, television contribute to the intellectual sophistication of today's children. Although television programming can be faulted on a number of grounds, and although television watching can become an escape mechanism, somewhat like a drug, the educational impact of TV on many young viewers has been enormous. Possibly, the current concern over the gap between the American dream and the American way of life is the result of television, although the programmers never intended their shows and commercials to produce this result.

To say that children are growing up faster does not, of course, tell us anything about a particular child. We have always had our early and our late maturers, our delayed "bloomers," children who were precociously sophisticated and those who were the opposite. The range of individual differences remains as broad as ever. As parents, we will be relating to a human being who does things at his or her own pace, not to a nonexistent statistical average. Still, we have to recognize that statistical averages affect the overall climate of the world in which our own child is growing up. Awareness of that climate makes us better able to help our child deal with it wisely, in the way that is right for him.

We will increasingly be required to make our own judgments about the flood of information reaching us as parents and citizens. The information explosion, combined with "instant communication," will continue to step up our exposure to varying viewpoints and seemingly conflicting "facts" about matters that directly concern families but cannot be authoritatively checked out with a specialist, such as the family doctor. When specialists disagree (as they do, for example, about the relative safety of the artificial sweetener saccharine, or the merits of breast-feeding), we must decide for ourselves what is the most sensible course for us to pursue. We will have to accustom ourselves to evaluating evidence, weighing alternatives, and reading the fine print on everything.

This might turn out to be all to the good. From having to pick our way through the morass of information relevant to living in today's world, we may recapture the self-reliance, the independence of spirit, and the feeling of being able to cope with our environment that earlier generations of Americans acquired through pioneering in the wilderness. That would be no mean gain.

We need to view new threats and dangers in proper perspective. We should not overlook the fact that significant progress has been made in some very important areas in this century. Life expectancy has risen from 49.2 years in 1900 to 70.2 years in 1970. The infant mortality rate has been cut by a third since 1930, dropping from approximately 65 deaths under one year per 1,000 live births to 22 per 1,000 in 1968. During the same period, maternal mortality has been cut from approximately 7 maternal deaths per 1,000 live births to less than 1. Medical advances have given us new drugs and vaccines that can protect us and our children against many diseases that were intensely feared only a few decades ago: pneumonia, scarlet fever, measles, polio, to name a few. Surgery has become correspondingly safer. And technology, for all its faults, has relieved us of many of the more burdensome aspects of running a home and rearing children. Although such gains have not been shared equally by all citizens, they are not to be dismissed lightly.

These facts do not minimize the threats that confront us today or the unknown ones that may confront us tomorrow. They merely put them in perspective. Pollution, violence in the streets, and all the rest must be faced up to realistically. While we work at identifying and treating their root causes, we must educate our children to avoid whatever hazards it may be within a child's power to avoid. Youngsters must, for example, be given pointers on navigating as safely as possible within their neighborhoods and environs. It may be helpful, to them and to us, to frame our teachings within the context that the world has always had its dangers and imperfections, and always will.

We will have to learn to live with more stress. Even if we manage within the next decade to stabilize the population, there will still be a lot more of us around by then, making for a lot more frustration.

There is nothing new about trains running late, mail being lost, banks making mistakes, or most other examples of institutional fallibility and/or technological breakdown that are the source of so much irritation today. Such frustrations have simply multiplied with the population explosion. To complicate matters, machines handle many large-scale operations today, and machines are, on the whole, sadly lacking in the ability to catch themselves up when they make an error.

A young father recently had his wallet stolen. The wallet contained his driver's license, which was very important to him, as his job required considerable traveling by car. He immediately notified the authorities and was informed that no record could be found of his ever having had a license, possibly because such records were in the process of being shifted from one type of machine to a newer model. However, he was assured cheerfully, if he were indeed a licensed driver, sometime before the end of the year he would automatically receive a renewal application, so that if he could afford to wait, all would probably turn out well. He could not afford to wait. It was suggested, then, that he apply for another license. This he did. In due time, the forms for renewing his earlier license arrived, as predicted, and he had to spend the better part of two days consulting with the authorities about which license he should keep, it being against the law in his state to have two.

This may seem an extreme story, yet nearly every day most of us hear from our friends and families similarly unnerving accounts of hours wasted coping with bureaucratic red tape, or inaccurate bills—or simply trying to get from one place to another.

Although some young people are trying to avoid these extreme contemporary pressures by setting up more primitive societies in isolated areas—in rural New England or the mountains of Tennessee or Colorado, or on the West Coast—for most of us there is no "getting away from it all."

Nor are there any magic recipes for living with modern stresses. A sense of humor, being able to laugh things off, helps. But one does not acquire that ability just by wanting to have it. On the other hand, some psychiatrists insist that we tend to become what we go through the motions of being. If this theory is true—and there is evidence to support it—then it might be helpful to cultivate the habit of joking about the frustrating dilemmas from which we cannot extricate ourselves. Jokes are known to be a psychologically useful way of letting off steam.

Certainly, parents can sustain their children through frustrating experiences, such as being caught in a traffic jam or waiting in a clinic, by making light of the situation—if it is quite clear that they empathize with the child's feelings. It is important that children not feel alone in their frustrations, or think that they are being laughed at, rather than with.

Often, too, our children can help us through stressful times, take our minds off our troubles. Since they are not always affected as we are by all the ramifications of a situation, their reactions can be fresh and cheering. A three-year-old, flying with her parents during a violent storm that was severely frightening most of the passengers, greeted each "bump" that the plane encountered with the happy squeal that she often gave when sliding down her backyard slide. Eventually one of the male passengers smiled weakly and remarked, "That child has to have been sired by a dive bomber." A few neighbors laughed. Soon, many of the passengers became so interested in the little girl and so intent on shielding her from their anxiety about the plane's safety, that they themselves felt better. The trip took on something of a carnival quality.

Parents sometimes, in various ways, let themselves in for more than the necessary amount of frustration and stress. A common way is through trying to "keep up with the Joneses." At best, bills tend to pile up during the early years of marriage, when husbands are just getting started in their work, and the presence of small children limits the ability of wives to augment the family income. However, persistent financial problems are often a signal that we need to rethink our values carefully and consider the possibility that our priorities should be reordered. Other attitudes that may subject us to potentially avoidable stress will be discussed from time to time in succeeding chapters.

It's Not All Up to Parents

A promising development in recent years has been the growing recognition that parents are not solely responsible for how their children turn out. Society shares that responsibility all along. Children, too, share in shaping their own destiny. Increasingly as they grow, they move into the community and make decisions that vitally affect their lives. The new view of child-rearing as an undertaking in which society, parents, and the child himself are all partners eases some of the pressure on parents and underscores the need for commitment to social change in high places. Although some families and some children are more victimized than others by the social problems of the day, we are all vulnerable to the ills of our times. No child is assured of having a healthy environment to grow up in until all children are.

It is not helpful to our children, to ourselves, or to society either to be prophets of doom, or to give up trying to change the world in which we live. Children do not thrive on a constant diet of pessimism or apathy. They need to see that we share their questions and concerns about conditions around us, to understand that many other parents feel as we do, and to believe that society can be changed to better meet the needs of all its members.

3
Preparing For A New Baby

NOT EVERY COUPLE is overjoyed when they realize they are going to have a baby. For some, of course, the event is urgently desired, perhaps long awaited, and as suspicion gives way to certainty, they walk with their heads in the clouds.

But others are annoyed—they would like to have children eventually, but not right now. Right now they have other fish to fry, and the coming of a baby is going to play hob with their plans. In the case of some, annoyance is too mild a word for the emotions engendered. They are enraged, or frightened. They simply cannot afford a baby, they think, or afford housing that would provide space enough for a baby, or their marriage is foundering, or the husband is about to be transferred to a job in a distant city, or the wife has just one more year to go to get her degree in medicine or social work or something.

Feelings Can Change

Often, couples who were resentful or worried at the start of a pregnancy come around to being delighted long before the baby is due. Together they hash out their feelings, go over the choices open to them, change some plans, rearrange some of their long-term goals, and gradually the future begins to look bright again, maybe even brighter than before.

A young mother of two children says:

> I was so upset when I got pregnant with my second child that I considered having

an abortion. My husband had quit his job the year before to go back to school and get his law degree, and I was working. He wasn't happy about my getting pregnant just then, but he dragged his feet about abortion. We stewed and argued for about a month, then things began to fall into place. His old company agreed to take him back and pay his tuition to finish law school at night. He'll graduate next spring, and our girl has been the apple of our eye ever since the day she was born.

As this mother's experience suggests, negative feelings about a pregnancy need not mean that you will be an unloving parent later on, or that your baby will be in any way adversely affected by the fact that for a period of your pregnancy you were prey to grave misgivings and doubts. Such feelings are extremely common. In fact, few prospective parents escape having *some* doubts somewhere along the line.

Talking Out Feelings

You shouldn't feel guilty about your negative feelings. The important thing is to talk them out. Pregnancy is a time when it is especially necessary that husband and wife be honest with each other, admit to each other their inmost thoughts and emotions. In sharing their private hopes, fears, and dreams about having a baby, each partner may discover new sides of his own personality, as well as his mate's. Self-doubts, never before admitted, may at last come out in the open, along with hidden ambitions, unexpected strengths, and unexpected tenderness and compassion for each other. There is opportunity for growth as a person, growth in marriage, and growth in one's relationship with one's own parents.

Dr. Paul Adams, a child psychiatrist, writes in a paper included in the book *Children's Rights:*

> Pregnancy . . . constitutes a kind of turning point in the relationship of the man and woman. Wonderment, joy, anger and irritation may all appear, presenting new opportunities for dialogue, for compromise and for self-assertion by both partners. A cosmic concern appears fleetingly even to the most blasé of young couples. They begin taking cognizance of their own origin . . . begin showing a preoccupation with their own parents. . . . It is as if they desired to set aright the relations with those generations which preceded them just at that moment when their own generativity comes to the forefront.

Women especially are apt to find that becoming pregnant puts them on a new footing with their parents, their mothers in particular. But men also may experience this. Even more than marriage or the first "real" job, knowing that one is going to have a baby makes a young person feel, "Now I am an adult." Parents, too, feel a difference. There is often a new ring of respect in the way they react with their children. Young people, on their part, may find themselves turning to their parents for advice—and taking it. The generations may become truly equals. When this happens, the closeness that it brings can provide a prospective parent with an additional, exceedingly valuable resource for talking through all his or her concerns, and often supply a tonic that has been missing: humor.

Serious Doubts

Sometimes talking out negative feelings doesn't cause them to diminish. The more husband and wife discuss the matter, the clearer it becomes that, for one reason or another, both of them are seriously distressed by the pregnancy. Both wish intensely that it had not happened.

In such cases, it would be wise for them to think about a legal abortion. Information about abortion and resources for securing it legally are given in Chapter 10. Through the tenth week of pregnancy, that is, up to about the point when a woman is missing her third period, a legal abortion is both very simple and very safe. After that it becomes more complicated, though still safe, through about the twentieth week. After the twenty-fourth week, abortion can no longer be performed legally. So this is a decision that should be made early. However, a couple has several weeks of leeway, after they first suspect the wife is pregnant, to think carefully about the possibility of having an abortion, arrive at a decision, and make plans before the wife is ten weeks pregnant.

Of course, for some couples abortion is out of the question. They reject it absolutely, on religious or other grounds. For them, some kind of professional counseling would seem advisable. A clergyman trained as a pastoral counselor or a psychologist or psychiatric social worker who shares their convictions may be able to help them with their anxieties about having a baby.

Couples who feel a conflict, who want an abortion but fear they may have guilt feelings about it later, would also be well advised to seek professional help in making their decision. Talking with the family doctor may be sufficient. If additional counseling is desired, the doctor can suggest where to go for it. The evidence suggests that guilt feelings about abortion are related to the climate of opinion to which a woman is exposed. Women in countries where abortion has been legal for some time and is taken for granted do not seem to be subject to guilt feelings after having an abortion.

Choosing an Obstetrician and Hospital

Good prenatal care is important to the welfare of both a mother and her unborn baby. Most obstetricians and prenatal clinics prefer to see a mother as soon as she has missed her second period. By this time, pregnancy can be confirmed or ruled out with a high degree of certainty. On the first visit, the mother's overall health is checked, and she is given some general instructions, often in writing, about diet and other matters to guide her throughout her pregnancy. She also is given the opportunity to ask any questions she may have on her mind. After the first visit, she returns for regular checkups, usually at monthly intervals.

Most women today live in areas where they have a choice of physicians and, often, hospitals. Perhaps you have already decided what doctor you want, or in what hospital you prefer to be delivered. If you have chosen a doctor, you will automatically be booked for the hospital where he practices.

If choice of hospital is crucial to you for some reason—perhaps because it permits "rooming-in" (discussed on p. 23) or is receptive to "natural childbirth" (discussed on p. 24)—you can either use that hospital's prenatal clinic or call and ask for a list of staff obstetricians engaged in private practice.

If you know nothing about doctors or hospitals in the area where you reside, you can call your city or county Medical Society and ask them to recommend an obstetrician or a prenatal clinic. You will be given several names. Every person needs to know this, in the event he faces a medical emergency in a strange community. But perhaps you consider it too impersonal a way to choose your obstetrician. You want to go to a doctor recommended by somebody you know. In that case, you might ask a clergyman for recommendations, or a neighbor whose judgment you trust, or your husband might ask advice of his boss. Personal recommendations, when the source is reliable, are always worth having. Another possibility is to contact a doctor in another area whom you or your parents know well and ask him for a referral. Although he may not personally know a physician in your area, he has resources for finding a reliable person and may supply you with a note of introduction.

Technically an obstetrician is a doctor certified by the medical profession as a specialist in obstetrics (delivering babies) and gynecology (problems related to the functioning of a woman's reproductive system). He has had advanced training in his specialty, passed certain examinations, and of course had a great deal of experience in the practice of obstetrics and gynecology. However, the term obstetrician is often loosely used to refer to any doctor who supervises prenatal care and delivers babies. General practitioners usually accept pregnant patients, and there is no reason not to feel thoroughly comfortable about putting yourself into the hands of one who has a large obstetrical practice. But if you prefer a specialist, check to see that the doctor of your choice is certified in obstetrics and gynecology. Ordinarily he will have a framed certificate attesting to this fact hanging on the wall along with his medical degree.

One final caution: On your first visit to your doctor or prenatal clinic, you will be warned against taking any medication, including aspirin, unless specifically prescribed. This is a very important rule that should go into effect at the beginning of pregnancy, even before you see your doctor. We have long known that some viral diseases, such as German measles, and some drugs, such as the tranquilizer Thalidomide (now banned), can damage a mother's unborn baby, especially during the first six weeks of pregnancy. Today, other viruses and medications are also considered suspect. It is wise not to take chances.

How Will You Feed Your Baby?

Whether to breast-feed or to use a bottle is a decision that husband and wife should make together. The hundreds of studies that have been made comparing breast-fed and bottle-fed children add up to one fact: It is not the method chosen, but how the feeding situation is handled, that matters. Babies need to be cuddled attentively when they are fed, by someone responsive to the cues they give about how the feeding is going, when they need to be burped, and when they have had enough. This can be accomplished with either breast-feeding or bottle-feeding. A woman should feel free to choose the method that appeals most to her and to her husband.

Doctors sometimes have rather strong opinions about which method is preferable. They may dwell on the advantages of one over the other. If you don't happen to agree with your doctor, tell him so. A good physician will respect a mother's decision on this subject. Most doctors recognize that a mother's feelings about how she wants to feed her baby are influential in determining the success with which she handles this crucial aspect of infant and baby care. Of course, if your doctor has a valid medical reason, in your particular case, for ruling out one method, accept his judgment. Remember that your baby will thrive whichever method you use.

If you are going to breast-feed, you should begin to prepare your breasts during pregnancy. Your doctor may offer suggestions. In addition, it would be wise to read up on breast-feeding, so that you will know what to expect during your hospital stay and during the early weeks after you return home with your infant. Consult the Bibliography for recommended sources.

Where Will the Baby Sleep?

Not all couples have an extra bedroom waiting to be turned into a nursery. If space is at a premium, parents may feel that the easiest solution would be to have the baby share their sleeping quarters. However, since a great deal of advice to parents warns against doing this, they may have qualms about it.

The only drawbacks to this arrangement for the first two years of a child's life involve the effects that his presence may have on his parents. Babies are restless, "noisy" sleepers. Having one in the room with you may seriously interfere with your getting a good night's rest. Additionally, parents may find that the arrangement is not conducive to their leading a healthy sexual life. After a child is two, the setup has potential hazards for him. It is generally agreed that a child as young as two can be emotionally disturbed by overhearing his parents' sexual activities, and children of this age are not always asleep when you think they are. Also, having his parents in the same room with him continually may be sexually stimulating Inevitably, it tempts the child to try to climb into bed with his parents, which is not advisable.

So by the time your child is two, you should arrange for him to sleep apart from you, and you may want to do this from the start, or at least before he becomes habituated to your presence in the room. Is there a part of a hallway, a corner of the kitchen, or other space capable of being screened or curtained off to accommodate the baby's crib? Babies and young children are not disturbed by diffused light or the noise of normal family activities. In fact, they may sleep the better for both, especially if they grow up accustomed to them. Another possibility, of course, is for parents to give their child their bedroom and sleep on a convertible couch or folding bed elsewhere

Choosing a Doctor for Your Baby

The concept of the "family doctor," a physician who handles all the medical problems of the families who are his patients, from delivering babies to treating sore throats, may be undergoing something of a revival—and high time, many people believe. Most women today, however, are likely to have their babies delivered by one doctor and looked after by another. If you plan to use some sort of a well-baby clinic, you will not need a private doctor for your baby. Otherwise, this is a choice that should be made a month or so before the baby is due to be born.

Ideally, your baby's doctor should examine your infant while he is still in the hospital, be involved in any recommendations about feeding or special care that the hospital gives you, and be available to answer any questions you have about the baby during the early weeks. When your baby is approximately six weeks old, you will take him to the doctor's office, or to your clinic, for the first of many regular checkups.

Any doctor who treats babies and children is often loosely referred to as a pediatrician. Technically, the term applies only to doctors who have had advanced training in this specialty and been certified by the American Board of Pediatrics. If you want such a specialist, check for this credential.

The suggestions offered earlier about choosing an obstetrician apply in general to picking a doctor for your baby. Since the relationship between parents and their pediatrician tends to be especially close, it is important to have a physician whose views about child-rearing you feel you would share on the whole. This can be determined through talking with other parents who have used the doctor.

Planning for a Mother's Return from the Hospital

For the first two or three weeks after a mother returns home with her infant, she will need full-time help with running the house and caring for her baby. Husbands have been known to take their vacation during this period and give wives the assistance they need. This often works out extremely well for all concerned. But if a husband is poor at housework or dislikes doing it, and especially if both husband and wife are inexperienced at handling a new baby and a bit nervous about the prospect, other arrangements will need to be made.

Many women want their mothers with them at this time. Mothers, mothers-in-law, and other relatives who have had experience handling an infant may be just the answer, if they offer their services. Since this is a period when emotions run high for the new mother, and often her husband as well, care must be taken to have help from a person with whom both husband and wife, and especially the wife, believe they will feel comfortable. A member of the family is usually, but not always, most likely to meet this requirement The couple need a fairly calm person who is willing to do things their way and not insist on imposing her ideas about housekeeping or infant care They require support, not bossing. Under some circumstances it may be wiser to go to the expense of hiring help rather than accept it from a relative.

On the whole, mothers usually prefer to care for their infants while somebody else sees to the housework. In interviewing a prospective employee or weighing a relative's offer of help, you will need to ascertain whether the person is willing to do the "dirty work" and leave the mother mostly free to feed and bathe her baby and to rest. You don't have to have a practical nurse, and so-called baby nurses often will not do housework. Friends, your doctor, or your prenatal clinic may recommend a competent person or sources for obtaining appropriate help.

You should make suitable arrangements for help several months before the baby is due to be born. Whatever arrangements you make, you may also want to look into the possibility that you may be eligible for help from your local Visiting Nurse Service. The nurse would come only briefly once or twice a week, but she might offer reassurance that things are going well, and she would be able to answer any questions that you might hesitate to bother your baby's doctor with.

If a husband foresees having to be away overnight during the first two or three weeks after his wife's return from the hospital, this factor needs to be taken into account in arranging for her help. It is unwise that she be left without another adult in the home (or readily available nearby) for more than a very few hours at a stretch.

Husband and Wife as a Team

A young couple expecting the birth of their baby imminently chanced to overhear — as they strolled down the street clad alike in jeans and workshirts and with their hair of similar length — some conversation behind them regarding the erosion of sex distinctions The young wife swung about suddenly and said with a grin, "Pregnancy lets the cat out of the bag."

It does, in more than just the obvious way. Many young couples today achieve in marriage a degree of sharing that is enormously satisfying to them and quite touching to observe. Either partner is capable of supporting the other financially, and over the course of the years they may take turns at this from time to time, to enable each to function optimally as a person. Either partner can soothe a crying infant, explain mathematical set theory to a fourth-grader, do the shopping at the local supermarket, prepare the evening meal, and correctly identify — and use — a socket wrench. But not every role, as yet, can be exchanged, and not every couple is dedicated to "sharing equally."

There are still men in their twenties who don't want to cook, change diapers, or be with their wives in a hospital labor room. In a pinch, they may *have* to do the first two chores — and hopefully will come through as gracefully as strong men have for generations. But there is no need for them to do the third if they really don't wish it.

We live in an age when both men and women should feel freer than ever before to be themselves. It would be a pity to limit this freedom by arbitrarily expecting every member of the "now" generation to share certain interests and characteristics. A couple awaiting the birth of their baby need to discuss honestly how they want to share baby care, household tasks, and all their other responsibilities. Frankness is essential to finding ways to accommodate the individual needs of both partners. Conflicts need to be brought out in the open and explored, so that reasonable compromises can be reached.

During the pregnancy a husband may be surprised, perhaps dismayed, to discover that his wife, who hitherto seemed quite competent and able to look out for herself, can be moody, demanding, "unreasonable." Pregnancy affects the emotions, as well as the body. This is caused by hormonal changes and the reality of the woman's situation. Having a baby may make her feel dependent upon others to a degree that she has not experienced since early childhood, and these dependency feelings can be hard for her to handle. Occasionally she may need to "test" the strength of her husband's devotion, much as a child sometimes tests his parents. Understanding this may help husbands to be more sympathetic. The problem is transitory. Soon after delivery, a woman usually becomes her normal competent self, often with more energy than either she or her husband knew before that she was capable of.

Wives, too, need to be sensitive to the fact that the prospect of having a baby subjects a man to emotional strains. He may feel not only that his powers as a breadwinner will be tried, but also that his standing with his wife is in some danger. They are no longer going to "mean everything to each other." The fluctuating emotional needs of both prospective parents will challenge their ability to continue communicating frankly and to support each other as partners in marriage, equal but somewhat different.

A Word About Equipment

The temptation to buy more baby equipment than is really necessary, and to spend more on necessary items than is required, is very strong, particularly when a couple are having their first child. This is sometimes sadly true of couples who can least afford it.

Of course, having a few pretty things for special occasions is fun. Life would be unbearably drab if we were always "sensible." However, the "fun" items often turn up as presents, so it is wise to go easy in this area at the start.

Baby garments made of machine-washable knits and other easy-care fabrics are one of the great boons of contemporary civilization. (Ask any grandmother.) They are often brightly colored and designed to make dressing the baby easy, rather than a chore. Sleeping garments will do duty around the clock in the early months, and you will need no more than three or four. A machine-washable sweater or two will be useful even in summer, except in very hot climates. As any friend who has recently had a baby will tell you, watch out for purchasing garments too small.

Many mothers find fitted crib sheets a convenience. If you plan to make your own crib sheets from worn bed linen, you may want to give them fitted corners. Good crib blankets can also be made by cutting down larger-size blankets that are worn in spots.

If you are going to wash the diapers yourself, you had better have at least three dozen. The fitted ones are easier to use, as they do not require folding, but they are sized and will be outgrown from time to time. If you would like to use a diaper service but don't feel that you can afford it, you might ask grandparents to consider treating you to this in lieu of some other present. Some mothers swear by disposable diapers. They find it is easier and no more expensive to use them than to use a diaper service.

It is on the large items of equipment that very substantial savings are possible. Thrift shops and Salvation Army stores offer bargains in used cribs and carriages (if hand-me-downs are not available), which often can be refurbished so that they look practically new. These are good places, too, to pick up a chest for the baby's belongings. Choose a chest that is the right height to serve as a dressing table when topped with a folded blanket or mattress pad (or, if you sew, a tailor-made cover).

A baby can be bathed in a kitchen sink lined with a bath towel for protection. However, inexpensive plastic tubs, in a variety of colors, are available.

More information about equipment is supplied in sources listed in the Bibliography. It is always helpful, too, to talk this over with other couples who have recently become parents, bearing in mind, of course, that your definition of "necessary" may differ from theirs.

Doing Your Homework

You will have a lot more time for reading before the baby comes than after. Now is the time to bone up on what is in store for you. In addition to reading and discussing the material in this volume, prospective parents are advised to read *Your Child's First Three Years* by Sara D. Gilbert. If this will not be your first child, see *Guiding Your Preschooler* by Edith G. Neisser for information on preparing older children for the arrival of a new baby.

"Rooming-in"

Some hospitals have facilities that permit the infant to stay in the same room with the mother, instead of in the hospital nursery. That is, they approximate what used to happen almost universally a hundred years ago and still does in primitive societies. The infant's crib can be rolled within easy reach of the mother's bed so that from the beginning she can comfort and feed him, play with him as often and for as long as it suits them both, and, in general, attend to all his wants, though a nurse can be summoned if the mother wishes assistance.

Rooming-in appeals to some mothers. They find it reassuring to know just what is going on with their infant at all times. If they are breast-feeding, they may especially like the freedom to feed "on demand" that this arrangement affords.

With rooming-in, visitors are limited usually to the husband and one other person—no substitutes allowed. This is considered necessary to protect the infant's health and the mother's emotional equilibrium.

If, after carefully weighing all the pros and cons, a woman decides that rooming-in is for her, her doctor will need to make reservations well ahead of time at a hospital that offers the service. The couple will have to select an obstetrician who is on the staff of such a hospital. In other words, their choice of doctor will be circumscribed by their choice of hospital.

"Natural Childbirth"

The concept of "natural childbirth" developed out of the conviction of a number of doctors that pain during childbirth is largely the result of fear; that if a woman understands how her body functions during the birth process, she will be unafraid, able to relax when that is desirable and to push when needed, and thereby to deliver her baby with a minimum of medication and of discomfort. Various authorities have devised exercises for the purpose of preparing a woman to function more effectively during childbirth. How one breathes during labor contractions is considered especially important, and breathing exercises are a major part of all such programs.

If you are interested in natural childbirth, talk it over with your obstetrician. You will need his approval in order to enroll in any formal exercise program. If you merely want to read one of the available books on natural childbirth and do the recommended exercises informally at home, your doctor is unlikely to have any objections, but it would be wise to discuss it with him anyway. Two such books are listed in the Bibliography.

When the natural childbirth movement first started, some mothers were so fanatical about rejecting all medication that the whole concept fell into disrepute with many doctors. Recent books on the subject, however, handle the question of medication more sensibly. If you are going to try natural childbirth, trust your doctor's judgment about what medication is needed and when. He has to think ahead. As one mother said, "When my doctor ordered a Demerol shot, I assured him I didn't need it. Half an hour later, just as the shot started to take effect, I was grateful for his foresight."

Understanding what goes on during childbirth is helpful to any woman, as is confirmed by many mothers who, in their words, "want all the medication I can get." Labor is a rhythmical process. The uterine muscles contract forcefully for about a minute and then relax for a period of time. The contractions come closer together as labor progresses, but between them many women experience no pain whatever. Lying on one's side during contractions and puffing out one's abdomen, by taking a big breath and holding it until the contraction ends, may alleviate discomfort.

During the first stage of labor, which is much the longest, the cervix dilates sufficiently to let the baby through. (See illustration.) For the first few hours of this

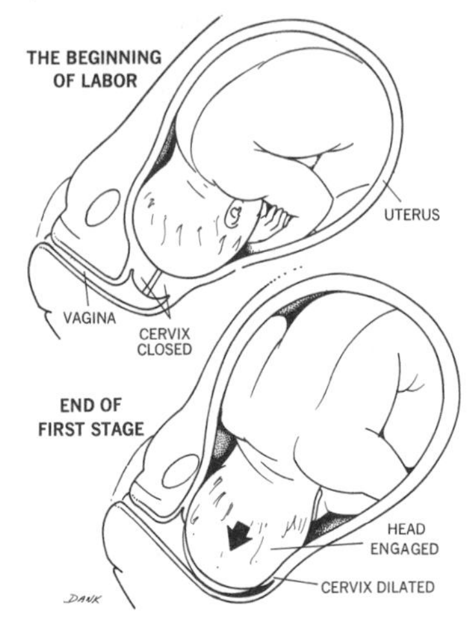

stage, a woman feels little, if any, discomfort. The only way in which she can facilitate the dilating process is by relaxing during contractions. She can be given some pain-relieving drugs, but not too much medication. Doctors do not want to deliver a drugged baby. The last half hour or so of the first stage of labor is generally the most uncomfortable part of having a baby. So it is consoling to know, when you are going through it, that soon the worst will be over.

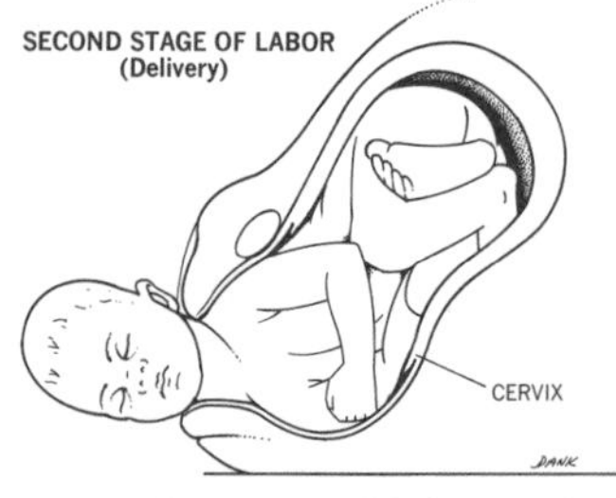

In the second stage of labor, which lasts only an hour or two, the baby is pushed through the birth canal and out into the world. (See illustration.) A woman can help by "bearing down" during contractions, which is not unlike straining to have a bowel movement. Her doctor has at his disposal a wide variety of anesthetics and other medications to make her comfortable, and there is less need for him to be stingy about using them at this point, for the baby will be born before being seriously affected by them.

After the baby arrives, the afterbirth or placenta must be delivered. This process constitutes the third and final stage of giving birth, and a mother is usually totally unconcerned with it. She is either asleep or wrapped up in admiring her new infant.

"Mother Love"

Since the perfection of spinal anesthesia, which blocks out all sensation in the pelvic area without putting a person to sleep, any woman can enjoy what is extolled as one of the greatest benefits of natural childbirth: she can be wide awake when her baby is born. Not every woman wants this, however. If you do not want to watch your baby being delivered and would prefer to wait to see him until after he has been all cleaned up, tell your doctor. Ordinarily, he will discuss with you, early in your pregnancy, what kinds of medication he might administer. He should be able to put you to sleep at the time of delivery if you prefer that.

Every mother is different. There is no reason to feel that not wanting to see your baby born implies that you might lack normal maternal feelings.

Mothers (and fathers) react differently also to the first sight of their newborn infant. A newborn is, at best, not pretty, except possibly to his own parents. The head of the newborn is likely to be rather startlingly pushed out of shape—elongated—by the birth process. (It will round out in a few days.) The legs seem pitifully thin and bowed. (They will straighten and plump out in a few months.) The infant's facial features are "scrunched together," giving him the appearance of an old man, and the skin is wrinkled and often blotchy (That, too, will be soon remedied.) All in all, it is surprising that any new mother or father should consider their newborn beautiful, but some do.

But probably the most unsettling thing that happens to some new mothers is the discovery that they are not overwhelmed with maternal feelings when they first hold their baby. Many women are, but not all, and this tells nothing about their capacity to be good mothers, or how much they will love their child later on.

In many mothers, and fathers, love for their child develops slowly, through ministering to the baby's needs and watching him grow into "a person." Some excellent mothers admit that they really do not care for infants at all. They did not begin to come into their own until their babies started to coo and gurgle at sight of them. Still others say the magic moment came even later, after the child began to walk and talk.

Some Goals to Keep in Mind

As you plan for the coming of your baby and make all the many decisions that this involves, here are a few general guidelines that may stand you in good stead:

Try to keep your options open. This means having alternative plans to choose from, remaining as flexible as possible. For example, it's the rare baby who arrives exactly on schedule. Most come a week or two before or after the estimated due date, and some are even earlier or later than that. That time factor must be taken into account in arranging the initial help that a mother will have and deciding other matters. Remember, too, that after the baby is born you may see some things differently from the way you see them now.

Don't expect too much of yourself. If you don't get around to painting the kitchen or the baby's chest before he comes home, he will never notice. Pregnancy is a good time to start learning how to cut corners judiciously, as you will need to do a lot of it when you have an infant to care for.

Watch your priorities. It is more important for a woman to get the rest and relaxation she needs during pregnancy than to keep her home in apple-pie order. Money spent on an unnecessary frill for the baby might be better used for groceries, so that the mother-to-be has the nutritious diet that she needs. Whether it is a matter of finances or work to be done, husband and wife need always to set their priorities thoughtfully, asking themselves what is truly essential, what is less so, and what might be dispensed with.

Trust your judgment. In the days and years

ahead you are going to be exposed over and over again to conflicting advice and pressures. It will be up to you to decide how you want to do things, after weighing the available evidence. This doesn't mean that advice should not be listened to. Quite the contrary. Your maiden aunt Sue may have a point. In any case, she deserves a courteous hearing. But you must decide how you will lead your life and rear your children.

Of course, when parents are young and inexperienced, they are often prey to doubts: "Maybe I should have listened to my mother, instead of to the doctor, about when to start the baby on cereal; Pat's baby is so much bigger than mine." You will have to remind yourself that however carefully you inform yourself, however intelligently you evaluate the sources of your information, you will inevitably experience some regrets, have some bad moments. But even infants are remarkably hardy little creatures. In time you will feel more secure about doing things your way.

4 *No Parent Is Perfect*

WE ALL MAKE mistakes, sometimes from lack of knowledge or experience, sometimes simply because we are human. "If only I had known about demand feeding when my children were infants," a mother says wistfully. Another mother regrets that she did not play with her first baby more and pick him up when he cried. With her second child, she had sufficient courage to find out for herself that such treatment does not cause "spoiling." Still another young woman wishes daily for more patience. She does not believe in physical punishment, but when she becomes angry she occasionally hits her children and finds it hard to forgive herself afterward.

Unavoidable Hardships

Then there are all the hardships and heartaches from which we are powerless to protect our children: painful surgery; an unsympathetic teacher; death in the family; the "unfairness" with which nature sometimes parcels out ability among brothers and sisters; budgets that will not allow for that special toy, or outfit, or experience that even the least demanding child occasionally sets his heart on; danger in the streets; living in a neighborhood that offers no really safe place for children to play and encourages precocious sophistication—all the "slings and arrows of outrageous fortune."

Life Is Like That

In this chapter we will offer parents a framework, based on the latest thinking about mental health, in which to view their limitations and their children's difficulties realistically, without undue guilt or anxiety, but without undue complacency either. As we shall see, children do not require perfection. They can adjust to the fact that their parents are fallible and, in the process, learn something about human nature and about living. Given adequate support, they can withstand even severe hardships—those experiences that it is not within our power to spare them—and still turn out well.

For several decades now, the pressure has been on parents to a degree that does nobody any good. We shall look at some historical and other roots of this excessive pressure. We shall also consider some recent psychological findings that may help parents face their job with more equanimity; to see it as a long-range enterprise during which, though things go wrong from time to time, there will be many "second chances" to help their children and themselves acquire the strengths that make for emotional health.

Our Role

One reason parents often feel more guilt than they should is that our society tends to blame parents, quite unfairly, for all their children's problems. If a child has trouble adjusting at school, or lands in juvenile court, or exhibits any other kind of problem behavior, it is commonly assumed that the fault lies with his parents. "They must have done something wrong," is the usual reaction. Few people stop to wonder what the

school, or society, might have done differently Almost nobody considers the possibility that the parents are doing the best job possible under the circumstances and that the problem results from a multitude of factors over which they have little or no control.

It cannot be repeated too often that parents are not solely responsible for how their children turn out. The nature of the society in which families live—employment opportunities, the quality of housing, education, and health care available, neighborhood conditions, the climate of the times—all these factors crucially affect what happens to children, just as they crucially affect the lives of parents. Also, children are not equally easy to rear. Each presents a highly individualized challenge, which may vary in degree of difficulty from time to time. And each, as he grows, is increasingly responsible for making the decisions that determine the course of his life.

This is not to imply that we should stop blaming parents only to start blaming society or the child. Assigning blame is, at best, an unproductive activity. We need to be aware of all the complexities involved in rearing healthy children in contemporary society, and to seek new ways in which families can assist each other and society can give to both parents and children the support needed to minimize their problems overall and help them through crises when they arise. What is required is planning not only for more mental health clinics but also for a more livable world.

Children's Vulnerability in Perspective

Another source of excessive parental guilt and anxiety is the failure of the general public to appreciate children's ability to withstand stress. This failure has roots in history. Early in the century, when psychoanalysis was giving us new and profound insights into human functioning, it was rather commonly assumed that an individual's problems as an adult could be traced back to a childhood trauma, or emotionally disturbing experience, usually involving his relations with his parents. Though this idea that a single traumatic event will inevitably scar a child for life has now been discarded, many parents still are frightened. They worry about every move they make, every frustration that their child is forced to endure, fearful that one false step or trying event might somehow spell disaster.

We now know that an individual is affected by all that he experiences, both outside and within the family over a period of many years. There are repeated opportunities for him to outgrow problem behavior, with or without the help of others. It is the long-run, broad-range picture that matters, the sum total of all that he is exposed to. The occasional "mistakes" that all parents make are weighed in with everything that we, and others, manage to do right over the years.

Children are capable of successfully weathering severe shocks, such as the death of both parents, and even prolonged stress, such as that engendered by physical disability or poverty, if there are enough positive factors in the picture. Conscientious attention from some trusted adult does seem to be necessary all along the line, but an interested teacher, community worker, relative, or other parent substitute, including a brother or sister, may alternatively fill this role at various stages of a child's development, as is attested to by the biographies of a number of well-known persons.

Toward a New Definition of Mental Health

Until recently, nearly all of our knowledge about emotional functioning was derived from the study of persons who had problems severe enough to require hospitalization or cause the person to seek psychological help. An enormous body of useful information has been acquired in this way, but, not surprisingly, as it filtered down to parents, it tended to make them extremely sensitive to all the things that could go wrong, and by extension, all that they might "do wrong." Since, in addition, it was widely assumed that an emotionally healthy person was one who had no clinically identifiable psychological problems, child-rearing came to be viewed as fraught with a staggering assortment of potential pitfalls.

One can, certainly, gain valuable insights into what makes people emotionally healthy through understanding the problems of those who are not. Today, however, a fresh wind is blowing in the mental health field. A number of psychiatrists, psychologists, and others in related professions have been acting on the hunch that it would prove fruitful to study persons who have never sought psychological help and are considered emotionally healthy by those who know them well. So far, this view through the other end of the binoculars has shown that the persons who pass for healthy among their peers are not without problems in a clinician's eyes. Their childhood histories indicate that they tended to have as many, and in some cases more, serious difficulties than a sampling of persons who have needed therapy of some kind at some point in their lives. What distinguishes the emotionally healthy persons is their ability to keep going in spite of their problems, to fight through their difficulties, whatever they happen to be, and eventually grow out of them.

We cannot as yet (and may never be able to) pinpoint precisely what it is that enables some people to cope successfully with the emotional difficulties that all of us have from time to time, while others either break down or require professional help in order to keep functioning adequately. In psychological circles, the phrase often used to sum up this critical quality is *ego strength*. Psychological theory has it that the *ego* controls conscious behavior, in contrast to the *id*, the instinctual drives that come with us into the world, and the *superego*, the "conscience" that we acquire as we grow up. The id and the superego are at work mostly in "unconscious" behavior—slips of the tongue, for example, or a man's erection, or the risking of our lives in a rescue effort. Ego strength implies the capacity to reconcile the often conflicting interests of the id and the superego and to do whatever will enable the person to function in a way that best serves the totality of his needs. From the layman's standpoint, a wide variety of strengths, such as self-confidence, flexibility, joyousness, and determination, appear to be involved. The healthy person does not necessarily have *all* the strengths mentioned. In fact, one alone may be sufficient to get him through a bad time. For example, a child who early acquires the feeling that he is somehow special may throughout life retain enough confidence in his powers so that he can come through difficulties that would be devastating to a person less sure of himself. Another individual may manage to weather his problems because he has a special talent for enjoying whatever there is to enjoy in life. He (or she) is the person who, even when his world is threatening to crash around him, will respond with delight to a spring morning, a child's laughter, an invitation to a party.

Using Our Leeway Prudently

When mental health is seen as being relative, and as having to do with strengths rather than the sum of our weaknesses, it becomes clear that parents have considerable leeway in which to operate safely. We need not feel that we are walking a tightrope. The journey is going to be a long one, and we will have many opportunities to help our children make the most of their potential.

Problem behavior is, of course, always a problem for the child and for his parents. It calls for intelligent attention from parents. If, for example, a seven-year-old boy, who is normally fairly easy to live with, becomes tense and irritable at home and bridles at everything his parents say to him, we do not dismiss his behavior lightly, assuming that he is simply going through a "phase" of some kind. He may be, but we would want to find out what is occurring in his life outside the home that might be causing the problem. Is he having trouble at school, with the work or with his classmates? Has he become as touchy with his friends as with his parents? What interests or strengths does he have that we might draw upon in order to help him feel better about himself and relate better to us? Can we arrange for more fun things for him to do, with us, or with others?

Often parents know right away what is causing a child's difficulties. In fact, they may have been expecting problem behavior to appear. The coming of a new baby, for example, or a stay in a hospital, a move to a new home, and many other such potentially stressful experiences are often accompanied by problem behavior. Given time and sympathetic understanding (not to be interpreted as suspension of sensible parental controls), the child tends to outgrow problems brought on in this way.

Sometimes, however, parents are completely in the dark as to what could be upsetting their child. Problem behavior does not always have readily identifiable precipitating factors. If none are easily apparent, parents had best avoid worrying about what may have gone wrong and just assume that something is going on inside the child that is none of their business. Prying into a child's private feelings is never advisable, although, of course, one needs to be open to confidences if the child makes a move in that direction. Difficulties of this sort also tend to be outgrown in time when they are accorded the same common-sense sympathetic handling given more "understandable" episodes of problem behavior.

As long as a child continues to function adequately in most ways and to develop overall as children of his age should—that is, he does not markedly *regress*, become decidedly more babyish in every way—parents can afford to conclude that he will in time outgrow his difficulties.

However, if months pass without improvement, during which parents have done all they can to help their child find satisfactions in his daily living, then psychological help should be sought.

"Second Chances"

Children often develop personality traits that cause their parents concern. Personality seems to be the product of both inborn predisposition and the experiences to which a child is exposed. When an undesirable trait appears, it is not profitable to worry about what we might have done as parents to ward off this particular development. Probably nothing. But there is a great deal that we can do over the years to help our offspring grow out of personality limitations.

For example, the normal rivalry that exists between brothers and sisters often leads to one child's becoming unattractively bossy, or touchy about losing, or undesirably fearful about competing for fear of losing. It is well to remember that such traits can just as easily be acquired by a child who has no brothers or sisters. Sibling rivalry may call parents' attention forcibly to a child's personality disabilities, but, on the other hand, when such traits come to our attention early, we have that much more opportunity to help our child modify his behavior.

The art of accomplishing this is a delicate one. Adult criticism is effective only if a child feels good about himself in general and if the criticism is worded sympathetically—"I know why you feel like behaving that way, but . . . ." Humor helps, when it comes naturally. Even with young children, there is a limit to how often criticism should be repeated. Once the child gets the message, understands that we do not find his bossiness or some other aspect of his personality pleasing, the change that we desire will have to come out of his own wish to change. All we can do is continually provide him with evidence that we are an admirer of his.

Whether the change that parents hope to foster is relatively limited, such as helping a small child curb his bossiness, or more all-encompassing, such as encouraging a youngster to spread his wings and be less fearful about making mistakes, we are more likely to succeed if we direct our efforts generally toward helping the child feel pleased with himself and find life as satisfying as possible, rather than making a big issue of his shortcomings. As we will see in the following chapter, children can often be browbeaten or frightened into obeying the limits that we set on their behavior, at least when we are present, but real personality change occurs on a deeper level and is never brought about through punishment.

If, for example, we try to root out five-year-old Andy's tendency to boss by punishing him whenever he exhibits the tendency, his frustrated aggression is likely to show itself in some other problem behavior of an even more troubling kind. To become less bossy, Andy has to see himself as a competent little person, recognize that there are more attractive ways to get what he wants, and feel supported in the effort to handle his aggression acceptably, not feel simply that he is always prevented from having his way.

"Second chances" of all kinds may come early in childhood or much later. For example, the mother mentioned earlier, who feels that her oldest child was shortchanged on attention during his first year, has found that as a preschooler he shows no signs of being the worse off for it. In the space of only a year or so, either his parents—more sure of themselves and of what small children need—have managed to give him whatever compensation he required in the way of extra patience and time in order to develop into a delightfully secure and inquisitive toddler, or other factors have combined to produce this result. On the other hand, another child who was handled similarly as a baby remained, much to his parents' chagrin, somewhat inhibited and cautious until adolescence, when suddenly he too blossomed. Whether the change is due solely to his parents' continuing efforts to bring him out, or whether it is at least in part the result of certain fortunate, rewarding experiences outside his family, nobody can say for sure. And it doesn't matter. Despite what both sets of parents now refer to as their shortcomings when their children were babies, the two children are doing well.

Learning from Mistakes

Parents are often understandably upset when they come across material that convinces them that they erred in how they fed, or weaned, or toilet-trained their child. They may hesitate to read about rearing children younger than theirs presently are, for fear of discovering that they did something wrong.

But, as we have seen, mistakes can be corrected or compensated for, once we recognize them. Each day offers fresh opportunities to affect the long-range picture. A parent who is aware of the various stresses that his child may have been under in the past, whether avoidable or unavoidable, is in the best position to recognize and make good use of all his second chances. For example, a father who did not realize, when his son was four and five, how strained father-son relations often are at this age and why, may, as a result of reading about the preschooler's sexual development, make a special effort to go out to his preadolescent boy and have the patience and understanding needed to maintain a sound relationship with him during the difficult years of adolescence.

The fact that we do not always live up to our ideal of what a parent should be can also teach us, and our children, how to make do within our limits. Parents differ, of course, in how much they can take in the way of whining, or sibling baiting, or messiness, or noise, or lack of sleep, but we all have our limits. For each of us there comes the point when we have had it. The sooner we learn to recognize when that point is about to be reached, and what frustrations are most likely to move us toward it, the better we will be able to function within our limits.

A mother who knows, for example, that she is at her worst on days when the weather keeps her children indoors might talk over the problem with her husband and friends and come up with some fresh ideas about handling the situation. Similarly, if there is a particular time of day when she is most prone to blow up, she can look into the possibility of rearranging the family's schedule with the hope of improving matters. If it is an aspect of the children's behavior, such as bickering, that triggers parental explosions, this can be talked over with the children. They may become better at keeping some of their disagreements out of parental earshot. They may also appreciate and learn to respect a timely warning, such as, "You know it gets on my nerves when you do that."

Knowing and trying to work within our limits in ways such as this will not accomplish wonders. Sometimes, however, it can improve the quality of daily living enough so that everybody feels a bit better about themselves.

Even explosions have their uses, if they are appropriately handled and do not become the major way of coming to terms in a family. They set the record straight about what each parent is like and can take. Nearly all parents, including those who do not believe in physical punishment, have occasionally hit their children in anger and done other things that they regretted. When parents can admit their regret to their children, say "I'm sorry," no lasting harm is done. Such incidents may clear the air and enable both parent and child to calm down and proceed more reasonably. The child realizes that even adults are fallible, that they lose their tempers and can be pushed into doing things that they do not really approve of. Knowing this may relieve the child of some of his guilt feelings about his own "bad behavior." A fitting apology assures the child of his parents' love and their respect for him as a person, however small or dependent on them he may be. It also drives home the importance of an apology, not only as a means of asking forgiveness of others and being restored to their good graces, but also as a way of forgiving ourselves for our failings. If we ask their pardon, children are generally quite touchingly quick to forgive us for mistakes made in the heat of anger.

Asking What We Should of Ourselves

We are entitled to be philosophical about our shortcomings and about the misfortunes from which we cannot protect our children, but they deserve the benefit of the strengths we have to offer. Knowing our strengths helps us to employ them well and also to see our weaknesses in perspective.

The fact that we take care of a child day after day, provide him with meals, clothing, and shelter, show concern for his welfare, monitor his comings and goings, is one such strength. Its importance is often underestimated by parents, and by children while they are growing up. The parents may wish that they had more money to spend on food, clothing, shelter, and recreation. If so, the child will certainly add to their frustration by asking for, or obviously wanting, things they cannot afford. And, since much of the friction that occurs in every family results from the fact that parents care enough about the child to monitor his comings and goings and other behavior, this, too, is rarely viewed by either side as a blessing while it is going on.

Yet there is ample evidence that children not only need but also appreciate our routine efforts to look after them, and parents who do the best they can with the available money get full credit for this. Rules and regulations formulated with a child's best interests at heart may be disparaged and resisted, but they are nonetheless correctly perceived as signs of love. Our concern for our child and the elementary daily care that we provide continually contribute to the child's sense of security and his all-around emotional health.

But beyond this, a child has other needs that should not be slighted. Parents can use their individual strengths in many ways in meeting their children's needs. Children need intellectual stimulation and enjoyable physical activities that help them become well coordinated, and they thrive on having fun with their parents. We always do a more effective job when we take into account what we do well and really like to do, along with the child's individual interests.

For example, a mother who is a great reader, and knows what exposure to books can do for children, discovered to her dismay that she intensely disliked her three-year-old's taste in books. When it became apparent that he felt the same way about hers, instead of dutifully rereading to him books that she detested, she fell back on an ancient device and asked if he would like her to tell him a story. He acquiesced. The first story, about a man shipwrecked on an uninhabited island, went over so well that it had many sequels. Storytelling came to be a popular accompaniment for mother and child while preparing meals, doing the laundry, even waiting in the doctor's office. By the time the boy entered school, his mother had delighted him with her freehand renditions of many of the classic adventure yarns and fairy tales. He had a large vocabulary, good attention span, and soon was reading facilely "for information," which was what interested him. He had been "intellectually stimulated," painlessly for all concerned, and apparently added to this his mother's enthusiasm for such activity. Quite beside the point, but worth mentioning, when the boy was twelve he came home from school one day and said to his mother with considerable consternation, "I guessed that some of those stories you used to tell me came out of real books, but I always thought you made up Robinson Crusoe."

As parents we have to be willing to extend ourselves frequently to meet our children's needs and further their overall development. Sometimes the challenge is cut and dried: a sick baby has to be held or rocked; the request, "Will you test me on my spelling words?" calls for just that. Often, however, we have some choice in deciding how to meet various challenges, and in these instances the child gains more when we are truly enjoying what we are doing.

Making and Living with the "Hard" Decisions

In the course of rearing our children we will inevitably be called upon to make decisions that involve choosing the lesser of evils, or weighing the needs of one member of the family against those of another member or against the needs of the family unit. Making these decisions is among the more trying experiences that parents have to endure.

For example, if for financial reasons the mother of a young child is suddenly forced to seek employment, she will need to keep down the cost of having her child cared for while she is at work. It is likely that she will be unable to afford what she considers ideal arrangements. She must choose the arrangement that appears to have the fewest drawbacks for the child, for herself, and for the rest of the family and hope that she has correctly evaluated the pluses and minuses of every option open to her. Similarly, parents may have to weigh the advantages of a husband's accepting a better job, involving an impressive rise in both position and pay, against the disadvantages of having to move away from a city where their seven-year-old deaf child has many friends and is attending an excellent day school for the hard of hearing.

Nobody can tell us what our decisions should be in circumstances of this sort There is no "right" choice. It is we who are in the best position to assess what price each possible course of action is likely to exact and what compensations each has to offer. We must be prepared for the fact that whatever our choice, we probably will not get home free. There will be regrets, second thoughts, times when we will have to eat our words. Occasionally, as with arranging for substitute parenting for a small child, we may find ourselves facing the same dilemma over and over again, with little to be learned from previous bad experiences except that our society does poorly by families in such straits. The best that can be hoped for is that when two parents are involved, they will provide emotional support for each other. Such support from a spouse, or relative, or close friend can make all the difference.

Once upon a time, nearly all parents rested secure in the conviction that, having made such difficult decisions to the best of their ability, the outcome was in the hands of God, who "read our hearts" and judged us by our efforts, not their results. This kind of assurance that one does one's best, then rolls with the punches, is enormously guilt-relieving and strength-providing. Here modern psychology joins hands with religion. We can do no more than our best for our children. Much is out of our hands. But doing our best should be, in itself, rewarding enough.

5
What Makes Johnny "Behave"?

WHEN WE ARE having trouble getting a child to take a bath, or leave his sister alone, or come to supper, or set out for school on time, or do any one of a thousand other things that we want him to do (with justification), we may tend to feel that discipline is all child-rearing is about. Everything else seems as nothing compared to the job of "making Johnny behave."

Discipline is indeed important. But it is a teaching process that encompasses a great deal more than policing a child's behavior. The core question is not "How do I make my child mind?" It is "What kind of person do I want to help my child become?" Only when we have our ultimate goals clearly in mind can we think discriminatingly about what limits to set on a child's behavior and how to enforce them.

Six major goals that need to be taken into account will be examined in this chapter: (1) keeping children safe; (2) nurturing self-esteem; (3) inculcating respect for the rights of others; (4) encouraging growth toward independence; (5) the development of good "inner controls" (that is, the child's ability to regulate his own behavior); and (6) building healthy attitudes toward authority. We shall see how keeping these goals in mind can help a parent function more intelligently in setting and in enforcing limits. Finally, we shall discuss some of the thornier issues that parents always seem to want to talk about, issues such as "permissiveness" and punishment, and look into how they are related to the goals listed above.

Keeping Children Safe

First of all, of course, we need to keep our children alive and in one piece, so the child's safety is always a consideration of paramount importance. It governs the amount of weight that we can afford to give to other goals, such as encouraging independence. Usually it begins to figure in parents' thinking about discipline very early, about the time a child starts to creep or crawl rapidly.

Parents not only seek to keep their newly mobile baby safe, but generally at this point they begin trying to interest him in helping with the job by teaching him to avoid potential hazards to his safety: stoves, hot-water faucets, and all the rest. This teaching picks up momentum as the baby becomes a toddler. Since he will, as he grows, take on more and more responsibility for keeping himself out of harm's way, parental teaching about safety is of critical significance. We do not want to make our children overly fearful or timid, but they must have a healthy awareness of the dangers that exist in their world.

If we are too protective, the child may not develop the capacity to properly assess potential hazards and become skillful at avoiding or handling them. He may lose his drive to venture and explore, to trust his judgment and try his wings Or he may rebel against the restrictions with which we hedge him about and grow deaf to all warnings. On the other hand, if we give him too much leeway and do not go to reasonable lengths to protect and instruct him, we invite trouble on two levels: he may seriously injure himself; and he may not acquire the respect for his person that every child needs to have.

From the very beginning, our efforts to keep our children safe tell them that we value them, and, by extension, this helps them value themselves and their physical well-being appropriately. Thus, while we are ensuring their safety, we are building their self-esteem. The correlation between these two factors is especially high and especially important during the first few years of life.

In addition to being realistic about danger and restricting our children enough but not too much, we have the job of helping them learn, at the appropriate time, how to handle certain potential hazards safely. The toddler who is prohibited from stepping off the curb alone will grow into the child who must be taught how to cross neighborhood streets and then busy intersections, and, finally, how to ride a bicycle in traffic. Sharp knives, matches, tools, a host of other useful equipment that he is initially forbidden to touch, he must eventually become skillful at using. Acquiring the skill he needs to be trusted with activities of this sort also contributes to a child's self-esteem and his growth toward independence.

Nurturing Self-esteem

Our approach to discipline affects a child's self-esteem in other ways. The manner in which we customarily enforce limits makes a difference here. If we are constantly harsh and punitive, show no respect for the child, he is unlikely to feel much respect for himself.

No child is too young to have his opinion and feelings respected, even when he must be prevented from acting upon them. Thus, a two-year-old bent on climbing the steps of the playground slide, or throwing sand at another toddler, or sampling the dog's dinner has to be stopped, of course. But he deserves to be given an explanation of why he is being stopped, not just yelled at or hit. After all, he is only doing what any two-year-old might do. We need to recognize this truth and somehow convey to him our awareness of it. He is not "bad," or "stupid," or "impossible to teach." He is simply a small child who has much to learn and needs a lot of patient help with doing it.

Many factors outside the realm of discipline also affect a child's self-esteem, notably the way in which feeding and weaning are handled and the overall quality of "mothering" a baby receives during his first year of life. However, the way in which limits are enforced exerts a continuing influence in this area, starting when parents first begin to "discipline" their children. Since genuine respect for the rights of others appears to grow out of esteeming oneself, it is desirable that a child's experiences during his early years contribute to building adequate self-esteem. Yet, parents always have the opportunity later on to help a child improve his opinion of himself. An understanding, nonpunitive approach to helping children operate within reasonable limits, however late parents get around to trying it, can do a great deal to heighten poor self-esteem.

Inculcating Respect for the Rights of Others

Parents actually begin much earlier than they may realize to help their child accept the need for limits. Even if they start out feeding their infant on demand, within a month or two they ease him into a more regular pattern of eating and sleeping, sometimes helping him wait a bit for a meal, sometimes rousing him for a feeding. This is the child's initial exposure to learning to adapt to other people's needs. Over the course of the first year, if the baby is sensitively handled—encouraged to make some adaptation, but protected, to the extent possible, against prolonged or severe frustration—he gradually becomes increasingly capable of accommodating himself to the needs of various members of the household. The groundwork is laid for him to accept many kinds of limits dictated by the fact that other people also have their rights.

During the preschool years, parents tend to put a great deal of stress on teaching their child to respect the rights and property of others. Sometimes they expect too much of the child too soon. A child needs time and sympathetic supervision to learn to share, to respect the rights of others, to wait his turn, and to resolve his conflicts with his peers fairly and nonviolently. Parents need to side with the child's desire to have his way, as well as preventing him from harming others and helping him see the legitimacy of other people's needs when their interests conflict with his.

We have noted already that until a child genuinely respects himself, he does not seem able to develop a genuine appreciation of the rights of others. He may make some superficial progress in learning socially acceptable behavior, and this in itself can contribute to his self-esteem. But to solidify such gains and stimulate further growth, he will need experiences that enhance his opinion of himself and his feeling that a fair proportion of the time he gets what he wants. Nature apparently decrees that our self-interest be adequately served before we can care deeply about the interest of others. This suggests that both the limits we set on our child's behavior and the methods we use to enforce those limits will affect our success in teaching him to respect the rights of others. We need to avoid pushing him too hard or too early to be "unselfish." We also had best avoid disciplinary measures that shame, or denigrate, or constantly enrage him.

Encouraging Growth Toward Independence

We have examined how concern for our children's safety circumscribes the goal of fostering independence. However, there are many ways in which parents can stimulate growth in independence within the boundaries set by the need to keep a child safe.

Becoming independent stems from having *adequate freedom to make choices*, as well as freedom to venture out into the world on our own. It is a way of *thinking*, no less than doing.

The more opportunities children have to choose between reasonable and safe alternatives, the better they become at problem solving and the more *independently* they are able to function overall. Even very young children can be allowed some freedom of choice about what they will eat, wear, and do: "Would you rather go to the store with me before lunch, or after your nap?" . . . "have a grilled cheese sandwich or peanut butter and jam?"

So, too, offering a child alternative courses of action, when he cannot be permitted to do things exactly as he wants to, is helpful: "I can't let you ride your bike to the movies on a weekday. Traffic is too bad. But I'm willing to give you bus fare. Or you and your friend could go on Sunday."

Protecting a child needs to be combined with giving him maximum independence and freedom of choice within certain understood limits. In this way he does not come to rely on his parents and others to do all his thinking and choosing for him.

Of course, it is important that limits be frequently reviewed as a child grows and becomes increasingly competent and responsible. Increasingly, too, the child can be involved in the family decision-making process. He is more likely to respect limits that he has participated in setting.

Mostly, children let us know as they become ready for increased independence. They strain at the leash. However, since some children tend to push for more freedom than they can handle, and others need to be encouraged to take on more than they push for, it helps if parents know what is generally appropriate behavior in this area at various stages.

The Development of Good "Inner Controls"

From the start, parents are usually aware that a crucial goal of discipline is helping their child to take over the responsibility for regulating his own behavior, that is, to develop what are often referred to as "inner controls." Increasingly as our children grow, we cannot be present to police all their actions, nor can we have the assurance that other adults will do so. We want to be able to count on their being as careful and decent when we are not looking as when we are.

The question of what makes Johnny "behave" when we are not around is an important and complex one. Partly, children normally have a strong desire to please their parents, and so, much of the time, they make a conscious effort to do as they have been told. Partly, too, they discover early that at least some of the limits we set on their behavior make very good sense. Though a toddler may not be able to understand that streets can be dangerous, the three-year-old sees that we have a point. As a child's own experience bears out parental judgments, his parents gain considerable credit with him as being generally trustworthy guides. This shores up his respect for all their warnings and prohibitions and reinforces his conscious drive to obey them on the whole.

But still another factor, a significant developmental process, will influence the child's behavior when his parents are not around. During the preschool years he begins to identify with his parents, to make their standards of behavior his own. He acquires a conscience, which, often, "speaks" to him much as his parents would if they were present. He feels guilty about sneaking money for a popsicle from his mother's purse after his mother has said "No" to his request for it. Even if his mother does not discover his misdeed, his conscience will not let him get away with it scot-free. Similarly, his conscience will reward him—he will feel good about himself—if he resists the impulse to steal or whatever the temptation may be.

Thus the "inner controls" that we all want our children to develop will grow out of their feelings about us, their opinion of our judgment, and our own behavior. This points up a further reason for avoiding harsh physical punishment in enforcing limits. Harshness will not enhance the child's natural desire to please us, which is a big factor that we should have on our side. And through the process of identification, the child who frequently experiences harsh physical punishment may become "brutalized," may tend to deal similarly harshly with other children. The significance of parental example, of which this is one instance, will be explored further in the next chapter.

The older a child becomes, the more capacity he generally gains to "think for himself." That is, standards of behavior acquired as a result of his parents' teaching and his early identification with them are reworked in the light of his experiences in the community and his exposure to other people he admires. His "inner controls" become, indeed, his. He matures into a product of his times, and also into his own creature, though he will continue to reflect many of his parents' values.

This, too, parents should want. Too rigid a "conscience," one that does not grow with the child, is not healthy. We want our children to use their capacity for reasoning to the fullest possible extent. We can help them do this by being careful to offer honest explanations for the limits that we set on their behavior. For example, we have every right to insist that our five-year-old stop bouncing on our bed, or the sofa, but we would be wise to put our reason in terms primarily of what this does to the furniture, rather than saying, "You'll hurt yourself."

Building Healthy Attitudes Toward Authority

War-crimes trials of the seventies have given many parents pause. We do not want to rear children who always follow orders blindly. Yet there are situations in which it is important for everybody concerned that "orders" be accepted immediately, with no questions asked. We don't argue with a fireman directing traffic. Also, if we see that our child unknowingly is about to shut the door on the cat's tail, we hope that he will heed our urgent "Hold the door open" and not hear from the cat what provoked our arbitrary-sounding command.

These two considerations are not incompatible. Children can learn that sometimes it is important to "hop to" immediately and ask questions later. And they can combine this with an awareness that questioning authority appropriately is not only a right but a duty in a democracy. Both society and parents need to teach them this.

A child's parents are the first authority figures that he encounters. If they are kindly and democratic, if they will hear out his side of an argument (though not necessarily be persuaded by it), he tends to respect authority generally but question it sensibly. If his parents do not constantly order him about as if they were drill sergeants—"Come here. Get to the table. Watch your brother."—a child soon learns that an "order" signals an emergency, and he tends to respond with alacrity. In a generally democratic household, children become sensitive, too, to changes in the tone of our voice, whereas in a home where they are accustomed to being continually shouted at, they seldom recognize when an adult voice conveys special urgency.

Much that was said about parents' role in helping the child develop sound inner controls applies to building healthy attitudes toward authority. The two goals are very closely allied.

"Permissiveness"

Exercising too little control over a child is quite as bad as going to the other extreme. Children need to have adequate limits set on their behavior for several reasons besides their safety and our sanity. They may interpret their parents' failure to exercise authority appropriately as lack of love. After all, it would often be easier to let children do as they please than to take the time and energy needed to enforce reasonable limits. Children know this, really. They recognize correctly that our efforts to control them mean we love them.

Then, too, children are aware of their inexperience and vulnerability. They know that the world can be dangerous. They are also often frightened by the strength of their own emotions, their rage, jealousy, destructive impulses. In order to feel emotionally secure, they need to know that we will not let them do anything that might endanger their own safety or hurt others. If we do not offer them guidelines for moving about safely in the world, plus assurance that we will prevent them from behaving destructively until they become able to control themselves, the world will seem to them an unduly frightening place. They may run wild, hoping in this way to feel stronger, less fearful—a variation on whistling in the dark. Or, interestingly, they may become extremely timid and inhibited, showing us in this way that they are setting on themselves the limits that their elders have failed to set.

The concept of handling children permissively, giving them more freedom of choice and whenever possible reasoning with them rather than laying down the law, originally grew out of an effort to remedy some of the problems caused by the kind of parental authoritarianism that characterized child-rearing practices of the late nineteenth century. "Authoritarian" parents were widely blamed during the early decades of this century for many of the ills that beset both their children and the world, ranging from inhibitions that interfered with healthy adult sexuality to war. Certainly, the authoritarian personality is not one that most Americans would wish to perpetuate. However, some conscientious parents misinterpreted early psychoanalytical insights to mean "*Never* frustrate your child," rather than "Avoid over-frustrating your child." This led to the commission of unfortunate excesses in the name of "permissiveness," including the failure, often, to impose reasonable limits and enforce them. As a result, the word "permissiveness" currently has a very bad *cachet*, though it is only "overpermissiveness" that should be avoided.

Labels are rarely useful. They almost always lead to oversimplification. It is clear, for example, that war is the result of many complex social forces operating on the international as well as the national level, and that to view it as the product of assorted child-rearing practices simply obscures the immensity of the problem. It is time to give up making scapegoats of parents when we encounter difficulty finding solutions to the complicated social ills that beset us. So, too, parents need to give up thinking of child-rearing in terms of labels. There is no one simple solution to the job of bringing up children. A vast variety of psychological principles are involved. We need to beware of extremes of all kinds and to avoid the temptation to look for simplistic answers or "sure-fire techniques."

Punishment

For reasons already examined, harsh physical punishment, at best, makes no contribution to a child's healthy development and, if often repeated, may interfere with the socialization process. Children can be cowed, through constant physical punishment, into staying out of their parents' hair at home, but this does more to encourage them to become clever at avoiding detection than to behave acceptably. Various studies of juvenile delinquents indicate that they tend to have in common a history of frequent brutal physical punishment by parents or other caretakers.

This does not mean, of course, that brutal physical punishment *causes* juvenile delinquency, but only that it is not a way of preventing it. Parents who beat their children are usually themselves hard-pressed not just by the child, but by their life in general. Having to cope with the child, or the children, is simply the last straw. Instead of blaming them, society needs to help them and their children. A pioneering effort in this direction is described in *The Battered Child*, edited by Ray E. Helfer, M.D., and C. Henry Kempe, M.D. The book is emotionally hard to take, but citizens interested in the problem of the "battered child" may want to read it.

One more point about physical punishment: slapping a toddler's hands to set up a conditioned reflex against running into the street or engaging in other hazardous activities is not brutal. Some parents find they must resort to physical measures such as this during the early "unreasonable" years. Also, as we have seen, the majority of parents will probably occasionally hit their child in anger, even though they may strongly disapprove of physical punishment. Although this represents an admission of failure on the parent's part, a temporary giving up on trying to resolve human conflict rationally, other things being equal, it does not damage the child.

Now, what about other forms of punishment? It is imperative that a child learn gradually to accept the consequences of his behavior, which means that "punishment" in one form or another probably has to be as routine a part of growing up as it is in the adult world. If an adult accidentally breaks a neighbor's window, he will either offer to pay for it or can be brought into court and forced to do so. If a child damages the property of another, he needs to understand that restitution of some sort is expected. If he cannot afford by himself to pay for the damage, he can contribute something from his allowance, if he has one, or perform a chore for his parents who will do the paying, or for the person whose property was damaged, or he may have to forgo an expensive toy or outing that he had been looking forward to.

Although we have to make every effort to prevent our children from committing some acts of which the potential consequences are serious—running into traffic, habitually being truant from school (or perhaps, habitually failing to do homework)—we cannot and should not protect them from the discovery that all of us must pay a price for our mistakes, our errors of judgment, our forgetfulness, stubbornness, and all the rest. However, parents need to set the price their children are required to pay for any given misdeed as instructively as they are able.

Ideally, the closer a punishment reflects the way things are in the adult world, the better. For example, if a child fails to get dressed in time to leave with his brother for the movies, it could be instructive for him to miss the movie. When adults are late for a train, they miss the train. On the other hand, we do not want to be unduly harsh with our children, and, besides, we don't *always* suffer when we are late. So we might content ourselves with a warning the first time, and the second. But if we are to be good teachers, when lateness threatens to become habitual, we must make the child accept the consequences of his dawdling.

If we simply spank a child every time he misbehaves significantly (especially if the spanking comes several hours after the deed), or deprive him of watching his favorite TV program, or lock him in a closet (which qualifies as inhuman treatment if the child is afraid of the dark), we may teach him more about our power over him than about the advantages he stands to gain through governing his behavior more maturely. Still, there is no perfect approach to the problem of meting out just punishment. It is an issue that troubles society no less than parents. Circumstances will force us sometimes to actions that, in hindsight, we see as too harsh, or too lenient, or totally wide of the mark. Nonetheless, if a good proportion of the time we try to be reasonable and fair, our children will give us full points in this area. And if, mostly, through our words and the punishments we impose, we make it clear that we are not exercising power arbitrarily, but attempting to teach, our child will learn what he needs to learn.

Helping a child avoid behavior that he might later regret is always better, of course, than seeing that he accepts the consequences of his shortcomings afterward. But it is not always possible. The best we can do is try to exact reparations for misbehavior that will help the child function more adequately in the long run, that is, truly "rehabilitate." Calling punishment by some other term, such as "deprivation of privileges," hardly makes the problem go away, though it may relieve some parents of their guilt feelings about it. And to say that we should never punish, but only "help children accept the consequences of their behavior," is also mincing words.

Standing Our Ground

Parents are often told to be "friendly but firm." That, too, is not always possible.

Pushed enough, any of us is likely to become for the moment quite obviously unfriendly, as the word is usually defined. Being forgiving is perhaps the quality that we most need to couple with firmness. It can wipe the slate clean after tempers cool.

Should we *never* give in, once a struggle over limits is under way? Well, it is hardly advisable to reward a child's temper tantrum or similar histrionics by letting him have his way simply because he wears down our resistance. We are inviting more trouble the next time around. Also, it is quite possible

that the fight the child is putting up springs from the fact that he is essentially in conflict about what he really wants to do and needs us to make the decision for him. If we give in under such conditions, he may be left feeling unprotected, frightened of his powers.

Still, every statement about rearing children has its exceptions. Parents always have to play each scene by ear. If they become convinced that they were too quick to say "No," they may decide to change course in midstream. But if this happens more than very occasionally, something is wrong either with their ability to say "Yes" or with their ability to stand their ground under fire.

Once in a while, every parent, out of weariness, or worry about more pressing matters, may say to a child, "Do whatever you please, just leave me alone." If this throwing in of the sponge is a rarity, the child will very likely be quick to sense that his victory is a Pyrrhic one; to get his way this once is not nearly so important to him as being ensured of parental protection in the future. He may ask, "What's wrong?" or "Are you okay?" or perhaps say, "I just changed my mind. I don't think I want to do that after all." In any case, no harm is apt to come anybody's way, and parents may gain the respite they needed but couldn't bring themselves to ask for.

Being firm should not be construed as antithetical to being flexible. There are times when limits need to bend or be forgotten altogether. Landings on the moon currently take place rather infrequently, and eclipses of the moon will, in the foreseeable future, continue to be few and far between. But events far more prosaic than these may warrant a temporary moratorium on accustomed limits. Children understand, even without being told, that exceptions are only exceptions. From the fact that we make exceptions, they also can learn that it is sometimes desirable to reorder one's priorities. As one parent said, "If we aren't going to allow our ten-year-old daughter to stay up to see what happens to her favorite baseball team when the game goes into overtime, then what are we telling her to expect of life? That enjoying baseball is for boys only? That you can't have fun except at the expense of jeopardizing your health or doing your duty?"

Mothers and Discipline

There has been a strong tradition in our society of relegating to fathers, or some other male, the job of dealing with children's misbehavior. This has often been coupled with the notion that women tend by nature to be rather more easygoing and lenient with children than is really good for them. Even today one hears it said that unless children have a man to keep them under control, they tend to be undisciplined. Is there any truth in this assumption?

Available research suggests that it is not the sex of the parent but his or her approach to the challenge that matters. There have always been women who, of necessity or by choice, assumed full responsibility for helping their children learn to behave and succeeded admirably. There have always been men who preferred to leave the job to their wives. There have always been couples who shared the responsibility equally, with admirable results.

An understanding of the process of discipline is the crucial factor. Women are potentially as capable as men of setting reasonable limits and standing firm on them. The idea that men are innately better suited to the job than women probably sprang from the false assumption that discipline requires the exercise of brute force, whereas in reality what is required is good judgment—and self-confidence.

Fortunately, the policy of pushing off onto fathers the unpleasant job of meting out punishment when children misbehave is becoming a thing of the past. Most couples today recognize that this policy is neither fair to fathers nor good for children. It inevitably prevents punishment from being the kind of learning experience that it should be.

In many situations, of course, two parents together will find the going easier than one alone. When a child is being difficult, two parents who see eye to eye can give each other a great deal of needed reassurance and support. But this does not mean that a single parent, of either sex, cannot manage. One important reason that some women when left on their own are inadequate in this area is that they are convinced that no woman is up to the job. Society has made them feel that they are doomed to fail. It is a cardinal principle of psychology that a person is unlikely to be successful at any task that he or she does not feel capable of handling. The implication, then, is that in one-parent families, that parent's opinion of his or her ability to cope with the challenge of discipline is of great significance.

Accepting the Need for Continuing Confrontation

It would be ever so lovely if there were a way to bring up our children so that they would always see the reasonableness of our demands (our demands would, of course, always be reasonable, since we have read up on child-rearing) and do their growing up without forever bumping up against us.

From what is currently known about psychology, children, in order to grow into healthy adults, not only need reasonable and caring parents or parent substitutes and a reasonable and caring society, but they also need to be able, while they are growing up, to bump against sympathetic teachers, to test with impunity the validity of all that is offered to them as their "culture," that is, the sum total of what humanoids have learned in the several million years since a thumb was first opposed to a forefinger and tools started to matter.

In primitive societies parents and children did not, and do not today, live in peace. Is a certain amount of friction between the generations somehow necessary to the evolutionary process, much as the opposition of thumb and forefinger seems to be?

Nobody knows for sure. But for now, it would be irresponsible to suggest that parents, by virtue of being better informed or wiser, could eliminate such friction altogether. The struggle over limits, or, in a broader sense, the friction engendered by the socialization process, is seldom absent for long in any household, and it tends to be especially intense at certain growth stages. Since parents are older and more experienced, it is up to them to prevent the struggle from becoming a running battle of wills, or a cold war.

6
Parental Example: How It Rubs Off

OUR CHILDREN PICK up a great deal from us indirectly, by virtue of the kind of people we are, or, as a psychologist might say, by virtue of how we function in our capacity as "role models." In the preceding chapter, we touched on the way in which a child's identification with his parents, especially in the early years, contributes to this process. But throughout childhood and even into adult life, our children will, consciously and unconsciously, model their behavior in innumerable situations on the example we have set them.

The more mature our children become, intellectually and emotionally, the more likely they are to evaluate our functioning as role models critically—in the best sense of the word. That is, they recognize that their parents are not infallible, and they accept us as useful models in some ways but not others. To a parent who bridles at the idea that he might have limitations, this can be threatening. Look at it this way: if all goes well, our children can become able to profit from our strengths and let the rest go.

What Is a Role Model?

"Wow," says eleven-year-old Mark, "I really admire Mr. Moore as a teacher. You know what a drag singing assemblies used to be. Well, he's got us all taking turns using instruments like drums and triangles and rattles, and everybody actually looks forward to it, even the worst troublemakers. He has this idea that everybody has musical ability, even people like me who can't carry a tune. I sure hope when I grow up I have his trick of handling kids."

Mark's admiration for Mr. Moore suggests that the teacher's approach to "handling kids" will be an important influence in Mark's life in the years ahead. Mr. Moore is a role model who may, for example, affect Mark's functioning as a parent, not to mention his attitude toward music and possibly the arts in general.

"I'm delighted to hear that Nina gets along so beautifully with Frannie's younger brother, but it surely comes as a surprise," Nina's mother informs the mother of Frannie. "If you knew what goes on here at home between Nina and her own brother, you'd hardly describe her as a 'born peacemaker.' Though things have improved since he started school, Nina still often acts more like a child his age than a nine-year-old. Some days I think I spend most of my time just trying to help them play together happily."

Here we have a familiar story: a child whose typical behavior at home does not fully reveal the skills she shows away from home, skills that reflect the influence of a parent as a role model. Nina's ability to play the "peacemaker" at a friend's house is an enormous tribute to the way in which her mother has handled the difficulties that inevitably arise between a brother and sister. Nina is not yet up to relating to her brother as if he were just another child. He is her brother. With other children, however, she functions as she has seen her mother function at home, exhibiting the same urge to help everybody "play together happily" and being unusually good at accomplishing it. Nina's mother's impact as a role model on her daughter's way of relating to other children is strikingly evident.

As we have seen, parents are not the only important role models in their children's lives. Teachers, relatives, family acquaintances, youth leaders, movie stars, close friends, any admired individual may, in this capacity, contribute significantly to our child's development, much as Mr. Moore is contributing to Mark's. For obvious reasons, however, parents tend to wield the most influence as role models.

What Rubs Off

Children see us whole. While Mark consciously admires Mr. Moore for "the way he handles kids" and will consciously learn from him something about that, much as one can learn about specific gravity through certain physics experiments, he may also pick up other qualities and mannerisms from his teacher. His walk, for example, or some of his gestures, or his taste in movies may, at least for a while, reflect Mr. Moore's. At one point in history, young people by the droves tended to move and talk like James Dean.

The influence of parents is also pervasive. Our children's behavior may mirror ours in innumerable ways, from how they talk on the telephone to their attitudes toward the political party in power. In areas that matter, such as political allegiance, the child will usually rethink his position in time, and, as a result, may change. He may consciously decide to modify other parental values, decide that one or both of his parents set too much store by neatness, or the social graces, and try to be less of a perfectionist in these areas.

But some very crucial attributes—such as flexibility, responsibility, regard for the rights of others, even traits such as wit, irony, a love of fun, a sense of "calling"—seem to be passed down from generation to generation, because the example of one parent or the other, or both, is irresistible—and because the child perceives what has rubbed off as a strength.

The Effectiveness of Models

As parents we spend a lot of time consciously instructing our children. We teach them how to use the telephone and the public transportation system, where babies come from, how to make change, make a bed, prepare a meal and clean up after it. We correct their manners, sometimes their homework, and over and over again their habits of dress and personal hygiene. Without in any way minimizing the value of all such teaching, it must be said that the example we set our children is at least as important, sometimes more so.

For instance, Nina's mother has probably done a lot of talking to her daughter about why the girl's actions sometimes irritate her brother, etc., etc. The mother apparently felt that the talk was largely falling on deaf ears. Yet the child, when away from the uniquely charged atmosphere that surrounds the nuclear family constellation, adopted with great skill the role she had for so long seen her mother play. So it often is with manners. A child whose etiquette at table leaves much to be desired when he is within the bosom of his family may do himself and us proud when visiting away from home, if his parents, through their behavior, have given him a clear picture of what good table manners involve.

When it comes to such matters as honesty or respect for the rights of others, parental example is especially crucial. A kindergarten teacher tells of a conference she had with the parents of a five-year-old who was unable to make friends because of his domineering behavior and quickness to hit. As she was explaining, as tactfully as she could, the difficulties the little boy was having in relating acceptably to his classmates, the father interrupted to say, "He knows better than that. We've taught him how to behave. You just have to be firm with him. At home if he doesn't do what we tell him to, he knows he'll get a licking." The teacher does not feel that she succeeded in indicating to the parents how their treatment of the boy was mirrored in his approach to other children. With her help, and the help of some of the children, he has learned to curb his tendency to bully, but she worries about what will happen to him when he comes up against the more impersonal, less sympathetic handling he is likely to encounter in first grade.

When Actions Speak Louder Than Words

"What did your teacher say when you told her you hadn't finished your social studies project?" a mother asks her fourteen-year-old son upon his return from school.

Somewhat sheepishly the boy admits having told his teacher that he had left his work at home but would bring it in, without fail, tomorrow. "It's not exactly a lie," he tells his mother as she starts to upbraid him. "I did leave my paper at home, and I will finish it tonight and get it in tomorrow. Besides, I usually hand my work in on time, and my teacher knows it."

His mother lectures him on the need to be scrupulously honest and to be willing to "pay for our mistakes," then grudgingly says that she will not report him this time, but that if she ever hears of his doing anything of the sort again, she will have to "take appropriate steps."

That evening when the boy tells his mother that Mrs. Bernard is on the phone and wants to speak to her, his mother says, "Tell her I'm not in. I know what she is calling about. She wants to know how my raffle-book sales are going, and I haven't had the time to sell any tickets yet."

Explaining Our Behavior

It happens that the mother in the preceding story recognized that there was some inconsistency between her handling of the "Mrs. Bernard incident" and her reactions earlier to her son's handling of the "social studies project incident." As soon as the boy had finished relaying her message as directed, she said to him, "I know you're busy tonight with that social studies paper, but I think I owe you an apology for some things I said, and didn't say, this afternoon. I'd like to discuss this further when you have time."

During the discussion that occurred the next day, mother and son hashed out all their feelings about "white lies" and "stretching the truth." At one point the boy said, "I know you're conscientious, Mom. You don't have to tell me." To which the mother replied, "I know you are, too. That's where I got off on the wrong track yesterday. I shouldn't have lectured you about honesty, just asked why you didn't ask your teacher for a one-day extension, considering that your work is usually done on time."

The boy allowed that he had taken the easiest way out and wasn't exactly proud of it. "Like me with Mrs. Bernard," his mother said with a smile.

"And I'm paying now, feeling a little guilty," the boy said.

"Me too," said his mother.

As a result of the talk, the boy came away not only with the assurance that he need not hide his peccadilloes from his mother, but also with heightened awareness of the ambiguity that pervades much of life. His mother turned what might have been evaluated by the boy as an instance of parental hypocrisy into a maturing experience. By catching herself in time and presenting a role model of a different sort, she conveyed to her son a great deal through her actions and also through her words.

This is not to say that parents need to be constantly on the alert to inconsistencies in their behavior and diligent about explaining them. Children tend to take our minor inconsistencies in stride, judging us by the long-run picture. The boy meant it when he told his mother that he knew she was conscientious. Explanations are useful, on the whole, only when they open the way to needed dialogue, as in this case.

Age Makes a Difference

Very young children tend to be purists, and literal-minded to boot. Our behavior around them may need to be adjusted accordingly. Although they have to be helped to progress beyond this point, such growth usually comes slowly. The ability to accept ambiguity does not begin to be much in evidence until about nine or ten. Even a rather trivial parental white lie may be confusing to a five-year-old. He has trouble viewing such an act in proper context. So, too, parents' "kidding" of each other, even when it really is all in fun (which it often is not), can confuse a young child. He takes all our words so literally.

Many a mother, as she dishes up her three-year-old's supper, will take a bite and smack her lips in evident delight, knowing this is an excellent way to trigger the child's interest in eating and encourage him to try a "new" dish. (A few years later the child will have become sophisticated enough to see through any dissimulation in this area.) Similarly, if we want to encourage a young child to react to his grandparents and other relatives affectionately and courteously, we are careful to talk affectionately and respectfully about them in the child's presence. Disparaging comments and criticisms, however merited, are saved for times when we are alone.

Do we really need to be such goody-goodies around our children when they are little? Well, yes and no. It probably helps to extend ourselves a bit through the preschool years: watch our language; avoid white lies and other actions that a young child might misinterpret; be meticulous about observing the rules, regulations, and customs that we want our children to observe; and yes, give Aunt Maude the benefit of the doubt. If it is all that difficult for us to practice what we preach well enough to gain credibility in a small child's eyes, then perhaps we need to question some of the preaching we do.

On the other hand, even young children do not need perfect models, and they can usually detect hypocrisy. All along we have to be honest with our children, respond to all their questions with truthful answers geared to their age and maturity. Often we are required to clear up, as best we can, confusions engendered by adult behavior, including our own. Life being what it is, our children will inevitably be exposed to ambiguous, or outright undesirable, role models before we feel they are "ready." This, when handled forthrightly, need not harm the child and may be a maturing experience.

A young social worker recalls that until she was ten her father never had a steady job, and the family was on welfare. She was carefully schooled to tell anybody from the Welfare Department who might appear at their door that she did not know her father's whereabouts, although in fact he lived with the family. She does not think the experience was corrupting. She shared her parents' conviction that this one lie was, regrettably, necessary, but that otherwise lying could not be condoned. Nor did she feel that her parents were not to be trusted because they were obviously deceitful in this one respect.

Normally our children let us know when we need to let our hair down with them a bit more: "Hey, Dad, we can cross now. There's not a car in sight." Or, "How can you stand Aunt Maude? I hate going to visit her." Or, "Johnny wants me to come to his house to play on Saturday and I don't want to. How can I get out of it?" Or, "Jesus, haven't you ever heard that word before?"

Little by little over the years, our youngsters have to come to terms with us and with life "with all the warts on." Insofar as we have any power to control that process, we play things by ear, catering as need be to the "purist" in our children in the early years and opening them up to ambiguity gradually as their behavior or experience dictate.

Sexual Identity

A great deal of serious questioning is going on these days about the extent to which differences between the sexes are culturally imposed, not simply biologically determined. Parents will naturally have their own ideas about how much differentiation between the male and the female role is desirable, but we need to be clear about the distinction between sex roles and sexual identity.

Boys and girls become aware by about age two of the anatomical differences between the sexes. If a child is valued by his parents the way he comes, he will ordinarily value his sex-determined attributes; that is, like being a boy, or a girl, along with liking himself as an individual, and look forward to functioning as a man, or as a woman.

However, the "if" in the above paragraph is a big one. Since boys and girls are customarily treated quite differently, both sexes get the message very early that being male or female involves far more than the anatomical differences with which we come into the world. When the doctor says, "It's a boy," or "It's a girl," the newborn is, in most cases, being assigned not only a sexual identity but also a rather rigidly defined role to play. This can complicate the child's journey toward accepting himself as a worthwhile human being who is also a member in good standing of the sex to which he biologically belongs.

Although from the moment of birth we rear our child as "a boy" or "a girl," the child does not begin to identify significantly with his or her sex for several years. Meanwhile, he, or she, is testing the temperature of the water: Is it good to be a girl? Is it good to be a boy? How are girls treated? How are boys treated? Are women nice? Are men nice?

The answers to these questions, which he obtains largely through observing his family, will affect how he comes to terms with his sex during the preschool years. From age three to five or six, the little girl ordinarily moves gradually toward identifying primarily with her mother or a mother substitute, and the little boy makes a similarly crucial identification with his father or some other male whom he admires. When this process goes well, the boy emerges proud of being male and able to appreciate women. The girl emerges equally proud of being female and equally able to appreciate men.

Both parents (or their surrogates) influence this process. In the case of a little girl, for example, her attitudes toward men are shaped not only by how her father reacts to her personally and to her mother, but also by what her mother thinks of men and how she relates to her husband. This same intricate combination of forces shapes her feelings about being a girl. Does her mother seem to enjoy being a woman and lead a satisfying life? Does her father not only make his daughter feel valued but also value women in general?

The sexes today seem in many instances to be moving toward a spirit of egalitarianism and mutual respect such as the world has seldom, if ever, seen before. It will be interesting to see how this affects the young child's coming to terms with being male or female. Will healthy adjustments be more often and more easily arrived at during the preschool years—and adolescence? Will the drama of the small child's attraction to the parent of the opposite sex be worked through with less strain on all involved? As sex roles become less rigidly defined, will the child be confused about his sexual identity, or simply relieved of unnecessary anxiety? Only time can give us the answers to such questions. All that can be said with certainty is that in order to achieve healthy sexual identity, children need to see, in the lives of the models they are exposed to, convincing evidence that one can both enjoy being a member of the sex to which one is assigned and appreciate—not exploit or fear or continually feel hostile to—the other.

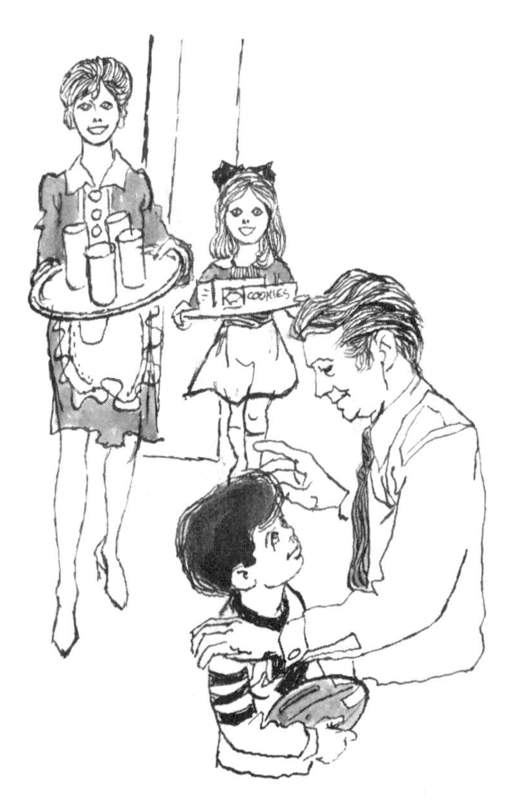

Hidden Assets

The ease with which children often seem to follow parental example can be disconcerting. As one young mother of two put it: "Sometimes I think what my children do is pick up all my bad habits and none of my good ones." It does sometimes seem that way, partly because we tend to be especially sensitive to irritating traits in our children that we recognize as present in ourselves.

Hearing our daughter muttering imprecations under her breath as she bustles about getting ready for a party, we go to her and inquire, "Is there anything I can do to help?" Back comes the answer, in almost the identical tone of voice with which we have so often responded to similar inquiries when we are bustling about the kitchen, annoyed at ourselves because something we were cooking was not going exactly as hoped for: "Yes. Leave me alone."

If we are wise, we do as requested, pondering the perversity of fate that robs our daughter, like ourselves, of the ability to be charming when frustrated by personal limitations. If we are lucky, however, we may receive from our child, as she is leaving, a hug and a kiss and a charming, "Sorry I was cross with you earlier. Forgive?" At least something good has been picked up with the bad.

Occasionally, our children's behavior may make us aware of aspects of our personality that we have previously been blind to. The annoying tendency of a five-year-old to weasel out of all his difficulties by blaming everybody and everything except himself suddenly has a familiar ring. When did we last hear something like: "It was Toby's idea to have a pillow fight and he missed the pillow so the window cracked"? Weren't we just this morning saying to that same child: "Now see what you've made me do; all your begging to have a friend over has got on my nerves so I've broken my favorite vase"? And how was it that we greeted the boy's father when he returned from work the evening before? "It was your idea to have stuffed peppers some time, so I hope you're not going to complain about dinner being late."

Although seeing how our example rubs off is sometimes painful, it may enable us to alter our own behavior as we try to help our children alter theirs. Our children are usually less interested in faulting us for our shortcomings, especially if we admit them, than in relating to us as positively as we make it possible for them to do.

The Whole Picture Counts

In the course of growing up, children are not only exposed to many models other than their parents, but they also have many opportunities to "unlearn" what they have picked up earlier from the example of parents and others. Parents themselves tend to grow in the process of rearing their children. This is often reflected in changes in the kind of example they set. A rather authoritarian young father mellows, learns to listen, and actually begins to enjoy it when his children show "spirit." Family relationships take on a new tone. An anxious "mother-hen" of a young wife relaxes gradually, discovers that her children seem remarkably able to thrive without being constantly fussed over, and loses her compunction about spending time pursuing her own interests. Her children show a corresponding lessening of anxiety, and of guilt.

Changes of another kind also occur. As our children mature, they become better able to build constructively on parental example in some ways, modify a bit here, look for a different kind of role model there, make allowances overall. Inevitably, they will be different from us in a number of respects, but this need not mean that they will no longer value our love or our opinion. Mutually rewarding relations between the generations is possible at every age. We will turn our attention next to how good communication facilitates this.

7
Is Anybody Listening?

SENDING MESSAGES IS nothing. We can do it any time, without even having to fall back on words. A raised eyebrow, a slammed door, lighted candles on the dining table *say* something. But will the message be received by the person for whom it is intended? Will it be correctly understood? Responded to? Will it invite further interchange, not simply punctuate an ending?

Communication implies, to use a currently much overworked word, some kind of *dialogue.* Even dialogue need not necessarily be verbal. The infant pushes the nipple out of his mouth, and his mother puts him on her shoulder for burping. This done, she offers the nipple again, and if the child still pushes it away, or merely toys with it, she assumes that he has had enough to eat for now. That constitutes very good dialogue, or communication. A twelve-year-old leaves his muddy boots on the rug just inside the front door, and his mother, after washing them off and drying them, deposits them on his bed. The next day the boy removes his boots before he enters the house, carries them into the bathroom, cleans them, and deposits them on the toilet seat. That is both efficient and rather witty dialogue.

Words Are Important

Still, man is a verbal animal. Nonverbal communication is almost always more open to misinterpretation than communication that offers us some verbal clues to go on. A young mother who believes in the significance of "body language" admits that she can hardly wait for the day when her infant will start to talk. "I read him fine when he's all smiles," she told her own mother, "but I feel so helpless when anything goes wrong. I'm just beginning to realize how marvelous it is to be able to ask, 'Where does it hurt?' and get some kind of answer."

Conceivably, the boy in the earlier anecdote might not have noticed that his mother *cleaned* his boots before placing them on his bed—some parents of fourteen-year-olds may be thinking it a miracle that a child that age should be so observant—and might have taken offense, rather than the hint. If this had happened, however, the mother could have explained her misinterpreted attempt to avoid being a nagging parent. And obviously it was only because the boy had been told many times, in words, what we do with our boots, *please,* that the nonverbal reminder worked.

As our children grow, spoken language plays an increasingly important role in our ongoing dialogue with them. Both we and they will continue, often, to respond to nonverbal cues. Parents need to be especially on the alert for such cues when relations are strained, as happens sometimes in any family. But ironing out conflicts and problems has to be a verbal activity. Therefore, from the time that the toddler is able to speak up, we need to do all in our power to encourage his feeling that this is safe and desirable for all concerned.

Children Must Feel Respected

Respecting a child is at the core of communicating well with him. Children can be easily discouraged from telling us what they think and feel. If they discover that we cannot brook any argument or questioning of our judgment, they tend to keep their opinions to themselves, at least when they disagree with us. They may sulk, visibly, but dare not go much further. A pattern of this sort established in the early years is hard to break later on, though not impossible if parents become genuinely eager to hear what their child has to say and can tolerate dissent.

Granted, it is often trying and not infrequently impossible to reason with a preschooler. There is a point beyond which it can become ridiculous to pursue the effort. Extended conversation about why it is time now to pick up our toys, or go home, or come to supper, or go to bed seldom serves any useful purpose. After offering the obvious explanation and pointing out compensations that may help the child make the desired transition under his own steam—supper will include a favorite dessert; going to bed will bring a story—we may be reduced to picking the child up and carrying him off to where it is time for him to go.

Such incidents, even when accompanied by tears, do not violate our child's feeling that, fundamentally, we respect him. Nor will they dampen his self-assertion or his insistence on being given a reason, however unpalatable, for being required to do this, that, or the other.

Granted, too, all parents have their off days. Any "why?" somehow seems one too many, and we fall back on the time-honored "Because I say so," followed by—if it is really a bad day—"Don't talk back to me," or "You'd better get a move on if you know what's good for you." As has been emphasized so often, it is what we are usually like at our best, not what we are occasionally like at our worst, that counts.

Children *know* when they are respected. At a very young age they can already sense when we empathize with their delights, their sorrows, their fears, their unwillingness to give in to superior strength, their hurt pride, and all the other signs of humanness that even the very young of the species are heir to. It is mainly through empathizing with a child's feelings all along, letting him know through our words and other ways that he is entitled to his feelings, just as we are not only entitled but required to ride herd on his actions, that we convey respect while standing our ground. Unless we provide this kind of climate, worthwhile communication between parents and children cannot occur.

It Takes Two to Tango

All along, too, parents must take the lead in avoiding useless wrangling. Four-year-old Janie is told that she may not go to the local playground with other children in the neighborhood unless an adult is to accompany them. Her comeback is the classic one, "You never let me have any fun." If her parents rise to the bait, mutual accusations are likely to be exchanged for quite some time. Almost any parent can write the script.

But suppose that Janie's mother and father ignore the child's provocative remark. Her father responds, "I'm sorry, Janie, but we both feel it's not safe at your age, since the playground has no attendant. You'll just have to be satisfied with going when your mother or I or one of the other parents can go along."

Oh, yes, Janie will probably put up a fight for a while, but if her parents refuse to argue the point, her disappointment and anger, lacking new fuel to feed on, will subside sooner than they otherwise would. One cannot do battle for long without a real opponent.

So parents are supposed to be saints? Turn down all those stinging challenges to square off that children of every age let fly when they are frustrated? Be deaf, alike, to the young child's "I hate you" and the older one's "Wow, you sure know how to muck up things!"?

It is, of course, more than any of us can manage all of the time. We sometimes cannot resist retorting in kind, rather than simply standing firm on an issue. We want our children's love *and respect.* It is hard for us to be eternally mindful of how their position, their dependency on us for so much for so long, can cause resentment.

Benevolent and democratic though we may be, we are still more powerful than they are. They are sensitive to this difference even when we are not, and it rankles. Our ability to take their verbal flak without returning it not only helps keep the lines of communication open but also moves our children toward mature tolerance for authority and a healthy view of how authority should be exercised.

Being Good Listeners

Not that we need submit to a tongue-lashing. The attempt to communicate rationally sometimes has to be suspended until a child calms down. A warning, such as, "Look, you're goading me," may help an older child collect himself. Younger ones may have to be temporarily isolated in a room by themselves. In some such fashion every child has to learn that our willingness to hear his side of an argument presupposes that he will exercise a certain amount of common decency in presenting it. There may be times, then, when children have to earn the right to be heard.

But family life should be made up of much more than heated confrontations. Being a good listener in general is crucial to knowing our child. What does he think of himself? Of others? Of life? He will usually tell us if we are available to listen. In the process we may be told more than we care to know about hockey standings, or the doings of some performer who has become the latest idol of the young. To dismiss his enthusiasms out of hand, however, never to try to share with him the excitement that he feels about the goal made in the last seconds of the game or the remarks made by his current television hero is to limit our chances of hearing what he has on his mind that we would very much like to know.

Why They Don't "Listen"

If a child begins to feel that communication with us is generally unpleasant, that is, consists mainly of fault-finding and admonitions, he soon tends to tune us out. Of course, every parent is occasionally perceived by his child as a nagging parent. If this is the exception rather than the rule, the child communicates his irritation to us in no uncertain terms: "Okay, okay, okay," or, "YES, Mother," or simply, "PLEASE stop nagging."

Messages of this sort suggest that it is time to take a different attitude, or a different approach, to getting those beds made, that room straightened up, or whatever else it is that we want done. Humor may help. Often it is the complaining tone of our voice, more than what we actually say, that our children object to. That they *tell* us they object implies that communication is not in real danger of breaking down, unless that is all they ever tell us.

A certain amount of necessary reminding has to go on in every household. However, the less annoying it is to the child, the more likely it is to accomplish its aim—and not just create resistance to doing anything we might suggest.

Sometimes children literally do not hear what we are saying because they are wrapped up in what they are doing at the moment. A child may even look up dutifully from his book or cookie-making or whatever the activity may be and nod acknowledgment of our message, yet fail completely to absorb it. Reprimanding the child later for his failure to "listen" is less useful than reminding ourselves to be sure we really do have his attention the next time we have something important to say.

Of course, children have their own opinions about what is really important. They may not, for example, "listen" to us when it comes to such matters as making their bed regularly or "wearing something more appropriate," yet they may value our judgment in other areas. When they do not respond to good-humored urging on our part, it is wise for us to do some reflecting of our own. Is the matter worth making an issue of? By pressing it, might we jeopardize our child's regard for our views on more significant problems, such as the value of education, or the hazards involved in using drugs.

The extent to which our child is influenced by what we say about issues that he, too, considers important will depend, in large measure, on the overall quality of our relationship with him. Too much carping about relatively minor things can impair the quality of that relationship.

Getting Our Message Straight

If our own behavior does not jibe with the messages we send, our children may not get them straight, or, if they do, may not set much store by them. Thus, if we tell a child when we return from a trip that we missed him, yet cannot find time to sit down with him and hear what he did while we were gone, even the souvenir that we picked up for him at the last minute at the airport may not convince him that he was much missed. Insisting that our children attend religious services every week, though we ourselves rarely, or never, attend any kind of religious service, invites confusion about our values, as well as the value of religion.

Since everything that we do with our children is essentially a kind of communication, children are not, as emphasized earlier, seriously misled for long by occasional minor deviations between what we say and what our behavior appears to indicate. Our children are not going to stop respecting the property rights of others altogether just because, once, we climb over a fence clearly marked "No Trespassing" in order to picnic on the bank of a nearby stream. Nor will they lose all respect for the law upon seeing us tear up a parking ticket issued to us in a foreign country that we are about to leave. Our deeds and our words are always viewed within the context of all that they know about us.

Still, it is important that we get our message as straight as we can all along. The trespassing and the tearing up of the parking ticket should be explained to the children on the value basis that we explain them to ourselves. If we find that we cannot do this in terms that the children can understand or accept, it may mean that such incidents should not occur, at least until the children are older. Sometimes, having to put our principles into words is a sobering experience.

Mixed Messages

Parents may, without realizing it, constantly send mixed messages that seriously confuse their children. For example, a girl of eighteen, the only child of parents who are schoolteachers, severely disappointed them by refusing to go to a prestigious college to which she was admitted. Instead, she has taken a job as a sales clerk and plans soon to move into an apartment with two girls she has met at work. She explained her decision this way to a longtime friend: "After I got admitted to [name of college], all I ever heard about was the sacrifices my parents were making to give me the kind of education they always wished they'd had. I was supposed to be so lucky, and so grateful. It started me thinking. They've had my future mapped out for me since practically the day I was born, and they sure never missed a chance to tell me all they were doing without so that I could lead the life *they* wanted me to. It took me a long time to realize everything was *their* idea—the music lessons, summer camp; they even picked the colleges for me to apply to. I have no idea yet what I want to do, except there aren't going to be any more sacrifices 'for Carol's sake'."

In the fall of 1971, the small town of Harrison, New York, was aroused by the mutilation and killing of thirteen animals in the Children's Zoo. The three high-school boys responsible for the killings were quickly apprehended. They turned out to be the sons of policemen. One father accompanied his son, sixteen, to the police station to surrender. The other two boys, brothers aged sixteen and seventeen, were brought in by detectives. Their father was quoted in *The New York Times* as describing his sons as "young and not that malicious." He went on to say: "The press should be ashamed of itself. Why don't they cover something important like the Vietnam War instead of a couple of rabbits getting killed?"

Nobody, of course, will ever know all the many factors that interacted to cause the boys to do what they did. One wonders if perhaps the atrocities of the Vietnam War, along with various sensational crimes such as the Manson murders, may have contributed by helping to bring about a social climate in which the "unthinkable" has become thinkable. Certainly, one admires the father who accompanied his son to the police station. That the other father seems to belittle the horror of the act in which his boys were involved gives the impression that these brothers may have been receiving mixed messages about where to draw the line. Obviously, far more is at work here than the possibility that a parent might have been sending mixed messages, but that possibility haunts the mind.

Getting Their Messages Straight

Children sometimes give us through their behavior important information that they cannot or do not put into words. If the parents of Carol, the eighteen-year-old mentioned earlier who has gone to work instead of to college, had been more sensitive to their daughter's behavior, they might have noticed that she always seemed a somewhat depressed child, and they might have wondered why being so "fortunate" did not make her happier on the whole.

The reading of behavior is especially necessary with little children, whose verbal facility is, after all, limited. A four-year-old, for example, cannot tell us, indeed probably does not realize, that she has been disturbed by a particular television program, but her behavior at bedtime says something is amiss. With only this clue to go on, we may make an educated guess about what upset her and eventually elicit a crucial question: "Why do Daddies hit each other, Mommy?" Aware that she calls every man a Daddy, we try to help her straighten out her reaction to an animated cartoon, and resolve not to let her watch similar programs alone for the time being.

With older children, the nonverbal messages that we pick up may be more difficult to decipher fully. The fact comes through that *something* is disturbing our daughter or son, but what? Since older children, with justification, tend to resent anything that smacks of prying, we can only be available for confidences if offered, and, perhaps, expose the child to opportunities to move in new directions. A mother reports:

Edith was really impossible the summer after she graduated from high school. We didn't know whether it had to do with boys or getting a summer job or what. We knew she followed up some leads on jobs that didn't work out. But we believed her when she said she liked the idea of being able to rest up before starting college and just do a little babysitting, enough to pay for a crafts course she seemed very eager to take. So we thought it was boys. But her father heard of an agency that specializes in getting jobs for teen-agers, so he told her, "I know you're probably not interested, but here's the name and here's the telephone number and here's how you get there."

The next day we had a new daughter. I could tell by the way she walked in that it was all right to ask what happened. "Well," she said, "I was scared stiff, but this woman at the agency liked me. At least, she set up some interviews for me, and I've got a job. It's not much money, and I can't take my crafts course, but I'll be a sales clerk in this great shop and help make some of the leather stuff."

The job didn't turn out to be all that perfect, but I think it was the answer for Edith right then. Any job might have been. She stuck with it. What floors me is how could she have been so scared of job-hunting after all those college interviews. I never thought of it.

Another mother has a somewhat different story to tell about getting a child's messages straight. She and her husband had decided that their fourteen-year-old son would not be permitted to go out for his school's football team, though they were willing to allow him to join the soccer team. They tried to explain to him their reasons for feeling that football was dangerous at his age, offering him several articles from medical journals to read, which he spurned. According to the mother, for two weeks during which they steadfastly refused to sign a slip permitting the boy to play football, he put up a battle such as they had never been through before. Usually rather easy to get along with, he was so nasty at home that she and her husband could not even say, "Dinner's ready," without receiving a contemptuous reply. Then the soccer season started, and things gradually returned to normal. The boy, always good at athletics, did well at soccer and seemed to enjoy it.

But the parents dreaded the approach of the next fall when once again they would be asked to sign the slip permitting their son to play football. They discussed whether, considering the way the boy was filling out as well as growing taller, they possibly should give in this time. The mother says: "If he had pushed for football, I'm afraid we would have signed." The father admits having asked his son, "You're not interested in football this year?" and receiving the reply, "Like you said, Dad, it's not worth the risks in high school." Both parents believe that their son was actually in conflict himself the first time around and had to make certain that it was his parents' doing, not his own, that kept him off the football team.

Children often battle their hardest when part of them does not want to win the fight. Parents are sometimes flabbergasted by the suddenness with which a child who has been fighting tooth and toenail to get his way may accommodate to a firm parental decision. Often this means that the child was being pulled in opposing directions and really needed his parents, whom he perceives as more experienced than he, to make the choice for him. The messages he sends do not mean, "Give me what I am asking for," but, "Help me make up my mind."

Getting Through to Each Other

Perhaps what good communication is all about is leveling with each other absolutely, not being pressured out of thinking what we think, yet always respecting each other even when we disagree. This way, though the chips may sometimes fly, we tend to stay in touch.

Some parents apparently cannot entertain the possibility that their children might be right and that parents could be wrong. On the other hand, some parents never seem to feel entitled to their convictions. In between, there are a vast lot of us who rock along with what we feel sure of and what we are unsure of; our children cause us to change our opinions sometimes, and sometimes we change theirs. Sometimes we agree to disagree. Always, most of us live with the knowledge that we are going to be old some day and will want them really to want us. We also live with the knowledge that, for their sake, we cannot afford to back away from our convictions in the hope of currying future favors. We keep trying to communicate honestly. The overall influence that our views have on our children will depend in part on them and in part on the world we rear them in. And that we have to live with, too.

8 *Tapping A Child's Potential*

PARENTS ARE LIKE mirrors constantly confronting the child with an image of what he is like and how he is doing. Naturally, the child always hopes the mirror will tell him he is the fairest one of all. If things go well for him during the early months of his life, that is pretty much the message he gets. Who can resist a smiling baby? Even the postman, the policeman at the corner, will have a try at showing off their power to evoke those delicious squeals and gurgles that make us feel we have a way with babies. Dozens of mirrors give the baby the word that he is the fairest. Then he becomes older and able to get into things and is evicted from Eden.

Of course he has to be. Each of us is only one among many, and we are no better than we are. Every child has to learn to go with that.

A Good Self-image Is Essential

However, as we help our children discover what they truly are and are capable of becoming, we need to remember that a child cannot learn to accept his limitations or discover and develop his strengths and talents unless, overall, he feels good about himself. The importance of nurturing children's self-esteem has been dealt with elsewhere, in another context, but it must be reiterated here. Those mirrors must at all times show the child that he is a worthwhile person, or he cannot make productive use of any other message they reflect.

To give just one example, a seven-year-old who is a poor sport needs to be helped to see how his behavior looks to others and how he has to modify it if he wants to get along better with his peers. His parents may find, however, that in order to help him change they must first ask themselves some questions: Why does the boy have so much difficulty with losing? What are the roots of his excessive need to "win"? Does he perhaps need help with arriving at a different definition of success? How can he be helped to feel good enough about his powers in general so that losing, when he has to, will matter less to him?

A father whose son had this problem found out that calling the boys' attention to his poor sportsmanship, no matter how tactfully it was done, accomplished nothing.

He and his wife talked the situation over and decided to try a different, indirect approach. They arranged for the boy to have judo lessons at the local "Y." At first their son tended to brag rather unattractively about the new skill he was learning, but they refrained from criticizing; they concentrated, instead, on finding opportunities when they could honestly praise the boy. His mother became aware that his coordination seemed excellent for his age and commented on this whenever the occasion arose. His father found time to take him and some other youngsters bicycling regularly, which considerably improved the boy's physical prowess and his social life. Although he still has more than the usual trouble with losing, he is making some improvement in this area and is more readily accepted by other children. His touchiness has diminished enough so that his parents are now able to talk frankly with him about being a good loser.

Knowing How Children Develop

Different as every child is, children the same age have a great deal in common. They tend to be coping with similar developmental challenges, and this means that their parents have similar kinds of behavior to contend with. In other words, there is a detectable master pattern in children's growth that, to some extent, every child hews to.

Being acquainted with this pattern helps us know what to expect of our children at every stage. Of course, through observing other children in the neighborhood, parents get some impression of what children of a given age tend to be like in general. Unless our experience with a particular age group is very broad, however, we may be led astray by some of the individual differences that we come up against personally.

Our Linda, at three, can count to three. Her friend, almost the identical age, readily counts to ten and seems to understand what the numbers mean. Is our child backward in this area? Should we work at teaching Linda to count? Actually, Linda is progressing as well as should be expected when it comes to understanding numbers. Her friend just happens to be a bit advanced.

How about Ronald, who at age four still expects his parents to dress him, although he seems bright enough compared to his four-year-old playmates? Should Ronald's parents relax and assume that the boy will begin to dress himself when he is ready? No, a four-year-old can and should do this most of the time. Ronald's parents need to look for more effective ways to encourage their son to take this step.

All along, we are required to make judgments of this sort in order to help our children progress at an optimal rate. Although children do seem to have an inborn push to grow not only physically, but in every way, it is now generally accepted that we do not just sit back and assume that a child will move ahead as he "becomes ready." Unless our expectations are appropriate—we neither expect too much nor settle for too little—healthy growth may slow down or stop altogether.

The Badge of Competence

But why does it matter, except to Ronald's parents who are stuck with dressing him, whether the boy learns to do this now or later? He seems to be progressing all right in other areas, and his playmates are unlikely to notice or care that Ronald is a bit behind in this one way.

It matters because every developmental step that a child takes adds to his sense of "mastery," or feeling of growing competence. This is crucial to his concept of his powers. The more he is able to do, the more he feels capable of attempting and learning.

Just as children know whether or not they are respected, so they know when they are functioning as well as they should be. Although Ronald's playmates may not realize that he still has to be dressed by somebody else, Ronald himself over a number of months has been becoming aware, in various ways, that his behavior in this respect is babyish for his age. No child is pleased with such a view of himself. Ronald may already have begun to reveal, as yet too subtly for his parents to recognize, that he is not really happy about himself.

While our children may cling desperately to some particular babyish behavior, part of them always wants to be helped to give it up. Their pleasure when they finally succeed is usually very evident, and, often, they become noticeably more mature in a variety of other ways as well.

Parents are often struck by the extent to which progress in becoming toilet-trained, for example, is accompanied by more mature behavior all around. "Jeannie even looks so much older now that she's mostly dry in the daytime," says the mother of a two-year-old. Every developmental step forward of this nature tends to be marked by similarly dramatic evidence of overall growth.

Keeping Expectations Flexible

Yet, all children tend to develop somewhat unevenly. And all have their ups and downs. What a child can do today he may not be able to do tomorrow, or next week. Parents need to take in stride a certain amount of unevenness and of occasional regressing, and be not too rigid in what they expect of their child in the way of age-appropriate behavior.

But where does that leave us when it comes to getting Ronald to dress himself? We have now been informed that he should be doing this, that he knows he should, and that the longer he is permitted to lag behind, the more chance there is that his concept of himself may deteriorate. On the other hand, we also have been informed that children tend to develop somewhat unevenly, and that parents are supposed to make suitable allowances for unevenness and for ups and downs.

Beautiful. If that is not an example of putting the screws on parents, what is?

Think. The two propositions are not mutually exclusive after all. The first suggests how a knowledge of child development helps parents set reasonable goals for their child, developmentally. The second indicates how they can go about helping their child attain such goals in a reasonable fashion. If Ronald were simply very slipshod about dressing himself, one would attribute it to "unevenness." That he never tries suggests that he is somehow blocked and that different approaches to the challenge are in order.

There is some evidence indicating that children tend to respond well to challenges that their parents, or other caretakers, view as unavoidable. It appears that, often, trouble arises because parents are unsure of their ground. Their own uncertainty is communicated to the child, who interprets it as meaning that he has a choice in the situation. Once Ronald's mother is convinced that it is actually best for her child that he start dressing himself, her changed attitude may have a decisive effect. Simply saying, "Your clothes are laid out on your bed. You're big enough now to put them on yourself," and then leaving the boy to his own devices may bring the desired result fairly soon.

However, Ronald's mother should be prepared to accept occasional backsliding gracefully, responding to his "You do it today," with "All right, I'll help." Children of every age (even after they are "grown") need the reassurance that they can, if they need to, retreat temporarily into more immature behavior and a more dependent relationship with us. Allowing them these breathers from time to time enables them, overall, to push ahead.

Knowing Our Child's Own Way of Doing Things

Each child weaves his own individual variations on the master pattern of development. Parents usually begin to get a feeling for this personal pattern rather quickly. Some children, for example, seem to develop at a consistently steady pace. They master new skills gradually. Other children grow in spurts. Just when we are beginning to believe that Danny will not be ready for some time to read, or ride a bike, or take on a paper route, suddenly he romps ahead as if all the while, when he seemed to be marking time, he was really somehow preparing himself for another leap.

There are fast starters and slow starters, quick-change artists and children who prefer to take their time moving from one activity to the next. And, of course, there are marked differences in the activity level of individual youngsters; some children, from birth, can keep on the go longer than others and appear to need less sleep.

Knowing our child's special way of growing and of doing things often affords valuable clues to how he can best be helped to fulfill his potential. Teachers frequently welcome such information. A Danny, for example, presents a somewhat different kind of challenge to teachers than the youngster who progresses at a steadier pace.

Knowing What Our Child Is Coping With

On the whole, children, like adults, can give their best to a new task only when they are not faced with too many other trying demands at the same time. Thus, if a child is adjusting to his parents' getting a divorce, it would not ordinarily be desirable to transfer him to a new school if it can be avoided. Similarly, one does not start trying to toilet-train a child immediately after he has acquired a new brother or sister.

Common sense tells us this. We do not allow difficult challenges to pile up on a child if we can help it. If a youngster is having to put up with some stressful experience such as moving, or hospitalization, or illness in the family, we try to protect him as best we can from additional, avoidable stress. We also tend to be protective when we can see that the child is going through a bad time, even though we do not know what it is in himself or his environment that is giving him trouble.

The instinct to be protective under such conditions is inherently sound. Yet there are times when a fresh challenge, which though trying in some respects might be very rewarding in others, can help a child in his struggles to handle unavoidable pressures. This is a little akin to fighting fire with fire, of course. So parents should always weigh the risks carefully and be prepared to react flexibly.

For example, four-year-old Martha was having a hard time adjusting to the birth of a baby brother. Her parents had deliberately decided against enrolling her in a nursery school, partly because of the expense but mostly because they felt it would be hard for her to adapt to being separated from her mother so soon after the arrival of the baby. However, being at home was not working out well for Martha. Her mother found it more difficult than she had foreseen to arrange to get Martha together regularly with other children, as she had done before the baby came. As September approached, Martha's parents were increasingly drawn by the idea of sending the child to nursery school, in spite of the obvious arguments against it. Finally they began calling the available schools, located an inexpensive church-connected one that would take Martha, and entered the child. "Martha had trouble letting me leave at first," her mother says, "but right from the start she loved having other children to play with. Her disposition at home was better from the day school began. I also think it was good for her to get away from the baby regularly."

Martha's parents took a calculated risk, based upon what they knew about their daughter and what she was up against. Another child in similar circumstances might not have found the opportunity to play with other children so rewarding—or have had Martha's ability to put her little brother out of her mind once he was out of her sight. It turned out that Martha was up to the challenge of nursery school and better able to work through her sibling difficulties as a result of the satisfactions gained through meeting the challenge. But whenever parents take such risks, they should stand ready to help the child retreat from the fray, if need be, without feeling any the worse for wear.

About Pushing

Life being what it is, children tend to be exposed in the ordinary course of events to situations that test them to the limit, emotionally, physically, and mentally. We do not need to create artificial challenges in an effort to toughen our children and prepare them for getting on in the "real world." As a matter of fact, children may see any such maneuvering on our part as a subtle form of punishment or a sign that we do not really love them.

In Chapter 1, we discussed the successful father who never gave his sons allowances in keeping with his means, hoping in this way to teach his boys the "value of money." We saw how his efforts misfired. The boys felt abused and viewed their father as stingy and unloving.

Along the same lines, a father who was worried because his son seemed physically "soft" decided to send the boy, at age sixteen, to a summer camp that afforded "experiences in surviving in the wilderness." The boy did not want to go, but the father insisted, asserting that if he were later drafted into the armed forces he would be grateful to his parents for having seen to it that he got himself into shape. After three days at the camp, the boy ran away. His parents, with some psychological help, eventually accepted the fact that the boy was not going to go along with any such efforts to toughen him up. At twenty-one, after graduating from college, this young man joined the Peace Corps and went to a remote village in Africa. His parents were sure that he would fall ill or tire of the life in short order, but he loved his assignment and adapted to primitive living conditions with no difficulty.

Nevertheless, our children do need us to help them properly evaluate and face up to the very real challenges that life presents them with. In the process, if we use our influence wisely, we can move them toward maximum development of their potential.

Why not just come right out and say that sometimes we ought to push our children? The point is that "pushing," to be effective, must come from within the child. We can do our best to help him see the desirability of trying this, that, or the other. But our efforts will come to very little unless the child decides to push himself.

Parents can, for example, expose their child to many different kinds of intellectually stimulating experiences that encourage a youngster to develop his mental abilities to the fullest possible extent. They can take him to museums and other cultural centers, see that he has a library card and a quiet place to study, be available to help with homework when requested, show interest in his school work, and talk with him about the issues of the day, books, television programs that the family watches together, and any other subjects that arouse his curiosity. However, in the final analysis, we cannot make our child exert himself intellectually. Only he can do that.

Evaluating Real Challenges

Children do not always want what they need, or even know what they want. Here is where parents can be extremely influential and helpful.

We mentioned a boy who resisted his parents' efforts to "get him into condition." Those efforts, while well meant, were obviously misplaced. Yet, one suspects that the parents missed some good opportunities to help the boy enjoy physical activity while he was growing up. Obviously, he had the potential for this, as most children do. Unfortunately, in our sports-oriented society, many children at an early age acquire a poor image of themselves physically and react by "not liking" many of the competitive sports that are popular with their peers. They tend to be wary of joining in any activity in which their performance is apt to be compared with that of the other participants. When they say, "I don't like baseball," or bowling, or basketball, what they often mean is, "I don't like my inability to play it as well as most of my friends."

Parents cannot overcome the culture single-handedly (though occasional small victories in terms of a school's physical education program may be possible). However, we can do a number of things to help our children view themselves as something other than bumblers and enjoy the uniquely satisfying experience of exerting their physical powers to the limit. Sports such as swimming and skating are less likely to invite unkind comparisons. If we help our child acquire minimal skill at them, he usually will enjoy them. Bicycling, hiking, and modern dance classes appeal to many. Often a child who is set against organized camping enjoys going camping with a parent, or the family, or good friends.

Children's resistance to testing their powers in any area—social, physical, mental—generally means that they have not come up against the right challenges under the right circumstances. Not that a child has to be well rounded in the popular sense of the phrase. Aiming specifically for that may hinder a youngster from finding out who he really is, and enjoying and developing that self. We must always respect our child's individuality when working to prevent him from locking himself into imaginary limitations.

Parents are often called upon, too, to help a child sort out conflicting challenges. Laurie has been invited to participate in an experimental foreign-language program in her school, but it would mean that she would be separated from her friends in all her classes, and Laurie does not make friends easily. Since she is only fifteen, her parents can play a crucial role in alerting her to all the pluses and minuses that might be associated with each choice, and in helping her live with the decision that she finally makes.

Real Weaknesses

Donald is very nearsighted and somewhat clumsy. Even with his thick-lensed glasses, he does not always see well enough to move about confidently and quickly. He hates organized athletics. The year he was ten he pestered his parents to ask his eye doctor for a slip excusing him from physical education. After discussing the matter, Donald's parents refused. They talked with him about possible ways of dealing with the teasing that his athletic shortcomings sometimes exposed him to, and suggested that, since nobody is good at everything, perhaps this was the time to come to terms with feeling inadequate.

Donald was not happy with that decision, but in time he stopped complaining about it. He has not since raised the question of getting excused from physical education. At fourteen, he has become, in his words, "the world's greatest loser—I had no choice." Recently, during a school field day, Donald's performance in the potato race gave rise to a few titters. As he crossed the finish line last in his heat, he shrugged his shoulders and said, "Well, you can't win them all." This brought a burst of appreciative laughter, and Donald walked off, as usual, with several friends slapping him on the back and cheering him.

Donald has learned to compensate well for his athletic limitations, without closing the door on the eventual possibility of lessening them to some degree. Last summer he had a job caddying on the local golf course, took a few lessons, and found he has a genuine knack for the game.

In helping our children accept and compensate for their weaknesses, it is important that we not rule out all hope of any improvement. True, there are disabilities, physical and mental, with which a child is born and with which he must learn to live as best he can throughout his life. Such disabilities must be viewed realistically by parent and child alike. Yet, nobody can foretell for sure the extent to which they might be compensated for in this way or that.

We do not want to push our children constantly into situations that will inevitably bring disappointment and defeat. Nor do we want them constantly to push themselves into such situations. On the other hand, we need to fish with a long line. We cannot afford to set a rigid ceiling on a child's potential in any direction; what he could not do yesterday, he just may be able to do tomorrow.

Parents and teachers need always to be ready to revise their estimation of a given child's capacity, and ready to offer him the opportunity to stretch himself. Shy, quiet Ruth, whom nobody ever thought of as having leadership ability, volunteers to chair an assembly meeting on racial issues that have been troubling her high school, gets the job because two other students give up trying to handle the meeting, and manages to bring some kind of order out of chaos. The teacher who had beckoned Ruth to the platform said later, "Sure I was as surprised as anybody else when Ruth volunteered, but I have a lot of respect for her, and I figured if she thinks she can do this, let's see."

Talents

Most people seem to think of talent as inborn, and that is at least partially correct. However, although there may be limits to what we can draw out of a child, it is clear that all children are, in their way, "creative." On the whole, we seem to know more about what puts a damper on that creativity than about how to encourage its flowering—in writing, music, art, science, or areas such as politics or business administration.

Is talent, then, synonymous with creativity? Both words stand for qualities that are hard to describe but immediately recognized when encountered. (The Austrian philosopher Ludwig Wittgenstein, in discussing the meaning of the word game, has called attention to this oddity in the functioning of language.) It may be that creativity is what makes "talent"—defined for the time being as a special aptitude of mind or body—matter. Perfect pitch, manual dexterity, and determined practice produce many a pianist capable of earning a good living as an accompanist. Without all three qualities, only two of which are inborn, Johnny is unlikely to get far as a pianist, although all through his childhood people observing the inborn qualities may say, "That boy has talent." Going a step further, Johnny may make it as an accompanist but fail to get beyond that point. He has the technical proficiency, but not that something extra that distinguishes an accomplished accompanist from the musician whose name goes down among the greats. And that something extra? It isn't the "ear," or the dexterity, or the hard work, but—for want of a better word—creativity.

So we do not try to make a musician out of a tone-deaf child—though we do operate on the thesis that music can be a lasting source of pleasure to any child who is appropriately introduced to it. And we do our best not to kill the creative effervescence, the free play of the imagination, that all children appear to bring into the world, though perhaps in varying amounts.

Some psychoanalysts, such as Dr. Lawrence Kubie, suggest that the educational process, meaning not only the educational *system* but acculturation in general, is inherently at odds with the child's creativity; some loss of spontaneity and imaginativeness may be the price we have to pay for becoming civilized. At the same time Dr. Kubie questions some standard educational practices, notably the idea that all children need to attend school throughout the school "day" and the school "year," and the deadly dullness of much drill, which, though it may be essential to learning, could be made more stimulating.

Many educators today are concerned with the stultifying effects of our lock-step system, which in the Western world, at least, has for several centuries been something of a sacred cow. Needed innovation may finally be in the offing.

Meanwhile, what can parents do to protect their children's natural creativity while helping them discover and develop their talents? Again, it seems to be a matter of leading the horse to water but accepting the fact that we cannot make him drink. Overloading a youngster with organized after-school lessons and other activities may deprive him of time needed to explore his world imaginatively and innovatively, as well as being hard on his health. Pushing a child, in music, art, or anything else, is not truly productive unless the child's interest is fired and he begins to move ahead under his own steam. Mozart's father, who is sometimes cited as an example to the contrary, did not begin to bear down on his son until the boy had exhibited both intense interest and extraordinary talent.

One can speculate for hours about how much talent goes undeveloped. That persons cast in the role of rejects by our schools and society occasionally manage, under the unlikeliest conditions, to educate themselves and exhibit remarkable brilliance—as in the case of Malcolm X or Eric Hoffer—should give us pause.

Society must work with families in tapping the potential of all children. Only in this way can we be assured that every child will be exposed to the variety of experiences necessary to enable him to discover his interests, strengths, and talents, and that he will have access to the facilities and adult guidance needed to cultivate them to the fullest extent. The indomitable geniuses among us may perhaps manage to surface regardless of the obstacles placed in their way. Even so, the scarring that sometimes occurs is appalling. That the obstacles are insuperable for some children seems clear and is a tragic loss for them and for society.

Nothing Succeeds Like Success

Having started with the assertion that a child must have a good opinion of himself, or a positive self-image, before he is able to accept and learn from criticism, we have now come full circle. The cliché that nothing succeeds like success contains profound psychological truth.

In any society, however, it inevitably raises the question of values. How do we define success? Though Americans are accused of being materialistic, few if any of us would define success totally in terms of the marketplace. Nor do we bring up our children to do so. This may account for some of the outrage that is evident among youth today. The discontented young have taken to heart what we told them was essential to the good life, and they cannot reconcile this with what they see in society and, sometimes, in their parents' own life-style. They want the world to conform more nearly to ideals that we ourselves instilled in them. Their impatience, though typical of the young, is also rather typically American. Both their nonviolence and their violence have been come by legitimately. In a country that was founded by, among others, Quakers and refugees from debtors' prison, that came into being by way of a revolution, that has bred slave traders and abolitionists, espoused slavery and outlawed it, many traditions and values, often conflicting, are as American as apple pie.

Within this welter of values every parent has to pick his way and come to terms with what constitutes success. Our children initially need to see themselves as successful in our eyes in order to keep growing. In the early years, especially, it is mainly we who confer the badge of competence on them, searching out, if we must, activities for them to succeed at.

What we value or do not value comes through covertly, as well as directly. If, for example, we secretly admire a child's ability to make his way with his fists in the world of his peers, he may, despite all our admonitions against fighting, see this as the road to success unless other role models convince him differently. If we value winning at any cost, competitiveness may become a crucial pressure in his life, though he may depart from our opinion of who the winners ought to be, or may even decide that it is evil to compete.

Still, in spite of the ambiguity involved in helping a child become what he is able to become, some principles emerge: we must help him feel good about his powers; we must help him see and accept the consequences of his behavior, serving as both mirrors and interpreters; we must give him all the opening-up experiences that it is within our power to expose him to; we must urge him on—but mindful of the hazards involved in excessive pushing—when, because he is young, he is sometimes too easily sidetracked; we must remember that society and the child himself share with us the responsibility for the ultimate outcome.

9
The Beautiful Times

HALLOWEEN? THE PARENTS of the girl who wrote the following letter were startled to learn that Halloween was a holiday that meant something to a seventeen-year-old.

> Dear Mother, Daddy, Lee, Win, Circus, Turtle and fish:
>
> Today for the first time since I've been here I am a little homesick. I woke up thinking about the house being all decorated, so after my morning classes I went down to Thayer St. and bought a pumpkin—very small, the big ones are so expensive!—but it looks cheery on my desk. This afternoon Rachel and I went out with two shopping bags and gathered oak leaves and spread them all over our floor! Our neighbors must think we're kooks, but our room smells delicious. Anyway, happy Halloween . . .
>
> —from a letter from a college freshman

Had they made that much of it over the years? A few cardboard skeletons that were practically as old as the girl herself, some rubber spiders hanging from ceiling light fixtures and in doorways—was that decorating? Of course there was always the pumpkin and the traditions surrounding it. The pumpkin had to be the biggest they could find. For a while, it had to be too heavy for the baby in the family to lift, but the youngest was now five, and that tradition had long since been outgrown. As for going trick-or-treating, the writer of the letter had given that up some years before she went away to college. *Halloween* mattered?

Much Eludes Explanation

All along we have emphasized the complexity of human nature and the multiplicity of factors that affect a person's reactions in any given situation. Nowhere is this more evident than in the capacity to feel joy.

In the foregoing letter, many currents of emotion can be identified: nostalgia; fondness for family, home, traditions, and holidays; a high opinion of spontaneity, individualism, having fun, being a self-starter. Yet who is to say that if we manage to rear children who value and exemplify these traits, we guarantee them their share of beautiful times?

And who knows all that was going on in the girl who wrote the letter? Obviously, memories of Halloween were not the only or even the major influence at work. They merely triggered feelings about home and about holidays in general, along with nobody knows how much else.

Then why try to discuss children's capacity to be joyous if it is so difficult to dissect? The reason is that it is widely recognized as a key factor in mental health. A characteristic of such significance deserves to be examined as best we can.

Is It Inborn?

In discussing creativity in the previous chapter, we suggested that all children are born with the capacity to be creative, though possibly they possess it in varying degrees. This also appears to be true of the capacity to enjoy life. Only sick or severely deprived babies are characteristically listless. In fact, listlessness in a baby who is receiving adequate mothering is often a sign of the onset of illness.

We have all witnessed the delight with which small children so often respond to the world around them. We know how easily they move from tears to laughter—as well as *vice versa*. The troubles of a healthy preschooler, intense as they may be while they last, are typically shrugged off as if by magic when pleasure beckons.

Is this because young children have short memories? Or because their native capacity to enjoy whatever is around to enjoy has not been diminished by guilt and other burdens that adults frequently bear? We do not really know. It could be a mixture of both factors.

We do know, however, that joyousness

can be all but extinguished in a child at a very early age. This is not something that can happen only later in childhood, or in adult life. Some decades back, Dr. John Bowlby and others called attention to the fact that children in institutions, whose physical needs were well met but who received no cuddling or other kinds of affectionate attention, were generally listless, failed to thrive, and often died—simply from lack of love. Institutions are now generally aware of this problem and make an effort to provide their charges with what they refer to as TLC, meaning tender loving care. Even so, more recent studies of young children in certain institutions in this country indicate that despite some improvement—apparently institutionalized babies are no longer dying from lack of affection—many such babies are remarkably joyless. They seldom smile and are noticeably slow to respond to an invitation to play. (Their intellectual development is also markedly slowed.)

Although this does not tell us how to nurture joyousness, it does alert us to some conditions under which it will almost surely be destroyed and documents the seriousness of its absence. Children without families, or with families so beset by problems that the child is deprived of adequate adult attention and affection, early lose an important ingredient of emotional health. There is some evidence that the process can be reversed, but only as the result of years of good "mothering" by a parent or parent substitute.

The "Happy" Child

From the beginning, hurt and frustration are a part of every child's life. There is a limit not only to our power to protect our children but also to the desirability of protecting them from everyday frustrations. Children have to learn to accept the consequences of their behavior, to respect the rights and needs of others, and to shoulder appropriate responsibilities. This is not always easy, to put it mildly.

Just as every child, however emotionally healthy he may be, experiences problems in the course of growing up, so he lives through a great deal of unhappiness. Yet if he can enjoy himself when the conditions are right for that, we correctly identify him as a "happy" child.

As children grow, they become more adept at concealing their true feelings from us. However, parents can usually tell when a child is basically happy and when he is continually joyless. During adolescence, moodiness is especially common. Yet, if in spite of this the child retains the ability to react with obvious, wholehearted pleasure to some aspects of his life, there is good reason to believe that he is coping adequately with his problems. Prolonged absence of any genuine joyfulness is grounds for concern, even if the child shows no other serious problem behavior. A depressed child may be as much, or more, in need of psychological help as a destructively rebellious one.

Spontaneous Delight

Some of the joy that we experience comes as a reward for effort and planning. The college girl whose letter was quoted earlier deliberately set out to cheer herself up. However, the beautiful times often come unexpectedly. Frequently, like sunsets and rainbows, they are beyond our willing. So, too, is our openness to them.

The spontaneous delight that small children are capable of touches a responsive chord in many of us. We enjoy the child's joy. For a moment the child may even enable us to see and feel freshly again some of the wonders around us that we long ago ceased to give thought to. Yes, the spider's web with dew on it is like fairyland. The steam shovel does huff like a great big bulldog. Night, when all the lights come on, is the most exciting time of day in the city.

When we can share our children's delight, both we and they gain. If we heed that request, "Come and see," we may return with renewed energy to our necessary duties. Our action enhances our child's special pleasure and also says to him that joy is an indispensable part of living.

Sometimes we may be the ones who are riveted by a sense of magic that escapes our child. "What's so great about walking under cherry trees? I want to climb the monument." "Please, can we stop talking history now and go swimming?"

We have the same right to our enthusiasms and excitements as our children have to theirs. If mutual sharing is not possible, mutual respect always is.

Of course, a child's age will affect his interests and attention span. There is a limit to how long a small child should be expected to bear with us while we enjoy the cherry blossoms. Still, even with small children, there is room for a certain amount of give and take in this area.

It is good for children to see us stop and linger with rapt absorption over discoveries that fascinate us. In this way, as role models, we reassure them that each of us is entitled to our own fun. Though our particular interests may not rub off on our children, our attitude toward life does.

Celebrations

Holidays and other occasions that are made much of in a family year after year have an enormous impact on children. Such family traditions probably matter a great deal more to everybody concerned than is realized at the time. The child's anticipation of the great event is evident all right—for days in advance. Sometimes it is so evident that adults are tempted to take advantage of the situation: "You'd better be a good girl or Santa won't come to see you."

It is easy to be a purist about such blatant attempts at bribery. Ideally they should not occur. Yet parents, tired and envious—yes, envious of the child's carefree excitement—sometimes yield to temptation. Eventually, of course, the child will realize the extent to which he was tricked through that particular device. But if he feels that the reward was always there, regardless, he will probably decide that his parents deserved whatever respite they gained through their ploy. Once more, it is the whole picture that counts.

The truly beautiful times that a family enjoys together tend to be relived over and over. In recollection, they often take on an added glow, a heightened power to bind us together. Minor disasters—the pumpkin pie that caught fire in the broiler and burned to a crisp, the homemade chicken paté that became the dog's Thanksgiving dinner before the family had a chance to sample it—such episodes achieve the status of conversation pieces in time. Their annual retelling adds to the shared warmth and festive spirit of the occasion.

As we all know, children often measure time in terms of holidays and other celebrations that they have learned to look forward to. The passing of the year is marked for them not so much by months, or seasons, as by birthdays and occasions such as Hanukkah or Christmas, New Year's Day, Valentine's Day, St. Patrick's Day, April Fool, Passover, Easter, Fourth of July, Rosh Hashanah, Yom Kippur, Halloween, Thanksgiving. One holiday is scarcely over before they are counting the days to the next.

And why not? Holidays are meant to be a time of joy for everybody involved. Though some of them are in part solemn occasions, even these are intended to include festivities and rituals that lift the spirits. Such celebrations have an honorable tradition going back to the dawn of civilization. They are particularly emphasized in primitive societies and among oppressed groups whose lives are conspicuously lacking in other pleasures and satisfactions, for example, first-generation Americans of various ethnic origins. Quite possibly, as some social psychologists have suggested, ritualized feasting is a saving source of emotional health for people who would otherwise have scant opportunity to experience joy.

One of the sad things that has happened to the affluent in our society is that, in some cases, they no longer really enjoy many of our traditional holidays. The commercialization of some, such as Christmas, has turned an entire holiday season into such a hectic, demanding period for adults that, often, the rewards hardly seem to justify the effort. For days on end, parents are too tense and tired to be happy. Children know when this happens, and a damper is cast on their native ability to be joyful.

Joy and Sorrow

We are all aware that joy and sorrow are not really opposing emotions, that, in fact, like tears and laughter they are often intermingled. As we sit listening to a favorite piece of music, reveling in the perfection with which it is being played, we suddenly find ourselves with a lump in our throat. Or, in the midst of a lovely day at the beach, the glow of happiness that we have been feeling is momentarily shot through with an inexplicable tinge of sadness, which somehow adds to our appreciation of the occasion. Could it be that the *most* beautiful times are those that evoke a spectrum of emotions?

Young children tend to be purists in this as in other areas. "Why are you crying?" the five-year-old demands when he sees tears spring to our eyes at the sight of the birthday present he has made for us. It will be some years before he will find out for himself, perhaps at a surprise party or upon receiving an unexpected compliment, that human beings often cry, or feel like crying, when they are very happy.

Yet every toddler and preschooler who is capable of being joyous is also easily moved to tears and anger. Their reactions in any given situation may be more simplistic than ours, but they are obviously capable of a broad range of emotions. Interestingly, marked joylessness is generally associated with what is technically termed "emotional flatness," that is, a blunting of the entire repertoire of normal human feelings. Such children (and adults) not only show less joy, but also less anger and all the other emotions.

Implications for Parents

This fact lends support to the assumption that the ability to enjoy life has complex roots. Certainly we should do what we can to provide our children with opportunities to enjoy themselves. We also need to put our seal of approval on pleasure by sharing their joys to the extent possible. However, still more seems to be called for.

What little we know indicates that it is important for us to make our children understand that they are entitled to *all* their emotions. Of course they have to learn to control their behavior. However, in the process of helping them accomplish this, we must be very careful not to imply that we blame them for how they feel. We need to assure Amy that we understand her feeling angry at her little brother. She has every right to be mad when he grabs one of her crayons and scribbles on her drawing. It is her *actions* that require controlling. We will not allow her to hit her brother on the head with her coloring book.

In our capacity as interpreters of how our children are doing and what they are up against, we want to be sure that we do not rob them of any of their spontaneous emotional reactions to life. Our job is to help them accept all their emotions, not feel guilty about them, while at the same time insisting that they handle their feelings in a socially acceptable fashion.

But what if we really do not think our child is entitled to feel as he obviously does? Then we express our puzzlement honestly, but in a way that does not pooh-pooh the child's emotion, or condemn it, or attempt to analyze it: "I see you're very angry with your teacher, Michael. What I don't see is why. The way you tell it, he had to send you and your friend out of the classroom in order to get the attention of the others. I'm sure you were being very funny, but he has his job to do. He must like the two of you, or you would have found yourselves in worse trouble." This sometimes invites our child to turn his anger on us, and he may do so initially. Through being accepting as well as honest, however, we give him the opportunity to think over his emotions without feeling threatened by them. As a result he may revise his opinion of his teacher.

Sometimes children may need us to help them admit what they are feeling. No matter how accepting we may be of tears, anger, fear, etc., our child may still find it difficult to acknowledge them. After all, parents are not a child's whole world. In some circles, as even a three-year-old usually knows, boys are not supposed to cry or show fear, and no child is supposed to feel angry at adults. In addition, some children may find it harder than others to face up to their real feelings. Perhaps they feel more intensely, which makes emotions potentially more frightening to them; or perhaps they have a stronger desire to please, or to be like, adults, and this seems to them to demand repression of strong feelings. Or unknown factors may be at work. At any rate, they become emotionally guarded and need us to help them keep in touch with their feelings.

A simple statement such as, "It must be hard on you when people make such a fuss over the baby. You're very nice about it," both compliments a child on his self-control and helps him acknowledge to himself that he feels resentment—and has a right to do so. In such ways we can give a child leave to feel angry or hurt or disappointed or whatever, while at the same time patting him on the back for behaving well.

One word of caution: parents are not supposed to be therapists. We do not say to a child, "Doesn't that make you fighting mad?" Such a question might undermine all his hard-won inner controls. We must always ally ourselves firmly with the child's control, or "better nature," when notifying him that he is entitled to whatever emotions may be churning around inside him. To reiterate, we never try to analyze those emotions, or argue with a child about what he is feeling. A therapist should be consulted if we think our child is seriously over-controlled. All we are supposed to do is acknowledge the possible existence of hard-to-handle feelings at the same time that we encourage socially acceptable behavior.

Face Up to Our Own Feelings

Again, some of the more important teaching that we do is through example. Parents' ways of handling their own emotions tend to rub off on their children. As indicated in earlier chapters, this can be disconcerting from time to time, as we watch our children mirroring aspects of ourselves that we do not admire. We need to keep reminding ourselves that over the long haul our youngsters will be exposed to many role models, and that there will be many opportunities for us and others to help them modify their behavior. The way young Sara now mimics the least attractive of our methods of dealing with our anger is open to change.

Children test parental self-control in innumerable ways. All of us lose our tempers from time to time, which, as already indicated, need not do any harm and may under some circumstances be salutary. Letting a child know when he is annoying us is definitely salutary. It may have a calming effect all around. There are times, though, when parents do not realize that they are annoyed with, or resentful of, their children because they have no "acceptable" reason to be so.

How dare we resent our children just because rearing children is a very expensive, time-consuming business? How can we possibly blame them for the fact that but for them we might be enjoying a carefree existence, going out nights when we felt like it, taking some of those fabulous trips advertised in the newspapers and on TV, quite possibly owning our own home by now, etc., etc. No, it is unthinkable that parents should entertain such selfish feelings, and obviously *we* do not. We love our children, have never for a minute regretted having them. If they do not always seem to appreciate everything that we have done for them, well, that's the nature of children.

It is true that we love our children and are glad we have them. Occasionally, however, our love may be mixed with resent-

ment or disappointment—through no fault of the children. If we can accept the truth that we, too, are entitled to our feelings, we are less likely to punish our children and ourselves unconsciously for our "unreasonable" resentments by playing the martyr or making life difficult for everybody in other ways.

Unadmitted resentment and disappointment have a way of leaking out around the edges of our self-control. The child feels that something is wrong, though he cannot put his finger on the trouble or how he may have contributed to it. He feels somehow at fault and does not know what to do about it.

Facing up to our difficult feelings is not guaranteed to make them go away immediately, but it does enable us to handle them more rationally. We catch ourselves being unusually demanding or picky or short with our child and say, "Look, I'm in a bad mood. It's not your fault. I'm sorry." The child senses that all three statements are true, and no harm is done. If, as often happens, he also concludes sensibly that this is a day to stay out of Mother's (or Daddy's) hair, we will probably be the better for it, and he none the worse. Children can cope with our off days if such days are not too frequent and if it is clearly understood by us and by them that they are doing us a special favor. In fact, such experiences can be maturing.

Fun and Responsibility

Just as the beautiful times have to be considered within the context of the entire range of human emotions, so fun is linked to responsibility—and not just in the minds of puritans. The two need not be antithetical. Ideally they reinforce each other.

When our children are very young we start teaching them that their freedom to have fun has certain well-defined limits designed to ensure their safety and that of others: no playing with sharp objects, no throwing sand. Gradually we go further and teach them to respect less obvious rights and feelings of others. We help them learn to have fun *responsibly.* If we are careful not to interfere with a child's fun capriciously, he accepts the value of such limits, even though he may not always abide by them. In time he also learns that he has responsibilities of various kinds—toward his school work, toward the functioning of the household—that take precedence over having fun.

As we help our child move slowly from playing responsibly to being a responsible person in every respect, we need to be sure that we do not, intentionally or unintentionally, rob fun of the status it deserves in our lives, turn it into a sort of second-class citizen. Joy, as surely as bread, is the staff of life. We must have both.

10
Having The Children You Want—And No More

PUBLIC OPINION POLLS conducted in recent years show that the vast majority of men and women in this country are in favor of birth control. We shall discuss some reasons for limiting family size and controlling the spacing of children; methods of birth control, including experimental approaches that may become available in the future; advances in treating infertility; and adoption as a means of having children when one is unable to conceive, or of enlarging one's family without contributing to the population explosion.

Family Planning as a Social Responsibility

Many scientists today are convinced that if voluntary family planning efforts do not bring about, within a very few years, a stable world population, governments will have to step in and limit, through some form of licensing, the right to give birth. This is not a pleasant prospect, but neither is the prospect of living with runaway population growth, as indicated in Chapter 2. Family planning, then, needs to be viewed as a social responsibility, as well as a matter of simply personal privilege.

Nowadays, numerous ecologists and others concerned about world population problems are recommending that couples have no more than two children of their own. Even this would result in a population increase in the United States for another decade or two. At present our population is composed of an unprecedentedly large percentage of young people entering upon childbearing years. The generation born during the so-called baby boom that followed World War II is now having its own babies.

Medical Considerations

There are many sound medical reasons for a woman to limit the number of children she bears and to control the timing of her pregnancies. Statistics indicate that, safe as childbearing has become, the risks it involves for both mother and child tend to increase with repeated pregnancies. They are several times higher for the woman having her fifth baby than for the woman having her second. After two or three deliveries, the uterine muscles gradually lose their tone and function less forcefully and effectively during the birth process. Other problems, such as varicose veins, anemia, hemorrhoids, and back troubles, also tend to be more common. Mortality rates rise for mother and child, and the incidence of birth defects is higher.

The spacing of children and a mother's age when she gives birth also make a difference. Obstetricians generally agree that the optimal spacing of children is approximately two years apart. This allows the mother's body time to recover fully from pregnancy and giving birth, yet her muscles still retain some of that extra capacity for stretching that a previous delivery gives them. As you would probably expect, statistics indicate that the incidence of problems of various kinds is significantly higher for mothers over age thirty-five. What you might not know is that this also holds true for mothers in their early teens. Mortality rates, for both a mother and her infant, are at their lowest when a mother is between the ages of twenty and thirty-five. Birth defects and complications during pregnancy and delivery are also lowest during this age span.

It would be a poor world, certainly, if we allowed ourselves to be governed entirely by statistics. They never take into account all the factors that enter into a given situation. For example, if you don't marry until your late thirties—or remarry then—there is no reason to fear having a baby as long as you are healthy and have good medical care. However, women (and the men who care about them) deserve to know the statistics relevant to making childbirth as safe and easy as possible, so that they can exercise as much freedom of choice as is available to them and evaluate their various options wisely.

Other Considerations

Many young couples desire to limit the size of their families for financial reasons. Children today are a luxury, especially if parents wish to provide their youngsters with "extras," such as summer camp, lessons in music or dance, a college education, and all the other experiences and equipment and medical care that can enable a child to develop his potential in all directions to the fullest possible extent. A young father was recently startled to discover that, in his words, "It's going to cost us as much to get our daughter's teeth straightened as it cost my parents to see me through braces and college both."

Another factor that may make parents want to limit the number of children they have is the growing awareness of the degree to which a child's intellectual development is affected by the amount and kind of adult attention and stimulation that he receives during the early years, starting right after he is born. We now know that "good mothering," by a parent or parent substitute, not only enables a baby to thrive physically and emotionally, but also plays a critical role in cognitive, or mental, growth. Babies and young children need the stimulation of being played with, talked to, reacted to, introduced appropriately to new experiences, and offered a change of scene from time to time in order to insure maximum development of their mental capacities. When there are many children close together in age, it is more difficult for parents to insure that each has the individual attention and constructive stimulation from an adult that is so important during the early years.

Then, too, an increasing number of young women are deciding that although they want the experience of being a mother, and possibly the experience of being a full-time mother for several years, they will want to pursue a career for most of their adult life. They are ready to drop out of the labor market long enough to get one or two children "off to a good start," but that is all the children they are interested in having.

Aren't Large Families Good for the Children?

There is no "ideal" family size. Though one often hears ominous warnings about the fate of only children, no available research indicates that, statistically speaking, they are any less likely to grow up emotionally healthy and be successful in life than children from larger families. A hundred years ago, when our society was still predominantly an agrarian one, an only child was quite often a lonely child. This may, in part, explain why some parents today still feel that they owe it to their offspring to provide him with a brother or sister, or several of both. But in our world today, playmates are generally easy to come by and provide the only child with the companionship and experience in relating to other youngsters that large families were once valued for.

Interestingly, studies indicate that two or three children is considered the ideal number by the great majority of people in all socioeconomic and ethnic groups. Many, however, have more children than they want, because of lack of access to effective means of birth control, or failure for one reason or another to use a reliable method regularly and as directed. Thus, some couples are in essence denied a choice; others take chances. One study indicated that 75 percent of women with large families had not wanted their last pregnancy. Many studies show that the burden of having unwanted children falls more heavily upon the poor than the well-to-do. All too often, poor women cannot afford effective contraceptives or do not have access to the kind of medical supervision that their proper use requires. All too often, also, poor women feel that available birth control programs are aimed at preventing them from having *any* children, not simply unwanted children. Changing this state of affairs will require concerted effort by citizens and medical personnel who are sensitive to the feelings of the poor, especially the poor who are members of minority groups.

The "Pill"

Properly used, birth control pills afford virtually 100 percent protection against pregnancy. A doctor's prescription is needed to purchase them. A month's supply costs around three dollars. They work by altering a woman's hormonal balance in order to prevent ovulation; that is, to prevent her ovaries from releasing an egg each month as they would normally do.

The pill was developed out of the knowledge that women do not ovulate when they are pregnant, because of hormonal changes that occur in the body following conception. Birth control pills simulate the hormonal conditions that exist during pregnancy. The pills are of two kinds: combination pills that contain both progestin and estrogen, and sequential pills in which initial doses of estrogen are followed by some progestin.

Both types are taken orally. Beginning usually on the fifth day after the onset of menstruation, a woman takes one pill a day for 20 or 21 days. For as long as she is taking the pill, her menstrual cycle is regularized; her period starts a day or two after she has completed taking her allotted series of pills. It is extremely important, however, that she take a pill each day during the required time. Skipping a day, even if she takes two pills twenty-four hours later, may allow ovulation to occur and thus make it possible for her to conceive. For this reason, women using the pill are advised to keep some other form of contraceptive handy—a diaphragm or a supply of condoms—and use it as a back-up measure during the remainder of any month during which they forget to take their pill one day.

Aside from its effectiveness, the pill is an appealing method of birth control because it is easy to use and dissociates contraception from the act of having intercourse. When a woman is ready to become pregnant, she simply stops taking the pill and, except in rare instances, she is ovulating regularly within a month or two.

But How Safe Is It?

Although oral contraception was first greeted as the "perfect" solution to family planning, some questions about its safety, especially if used throughout a woman's reproductive years, have since been raised. Statistics indicate that there is a significantly higher incidence of blood-clotting problems (thrombophlebitis and pulmonary embolism) in women using the pill than in women the same age not using it. Still, the mortality rate from such problems among pill users appears to be very low, about 8 per 200,000, which is less than the mortality rate associated with pregnancy. Even so, women with a history of circulatory problems should certainly not use the pill. When a woman goes to a doctor for a prescription for an oral contraceptive, the doctor is supposed to take a careful medical history, in addition to giving a thorough medical examination. Both should be insisted upon.

There is no evidence to date that using the pill makes a woman more susceptible to breast cancer. In regard to cervical cancer, the statistics are more ambiguous. Some studies indicate that there may be a slightly higher incidence of such cancers among women who use the pill. However, this kind of cancer has a cure rate of approximately 100 percent when diagnosed in its early stages. Thus women using the pill who go to their doctors every six months for checkups, as they are supposed to do, may actually have less to fear from cervical cancer than do women who have a "Pap smear" test (the standard test for cervical cancer) less frequently.

In addition to the possible risks mentioned, the pill may produce certain unpleasant side effects in some users. Some women complain of nausea, though this usually disappears after a few months. Others experience breast enlargement and tenderness, annoying vaginal discharge or vaginal itching, periodic "bloating," weight gain that they are unable to control, or tension similar to premenstrual tension. Individual differences enter in markedly. Often an astute physician can eliminate all, or nearly all, the unpleasantness of which a woman complains by prescribing another brand of pills. The various brands affect different women differently. But occasionally switching brands does not help, and a woman and her doctor may conclude that some drawback, such as weight gain or nervous tension, makes it desirable for her to give up oral contraception.

Because the pill is relatively new, we do not know what its long-term risks may be, or whether, for example, a woman should make it her choice of contraception throughout her reproductive years. Many women are understandably nervous about altering their hormonal balance over a long period of time. More research is needed to give us the answer. Some young mothers now using the pill say that after they have had the children they want, they intend to be sterilized, have their tubes tied.

It is quite possible that the next few years will see the development of a form of contraception that is as effective as sterilization or the pill and more appealing than either. Meanwhile, on balance, the benefits of oral contraception appear to outweigh all its possible risks and other drawbacks. Having good medical supervision is a must, though. It keeps the risks minimal and usually enables a woman to avoid the more unpleasant side effects.

The IUD

The intrauterine device is a delicate, flexible "loop" or "coil," generally made of plastic, which is inserted through the cervical opening into a woman's uterus or womb. Insertion and removal must be done by a doctor. For as long as the device is in place, it affords almost complete (about 98 percent) protection against pregnancy. A woman continues to menstruate normally. When she is ready to have a baby, she simply has the device removed.

It is not known exactly how the IUD works. Probably an egg can become fertilized, but it is somehow prevented from nesting in the womb's lining and developing further.

This kind of "one-shot" approach to contraception—once the IUD is inserted, you are protected for as many months or years as it remains in place—has an obvious appeal. Again, however, there are drawbacks for some women. On the whole, the IUD is not suitable for women who have never been pregnant, especially if they are under twenty. In some women, it causes cramps or bleeding severe enough that the device must be removed. (Most women have some side effects for the first few months.) It is estimated that this happens in 10 to 15 percent of cases. Somewhat less frequently, the IUD is expelled spontaneously, that is, comes out of itself. If this occurs without a woman's knowledge, she is, of course, subject to becoming pregnant. To guard against this eventuality, IUDs today are equipped with a fine nylon thread that extends through the mouth of the womb into the vagina, so that a woman can check to make certain that the device is still in place.

There are no aftereffects on a woman's womb once the IUD has been removed. Other things being equal, she is as likely to become pregnant after using the device as she was before. In the rare cases in which pregnancy occurs despite the presence of an IUD, there is no evidence that the resulting infant will suffer any abnormality. After the baby is born, the IUD is delivered along with the placenta.

For the woman who can retain an IUD, it is a very easy, inexpensive, and almost foolproof method of contraception.

The Diaphragm with Spermicidal Jelly or Cream

The diaphragm is a shallow cuplike device of rubber with a thick springy edge, designed to fit snugly at the far end of the vagina, holding a spermicidal agent over the cervical opening and preventing sperm from entering the womb. (See illustration.) When properly fitted by a physician, and used in conjunction with a spermicidal jelly or cream according to the physician's directions, it is very effective in preventing fertilization. Some authorities assert that the only "accidents" that occur with a diaphragm are the result of "human failure." Others consider the method only about 96 percent effective, at best.

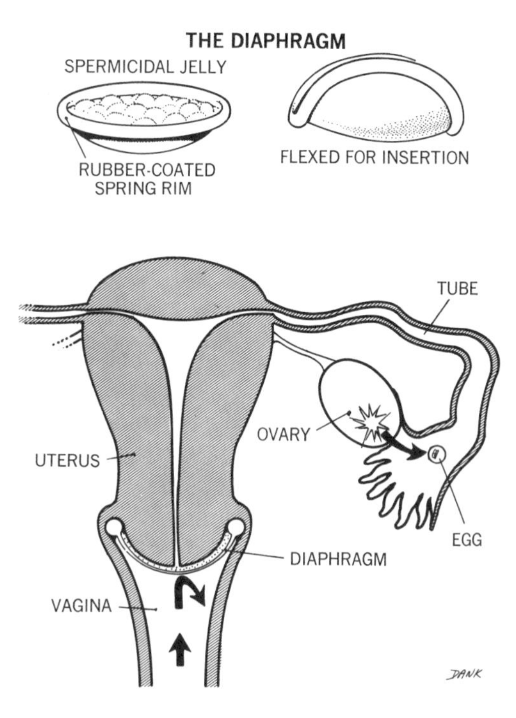

Unquestionably, using a diaphragm correctly can be a bother, and couples may sometimes be tempted to take a chance. A woman must insert the diaphragm before having intercourse and leave it in place for at least six hours afterward. If intercourse is desired more than an hour after the diaphragm has been put in place, its position should be checked and additional jelly or cream inserted. The fit of the diaphragm should be checked by the doctor who prescribed it two or three months after a woman is initially fitted. Refitting is also necessary after she has a baby. Normally a diaphragm holds up for several years, but it should be replaced if the rubber shows any signs of weakness.

From all this, it is evident that a couple

need to be highly motivated in order to make the most of the protection that a diaphragm can afford. Still, the fact that it does not necessitate manipulating the body chemistry and has no side effects makes this method, in the opinion of many, worth the trouble it involves.

The Condom

Condoms can be bought in a drugstore. No prescription is needed to purchase them. Sometimes called a "rubber," the condom is a thin elastic sheath, several inches in length, intended to be pulled onto the man's erect penis just before intercourse and to contain his semen after he ejaculates, so that no sperm are deposited in the woman's vagina.

Condoms today are made of tougher material than they were some years ago. They are newly designed, too, with a marked pouch at the tip to show the user precisely how far to pull the sheath and leave adequate space to accommodate his ejaculate.

These improvements have greatly enhanced the effectiveness of condoms. Again, some authorities believe that a condom gives close to 100 percent protection if it is used correctly. Protection is enhanced if the woman uses a spermicidal foam.

The condom should be pulled onto the erect penis carefully, to ward against weakening the sheath. At time of withdrawal, the man should hold the rim securely with both hands to prevent any slipping or leakage. It is then discarded. A fresh condom is used each time a couple have intercourse.

Vaginal Foams, Creams, Jellies, and Foaming Tablets

All these contraceptives are available in drugstores, without prescription. They are intended to coat the cervical opening with a spermicidal agent—a substance that kills sperm—in order to prevent fertilization. As indicated earlier, a spermicidal substance used in conjunction with a diaphragm affords very good protection. By themselves, however, these agents are considerably less reliable. The data regarding their effectiveness are conflicting, but even the foams, which are perhaps the best of this type of contraceptive, appear to be less than 80 percent sure. Foams have an advantage over creams and jellies in that they are not messy. However, they must be applied no more than thirty minutes before orgasm, which means that reapplication in the midst of foreplay may be necessary. Care must also be taken to insure that the foam, from spray container or tablet, adequately covers the cervix and is not wasted elsewhere in the vagina. (See illustration.)

CONTRACEPTIVE FOAMS

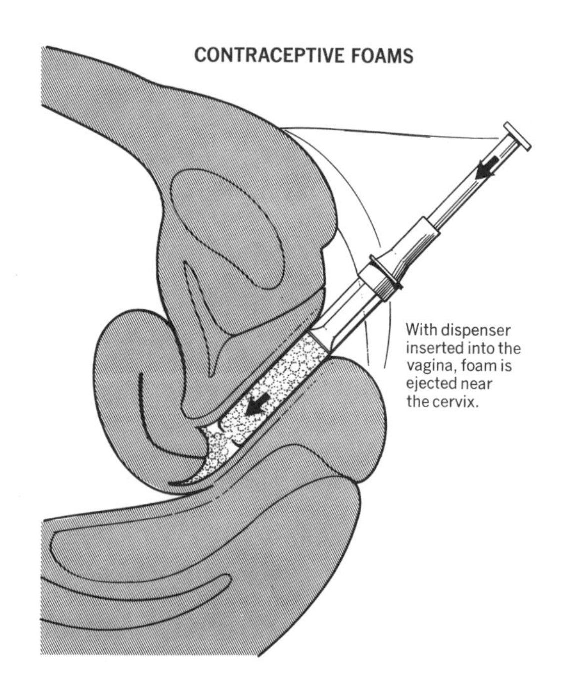

What the Future May Hold

Attempts are being made to develop once-a-month oral contraceptive pills and to perfect methods of injecting hormones that have a long-lasting effect, as long as several months. Another possibility may be to implant such hormones under the skin in a way that allows them to be released gradually over an extended period of time.

We already have what is known as a "morning-after" pill, which averts pregnancy when treatment is begun within a few days after sexual relations have occurred. This is useful in cases of rape and other incidents involving one isolated sexual encounter. However, the treatment, which involves taking large doses of estrogen orally, can cause extremely disagreeable side effects and must be carried out under a doctor's supervision. Obviously, this is not a practical approach to contraception for couples having intercourse regularly.

It is known that small amounts of progestin placed in a woman's cervix will cause her cervical secretions to thicken sufficiently to prevent sperm from entering her womb. The amount of progestin needed seems to be so small that it produces only this local reaction and does not otherwise affect her body's functioning. Efforts are under way in two directions: to ascertain the precise dose of progestin needed to work, and to design a suitable device to hold it in place.

What about a contraceptive pill for men? This is also being investigated. Research has been centered mainly on interfering with spermatogenesis, the production of sperm. Some promising leads have had to be abandoned because the experimental pill produced proved incompatible with the consumption of alcohol.

Meanwhile, researchers continue to try to improve the contraceptives presently available. The dosage of hormones in oral contraceptives has been steadily lowered ever since the pills came on the market, without reducing their effectiveness. Still further progress may come in this direction, which would lead to further reduction of unpleasant side effects and possible risks.

Rhythm Method

For couples who have religious scruples against using other methods of birth control, the rhythm method, which requires abstaining from intercourse during a woman's "fertile period"—the period just before and after she ovulates—can now be practiced with somewhat more hope of success than formerly, though the failure rate is still discouragingly high. The crucial factor in the rhythm method is, of course, to determine exactly when a woman will ovulate—and this is important to couples who *want* to have a baby, as well as to those who do not. A woman is fertile for no more than two days before the ovum, or egg, leaves the ovary (two days being the maximum length of time that sperm are capable of fertilization after ejaculation) and for no more than two days following ovulation (that being the maximum time that the ovum remains fresh enough to be fertilized).

Most women ovulate around the middle of their menstrual cycle, or about fourteen days after the onset of menstruation. But that statistic is of no help in avoiding or fostering conception. Each woman has her own brief fertile period, which may vary from month to month. The time of ovulation can be determined with impressive exactitude if a woman has the patience and knowledge needed to keep a daily chart of her basal body temperature, a technique described in detail in *A Woman's Choice: A Guide to Contraception, Fertility, Abortion, and Menopause* by Robert H. Glass, M.D., and Nathan G. Kase, M.D.

A woman's temperature rises detectably at the time of ovulation. (See page 72.) To avoid pregnancy, however, or to become pregnant, a woman needs to know two days before she ovulates that this event is impending. The Basal Temperature Chart may offer a clue to this, too. Generally a woman's temperature drops a day or so before the rise associated with ovulation, but this warning probably comes too late to enable a couple to avoid conception with any degree of certainty. More help is provided by the fact that the chemistry of a woman's cervical secretions changes several days before ovulation. Nature makes her reproductive tract more hospitable to sperm. The cervical secretions become more watery, abundant, and alkaline, providing an environment that prolongs the life of sperm and makes it easier for them to get through the mouth of the womb. Kits that enable a woman to test the chemical makeup of her cervical secretions, and in many cases determine accurately several days ahead that she is due to ovulate, are available in drugstores. These kits do not make the rhythm approach to birth control anywhere near foolproof, but combined with the use of a temperature chart, they help.

Some women find, after keeping a temperature chart for a year, that their pattern of ovulation is quite regular. They may be tempted to assume that they know when their fertile period is and give up checking in other ways each month. This is risky, for

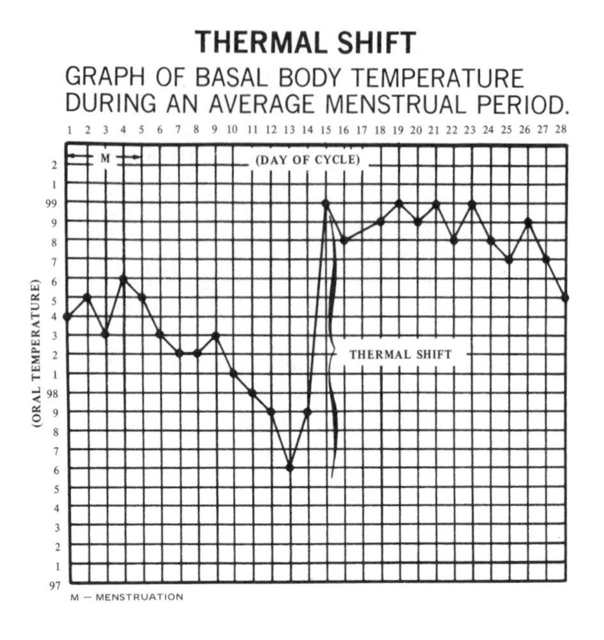

the most regular cycle occasionally changes unpredictably. Women who are irregular, of course, cannot hope to achieve any protection unless they keep a temperature chart and test their cervical secretions—or abstain from intercourse for most of the month.

Sterilization

This procedure can be performed on either a man or a woman but is much simpler for the male. The operation for the male, called a vasectomy, involves cutting and tying the vas deferens—the tube that carries sperm from the storage area to the penis. (See illustration.) It can be done in a doctor's office in less than half an hour. Cutting and tying a woman's Fallopian tubes is major surgery, requiring an abdominal incision under anesthesia. (See illustration.)

Neither operation affects the hormonal functioning of the person involved. Sexual desire and performance need not be in any way affected. The result is simply, in the case of the male, to eliminate sperm from the ejaculate, and, in the case of the female, to prevent eggs from being fertilized. Both operations are sometimes reversible—in perhaps half of all cases for men, less often for women. But a person should not take this step if he or she has any lingering doubts.

For a couple who have had the children they want, sterilization may be the perfect way to eliminate all worry about unwanted pregnancies. It is sure, and, when the man is the partner to be sterilized, simple. More and more young fathers today are having a vasectomy as an alternative to allowing their wives to have their tubes tied.

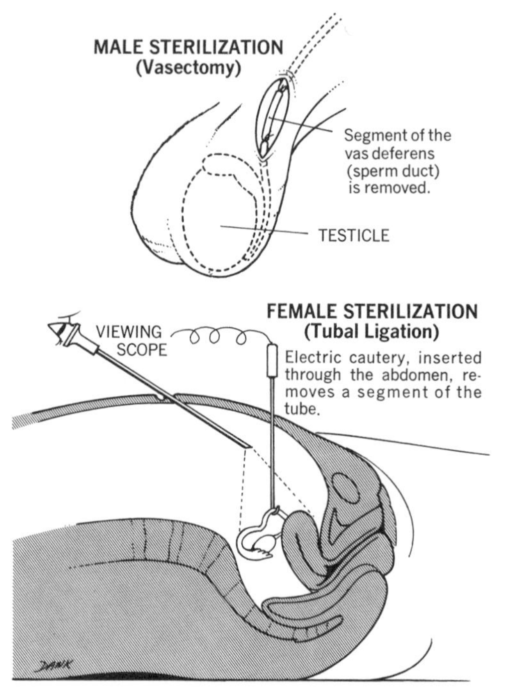

Abortion

Nobody advocates legal abortion as an alternative to contraception. But numerous thoughtful persons, including many doctors and clergymen, consider it preferable to an unwanted child. It is obviously preferable to the dangers that illegal abortion poses.

The widespread practice of illegal abortion in the United States, which has caused the death of thousands of women, has been one factor contributing to the recent push to reform abortion laws in many states. It is now possible for a woman who wants an abortion to obtain one legally in this country, though she may have to go out of her state to do so. Information about costs and referral to a doctor or hospital is offered by two national agencies: Planned Parenthood—World Population, 810 Seventh Avenue, New York, N.Y. 10019, telephone (212) 541-7800; and Clergy Consultation Service on Abortion, 55 Washington Square, South, New York, N.Y. 10012, telephone (212) 477-0034. The Bibliography includes a pamphlet that lists, by state and city, local agencies that provide such information and referrals.

The earlier in pregnancy that an abortion is done, the better. Some states permit an abortion to be performed through the twenty-fourth week, but many doctors refuse to perform the operation after the twentieth week except in very special circumstances. The optimal time is through the tenth week, that is, up to the time when a woman is due to miss her third period. Up to this point, abortion, when done legally, is extremely safe, safer than normal delivery.

Early abortions are of two types: the D & C (dilatation and curettage), which is done under anesthesia and involves scraping the lining of the womb clean; and the Suction Method, in which a small tube is inserted in the uterus and draws the pregnancy out. Neither of these methods usually requires an overnight stay in the hospital or clinic where it is done.

Later abortions are more complicated and generally require a stay of two or more days in the hospital where they are performed.

Treatment for Infertility

A couple should seek treatment for infertility together, for a very simple reason: it is much quicker, easier, and less expensive to evaluate a man's fertility than to evaluate a woman's. Most gynecologists can do this, though if the husband requires treatment, a urologist will be consulted. If your own doctor does not handle fertility problems, he will recommend a specialist, or a clinic, that does.

The evaluation of a man's fertility is made through microscopic examination of a semen specimen, ordinarily obtained by masturbation. The specimen must be examined within two hours after ejaculation. The doctor needs to know whether the man's sperm count and the number of abnormal-appearing sperm are within the normal range.

Another test done early in the course of infertility treatment, because it is simple, is examination of the woman's cervical secretions following intercourse. This reveals the extent to which sperm can survive in her reproductive tract and indicates whether or not her secretions are unusually hostile to them.

Testing to see if a woman is ovulating normally, and if not why not, takes time. The doctor will check on ovulation by having her keep a basal body temperature chart (See page 72) for several months and perhaps also by performing an endometrial biopsy—removing a bit of tissue from the lining of the womb and examining it under a microscope. This not only tells whether ovulation is occurring but also reveals whether progesterone production is adequate. Tests will be made to determine if the Fallopian tubes are open and healthy so that the ovum is accessible to sperm and the fertilized egg could make its way, at a normal rate of speed, to the womb.

A very few women cannot conceive because they are allergic to their husband's sperm. (This is not the same as having cervical secretions that are hostile to sperm.) There is now a way to test for such allergy, and it can be treated.

If you wish more information about the many tests available to pinpoint infertility problems, consult the Bibliography. Improved testing has probably contributed as much as advances in treatment to the ability of modern medical specialists to help parents have the children they want.

The most publicized recent advance in treatment has been the development of "fertility drugs," notably Clomid. Clomid, which is taken in pill form under a doctor's supervision, stimulates ovulation, apparently by causing the pituitary gland to produce more of the hormones a woman needs to ovulate. Though Clomid is much less potent currently than it originally was, a woman still runs the risk of multiple births when she takes it. Clomid has also been used to treat men with a fertility problem, but it is not always successful in improving the quality of semen.

There are other recent approaches to hormonal therapy for women. Commercially prepared hormones may be given in doses that approximate what nature intended, to trigger ovulation. Since much has been learned in recent years about hormonal functioning in both men and women, doctors are better able to detect and compensate for an individual's lacks in this area. Some doctors have reported that up to 70 percent of their women infertility patients treated in this manner became pregnant. As with Clomid therapy, however, a woman's ovaries may sometimes be "overstimulated," and multiple births can occur.

"Fertility drugs" are an exciting development in the treatment of infertility. As this type of therapy becomes increasingly refined with time, it should involve fewer drawbacks for women and perhaps offer more help to men. It will never be a cure-all, however, since there are problems, such as malfunctioning tubes, with which it cannot help. When a couple seek help from a competent fertility specialist, they should be prepared to accept his decision that he has done all that can be done. When that point has been reached, they would be wise to set a deadline for themselves, after which they will give up working at trying to conceive and investigate adoption or devote their energies to achieving other satisfactions in life.

Adoption

Professionals who work with families agree that parents should consult a licensed adoption agency if they want to adopt a child. This is not just a matter of "experts sticking up for each other." Although non-agency adoptions sometimes work out beautifully, and agencies occasionally make mistakes (in addition to requiring a lengthy investigation), agency adoptions have a number of advantages: (1) prospective parents receive counseling about child-rearing and the problems that adoptive parents are likely to encounter; (2) agencies are prepared to deal with such eventualities as an unexpected pregnancy after a couple have been promised a child; (3) agencies offer parents support and advice during the early months when they are adjusting to their child; (4) the natural mother is less likely to change her mind and try to reclaim the baby when an adoption is handled by an agency; and (5) agency adoptions, even if the agency is a private one, are on the whole considerably less expensive.

Unfortunately, there is today a growing black market in the adoption field. This is because the supply of adoptable white babies has shrunk markedly in recent years.

One of the largest United States private agencies, which in 1968 arranged 1,903 adoptions, expected in 1971 to arrange less than half that number, or 888. As of June 1971 the agency stopped accepting applications from couples who want only white infants.

This trend is thought to have three main causes: the increased availability of contraceptives, especially the Pill; liberalized abortion laws; and a dramatic increase in the number of unmarried girls who decide to keep their babies. At the same time, the demand for babies appears to be increasing, partly because a number of couples feel that, in view of the population explosion, they should have no more than two children of their own and adopt any more that they want.

One good feature of all this is that many children who a few years ago would have been slated to spend their lives in institutions or foster homes are now being adopted. Interracial adoptions are on the rise, as the supply of babies of minority-group origin still greatly exceeds the demand for them by couples of like origin. What evidence we have to date indicates that interracial adoptions are as successful as any other kind, for everybody concerned. But there is a lack of long-term research into this.

Older children and children with handicaps are also being adopted in increasing numbers. There have always been a few such adoptions. One recent study of a number of them *Adopting Older Children,* by Alfred Kadushin, indicates that here, too, the success rate, judged in terms of parental satisfaction, compares very favorably with that of more conventional adoptions. When older children are adopted, they tend on the whole to "show gratitude and not complain," and to "try hard to be good"—to quote some parents surveyed in the foregoing study. This is understandable; such children have tasted what *not* having a family means. It does, however, point up the fact that parents who adopt older children, especially from an institution, may need to help the child feel comfortable about expressing normal irritation and resentment without fear that this might jeopardize his relationship with his adoptive parents. Couples considering this kind of adoption (and perhaps interracial adoption also) should be certain that they are motivated by concern for the child's welfare, and not just narcissism. Children deserve the right to be thoroughgoing ingrates occasionally and not have to appreciate us all of the time.

Young marrieds today are showing a heartening concern about having only as many children as they, and the world, can accommodate adequately. This, combined with their rejection of pigeonholing people according to race, should mean that in the decade to come there will be fewer unwanted babies and that every child born will have a better chance of enjoying the advantages that should be the birthright of all children.

---

11 *Our Needs In Perspective*

IN BECOMING PARENTS we do not cease to be people, with lives of our own to lead and needs which, whether we are male or female, cannot be totally satisfied simply through having and rearing children. That statement is a truism. Yet many parents feel uncomfortable with the idea that their own needs are always important, should always be taken into account, and sometimes deserve to take precedence over some of their children's needs.

Partly, this is because many of us are imbued with the notion that it is selfish to pay any attention to our own self-interest. That is untrue. One of the basic tenets of psychology is that unless a person's own needs are adequately met he is not capable of properly assessing and ministering to the needs of another.

This principle was examined earlier in the discussion of how children learn to respect the rights of others. It applies to us as well as to our children. If we continually do violence to our own self-interest, our children will be made to pay for it in one way or another. Often in middle-class circles children pay through being saddled with an almost unbearable burden of guilt. In other circles, when parents are insufficiently fulfilled personally, the young may be beaten viciously, or their care may be relegated almost exclusively to hired help.

Another and perhaps even more important reason that we frequently hesitate to weigh our own interests as carefully as we should is that we somehow feel that meeting our own needs adequately will inevitably result in slighting our children's. This is also fundamentally fallacious, the result of viewing the interests of parents and their children as being diametrically opposed. Actually they often go hand in hand. When conflicts arise, the interests of one party do not usually have to be totally overridden in order to insure the well-being of the other. A variety of adjustments and compromises are nearly always possible.

The Trap of Thinking in Terms of Opposites

It is not surprising that we often think in terms of opposing extremes rather than in the round. The adversary approach is endemic in our culture. It does not really come naturally to us to size up all the possible options available to us in a given situation.

Linguists have commented on the extent to which Western languages, unlike Eastern ones, both reflect and encourage a tendency to think in terms of opposites, or mutually exclusive choices. Either/or. You can't have your cake and eat it too. He who is not for me is against me. Take sides. Crossing the Rubicon. All or nothing.

The more skillfully we avoid this way of sizing up our options, the better off we and our children will be. In rearing our children and in leading our own lives we must, of course, constantly make decisions. But each decision is only one step in a very long journey. It will shift us away from some possibilities, at least temporarily, yet at the same time it also opens up new ones. Before making any decision, we should survey the full circle of moves available to us. We need not lock ourselves into viewing the situation as affording only a few mutually exclusive choices. And after the step has been taken, and our perspective has been changed by that much, it is again important to survey the full circle of moves available to us.

How Our Way of Viewing Problems Matters

There are times when our children's needs must clearly take precedence over our own. A sick child needs attention, regardless of how tired we may be. Yet, even here, if we define the problem accurately as seeing that the child has the attention he needs, we may discover that the possibilities for handling it are more numerous than would appear at first glance. The mother of a three-year-old reports:

> George had a very rough case of chicken pox, and I was going out of my mind because my husband was away on business and there was nobody to spell me at night. When Judy, my best friend, called, it must have been evident what a state I was in. She said she would get her mother to stay with her kids and would be over shortly to take care of George so I could get some sleep. I protested, but she insisted. She said she'd had chicken pox and George liked her and wouldn't I do the same for her? She arrived within an hour with a note from her mother to me, saying Judy was to stay as long as needed —everything under control at the other end. Judy stayed two days, until George was comfortable enough so I could manage alone. As a result of that experience, Judy and I started a cooperative babysitting setup among our friends which covers emergencies as well as the usual. Like our group knows which parents have had which children's diseases, and we will take on each other's crying infants if one of us is desperate for sleep. The men suggested also including help with crying infants. Sometimes having a new person aboard really calms things down, and some of our best infant soothers are fathers.

Often it is in the financial area that our children's needs conflict with ours. Willie's need for orthodontic care obviously takes priority over our plans for a second honeymoon. But does meeting his need for braces really exclude meeting our need for a vacation alone? Have we considered the possibility of having Willie treated in a clinic rather than by a private orthodontist? And have we considered all the possible ways in which we might manage a second honeymoon fairly inexpensively, including arranging for our children to visit relatives while we stay home? Another mother says:

> Bill and I had been saving for several years to go to Europe together the summer of our fifteenth wedding anniversary. Bill would be due for four weeks' vacation for the first time, and his parents had offered to keep our three kids for us. Then the winter before we were due to go, Bill's father had a heart attack and our Jill had to have an appendectomy. Our plans were blown sky high. Jill's surgery took a big bite out of our savings, and we knew Bill's parents shouldn't take on our kids even if they offered to. We also knew that with Bill's father not entirely recovered, it wasn't the time to leave the country. We were pretty disappointed, and our friends and the people Bill works with knew it. One of Bill's co-workers mentioned that he had taken a very large house on the beach for the summer. It was really too expensive and too big for his family, and he was looking for somebody to share it. He suggested that if we went in together on the house for the season and we got along with each other's kids, maybe we could swap off caring for the lot so that each couple could go away on a vacation alone for a week or so. We took him up and it worked. Our kids adored being at the beach all summer, and Bill and I spent two great weeks alone together on a camping trip in the mountains. I can't say it was like going to Europe for Bill and

me, but it was a better vacation for all of us than I'd thought we could work out.

It Is Not Always So Easy

There is no question but that sometimes conflicts of interest between parent and child cannot be resolved, or even alleviated much, through tickling them with all the available feathers. Cooperative arrangements for caring for children, for example, are not a possible option for us if we do not know some other parents fairly well or if our child is not agreeable to such arrangements. Then, too, some parents simply do not find the idea appealing. If we are not by temperament suited to being involved in cooperative enterprises, we certainly should not push ourselves in this direction, at least not until we have exhausted all other options.

As for money, there are times when it simply runs out. We are left with no leeway for juggling expenditures. Everyday necessities consume all we have to spend.

In large matters and in small, parents often have to make sacrifices for their children. Generally we do it automatically, because we care about our children. Their well-being and their happiness matter more to us than our personal comfort. We do not expect them to notice and be grateful for all the ways in which we extend ourselves to meet their needs, though, of course, the occasional expressions of gratitude that we do get are heartwarming.

Sacrifices made in this spirit do not really violate our self-interest. Like the experience of walking the floor in the middle of the night with an unhappy baby and feeling him finally relax in our arms and drop off to sleep, they are their own reward. It is only when we begin constantly to resent our lot, when meeting our obligations as parents is continually felt as more of a burden than a pleasure, as inimical to our personal fulfillment, that the atmosphere becomes tainted and children and parents alike suffer.

Avoiding Unnecessary Resentment

Such a state of affairs is often due to demanding more of ourselves than is really required, or underestimating our children's ability to adjust their needs to accommodate ours. A six-year-old, for example, does not have an inalienable right to skip rope or bounce a ball in the hall if it gets on our nerves. Granted, the activity is pleasurable for him and does not harm the hall and does not get on every parent's nerves. But if it bothers us, we had better say so, not grit our teeth and suffer in silence.

As indicated all along, children whose rights are appropriately respected usually show surprising ability to heed a peremptory, "That noise is driving me nuts. Please find something else to do." Or, "Get those toys out from underfoot PLEASE." At an early age they can accept the fact that there are limits to our ability to tolerate noise, messiness, and such. They may not empathize with our limits. Grown-ups are a strange breed to children. Our ideas about what is important often seem peculiar to them. Yet the child is usually willing to honor his elders' peculiar needs if they are not too numerous and are clearly enunciated, and if he is thanked for it, and he knows that his own idiosyncrasies are respected even when they cannot be honored. That is a lot of "ifs," but they are all important.

In middle-class households a common cause of much parental irritation is the fact that children have a way of standing around and watching grown-ups work without feeling any urge to lend a hand. Wrapped up in regaling us with tales of their latest comings and goings, they may possibly step out of the path of the vacuum cleaner without being asked, but it will seldom occur to them to lift a finger to move a chair or any other piece of furniture. We tend to suffer our exasperation in silence because we want very much to be privy to their doings, and we do not need their help that much. They, in their turn, do not really comprehend why we become somewhat short-tempered. They know that we like them to tell us about their affairs, don't we? They have not been taught the lesson that less privileged children learn very early: Stay out of the way when grown-ups are working hard; otherwise you will be yelled at or roped into helping.

"Damn it," a father said to his eleven-year-old daughter who was accompanying her parents around their home, chattering happily, as her father and mother set about installing speakers for their newly acquired stereo, "don't you realize how infuriating it is to watch somebody taking it easy when you're working your head off?"

"Damn it," the girl responded with equal heat, "if you want me to help or to shut up, why don't you just ask?" In the ensuing conversation, the parents admitted that they should have expressed their feelings honestly right away, should have told the girl that while they wanted very much to hear what she had to say, this was not the time for an extended conversation. And the child admitted that it was understandable, once you stopped to think about it, that people would get annoyed at having you standing around running off at the mouth when they were hard at work. She had never before thought about it.

Middle-class children frequently are confused about when and how to lend a hand, and how to avoid irritating us when we are busy and their help is not needed. Too often, we fail to give them the specific guidance they need in this area. This does *them* a disservice, as well as ourselves, for it fosters habits of behavior that may make them seem spoiled in the eyes of many people.

Overprotection

Another source of unnecessary parental resentment is our natural tendency to spare our children many of the worries that we wrestle with. There are times, of course, when this is justified. Children should not be burdened with all our adult concerns about matters of health, finances, and the future. When we are deeply worried, however, it is wise to share this fact with our children in a fashion that is suited to their age and understanding.

For example, if a husband's job is in jeopardy, the strain that he and his wife are under will probably communicate itself to children as young as six or thereabouts. They sense that their parents are somehow different, harder to get along with. It may actually come as a relief to them to be told, "Daddy is worried about his job. He's afraid he may have to get another one. This makes him act cross sometimes, and me too. It isn't going to be like this forever, but we want you to know why we're upset, so you won't think it's your fault."

We need to remember that our children, even after they reach adolescence, think of us as being far more powerful and able to cope with the world and to protect them than we actually are. They simply do not worry, as we do, about what could happen if Daddy or Mommy lost their job. They assume that we will somehow continue to manage in the way that we have heretofore. This is just as well.

They can make allowances, often quite touchingly, for our behavior if they have been informed that we are under stress. But when no explanation whatsoever is offered, they tend to become difficult or withdrawn in response to our moodiness, and perhaps feel guilty about the situation, thinking they have brought it on somehow. This adds to the stress we are under already.

In sharing the truth with our children, we try not to frighten them or worry them needlessly. We withhold information that they cannot handle, though without resorting to lies. Certainly a father does not tell his children that, given his age, he is afraid he will not be able to find another job as good as the one he now has. If they question him about his plans, as young children may do, out of curiosity more than real anxiety, an "Oh, I'll find something" will settle the matter reassuringly and is an honest declaration of intent. Similarly, if a member of the family is gravely ill, a child has to be told the person is ill, so that he can handle our tension. However, he does not need to know how serious the illness is. If he asks if the person will get well, and if the circumstances demand that we be reassuring (which would certainly be true in the case of a parent's or a sibling's illness), we can respond that everything is being done to insure this and that we do not want him to worry. Again, the child's faith in our power to move mountains works to our advantage. Some such statement usually reassures the child under eight or nine and many older children. If it is apparent that a youngster, because of his age or temperament, still worries, we allow him to share his pain and anxiety with us, answering his questions honestly, though putting the best face possible on matters. By treating him as an equal, we let him experience at least the comfort of closeness with us.

Leveling appropriately with our children about what the family is up against is healthy for us and for them. It enables us to "ventilate" some of our feelings, so that pressure does not build up to an intolerable point. It guards against the possibility that our children may feel unnecessarily to blame for tensions that they detect in us. Finally, it encourages our children to face reality and to function as responsible members of the family who are expected to contribute what they can to the well-being of the household.

Trying to insulate our children from life as it is seldom makes any lasting contribution to their happiness and may seriously interfere with their maturing. As emphasized previously, we do not have to create artificial challenges in order to help them grow up. Life itself offers real challenges enough, even for the most fortunate. However, when challenges do arise, our children should be expected to face them to the extent of their ability.

The Temptation to Live Through Our Children

If parents do not take their own personal needs sensibly into account, they also greatly increase the ever-present risk that they will look to their children to provide them vicariously with the emotional satisfactions that every person craves. All of us identify to some extent with our children. We are buoyed by their successes and saddened by their failures. This is as it should be, so long as at the same time we maintain a healthy awareness that our offsprings' successes and failures are indeed theirs, not ours.

Self-fulfilled parents have that awareness. When Jane runs for president of her high school and makes it, we share her elation, but we do not see it as a victory that we have somehow personally wrought and can take credit for. It is her doing. Likewise, if she loses, we do our best to help her be philosophical about it. But we do not take the defeat personally, as if the outcome had depended on us and in some way diminishes us.

Being proud of or sad with our children is one thing. Trying to live through them is quite another. We have all known parents so determined that their children be or do what they themselves were never able to be or do that they run roughshod over the children's own feelings and interests. Parents who never went to college may become so obsessed with having their children go that they are blind to what kind of education would be best for the individual child concerned. A father who was never good at athletics may be determined that his son become an athlete, regardless of the son's interests. A mother who was never particularly popular may push her daughter socially, bent on having the child gain the kind of recognition the mother always wanted, even though the child is drawn to more introspective friends and activities. Some of the pressure that young people are under to gain admission to prestigious colleges is undoubtedly the result of parental needs rather than the needs of the young.

Of course, children are also often pressured to follow in the footsteps of parents who have achieved obvious success in one area or another. The mother who was a great belle pushes her daughter to be the same; the doctor father presses his son to go into medicine. Although it is natural to want one's children to do what one has found satisfying, empathic parents stop pushing when the child resists or shows differing habits. If pushing persists in the face of determined resistance, here, too, it is apparent that although the parents may seem to be self-fulfilled persons, they view their children as extensions of themselves rather than separate individuals with lives of their own to live. The parents cannot feel truly successful unless their children achieve success as the parents define it. A variety of factors may contribute to this, including on the part of one or both parents a limited concept of what constitutes the good life. The net result, however, is to place children in the unfair position of being instruments through which their parents attempt to achieve needed satisfactions. The parents should be paddling their own canoes.

Our children need us to guide them, to give them the full benefit of the wisdom that experience ordinarily confers, to point out the pitfalls of which the young are often unaware. But in the final analysis, our children must decide what they want to do with their lives. If we look appropriately to our own fulfillment as individuals, we are more likely to give our children their heads to the extent we should.

Fulfillment in Work

There are many men as well as women who view working with children as the most challenging and satisfying of all possible tasks. We have pediatricians and child therapists and teachers and full-time mothers who love their work and find it deeply fulfilling. Today there is a tendency in some circles to denigrate the job of full-time mother, unless a woman is being paid to mother children other than her own. This is as silly as the tendency not long ago to denigrate any mother who worked outside her home.

The only real problem about the job of full-time mother—if you like it, that is—is that unlike being a teacher, pediatrician, or such, it has a limited future. By the time you reach your prime, or earlier, you will be—perhaps *should* be is correct here—in the market for another job. Once all the children are in school for most of the day, they no longer require full-time maternal attention. If at that point a mother does not have some other interests to engage her energies, both she and her children may suffer.

Every woman has to resolve her need for fulfilling work in her own way. A wider range of choices is open to her now than ever before. More women than ever before are combining rearing children with holding down a full- or part-time job. More men are eager, not just willing, to share in all aspects of child care from the moment their babies arrive on the scene, which makes it easier for mothers to work. A growing number of fathers are willing to arrange their working lives so that they can take on the care of their children while their wives secure professional training or get started in a career. For the woman who does not need to work for money, there is a greater variety of opportunities to be involved in stimulating volunteer activities in the community than ever before. Also, society at large is more open to the idea of enabling women in their middle years who have reared their children to return to school or find jobs that utilize skills learned through running a home and bringing up children. On-the-job training is coming back into vogue.

Nevertheless, if a woman wants to work, or has to work, when her children are small, she is likely to find the going rough occasionally. The major concern of most working mothers is the kind of care their children receive in their absence.

Then, too, as one working mother says, "Don't tell me it's the *quality* of the time you spend with your children rather than the amount that's important. Both are important." Working mothers with small children, and even school-age ones, had best accept the fact that they will be pulled in conflicting directions from time to time. But that also happens if a mother stays at home. Increasingly, professional people who work with children and families are coming to the common-sense conclusion that if a woman really wants to work, she and her children will be better off if she does, and that society should assume the responsibility for providing first-rate facilities for the care of children of all working mothers during whatever hours the mother is at her job. This may soon come about, though the care will probably not be free for all mothers, as some groups have urged. Still, it should be relatively inexpensive compared to employing household help.

What about a father's right to fulfillment in work? It is becoming increasingly apparent that many men with jobs that pay very well are not happy in their work. They feel locked into their jobs by the need to support their families (and themselves) in the fashion to which all have grown accustomed. This, too, seems to be changing somewhat. The number of young men who are more concerned about how interesting and socially useful a job is than about how much it will pay appears to be growing. Some corporations are sending out long-haired recruiters to college campuses in the hope of influencing greater numbers of the better-qualified graduates to consider going to work for them. One such recruiter says, "You just wind up listening to guys trying to persuade you to go into elementary school teaching, or police work. *Police work.*"

The crumbling of stereotyped attitudes toward work (or anything else) is a heartening sign. If it enables more members of our society, regardless of sex, race, or class, to arrive at more innovative ways of reconciling their personal interests, their financial needs, and their children's needs, society as well as the families concerned will be strengthened.

Fulfillment in Marriage

Some members of the women's liberation movement are warning women nowadays that children can interfere with having a satisfying relationship with a man. This is not news. Psychiatrists have been pointing out for years the ways in which children test the strength of a marriage and the emotional maturity of both partners. They have always cautioned against having children in the hope of saving a shaky marriage.

Nevertheless, if a marriage is sound to begin with, children can strengthen the bonds between a man and a woman and add new dimensions to their relationship. The birth of a baby is a kind of emotional high-water mark, like falling in love. Mature partners who have shared these two experiences are linked by bonds capable of withstanding a great deal of rough weather.

Yet children can put a strain on the personal relationship between man and wife in two ways. They consume a great deal of the time and energy of both parents, especially during the child's early years. In addition, their presence tends to reactivate any problems that either parent once had with his or her own parents or siblings—and all of us once had some.

About the matter of time, husband and wife will have to learn to budget it carefully, so that they still have time to be themselves and time for each other, as well as good times with their children.

The sexual relationship is a crucial factor in the health of a marriage, though partners who have earned each other's devotion have much in addition to hold them together.

The so-called sexual revolution of today

has not really taught us anything about sex that was not known already. There is nothing new about sex outside marriage, or the desire to experience unrestrained sexual pleasure without guilt. Available research makes it clear that the vast majority of men and women, including the sexually "liberated," still hope to find sexual fulfillment within the context of some kind of continuing relationship. Couples should not need a marriage counselor or psychiatrist to tell them that this happens only if both persons involved give careful, considerate attention to making it happen—at least if the relationship lasts any length of time.

Yet, there is clinical evidence that many sophisticated young men and women who start off together with excellent sex let it dwindle away gradually because both keep waiting for lightning to strike, as it did constantly when they were first getting to know each other. Lightning *can* strike surprisingly often, even after years of being married and rearing children. But not unless both partners carefully nurture the spark, through all the days and nights when there are babies to walk the floor with, toddlers to run after, preschoolers to be helped to get over their fear of the dark, homework to be supervised, bills that somebody has to earn the money to pay, teen-agers to sit down with at the oddest hours, when they just happen to show an inclination to let down their hair and talk, and talk, and talk, as if for the first time in their lives they thought we knew something they did not know.

A good long-term sexual relationship, like any work in progress, sometimes streaks ahead under its own steam. At other times it proceeds more prosaically. The artisan works at it faithfully, knowing that if he neglects it too often or for too long a spell the initial inspiration will be hard to recapture.

The presence of children can activate a parent's ancient history at any point in a marriage. A father feels jealous of his baby's claim on his wife's attention. A mother feels left out as she watches her husband and their teen-age son planning a fishing expedition together. Parents find themselves in competition with each other for the affection or admiration of a child—or in competition with their own youngster, striving not to be outdone in this, that, or the other. Petty. Childish. But we cannot help how we feel.

The minute there are more than two people in the family picture, our old reactions to being just one among several, rather than the favored one, are likely to be triggered. We may compete, or withdraw, be jealous, hurt, angry, whatever, not so much because of what is specifically being done to us in the present, but because the present setup hooks us into how we reacted to similar setups in the past. Parents who are aware of the subtle ways in which children can bring out in us the child we once were are in a better position to avoid relating immaturely to their children and to each other. They tell each other honestly when they feel hurt or left out or angry, and work things out in terms of what is going on now. The ghosts of the past are more likely to be laid if we cope with the present forthrightly. Again, we do not try to analyze each other, just be honest about what we are feeling.

Divorce

Some marriages cannot be made to work. Responsible persons generally find it difficult to break off any relationship that has once meant something. If the relationship is a marriage that involves children, breaking it up is even harder. However, it sometimes needs to be done. The weight of the evidence convincingly supports the idea that children are better able to cope with divorce than with living in a home where parents are hopelessly at odds.

This is not to say that divorce is easy for children. As with other difficult challenges, however, children can manage if they are given adequate support from adults who matter to them. It is important that they not feel somehow to blame for the divorce, and that parents not deliberately attempt to undermine each other's standing with their children.

Grandparents and other relatives can be enormously helpful to children when parents divorce. Being a part of an extended family reassures a child that come what may, somebody will take care of him lovingly. That can remove what is perhaps the greatest threat that divorce poses for children: the fear of being left without any loved and caring adult to look after them. A child can get over losing, partially or completely, someone he loves if others whom he loves remain reliably in the picture. A selective list of materials on divorce is included in the Bibliography.

One-parent Families

Attitudes toward the one-parent family appear to be changing. Many professionals are pointing out that it is the overall quality of a child's home life, not who rears him, that matters. A recent roundup of all available research on children reared by one parent indicates that they seem to turn out as emotionally healthy as children from intact families if the person who rears them is aware of their special needs. All children do need to have close ties with adults of both sexes, but opportunities can be found for a child with only one parent for some such ties outside the immediate family circle, if this need is understood.

One sign of changing attitudes is the fact that some respected adoption agencies now permit single persons, male as well as female, to adopt young children. Of course, a single parent may often be subjected to extra stress simply because she or he is solely responsible for meeting the everyday challenges of living with a child. When a child is in a balky mood, or wakes up in the night with a fever, two parents have more going for them than one. Financial strains on the one-parent family also tend to be more acute, and if the parent works, seeing that the child is at all times and under all conditions adequately looked after is more continually a worry than if there were two to share the responsibility.

Thus, while single parents can succeed as well as any if they understand their children's individual needs, they are more likely to require support from friends, relatives, and the community. In many instances, appropriate support from the community is not forthcoming, although outstanding exceptions are often found in black communities. Similar exceptions can also be found in the military services, where there is special sensitivity to the problems of women separated from their husbands for extended periods and required to function as single parents.

The emphasis throughout this series is on the kind of care that *all* children need. When developmental challenges, such as the preschooler's need to identify with members of his own sex, might pose special problems in a one-parent family, single parents are alerted to this possibility and to ways of handling the challenge in their particular circumstances.

Disappointments and Lasting Difficulties

No matter how fulfilled we are as individuals and how successfully we resist the temptation to live through our children, we will have our share of parental disappointments. There will be times when our children's choices are not what we hoped for, but we must accept their right to choose. Watching a youngster move in his own directions is occasionally quite painful (as well as often exhilarating), as it inevitably involves some learning through trial and error and some breaking away from our views and priorities. Yet such hurts need not be lasting if we keep open our lines of communication with our children and relate to them as individuals with lives of their own to lead.

Then there are the disappointments that nature deals us. These are harder for even the healthiest parents to handle. Brilliant parents sometimes have quite ordinary children; not all boys are big and strong; not all girls are pretty; some children are born with pronounced physical or mental handicaps.

There is a profound difference, of course, between having low-normal intelligence and being retarded. There is an equally big difference between being "plain" and being deaf. Yet a child of low-normal intelligence in a bright family and an ugly duckling in a handsome family can subject parents to lasting strains on the order of those felt by parents of many children designated as handicapped.

It is all very well to assert that we should not be so concerned about boys being big and strong, girls being pretty, and children of both sexes being "bright." Of course, as parents and as a society our goal should be simply to enable every child to be accepted as he is and to develop to the fullest whatever potential he brings into the world. However, it is of no help to disappointed parents (or their children) to say that they have no right to be disappointed. The first step in working innovatively with our children is to face up realistically to the situation and all our feelings about it. That done, we are in a position to look for positive factors and build well on them.

Every handicap presents its own special challenges to the child and to his family. It may necessitate special training of one kind or another. Sometimes it requires institutionalization. Depending on the severity of the handicap, the child may or may not be expected eventually to lead a relatively normal life. Coming to terms with what can and cannot be expected is frequently difficult for parents and may require expert counseling.

There may be a temptation to go from professional to professional with the hope of hearing a more favorable prognosis or turning up a new treatment—surgical, psychological, or medicinal. There are times when getting another opinion is justified, but this is not a course to pursue indefinitely, even if one has the money to do so. Generally one is much better off if, when a new professional is consulted, arrangements are made for the new person to have access to the records and opinions of all professionals who have been seen previously.

Accepting Our Children and Ourselves

There is a difference between accepting people the way they presently are and settling for this as being the outside limits of what they can ever become. A paramount aim of this book has been to try to help parents feel this distinction in their bones.

Tomorrow is always another day. People change, even after they are well into middle years. Circumstances also change. It is self-defeating to expect miracles of life or of any individual, but it is equally self-defeating to assume that the way things are now is the way they must always be.

Our needs and our children's needs mesh differently as we and they grow. In general, our children should become able to do and to give more with the passage of time. Yet there will be exceptions that we and they will have to ride with. They may sometimes be asked to give beyond their years, which can make them proud. We may sometimes need to find depths of patience that we did not think we had or feel we had to have, which can enlarge us.

Nobody can promise anybody a rose garden. Much that happens to all of us will depend upon the society in which we live. Yet if we and our children can manage to be accepting of each other, and of ourselves, ask enough but not too much of each other, and of ourselves, family life will be a more stimulating and growth-provoking experience for all concerned.

Useful Guide to Child Behavior Ages 1 Through 5

HOW AN AVERAGE ONE-YEAR-OLD BEHAVES

Each child sets his own pace of growth, but knowledge of children in general, as shown in this typical day in the life of a one-year-old, is valuable in interpreting individual behavior and rate of development.

WAKING

Usually early wakers. May call out or cry. Happy to see Mother.

Needs changing. Cracker may satisfy immediate hunger.

BREAKFAST AND DRESSING

Usually is hungry at breakfast. May want his bottle even though he drinks fairly well from cup.

Frequently has an after-breakfast bowel movement. It is generally advised not to start toilet training before 18 to 24 months.

May cooperate in dressing by putting arm in sleeve or holding out leg for pants. Practices undressing himself.

MORNING ACTIVITIES

Likes to climb and cruise, pulling things out of shelves. . .

Likes to toss things out. May want Mother to be his retriever. May be happy in playpen for a while.

MORNING ACTIVITIES

Loves to explore. Full supervision necessary to prevent shocks, burns and accidents when he is freely roaming about.

Likes toys that fit inside each other, clothespins and basket.

NAPTIME

Naptimes may vary. May skip a nap one day and need more sleep the next.

AFTER NAP

May need diaper change or toileting, if ready. May show interest in procedure and product.

LUNCH

Appetite varies due to teething and other growth factors. If self-feeding, may want help for part of meal.

May be finicky about food. Introduce new foods in small amounts. May refuse to eat unless allowed to feed himself.

Likes to eat with his fingers. Developing ability to spoon feed himself. Will grab the spoon and try to use it.

AFTERNOON ACTIVITIES

Wants to be on the go. Impatient for an outing if he does not nap after lunch.

Loves to get out of doors. Watches cars and people with interest.

Likes to watch other children playing. But isn't yet ready to play with them.

Apt to wary of strangers. Will warm up to people gradually. Doesn't like to be rushed.

EARLY EVENING

Ready for play with Daddy. Delights in peek-a-boo, being chased and hiding.

Likes to practice walking with his hand held. Most children learn to walk alone between 12 months and 15 months, but may still creep part of the time.

BATHTIME

Enjoys his bath. Likes to play with washcloth, soap and water toys.

EVENING

Uses "mama," "dada," and a few other words.

Light supper is frequently favored. May want a bedtime bottle.

May go right to sleep, play a bit or resist falling asleep.

WHAT TO EXPECT OF A TWO-YEAR-OLD

In this typical day in the life a two-year-old, based on hundreds of different observations, it is possible to trace the abilities and behavior traits which tend to appear in many children of the same age.

STARTS DAY

May play happily in crib for half an hour after waking. Glad to see his mother.

Most children are wet in the morning.

Usually eats small breakfast. May still need a little help feeding himself.

Gaining good control of elimination. Begins to take responsibility for toileting himself.

MORNING ACTIVITIES

Interested in dressing and undressing, but still needs help. Can put arms into armholes, feet into pants.

Likes to imitate and tries to help with chores.

If left unsupervised, can turn room topsy-turvy.

Uses 2 to 4 word sentences. Refers to self by name. Vocabulary grows by leaps and bounds.

BEHAVIOR TRAITS

May enjoy playing near another child, but not actually with her.

May grab other child's toys, but refuse to share his. Doesn't yet know what sharing means.

Likes to feed himself—still spills a lot. May ask to be fed.

AFTERNOON

Usually naps but with some difficulty.

Builds tower or train of several blocks. Likes to play with action toys. Enjoys painting, clay.

Likes stroller, car rides, walking on curbs and low walls.

EARLY EVENING

Enjoys time with Daddy. Likes to point to and name objects in picture books.

Relishes rough-and-tumble, though best not to overstimulate him before bedtime.

EVENING

Some children find it hard to be with both parents. May want attention, interrupt parents absorbed in conversation.

Affectionate toward mother. May whine and cling to her.

If mother is pregnant, and child notices bulge, wise to tell child baby is growing inside her.

Likely to be upset if a member of the family is absent for a few days or if family moves.

Shows both jealousy and love toward new baby. Good to get jealousy out in the open. Reassure him through extra attention.

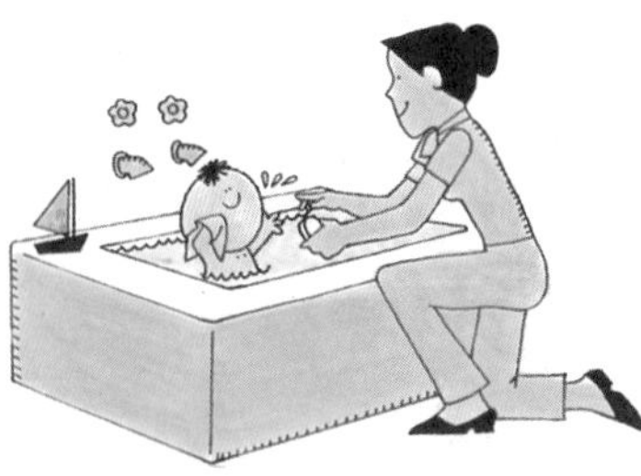

Helps wash himself in bath. Usually loves water play.

SUPPER

Likes to help mother in the kitchen. Responsive to praise and encouragement.

BEDTIME

Often finds it hard to fall asleep. Many demands. May come out of room.

Resists being picked up at night, though may wake self for toileting. Waking child for toileting rarely helps in nighttime control.

INTRODUCING THE THREE-YEAR-OLD

Three is a delightful age. A child has greater self-control, is friendly and cooperative, and is learning to manage social relationships, as can be demonstrated in this typical day.

MORNING ACTIVITIES

Frequently whines and fusses upon awakening. May drowse off after getting mother's help in toileting.

Cheers up when fully awake. Usually likes to frisk around parents' room before getting dressed.

May need or want some help with dressing.

Appetite may be good at breakfast. Feeds himself skillfully—not much parental help is needed.

Will cooperate if asked, in small tasks like clearing the table, tidying his own room.

Sometimes creates imaginary playmates, pets, or pretends that he is an animal.

Alternates between pestering brothers and sisters and getting along with them.

Learns to ride tricycle. Likes to go marketing with mother.

LUNCH

May have definite likes and dislikes in food.

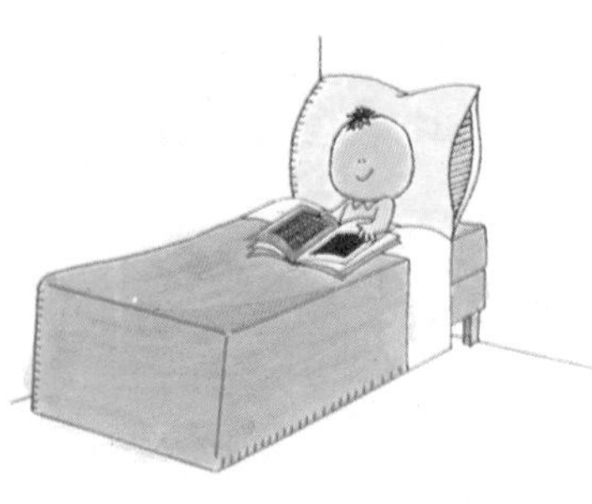

May rest at naptime but frequently does not go to sleep.

Begins to play with other children, as well as beside them. He has definite choice in friends.

Needs guidance when play gets quarrelsome.

Notices sex differences. Questions should be answered simply, truthfully.

May handle genitals. Can be quite matter-of-factly distracted from sex play.

Enjoys painting, crayoning, modeling with clay. Results seldom resemble what he calls them.

Likes music. Recites short rhymes, sings part of songs, usually off key

EVENING ACTIVITIES

Likes to have familiar stories read over and over. Enjoys explaining pictures.

Welcomes playtime with his father. Enjoys simple guessing games and puzzles.

Listens to adults. Wants to please and enjoys praise. Likes to master new words.

Affectionate toward parents. Mother is generally the favorite.

Enjoys meals with the family.

Likes to help prepare his bath, wash himself. May get out unwillingly.

When he knows parents are going out, he may say good-by cheerfully. Or he may protest.

BEDTIME

May play in bed for half-hour or so. Usually goes to sleep without too many demands.

May want bathroom privacy and need little help in toileting.

Outcropping fears: of the dark, dogs, other animals, noise. Needs reassurance.

Begins to talk about his dreams and may occasionally be awakened by a bad dream.

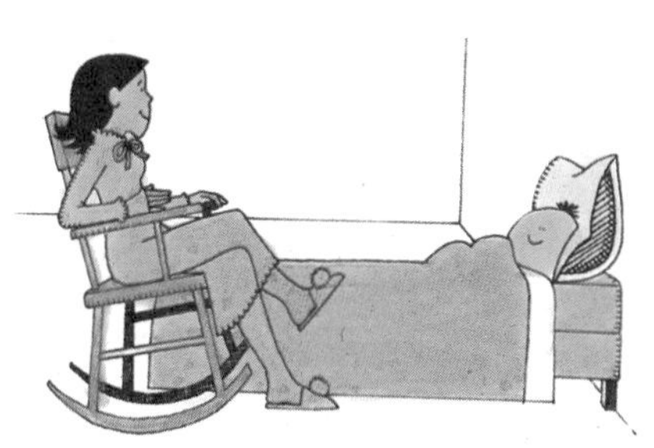

May want to get in bed with parents. But can usually be diverted if parent stays with him a while.

A PICTORIAL GUIDE TO THE FOUR-YEAR-OLD

Every four-year-old is different; yet studies of thousands of children of this age show that they have certain abilities, interests and characteristics in common. It is a help to parents to know what in general to expect.

MORNING

Generally wakes in the morning in a cheerful humor. Takes care of own immediate needs.

Can almost completely dress himself if clothes are easily at hand.

Sandbox, swing, climbing apparatus are popular outdoor equipment.

Enjoys nursery school or a play group, since he usually prefers play with others to solitary play.

Verbal ability grows. Quarreling, tattling, boasting are common.

Is continually asking questions —both to get information and to make conversation.

Play still needs some supervision. Quarrels may lead to too much hitting, kicking, throwing.

He begins to understand rules and restrictions. Blocks are for building as balls are for throwing.

A calm reaction works best when a child rebels.

May frequently annoy older brothers and sisters and bully younger ones.

He has definite likes and dislikes in food. Eats skillfully.

AFTERNOON

Frequently wants toilet privacy but may still ask for help with difficult clothing. Controls daytime urination well.

May rest briefly after lunch, but seldom naps. May play quietly with books, toys.

Vivid imagination is frequently expressed in dramatic play, imitation of adults.

Boys may play with dolls, girls with boyish toys. Playing "house" is a favorite joint activity.

Likes to paint and crayon, though he may change theme in the middle. Details are crude.

Likes to try musical instruments, play records. Takes part in singing games.

EVENING

Makes intricate buildings with blocks. Admires his own work. Likes to have father help.

A peak age for crying and whining if bored or hurt. Needs comforting, then distraction.

EVENING

Listens with interest to verse and action stories. May have increased attention span for those explaining how things work.

Frequently clings affectionately to parents. Likes to be cuddled. Enjoys tumbling.

May want to be told more than once how babies are born.

Bathing, toileting of both sexes together offers healthy ways to observe sex differences.

Can bathe himself if mother supervises.

Enjoys eating with the family. But should be excused from table when his appetite is satisfied.

BEDTIME

May be fearful of the dark, animals, fire engines, old people, but may try to hide his fears.

Goes to bed without serious objections—especially if he can recognize bedtime hour on the clock.

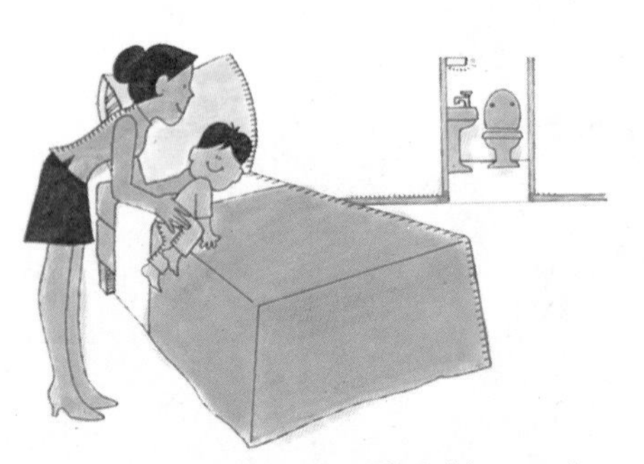

May wake to go to the toilet. May want Mother to see him back to bed.

PORTRAIT OF A FIVE-YEAR-OLD

Early childhood is almost over when a child is five. Here is a self-reliant individual who enjoys groups. Although all "five's" differ from each other, they have traits in common, and it is helpful to parents to know what in general to expect.

TYPICAL ACTIVITIES

Can dress himself efficiently if his clothes are put out for him.

Plays well in group, often in cooperative projects. Adult needed as distant patrolman, rather than close supervisor.

Likes to go on expeditions with Father. Enjoys helping Father with household repairs.

Usually adjusts easily to Kindergarten. May want Mother to stay with him a short time.

Likes to build with blocks. Usually finishes a project he starts.

Likes to paint, draw, cut and do collage. Has become definitely right- or left-handed.

Very energetic. Adept on tricycle and climbing apparatus. Can handle some simple tools.

TYPICAL ACTIVITIES

Talks a lot and clearly. Can tell a story, enjoys talking on the telephone and can take a simple message.

Enjoys having parents read to him. Memory enables him to "read" to younger brothers and sisters. Some are actually able to read.

Likes to play simple counting and alphabet games. Knows penny, nickel, dime.

Likes to play records, dance, listen to radio and TV. Some can pick out tune on piano.

BEHAVIOR TRAITS

Washes efficiently before meals, if reminded.

Feeds self skillfully and likes company at meals.

Usually wants to please and help Mother, but may become angry if thwarted.

Begins to understand time words. Interested in clock and calendar.

Will usually cooperate in plan to give up thumb-sucking.

Two play best together. If there are three, two children are apt to gang up on one.

Both boys and girls interested in playing with dolls. Both express desire to have own babies.

Becoming bashful about letting others see him undressed. May insist on privacy in the bathroom

BEHAVIOR TRAITS

Enjoys visiting his grandparents, hearing their stories about his own parents' childhood.

Likes Sunday school (though it's too much to expect him to sit through regular church services).

BEDTIME

May be afraid of thunder, and sirens at night. Afraid that Mother will go away and not return, or not be there if he awakens.

May have nightmares and have trouble getting back to sleep.

Comforting and reassuring the child will help him conquer fears. Logical arguments and ridicule won't help.

BOOK TWO

Your Child's First Three Years

By SARA D. GILBERT

Introduction

NO ONE CAN tell you how to raise your children. Every adult is unique, and every child is, too. It is the aim of this book to encourage you to get to know your baby and to explore your own personal strengths and weaknesses so that you can be self-confident individuals guiding your baby in his first explorations of the world during his first three years.

Understanding the basic patterns of human physical growth and psychological development can help you know what to expect when.

New research on learning, intellectual growth, and social development may give you an idea of what physical and mental feats your child will accomplish during his first three years.

Sharing experiences that other parents have had with the routines of baby care and child management may suggest new ideas to you and encourage you to think through your own child-rearing techniques.

This book is not broken down by age limits, because babies do not grow according to timetables. Instead, the chapters are organized around a general topic and arranged in the order in which you'll probably meet an interest. The first is a general outline of the first three years. The next two cover matters usually raised during the first few months. Chapters 4, 5, and 6 take you through the first year and examine issues that have important implications for the future. Chapters 7 through 10 deal with crucial challenges of the second and third years. Chapter 11 covers the not-so-terrible twos saying their good-bye to babyhood, more or less. Chapter 12 raises questions you may ask at any time, and the final chapter again takes up the period as a whole and looks to the future. To check on specific topics, you can consult the index.

Although this volume contains some information on infant-care routines and general health care, its limited length does not allow provision of detailed technical how-to or medical advice.

Instead, the book outlines the experiences and challenges you and your baby will share during his first three years and suggests ways of meeting them.

Many books written during this era of surging "woman power" need to state a defense against charges of "sexism," and this one is no exception. Although the tradition may change, "he" is still the customary pronoun to use when referring to either sex. If your baby is a girl, please feel free to prefix an "s" to every "he." You may also notice the assumption that the infant's chief caretaker is Mommy, not Daddy. A small but apparently growing number of American families have arranged their lives around a working wife and a home-keeping husband. Since they are still a minority, the male homemakers will hopefully not take offense if this volume calls them "Mommy."

1
Your Baby Will Grow Up

ALL KIDS START small and get bigger. They do it so fast in their first three years that the mother of a three-year-old can hardly believe her child was ever a tiny, helpless newborn. Yet when she first brought her baby home, she may have thought he was the most remarkable creature she had ever encountered. A new mother cannot imagine her infant actually growing up; after three years she will have almost forgotten how a newborn behaves.

The human growth process is especially noticeable in the first years of life. Beginning as a not-quite-complete organism utterly dependent on his mother for survival, a child becomes a fairly independent person who is able to walk, feed himself, talk a little, and usually use a toilet instead of diapers.

Each child goes about growing in his own way and at his own pace. At first, a baby may look a lot like all the others in the hospital nursery, at least to a disinterested observer. But he is a unique being. The combination of characteristics contained in the chromosomes and genes that were passed on selectively from his parents are his alone. His body, mind, personality, and behavior probably carry his own special brand even from before the moment of birth.

Our baby is as different from other babies —and from each of us—as any person is from another. By the time he is three, as this individuality interacts with his environment and with our personality, we will see him become even more definitely "himself."

Still, our baby's development will follow certain patterns common to the entire human species. By the end of his first three years, a healthy baby will have reached a stage of development generally similar to that of other healthy three-year-old human beings. It may help a new parent to glance at how an infant progresses from birth to age three. For when we are in the throes of diaper-changing, burping, and 2 A.M. feedings, we may be unable to believe that the child will ever be able to do anything for himself. Indeed, we may occasionally wonder, "Why did I get myself into this?"

Young parents can easily forget the point of it all. It is often reassuring to view our infant in the context of his probable overall development during these first three years. This may even enable us to better understand him as an individual and help him follow his own developmental path, rather than doing battle with him all the way along it.

By the end of about 36 months, with a little luck and patience, we can look forward to having a child who, in his own manner, has become weaned from bottle or breast and strained food, who can walk and talk, and who has some degree of control of his bowels and bladder.

Convenient as these achievements are, they are, in a way, only the more striking outward signs of spectacular, though not always obvious, overall growth. Weaning, walking, talking, and toileting can be seen as results of many basic advances our baby makes as he develops from infancy into childhood—advances that may be classified as *physical, sensorimotor, cognitive,* and *psychological,* or "emotional."

Physical Growth

The most obvious area of early development is, of course, actual physical growth. Our baby's weight will generally increase from an average of 7 pounds at birth to between 30 and 35 pounds at the end of his third year. (Incidentally, birth weight offers an example of individual differences: our baby probably did not weigh 7 pounds. He may have weighed under 5, or well over 9. And as if asserting his independence already, he probably did not weigh what we and the doctor had predicted.) From an average length of 20 inches, he will stretch to a height of over three feet.

Earliest growth will be the most rapid; the rate of growth will slow down near the end of the first year. Birth weight will triple in the first year, for instance, then slow dramatically. And our baby probably won't grow steadily, but in spurts.

In the two years following our baby's seventh month or so, approximately 20 teeth will sprout in his little mouth. His head, molded oddly by his trip through the birth canal and probably bald soon after, will round out and grow a good crop of hair. His hair and eyes are likely to shift from their birth color to shades he has inherited through our genes. His very shape and proportions will change, from that of a curled-up, top-heavy polliwog at birth to that of a pudgy, miniature human being after he starts to walk.

Sensorimotor Development

As our baby's body grows, his senses sharpen and his muscles gain strength and skill. The growth, integration, and coordination of the senses, nerves, and muscles is called sensorimotor development.

A healthy newborn, or neonate, has the use of all five senses in that he can see, hear, feel, smell, and taste. *What* he perceives through his senses, however, is probably quite limited. Exactly how fuzzy or precise a newborn's sensory perceptions are is a subject that has long interested child psychologists and other scientists. Research has shown that the newborn's eyes respond to bright lights, color, and moving objects. Most newborns startle at loud noises, and some will turn their heads in the direction of sounds. The senses of taste and smell are difficult to test, although investigation has confirmed what common sense would suggest—that neonates prefer sweet tastes to sour or salty ones and vigorously dislike such pungent, irritating smells as that of ammonia.

Probably, a neonate is most responsive to tactile stimuli—those related to the sense of touch. For instance, he shows discomfort when he is too warm or too cold. (And he is more vulnerable than adults to changes in temperature, because his internal temperature regulator does not function very efficiently at first.) A newborn also likes being held close, although there is more to that than the sense of touch.

The newborn can feel such externally caused pain as pinpricks, though apparently not as intensely as does an adult. The baby is especially sensitive to touch on his face, particularly around his mouth. Stroking an infant's cheeks or lips will stimulate a searching and sucking motion, "rooting" for a nipple. This sensitive response to touch is a major factor in the infant's primary task—finding food and thus staying alive.

When the baby is first born, he has some "survival reflexes," which, according to some theorists, are leftovers from earlier levels of evolution. The neonatal "grasp reflex" enables many newborns to grasp a bar tightly enough to support themselves. The "Moro reflex," which occurs when an infant is startled, is a tight pulling-together of all the limbs after they have suddenly been outspread, seemingly a "grabbing-on" reaction. If man were still a monkey, he would need these two reflexes to keep from falling out of trees. Likewise, he would need the newborn's "swimming reflex" if he still lived in water.

Whatever their original purpose, these involuntary reflexes disappear soon after birth, to be replaced, a little later in life, by learned, or voluntary, activities that appear similar. Some tiny babies, for example, seem able to creep across their cribs because they straighten out their legs and automatically push when their feet touch a resistant surface. This early "creeping," which may be part of an infant's unkinking process, precedes by many months intentional locomotion.

A newborn is capable of more than reflex activity, of course. He can deliberately move his entire body, although he generally lacks the spinal strength to lift his shoulders and head enough to turn his face when lying on his stomach.

At birth, he is a much more complex and capable creature than he appears. As soon as he enters the world, his senses and body begin reacting to and interacting with the stimulation offered by his environment. His perceptions grow sharper and his movements more purposeful, and he learns to coordinate the two. Some babies make quicker sensorimotor progress than others within the broad range of normal development.

Growth Trends

Babies develop from head to foot: the closer a sense organ, muscle, or nerve system is to the head, the earlier it will mature. A newborn's head is the most active part of his body: his mouth and throat are the busiest—crying and sucking, smiling, grimacing and yawning—but his eyes are active, too, and he can move his head purposefully in all directions. As the childhood specialist Arnold Gesell puts it, "The infant can lift his head in the first week of life; not until the end of the first year does he stand on his feet."

At the same time, a baby develops outward. This proximodistal, or near-to-far, trend means that a baby can move his neck, torso, and other close-in body parts well before he can effectively operate his fingers and toes.

A third trend common to all babies is from bilateral to unilateral, or two-sided to one-sided. This means that at first an infant is equally adept, or equally awkward, at using both sides of his body. Gradually, however, he comes to prefer one side. Some children reveal their "handedness" early in the first year; others alternate between left- and right-handedness throughout the second year and even longer. The origin is not yet completely understood. It is known that it is not "better" to be right-handed and "worse" to be left-handed. What does matter is that a child choose one or the other eventually, because confusion over handedness is often associated with a variety of psychological and emotional difficulties. We may be able to encourage a choice of hands without forcing if we consistently hand a baby objects to one hand rather than the other. The right hand is probably preferable, since this is a right-handed world.

The baby will gain control of his large muscles before his smaller ones. The coordination needed to make precise movements comes slowly; a five-month-old can grab a large wooden ring out of his mother's hand, for example, but it takes a lot more maturation before he can slip the ring over a stick.

Eye-hand Coordination

The coordination of the senses plays an important role in such reaching and grasping. Automatic as it may seem to a grownup, picking up a nearby object is a very difficult task. A baby must be able to focus clearly on the object, and he must have learned some of the visual cues that help him tell how close the object is. Then, he must be able to move his arm to the proper distance in the right direction and to manipulate his fingers well enough to grasp the object. Such simple but crucial eye-hand coordination is usually achieved, after much trial and error, by most babies in the fourth month.

Thus, we see how hard a baby must work to grow up. He will barely have mastered one feat before he is pushing on to the next. Why healthy babies work so hard to mature is a mystery. Some psychologists call it a *drive,* an inborn push, toward maturity. Whatever it is, it makes watching our baby an exciting adventure every day as he works toward the four major achievements of his first few years: walking, weaning, talking, and bowel and bladder control. These accomplishments are not simply physical feats. Their psychological, social, and emotional aspects are discussed later. Still, before he can manage each of them, his sensorimotor development must have reached a certain minimum level.

Walking

The baby's first progress on the way to walking involves his spine: he learns to turn his head when lying on his stomach. Then, around the fourth or fifth month, he becomes able to push his head and shoulders up while lying prone and to hold his head steady when held upright. During the next few months he will become able to sit unsupported, and in the second half of his first year he will be getting himself into a sitting position. By about the middle of his first year, he will be able to roll over and back, and soon he will be scooting around on his belly or back. In the second half of his first year, he will probably get himself to a hands-and-knees, one-hand-one-knee, or hands-and-feet position and be able to creep or crawl around. Near his first birthday, perhaps, he will be able to pull himself to a standing position and stand unsupported. By the middle of his second year he will probably be able to walk on his own.

Weaning

Weaning and self-feeding require control of mouth and hands. A newborn's hands are almost always fisted. When a baby first learns to hold things, during his fourth month or so, he uses all five fingers in an awkward, paw-like manner. By his ninth month, however, the baby will probably be using that uniquely human piece of equipment, the opposable thumb: he can coordinate his four fingers with the separate action of his thumb to pick up and manipulate small objects. During the first half of his second year, he will be able to use index finger and thumb alone for even greater precision. At first, he will probably use only one hand at a time, clutching something in the inactive one to keep it out of the way. Around the beginning of his second year he will discover that both hands will cooperate for a greater range of activities. As his manual dexterity increases, he can learn to hold a cup, finger foods, and eventually a spoon and fork.

Before a child can feed himself, he must be able to coordinate the muscles of the mouth, tongue, and throat. A newborn can use his mouth for crying and for a kind of continuous sucking-swallowing motion. After two or three months his muscles are capable of other movements, and he can take in other than liquid food. By his sixth month a baby can use his mouth for foods that are not all mush. Some babies have teeth by then. They are not much good for chewing until later (although they are a good reason for weaning from the breast), but the baby, toothed or untoothed, can use his gums to mash his food.

Talking

Talking is an oral achievement that is social and intellectual as much as physical. But learning language requires sufficient development of the mouth and throat, as well as good hearing. During his second or third month the baby will probably begin to make noncrying noises. These increase in scope and complexity until, by the end of his first year, he may be saying real words as well as sending forth a constant stream of "babbling": conversation-like, meaningless sounds. During his second year, the baby will probably begin to talk in words and short phrases, though some children put this off until a bit later. In his third year, the child's vocabulary expands strikingly. He has probably begun to decipher the grammatical structure of language—a remarkable feat—and is talking in sentences, especially sentences that end with a question mark.

Toilet Training

Toilet training, too, depends on the interaction of many factors. This is discussed further in Chapter 10. At this point, it is enough to note that toilet training cannot be effective until a child's body is ready, until the muscles that control the bowels and bladder are mature enough to function. The average baby cannot physically control these muscles until late in his second year.

Interrelated Development

It is important to have an idea of sensorimotor timing, so that we will know how much and how little to expect from our baby. It does not matter at what age he achieves his developmental goals, as long as he seems to be moving along from one stage to another. If we become concerned over his rate of development, we can check with the doctor. But most babies do progress from one achievement to the next at a pace and in a manner that is uniquely their own. The ages at which the baby masters the various challenges will depend in general on his strength, coordination, and size as well as on his own temperament and personality.

None of his sensorimotor development occurs in a vacuum. Not only does each area of physical development overlap and interrelate with the others, but the child's physical growth interacts with his intellectual, social, emotional, and psychological development.

Cognitive Growth

Cognitive growth, the development of the ability to learn, is either a cause or an effect of an individual's intelligence, depending on what theory we accept. In short, infant intelligence is difficult to study or explain. *Our* baby, of course, is quite bright. But how do we know? And what is "intelligence" in an infant, anyway? It seems so completely connected to the rest of his abilities that it is hard to isolate.

Today parents would be dissuaded from having their baby's intelligence tested until well past his third birthday, no matter how eager they are to show how smart he is, because no reliable tests have yet been devised for measuring mental ability before then. This is not to say that the baby learns nothing. Far from it!

As one young father comments, "It's amazing to me how much my six-month-old *knows* already." That is not just the pride of a new parent; it is true that babies learn a fantastic amount incredibly early. In the past few years, psychologists and educators have "discovered" what that young father meant: that young children, even tiny infants, *can* learn, and in fact that the first few years of life may be crucial learning time.

Experiments have proven that newborns *can* learn. Just *what* babies can learn is more difficult to discover, although recent research has developed new and effective study techniques. As for *how* a baby goes about learning, from the moment of birth and even before—this is a question that is far from being answered.

What is known is that an infant's learning is almost completely interwoven with his physical development and emotional state, as well as, we assume, with his heredity.

How the Baby Learns

At first, a baby has best use of his eyes and his mouth, and it is through these organs that he first begins to take in information. His mouth's repeated experiences, for instance, teach him in the first few months that when he cries he gets a nipple to suck, and when he sucks he gets milk that soothes his hunger. His eyes, which at first may be open only at feeding time, show him a face that appears at the same time as this miraculous nipple. He associates pleasure and satisfaction with the face, and soon he is interested in what else his eyes can see. He finds that by moving his head and eyes he can see a lot of bright, colorful shapes that move, disappear, and reappear as he turns and blinks.

In this way, during his first two or three months, the baby is learning that a world exists. More accurately, he discovers a context in which his needs and curiosity are satisfied, for it will be a long time before he realizes that there is a world outside of himself.

In those first few months, the baby is just getting his land legs; his body may not be operating well enough to cope with much more than sleep and digestion. Still, he is beginning to create a memory, to feed his intelligence, and to establish landmarks of his existence: nipple, mother's face, crib toy, light. His experiences with these first discoveries are important in determining whether he finds the rest of his world worth exploring.

If he is led to feel that it is, he will try to reach out for the world when his senses sharpen and his muscles strengthen enough to allow him to raise himself and direct the movements of his arms and legs. He learns that there is something to learn.

As he is able more actively to grasp and to move around, he will learn *how* to learn, by exploring, feeling, and comparing. He may learn, too, that he can make an impact on his world, can make it do things.

By the middle of his first year of investigation, the baby will begin to form the concepts of "me" and "not me." He will find, for example, that his feet are attached to himself. And he will realize that Mother is not a part of him and that she can disappear. This will upset him, but because she comes back, he is led to the important concept that things exist even when he cannot see them.

By this time, the baby will be a social being. From the moment he learns that "face-brings-food-makes-me-happy," he will enjoy faces and the people who go with them. He has learned to make social sounds, too. He keeps working at them, and he is on his way to learning the language. Language spurs cognitive development. Words help him to label and classify the objects and people he discovers in his world, which grows ever bigger during his second year, when he gains mobility and manual ability, and during his third, when he becomes an increasingly independent being.

A child's primary cognitive tasks during his first three years are to absorb experience through his senses and to begin to sort it out. The kind of experiences the baby has during his first few years may determine how well he will think and learn later in life. Does the world seem a happy place? Or distressing? Interesting? Boring? Responsive? Or silent?

The answers make a big difference to his mental growth.

Development of "Human Feelings"

The baby's emotions are closely linked to his earliest learning. His first lesson is either "The world makes me feel good. It is a nice place. I want to know more about it," or "The world makes me uncomfortable. It is a bad place, and I want little to do with it."

Childhood specialists have tried to examine newborns' emotions and have been able to isolate only two states of feeling, "pleasant" and "unpleasant." If he is full, dry, and warm, the baby is in a pleasant state; if he is empty or gassy, wet, or cold, he is in an unpleasant state. When he wakes and the nipple is not immediately in his mouth, his screams are not, the experts insist, those of rage, no matter how they sound to a harried mother, but simply screams of distress over his stomach's unpleasantly empty condition. His smile does not necessarily indicate joy or friendliness, but simply his feeling that all is right in his little world. Because of the response he gets to these early emotional signals, he learns to use both screaming and smiling as social tools.

During his first three years, as he grows in his awareness of how the world operates, the baby begins to acquire the full repertoire of human emotions that are implicit within the two basic infantile states of feeling. He learns to feel and show affection for those who make him feel pleasant, for instance, and anger at situations that unpleasantly frustrate him.

Learning and emotion, like physical growth and learning, interact. If a child's emotional environment is too unpleasant, he may not risk exploring it. In addition, the emotional weight attached to his major early learning experiences—weaning, talking, walking, and toilet training—can influence his approach to comparable tasks later on.

Psychological Development

"All that is very interesting," we may say, "but . . . ," as we change a diaper with one hand and pour a formula with the other. A new parent probably is too busy to think about such far-off events as weaning and toilet training (beyond wishing they were inborn traits!).

The underlying theme and goal of all the activities that we and our baby are going to be busy with over the next few years is worth remembering, and it is easily summarized. Psychologist Erik Erikson calls the main job of the first two years "the formation of basic trust." The most important thing our baby needs to learn in these years is that we, himself, and the world are worthy of trust. He needs the security of feeling that his world is a safe one, to have confidence that those who care for him *will* care for him, and to trust that, somehow, whatever he needs he can get. As he leaves the first two years, if he has learned to trust the world, he will begin to build what Erikson calls autonomy, the sense of himself as an independent, worthy person, capable of managing himself and coping with the world.

All that a baby is—even a food-messing, no-saying, tantrum-throwing 14-monther; even a walking, talking, grown-up-seeming two-year-old—is what one new parent calls a "bundle of needs." It is our job as a parent to fill these needs and, in doing so, to create a feeling of trust in our growing child. Once he learns to trust, he is open to learning almost anything. Without that security, he will be afraid to learn anything; he is likely to assume that all future learning will be only painful, and coping happily and independently with his environment will be well-nigh impossible. It is on a foundation of trust that our baby takes on the second task of his psychological growth, achieving independence.

2
Getting To Know Your Baby

A BABY BUILDS on trust, and the basic way in which the baby gains that trust is by learning that grown-ups tend to him lovingly, carefully, regularly—and particularly in the *special* ways that he alone needs.

It is true that every baby needs to be fed, changed, bathed, and loved, of course. But every baby has his own style, his own way of going through daily life in his small world. Before our baby arrived, we may have wondered how we would ever be able to figure out when he was hungry, tired, happy, or unhappy. But mothers often tune in on their babies' styles so quickly that they don't even think about it.

Not long ago some doctors in Boston spent a number of hours observing four pairs of newborn identical twins and recording the ways in which the "identical" babies differed from each other. After compiling an impressive list of differences, the doctors compared their impressions with notes made by the mothers of the twins, who had been asked to record their feelings about their babies after holding them for twenty minutes on the very first day. According to one of the doctors, Dr. T. Berry Brazelton of the Harvard University Center for Cognitive Development, the mothers had picked up all the differences that the doctors had noticed —in a fraction of the time. The mothers showed remarkable insight into the individual style of each of their babies and responded to it intuitively right from the start.

Because our baby is an individual and needs to be treated like one, the routines of baby care, which we may have studied carefully while waiting for the baby, need to be bent a little. It may take us a while to realize that we don't have to follow rigidly anyone else's rules—whether prescribed by book, course, hospital nursery, or mother-in-law—in caring for *our* baby. Believe it or not, all that ritual of changing diapers, making a bottle, giving a bath, will come naturally after just a few days of following it. What is more important is tuning in to our baby's style and adjusting ours to his.

Maybe we haven't thought of our baby as being all that unique a little person, or ourself as being such an authority on what he is like. But let's stop for a minute and consider the way he eats. Maybe he tackles the breast or bottle impatiently and takes his meal very fast. Or he may be more deliberate but suck steadily. Perhaps he eats in fits and starts, stopping from time to time to look around, tongue the nipple, or drop off to sleep. And we do tune in, automatically: if he is a fast eater, we try to slow him down a bit without frustrating him; if he is a slow eater, we may encourage him to pick up the pace without making him angry.

These accommodations that we instinctively make to our baby's preferences contribute importantly to his overall well-being. Research evidence shows that even at this early age a baby thrives on being allowed to "do things his way" as much as possible.

"Self-regulation"

Just as healthy infants come in a variety of sizes and body builds, from a fragile 5 pounds to a chunky 15 pounds, so they also differ vastly in how active they are. Some seem to be in motion most of their waking hours, whereas others are often content just to lie quietly, staring. A moment's thought will indicate that these different types of babies must have different needs, so the rules that apply to one baby will not be appropriate for the next. Nor will one day's routine necessarily fit the following day, because during the first few weeks our baby is changing and growing every day. In fact, we may feel that the baby we pick up in the morning is almost a different child from the one we put to bed the night before, so rapidly do newborns develop.

For these reasons, most parents today do not follow a strict schedule in feeding and caring for their babies. Instead, they feed, change, cuddle, and play with the baby when he "demands" it—that is, when he indicates that he is ready by the only means he has available: crying. Until recently, mothers in America did follow a rigid three- or four-hour schedule in feeding their infants. Most nurses and hospitals still stick to such a routine, because, for one thing, it is more convenient for the grown-ups than the "demand" system. The label "demand feeding" tends to discourage a lot of adults who are used to having *their* way. "Self-regulation" is actually a more accurate term for the method of caring for a baby in a flexible way that fits his needs. The approach has much to offer mothers, as well as babies, if it is handled sensibly.

We need not go to extremes. Our baby probably won't mind being waked up for a feeding after three or four hours of sleep, for example, if it is more convenient for us and the family to feed him then rather than wait for him to rouse himself. (If he *really* wants to sleep, he just won't wake up enough to eat.) Mothers often do this in the evening, just before they retire, in the hope that their baby will then sleep for a good long stretch during the night.

Also, we should not jump too quickly to the conclusion that hard crying means that the baby needs feeding. If he was fed only an hour or so earlier, he is more likely crying because he is tired, bored, tense, or uncomfortable for some other reason. We will probably be able to distinguish his various cries quite quickly, and if he doesn't sound hungry to us, we can try to console him in other ways—with a pacifier (more about this a few pages further on), rocking, or playing—to see if we can postpone feeding him. Sometimes an unhappy baby will, if urged, take food that he really doesn't need, because eating is associated with comfort. Ordinarily, the worst that happens is that he spits up later. But if he is regularly overfed, his body may adapt to this. Recent evidence suggests that chronic overweight in later life may be established as early as the first year if a baby is continually encouraged to overeat.

The "self-regulation" schedule allows parents more freedom to use their judgment than earlier, rigid approaches to infant care did. Most young parents find this makes their job easier and more satisfying. Even more important is the trust and self-confidence an infant feels when his needs are met on his terms. And gradually, some sooner than others, all babies settle down into their own pattern of regularity.

Handling Feeding

You may read and hear a lot of argument about whether it is best to breastfeed or bottlefeed your baby. The decision is up to you. (And if your doctor or hospital exerts pressure against the method you select, you can use your own common sense or switch "experts," if possible.) Babies thrive on either the breast or the bottle. It is not the method you select but the way in which you handle it that matters.

Feeding is an infant's most significant experience. During the feeding, he gets his most vivid impression of what the world is like. He needs more than food; he needs

affection and the chance to socialize as well. This we give by snuggling him, talking or singing to him, and responding to his facial expressions. Of course, if we are breastfeeding we can hardly avoid giving our baby the snuggling he needs along with his meals. If we are bottlefeeding, cuddling him during the feeding will make mealtime always the warm, emotionally satisfying experience that it should be.

Mothers with several children sometimes feel it necessary to prop an infant's bottle and let him eat alone. Since the newborn gains his most important impressions at feeding time, it is better to make other arrangements, at least for the majority of feedings. Mealtimes are especially important if our baby is not awake between feedings, for they become the only times when we get to know our little character.

Feeding can be a pleasant, restful experience for us, too, if we plan ahead. If we are using bottles that must be prepared in advance, we should be sure to have at least one in reserve at all times. We can choose a comfortable chair (one with arms helps support the baby close, in the crook of our arm) and place it in a pleasant place, near the telephone if possible, in case it rings after we have settled down. This is a chance to relax and get a load off our feet! If the baby is not alert during the whole feeding, or if we tend to get restless, having a book or magazine handy can keep us from becoming impatient or tense.

Fast Eaters

Of course, we may not have time to do anything but pay attention to the baby. Some infants seem to want to eat more rapidly than is good for them. They gulp their meals down avidly without stopping and then spit up while being bubbled, or a while later. In bottlefeeding, this can be controlled by buying nipples with a smaller opening, or purchasing ones that have no opening and making the hole by piercing the nipple with a hot needle.

If this smaller opening annoys the baby, enlarge the hole slightly and try to slow him down by other methods. Holding him in a more upright position while he sucks may discourage spitting up. Talking or singing to him may slow him, too. And with a fast eater, we should be extra careful to replace nipples before they get so old that the holes enlarge. With any baby, checking the nipple opening before a feeding is a good idea.

Ordinarily, a breastfed baby cannot get his meal faster than is good for him. He may occasionally choke over the first mouthful or so, since breast milk sometimes comes out rapidly for the first few seconds. If this happens often, and if the baby seems satisfied after less than ten minutes of sucking, it may be wise for the mother to press out some milk with her hands before putting the baby to the breast.

Slow Eaters

A slow eater is a problem, too—to his mother and family more than to himself. But parents have their rights and needs just as babies do. Although a new mother may, of course, let her baby take as long at meals as he wants, she is busy and easily tired, and she may find that too many demands, even from her own child, make her impatient and irritable. She need not spend an hour with each of her infant's six to eight meals; thirty minutes' sucking should suffice. In that time a baby should have taken all the formula he is interested in, or emptied both breasts, if he is encouraged to suck steadily with only a brief intermission for bubbling the first time he pushes the nipple away or begins to play with it.

If the baby stops sucking intermittently because he is drowsy, he can be roused by jiggling the nipple, by thumping the soles of his feet gently, or by stroking his forehead with a cool cloth. If this does not do the trick, let the baby sleep, but try to keep the time between feedings as long as possible.

How does this fit in with all the talk about adapting to our baby's style? To best serve her child, a mother needs to approach the job of feeding him in a relaxed, eager frame of mind. If she is concerned about how long the task will take, or whether her baby will get enough food, she will tense up. Her body will inevitably communicate this tension to the baby. So it makes sense for her to try to influence her baby's way of doing things sufficiently to accommodate her own pressing needs. Healthy parent-child compromises are possible very early.

Pacifiers

Feeding satisfies more than an infant's hunger. Babies seem to need a certain amount of sucking for its own sake. If a baby fusses or roots around as if he were hungry soon after he has eaten, it may mean that he needs to *suck* more, not to *eat* more. If a baby eats very fast, he may need some extra opportunity to suck; if he eats very slowly, it may be because he is more interested in the sucking than the food. Many babies bring their own fingers to their mouths to satisfy their sucking needs. If ours doesn't, we can try a pacifier. Our older relatives may be horrified, for pacifiers once were regarded as being almost immoral. But recently doctors have realized that they can perform a necessary function for some babies during the first few months. The sucking drive diminishes after the fourth month or so, and a baby who continues to suck on pacifier or thumb later in his first year is doing so for another reason—but more on that in Chapter 6. For the first few months, our baby needs as much sucking as he can get.

Food Intake

"Is the baby getting enough to eat?" is a question that all mothers ask themselves at one time or another. It is almost impossible for parents to be objective about this issue when their baby sucks his fingers a lot, or is crying inconsolably, or has just spit up what looks like a tummy-full.

The baby is an excellent judge of how much he needs to eat. Parents just need to remember that what happens at one feeding is not the whole picture. The amount of nourishment that an infant requires will vary from feeding to feeding—as with an adult. If a baby eats less than usual at one meal, he tends to make it up the next time around, by asking to be fed sooner or eating more heartily.

If a baby is really not getting as much nourishment as he needs, he will let us know. He may consistently empty breast or bottle quickly and completely and continue to suck and root. He may continually wake up hungry, demanding to be fed sooner than we expect him to at all times of day, not just occasionally. (Breastfed babies predictably want to nurse frequently during the day and then sleep for long stretches at night, but they are getting enough food in their way.) If our baby always finishes his formula or sucks well for twenty to thirty minutes at the breast and still wakens at less than three-hour intervals, we may want to consult with our doctor or clinic about giving more food—but we should not take the step automatically. Too much food can be as damaging to an infant as too little.

Weight Gain

A healthy baby begins to gain weight after the first week or so of life. But every infant does this at his own rate. Some babies may gain half a pound a week during the first few months, whereas others, equally healthy, may gain only half that rapidly. Even babies who are gaining at nearly the same rate may not look as if they were. Some infants put on weight where it shows, but others don't. The baby's weight will be checked at each periodic medical examination, but if a mother feels she must weigh him between his regular checkups, once every three days or once a week is plenty. Daily weighings are unnecessary and may cause parents needless concern.

Bubbling the Baby

Babies swallow air as they suck. Bottlefed babies also swallow air from inside the bottle (though some of the disposable sack-type bottles, which are handy, give less air), and they need to be bubbled more frequently or may burp more impressively than breastfed babies. Bubbling at the end of a feeding only is usually sufficient for the breastfed infant.

A baby may be positioned in several ways for bubbling. The mother may hold him upright against her chest, with his head resting on her shoulder, and massage or pat him gently on the back. She may support him in a sitting position on her lap, or she may place him on his stomach, across her legs, for bubbling. She will soon discover what works best for her and the baby. She will also quickly learn the reason for placing a clean towel or diaper between her and the baby.

If the baby needs to be bubbled in the middle of a feeding, he will usually announce the fact by squirming, drawing up his legs, pushing the nipple away, or, occasionally, crying. The bubble of air in his belly makes him feel either full or uncomfortable. Even if he gives none of these cues, if he is a very fast eater or a spitter after meals, it is wise to try interrupting him midway for a bubbling attempt. He may resist such an interruption until we become skillful at soothing him by talking or singing.

When we do bubble him, there is no need to keep pounding him on the back indefinitely. Not all babies need to burp. If they do, most will do so rather quickly. If our baby cries and squirms during feeding and does not burp after a few minutes' bubbling, we should check for other problems: is he in an uncomfortable position for eating? Are we and he tense? Is the milk flowing well? "Gas" is not the only cause of mealtime fussiness.

Elimination

Daddy, changing his baby's diaper, marvels over what such a tiny creature can do with applesauce and cereal. Mommy thinks it still looks like the applesauce and cereal that went into his mouth. Adult stools are not good criteria by which to judge an infant's stool. Healthy babies may have green or yellow stools from time to time, especially in the early months. This, and other deviations from the expected, such as an occasional very loose stool or a very hard one, need not concern parents. And any change in diet can change the stool temporarily. Of course, if any of these conditions persists without interruption for more than a day or so, it is wise to check with the baby's doctor or clinic. Any diarrhea in an infant—very watery, frequent stools—should be reported to a doctor *immediately.*

Many pediatricians say that they have never known a breastfed baby to become constipated, although such babies will often go for more than twenty-four hours without passing a stool. So a mother who is nursing her baby need not worry about the absence of a daily bowel movement, as long as he seems otherwise healthy.

All babies may occasionally "strain" noticeably, or even cry, just before or while moving their bowels. If the resultant stool is not overly hard, this can be considered normal. However, if a baby goes through several consecutive episodes of straining without passing a stool, or if his crying indicates that he is in pain, the doctor should be called promptly. Problems more serious than constipation can cause such symptoms.

Colic

For some babies, a full stomach is not the passport to contentment that it usually is for most. After a meal, and sometimes during it, these babies may squirm, curl up, spit up copiously, fuss, or otherwise show discomfort. This happens to all babies once in a while, but when it is the rule rather than the exception, and when the doctor has eliminated any other problem as causing the infant's distress, the sufferer is called "colicky." Nobody knows what causes colic. Not all fussiness *is* colic. For a case of real colic, time is the only proven remedy. Fortunately, the condition generally begins to clear up around the end of the third month. This has led many doctors to conclude that it takes some babies longer than others to get their plumbing into good working order.

It may be reassuring to worried parents to know that colicky babies seem to gain and thrive at least as well as other infants do, and that the problem usually clears up spontaneously. So parents need not worry about the baby's future over the long run—for what that is worth when constant crying wears down their nerves and eats at their sleep. Meanwhile, a pacifier may serve to take the baby's mind off his troubles and reduce the amount of fussing. Also, some positions, such as lying on his stomach across his mother's knees with legs dangling, may help ease the discomfort. Working extra hard at bubbling a colicky baby is always worth the effort.

Crying

All healthy babies do their share of crying, as any new mother must know by now. Most adults react instinctively to a baby's crying by trying to comfort him. This instinct is sound. Crying is the new baby's only way of communicating distress. Responding to those distress signals promptly may be crucial to his physical well-being, and it is always important for his emotional welfare. Even if he has no immediate physical problem—hunger, dirty diapers, pain—a quick and compassionate response to his crying teaches him gradually that the world is a friendly place. It helps to nurture his "sense of mastery," the important emotional strength of feeling able to cope with things.

If a crying baby seems drowsy, a brief period of being held, patted, rocked, or crooned to will usually calm him so that after a spurt of "last gasp" fussing he drops off into needed sleep.

If he is wide awake and seems to be crying for companionship, we should offer it to him. Babies don't like being bored any more than grown-ups do. We can play with him, or allow him to be near us or the others in the household by moving him around in a carriage or infant chair. Even very young infants enjoy and need a change of scene and a bit of entertainment. Just being able to watch us may entertain him—and teach him things, too.

If our baby is quite fussy and we are quite busy, it may help to carry him close to us in one of the several kinds of baby carriers or slings now on the market.

"Swaddling"

What do we do if our baby persists in crying and the techniques we normally use won't work?

Occasionally such spells of crying can be stopped by placing a baby's arms close to his sides and wrapping his body very snugly in a receiving blanket. This practice, called "swaddling," is an ancient remedy that is still used in many parts of the world. Swaddling serves to stroke the entire body at once, and it may work for another reason, as well. When a baby cries hard, his body movements set off a continuous startle reaction, the Moro reflex, which keeps the crying going. This reflex is in operation when a baby's head arches back and his arms and legs vigorously thrust out. If it is interrupted by swaddling or holding him snugly, he may calm down dramatically.

However, this is something of an emergency method. Many doctors frown on swaddling a baby routinely when putting him down to sleep. They feel that physical development is furthered by leaving the baby unencumbered, most of the time, to move his arms and legs freely. Also, some babies resent being swaddled, and the technique will not work for them.

Of course, some perfectly healthy babies cry more than others. Some well-meaning people may say that a "good" baby is a sign of "good" parents. But crying has nothing to do with a baby's "goodness" or "badness" and is not a reliable indicator of the competence or concern of his parents. Some babies simply have a greater need to cry than others. Doctors agree that crying is useful to a baby for reasons other than communicating distress. It may aid lungs, circulation, and general body functioning. It enables active or tense babies to work off energy and relieve tension. Many thriving babies may have one or two difficult periods each day, which parental attention cannot prevent. These periods usually come at a predictable time of day, most often in the late afternoon. Hard crying may alternate with brief, fitful intervals of sleep as exhaustion takes over.

Every baby differs in the amount of crying he needs, depending perhaps on his physical and emotional makeup. For one, a "crying spell" may last 15 minutes; for another, an hour or so. Once we have taken care of our baby's basic needs and made sure that he is healthy, we need not go to extremes in trying to prevent crying spells.

Bathing the Baby

For some reason, "baby's bath" has always held a special mystique. It needn't. We can keep our baby clean without making an elaborate production of giving him a bath at a certain time every day. Of course, if he enjoys being in the water, as many babies do, we will probably look forward to giving him a daily bath in his tub or in the kitchen sink, and to stretching it out for as long as he likes it. As he grows older, he may count on having it at a certain point in the day's routine, and even later, a bath may serve to calm him down for sleep. But if our baby hates being put in his tub, a sponge bath two or three times a week is all he needs, as long as we are careful about keeping his diaper area clean and also the area affected by his spitting up. A cloth, soap, and a bowl of water within easy reach of where we change him makes this simple. Water used for sponging or bathing a baby should be about the temperature of the body—that is, if we dip an elbow in, it should feel neither hot nor cool.

Obviously, on an unusually busy or demanding day, the bath is a routine that can be skipped. Also, though it is sometimes said that a baby should be bathed before, not after, mealtime, there is no good medical reason for this. It will not interfere with the baby's digestion to bathe him after feeding, and it's more efficient, since eating makes him messy! Many babies prefer eating first. Since they generally wake up because they are hungry, not because they are dirty, they may, understandably, object strenuously to being bathed between waking and mealtime, no matter how much they enjoy their baths on a full stomach.

Dressing and Undressing

Most mothers—and grandmothers—love dressing up babies. A new mother usually receives a lot of cute outfits for her baby, and she may be tempted to buy more every time she passes a children's store. This is fine and fun, but not really necessary. All a small baby really needs to wear is a diaper and an undershirt. If his home is cold or drafty, he will need to be covered more. The one-piece stretch suits that unsnap completely are the greatest invention since skin. When shopping for baby clothes the mother needs to consider several factors: the baby's comfort and freedom of motion; her own convenience in getting him into and out of the clothes and washing them; and expense.

Modern mothers even have a wide choice of diaper styles. Some prefer cloth diapers; some swear by disposables. Each kind has its advantages and disadvantages; cost and a mother's convenience should be the major considerations. If she has easy access to a washing machine and dryer, old-fashioned cloth diapers—prefolded or flat—are the most economical. If not, she may want to consider a diaper service or disposables. Some of the disposable types work well and are comfortable, and in some areas of the country they cost less than a diaper service.

When and how often the baby is diapered depends on his elimination schedule, of course. If he constantly has diaper rash, he may be wet too much of the time because he is not being changed often enough. (Older babies develop rashes more quickly, as the chemistry of the urine grows harsher.)

A good way to prevent or cure diaper rash (and the easiest way to dress a baby in warm weather) is to leave the diaper off and let the fresh air work on the rash. Just put an extra pad under him, and let him enjoy the freedom of his natural state.

Sleep

A healthy baby will sleep as much as he needs to—no more, no less. For about three months, or even longer, many babies sleep for the whole time between feedings, barring a difficult period or two daily—and these tend to seem longer than they are (try timing them sometimes!). Others, right from the start, are content to be awake far more of the time. This is just another example of individual differences. Parents need not worry about their baby's getting enough sleep until he is many months older and open to overstimulation.

Most parents soon begin to recognize when their infant needs to go to sleep. He is unresponsive to invitations to play, or he responds frantically between cries. He fusses, closes his eyes briefly, then startles into wakefulness and fusses again. We know that the time has come for him to rest. We put him down into his favorite position for sleeping. Some prefer their backs, some their tummies (and it's perfectly safe to let him sleep on his tummy), and a few their sides. The major dangers to a sleeping baby are a mattress that is too soft, a pillow, or a too-soft crib bumper, all of which could suffocate an infant. If he does not drop off right away, we soothe him or rock him for a bit.

"Spoiling"

Some mothers worry that they may give their babies too much attention. Won't he become spoiled, they wonder, if they continually try to cater to his needs, rocking or patting him off to sleep, rushing to check on him whenever he cries, playing with him when he seems to want to be played with?

The answer is no, not at this stage of the game. A good definition for spoiling is "doing for a child what he can do for himself." An infant can't do anything for himself; therefore, we can't spoil an infant. The baby relies on his parents for the satisfaction of all his needs, and for reassurance that life is good. During his first three months or so, adjusting to surviving outside the womb is challenge enough for him under the best of circumstances. He can use all the compassionate attention that his parents are able to give him.

Later, as he begins to "shake down," around the start of the fourth month, we will gradually help him learn to wait a bit for a meal or other attention when we are in the midst of something else.

Stimulation

A small baby can use a lot of emotional and intellectual stimulation. In fact, if he receives only essential physical care, he will not thrive. Some years ago researchers noted that infants in institutions who were physically well tended but otherwise ignored sometimes even died, for no immediately apparent reason. They discovered that if the babies were held for only a few hours a day by hired "mother substitutes," they escaped death and came closer to developing normally. Since then, evidence has been piling up of the importance of loving attention and stimulation in promoting an infant's healthy growth. This means that babies should not be simply fed, changed, and left alone. Being handled, cuddled, played with, and talked to is as important to a baby's development as being offered the food he needs.

It can do no harm to surround our infant with bright, attractive pictures, mobiles, lights, and colors, even before we think he "can see" them. Many young parents find that their infants respond to stimulation long before the scholars say they "can." Even if our baby wakes only to eat, we can take the trouble—and pleasure—to talk, sing, smile, and play with him as we feed him. It will be worth it! If he does enjoy being awake, we can keep him with us and the rest of the family in an infant seat or baby carrier. We need not force ourself to do more than we feel up to, but when we do have time and energy for playing, it is good for both of us.

He'll probably like visitors, too, and we will probably enjoy showing him off. Naturally, we don't wake a baby up from a sound sleep to exhibit him to guests, or turn on a bright light in the room where he is sleeping so that a vistor may have a better look at him. But if he is awake and likes being fussed over, passed from hand to hand, and otherwise involved in the general hum of household activity, the stimulation is good for him.

"Baby Blues"

The new baby can probably "turn off" overstimulation, but his parents can't, and their first few months in their new roles are a very stimulating time. Their baby is changing dramatically in his first months, and so are they. They both have been looking forward for a long time to this baby, and they should be prepared for some, perhaps unexpected, changes in their lives.

New parents probably have been warned, for example, that mothers may sometimes have spells of feeling depressed or being tearful, which seem to come on rather suddenly and without obvious provocation. It often happens.

"Baby blues," postpartum depression, or heightened emotionality—whatever we wish to call it—is partly due to the hormonal readjustments that take place in a woman's body after she gives birth. In somewhat the same way that premenstrual tension may cause a woman to behave in ways that take her by surprise, the postpartum period may produce mood swings. (This also happens to mothers who adopt babies, and the possibility that adopting an infant may trigger hormonal changes similar to those brought on by giving birth has not been ruled out.)

There is not much she can do about this, except to know that it happens and to get the rest that every new mother needs, especially if she is nursing. She may have felt that by the time the baby was two weeks old, the mother was altogether herself again, but her body will not have returned completely to normal until six weeks or more have passed. Many modern young mothers, especially those who have used natural childbirth, come home feeling they are fit to cope with anything. They return to their old pace without the help from relatives and friends that people had back when "natural childbirth" was the only method available. Some of these young women may still be short of recovering their strength when their babies are learning to walk. Not only is a new mother apt to be tired when she comes home from the hospital, but her responsibilities have increased considerably in the week she has been gone. It is important that she pamper herself. She should rest when the baby sleeps; cut corners with housekeeping; and make meals that are simple to cook and clean up after, as well as tasty and nutritious, even if it means spending more money on food for a while.

In addition to her physical load, she may, secretly, have misgivings about her infant. He is not what she expected, or really wanted. Having a baby is so different from *thinking about having* a baby. Apart from all the physically exhausting work involved, and the lack of sleep, she worries that she can't love her infant the way a mother ought to love her child.

Such thoughts are common. Many mothers, as well as fathers, are plagued by these and other disconcerting emotions during the early weeks. Fathers are proud of their offspring but may find themselves in competition with them—and feeling guilty about it. Most worried parents tend to underestimate one very important thing that they—and their infant—have going for them: their baby's ability to worm his way, slowly but surely, into the affections of the man and woman who take care of him. So they shouldn't worry about their worries. They are natural and will, most likely, work themselves out.

3
You And Your Baby Meet Life As It Is

THE HECTIC EARLY weeks of parenthood are exciting, exhausting, exhilarating, and centered almost completely on the new baby. Then, sometime during the first few months, when it seems that life will never settle down, things begin to get back to normal.

The Six Weeks' Examination

That goes for a new mother's body, too. About six weeks after giving birth, a mother should return to her obstetrician for a checkup. She may have arranged an appointment before she left the hospital. It is an important date. By the end of six weeks, the uterus should have returned to its normal size and the birth canal should have healed, so that sexual relations may be resumed; but until the doctor has checked, it is not safe to have sexual intercourse, and it could prove painful as well.

Before new parents resume sexual relations, they should make some mutual decisions about contraception. A woman is not necessarily sterile while she is nursing. Plenty of babies have been born to nursing mothers ten months after their brothers or sisters. Decisions on contraception must be made by each couple according to their individual and mutual consciences.

For now, one baby is all we need. At the end of about six weeks, with our household, hopefully, settling down and our married life returning to normal, our baby passes a landmark, too. He is no longer a mere appendage of his mother. He can begin to grow *up,* as well as just grow. We can start helping him adapt to family life and needs. He can move to a room of his own now, if he has been sleeping in ours. If there is no other place to put the baby, we can at least screen off his crib from our bed. The effect on children of exposure to their parents' sexual life is of concern to psychologists, though it is certainly questionable whether a child is aware of this before about age two.

(For more on the subject, see *What Makes a Good Parent?* by Mary Hoover.) Still, parents and baby are probably better off with more privacy than is fostered by sharing a room. As our baby becomes more mature, he can benefit from having a place that is his alone, however small that place may be. Also, of course, we are very sensitive to his sounds and movements and may tend to waken when he only stirs.

Visiting the Baby's Doctor

At the tender age of six weeks, our baby will get a rather rude introduction into the grown-up world: his first shot at the doctor's office. Although his pediatrician may have already checked the baby over while he was in the hospital, it is not until the six weeks' checkup that he will give the first inoculation, an immunization against diphtheria, whooping cough, and tetanus (abbreviated DPT). Young mothers may have heard that a baby is automatically immune to disease for the first few months and that breastfeeding prolongs the immunity. A mother does transmit some of her own antibodies, and breastfeeding *may* prolong this natural immunity (though that is not certain). She cannot, however, protect her baby from all diseases, so getting immunizations is one vital reason for regular visits to the clinic or pediatrician, beginning when the baby is about six weeks old. A chart outlining the course of immunization that most pediatricians follow is given in Chapter 6.

Our baby's first shot—perhaps the whole visit to the doctor—may not be a pleasant experience. It is going to hurt and frighten him. We can help, on this and all other trips to the doctor, by having a relaxed, friendly attitude and by allowing sympathetically for any extra crankiness on the baby's part. We may be terrified of shots ourself, for example, but if we can keep a smile on our face and our muscles relaxed while we hold our baby for his injection, maybe he will be able to take them in his stride. Maybe, also, seeing him through this experience will help us get over some of our own fear of shots.

Many young babies have "reactions" to shots: a few hours after being inoculated, they become fussy and irritable and may run a slight fever. We can ask the doctor if this is likely to happen with a particular injection, and he will advise us how to cope with it. The baby may need extra attention to help him through this uncomfortable time, and usually doctors will recommend a baby aspirin to ease the fever and discomfort. We need not be surprised if our baby sleeps longer or more heavily after a shot, but if the reaction seems extreme in any way, we should check back with the doctor.

It is useful to start a medical record for our baby by jotting down what shots he gets at what age and keeping track of other important medical treatment. We should note on it any childhood diseases he may have that confer immunity. The chart in Chapter 6 can be used for this purpose.

The first visit to the baby's clinic or doctor is our first opportunity to really get to know the person, or team, who will be playing a very important role in our life for some time to come.

If we live in an area where we have a choice of pediatricians, we probably will have selected our baby's doctor before or immediately after giving birth. If we have no choice, we can still get to know our clinic or doctor—at least the office location, hours, and phone number—well before we need them.

To choose a pediatrician, we can get recommendations from our obstetrician and family doctor and ask our friends and neighbors about their children's doctors. The comments of friends about a doctor's personality and views on child-rearing can help us select someone whom we are likely to find compatible. If we are new in a community, the local medical association will supply the names of several baby doctors to choose from. It is a good idea to find out about the hospital that a doctor is affiliated with. Does its pediatric service—the staff and wards that serve children—have a good reputation? Would we be allowed to stay with our baby if he needed hospital care? Ideally, the doctor's hospital would be the one nearest to our home.

But more important than the hospital is the pediatrician. He is a major figure in our baby's life and ours. He will have a big influence over a lot more than our child's physical health: he tends to our baby's emotional, psychological, and social growth as well.

We should keep in mind that pediatricians are human, too, although many young mothers tend to take all their pronouncements as holy scripture. As one baby doctor puts it, "Every doctor has his own ideas about a lot of nonmedical matters, and mothers need to remember that they're *only* ideas." We can assume, of course, that our doctor is competent in medicine. In the nonmedical aspects of child-raising, we should be able to trust and respect him. If we don't, we would do better to change, if we can. In any case, we must remember that parents do not abdicate to a doctor their responsibility for using their own judgment.

Fitting Baby's Schedule to the Family's

It is the doctor who will provide specific advice on meeting our baby's needs as he leaves his newborn status behind and grows into babyhood. The baby who appears for his six weeks' examination has made remarkable progress since his birth. He probably looks a lot more like a "picture-book" infant than when we first made his acquaintance. He may smile when we play with him. His senses are fairly sharp, and his digestive system works much more efficiently. He is ready to begin easing into "life as it is" by adapting a bit to family routines and needs.

We may notice that his cries for food are less intense, less desperate. Around the third month, he may awaken without immediately calling for food. By this time, too, if he is not doing it already, he will begin to stay awake for longer periods when he isn't feeding, so we can begin adjusting his schedule to ours, if we like.

We will not, of course, want to announce to him on his three-month birthday that from now on he gets fed only at 7, 1, and 7, but we can gradually work him into a new eating pattern. First we might set a general plan of the kind of schedule we want him to follow, whether we want to aim toward three meals only at this point, or in addition to three daytime meals continue to offer him the breast or a bottle in the evening, just before retiring. We can decide roughly at what hours we want him to have his meals, and then not rush to feed him as soon as he wakes, but play and talk with him for a while. Gradually we can help him to lengthen the time between feedings and to eat at approximately the hours we prefer.

Some babies make these changes on their own. Some will adapt more readily than others to outside influences on their schedules and ways of doing things. If ours is particularly adamant about sticking to his own patterns, we should not force the issue, but just continue to encourage as much adjustment as he is agreeable to. More important than our convenience is his learning that he can count on us to fill *his* needs. Eventually, with patience, we can work him into the family's way of life, and in doing so, "teach" him that there are others in the world who have needs, too.

Introducing Solids

As to when to begin feeding solid foods to our baby, that is up to us, our pediatrician, and our baby (especially the latter two). Babies have grown perfectly well and strong for generations on nothing but milk throughout their first year—or longer. In American society, in fact, until rather recently children were walking around on their own before they were eating "real" food. Lately the

fashion has been to start feeding solids very early. It has been shown that babies can make some use of solids at a young age, and there is a desire to help babies grow up faster than they used to. Many doctors recommend beginning solids around the third month, if not before, but some are reverting to the older idea of delaying solids. Again, we can take our cues from the baby. If he empties both breasts or consistently drinks more than his quota of formula and still seems hungry, we can talk to the doctor about beginning solids.

The doctor will advise that it is a good idea to introduce only one new food at a time and to wait several days or a week before offering another. In this way, if the baby has an allergic reaction to a food, we can easily figure out which one caused the problem.

When we start on solids, we have a wide variety of commercially prepared baby foods to choose from. These are convenient and easy to store. But with an electric blender, we can easily make our own baby foods from fresh meats, fruits, and vegetables. (And we can always use any "grown-up" juice that is thin and smooth enough to pass through the nipple.) Our own preference and the amount of time we have at our disposal will dictate the decision. When we do use commercially prepared baby food, we should read the label carefully to make sure that the jar contains no ingredients that our baby has not started on. A jar marked "Bananas," for instance, may contain tapioca and orange juice in addition to bananas.

No matter what solids we feed our baby, or when or how we introduce him to them, we should take it easy. This is a big step for him. And, like all other new activities, especially ones involving eating, it is a vital learning experience. If he is on the breast, for instance, being spoonfed may give him his first real inkling that a world exists beyond his mother and himself. Many mothers find that feeding their baby juice from a spoon accustoms the baby to the technique and helps prepare him for the challenge of eating solids. The physical sensation of swallowing without sucking is a new one for a baby, and the texture and taste of the food are, literally, like nothing his sensitive little mouth has ever experienced before. The techniques, attitudes, and timing surrounding this great event may heavily influence his eating patterns for a long time, so it is important that his first experiences be pleasant ones.

Because this is such a big step toward growing up, we will want to "baby" him during the experience. At least at first, we can keep feeding time the warm, cozy experience it has been with breast and bottle by holding him in our arms as we feed him from a spoon, just being sure to wear an apron and to sit where mess won't matter. (He *will* be messy! His tongue does not work too well, and he may squeeze half the spoonful out of his mouth instead of down his throat at first.) It is best to put just a small amount on the tip of the spoon and be ready to scrape the excess off his mouth and chin. Later, when he is more active, we can feed him in an infant seat. But for now, the snuggling is almost as important as the food, even though he is big enough to eat "like a grown-up."

As for which should come first at each meal, the bottle or the spoon, opinions differ. Some mothers say that if the baby is given his bottle first, he doesn't eat the solids. In that case, maybe he is not really ready for the solids. Even if he wolfed them down last week, maybe this week he'd like a break from them. The baby may happily take the spoon first. If he doesn't, and we make him wait for his bottle while we shove a spoon at him, he may come to resent the spoon. If we give him the bottle first, he need not empty it before he eats his solids; we can offer the spoon when he stops for a breather from sucking or slows down. Whichever way works best, he needs to have plenty of sucking time, because sucking is still more important for him than solids. And he needs time between spoonfuls; the food may look like mush to us, but many babies seem to need to "chew" each mouthful. He may not eat steadily. He may, especially as he approaches his fourth month, stop, "talk," look around, and seem to play in the middle of the meal. Fine! We can talk and play right back. This is *his* time—the time when he is most alert, taking in things through all his senses as he takes food into his mouth.

He will let us know when he is ready to stop for good by spewing *everything* out of his mouth instead of just half of it, and soon he will learn to close his mouth tight when he has had enough. When he wants to stop, we should let him. Pushing food at him can do no good and, as mentioned earlier, may encourage a longlasting tendency to overeat.

What if our baby does not like the whole idea of a spoon, even though he is hungry enough to eat two portions of formula? We need not force him. We can try introducing the spoon when he is very hungry; try at different times of day; try different kinds of foods. If he is steadfast, he just is not ready for the spoon, even if all the other babies in the neighborhood are.

There is really only one "rule" to follow regarding a child's eating, from birth into childhood: if the baby does not want to eat a specific food, or any food, we should not try to force him, and we should not complain to him about it. It is impossible to force a child—or anyone—to swallow something he doesn't want to. Our tension and anxiety about what is, for him, a major daily experience can only have a negative effect. All sensible young mothers pay lip service to this rule until they are confronted with a problem. Faced with a non-eating baby, they may panic and in trying to make him eat succeed only in making him more stubborn.

On the other hand, we need not cater to his eating whims, and we should not let him fill up on snacks. He will eat his meals when he is hungry, and by the time he is three months old, we should be well aware that he lets us know when he is hungry.

He will also eat as much as he needs of the foods he needs. In a now-famous study made in the 1940's, Dr. Clara Davis showed that babies, given free choice of a variety of foods, would eat a well-balanced diet over a week's time, even though they might do so erratically, eating nothing but one kind of food for a day at a time. Also, it takes less food than we may realize to give a baby proper nutrition. The doctor can reassure us that what looks like a few mouthfuls to us can keep an infant going for a long time. We can take his word for it when he says our baby is thriving. He may prescribe a vitamin supplement to make up for anything our child may be missing.

Getting Fresh Air

A baby can get the nutrition he needs in small amounts, and the same applies to "fresh air." Giving a baby a certain amount of fresh air is sometimes as rigid a ritual as giving him a bath at a certain time of day. Both should be flexible factors in a baby's routine. Babies need, and most babies enjoy, fresh air and sunshine.

In judging the weather, a good rule of thumb is whether *we* feel like going out. If the thought of opening the door onto all that heat makes us feel limp, or if three layers of wool won't keep out that winter wind, then our baby is not going to like it outside very much, either. One thing that is harder to judge is the amount of air pollution. Many modern pediatricians feel they must warn new mothers against taking infants out in smog. Air pollution has been shown to increase sharply the rate of bronchial disorders among babies and young children. So if we live in a high-smog area, we should check the daily radio or newspaper report on pollution, and take into account the fact that on some days the "fresh air" may not be so fresh.

In general, however, an outdoor period should be part of our baby's daily routine, for it stimulates his body and his mind. If we have our own outside space—porch, patio, or yard—we can dress the baby appropriately and put him in his carriage, playpen, or portable bed where he will be safely out of wind and direct sun.

"Dress him appropriately"—there's the catch. Gone should be the days when an infant was swaddled in wool within an inch of his life on the warmest day in May. His clothing needs to be simple enough to allow him freedom of movement and only warm enough to maintain his body temperature. The indoor temperature will affect the baby's reaction to the weather outdoors. If it is hot inside, he is bound to need extra protection against the cold outside. A baby's room, however, should not be over 70° F. Babies take a while to develop good internal temperature regulation, and if his room is overheated, it will take even longer. Since an infant's circulation is sluggish, cold hands and feet do not mean that he is too cold all over.

A mother's best criterion for how to dress her baby is her own comfort. We can assume that our baby enjoys being just as warm or as cool as we do. (That goes for air conditioning, too, except that he needs to be protected from abrupt temperature changes.) We should put as many layers of the same weight clothing on him as we do on ourself, but keep wool away from direct contact with his sensitive skin and allow for the fact that we may be generating more warmth by moving around than he is. In addition, a young infant should have a hat to protect his head from hot summer sun. We must be prepared for innumerable comments from relatives and passersby, no matter how we dress the baby. One will tell us that he looks hot; the next, that he looks cold. If our baby is happy and we feel he is comfortable, we can ignore the sidewalk superintendents.

We need not feel that we *have* to take him out in all weather. Blustery winds especially may bother him. Still, why keep him out of all inclement weather? Properly protected, he may enjoy a rain shower or snowfall, for instance. And if we don't make a big deal out of it, he will grow up to be matter-of-fact about the weather, which is a healthy attitude toward something one cannot control.

If we live in a city apartment, we may have to go for a walk with our baby to air him. Even if we don't *have* to, we might enjoy walking him every now and then. It is a good break from a busy schedule, and it helps tone and relax the muscles.

Taking Baby Visiting

When a baby can go out, he can go visiting. Of course, we have been showing him off to family and friends who have come to pay homage since a few days after he was born. (Hopefully, they have been thoughtful about the length and timing of their visits.) By the third month, if not sooner, he is probably old enough, and we are organized enough, to take him calling. If the weather is bitter cold or scorching hot, we should put off any excursions. And we should remember that it is not rude to check and make sure that the people we are visiting are healthy.

At first, we will probably make quite a production of going out, loading ourself down with enough diapers, food, and other baby equipment for a safari. Pretty soon, we will learn what equipment we really need to take along and how to make do when visiting households that don't have needed supplies. It is wise not to make going out too much of a chore, for visiting should be fun for both of us.

Even when he is just a tiny thing, he will probably enjoy a change of scene and new faces in small doses. At least he will *notice* the change; some less adaptable babies may become noticeably uncomfortable in strange situations even when they seem "too young to know the difference." Laboratory research indicates that even newborns are aware of a change in their surroundings. If our baby does react negatively, we should try protecting him as much as possible from the change by taking as many familiar things as feasible when we go calling and encouraging others to go easy in making overtures to him. If it becomes too much of a struggle, it may be better to leave him at home; he'll get over his nervousness before too long.

Even a baby who seems to enjoy new faces and places may have some difficulty in going away from home. He may sleep an extra amount, or a lot less; his eating or digesting may be disturbed. Too much traipsing around will wear any baby out; even being carried can get tiring. So we should avoid trying to do too much in one day, and we should not hold it against the baby if he spends our entire first visit to Aunt Mary screaming from exhaustion. The more we can bend to his needs, the more fun we will all have traveling, whether for long trips or short outings.

Dealing with Baby-sitters

The time will come, later or sooner, when the grown-ups in the family want to go out and can't or don't want to take the baby with them. Well in advance of this time, we will want to have given thought to finding a competent, trustworthy baby-sitter. (Grandparents think sitting is fun, once in a while, but it is not fair to count on them all the time even if they live nearby: they have already raised their children, or so they thought.)

How we find a sitter and whom we get depends on our situation. We may live in a secure suburban community next door to a young teen-ager whom we've known all her life. If she is mature and responsible, we won't think twice about leaving even a tiny baby with her, especially since her parents will be close at hand. If we are not so lucky, we may hire a girl we know less well, an older woman, a student at a college or nursing school, or a professional from a baby-sitting service.

Whomever we hire, we will want to learn as much as we can about her. If we are not using a service, we should talk with her at some length before employing her and talk to others who have used her to learn how they liked her, what she did with the children, and how she handled any emergencies. We should engage her to come fifteen minutes or so before we plan to leave the baby with her, so there will be ample time for getting acquainted and giving instructions. It is a good idea, if possible, to leave the baby with a new sitter for a short trial run, perhaps for a few hours in an afternoon, to see how it works out.

Suppose we can't afford to hire a sitter. We may find or organize a baby-sitting exchange, or "sitter bank," in our area. Under such a system, parents take turns caring for each other's kids. It benefits everyone, and nobody pays. (See the book *Guiding Your Preschooler* for more on setting up such a system.) If there are too few young children close by for a formal setup, we might arrange with one other young family to switch off baby-sitting each other's children.

If our sitter comes early enough, we won't be in a rush while we fill her in completely on where the baby supplies are, what the baby will need while she's in charge, and what his quirks are. We should leave her the doctor's, hospital's, and other emergency phone numbers, including the one where we can be reached. If possible, the baby should be awake so that he can "meet" the sitter. Even if our infant is tiny, it is courteous to him to do this, and the technique will become very important when he is a bit older.

Making sensible, careful preparation for a sitter ahead of time allows us to go out relaxed and happy. The less of a production we make of leaving, the less it will disturb our baby. We should get in the habit, from the beginning, of giving a quick "bye-bye" and kiss, then going straight out the door. Even if our baby has been fussy all day, he will probably benefit as much from a new hand at the switch as we will from a night off.

Beginning to Play—and Learn

Think of all that our baby has learned in his first few months! To the uninitiated, he may seem little more than a plumped-out newborn, but we know better. If we need expert support for our opinion of his cognitive growth, we can remember that recent research has shown that infants are capable of acquiring knowledge from the earliest weeks of life. In fact, as already emphasized, these recent studies indicate that early learning may be a crucial factor in what and how children learn later in life. They learn more than to feel secure or insecure, confident or fearful even in the first few months; they take in information.

We can help our baby learn about his world and, more important, learn to learn, by encouraging creative and stimulating play and by providing toys that capitalize on his beginning skills. If our infant seems content to lie and stare at the wall, we must not assume that he is not ready for learning. It is especially important to encourage such a quiet baby to engage in more active play. A baby is never too young to have interesting things to look at. When we are fixing up a place for our baby, we can hang a few bright pictures around the crib and attach stick-on decorations to crib bumper and carriage. Of course, we will always want to make sure, even at the earliest stage when a baby theoretically "can't" hurt himself, that anything we put within reach of him is nontoxic, unbreakable, and without sharp edges.

A rattle is a traditional baby toy and a good one, because even before he can grasp it, he likes the sight and sound of it and therefore is motivated to reach for it. The same goes for mobiles or cradle gyms that can be suspended over and across the crib and carriage. A variety of these are available, ranging in price from quite cheap to very expensive. For even less money, eye-catching mobiles can be made by hanging painted spools, measuring spoons, cutouts—almost any bright, safe objects—from ribbon strung across the crib. Store-bought or homemade, a crib toy should include bright things and noisemakers to catch and hold even the tiniest infant's attention.

First he will be able to "play" only with his eyes, but soon he will try to reach out for what he sees. As he bats the objects hanging above him and makes them move or jingle, he will try harder. At first he will set his toy in motion by accident. Soon he will be deliberately trying to and will be putting several activities together. The more he does this, the better his eye-hand coordination becomes. More importantly, he learns he *can* affect his environment, and he is stimulated to do more.

Many babies can entertain themselves with such crib toys for part of their waking time. We may notice, too, that our baby seems happy to see his crib companions when we bring him to bed, so crib toys are as good for us as they are for him!

The baby can benefit from play with people, too. (This is where a sibling, well versed in how to be careful, and judiciously supervised, can help.) The baby will like it when somebody is there moving a rattle or toy for him to watch and reach for. Some babies when they are tiny enjoy *gentle* physical games like jiggling, or moving their hands and feet in rhythm.

And there is no "game" easier for us or better for our baby than a good conversation. Whether we are bathing, feeding, changing, or playing with him, or if he is just propped up in his infant seat while we are cleaning or cooking, we can talk to him! We may feel silly at first, but we will be helping him become familiar with the sound and use of language, and he will like the plain old attention, too.

Through these earliest games and simplest toys, our baby begins to put together the pieces of this puzzling world. He learns to use, and to enjoy using, his senses, his body, and his mind. And he may—who knows?—start to get the idea that we, the miraculous grown-ups who fill his needs, think learning is important and fun.

4
Building The Bonds Of Love

LEARNING TO LOVE is one of the most crucial tasks of a baby's first year. What does "love" mean to an infant?

Grandma adores her toddling grandchild. Whenever she's around him, she snuggles him, keeps him full and happy, and lets him do just about anything he wants. But as soon as Mommy comes into the room, the baby wants only her. Why does a baby love his mother?

Babies do not automatically love their parents. During his first six months or so, the baby probably feels no real emotional attachment to either parent—or anyone else—as individuals. To an infant, the world is little more than an extension of himself; he is at its heart. If *he* is hungry, *he* is fed. If *he* is wet, *he* is changed. When he opens his eyes, fascinating things appear to entertain *him*. Nothing exists beyond his needs and the fulfillment of them.

The baby learns quickly to associate certain objects, sounds, activities, and faces with the food and attention he demands. But during a baby's first few months, he does not care about the source of that food and attention; as far as he is concerned, any competent caretaker will do. An infant probably does not "love" these caretakers, as grown-ups understand the word. Even if they are his parents, they are to him as hands or eyes are to adults, necessary for normal existence but not objects for emotional attention. (This does not mean that an infant can thrive on being looked after by a multitude of caretakers—far from it. But more on that later.)

Forming the Mother-child Bond

Sometime during his first year, the baby will begin to "love": he will form an emotional attachment for the person or persons who care for him. Exactly why and how this bond develops are questions that psychologists, philosophers, theologians, and other thinkers have long pondered, with mixed results. Several theories have been popular in recent decades.

Some psychologists of the Freudian school have maintained that a baby feels attachment for its mother primarily because it wants to return to the safety and comfort of her womb. (This may be, but adopted children love their adoptive, rather than their biological, mothers.)

Others have held that the baby's attachment is for the "breast" and arises out of the infant's sucking drive, although bottlefed babies love their mothers, too.

Some have maintained that a baby becomes attached to its mother through its need for "contact comfort"—the comfort of being touched. Contact comfort is indeed important to an infant's well-being.

The simplest and perhaps most widely held explanation of why a baby forms a bond with his mother is that he comes to love whomever fills his needs. He associates being in a pleasant emotional state with the person who created that state by feeding, warming, and changing him. As he grows, a specific feeling of love develops from the primitive state of pleasantness and is directed toward a specific person. This theory would certainly explain why an adopted child is attached to his adoptive parents, and it would also encompass the "breast" and "contact-comfort" explanations for the mother-child bond.

But the love bond may be even stronger and more essential than that latter theory suggests. Quite recently, research has indicated that the formation of the mother-child bond may derive from a need deeper than any creature's unwillingness to bite the hand that feeds it. For example, John Bowlby, a British psychoanalyst, has proposed that the need for attachment is an innate drive itself, not directly connected with feeding or other care.

Bowlby's theory that the "need for attachment" is an inborn drive distinct from other basic drives for survival is controversial, but provocative.

The formation of the love bond in humans probably depends on a combination of many factors, innate and learned, although scientists continue to debate its prime cause. What they do know with certainty is that babies raised without a warm, consistent "mother-figure"—one person who cares *for* them as well as takes care of them—encountered serious emotional difficulties during their formative years and later in adult life.

In order for a baby to grow independent, he needs to feel that there is at least one person on whom he can count and, as he gets older, run to when things get upsetting. To a child, parents are what psychoanalyst Selma Fraiberg calls "protectors against danger." The small child views his parents as a great deal more powerful than they really are. Most people can remember times, during thunderstorms or bumpy airplane rides perhaps, when they would have been terrified without Mommy or Daddy, even though their parents could have done nothing actually to protect them. The presence of the parent, per se, reassures the child that all is well.

This kind of confidence in parents is learned, and it is vital to a child's feeling of security. In his first six months or so, the baby has learned that he can rely on his parents to meet his basic needs. From the middle of his first year through his third year, he should come to feel that he can rely on them for *anything,* that they are good people to be "attached" to.

If his parents, the people he first loves, prove reliable, then he feels secure enough to reach out and respond to other people in the world, and as he grows he will be able to enter into relationships of friendship and love with them. Should the bond with his parents be *too* protective, of course, he may have difficulty letting go as he grows. Sometimes parents, out of their own need for love, bind their children too tightly to them. Nevertheless, during the first two or three years, it is better for a child to be overly attached to his parents than not enough so. If in the first six months of life or thereabouts a baby does not attach himself to a loved person, or if the person with whom he forms his first emotional bond proves unreliable, he may be unable to stand on his own and also afraid to enter into significant relationships with others as he matures.

Learning to Love

Early attachment leads into a true loving relationship, as a child gradually comes to experience the happiness of giving and receiving love for its own sake. Once attached to a loving person, the baby begins to learn to feel and express the same kind of love he receives from his mother, or the person who mothers him. This usually happens sometime during the latter half of his first year. Of course, it will be some years before he is capable of selfless concern for those he loves, but he has begun to feel genuine affection.

In much the same way that our baby learns to love us, we learn to love him—and it may take longer than we expected. Alice Johnson and her husband adopted an infant. The baby was in their home several months before Mrs. Johnson could honestly say that she *loved* him as an individual. In discussing this with the "natural" mothers in her neighborhood, she found to her surprise that most had felt the same way about the children they had borne themselves. They had felt joy and pride when they brought their babies home from the hospital. They knew from the first, just as Alice Johnson knew, that they wouldn't want to part with their babies and would protect them against any harm, but a real feeling of love took a while to grow. Most agreed that their love for their offspring began to deepen when their babies started responding to *them* as individuals. The bond, those mothers felt, strengthened as the babies grew to express love for them. Loving is a mutual experience.

Only after learning to love his mother (or some mothering person) and to feel sure that she loves him, can he begin to love others, as emphasized earlier. The mother is the child's interpreter of the world. Only through her can he learn that the world can be a loving place. The bond between mother and child is the first link in what could be a chain of loving relationships for the baby. If the first link is weak, the rest of the chain will be shaky. We can nurture our child's ability to love during his first three years by meeting his early needs with affection and by making sure he always has someone—mother, father, or a loving mother-substitute—to rely upon.

Sharing Love—and Mother

By the time a baby gets to the stage of knowing, in his way, that his mother loves him and he loves her, he has probably become aware that there are other demands on her affection. Brothers or sisters, Daddy and friends all seem to be competing for her attention.

Jimmy, barely six months old, surprised his mother by pulling her arm away as she was feeding a neighbor's newborn. Sally at eleven months manages to raise a ruckus whenever Mother is on the phone. Fourteen-month-old John frowns whenever Mommy gives Daddy a hug and a kiss—then runs over to get his share. Two-year-old Mark, who by now usually adores being with his father, sets up a howl when his mother, busy with Mark's older sister, suggests that he get Daddy to untangle his "Slinky" toy.

A mother cannot—and for her child's own good, should not—make Baby the exclusive focus of her affection. He needs to learn to share her. Our baby will gradually learn to share our love and attention if he gets as much of both as he needs when he needs them. Once he begins to prefer us to any other caretaker (around the sixth month), when we must reject his demands or deny him immediate attention, we can give him some sort of reassurance at the same time. If he is jealous of the phone, we can hold him on our lap as we talk and let him listen a bit. If we are caring for a sibling or a visiting child when our baby starts nagging for attention, we can give him a hug, try to distract him calmly but firmly by offering a favorite toy or snack, and be sure to spend a little extra time with him soon after.

Better yet, help him to become involved satisfyingly with us in the situation that is causing him distress—by, for example, encouraging him to remain close to us, reaching out to stroke him occasionally, and talking about how "we are washing sister's hair."

For our child's own future ability to love, it is important for him to learn that it is possible to love more than one person. We teach him this by showing him that there is plenty to go around, that we can give a great deal of loving care to siblings, pets, and Daddy and still have lots of gentle affection for him. He may learn that sharing mother can mean *more* love for him, too, when those brothers, sisters, daddies, and friends all shower him with affectionate attention.

Clinging and Separation Anxiety

As a child gradually grows out of being a helpless infant, dependent on his parents' goodwill, into being a demanding individual, many mothers encounter periods and situations in which it is exceedingly difficult to be loving.

Stevie, who used to be a happy, self-sufficient baby, has suddenly started whining, whimpering, and screaming when Mother goes away and clinging to her desperately whenever he can. "He's driving me crazy!" his mother complains. "What happened to my nice, happy little boy?" Such irritating spells are times when the baby most needs the calmest, warmest, most loving attention from his mother.

"Separation anxiety," "eight-month anxiety," and "infant adolescence" are terms that child specialists use to describe these difficult periods that begin to occur, for a variety of reasons, during the second half of the first year. Not all children undergo them. When they do happen, parents need not fear that they will last forever. Such difficult-to-deal-with behavior in an otherwise adaptive child may last only a few days or a few weeks, but it needs to be handled carefully.

Barbara has been a smiling, happy baby for most of her seven months. She could entertain herself for long periods in her crib or playpen, but she has always enjoyed socializing with Grandma and the neighbors as well as her parents. Suddenly, at seven months, she screams when Mommy puts her in the playpen. When Grandma or a neighbor try to entertain her so her mother can get to the housework, she only shrieks louder. Only Mommy can soothe her; as soon as Mommy tries to put her back down, the screaming starts again. Barbara is only happy when held by her mother, and Mommy is getting worn out.

It may be hard for Barbara's mother to feel flattered, but she should. Barbara has learned to want Mommy, not just satisfaction of her needs. She has also learned that Mommy sometimes disappears, and the implications of that terrify Barbara. Doctors call this "separation anxiety." Barbara realizes for the first time how painful it would be to lose her mother and worries that she might. Right now she needs a lot of patient, loving reassurance. During the day she needs to be with Mommy as much as possible—in the same room, or if that doesn't do, in a sling that nestles her against her mother's body while her mother does household chores. Her mother should try not to leave her with sitters until she has grasped the important lesson that "Mommy Always Comes Back." Playing peek-a-boo with such a baby might help her learn this lesson; some psychologists feel that making Mommy, or baby, "disappear" then "reappear" points up the fact that being temporarily out of sight does not mean being gone forever.

Another form that separation anxiety takes in some babies is fear of strangers, or anybody outside the immediate family, even when Mommy is present. Linda had always been a joyously sociable baby and loved to be passed from arm to arm at family gatherings. She giggled with glee when her grandparents came to visit when she was just short of six months. Only one week later, when Grandma walked in the door and picked her up, Linda shrieked with terror and could be soothed only by her mother.

For many babies who have learned to differentiate Mommy from others, it is not enough simply to have her there. They want nobody else there, either. Some babies are even afraid of Daddy for a while. If we see our baby reacting this way, we should protect and reassure him as much as possible. Visiting friends and relatives should be warned to wait until the baby comes to them and not to be insulted if he refuses to have anything to do with them at first. We should let the baby stay close to us as long as he wants, but let him know that other people are okay, too. This is not the time to take a baby traveling, to introduce him to new situations, to leave him with a new sitter. Soon, when the baby learns there's no danger that we might desert him, and that it is safe to trust us and the people we trust, he will be happy once more to get acquainted, or reacquainted, with the other people in his life.

Bobby takes strangers and daytime separations in stride, but he has a problem that is actually no different from Barbara's and Linda's. He had been sleeping through every night for several months until one midnight shortly after his six-month birthday, he woke up crying hysterically. His parents comforted him, only to be awakened two hours later by screams—and then again at 4 a.m., and then 6. When this went on for a few nights, they took him to the doctor. He found Bobby to be in good health and explained that night waking is one form that separation anxiety takes in children about Bobby's age. He advised them to comfort Bobby whenever he cried until he got over his terror at being alone. It would be exhausting, the doctor admitted, but the phase would probably last only a short time. A couple of rugged weeks later, Bobby started sleeping through again.

Some child specialists still recommend letting a baby this age "cry it out," knowing that he does not wake from hunger or discomfort. However, if a baby's separation anxiety takes the night-waking form, the mother probably will *want* to reassure him—his cries are so heartrending. The weight of the evidence supports following the instinct to go to the baby. At first when his mother comforts him, she may have to rock him back to sleep, and it may take a while. Gradually, her presence will be all he needs. As he is beginning to learn that she is always available when needed, he will quiet down with a pat on the back and an "I'm right here." Having a nightlight may help him; most children need, and deserve, this reassurance.

Whenever a mother does respond to night crying, however, she should be careful not to make it such a pleasant experience that the baby keeps waking up just for company or a snack. She can leave him in bed as she comforts him, if possible, and leave the lights off if she can manage with only his nightlight. She should not play with him or offer a bottle. If he is really suffering from separation anxiety, he probably would not take food anyway. She should never succumb to the temptation to take him to bed with her; that move will create more problems than it solves in the long run.

A baby who is excessively clinging may be suffering from separation anxiety. If he is old enough to crawl or walk, he never seems to be able to leave Mommy alone, but is constantly hanging onto her, climbing up her legs, begging to be picked up. It can be very irritating until Mommy realizes that he's going through a developmental stage and needs extra love and reassurance. If she gives him lots of it—rocking, hugging, playing, and snuggling (and even babies who are not normally the cuddly type will accept a lot of contact comfort during these anxious times)—she can help him through this unhappy period. (A good long rocking-chair ride can often soothe a cranky baby and relax a tense mother's nerves, too.)

All these rather umpleasant and annoying symptoms can occur under still another set of circumstances, also related to anxiety. Little Jimmy was trying with all his might to crawl. As his mother watched him push himself up and rock back and forth, she could almost feel how much he wanted to move himself somewhere. He was *terribly* cranky for a while. Then, as soon as he figured out how to locomote, he regained his old cheerful personality. So, a few months later, when Jimmy was learning to walk, his mother understood why he once more turned into a cranky little monster. She only hoped he would begin walking quickly. When he did, he was all smiles again.

Jimmy's doctor called this behavior "infantile adolescence," another version of separation anxiety. Like teen-agers, many babies at this stage are aching to go off on their own before they are really able to, and they're a little afraid to leave Mommy, too. They need reassurance that she will still be there when they finally do push off. For every five minutes they spend on their own, they spend one minute getting back in touch with Mother. This kind of pre-mobile crankiness is often made worse by teething discomfort. A baby may simply be irritated all over. Knowing this may not make a mother happy coping with these hard spells, but it may give her added patience.

Some experts call separation anxiety "eight-month anxiety," because this behavior was once thought to be worst around that age. However, it can occur at any time from four months through eighteen months. Some babies go through separation anxiety several times and some not at all, or at least not noticeably. Whenever it happens and however it shows itself, a baby's anxious behavior is his cry for love and help as he pushes from one level of development to the next. When he is at his crankiest is when he needs the most understanding.

But maybe our baby becomes clinging and fussy when there seems to be no developmental reason. Our doctor tells us that he is healthy. He is not teething, not impatient to start walking, not involved in learning to let Mommy out of sight—just maddeningly cranky. We might ask ourself what else has been going on. Has Mommy or his usual caretaker had to go away or change her schedule drastically? Has Daddy been away from home or working a different shift so that the baby misses him? Has he suddenly been weaned from the bottle or strained baby food? Is there a lot of tension in the air resulting from some family upset? Any major change in a baby's life can make him temporarily clinging. He seeks reassurance in times of stress. We give it to him by giving him extra love (if possible, before he whines for it) and by keeping his routine and surroundings as familiar as possible. We protect him as best we can from avoidable sources of stress, such as long visits, and are extra cautious about where, when, and how we leave him with others, or alone in his crib or playpen.

Backpacks and slings come in handiest when baby is at his most clinging and anxious. If we can wear them around the house, we can get our chores done while giving baby the contact comfort he needs. And our clinger *will* get over this unpleasant and uncomfortable stage. In a way he needs proof that we love him even when he is at his most *un*lovable. The more love and reassurance he gets when he's feeling wretched, the better.

When Mother Leaves Home

A baby needs a lot of mothering, not only in times of crisis, but all the time. That doesn't mean that Mother has to hover over him every minute. And it doesn't mean that only Mother can give mothering. If a mother must or strongly wants to work outside the home, there is no reason why, for the baby's sake, she shouldn't, as long as she plans for his needs with the same loving, intelligent interest she would give those needs if she were at home.

There are many reasons why a mother might want to go outside her home to work after she has a baby. She may simply need the money. Or she may have found, like many modern women, that though during pregnancy she looked forward to being a full-time mother, the constant demands of a baby make her irritable, and the experience of being housebound makes her restless and depressed. Getting out of the house at least part of the time for a job, volunteer work, or a hobby may benefit both her and her baby. A woman who really wants to continue a promising career that she interrupted to have her baby may resent the baby if she stays at home. Woman's place is no longer necessarily in the home. Because of the availability today of many effective methods of family planning, women have great choice in their life styles and can plan in advance to combine work and motherhood to their satisfaction—and their family's. A mother does have an extra responsibility, though, to the small being she brought (hopefully by choice) into the world.

A mother needs to weigh many pros and cons before deciding on outside work. If she is planning to work for money, will her job bring in enough income to pay for the extra expenses—lunches, carfare, taxes, clothing, baby-sitter—that it will require? She must balance her own peace of mind with her worries about the baby: if she is too concerned for his welfare to enjoy her job, she might as well stay home. Unfortunately, she may also have to face the disapproval of family and friends who believe that working mothers are neglecting their children. If she feels strongly enough about getting off on her own, she should manage somehow to do it, for everyone will be better off. She can meet her responsibilities as a mother by planning carefully for her baby's welfare.

Choosing a Mother Substitute

Unless it is absolutely necessary for financial reasons, a mother should not take on an outside job during the first few months of her baby's life. For one thing, she should be taking it as easy as possible. Also, she will probably want the chance to get to know this baby she has awaited so long. Even after the first months, for mother's and baby's sake, part-time work is probably more sensible to start with, especially if a mother has to keep house.

For those for whom financial difficulties make a job vital, many public and private organizations now operate day-care centers. But these, unless they are extraordinary, are not for infants. Infants need individual attention. If a baby cannot have his mother when he needs her to be an interpreter of his new world, he needs a substitute mother: one individual, loving person on whom he can depend for the personal, special care he has a right to expect.

Before a mother goes to work, she will want to find some such person. She will have her own criteria, but there are some basic requirements. A mother-substitute need not be young, but she should be spry, even if the baby is not yet a toddler—he will be before very long. She should be competent and dependable, of course, and have good experience in caring for infants and in dealing with emergencies that might arise. She should also be a warm, loving person who cares about this baby, who can give affection and stimulation, and who agrees with—or agrees to follow—the mother's ideas about child-rearing.

If a mother is very fortunate, she will have a relative or close friend who is handy and available for this kind of service. She may be able to work out a trading arrangement with a trusted neighboring mother, if both of them work or get out only part time. More likely, she will need to hire someone, which she will go about in the same way as she would hire a baby-sitter, only much more so. She will want to get to know very well the woman who will act as mother's stand-in. And, she will be sure that this woman understands her directions and likes the baby.

When hiring a mother-substitute, it is a good idea to be quite specific about the details of the arrangement, beyond salary and hours. What meals and transportation expenses are included? Will her duties include anything other than strictly baby care: preparing formula? washing baby's things? cooking any family meals? playground duty? any household cleaning? shopping?

Both parents should be completely satisfied with this important person, and she should like both if the arrangement is to work at its best. Such mutual admiration is necessary for the parents' peace of mind, and the baby needs to realize that they like and trust this person. She will become another member of the family, even if she comes only a couple of days a week.

Once the new routine is established, the mother should find time to talk with her mother-substitute often to share ideas and information about the baby. She will also want to arrange the baby's and her own schedule so that she can spend some special time alone with him. If a mother is happy in her own life, the quality of attention she is able to give her baby will increase, even if the quantity is less than that of other mothers.

What Is a Father?

Of course, Mother, or her stand-in, is not the only person in the baby's life. A father is pretty important, too, as can be seen from the way the baby gets himself to the front door by any means available when Daddy announces his arrival from work. Kids have probably always been pretty impressed, one way or another, by their fathers, even from a very tender age. But recently Daddies have been changing, or at least thinking of themselves in a new way. Perhaps there are fashions in fatherhood just as there are in other aspects of child-rearing.

For one thing, Americans' rules about what is "woman's work" and what is "man's work" have been relaxing over the past decade. Men do not seem so nervous about helping around the house or having their wives leave the home for work or recreation. Fathers today seem to be getting over the idea that it is sissy to be sentimental about their kids or to get involved in any way other than paying the bills. Fewer fathers apparently feel the need for strict and immediate obedience from their children. The image of Dad as a tough, aloof, godlike creature is long gone. The "pal" syndrome is disappearing, too: today most parents would agree that children need to be raised by adults, not buddies.

Sometimes there is more pressure than is realized on a man to conform to standards of what a good father "ought" to be like, whether the ideal image is that of a stern disciplinarian or of a birdhouse-builder. The trend among today's generation of fathers is to ignore what a father "should" be in favor of being themselves and enjoying their children in their own unique ways. They certainly are much more active in making decisions regarding their kids and in actually caring for them, beginning when the baby comes home from the hospital. Even a father's traditional role of supplying the financial and moral support for the mother is changing these days. In more and more families, the mother brings in some if not most of the money, and husband and wife, as partners of equal standing, share decision-making and work out their own untraditional division of household and child-raising duties.

Even so, a father does bring something special to a baby. It is often said that children need both love and discipline, both softness and firmness, to grow up healthy and able to cope with life. Most societies give the tough role to the man—either the baby's father or some other male—and the tender role to the woman. In America's fast-changing social structure this is still usually the case, although there are exceptions—and always have been. Why does this happen? Who knows? It may be the nature of the beast, or simply learned tradition. A deeper, louder voice, being away from home most of the day—*something* gives most fathers more authority over most children, even young ones, than most mothers can muster.

When Jimmy's mother tells him to sit down in his high chair, he just giggles until she gets mad. When his father tells him to sit down, he sits down. He squirms when Mommy changes his diapers, but lies quietly while Daddy does it. He obeys, surprised, when Daddy tells him not to touch something Mommy has been trying to keep him away from all day. Yet Daddy has never been rough with his child, and Mommy thinks of herself as being reasonably strict. What is it? Maybe anyone who is out of the picture most of the day would have the same effect, and in most households that is Daddy. Maybe a child is naturally able to accept authority from one caretaker as long as the other one is something of a pushover.

Of course, daddies are not only for discipline. A father also brings fun, for the practical reason that the mother of an infant is usually too tired or busy to play the strictly fun games (no let's-learn-to-read toys for Dad!).

Whatever role a father plays, childhood experts feel that, if there isn't a daddy around, a child, even in the first three years, needs a "daddy substitute." Both boys and girls can use a grandfather, an uncle, a big brother, or some other male to occupy that special place reserved for daddies.

5 *Your Baby Is Special*

EVERY FAMILY IS different, and even within families, every child is unique. A baby may seem "just like Daddy," or "the image of her mother," or a "carbon copy of Aunt Susie." He may have "Grandpa's temper" or "Grandma's good nature," but he has his own personality. He inherited some characteristics, and he has picked up some as he has grown. The interaction of his special self with the world around him, plus what he has picked up, have come to equal a markedly individual being. Yet even after a year or two of growing, he is probably in many ways the same as he was when you brought him home: placid or impatient; energetic or lazy; easygoing or tense.

Infant Character Types

Does nature endow a baby with his psychological makeup, or is it nurtured by society? This so-called nature-nurture controversy is one that continues to engage scientists. Psychologists once thought that a baby at birth was without any ingrained disposition; that he gained all his personality characteristics from his experiences with the environment.

Recent studies, however, have lent a lot of weight to the idea that each baby has a strong individual personality at birth or even before.

Observing a number of infants from birth, Dr. Stella Chess and other New York pediatricians and psychologists have described three general types of babies. They label these "easy," "slow-warmer-up," and "difficult." On the basis of infants' activities and reactions, these researchers found that they could divide the babies' behavior and personality into a number of different categories: activity level, adaptability, attention span, and mood, among others.

According to their findings, an "easy" baby is very regular in his habits, moderately active, highly adaptable, moderate in his reactions to stimuli, and positive in mood and sociability. A "slow-warmer-up" is just that—his reactions are negative at first and his initial activity level is low, but he gradually becomes more positive toward new situations. "Difficult" babies have extremely intense reactions to stimuli, generally negative moods, slow adaptability to changes, and a tendency to withdraw from things or people.

These findings support what parents have always felt: that there are "bad" babies—difficult—and "good" ones—easy. For many years mothers were blamed for whatever difficulties their baby might have in coping with the world. But some babies do seem to be "just born that way." This does not mean that parents can have no influence on difficult babies. The Chess findings indicate that once parents get to know their baby's strong and weak points, they can help him cope by avoiding demands that clash with his personality and by giving support in situations that are hard for him.

Handled appropriately, any baby can achieve his full potential. The uniqueness of every baby is complicated by the uniqueness of every mother. In a study of mother-child interaction from infancy into childhood, Sylvia Brody and Dr. Sidney Axelrod identified six types of mothers, according to their empathy with their children, their control of them, and their efficiency in accomplishing their stated goals. They found that a tense, cold mother can turn an "easy" baby into a "difficult" one, whereas a warm, firm mother can guide a difficult one to a state of satisfaction with life. These results indicate that a baby's birth character can indeed be changed—for better or worse—within broad limits. Extremes in the environment, too—brutality, isolation, marked tension, or disease as well as rich stimulation—may of course make a child different from the one he at first seemed slated to be.

Still, if the baby we brought home from the hospital was a voracious eater, demanding of attention, sleeping little, and in constant motion, it is doubtful that during his first year he will have turned into a quiet, lazy observer of the human scene. If our newborn was placid, easily contented and sleepy, a delicate eater, the tense, screaming problem she may have become at 12 months probably will not last.

What Is Normal?

If every baby is so different, what *is* normal? At a year, Johnny is walking, but Sam still crawls; Jean talks—she says many recognizable words and phrases, but Alice barely babbles; John is almost three feet tall, Bill is hardly over two feet; Mike weighs 30 pounds, Allen only 18; Stevie can work a simple puzzle, Dave can just manage to clap his hands together. All these children could be called "normal."

Perhaps the most useful standard by which to judge a baby's behavior and development after the first year or so would be: Is it normal for *him?* Does his emotional state or physical activity fit into his *own* pattern?

Understanding our baby's unique personality characteristics eases the task of caring for him. By now we have come to know what is typical of our own baby. He is husky or delicate, short or tall, relaxed or tense, limp or well-toned of muscle, an eager eater or a picky one, predictable or unpredictable. We are familiar with his activity level, too. His activities have changed as he has grown, but his way of going about them is the same. As a newborn he never stopped flailing his arms and legs, and as a toddler he is always on the go.

We have an idea, too, of what motor skills we can expect of him. Some babies are well coordinated and agile from birth; some are strong but clumsy; some have excellent control over their small muscles and can manipulate tiny objects from a young age but show little interest in pursuits such as crawling or walking that require cultivating large-muscle control.

Variations in Sociability and Adaptability

Does our baby like people and enjoy being with them, or not? Some infants like nothing better than a party; some are such loners that they occasionally push even their parents away in favor of privacy. Given a change of routine or surroundings, some babies relish the new scene with enthusiasm and excitement; others cling in terror to their mothers. Some babies develop steadily; some in spurts, seeming to take two steps forward followed by one step backward.

Such normal differences are not necessarily connected with a baby's parents, either. The same family can bring two, or more, completely unique personalities into the world. A mother whose first baby was "easy" and adaptable looks forward with nonchalant happiness to her second, who turns out to be a screamer. Another whose first was a decidedly "difficult" baby dreads the arrival of her second and is surprised with a gentle charmer. (Individual differences are just another reason for spacing one's children so that each gets the special handling he needs, rather than an assembly-line job.)

To keep an effective eye on our child's development, we need to know what is normal for him, and that takes time and care. Despite the rule of thumb, "Is it normal for him?," if anything in a baby's behavior or development concerns or puzzles a mother, she should never hesitate to check with the doctor. Curing a problem early is almost as good as preventing it.

Tuning In to the Baby

The better we can get to know our baby now, while his his life is relatively uncomplicated, the better we will be able to understand and help him as he develops. If we can size up his abilities, his difficulties, and his relationship with the world as a baby, we can be a more constructive influence in his life when he leaves infancy and must deal with other children, school, adults, and eventually his own family.

By understanding what is normal for our child at this early stage, too, we can start encouraging his strengths and helping him outgrow or compensate for his weaknesses during these crucial first years.

If our baby is "difficult," for example—if he reacts in an extreme fashion to any excitement or frustration, if he is terrified of new situations—he could use our steadying hand now to help him calm down and get control of himself before he toddles off into the world. He will need our watchful eye as he grows and faces new stimulation. If our baby is very active, now and later we can help him direct his energy and can find ways of keeping him in one place so that he can explore the quieter aspects of life. If our baby is very placid, we will want to try to interest him throughout childhood in moving about more while giving him plenty to stimulate him where he sits still. If our baby is afraid of new people and things, he will always need extra encouragement to begin new ventures, and he will always need reassurance that we are there when he needs us.

Our baby need not fit into any kind of mold, of course; there are so many factors to his personality that he *is* unique and not easy to categorize. However, by the end of his first year, he will have settled down, probably into some regular habits, and we, hopefully, will have a few more moments to sit back and observe him.

This is the time to do it, if not before. A baby spends his first year or so laying the foundations of love and trust. During his second year, he begins to build on those foundations. He starts to learn and accomplish in earnest, and he needs our understanding help. The second and third year of life is a time when, child specialists say, parents can have a dramatic effect on their child's future intellectual development and social achievement.

Tuning Up and Tuning Down

Since our baby's first days, we have been trying to tune in to his style, but as that style becomes increasingly definite, we may find that we need to "tune up" or "tune down" his personality.

Beth had always been a quiet, placid infant, content to lie in her crib for hours, playing with her hands or staring at a mobile. When the neighbor babies her age began to crawl and to grow more active every day, Beth still seemed to enjoy just watching the world go by. At first, her parents worried, but their pediatrician assured them that she was physically and mentally normal.

They sought ways to encourage greater activity. Prodding her to play and walk only made her quieter; roughhousing frightened her. Instead, they found they could tune her up in quite simple ways. Rather than fetching her, they called her to come to them. They asked her to get things for them. They played gentler physical games with her, such as tickling and a simplified version of hide-and-seek, and gave her a few action toys she enjoyed—a pull toy and a doll carriage. They made sure she spent lots of time with other children, although at first she only watched.

At the same time, Beth's parents capitalized on her strong points. She loved books, dolls, and small toys she could play with quietly, so she was given plenty of those. Well-behaved and observant, Beth was a dream to take to the zoo or the museum, and such activities seemed to stimulate her. Most important, perhaps, her parents learned to pay lots of attention to her even though she did not demand it. They played, read, and talked with her to be sure that she didn't miss out on stimulation. Gradually, Beth opened up, gained confidence, and began to display, to her parents' delight, all that she had been quietly absorbing.

Jim had been a boisterous baby since the day he was born. He was a vigorous child, an early walker, full of energy and devilment. Once he became mobile, he could have kept going continuously till he dropped from exhaustion, but neither he, nor his parents, nor the family home could have withstood that pace for very long. And in a way Jim could have missed out on a lot of life simply by going through it at top speed. His parents felt a need to "tune him down." They made sure he had plenty of strenuous activity, outside and with friends when possible, to burn off some of his energy. They took him to a variety of play areas in the hope that differing environments would encourage him to explore. They also tried to find entertainment that could slow him down and give him time to think. After several tries they found some toys and games—large blocks, water play in the tub—that occupied him relatively quietly. Since managing his routine was sometimes a problem, Jim's parents maintained firm rules for naptime, bedtime, and mealtimes. Gradually, Jim grew able to tune himself down and impose some order on his own life.

In learning to deal with their children's personalities, parents sometimes need to tune in to themselves, too. The Packards, for example, an exuberant, energetic couple, gave birth to a quiet, retiring child. In their efforts to encourage their baby to greater activity, they succeeded only in overwhelming him. They had to learn to tune themselves down to give their son the kind of stimulation he needed without overdoing it.

The Wyeths, on the other hand, were a settled, subdued, older couple when confronted with their extremely bouncy baby girl. As a toddler her zest for life was on the verge of being completely inhibited by her parents—and they were nearly nervous wrecks—when wise counseling encouraged them to loosen up a bit and join in directing some of their daughter's energies. They had to tune themselves up a little.

The Trap of Pushing or Comparing

Tuning in to a child's wavelength and fiddling a bit with the controls is different from *pushing* a child. Some parents try to force their children to fit a preconceived notion of what they "should be." This is a normal reaction perhaps, but likely to be frustrating for all concerned. A baby may not be growing into the kind of person his parents expected. He may be like neither one of them, but he has a right to be himself. We push a child when we try to make of him something *we* want but *he* is not. We *encourage* a child when we give him the opportunity—even from these early years—to fulfill his own potential.

Parents may push children after comparing them with other kids the same age. "How come Jimmy can crawl and you can't?" they may begin to ask their six-month-old, and they'll start egging him on toward crawling. If ten-month-old Susie down the street has given up her bottle, year-old Johnny's mother starts putting pressure on him to use a cup.

This is not to say that it isn't a good idea to compare notes with other parents of young children—it is. Their ideas and experiences can often help us if only by encouraging us to think through our child-rearing practices. But it is not wise to start applying other people's opinions to our child before analyzing the whole situation. Does little Susie-down-the-street suck her thumb a lot more now that she is weaned, or grab for other babies' bottles? Then maybe her mother rushed the cup. Is Johnny in the throes of learning to walk? Then now is not the time to introduce him to the cup, or anything else new.

It is inevitable that we will compare our baby with other people's, but we must remember to take our own pride and others' criticism with a grain of salt. Each baby is different—and if we really look, we will probably find that almost every healthy, reasonably happy baby we hear about, including our own, is "advanced" in some areas and "backward" in others. We must remember, too, that we must fit every baby's outward achievements into the entire context of his personality. Things that are easy for some infants are hard for others.

6
Coping With Common Concerns

WHEN A MOTHER gets to know other parents of young children, she may quickly notice that their conversation usually turns to their children and common problems that concern them all. Perhaps the most constant worries among parents of babies and toddlers are injury and illness that may befall their children.

Accidents

Some parents worry about accidents more than others. Some kids seem to get hurt and sick more often than others.

Ellen is one year old and still unscathed. She has never so much as bumped her chin on a table edge. Fred is continually covered with scratches and bruises, and the trouble didn't begin only when he started walking. By the time he was four months old, he had been back to the hospital twice—for hernia and a dislocated shoulder—and he was always rolling off his changing table, even when he was tied down.

"Accident prone" would seem a strange term to apply to a child at such an early stage in life, but kids from a very young age do seem to differ in the vigor with which they bump their way through the world, even given parents of the same degree of common sense and carefulness. How should a parent cope with accidents?

Try to prevent them, of course, but without brooding or overprotecting. It is a good idea to practice the safety consciousness that is the basis of babyproofing the home environment long before the infant is capable of swallowing a pin and long after the child *seems* able to take care of himself. (A detailed discussion of accident prevention may be found in Chapter 7.) Still, a child who *never* had an accident would be one who never did anything else, and there are accidents that no parent can foresee.

Against such misfortunes the best remedy is a certain calm attitude on the parents' part, and as new parents we might do well to decide ahead of time how to react. Our automatic reaction to a fall or a bitten lip may be to gasp and clutch the child, but if we make up our mind ahead of time to keep calm, we can have extra energy to spend on taking care of the child. Parents need above all to be—or to *appear* to be—calm when an accident befalls their children. A child can withstand almost anything—from scraped knees through major operations—if Mommy and Daddy are cool and steadfast. If an infant rolls off a bed, or a toddler falls off a slide, the tumble is upsetting enough. If he sees that his parents are panic-stricken, he'll really become frightened. We needn't make so light of an accident that we seem unsympathetic, but it is enough to say simply, "Oh, my, you fell down," as we pick him up and give him a hug. If the child is seriously hurt, he will let us know by crying for an unusually long time, by passing out, or by displaying other unusual behavior. We can keep an eye on the child after any mishap without making a production of it. A baby needs calm reassurance that he is all right, but he does not need to learn that getting hurt gets him extra attention.

Disability and Disease

Disease is another common concern among parents. Like accidents, many illnesses can be prevented, but children cannot be protected against all of them.

Some babies are born with physical problems. Birth defects are sometimes a big worry for expectant parents. Doctors are devoting a great deal of research to preventing and locating such defects before birth. To help prevent possible problems in apparently normal newborns, many obstetricians routinely give eye drops, "PKU" tests (to check on a certain kind of metabolic difficulty that can lead to mental retardation), and other preventative care immediately after birth.

Congenital defects still do occur, however. Most of the more common ones—weak eye muscles, turned-out feet, certain blood maladies, even cleft palate and harelip among others—are now remediable. At the proper time in a child's development they can be effectively overcome through relatively simple treatment.

A mother may have heard or read about—and been frightened of—rarer disabilities and genetic defects that doctors are only now discovering. The existence of such problems makes it important that she pay attention to her child's development and behavior. Rather than be afraid to admit that she sees a possible disability, she should consult with her doctor. Prompt treatment of a defect can often do wonders, since young children have remarkable powers of recovery.

In dealing with birth defects, parents, in addition to remaining as unflustered as possible, must give their baby the kind of love and relaxed assurance that will help him gradually learn to accept and live with his disability. They need also to overcome any feelings of guilt about the problem. Such guilt feelings are understandable but will only do them and the child harm.

Even if our child, like most children, is born healthy and normal, all the medicine and hygienic practices in the world won't keep him from being sick occasionally. Colds, flu, and other minor maladies are simply part of life that any child learns to weather. Ours may catch his first cold at four months and, depending on the season, seem to have a runny nose till he gets to high school. We can and should keep a child away from people with dangerous infectious diseases, but we can't, and we wouldn't want to, isolate him from every child with a sniffle.

We can prevent many of the more dangerous common diseases by providing our child with proper immunization at the right time, including booster shots. Parents today need have no further concern about polio, smallpox, measles, mumps, German measles, diphtheria, whooping cough, tetanus, some

IMMUNIZATION CHART

	Birth	6 Weeks	10 Weeks	3 Months	6 Months	9 Months	1 Year
DPT*		X	X	X			
Smallpox							X
Measles							X
Polio—oral* (or, more rarely, injection)		X	X	X			
PKU test	X						
TB test						X	
German measles**							
Mumps**							

Certain childhood diseases are presumed to confer lifetime immunity. If your child contracts one of the following, record the data on this chart.

Chickenpox
German measles
Measles
Mumps

* DPT (diphtheria, pertussis [whooping cough], and tetanus) and polio immunization must be renewed by boosters several times during childhood. Note dates of boosters on the chart.

** Doctors differ about age to give these vaccines—usually not administered until preschool years or later, as the length of the immunity conferred is debatable.

Note: Doctors will not give vaccines to a child who has a cold or other illness, and the smallpox vaccination will not be given in hot weather or to children with rashes.

types of influenza, and other serious and often fatal illnesses that once afflicted children and their families—*as long as they have their children immunized.* The baby's doctor or clinic will give him the necessary shots if he is brought in regularly. The chart shown above summarizes the immunization series and its usual order. In addition, if a child is exposed to any serious contagious disease, the doctor should be consulted immediately to obtain treatment that might neutralize or weaken the infection.

Teething

Children must endure certain inevitable growing pains. For some babies the onset of teething may be the first indication that the world is not entirely a rosy place. He hurts, and there is nothing anyone can do about it. Nobody knows exactly how much pain accompanies teething, and it surely must differ from child to child. From the third month on, many parents blame any crankiness or sickness on "teeth." It is rare, however, for teething to be the source of any prolonged, intense discomfort, and it does not *cause* illness. Since teething usually begins at the same time as solid food is introduced, when the baby is meeting new people, and when whatever natural immunities he may have had are gone, these other factors are more likely than teething to be the cause of stomach upsets and colds.

Teething may simply be the final straw in an otherwise difficult period. Its onset coincides with some major events in the baby's psychological and emotional life. Until his third month or so, he is a passive, sucking creature who takes in anything that is presented to him without using initiative to *get* things. When teething begins, he has a natural urge to bite and to take, not just to receive. At the same time, new mobility enables him to be more aggressive in going after things with the rest of his body. Some psychologists theorize that the two modes of behavior—biting and aggression—are directly connected. Whether they are or not, their onset is often simultaneous, and whatever discomfort the baby feels from his erupting teeth may accentuate his eagerness to get at the world and his frustration at not being quite able to. If he is trying to crawl at the same time his first teeth are poking through, his frustration could be maddening.

Also coinciding with the sprouting of the first two teeth is, for many breastfed babies, weaning from the breast. An infant may feel a double shock when "Gremlins hurt my gums, I bite Mommy, Mommy goes away . . . ." Sometimes it almost seems that a fussy teething baby is testing the world, saying, in effect, "Even my own body is attacking me—prove you still love me!"

All of which is simply to say that teething is a big step for a baby. It does cause discomfort for a variety of reasons and requires extra understanding of more than swollen gums. The gums do sometimes need soothing. Patented anesthetics are available for them, and rubbing whiskey on them occasionally helps numb them. Most doctors today discourage the use of paregoric, a traditional remedy, because it is a narcotic. The doctor may recommend giving aspirin, but a mother should check with him; it seems wiser for many reasons not to respond automatically with a pill.

Teeth may not be quite the villains they are made out to be, but they can cause some physical symptoms. A teething baby will probably drool and may have a runny nose with no other signs of a cold. He may rub his ears as though they hurt, but if there is no fever and the rubbing does not persist, he is probably responding to pain in his jaw, not his ear. Many teething babies have bouts of diarrhea. During teething an extra supply of saliva is produced, which helps to overdigest a child's food. This is most noticeable immediately before a new tooth pushes through. Of course, if diarrhea persists or is extreme, the doctor should be consulted and the baby should have plenty of fluids to counteract the dehydration that diarrhea can cause.

Some babies breeze through teething as though nothing were happening, quickly and efficiently producing teeth at the "proper" time and in the "proper" order, whereas some take forever and agonize over each addition. If our baby does not sprout his teeth in order or "on time," we needn't worry, of course. He can learn to chew and talk without teeth. His doctor can take a look at his gums at each checkup to make sure they are healthy. Eventually our toothless wonder will be toothless no longer.

Thumb-sucking

Parents sometimes worry that their baby's teeth will grow in crooked if he sucks his thumb. Pediatricians and dentists can reassure them that any effect on the baby teeth does not influence the development of the second set of teeth. Thumb- or finger-sucking after the first four years or so may

affect the alignment of the second teeth, but that is something to deal with later.

Some parents worry about thumb-sucking simply because they think it is "wrong" or "bad." When a baby sucks his thumb or hand before his third or fourth month, it is a function of his sucking drive and will probably disappear. Babies who suck their thumbs after the sixth month do so as a security measure in the anxious period when they discover that Mommy can go away. There is no reason to stop a baby from doing this (and no way, either).

Thumb-sucking may upset a mother's older relatives and friends. Previous generations disapproved of it so strongly that they resorted to bizarre methods of keeping tiny thumbs out of tiny mouths. Thumbs offer solace to baby as reminders of the cozy comfort mother and the nipple used to bring on demand. When looked at that way, it seems cruel to force a baby's thumb out of his mouth.

A baby may continue to be a thumb-sucker throughout his first year, toddlerhood, and beyond. He will probably gradually give up sucking his thumb during the first three years, but he may revert to it later in times of stress (many adults, under strain, continue to bite their nails and cuticles and play with their mouths). As he enters the preschool years he will learn that it is not socially acceptable. Then we can talk to him about it and try to discover why he feels a need to suck his thumb. For now, it need not concern us. If it does, we can make sure the baby is getting as much direct affection and contact comfort as he needs and be sure not to punish or shame him for something that is so important to his contentment.

Pacifiers

A pacifier serves the same function as the thumb in both the infant and the older child, but it is easier both to abuse and to wean from. Some children will have nothing to do with a pacifier in infancy, although most modern parents would find it preferable to a crying baby. Babies who do accept it during the first few months do so from their drive to suck. The sucking drive usually diminishes by the fourth month. Many babies who have avidly sucked the pacifier until then actively refuse it when it is offered after that. In other cases parents can take the initiative by not offering the pacifier to the baby after the third or fourth month. It is easier to wean a child from a pacifier than from a thumb, since the pacifier can be "disappeared." This may prove difficult at first, but after a few days, if the baby's sucking drive is really tapering off, giving up the pacifier will be simple.

It is also easy for parents to use the pacifier as a plug: the minute a child starts fussing, his mother may stuff the pacifier in his mouth to quiet him. Used in this way, the pacifier becomes the routine source of comfort, perhaps even more so than when a child simply attaches himself to the device for security. To see toddlers and older children sucking on a pacifier in the market or on the street is offensive to some adults, but the habit is still very important to the child and needs to be broken with tact and caution.

Many parents have weaned their toddlers or two-year-olds from the pacifier by, first, not using it as a plug, and second, limiting the times or areas in which the child may suck on it. When the child is capable of understanding what is being asked, he is usually at the point of wanting to be grown-up and will respond to "Now that you're a big boy, you'll only need to use the pacifier in the house, okay?" Soon it can dwell only in the baby's room, and then it can function only at nap and bedtime. In this way, the baby will get the idea that it is more grown-up not to have the pacifier. He will also learn that he has his mother's support in his effort to grow up and her understanding of how important the pacifier is to him. So she and he will be working together, gently, to help him mature.

Security Blankets

Babies adopt "comforters," "loveys," or security blankets for the same reason that they suck thumbs or pacifiers. The comforter plays the role of a substitute mother that never leaves him, never scolds him, and always bends to his needs after he has found that Mother is not quite so cooperative. Some babies who suck their thumbs also involve comforters in this activity. Some who adopt loveys never suck their thumbs.

Having a comforter can prove handy because it offers the baby security in times when Mommy has to leave him. And it doesn't necessarily mean that the baby has been deprived of adequate mothering. If our baby has selected something anonymous, like a diaper or a receiving blanket, for security, we're lucky. If he prefers a favorite doll or teddy bear, we should try to get in an extra supply before he wears out the first one, because comforters are things that it's difficult to separate a child from. If our toddler drags one around everywhere, we needn't worry; he'll eventually grow out of it. He will be able to understand that it isn't suitable to carry a ragged diaper to nursery school or that there is no place for a teddy bear in the playground, even though in his own room it may be difficult to accomplish the split. We may know people who find it hard to get rid of their childhood dolls even in adulthood.

Weaning

Growing out of comforters, pacifiers, thumbs, and teddy bears are hurdles to maturity that, with diplomacy and love, can be taken one by one as a child grows. Weaning from the breast or bottle is something that definitely must be accomplished, but it must be handled with the greatest of care and understanding, for both mother's and baby's sake.

However long a mother has been nursing, whether for several weeks or many months, weaning is a big emotional step for both her and her baby, even though she may have introduced the baby to solid foods before she started weaning.

Babies will indicate a willingness to leave the breast at three months, about six months, and again at nine months, so it is at these general times that most mothers wean. Mothers who wish to go back to work, or who have trouble nursing, wean early; those who do not wish to be bitten by baby's teeth wean at about six months; and others who find the experience satisfying and convenient may continue nursing, generally while giving other foods, till the ninth or twelfth month.

Depending on when she weans, she will graduate her child either to the bottle or to the cup. If the baby is old enough to drink from the cup, she can save an extra step by going immediately to it. Her doctor can help with the technical details of weaning, and the baby will give her cues on when and how to go about it. She will notice that the baby is less eager to nurse at some meals than others; those are the times to offer milk or formula in cup or bottle along with his solid food. Gradually the baby will take the bulk of that meal's milk from the cup or bottle and will in time be happy to extend the practice to other meals. At the end of the meal she can breastfeed a bit, which allows the supply of breast milk to taper off comfortably as the baby graduates to other ways of doing things.

Whether a baby is weaned from bottle or breast, it should be done gradually and warmly. The nipple has, in effect, been the baby's main connection with the world. He needs reassurance that even without that connection the world is still a friendly place.

If a family crisis arises, or sometimes for a mother's own convenience and peace of mind, the baby may have to be weaned quickly. If nursing is difficult, physically or emotionally, for the mother, it won't be the kind of experience for the baby that it should be. A baby may fight sudden weaning from the breast by refusing other food, mostly, for a day or so. But given enough cuddling and comforting, he will make the transition and not be harmed, physically or emotionally, by his "fasting." It is best not to push bottle or solids on the baby when he resists. Console him in other ways and let him come to eating differently in his own good time.

On the other hand, mothers sometimes keep their babies nursing because, unconsciously, they are unwilling to give up the close bond that nursing can create. Even mothers who are not happy nursing may not be prepared for the sense of loss that weaning can create. They sometimes experience a depression similar to post-partum blues as their body's hormones return to the nonnursing state. Weaning has considerable importance for mother as well as child, and the mother should be aware of her own feelings when she begins to ease the baby from the breast.

Weaning from the bottle has no such hormonal implications for a mother (as far as we now know), but some women still find it difficult to let their babies move from bottle to cup because they so enjoy babying them. This is not to say that leaving the bottle is easy for the babies. To them the bottle's nipple and the sucking experience have the same significance as breast suckling.

For the past few decades the popular rule has been to take a baby's bottle away as soon as possible. Many doctors recommend starting the cup at four months and having a baby completely off the bottle six months later. More recently, some pediatricians and mothers have worried less about taking the bottle away and have left the time of weaning more up to the baby. Some babies are ready to give up sucking as early as six months, but some seem happier to keep working at a bottle, if only occasionally, well into their second year.

The baby might start exploring a cup at about his fourth month, or as soon as he is sitting up by himself for meals. He will need to understand what it is and get the feel of it long before he is comfortable drinking milk out of it. (He may have been taking juice out of a cup for some time, but somehow milk is a different experience, even to a child who is not breastfed.) If he has been able to satisfy his curiosity about the cup early, it will be easier to persuade him to drink, not to pour, from it. A variety of cups are available equipped with drinking spouts so that the beginning drinker can't spill the entire contents before he gets it to his mouth. Spills should be expected, though, and the floor protected from them if necessary. We probably can't say that the baby is spilling on purpose (and the time will come when he does) until he is past a year. When that happens, cup-throwing can be made a "no-no."

During the second half of his first year, the mother starts putting a small amount of milk in the cup and offering it to the baby along with his bottle. She will notice that at some meals (for many babies, lunch) he will have decreasing interest in the bottle, and at that meal she can give him the cup only. Eventually, if she is persistent and consistent, he will be drinking from the cup at every meal. Many babies are also perfectly willing to have their between-meals juice from a cup, but some find bedtime bottles the sort of solace that only sucking can offer. Since nighttime bottles serve the function of comfort as well as feeding, they may take the longest to wean from.

If a mother has been wise and/or lucky, she won't have put her child to bed with a bottle. This practice does not indicate wickedness on the parents' part, but it may, in time, prove a mixed blessing. Bedtime bottles have long been a bugaboo in some circles on the theory that the bottle becomes an unwarranted security device, since sleeping and eating should not be confused. It is probably best for the long term not to start babies on the habit of taking a bottle to bed.

It may be easier to separate the baby from his bottle if his bottle-beverage is limited to juice and the juice is gradually thinned out until he is having plain water (we needn't worry about his not getting "enough" milk from his cup; once he is on solid foods, he will need very little milk).

Perhaps the most important thing to be remembered about weaning, as about other areas of child care, is that attitude is more important than timetable and technique. Despite what we may read or hear, common sense would indicate that there are no "shoulds" in weaning—no absolute age limits before or after which a baby must have been weaned if he is to be a respectable human being—so we can afford to be relaxed. Still, the baby does need to grow up, and he *wants* to. He needs firm guidance and loving support in giving up the ways of babyhood without sacrificing the warmth he has enjoyed as a baby.

Self-feeding

Feeding himself is also an important milestone in the baby's growth. Most babies make it clearly known when they are ready to feed themselves: sometime between six and fifteen months they simply refuse to be spoonfed. At that point, a mother must use her ingenuity in selecting foods that her baby is capable of feeding to himself and that are nutritionally valuable to him. Forcing a spoon into the mouth of a child who has decided he wants to feed himself may serve to turn him away from eating altogether.

To encourage the baby to feed himself and grow out of baby foods, if he doesn't do it on his own, his mush can gradually be converted into roughly mashed or chopped foods that require some chewing. By the fourth quarter of his first year, he will be able to digest almost any type of food and will no longer need to have everything puréed. In fact, if he is offered hard foods that he can gnaw during his sixth month, his teething gums will appreciate it. He will be able to mash and digest a lot more than one might imagine.

Sometime after the middle of his first year, the child will probably start grabbing the spoon from his mother, trying to play with his food, and otherwise indicating that he would like to embark on this adventure of eating all by himself. When this happens, she should have two spoons ready, one for her and one for him. She should explore her own attitudes toward food messiness at this point. If she punishes him for playing with his food, or expresses disgust at the inevitable mess, she will only bewilder him and maybe cause him to give up the self-feeding project completely.

Babies—even very young and completely toothless babies—can eat many foods that are less messy than puréed ones. As soon as a child shows an interest in feeding himself, his mother should stock up on commercial "finger foods" as well as hot dogs, bologna, cheese, crackers, eggs, hamburgers, bread, peas, carrots, stringbeans, potatoes, rice, spaghetti, dry cereals, and almost any fruit. At first the little experimenter won't seem to be getting much into his mouth, but he'll take in enough to keep from starving.

The beginning eater should be allowed to go about this vital leap out of babyhood in his own way. If that means slowly, let him take his time. If that means messily, give him a protected corner and let him go at his meals without getting the idea that mess is bad.

A worry shared by mothers of both late and early starters is that their small eater is not getting a balanced diet. Just as he may have done as an infant, the toddler may eat nothing but stringbeans for three days, then nothing but bologna, or go on and off milk every other week. In the long run, though, his diet will balance itself, and if he is offered enough foods, he won't let himself starve. Nutrition experts point out that even an active toddler needs only about 100 calories of food daily for every kilogram, or 2.2 pounds, of weight, or between 1000 and 1500 calories daily on the average (when we eat that little, we're on a strict diet!). Several cups of whole milk (or the equivalent in cheese or pudding), an egg, some whole-grain cereal or toast with butter, a little meat or fish, a few carrot sticks or peas or other vegetables, and some fruit and juice can make up that amount easily. If we are seriously concerned about our child's nutrition, we can ask our doctor to recommend some vitamins and we can mix some raw egg and sugar with his milk. If he is not eating much at meals, he should not be allowed to snack in between. If he absolutely needs to nibble, he can have fruit, vegetables, or cheese.

"Don't get upset" is the basic rule for mothers of late and early starters, over- and under-eaters, to follow. Concern over a child's eating will only aggravate the problem. In an atmosphere of calm acceptance, the baby can work his way gradually from pablum in the high chair to grown-up food at the dinner table.

Sleeping

Just as the baby, assuming he is healthy, will get the food he needs, so will he manage to get the sleep he needs—up to a certain age.

Some babies are reluctant sleepers from birth. Others have gone to bed with no fuss at all until they became mobile and were eager to keep going at the world, or until they became verbal and wanted to stay with the "other" grown-ups. When he was tiny and fussy, we either rocked our baby till he fell asleep or tried to help him in other ways to drop off. (After the third month or so, we may have let him cry himself to sleep when it was apparent that he was "winding down.") Now that he is bigger and a bit more complicated, we need to watch for subtler signs of fatigue and, sometimes, deeper causes of wakefulness.

Many babies, once they start moving around by themselves, become so involved in their new discoveries that they are unwilling to take a sleep-break. So we must impose rest on them when we see that they need it. Some children get cranky and groggy with fatigue; others actually seem to perk up and get giddy and silly when really they are ready for bed. By now we know our child's sleep-signs, and we will need to follow them up.

When a sufficient time has elapsed since his nap, when the hour is late enough and the grown-ups have had enough, then is the time to have the baby say night-night. Sleep may come more easily if it follows a regular familiar routine. Napping the baby *right* after lunch, and bedding him *right* after his bath serves to calm him and prepare him for sleep. Children who find life too exciting to sleep through need to be guided into quieter activities before nap or bedtime. A young child may want a bottle and a period of being rocked in a rocking chair, an older one a snack and a story. Most of all ages will play or perhaps fuss for a while after being put to bed, but unless ours screams hysterically for what seems to be an unreasonable time, we should let him settle himself down. He'll appreciate it, because, with all his new challenges and stimulation, he needs his rest.

Sometimes a child fusses because he simply is not tired. Just because 7:30 has always been bedtime doesn't mean that it's an absolute. His internal timetable is changing, and rather than struggle for an hour to get a wide-awake baby to sleep, we might do better to postpone bedtime till later.

Naptime fussiness requires the same kind of firmness-plus-flexibility. Some toddlers know when they need a nap; others need to be just put in bed. The previous night's sleep and the day's activities will influence the child's need for a nap, so we should stay flexible and keep an eye out for our child's signs of fatigue.

This does not mean he is growing out of his need for a nap; most children (and their mothers!) require some daytime rest until well into the preschool years. But schedules do change. Around the age of one year, for instance, many babies are in the process of working themselves down to one nap a day. Often they begin to get groggy in the morning, but if they are to take only one long nap a day and go to bed at a reasonable hour, their mothers may find it best to gradually help them move their sleep time to immediately after lunch. If we can gently stimulate our baby to stay awake for as long a stretch as possible before giving him lunch, he will take a good solid afternoon nap without fuss.

Persistent wakefulness or extreme bedtime fussiness in a child past 18 months or so is something to be looked into carefully. As a child grows out of babyhood he may grow into nightmares, worries, and fears that interrupt his sleep. If an older toddler develops sleep troubles, we should examine the environment, atmosphere, and activities for factors that may be troubling or overstimulating him and eliminate them, or modify what we can. A discussion of the deeper sources of nighttime fears and approaches to handling them is given in *Guiding Your Preschooler* by Edith Neisser.

Stimulation

Wakefulness and bedtime fussiness may be simply the product of overstimulation. Some children have so many things to do and so many people to do them with that they hop from one to the other and then end up in exhausted frustration. When our baby can get around on his own, he will find plenty of exciting things in the world to interest and absorb him. If we make sure that he has access to some appropriate, if informal, toys and play materials and that he has the freedom and safety to roam, if not his whole home, then a good part of it, that is probably all the stimulation he needs.

Our baby may be perpetually cranky and irritable, now that he is out of the immobile stage of infancy, because he doesn't have *enough* things to play with or enough area to roam. We can try giving him more playthings (or more interesting playthings) and babyproofing a larger area, to see if his fussiness was not simply due to boredom. If we live in a small apartment, we can try to get him to the playground or park as often as possible; that automatically enlarges his territory and increases his stimulation.

Some understimulated babies, on the other hand, don't complain about it. The understimulated child may seem less of a problem to a busy mother because he's so "good." But all babies need to explore in order to learn, to exercise their bodies, minds, and wills. Some need to be encouraged to do so. If our baby is a late walker, we will want to make sure he has lots of things to investigate without walking. If he simply seems happiest sitting by himself and doing nothing, we can entice him to play, find toys or other play materials that he seems to enjoy, and play with him more than we would with a more active child. If possible, we should get him together with other children his own age. At first he may just sit and watch, but even that is stimulation, and he soon may join in. Taking a quiet baby to the store or other places is a good way to stimulate him, and simply talking to him or playing music when he does not seem interested in anything else will give him something to pay attention to.

An appropriate amount of stimulation—not too much and not too little—is more than a way to occupy our baby and keep him out of trouble. Research continues to demonstrate that it is vital to his cognitive growth.

7
How Your Child's Mind Develops

BABIES AND SMALL children learn so much so fast that one can almost watch their minds become increasingly sharp. The pace picks up with every day and week of their first few years. It was once thought that children did not really begin to learn, and didn't need to, until they went to school. Now it is recognized that learning begins at birth if not before, and that early mental activity strongly influences later ability to think and learn.

Although we may not be able to put our finger on our child's intellectual achievements, we know that they have been great. We have watched him smile at his crib toys, then reach for them. We have seen him discover his hands and what they can do. We have noticed him studying us as we take food from the refrigerator, then pounding on the fridge door when he wants a snack. We have seen the glee with which he pulls away a pillow when he figures out that we have hidden a toy behind it. He has learned that a cry of "Daddy's home!" warrants a race to the front door. We know that when he hauls his jacket in from his room, he wants to go outdoors. When he thinks he is not receiving enough attention, he has become very knowledgeable about how best to attract it.

In these ways and many more, we have observed our baby's "cognitive growth." We have watched him learn to use his mind and piece together an image of the world. For the doubters, scientists have proven that babies *can* learn. Until surprisingly recently, many experts thought that all infant behavior was "reflex activity." It was even once believed that babies were little more than turnips until they started to talk and began to learn "real things" like words and numbers. That was partly because researchers had not developed methods to measure learning in a creature that cannot communicate in language. Now, however, child specialists have evolved ways of studying learning in even the tiniest babies.

One technique, employed at the Harvard Center for Cognitive Studies, uses the ability of two-month-olds to suck on pacifiers. The infants learn that sucking turns on a board of colored lights. When a particular pattern of lights appears, a movie screen is activated, and the babies have learned to turn their heads to watch the screen as soon as they see the telltale light pattern. A turnip could hardly master such a complex thought process! Using the powers that a small infant does possess, the child specialists at Harvard have shown that an infant can grasp an idea, gather information, and achieve a goal he has decided on.

Studies like this one and others that illustrate learning in infants show not only that they can learn, but that they are born with the ability to learn. It was once thought that an infant's mind at birth was like a blank page. All knowledge, it was believed, was written on that page by the baby's experiences with his environment. Now research indicates that a baby comes into the world with complex learning abilities, and that learning and mental development are dynamic processes: an active mind and a stimulating world interact.

How Your Baby Learns

How a child—or anyone—learns is a subject of dispute among scientists. It is known that learning is basically a biological activity. Each new stimulus seems to create complex changes within brain cells.

From the first few minutes of life, human learning is a process more intricate than the workings of the most sophisticated computer. A baby comes into the world with the ability and perhaps the drive—an innate push, like the drive to satisfy hunger—to learn. His brain is not completely finished at birth, but continues to develop as he grows. Each impact with the environment establishes a pathway—a connection, so to speak—in his brain. In this way, every bit of information he takes in through his senses is stored and enlarges his brain power. With each new pathway or connection, he has a new instrument with which to receive and sort information from the environment. His mind and the information it receives continually interact, creating new connections, which in turn are capable of interpreting new information. This process continues constantly, indefinitely, as his mind and his environment interact. As his senses mature and his experience widens, the information to which he is exposed grows more complex, and so does his processing mechanism. The brain's connections begin to interconnect. His knowledge grows, the interconnections increase, and his abilities to deal with new information multiply. Early-learning experts feel that the more environmental stimulation of the right kind at the right time that a baby encounters, the stronger and more agile his mind will become.

What a Baby Learns

Cognitive development—the growth in the ability to learn—has two fundamental aspects: accumulating information and learning to learn. In his first three years, a child's mind absorbs an almost incredible amount of information. He also learns to learn by exercising his brain's mental connections.

A hungry newborn learns that crying brings food. Soon he associates food with breast or bottle. This is probably a baby's first and best-learned lesson, creating a basic mental connection. It is important that this first learning experience be a rewarding one, because it tells the baby whether the world is a place worth finding out about or not; it can either encourage or discourage further exploration. From these and other early associations of facts, a baby learns that he *can* learn: that he can connect such things as a feeling of hunger with a demand for food. He also gains from this early encounter an important factor in cognitive growth: a feeling of mastery. If he can get or see what his mind tells him he wants, he learns that he has the power to effect his own comfort and shape his environment: crying makes food appear from somewhere outside himself and it makes himself feel better.

Concepts

Learning that he can learn and can master his environment lays the basis for curiosity, which in turn leads to more learning. This desire to explore is vital to learning, because a child has an entire universe to discover from scratch.

The details of what a child learns—the specific facts he takes in—depend, of course, on what is in his world, but the facts are less significant than the concepts he learns to build from them. We may be able to get a child to memorize and recite the alphabet as soon as he can barely speak. He can learn this kind of trick by what is known as rote because he wants to please his parents. Still, he will not be capable of the thought it takes to understand what the letters mean or to put them together into words. A baby can learn the trick of putting a certain block into a certain hole, but until he figures out that other blocks go in other holes, he is not using thought. The memorization of facts is only part of the more important process of learning to think. Thought relies on *concepts,* generalized groups of facts or ideas. During his first three years, the child will develop a variety of important concepts, among them the concept of himself, an understanding of the interrelatedness of aspects of the world, and the very idea that things do have labels and can be sorted into general groups.

The formation of concepts begins in a primitive fashion. At first, a baby takes in only individual pieces of information: "hunger," "food." Then he begins to connect the information in basic chains: "hunger brings food"; and more complicated ones: "hunger-bottle-food-mommy." Later, he attaches associations to this chain: "hunger-(mommy fixing lunch with pots and pans)-(sit in chair)-food." If a child had to learn about the entire world in this piecemeal fashion, he would need a lifetime simply to find his way around his own house. That is why his mind must learn to generalize, or form concepts.

The human mind copes with all the information it takes in by sorting it out, grouping and regrouping it according to a variety of common characteristics. An automobile, for instance, fits into many different mental slots or concepts: four-wheeled vehicles, power-driven machines, means of transportation, dangers to watch out for, expenses to pay. An adult knows this only from years of having his mind absorb information, break it down, and reorganize it to fit with other bits of knowledge. A child must learn to do all this.

A toddler, playing with an assortment of plastic containers, will learn by trying that the little blue one will fit into the big red one, but that the big red one won't fit into the little blue one. To find out if the even bigger yellow one will fit into the little blue one, he has to make a new experiment. An older child will have learned that the biggest one won't fit into the little one, but until he grasped the concept of "big" and "little" he had to perform the operation in order to discover the answer, or "learn by trial and error."

That is how a child learns to form any concept: after enough experimenting, enough trial and error, he is able to formulate the rule or generalization that applies to a particular task. As he grows and explores more, the rule, or concept, will be applied to other situations. At first, his concepts will deal with such concrete objects as boxes and blocks; more abstract subjects will not occupy his mind until his third year or later, but he is working up to such complexity from the moment his mind starts functioning.

Intelligence

The skill with which a child learns to think probably depends upon something called "intelligence." No one knows precisely what intelligence is or how to measure it with accuracy and predictability (especially in young children), although many theoreticians and child specialists over the years have claimed to have a definition. Perhaps the easiest and most practical definition of intelligence is "the ability to use the mind to cope with life."

"Where does intelligence come from?" is an even harder question than "What is intelligence?" Fashionable explanations of the source of intelligence change with time and have always been a subject of controversy. Some scientists and philosophers have maintained that a child's experiences alone fill his mind with intelligence. Others have held that a baby's level of intelligence is inborn and unchangeable. Today, some scientists are again stressing the importance of heredity over environment. The two factors are probably combined in some ratio; one way to think of their relationship is, "Heredity sets the outside limits on intelligence; environment determines how close to those limits intelligence will grow."

If we think of intelligence as "the ability to use the mind to cope," it is easy to see how great a role both heredity and environment play in shaping a child's intelligence. The human mind learns—receives, stores, and processes information—in its individual brain cells. These cells, in turn, are fed information along the nerve paths from the body's sense organs. The cellular makeup of an individual's body is determined by genes transmitted from his parents. Therefore, his heredity determines the structure and perhaps the function of his brain cells, his internal learning machinery. At the same time, however, his ability to use his mind depends on his relationship with his external environment. A child whose world leaves him hungry, afraid, and understimulated will not be able to learn as much as a child whose environment is secure and stimulating. All the brainpower in the world is worthless if it is unused.

The Pattern of Cognitive Development

No matter how "bright" a baby is, his cognitive development will probably follow a pattern similar to that of other children. Just as with his motor development, he may proceed faster or slower than other children from one stage to the next, but his progress will be orderly. As he probably couldn't stand before he could sit, so he won't be interested in working a puzzle until he has learned to manipulate a lot of simpler materials.

The pioneer work of Jean Piaget, a Swiss psychologist, lays the groundwork for much of the current investigation into children's intellectual growth. Although some researchers dispute details of Piaget's methods and theory, most agree that his general outline of how a child's mind progresses from one stage to the next is valid.

Piaget calls the first stage of cognitive development the "sensorimotor period," because an infant and toddler must rely primarily on his senses and his body, rather than on words or other symbols, for his learning. He manipulates his environment and takes in information with his hands, eyes, and mouth. In the next stage of mental growth, he will begin to explore it with his mind.

By the end of his second year, he will be using sounds for many objects and activities. From then on, his symbols will be less physical and more mental, as he internalizes images and his ideas about the world. He may no longer need to shake his head as he contemplates a "no-no" but he may be saying "no-no" in his mind. By the end of his third year, he will be using words to label and sort out the objects of his world, instead of having to deal with them physically.

Because a young child's mind deals with concrete objects, things that to us are imaginary are real and alive to him. A child, for example, does not know what a dream is. He does not differentiate between what occurs in his mind and what happens in the outside world—it is all part of a single whole. When an infant's mother leaves the room, he doesn't *know* that she will come back. A toddler's comforter is as alive to him as the child is to us. A two-year-old does not know that the bear in his nightmare is not real. Parents often need to remind themselves that a child needs years of mental growth and intellectual exercise to sort out the world and his place in it before he is capable of logical thought and reason.

In order for a child to achieve logical thought, to make effective use of the facts he is discovering about his world, he must grasp a few very basic concepts about how the world works. Piaget lists four: "object permanence" (the idea that things exist even when they are out of sight); space (the idea that things occur in a definite physical environment); time (an understanding of past, present, future, and continuous time); and causality (the idea that one event causes another). To adults, these concepts may seem ridiculously obvious, but it took us many years to grasp them fully. Block by block, a child builds toward these concepts, and each row of blocks must be in place before the next one can rest securely on it.

How Parents Influence Cognitive Development

The fact that our child's mental ability develops gradually and in stages does not mean that we cannot affect his intellectual growth. We can help him grasp the concepts he is ready for, and we can encourage him to enjoy learning. We helped him to stand by giving him opportunities to practice, and there are many ways in which we can give him appropriate opportunities to exercise his mind. A stimulating environment can help our child cultivate his intelligence to its limits. If the many recent studies of infant learning have shown nothing else, they have pointed out that the right amount of the right kind of stimulation during the earliest years of life can increase a child's mental agility and his ability to cope with the world.

Obviously, kids were growing up bright and happy for many generations before adults ever heard of "special stimulation" or "educational toys." The kind of stimulation children need has probably always been provided "instinctively" by caring parents and relatives. It certainly is not necessary—or helpful—to teach a baby such tricks as reading, counting, or reciting poetry. These skills any child with a reasonable amount of security and self-confidence will eventually acquire. Still, there are many simple and enjoyable ways (many of them time-honored) in which we can help our baby develop confidence in his ability, so that he enjoys learning and wants to do more.

Children learn through what grown-ups call play. In addition to creating a pleasant and interesting environment and providing appropriate play materials for their children, parents can play a number of simple games that help even the youngest child to learn and want to learn more. Watching mother move a rattle back and forth is exciting to a tiny infant. Older ones enjoy pat-a-cake, peek-a-boo, or "this-little-piggy." Toddlers like music and "dancing" and can endlessly fill and empty boxes and sort and re-sort blocks or bottle tops. Older toddlers like imitating Mommy and Daddy—cooking, washing, hammering, shaving, reading. All these activities take on added interest when a grown-up introduces them and participates.

Parents can probably think of many more games. The idea is simply to stimulate a child's mind through those receptors he has use of at a given level of development: an infant's eyes, mouth, and ears; a creeper's hands and body; a toddler's body and understanding of language.

Of course, some of the easiest "games" are ones that Mommy does not *have* to be involved in. If a child is encouraged and allowed to explore in a safe house or yard, for instance, he will be working toward fulfilling his potential as surely as if he were enjoying an organized activity or educational toy. Exploration encourages the child to be curious about the world and want to learn more about it.

Busy mothers arouse small children's curiosity without trying to: what goes on in that cupboard she's always opening? Why does the bucket fill with water when the faucet is on? Making a child wonder what is in a pot or where a toy is hidden is an almost automatic way of distracting him when he is bored or bothersome, and it exercises his mind as well.

A young child can get plenty of stimulation from the world around him. Although parental attention, interest, and participation are important, we should be careful about overstimulating him by giving him too much to deal with. If a child is enjoying what he is doing, leave him alone! An important part of learning is being able to complete a task once it is started, even if to grown-up eyes the activity does not look very interesting. Being able to accomplish, to achieve a goal, plays a big role in giving a child that all-important sense of mastery.

The opposite of mastery is frustration. A child who is prevented from doing everything he tries, or is completely ignored, or is not allowed to explore, gets the idea that nothing he does has any value or impact on his world—so why should he try? If we try to get a child to do things he is not ready for—have a one-year-old play catch, or a two-year-old work a complicated puzzle—he will feel frustration. If this happens too often, he may get the idea that nothing he can do pleases us, or that our standards are too high for him to meet.

When we are planning activities, or buying toys, or putting together playthings out of odds and ends, we should keep in mind our baby's interests and abilities. Since each baby has his own style, he has different tastes, too. A quiet, thoughtful child will enjoy different toys and games from a vigorous, active one. Some children are organizers, putters and takers, rearrangers; others are bangers and stompers. Some have almost frighteningly rich imaginations; others are hard-headed realists.

We must remember, too, that physical and mental development do not necessarily keep pace with one another. In some ways, the two are often connected in the first few years. An early walker, for example, may learn some words and games sooner than a late walker, because he had a head start on exploring. But a late walker will eventually catch up, and he may also have gained advantages from having spent more time sitting and thinking. A toddler's mind may understand the principles of putting a simple puzzle together, but if his manipulative ability and eye-hand coordination are not yet well developed, he won't be physically able to work the puzzle.

Language Development

One of the most important "games," and one of the easiest, is conversation. Talking to our child helps him learn to talk.

At first, the only sound our baby could make was a cry. Responding to these cries of hunger or discomfort was important for many reasons, including his language development. Our response taught him that he could use his voice to communicate.

By his fourth month or so, a baby is making sounds other than cries. He needs response to these first "talking" sounds, too, to get the idea that talking is good. But he needs more than just to have a response from us. The more he is spoken to from his earliest days, the better he will be able to use language as a means of communication and thinking.

For language is more than a means of communication. At first a baby uses sounds simply to express his feelings and make his needs known. This is a function of language that he will retain, of course, throughout his adult life. Words are also the basic tools of abstract thought.

As was mentioned in the discussion of cognitive development, the formation of concepts and the use of symbols are vital to the brain's ability to sort out and piece together information. Words are the primary symbols, standing for things, ideas, and feelings. Thought without words would be like mathematics without numbers. The better our baby's use of words—his verbal ability, as the aptitude tests call it—the better may be his thinking power. He can learn only by example that words stand for things. That is why it is so important to talk to, at, and around our baby.

To most mothers, talking to their babies comes naturally. We may have found, for instance, that talk helped calm our infant when he was upset, entertained him while we were changing him, and kept his attention at mealtimes. Occasionally, a mother is so tense, depressed, exhausted, or just plain busy that she almost never converses with her infant. She might feel, too, that it is pointless to talk with a creature who can't talk back. We may feel a bit silly jabbering to a chubby blob in an infant seat about what we are fixing for lunch, or chatting with a lump under the carriage blanket about what a nice day it is, but it's good for him to hear us talk, and it accustoms us to communicate with him in words.

Soon we will want to be able to use words to guide and control our child. A hungry toddler may be able to wait just a minute more for food if Mommy says, "I'm fixing your lunch, and it will be ready very soon." A one-year-old may not be able to say, "Mommy's going to put my shirt on now," but if Mommy says it before she does it, he may squirm less when it goes over his head.

Of course, there is such a thing as too much talk. A constant stream of words from grown-ups can prevent a child from getting a word in edgewise and may make him give up trying. So instead of a lecture, we can make it a conversation. When the baby makes a sound, we can respond to it. Repeating the same sound an infant makes helps him to get the idea that he is on the right track with his vocalizations. Later, when a toddler is trying to say a specific word—"bah'ty" for "bottle," for instance—saying, "Yes, that's a bot-tle," will encourage him to keep trying for the right pronunciation. When a two-and-a-half-year-old's "What's this, Mommy?" nearly drives us to distraction, we should remember that he is really only trying to add words to his growing store of ideas.

Speech development is a long process, intellectual as well as physical. A child's speaking mechanism—his tongue, mouth, throat, larynx—will not be fully developed and functioning until he is about seven years old. A baby is capable of producing any sound or series of sounds in any human language. During his first year, according to speech experts, he vocalizes all of them. It is our speaking to him in our language that helps him sort out from all those sounds the ones that he will need and encourages him to work on those.

Children learn to speak primarily by imitation. (That is why it's silly to use "baby talk" with a child; he needs to imitate grown-up talk.) After we have been talking to our baby for a few months we will have a moment of delight when he repeats a sound we have just made. We may be singing in the kitchen and hear a strange hum from the infant seat—singing! Or we may have "Here's Daddy" echoed by "Da." Slowly these separate symbols will play a greater role in our baby's happy sounds. Ma, da, ba, and ga are probably the most common ones at first, and we will hear our baby repeat them endlessly as he tries them out and strengthens his speaking equipment.

At first, these sounds have no meaning. It is the response to them that gives them their symbolic significance. A baby will learn, for instance, that "ma" brings a delighted Mommy, "da" Daddy, "ba" a bottle. At this point, his definitions are very general: "ma" may stand for anything Mommy can do for him; "da" may mean "Let's play." Gradually, our response will help him firm up his definitions as he improves his pronunciation of these first words. Soon his vocabulary will explode. He may imitate words we use while talking or playing with him. As we describe out loud what he is doing or touching—"Bill is climbing the steps," "Yes, that's the television"—he absorbs these new words and eventually will use them.

By the time he can say a few words, he can understand many more. He may surprise us by climbing into his seat when we say, "It's time for lunch," or by getting the ball when we say, "Go get the ball." He will soon be saying many words we don't think he has ever heard, because once he starts, he is like a sponge, soaking up language constantly and figuring out the complexities of grammatical structure. This phenomenon has led some researchers to theorize that language is not learned completely by imitation, but perhaps may be the result of some drive or brain function of which nothing is yet known.

It takes a while for a child to talk in real sentences. At first, each word represents a complete thought—"ma" may mean "Mommy, come here." (Does that ever change?) As he adds more words, he can communicate more needs and feelings. He will probably begin with a collection of nouns, names of things he has been attaching labels to in his explorations. To these will soon be added other types of words: out, up, down, go, get, give, nice, no are some of the basics. Pronouns probably won't come until much later: he'll say, "Jimmy go out" instead of "I go out." When he begins to put together two words to make a sentence—"get ball," "give bottle"—he is well on his way to piecing together a grammar that will grow more complex, paralleling his increasingly complex thought processes.

Most children say their first real word sometime around their first birthday. By their second, many are able to use two-word sentences. By their third, they may be talking in more complex sentences, giving a running commentary on the activity they are engaged in. Some children start earlier, some later; girls are generally more adept at first. There are numerous examples of children who did not speak till age three but grew into adults with such highly verbal occupations as writing or teaching. If parents are worried about a baby's language development for any reason, they should check with their doctor to see if there is any physical problem retarding speech (and read the section on late talkers in Chapter 12).

Child therapist Selma Fraiberg points out that it is as hard for a child to learn the name of an object without being able to touch it as it is for an adult to remember the name of a person he has met only once. For language development, as for cognitive growth, physical health, and psychological strength, children need to explore. This fact raises the problem of creating a touchable environment for our child—one that is both safe and interesting for him to investigate.

8
It's Your Home— And Your Child's, Too

WE MAY AGREE with childhood experts that our baby needs freedom to explore for the sake of his language development and overall cognitive growth. We may recognize that encounters with his environment stimulate his curiosity and exercise his mind. We can see that his body needs exercise, too, for good motor development. The more he can move about—creep, crawl, stand, walk, climb, put, take, push, pull—the stronger his muscles and the sharper his coordination.

But—days will come when we wish we could just tie the kid to a hitching post and the devil with cognitive and sensorimotor development!

On those days, it may extend our patience to remember that a baby gains other vital, if less tangible, strengths from exploration. He will grow into independence more quickly and surely if he learns early to use freedom within limits. Even more important, he needs such freedom to build what psychologists call "ego strength." This sense of *himself,* separate from the other objects of his world, as a worthwhile individual who can learn, grow, and accomplish is basic to success in all other areas of achievement.

We help our child develop ego strength by letting him be on his own within certain boundaries while showing our interest in the safety of his physical self. Remembering all that, we might find it easier to take a deep breath and let him go on emptying the cupboard. Still, though our child needs to do things a tidy housekeeper might wish he wouldn't, he does not need to be allowed to run completely rampant. We, he, the family, and our home need to make adaptations to one another.

His home is the universe, and he is a junior Columbus off to find a route to the Orient. While he was being carried around, he had no idea how to begin, except to cry till he was picked up and moved. Our seven-month-old may sit in the living room and bawl when we go around the corner into the kitchen. We have disappeared into the unknown. Then he decides to see what happens if he tries to go around the corner. Will he fall off the edge of the earth? He crawls and belly-flops toward the door, peeks around it, and what a surprise! There are Mommy and Daddy, and he can get to them, all by himself. His face bears an expression of delight and of "So this is where you've been hiding from me—but you can't any more!" With barely a pause, he is off down the hall to see what other mysteries he can unravel. He has added one piece to his puzzling globe, and he wants to add more.

Playpens

Our child has been exploring all his life, of course, but as an infant he used only his eyes, mouth, and ears. When he was tiny, we probably kept him near us or the rest of the family in his carriage or infant seat.

How fascinated he seemed with the slightest activity around him!

As he becomes more mobile, we will want him to have the same kind of opportunity to keep in touch with the household and to entertain himself, but he'll need to be safe. That is what playpens are for.

Some contemporary parents have an aversion to playpens. "I won't have my baby cooped up," they say. Misused, a playpen *can* be a cage. If one is not used at all, parents of a normally active baby may find that they are driven to distraction worrying about his safety and keeping him entertained. They may end up restricting the baby's freedom much more than if they used a playpen wisely. Some families go to the other extreme and expect a child to stay in his playpen all day. They use it to keep the baby out of Mother's hair or to get him out of the way when he is cranky, and of course the baby resents that.

Some parents, even with quiet babies, have to give up on using a playpen quite soon after they start, while others, even with active children, make good use of it for a year or more. What is the secret? Successful playpen users work it so that the baby comes to love his pen as his special place, a refuge from the sometimes overwhelming buzz of family life without the isolation of being in his crib in a room by himself.

If we want to do the same, we must start early. We can plan on getting a playpen when the baby is about four months old. As soon as he can roll over and lift his head and chest, he is ready for it. It is at that point that he can entertain himself by moving and reaching, and it is at that point that we begin to worry about his safety when he is on a blanket on the floor. If we wait until the child has really gotten the feeling of moving around on his own, the playpen is more likely to seem a restrictive prison. And if introduced to the pen before the onset of any separation anxiety, he can get used to it before he is terrified of being temporarily out of sight of Mommy. Also, well before a baby is mobile enough to get into big trouble, he can do himself serious damage in small ways: swallowing bits of metal, paint, or dust, for example, the miscellany that is on even the best-kept floor or rug.

The playpen should be as large as possible. Even if it means a drastic rearrangement of family living space, it won't last forever and it is worth it. If expense is a problem, playpens are one baby supply that people are more willing to lend than store. The pen can be in the corner of the living room, family room, kitchen, or wherever most of the household's activity goes on. If the apartment or house is very small and there just is no room for a playpen, one centrally located room or hall—or a corner of it—can be turned into a safe play space by blocking it off with baby gates, "babyproofing" it to the extent possible, and patrolling it regularly for hazards. If the house is very large, a whole room that is near to family life might be cleared out and made a play area for the baby.

The pen should be a pleasant place, with mobiles or other dangly toys hung across the top and a brightly patterned cover on the bottom. A playpen is a good place to collect all his playthings: favorite rattles, balls, dolls, and other toys. That helps consolidate the mess and makes the pen *the* place to have fun.

It is wise to wait till the baby is full, dry, and happy before putting him in. Showing him all the things there are to see and do, we can let him explore this new place on his own. Most four-month-olds enjoy this change of scene and the freedom it offers compared with the infant seat or crib or carriage.

Later on, when our baby gets more independent and self-assertive, we will need to adapt our use of the playpen. Some kids seem happiest there when their mother is in the room, or at least within seeing and hearing distance. Others play very happily *until* Mommy appears and then ask to get out. If we want to be able to continue using the pen, we should keep putting our creeper in it at a fairly regular, happy time each day. If the goal is to keep him out of the way while we are doing household chores or other projects, we can plan accordingly: work in the same room if our baby prefers it; busy ourself elsewhere if he is most content alone.

Since any baby would usually rather be with Mommy—playing with her, sitting on her lap, and getting all her attention—most will protest playpen duty at times. If we take such protests seriously and immediately remove him, he will never be satisfied to stay in the pen. If we interest him in a toy or game and then leave despite his protests, he will learn that he might as well amuse himself there. When it is obvious that the baby has had enough—he protests vigorously and won't be put off—it helps to wait till he stops complaining briefly, or distract him into a happier mood, before taking him out of the playpen. That way, he *may* not learn that he can get out by crying. By the same token, we won't want to put our child in the pen when he is crying or unhappy, and never as a punishment; it's supposed to be a nice place. If we handle a playpen sensibly, our baby may regard it as such a good place that when things get too hectic on the outside, he'll go over to it and ask to get in.

When our baby has become an expert crawler and is standing and tentatively walking, the playpen era is ending. He may be happy there occasionally if he has always liked it, and it may be handy during emergencies or busy times, but it should not continue to be in regular use when he is a toddler, because he needs to move around.

Babyproofing

We need not wait until our child has given up the playpen to babyproof our home. When our baby was new, we made sure that the area around his bed was safe, and that is not too early to start taking care of the hazardous temptations in the rest of the house (kids always seem to be able to get into things at least a day before you expect them to!).

Babyproofing has several aspects, but the basic consideration is the child's safety. The following are some suggestions for babyproofing a home against certain common dangers.

• Cover electrical outlets with tape or with plastic inserts obtainable from the hardware store. Try to get electrical cords and wires out of reach and out of sight; where possible, plug lamps and other equipment into outlets that are high up or behind heavy furniture. A pediatrician can tell horrifying tales of electrical burns resulting from babies' licking outlets or chewing wires and plugs.

• Rearrange cupboards and closets so that all cleaning supplies, light bulbs, plastic bags and wraps, matches, sharp tools, and medicines are on high shelves, preferably behind doors that even a curious two-year-old could not open. Put nontoxic items on lower shelves. Use no kind of rat or insect poison; find another way of controlling pests. Remember also to be careful about where cleaning solutions, pincushions, and the like are left while they are in use. Could the baby reach the scissors or pull the iron off the ironing board while we were answering the phone? Get in the habit of picking up any small, potentially dangerous objects on the floor—pins, staples, bits of plastic, toothpicks, bobby pins. Put gates across any stairs or windows the baby might fall from.

• Look for any special hazards the home contains. In an old building, for instance, watch out for falling paint chips: all paint was formerly lead-based, and eating lead-based paint can damage a child's brain. (If you think your child may already have eaten some paint chips, ask your local health department to test him for lead poisoning. Early treatment can ward off serious damage.) Scrape any peeling surface and recover it with a nontoxic paint—one without lead in it. Be sure that access to wells, pools, streams, or other bodies of water is blocked completely, and don't leave tubs of water where a baby could tumble in. If you live on a farm, make sure that your barns are babyproofed, too, or don't let a child go in them unescorted.

• A vital and often forgotten part of babyproofing is knowledge of first aid and other emergency procedures. (Would we know how to stop a baby from choking? or to give mouth-to-mouth resuscitation? or neutralize poison?) If a mother has ever taken a first-aid course, she might want to brush up before her baby arrives. If not, she can get a book—the Red Cross sells a good one—and study up. Keep some simple and up-to-date material on first-aid techniques and poison antidotes where it can be found easily in a hurry. Maintain a good supply of bandages, disinfectants, and such. Keep emergency phone numbers—the doctor's, the hospital's, the poison control center's, the rescue service's—taped to the telephone. In any emergency, call one of these experts as soon as possible.

Of course, most of the bumps, scrapes, and cut lips a toddler incurs won't be serious and will heal almost before we can treat him. But since we probably can't prevent *all* accidents, it is best to be prepared for the bad ones.

So much for the safety basics. In childproofing a home, each family seems to have its own approach. Some toddlers are given free run of their homes. They can do whatever they want, but the rooms are so barren of "no-no's" that there is nothing the kids *can* do. Another house may be so full of toys that the entire place looks like one big playpen for Junior. Some families may have lovely collections of furniture and bric-a-brac and an 18-month-old who is confined to his own babyproofed room. Others are so confident that they have trained their children what they may and may not touch that they don't even lock up their cleaning supplies.

"Creative Babyproofing"

Is there one right way to babyproof? The answer to that depends partly on the definition of the term. In some households, babyproofing means protecting the house from the toddler; in others, it means protecting the child from his surroundings. Some people proof *against* babies; some *for* them.

A middle road might be called "creative babyproofing." That is, some things are left within a child's reach not only because they are safe for him to get at, but also because they are good for him (some children have learned to read from the labels on food cans stored at their level). At the same time, the house still looks like a home—interesting for a youngster to explore and pleasant for the rest of the family, too. It might seem easiest simply to clear away every possible temptation, but that would make living in the home boring for the rest of the family and would create an unreal and uninviting environment for the little explorer.

We can probably glance around our home and think of many ways in which we can accommodate all these needs. If there are smokers in the family, we can substitute metal or plastic ashtrays for breakable ones and keep them at levels convenient for grown-ups but not for little ones. If we don't care for the game of junior TV and radio repairman, we can put these fascinating objects where the child can't reach the knobs. Tuck wastebaskets under or behind furniture, stabilize tippy tables or chairs or put them in an out-of-the-way corner. As a substitute for an unstable coffee table, we might use a big chest—it's handy for throwing toys into at the end of the day, too. Wedge prized books tightly into bookcases so that they are not always on the floor, but leave a shelf of his books or our old ones loose enough for a baby to get at—we don't want him to get the idea that all books are "no-no's." When our child starts to climb, we may need to rearrange the furniture so that he can't get up dangerously high on his own. Babygates that close off stairs or other danger spots can be folded out of the way unobtrusively when the climber is in bed.

If we are lucky enough to have a lot of space, we might declare one room off limits to all but grown-ups and older children, provided that there are other areas for baby to be himself in. Even if daddy and mommy and siblings cannot have their own room, keep some places—drawers, shelves, closets—especially "theirs." If the baby has a place for things of his own, he can begin to learn that some things and places are other people's. Rather than keeping him out of *everything,* we can make sure he has some drawer or shelves that he may empty and rearrange.

The kitchen can be a great place for kids to explore. It is relatively easy to clean up, it is usually close to Mommy, and it is full of all sorts of fascinating things like pots and pans, dishrags, canned food, and other unbreakable containers and utensils. We can be sure that the dangers are out of reach, and then, if we can stand a certain amount of disorder in our cupboards, our baby can entertain himself happily there. Lid-banging is sometimes a noisy occupation, but most mothers prefer it to whining.

A bathroom can be a dangerous place for a child with shaky legs if it is all tile and metal. It might just as well be a complete "no-no" to a little child, but if that is not possible, we can at least be sure that medicines and toiletries are really out of reach.

Indirect Babyproofing

If we want to be able to live in our own home, we won't be able to move every temptation out of our child's way. Instead, we have several indirect babyproofing techniques available. The word "no," for example. As soon as a child can move on his own, he should begin to learn what "no" means. It is not difficult to teach, because our baby wants to please us. When he is doing or about to do something dangerous—playing with an electric cord, for instance—we can go to him, remove his hand, say "No" firmly, and present him with something else to do. Some babies don't need to be told more than once. Most are less easily distracted. If he heads right back to the "no-no," repeat the procedure. If he keeps it up, and it is something dangerous, a single slap on the offending hand should demonstrate what the word means. He may be insulted, but better that than an electrical burn. Even experts who frown on ever spanking a child admit the usefulness of a warning slap, at the crucial moment, to reinforce the meaning of "no" during the first two years or so. Our baby is not being good or bad; he is just exploring, and he cannot legitimately be punished for that. A handslap, however, given not in anger but in concern, may effectively warn him off dangerous activities. (Our frightened tone of voice when he is really in danger may be equally effective. For more on this see the following chapter.)

In this context, the hitting is not a punishment, but a part of the lesson that some—not all—babies need in addition to being distracted. Also, many parents have almost automatic warning signals that show when they mean business: a vigorous shake of the head, a hard frown, a raised index finger. They may be amused to come upon their toddlers looking squarely at a "no-no" and shaking their head or finger, frowning, or saying "No" in exact imitation of Mommy or Daddy.

As our baby is learning about "no" and finding out that there are certain places he may not go and objects he may not touch, he may crawl over to "no-no's" and ponder them. He may reach out toward them, looking at us as though he were testing us. At first, he is probably not testing but trying to remember what it is about this fascinating object or place that is special. We remind him by repeating "No." Even when he seems to have learned the meaning of the word as it relates to specific activities, he won't understand (or heed) it well enough to obey when we tell him "No" from across the room. We will need to continue going to him and removing him from temptation or distracting him as we say "No" for a good while.

"Hot" is another remonstrative word a child can learn early, because he can feel what it means and teach himself to stay away from stoves, radiators, or coffee cups.

Some things we may want him to be careful of without avoiding completely—pets, for example, or other children. We don't want these to be "no-no's," but if we say "Gently" or "Careful" and show him what we mean, we can encourage even a small toddler not to pull hair, poke, or punch too hard. (An easy way to release a baby's grip on a dog's tail, a child's hair, or a breakable valuable is to squeeze his forearm, which forces his hand to open without doing further damage.)

If we find ourself saying "No" to most of the things our baby goes after, we either need to babyproof our house again or rethink our decisions on what matters and what does not. A constant stream of "No-no's" can be a much more damaging restriction on a child than a playpen.

Besides, it can drive parents crazy. Both should discuss and agree before the child is mobile on what will be considered absolute "no-no's" and what will be simply "I-wish-you-wouldn'ts." If we can limit the absolutes to dangerous places and objects, like electric cords or fireplaces, fine. "Wish-you-wouldn'ts" might include the television, pet's dishes, bookshelves, toilet paper, toilet, the telephone or other things that can create annoyances for us, but are not hazardous to him. When he goes for such things, the best approach is to distract him by steering him to another activity that he enjoys. If something similar can be offered in exchange—his own toy telephone, his own bookshelf, his potty chair, his own pan and spoon—he *may* be easier to distract. Or ingenuity may lead a parent to hit on a fascinating, hitherto unthought-of substitute activity.

Another obvious way to keep a baby away from "wish-you-wouldn'ts" is simply not to call his attention to them. If we don't want him exploring the toilet bowl, we need not clean it while he is watching, since he loves nothing better than to imitate.

No matter how we babyproof, our home won't be entirely free of mess all the time (if it is, we're probably not letting the child explore as much as he needs to!). Pans, books, and toys will inevitably be scattered on the floor, and it would be too much of a strain on both parent and baby to be picking up all day long. Still, Mommy and Daddy need a pleasant environment, too, and it is hard to relax in a room strewn with toys or take a shower in a sea of rubber ducks. We may want to keep one area that is always messy, where a child can do almost anything without being nagged. Or we may have one room that is sacred to grown-ups. If we haven't that kind of space, we can easily make sure that there are some times when the house belongs to the grown-ups with a minimum of effort on our part.

We can save tidying up for the end of the day, and then toss all the toys in that chest we have found for the hall or living room or a large basket that we can stow near or underneath the baby's crib. We can hang a net bag near the bathtub for bath toys. And we can decide not to worry for the time being about what our cupboards, drawers, and closets look like, as long as the mess is out of sight and we can feel for a few hours each evening that our home is ours alone.

If we can take the care and patience to babyproof creatively, so that our child feels that he is at home in his own home but that he also shares it with other people, then he is on the way to learning that he is important as an individual, but that there are others around with their own tastes and needs.

9 *When And How Does Discipline Begin?*

A CHILD NEEDS to learn to live in the world with others, for society's sake and his own. To socialize children, parents use discipline. "Discipline" means "teach." When we teach our toddler not to throw his cup off the high chair, not to dump wastebaskets inappropriately, or not to pull his friend's hair, we are disciplining him. We are teaching him to live in a society where cups are not thrown, trash stays in wastebaskets, and hair is not pulled. More broadly, we are teaching him that society has certain rules of order.

We may not be conscious of doing anything so grand during our child's first three years. We may not think of the guidance we give him as discipline. But his first view of society is his family, and the first social rules he learns to follow are family rules. Our earliest limits on his behavior lay the groundwork for the entire socialization process.

When our baby was a few months old, for instance, we began asking him to wait a little while before getting that food he said he wanted instantaneously. We didn't get angry at him for crying, or frantic about fixing his meal. We probably gave him something else to comfort him, letting him know, calmly but firmly, that we would feed him soon but that he was big enough to wait a bit. When we felt it was time for sleep, we put him in bed. When he let us know he didn't agree it was bedtime, we left him and usually he soon fell asleep, accepting our judgment in the matter.

Our baby accepted these new rules, partly because he had no choice. But he was willing to put up with the whim of these parental gods partly because, in his own way, he had learned during his first few months that we would care for him and that he could trust us to meet his needs. That is the basis for all discipline—trust and respect for the people making the rules. From these first lessons he learned that he does not expire when his demands are not immediately met, and that the world does not crumble when his parents say "No." Upon these simple beginnings, we build future discipline and teach him that it is possible to accommodate his needs to the needs of others.

As our child grows and changes, the areas in which discipline is appropriate will, too. When a five-month-old is throwing a screaming fit, it does no good to say, "Mommy would rather you didn't do that right now," and tell him to calm down. When a two-year-old is having a tantrum because he didn't get the cookie he wanted, he can comprehend when we tell him "Not till after dinner" and ignore his protests.

Setting Enforceable Rules

An understanding of human development and of our own child's nature and temperament will let us know what to expect and demand when. If we ask too much too early, both parents and child will be frustrated, angry, and bewildered. There is no point in demanding that an active toddler sit still in his high chair during a long family dinner. If we lose the tense power struggle that would ensue, we have lost some of our disciplinary authority and become a nervous wreck besides. If we win struggles like these consistently, we do so at the expense of winding up with a cowed, frightened child who will grow up wishing he could get back at us somehow. Actually, everyone loses in such parent-baby power struggles. A useful standard to follow in discipline is to make only those rules that our child can cope with and that we know we can and will consistently enforce.

On the other hand, if we ask nothing of our child, give in to his every whim and demand because he is "only a baby," he will never be anything but a baby. If our child as a toddler and two-year-old learns that he can get or do anything, even "no-no's," if he puts up a fuss, he will never have faith in our authority or learn to control himself.

Our daily disciplining will be in response to individual situations—"No more cookies," "Don't punch the cat," "Time for a nap." But to be effective, it should be more than that. We will need a philosophy of discipline, a long-range goal for our child-rearing practices. Although the specifics of disciplining our child will change, the goals and approach will remain constant throughout childhood. Each family will follow its own pattern, but it is a good idea to think and talk out our ideas about discipline early, perhaps before the baby is born. Parents may be surprised to find that they have different approaches, and they would be wise to work out a common ground ahead of time.

What do we want out of discipline? This question really asks, "What kind of person do we want our child to be?" Many parents would answer by saying that they want their children to be independent adults with enough control over themselves to achieve the goals they set for themselves in life. To do this, a child needs to learn to discipline himself. He needs to internalize acceptable rules and ideals, to incorporate them into his own conscience and behavior. He will be an adult before he completes this feat, but he will make a start during the earliest years of life.

When our baby says "No-no" as he reaches for a "no-no," that is a form of self-discipline; he is beginning to internalize our external controls. When he waits for his supper without whining or clinging because he knows it is on the way, that is a sign of self-discipline.

If we want our child to incorporate the controls we impose on him—make them his own—he will need to trust and respect our judgment and know that our discipline is based on love and reason. The kind of discipline that boils down to "Do as I tell you because I tell you" will produce a person who is easily swayed by outside forces and has little inner strength to rely on.

If we think of discipline as "guidance"—guiding our child along the way we hope he will follow in life—we will have a concept we can employ from his infancy through his adolescence. Parents guide children by pointing the way and setting limits along both sides of the path to maturity. We need to decide first what limits to set, and then how to enforce those limits.

What Limits to Set

The basic boundaries, especially during a child's first few years, are set for his own safety. Additionally, after the first few months, he can learn to be limited somewhat by the demands of the rest of his household.

Many of the earliest disciplinary limits are actual physical boundaries. At eight months a child plays in the playpen; at eighteen months he can roam the backyard. As he grows, his world expands, to his block, then the neighborhood, then the whole city. Another space limit might be where a baby may intrude and where he may not. Mommy and Daddy, brothers and sisters deserve to have their possessions and privacy respected.

Bedtime

Babies need time limits, too, for their own sake and that of the rest of the family. They need to take naps, and they need to sleep at night. So bedtime involves discipline.

When a baby is mobile and into the stage of not automatically going to sleep when he is tired, he may need some convincing that it is bedtime. Some parents set a bedtime for their children to suit their own needs. Others adjust more to the baby's needs. Both types of families should try to keep the routine fairly regular and relatively painless. When the time set arrives, and the baby is ready for bed—clean, full, and well-loved—he should be put in. Most babies protest, if not every night, then at certain points in their growth. When a baby is going through separation anxiety, for example, bedtime may be terrifying and require special handling. Even under normal circumstances, children will often fight going to bed and fuss once they are there. They would rather be out of bed with the folks.

This is a time for "guidance." We can leave a nightlight if our child wants that, leave the door open or closed, whichever he prefers, say good-night, and leave him. He may cry for a while, but he'll usually settle down. Just as some infants need to cry to let off tension, some toddlers cry to burn up energy and to unwind before going to sleep. Parents will know by now when his cries are desperate and terrified. Those cries require special response. But run-of-the-mill complaining deserves patient ignoring. Different babies will fuss for longer periods and for more nights in a row. Parents have to use their own judgment, on the basis of their knowledge of their child's habits, about how long to let a child "cry it out." Many young parents who are firm and loving are surprised at how quickly their babies learn the lesson that bedtime is bedtime and there's no point in arguing. Except for unusual circumstances, the most workable rule is "Once in bed, stay in bed."

Although bedtime may be difficult sometimes and is a major test of our disciplinary skill, it need not be a continuing struggle. Our common sense will indicate some practical ways to make it easy but definite. There is not much point in trying to bed a baby who just is not sleepy, for example. Some children play happily in bed until they fall asleep, but others resent being cooped up when they still have lots of energy left. Into his third year, our child's internal schedule is still changing considerably, though not as rapidly as it did during the early months. He may get tired later or earlier one week than he does another, and if we insist on keeping rigidly to our schedule, we will have a power struggle on our hands—our will against his. On the other hand, a mobile child wants to keep moving and will until he collapses, unless we step in. So for the least friction at bedtime, it is a good idea to pick a time when the baby is sleepy but not overtired.

If our child senses that we are doing what is best for him and he knows that we mean business when we say good-night and that he won't get sprung from his crib by crying, bedtime can be much easier for both of us.

Mealtimes

Mealtimes often can be times of stress. Babies throw cups, dump plates, stand up and wiggle out of high chairs, refuse to eat, mash their string beans. We can't get mad at a baby for making a mess when he is just doing what is natural for him. If we try to force him to eat what and when he doesn't want to, we will only do ourself and him harm. But we don't have to put up with escape attempts that endanger him, plate and food throwing, or purposeful mess.

How to Enforce Limits

We can't limit all our child's behavior and activities. If we find that our discipline in any area is having no effect, perhaps we have set a limit that our child is not ready for or does not need. Granted that we have set sensible limits, how do we enforce them? We cannot reason with an infant or a small child, no matter how grown-up he may seem. Beating a baby will have no constructive effect. We don't want to shame a child into submission either. We can only be firm and consistent. This does not mean rigid. It means that we have certain basic rules regarding safety, parents' rights, and general household order within which the daily routine fits—bedtime, mealtime, playtime. We use our judgment, and our child learns to use his. (Of course, at this age we can pick our child up and remove him from many forbidden situations, if need be.)

Effective discipline is based on love and respect. We love our child enough to want to guide him well in life. We respect his independence by taking his needs and personality into account in our guidance and by not making capricious rules. Our baby trusts and feels our love enough to respond to our guidance and incorporate it into his own behavior. On that basis, he gradually learns to discipline himself appropriately.

Effective discipline also derives from a parent's own self-confidence. Our friends and relatives may impose rules and use methods that make us uncomfortable. We may waver between their way and ours—but if we try to use others' methods to achieve others' goals, we do ourself and our child a disservice. If a parent is unsure of himself and on the defensive, he may respond to what he sees as a threat from his child by lashing out. Or he may be afraid to say "No" and fail to discipline altogether. If a parent is sure of himself, aware of his goals, and conscious of how he is going about achieving them, he will have a minimum of difficulty in disciplining with firmness, love, and consistency.

If we have decided, for example, with good reason, that we don't want our child to snack on sweets between meals, when he asks for a cookie before lunch we are firm in our "No." When he persists, we remain firm in our "No," explain why, and try to distract him or offer an apple or carrot instead. If he is a tantrum-thrower, we let him throw one—he has a right to protest in his own way. But if we give in, the whole point will be lost. In the same way, if we are inconsistent in our rule—if we offer him a cookie one day and refuse him one the next—our discipline will have no effect.

Firmness, however, does not mean anger. Before the birth of a baby, parents may have wondered how anyone could get angry at such cute little creatures. By now, they probably know. If we find that we are getting irritated too fast too frequently, we should stop a while to analyze the situation. Maybe we are making too many unreasonable or unenforceable rules. Maybe we need to find a way to get more rest or more time off. If we always "discipline" in the heat of anger, we are not really disciplining, but venting our own frustrations or punishing a person who is too small yet to learn the lesson we are trying to teach. We will dull the effect of our guidance in general.

Too much parental anger can terrify a child. We may know how human we are and be conscious of the fact that we are just having a cranky day. But to our child, we are the faultless gods of his self-centered universe. Even when something other than our child has angered us, he will always tend to feel—since he feels that he is the center of the universe—that it is his fault. Frequent bursts of capricious anger may make him afraid to do anything, for fear of a misstep that will bring the wrath of the parent-gods down on him. Our disciplinary ideal might be, "Don't get mad, but don't give in."

We won't always live up to this ideal. Times will come, more or less frequently, depending on our personality and our child's, when we simply can't stand his behavior any longer: we just get *mad.* When that happens, it won't help to feel guilty or to rebuke ourself, although if we are angry a lot of the time, we might want to examine our own attitudes and feelings. If we consider how to handle our anger before we have to, we may think of ways to express it without overwhelming our child. When we feel our own tension mounting, we can take a deep breath and a good look at him: if it's *our* crankiness, his very cuteness might calm us. If it doesn't, we can try saying to the child, "Mommy is getting *very* angry with you!" or "I have just about reached the end of my rope!" Much misbehavior is a child's way of testing where his—and our—limits are, and our warning may tell him all he wants to know. Even the youngest and most recalcitrant child will often shape up, sensing that he has gone almost too far.

If we have already reached the end of our rope with a toddler, we can try sitting him down firmly on a couch or chair (not bed, playpen, or other hopefully happy place) and making him sit there for two minutes. Even the most rambunctious child will most likely do it, faced by an angry parent. Those two minutes let him know we mean business and give us both a chance to cool off and avoid a violent solution to our conflict.

This is not to say that physical punishment should never enter into discipline. Spanking is a highly controversial subject. Various highly respected child experts advise with equal vigor everything from never employing any kind of physical punishment to spanking a child for every mistake. Our methods are our decision. Slapping a young hand that is headed for danger seems sensible to some parents but not to others. Swatting the well-diapered bottom of a child who has been asking for it all day offends the beliefs of some, but not others. It is difficult to imagine a situation that would call for really spanking a child under two with premeditation. And spanking an infant in anger seems unjustifiable cruelty. Once a child has begun to understand what is permitted and what is not, and has learned for sure that our "No" means "no," he is not going to suffer from a smack that comes after he has tested that "no" too often, as long as physical punishment is the exception and not the rule in his relationship with his parents.

Parents can probably do worse violence with words. If they attack, shame, or tear down their child's self-image while "disciplining" him, they will do more harm than good. They, the gods of his universe, can hurt him badly by calling him names—"stupid," "clumsy," "slob"—when he makes a mistake.

So we should choose our words carefully (and take a deep breath while doing it) before we use them. Do we say "No," or "Bad," for instance? A small child is not *bad* when he dumps the trash or fools with the record player; he has merely done a "no-no." "Bad" tears down the child; "No" simply condemns the act; and it is the act, not the child, that is unworthy. The difference may seem slight, but it represents an important difference in attitude. Even if our baby cannot yet understand the meaning of the words we use, he will be able to soon, and we might as well get in practice.

Just as firmness does not mean anger, so consistency does not mean rigidity or narrowness. As our child grows and changes, we will want to expand the limits on his behavior. As long as our baby has plenty of freedom within the limits we set, he can respect those limits and learn acceptable, safe ways to push them outward as he matures. If we made the staircase out of bounds at first, when our toddler gets firm on his feet he will push us to let him go up and down it on his own. Initially we will permit this only when we are there; then, after a while, out go the baby gates. Nor is it inconsistent to change a rule when it seems unnecessary or too limiting. We may wish our child would not eat between meals, but if he goes through a growing spurt, he may well eat at meals but still need a snack. By being flexible enough in these small ways and in more significant ones, we allow our child to expand his own limits as he grows. We show that we respect him by considering his needs. He will feel that respect and return it by obeying our reasonable rules. More importantly, he will develop self-respect. With self-respect, self-discipline will come naturally to him—and that is the goal of all those "no-no's."

---

10 *Toilet Training And Other Progress*

TOILET TRAINING WILL probably be our child's first major experience with self-discipline. By himself, he must be able to realize when he is about to urinate or have a bowel movement, to stop whatever he is doing, and to get on the toilet. That's some challenge! Toilet training is also a prime example of how parents guide their children toward self-discipline. Bowel and bladder control is a very significant sign of our child's progress toward independence and maturity. It has practical benefits as well, as any diaper-tired mother can testify. Toilet training is, in short, an important experience for both mother and child.

It is possible, of course, to attach too much significance to the process. Some psychiatrists have claimed that they could trace any of dozens of character and personality traits, good and bad, to the toilet-training experience. Some parents make toilet training a matter of pride, a feat to be achieved as early as possible.

Toilet training *is* important. But rather than a crisis to be worried about or an achievement to be gloated over, it is a learning experience that prepares our child for many similar ones to come. Nor can it be isolated from the rest of his past or present life. All the attitudes he has been learning about and from us and all the discipline he has been exposed to influence how he will respond to toilet training.

Smearing

Someday we may walk into our baby's room after his nap and be stunned to find that he has had a bowel movement and has smeared his feces all over the wall next to his crib. We won't like it, and we don't have to. Babies who do this (and not all do) are again just exploring; they have found something interesting and are seeing what they can do with it. They have no way of knowing that their behavior will disgust us. We shouldn't punish a baby for smearing, but we can let him know in a friendly way that we don't like it and don't want him to repeat it. Most likely our expression alone will get this message across, even if he is only six months old. Once we discover smearing, we can make an extra effort to keep the baby's diapers clean and to diaper him securely. Putting pants—waterproof or other snug-fitting ones—over the diapers may discourage smearing until our baby gets over the urge to do it. (If the behavior does not stop, or recurs frequently after our child is more or less toilet trained, we should consult our doctor about the desirability of getting some psychological counseling.)

How to Begin

Methods and timing of toilet training have their fashions in different eras and different cultures, as with weaning and feeding solids. There was a period, not too long ago, when mothers in our country started putting their babies on potties at the tender age of four or five months. If the baby was regular in his habits, or if the mother had extraordinary patience, the method "succeeded"; that is, the baby had all his bowel movements on the potty. But it was the mother who was trained, not the baby. The baby was not trained in the sense that he could let his mother know when he needed to use the potty and could control his bowels until the appropriate time.

A few parents still try this approach, but it seems an awful lot of work, since the baby is probably not trainable for many months more; and if a tired mother gets annoyed and frustrated when her infant doesn't "succeed," she may make such an unpleasant impression on him that he delays training himself even longer.

Some parents start when their baby is a year or so old and beginning to be able to communicate. They put him on the potty and wait until he has a bowel movement. Sometimes he does. Mommy is pleased, and he tries to figure out what she is pleased about so he can repeat the experience. Sometimes, he doesn't. Then Mommy may say, "Sit there until you do something," and the potty becomes a battleground, with Mommy getting angrier and baby getting more stubborn until the whole event takes on a significance far beyond its worth.

For these reasons, many pediatricians today recommend that parents not begin serious toilet training until their children are about two.

This does not mean that we need ignore the whole subject until our baby's second birthday. He needs to have an interest in it and a vague idea of what it is all about before he is put on the potty. Indeed, if we interest him and tell him enough, he will sit himself on it with little further help from us. Well before our baby is trainable, and before he *seems* able to understand, we can start talking to him while we're changing him, explaining what he has done and what we're doing. We might comment, "Oh! You've had a b.m. We'll clean you up and flush it down the toilet." (We can use whatever terms we're comfortable with, though it seems sensible to choose neutral words that express neither distaste nor disgust.)

When we notice that the baby is having a movement, we might comment casually on that, as well. "Catching" a few b.m.'s—putting him on the potty just before he has a movement—is another way of introducing him to the idea of training. But it does not count as training until *he* gets himself to the potty, and it is worse than worthless if we force him to sit or otherwise make it unpleasant. He will begin to associate our announcement that he is defecating with his physical experience of doing so, and his training will come more naturally. When he sees that we are interested in what he is doing, he will be, too.

When he starts to explore the toilet, as all babies seem to, we might explain that this is where Mommy and Daddy, or brother and sister, have b.m.'s, and when he is bigger, he will, too. Seeing his older friends or siblings using the toilet will increase his interest in being grown-up. For a boy to watch Daddy or a girl to watch Mommy is also useful, as long as the child does not seem to feel put down by the parent's more impressive genital equipment. (Boys may be more vulnerable in this respect than girls.) If splashing in the toilet displeases us, we can get our child a "toilet of his own"—a potty chair. Potty chairs are better than the seats that attach to regular toilets because the height of such a seat makes it hard for him to reach. He can explore his potty in the same way we let him investigate a cup long before he was ready to use it appropriately. In all these ways we can make it possible for our child to have an interest in training himself, so that the rest is relatively easy.

When we see that our baby is about to have a b.m., or when he gives us his own signal, we take him to his potty chair. (It is probably best to have it in the bathroom, where the rest of the family goes, but if another place is more convenient, okay.) We take off his diapers and sit him down, explaining all the time what we and he are doing. We stay with him and chat, if he seems to want companionship, give him a toy or book to keep him busy if he seems restless, and wait until he has a movement or until he refuses to sit any longer and our patience is ebbing, too. We talk to him encouragingly about what is happening, about how grown-up he is being, doing what Mommy and Daddy do, but we should not force him to sit beyond his endurance. If he has a b.m., we express our satisfaction. If he doesn't after a reasonable time, we put his diaper back on and send him about his business, expressing confidence that there will be another time. When he seems to be in control much of the time, we can start substituting training pants for diapers and show him how to get in and out of them, as the next step toward being a grown-up.

When It Happens

At what age this kind of real training, or self-training, occurs depends on mother and baby (girls seem to get the hang of it younger than boys, if only because their bodies mature earlier). Many children show a readiness to train themselves well before their second birthday.

Many mothers simply don't brood over the psychological significance of toilet training and train their babies matter-of-factly, with great success. The clue is the matter-of-factness. Some mothers delay toilet training longer than is necessary for their particular child, or give up after some false starts, because they expect a hostile and negative reaction. This is like a salesman whose line is, "You don't want to buy this vacuum cleaner, do you?" Of course it doesn't work.

When we do start serious training, any pressure, anxiety, or anger will only be self-defeating. Some parents, for instance, shift to training pants too soon, in the hope of making the child so uncomfortable that he will have to use the toilet. The person most inconvenienced by this technique is usually Mommy. A more subtle kind of pressure is, "Do it for Mommy" and "Oh, Mommy's so pleased," with the implication that Mommy would be offended if he didn't. If he does not, he feels guilt on top of his embarrassment. He should never be made to feel that he is a *bad* boy because he didn't succeed, or a *good* one when he does. Calm, rather than effusive, praise for the act, not the person, is the order of the day for toilet training. "That's fine—you had a b.m. in the potty," or "Oh, we didn't make it in time. Next time I'm sure you'll try to let me know sooner."

Urine training—teaching the child to control his bladder—is accomplished in the same way as bowel training. Children usually gain control over the bowels first (though some boys may achieve bladder control first). Urine training progresses rapidly after the child has attained bowel control, because of his experience with bathroom procedures and frequent opportunities to practice. But the less urgent call of the bladder may often be ignored when a child is otherwise enjoying himself.

If toilet training can be so easy, how come so many problems are attached to it? Some childhood specialists point to various psychological aspects of the toilet-training procedure that might not occur to a layman. According to many psychologists, a child is proud of his feces as something he has created. This may be the first thing that he has ever produced, and what is more, when deposited in the right place, it's a gift for his mother, who may seem very pleased with her child's creation. Not every child actually appears to have this attitude toward his bowel movements. Those who do may present a seemingly minor but intricate psychological puzzle to their parents. First of all, they may be very possessive about their feces, this product of their bodies; they may want to explore their production, or keep it. If our child does this, we should try not to express disgust, but explain that his b.m. is something that his body has made of things it couldn't use and had to get rid of. It was meant to leave his body, and where it belongs is in the toilet, which he is welcome to help us flush.

That brings up the toilet-flushing phobia. Many young children, experts say, are terrified by the flushing of the toilet. They don't like the noise and turbulence, and they are afraid that they somehow might disappear down the toilet. Some children show they are indeed afraid of toilet-flushing. If ours seems to be, we can wait until he is out of the bathroom before emptying his potty. He will grow out of his fear if he isn't ridiculed and he discovers, with the help of our gentle explanations, that his mother, father, brother, and sister flush the toilet without disappearing into it. On the other hand, many children are not afraid of the flushing. If ours is not, having him dispose of his own stool or "help" us flush it away may be a good way to satisfy the possessive interest he may have in his bodily product.

Nor do all children show this possessive interest. Whether or not it is present in all children as a natural psychological phenomenon cannot be stated for sure, but it is wise—and easy—to avoid playing up to it. We should avoid overdoing our praise or excitement or phrasing it in terms of, "What a wonderful thing you've done for Mommy." If we praise the *behavior* rather than the child or the product, we won't puzzle the child when we flush the b.m., or give him a distorted idea about the value of his production.

In short, with toilet training as with everything else, we use our common sense and our understanding of our own child. It is good to be aware of potential problems—some children are afraid of the toilet; some are not physically mature enough until their third year—but we need to take our cues from our child.

Toilet training need not be a difficult or painful process, but it will be a long one. Whenever we start, it will probably take at least a year from the first suggestions to the time when our child is able to keep clean and relatively dry on his own. For a year or so after that we should be prepared for accidents under some circumstances. Bladder control usually takes longer to achieve than bowel control, and even a child who stays dry all day will not stay dry at night for some time to come. Nighttime dryness is primarily a matter of the bladder's being of sufficient size and maturity to retain urine for long periods and to respond to fullness by contraction rather than relaxation. Our baby will have grown well into childhood before he can always sleep dry—or qualify as a problem bedwetter.

What It Means

Whether the experience is painless or painful, our child will learn much more from toilet training than how to use the potty. If we handle it right, we will gain more from it than the end of diapers and the privilege of boasting to our mother-in-law.

Toilet training makes use of all the respect and trust for us that we have helped our child build since his birth. If he loves and admires Mommy and Daddy, he wants to be like them. If he has learned to feel that we do what is best for him, he will be willing to accept our authoritative word that it is time now to be more grown-up. If his early lessons in discipline have been good ones, he will be able to take in stride this major step in becoming self-disciplined. During his toilet-training experience he will learn that we will help him be the grown-up he wants to be while still caring for him as we always have, so the bond of love between us can be strengthened.

Toilet training also has significance as our first shared teaching-learning experience, and in many ways it is exactly like all the future learning he will do at home, in school, and on his own. To learn any skill, a child—or anyone—must understand what is required, must want to learn, must be capable of learning it, and must have lots of practice at it.

Toilet training can be compared with learning to ride a bike (and the time will come, all too soon, when we are teaching our child to do that). The goal is to be able to start, ride, and stop unaided a piece of machinery with a very narrow base. We will have to show our child how to hold on, steer, pedal, balance, and brake. We may need to explain some of the principles involved: why it is easier to balance when we are moving than when standing still, for example. He may have to topple over several times to lose his tension about falling. His desire to learn to ride will have to be greater than his fear of looking silly or falling down, so it will need to be his own desire, not a whim of Daddy's, if the lesson is to succeed. And he must have the physical capacity to reach handlebars and pedals at the same time and to maintain balance. Finally, the more practice he gets, the better rider he will be.

If we run out of patience, decide that "Darn it all, it's time that kid was out of diapers!" and try to bring all the weight of our authority into the situation, we may learn a surprising lesson. During toilet training, for the first (but not the last) time, our child is essentially in control of the situation. There is nothing we can do to force him to do a b.m. in the potty. If he decides he does not like the way we've been treating him, or that we don't know what we're talking about when we tell him it is better to be out of diapers, he will simply refuse.

Children may refuse to eat when parents make an issue over food, but eventually they will get hungry and have to "give in." But children *never* have to use the potty if they don't want to. They have to want to. Children who have developed a loving, trusting relationship with their parents want to please them in this as in other ways and be like them.

It's difficult for some parents to let the children grow up. They like the warmth and dependency infants show; they like, perhaps, the absolute control they have over a baby. It may be hard for them to let their children leave babyhood. By the time a baby is ready for toilet training, he is ready for independence in other areas as well; and it is a parent's function to guide him to maturity while still giving him, in different ways, all the love and support he had as an infant.

Few children have to be forced into growing up; they want to, and they show that they do by imitating Mommy and Daddy. Mommy may be cleaning and suddenly find her toddler next to her, "scrubbing" away with a bit of rag. Just after Daddy has left for work, Junior may appear with a hat on, plant a wet kiss on Mommy, say "Bye-bye," and head for the door. A child who has not yet been taught to blow his nose may clamber up for a tissue, put it over his face, and snort, like Daddy. While Mommy is cooking, her small daughter may insist on a spoon and pot to "cook" with, too.

Self-feeding and Dressing

Children learn to feed themselves through wanting to be independent and by imitating the grown-ups. When a child starts trying to grab the spoon from his mother, that is the time to get an extra spoon and let the baby "help." Even if he makes a mess, it is something that even the tidiest mother needs to steel herself against if she wants her child eventually to feed himself. In fact, the more he is permitted to help, the faster he will learn to eat on his own. He can learn to feed himself if he learns that we don't get mad when he makes a mess, that we give him foods he can manage, and that we help him get gradually less messy and more efficient.

Our child will probably not be dressing himself consistently or very skillfully by the time he is three, but he will have made a good start if we give him a chance.

During the third year, when he begins trying to dress himself, we praise these efforts, not ridiculing failures but encouraging his grown-up success. We can give him buttons, zippers, snaps, and ties to practice with, if he is interested, and when we do remedy his dressing mistakes try to do so tactfully, so that he will know we are glad he is trying to be grown-up.

Other Signs of Independence

When he is into his second year, our baby may show his independence and growing self-confidence in other ways. After a clinging period it seemed would never end, he may start playing on his own again, without Mommy or Daddy in attendance. We encourage this new development by letting him do it without hanging over him and by letting him finish his projects before whisking him off to bath or nap.

Not all toddlers take the initiative toward independent play, and they need our help. If he is timid about going off on his own, even if it's only to the yard or another room, we can encourage him by taking him to the play area and getting him interested in some toy. Perhaps we will sit nearby for a while; eventually he will be willing to have us go away completely. Once he is able to play on his own, we shouldn't keep going to check on him or urge other activities on him. He'll come to us or call us when he needs us. Many toddlers will pop in on Mommy for a quick hug, then, with their emotional batteries recharged, so to speak, return to play on their own. If we find that we have a hard time leaving him alone, maybe we are not so anxious to have him independent as we thought we were.

During his second year, if not before, our child will probably enjoy playing around other children. It may be a while before he really plays *with* others, but even toddlers get a lot from the experience of playing in each other's company. Although many child specialists say that kids this age don't form attachments to each other or get involved in real social interchange, mothers who take their very small children to the playground or have other children over find that the kids enjoy it and gain a lot from the experience.

But He's Not a Grown-up Yet

In many areas—toilet training, playing, eating, dressing—he will make marked progress toward independence, but probably not steadily. When we wonder whether our child is ready for a new step toward independence, we can give him the benefit of the doubt and assume that he is. We should not refuse to let him have a cup or a spoon because he "isn't ready for it"—he might surprise us.

By the same token, we won't want to be angry when he doesn't use the opportunity we've offered right away, or be annoyed when his progress slips a little.

We must remember, too, that though he may want to grow up, he can't do it all at once. When he is learning to use a potty, that may be enough effort for the time being. It is not the moment to make an issue over giving up a bottle or using a spoon. If a mother is expecting a new baby, she might postpone toilet training the older child; he will have enough to cope with for a while. If a baby—and even an almost-three who looks and sounds very grown up is still a baby at heart—feels the pressure of too many demands, he may panic about leaving babyhood and give up on all fronts. If a child is allowed to take one hurdle at a time, the satisfaction gained from one achievement will make the next goal that much easier to reach.

11
Your Baby Becomes A Child

ONE MORNING A few months after her second birthday, Ellen claimed for herself the drinking fountain in the playground. Just tall enough to reach the water, she played with it happily for a few minutes—until another child came over to get a drink. "NO! MINE!" said Ellen with enough authority to drive the other child away. Her "No!s" and "Mine!s" scared away a number of other thirsty children and resulted in some vigorous tussles as well. Nothing Ellen's mother could say would convince her child that the fountain was for everyone, or that she might at least let the other children have a drink from "her" fountain. Finally Ellen's mother dragged her, screaming wildly, away from the fountain and toward home. After several days of Ellen's violent occupation of the water supply, her mother looked for a playground without a fountain.

Thirty-month-old Jeffrey was *always* hungry, but when his mother tried to sit him at his table for lunch one day, he refused her invitation with "NO! NO WANNA!" Encouragement only produced a louder and firmer series of "NO!s". Surprised, she put his plate in the refrigerator. This well-intended act created a stormy tantrum. "ME WANNA! ME WANNA!" Jeffrey screamed, pounding on the refrigerator. As soon as his plate appeared again, he carried it to his table, sat down calmly, and ate a huge lunch. It was the first of many similar difficult mealtimes.

The "Terrible Twos": this pattern of "negativism" and unreasoning, unreasonable temper is all too familiar to many parents.

But "terrible"? Is it really? That depends on how we look at it. To the mother of an Ellen, unused to her daughter's new toughness and violent disobedience, it may seem terrible. The contrary and contradictory behavior of a Jeffrey may leave a mother bewildered and annoyed. On the other hand, Ellen is showing that she knows she is an individual, capable of having possessions and making a stand for her rights. In this case, she made the wrong stand for a nonexistent right, but she learns through such trial and error what limitations she needs to place on the concepts of "her" and "hers." Jeffrey is simply saying that he is able to make his own decisions and doesn't need to be told to do something—even things he *wants* to do.

If we take such behavior as the symptoms of malicious rebellion intended to undermine our authority and overthrow our household, it would indeed seem terrible. But if we can see it as evidence that our child is vigorously pushing away from babyhood toward maturity, then it seems less so. After all, we shared the baby's delight when he discovered his hands and feet and his pride when he took his first step. "NO!" and "MINE!" may be harder to take, but they are just as surely signs of progress toward independent selfhood.

Some children seem to show symptoms of turning into a "terrible two" quite a while before their second birthday; some a bit later: each child will follow his own growth pattern. Whenever he enters and leaves this stage, he will spend about a year in it, letting go of babyhood and moving into childhood.

Progress Report

Of course, in many ways our child between two and three is a pretty admirably independent character. He will probably be pouring out a flood of language, adding new words and more complex grammar at an incredible pace. By his third birthday, most people will even be able to understand much of what he is saying. His growing language skill is a big boost to a child's independence, because he can easily make his needs and feelings known. Language also helps parents in managing him—and there are times when we'll need all the help we can get! Some two-year-olds speak so well, so clearly, with so many words and such intricate grammar, that it it precariously tempting to think of them as more grown-up than they are. Even the most articulate two still needs babying.

Most twos make good progress in toilet training (language helps here, too) and may manage to stay clean and dry daytimes at least. Of course, a "trained" child can be a trial to parents at first: when he has to go, or says he does, they have to drop everything and help, or find a bathroom if they're away from home, because once he's able to toilet himself, it is a source of great pride to the child.

He will probably be fully weaned, too, although some children need to cling to at least a sometime bottle through their third year. Our child is probably doing pretty well at feeding himself and can eat, if he will, the same food as the rest of the family. He may enjoy eating with the "other" grown-ups sometimes.

He will want to dress himself, and we will want to let him practice, even if it means backward shirts and reversed shoes. A cloth, a board, or a doll with buttons, zippers, snaps, and ties might prove a useful toy for an overambitious dresser.

Physically, our two-year-old will be about one-half his adult height (figure it out!). The third-year growth rate is generally much slower than that of the first two years, and growth may show itself more in changing proportions—longer legs, a slimmer torso—than in increasing size. The last of his baby teeth will push through this year, so the teething problem is over until they start loosening up and coming out in a few more years (not usually painful).

Our child will be quite sure on his feet, and his physical coordination will be good enough to allow "dancing," hopping, high climbing, and (endless) running. His posture will be more erect than a toddler's, and he will move more with the rhythm of adulthood than the stiff bounce of babyhood.

Discovering Himself

The two is ready to meet the world—sort of. Some childhood specialists call this period "first adolescence." Like adolescence, it is a time of major personal and social transition. Like the teen-ager, the two-year-old is struggling for independence and experimenting with using it, but at the same time he is somewhat fearful of giving up his dependent status. And like the adolescent, the two-year-old is exploring the powers of his mind and getting to know his body and what it can do. He is discovering his identity and encountering society and learning to place himself in it.

His Body

His physical self will become very important to the child during his third year. By now he can probably name or point out most body parts on himself and on other people, dolls, and pictures as well. More significant is his conscious realization that these physical attachments are *his* and make up himself.

Two-year-old Jim squealed with delight when his feet reappeared from his shoes at the end of the day and his hands escaped from their mittens—as though he were just getting the idea that they were there all the time, even when he couldn't see them. A little later he figured out that he could find his missing bellybutton by lifting his shirt. Soon he was undressing himself completely several times a day—often at moments embarrassing for his mother. A two-year-old disrober may be partly practicing his new dexterity with clothing. But he may also need to reassure himself that his body—that very important part of "me-ness"—is still there and want to free it from the foreign matter hemming it in.

Sylvia seemed to spend most of her thirtieth month in front of one mirror or another. She played beside the long closet mirror, stopped to stare in glass storefronts, and climbed onto sinks and dressers to get a glimpse in a high mirror. Sometimes she talked to her reflection; sometimes she just studied it. Mirrors are fun for even tiny babies, but they become very important for a child of any age who is trying to get to know the person he sees reflected. By two, he understands that, somehow, it is himself he sees, and he may work hard at learning how he is put together and how he compares with other people.

The two-year-old may begin to express the importance of his physical self in other charming ways. For some, two is the start of the "Band-Aid age." A few hours after little Sam sees Daddy patch up a shaving nick, he stubs his toe, and nothing will ease the pain but an adhesive bandage. In not too long every nearly invisible scratch and freckle needs bandaging. This is more than just cute; it is a sign of Sam's concern for the integrity of his body. With the conscious discovery of his physical self, a young child begins to be aware of its vulnerability. The child will probably not have an occasion to become fearful of such major threats to his body as serious accidents or surgery until he is a bit older. But in his initial stages of body-consciousness, he will show that he likes all his pieces in place and intact.

This interest in intactness may extend to experiences beyond his own body. Twos are surprisingly quick to notice flaws in things around them. Janice points out holes in her mother's stockings before her mother is aware of them; Stevie won't wear the pajamas with the hole; Sandra won't even eat a banana or a pretzel that is broken. For a while after a small child realizes that things, including himself, *should* fit together and be whole, he isn't happy unless they *do*. This is an area in which parents can safely, easily, and lovingly humor a child. And the fact that Mommy or Daddy can "kiss and make better" practically anything shows the important role they play in holding a two-year-old and his world together.

His Mind

It is not only his physical self that our two is getting to know: he is discovering his mind, too. Our child has always had a mind, of course. He has been using it and developing it since birth. But when he reaches this stage of twoness, it becomes a powerful force. He becomes aware of his mental skills and actively uses them to manipulate the world and the people around him. His mind is capable of complex thought, as his use of language or his ingenious mischief may demonstrate.

A two-year-old is bursting with imagination, dreams, and fears. He still cannot separate his fantasies and dreams from external reality. Sometimes his imagination voices what he wants reality to be. "Grammy home! Grammy home!" Sally insists, trying to drag her mother away from the grocery store. She wants to see her grandmother; she wants to leave the store; therefore Grammy must be at home and Sally must go there right now. Sometimes imagination expresses what the child does not want, what he fears. The dragon under Ricky's bed is very real to Ricky and should not be laughed at. Such a "dragon" may represent Ricky's fear of being left alone in the dark at night, and it should be dealt with as such.

Many children begin to have nightmares during their third year. If our child usually sleeps well but wakes up one night screaming in terror, a bad dream may be the cause. If nightmares frighten adults, who know that they are dreams, think what they must do to a child who believes they are real! We should try to find out what "happened" in the child's mind, comfort him, and reassure him that it wasn't real.

Good dreams also seem real to a small child. Mary, just going on three, loved nursery school. After her nap on a non-school day, she told her mother what a good time she had had at school and gave details of her activities. Her mother tried to explain that she had not been to school, that she had just dreamed about it during her nap, but Mary remained unconvinced.

It is during the third year that some children meet up with an imaginary playmate, although some wait until later, and many never create these mythical sidekicks. Becky, going on three, "brought home" a very large dog named George. Nobody else in the family could see George, and he never needed to be fed or walked, but he was very important to Becky for a while. He didn't hang around all the time, Becky explained to her curious parents; sometimes he ran off and played with other dogs. But George was always by Becky's side when trouble threatened: when Mommy went away for a while; when bigger kids grabbed her toys. And always always George stood watch by Becky's bed at night.

Alan had an invisible chum named Herbert during his early childhood. Alan liked Herbert a lot, even though Herbert was always getting into trouble: Herbert hit Alan's little sister every now and then, or wrote on the walls, or pulled the dog's tail.

A child who invents an imaginary companion does it to cope with the sometimes frightening complexity and inconsistency he is just becoming aware of in both his internal and his external life. Like Becky's dog George, he may be a protection against fearful situations; like Alan's friend Herbert, he may be a scapegoat for all the less-than-perfect behavior of a small child. It seems likely that he is also an expression of a child's attempt to resolve his confusion over the inner conflicts that everyone eventually learns to live with. "I know there's nothing to be afraid of at night," one part of Becky's mind may argue, "but then why am I scared?" No matter—let George worry about it. "I know I'm supposed to be good, so why can't I always be? I know I love my sister, but sometimes I have to do mean things to her": these thoughts may bewilder an Alan. Since the small child cannot see how two contradictory impulses can come from him, he figures that someone else, some little person inside him or some imaginary person outside him, is responsible. Imaginary playmates must not be ridiculed: they are as real and important as those nightmares and, unlike nightmares, often useful to the child.

Parents whose child introduces an invisible house guest will want to humor the child somewhat. But to encourage it and even embellish on the imaginary creature because it's "cute" is to miss the point. As with any puzzling behavior, parents need to look for the cause and deal with that rather than with the symptom.

Becky's parents would not want either to banish George from the house or to rely on him completely to protect their daughter from her nighttime fears. Rather they would let George hang around and they would work on the cause of Becky's worries while reassuring her that such fears are normal.

Alan's parents might ask themselves if they are putting too much pressure on Alan to be "good" or being too harsh with him for his little-boy aggressiveness. He might want to blame Herbert for his misdeeds because he is terrified of being blamed himself. Until he learns that he is not wicked or unworthy when he does a "no-no," that it is possible to be both "bad" and "good" at the same time, and that Mommy and Daddy won't withdraw their love as punishment for a misdeed, he is going to need Herbert around.

Finding His Place in the World

While he is finding himself and fitting that self into the world, he may also need for the world to be intact and strictly organized. Many twos are enthusiastic proponents of routine, ritual, and domestic order. Cindy is on constant watch to see that every household chair and table is in exactly the "right" place. Mike won't eat if his high chair is in any but its customary corner. Julie can't be put to bed without going through a specific ritual of books, songs, etc. Seasonal change often upsets a two; if he is used to wearing his winter jacket, he won't go out in just a sweater, no matter what the temperature. To a mind that is still incapable of balancing much more than two extremes, anything that isn't correct or customary has to be wrong. Familiar habits and patterns offer a great deal of security to a small child who is just beginning to realize how complicated and changeable he and the world can be.

Sociability

Becoming consciously aware of the world outside himself helps the two build his identity in many ways. Learning about other people, he can compare and contrast himself with them, assimilate their definitions of him, and find the limits that the world of people places around his me-ness.

The two has been able to benefit from contact with other children for some time, and he has probably enjoyed the chances he had for companionship. But two-year-olds *need* such contact.

When young children first enter the social world, they engage in what childhood specialists call "parallel play"; beside other children, they do their own thing without actively participating or cooperating in play with another. They may not even mind when other children take their toys or get in their way. Gradually, they begin to interact and to enter into joint activities. The two-year-old's interest in and ability at playing with other children will depend on how much practice he has had. Two is the time to really encourage social activities, and by his third birthday he will be giving and taking both good and bad with the best of them.

A two-year-old may sit in the sandbox with other kids, filling and emptying his bucket all by himself, apparently paying no attention to the others, or he may sit on the living-room floor "reading" a book next to a playmate who is "reading" another book. It may seem that he might as well be on his own, but he will let us know he prefers company by being unwilling to entertain himself in these ways when he is not with other children. Watching twos play, we may see them babbling at each other, or, more often, babbling to themselves in unison. Eventually their babbling will become a conversation, or even a game. We may soon notice one jabbering "instructions" and encouragement as the other climbs the kitchen shelves to get the cookie box. When a two starts banging his shoes on the top of the slide, soon every two is doing it, and they are all laughing gleefully over their joint-but-separate fun. As the small child gains confidence in himself and experience in dealing with others, he will enjoy easy group games and sandbox or block play that requires cooperation with another child. Even in a large group, two-year-olds tend to play two at a time. One other child is often the most a two can cope with at first, though he may like to have others in the background.

Aggression

Some two-year-old's—or most kids at some stages of twoness or later on—are very aggressive in their play. Without provocation, Mary Anne at two and a half pushes, slaps, and throws things at other children in the playground. Her embarrassed mother may feel the need to punish her more severely than she ever has, but be dissuaded by other playground mothers of twos and threes who understand, since their kids have gone through this, too.

This kind of aggression—like the words "NO!" and "MINE!"—expresses Mary Anne's need for independence and her developing sense of self. It is extreme because, perhaps, she isn't quite sure of herself and is putting on a front to convince others and herself that she is capable of acting on her own.

Her aggression does need to be restrained. For one thing, she is asking, in her own way, for a limit to be set on her feelings and behavior. That is one way she will gradually learn where she stands in relation to others. For another, of course, she must not be allowed to do real damage. But the action probably doesn't call for severe punishment, rather for a firm "No" and an explanation of why. We don't want to completely squelch our two's new ability to assert himself—he's going to need it later in life! But we need to help him redirect it into less harmful activities. If he is grabbing other children's toys or intruding violently into others' play, we can help him play with his own toys and games. If he can't seem to stop pushing and hitting, it might help to give him a punching toy or let him wrestle with Daddy or big brother.

Two-year-old aggression may also be verbal. Many small children are exceedingly and often comically bossy with their playmates, pets, and toys. They are bossed around a lot themselves, and they just want to show that they can give as good as they get. They are also bossy to themselves. We may hear ours giving himself rules and criticism as he learns to manage that very difficult "me." At first he may be tough on himself, and the toughness sometimes spills over onto others.

What about aggression against parents? Some parents adamantly refuse to allow even the youngest children to push or hit them or say hostile things to them. Others go to the opposite extreme and allow themselves, without protesting, to be pummeled by tiny fists and cursed with preschool curses.

It is understandably difficult for parents who are used to being the boss to accept hostility and aggression from their children. But if we find that the "no's" and "won't's" and occasional angry smacks from our two-year-old infuriate us and arouse our own strong hostility, we may be feeling unduly threatened by this tiny insurgent. He needs to be able to test his independence directly, and that is all he's doing. He is not attacking us; he's expressing himself. If he is literally or figuratively slapped down for that too often, he may give up.

On the other hand, he needs, now as always, the strength of his parents' special authority. If he finds that he can beat up on us without criticism, he may end up just as bewildered as if he were forbidden to express any anger toward us.

It is possible to follow a middle road in dealing with this "first adolescent" rebellion.

As the parents of one vigorous two-year-old put it, "We let Richard get mad at us in his own way because he has a right to be angry sometimes, and because if he has to hit someone, we'd rather he hit us than anyone else. Still, he knows there are limits." That is the voice of parents who are confident that they understand their child and that they are masters of the situation. They don't feel the need either to run scared or to fight back.

A child needs to know that he can let out his negative feelings at his parents, but he also needs to know that he can't get away with murder. This is the time, too, to encourage direct, nonviolent expression of these feelings. When little Stevie wants a cookie and is refused, he may throw a tantrum. He may even hit Mommy or shout at her. She can say, "You may not have another cookie because you've had too many. I can understand that you feel angry, but if you hit me so hard again, I'm going to have to put you in a room by yourself until you calm down. Mommy doesn't like to be hit any more than you do." He will appreciate her understanding, and he may learn soon to leave his protests at "You make me *so* mad!" and accept his own angry feelings as normal.

We don't want our child to hurt us (and those little shoes *do* hurt!), and we want even less to have him hurt other children. When his sense of self takes aggressive expression in the form of pushing, hitting, pinching, or biting his siblings and playmates, he needs to be stopped. He doesn't need to be punished or frightened into submission, but he needs to be told firmly that "We don't hit people, because it hurts. See, your friend is crying" and removed from the situation if necessary. The Golden Rule has no appeal to small children, but there is no harm in reminding him when *he* gets hurt that *no*body likes being punched. If the aggression persists, a smack on bottom or hand might be in order, but there is something illogical, if not ludicrous, about really spanking a child while shouting, "I can't stand your violent behavior!"

Timidity

Not all two-year-olds are aggressive (and most aren't all the time). Some go to the other extreme of great docility. Little Andy is pushed and hit; his toys are snatched and he rarely ever protests to Mommy about it, let alone fight back. He also tends to be a lot more clinging and cuddly than his playmates. Andy is going through the same internal emotional conflicts as his more aggressive friends, but his discovery of himself and his capability for independence seem to frighten him. He feels unsure of himself, but rather than put on a front as his friends do, he retreats, as if clinging to the comfortable dependence of baby status.

He needs to be encouraged to stand up for himself more actively, because it is only by trying out his wings that he will develop self-confidence. His parents should not fight his fights for him, but they should urge him to go after his stolen toys, and if not to hit back, then to say "Stop that!" His parents need to be extra careful that their reactions to any aggressive behavior on his part are ones of guidance, not punishment.

His clinging should be taken as a request for reassurance that he can still be a baby even if he does want to be independent. Even the most aggressive twos go through intense clinging periods, because of the conflict between their desire for dependence and their need for independence. Some suffer extreme attacks of separation anxiety, as their new feeling of self-sufficiency may raise the fear that they might be left on their own altogether. A child who has survived earlier bouts of separation anxiety, or who has had experience parting for a few hours at a time with his parents in the past, may not be subject to such anxiety in the third year. But those who are, usually at the midpoint of their twoness, violently resist being separated from Mother, perhaps Father also, for even a little while. This, too, will pass.

Imitation and Cooperation

Twos need Mommy and Daddy more than just in times of crisis. This is an age when children worship the parent-gods with absolute devotion (despite what they say in the heat of anger!). Since the two-year-old's world is still primarily his family, mother and father, brothers and sisters are vital in his effort to discover and build his own identity. They demonstrate appropriate roles for the child—as male or female, child, and sibling.

Also, by showing him how he is the same as or different from each of them, they give him an idea of who he is and how he fits in.

Most children this age, boys and girls alike, love to watch Daddy shave and Mommy put on makeup, to help Mommy clean house or Daddy fix the car. Nobody can write a letter without providing "writing materials" for the two-year-old; when Mommy or Daddy sits down to read a magazine, so does the two. Our child is learning by such imitation how to be a person in this society.

We will find that our two, because he wants to be a grown-up, can often cooperate and actually help with grown-up tasks. With our patient encouragement, he can be useful in picking up his toys, sorting laundry, or carrying out trash.

On the less positive side, we may find him repeating old "sins"—doing things he accepted long ago as "no-no's." He is not being wicked; he is just asking to learn the rules in a new, more adult way and checking the limits on just how grown-up he really is. He may throw uncontrollable tantrums over seemingly minor matters. We don't have to like these scenes, but we can understand them: he feels so big, but he looks around at Mommy, Daddy, and siblings and realizes that he is really very small. How frustrating not to be able to be as grown-up as they are and as he feels. All he can do to vent the frustration is to stamp his feet and scream. If we ignore it for a while, it will stop or turn into a genuine cry for comfort. Babying our tentatively adult two a little can work wonders. If he is having a bad day—getting into one kind of trouble after another—offering him a snuggle can do us both a lot of good.

Even on good days, he may be happier dealing with one parent at a time than with both together, perhaps because he has enough conflict inside of him without trying to get along with two authority figures at once. This is an age when children begin to be more fun than work, and it can be a pleasure for a parent to spend some relaxed time alone with his two-year-old.

Social-sexual Identification

Many two-year-olds seem closer to the parent of the opposite sex. A little girl may worship Daddy and care about Mommy only at mealtimes; a boy may not even look up from his toys when Daddy comes home, even though he should be bored with Mommy's company by that time. Whether this is the case with ours or not, both boys and girls need a male and a female model during this period of self-discovery. Learning about the role of the opposite sex helps them delineate their own role by showing what they are not, and helps teach them how to deal with the opposite sex.

It doesn't matter that little Joanie will never have to shave her face; she adores watching her Daddy do anything and in doing so learns more about him—and about men in general. We need not worry that two-year-old Donald is a sissy if he wants to help with the housework: Mommies and what they do are very important to all children. Similarly, young children of both sexes enjoy playing with dolls. The doll is the baby—himself—and by giving it the kind of care and treatment he gets, he finds another way of working out who he is.

A boy's fascination with cosmetics or a girl's with shaving should not evoke an alarmed response in us. If we feel the need to make a point, we can comment, "I see you're powdering your nose, like Mommy. Powder is for Mommies and girls," or "It's fun to watch Daddy shave, isn't it? Even though girls and Mommies don't have to shave their faces." One approach *not* to take is, "You *may not* help cook. Boys can't cook; that's for girls," or "You *may not* use the hammer. Girls can't hammer; that's for boys." It is that kind of rigid "sexism" that many women (and men) rightly object to today. Children need to learn to do anything that interests them. More important than being a male or a female is being a person.

Still, children need a strong sexual identity to grow up healthy in this society. Part of the "me" that our two is working so hard to build and discover is his sexual self.

It may be that our baby developed some sort of consciousness of himself as a boy or girl during his first year. Some parents say they sense such early identification, though they may be reading a lot into their infant's behavior: the treatment of boys as boys and girls as girls from birth on fosters social-sexual identity. But it is usually not until the child is in his first adolescence that he becomes consciously aware of sexual differences and of the existence of this aspect of life.

Our child may first notice his genitals as something special during toilet training, for example. He will be curious about this part of him that does such magic things. This is a time to talk casually about our child's reproductive and excretory organs, although he is hardly ready for a complete course in the birds and the bees.

Jennifer notices that her brother has a penis and she does not. Little David observes that his friend Donald has a penis but his friend Liz does not. We will be able to tell that our child is aware of these things, even if he cannot ask about them (and many twos can). We can explain that girls are born with a vagina and grow to be like Mommy, that boys are born with a penis and grow to be like Daddy.

It is good for kids to get an introduction to these basic physical differences by seeing their friends and siblings undressed. The child may also learn about physical differences from observing both of his parents. Family nudity is a controversial subject and one about which parents must make their own decisions. Some couples never allow their children to see them naked or even partially unclothed. Some go out of their way to be nude in the home, feeling that it is healthy for children to understand and accept the body. Some don't make a point either way. A good rule of thumb when our children are this age is: do whatever feels natural and comfortable. "Natural and comfortable" might encompass anything from bathing with children, within limits discussed below, to simply not making a scene when the child accidentally encounters us dressing.

Whatever our feelings on the subject, we would do well to examine those feelings carefully. If we are of either the completely modest or completely open ideology, can we think why? We may have hangups of our own that need not be inflicted on our children. Even when we are aware of our own motives, we won't want to behave in a way that makes us uncomfortable, for we will communicate that feeling to our child, making his earliest awareness of the adult human body disturbing and confusing.

Whatever pattern we follow, many psychologists would urge us to realize something that may be hard to comprehend: that children, even at two, can be sexually stimulated. They have such a passionate emotional attachment to their parents that the addition of any sexual element can be potentially disturbing. Although exposure to the parent of the same sex in the nude may help strengthen sexual identification, continually seeing the parent of the opposite sex undressed may interfere with healthy development. We must keep in mind that our two, who still looks so much a baby, is almost as full of intellectual and emotional complexity as an adult but lacks the adult's experience in coping with that complexity.

What Do We *Do* with Him!

Sex, self, mind, body, society—pretty big topics for such a little creature to be concerned with. It is easy to understand why twos sometimes can be so terrible—for themselves and for their parents.

Two *can* be a marvelous age, once we understand what our child is going through and can see some of his more annoying behavior in the light of its developmental implications. A two is still baby-cute, but he can talk and respond, and he is less work because he is at least partly toilet trained and is eating "regular" food. His attention span has lengthened so that he enjoys playing and going places. What's more, he adores us. He can be fun to be with and exciting to watch, as he seems to be learning something new every minute. Still, he can be a trial, no matter how well we understand him. How do we manage a child who is fighting our management and working his clumsy way toward managing himself?

• *Be tolerant of him, but give him firm guidance.* He may throw tantrums, for instance, from sheer frustration at not being able to do for himself and having to submit to us; at not being able to do all he feels he should be able to do; at feeling so large and realizing he is so small. But that doesn't mean we should take the tantrums seriously, or give in to his whims just because he expresses them so loudly.

• *Let him be as grown-up as he can, but don't push him out of babyhood too fast.* Many twos want to cooperate. Let them! They can help us unpack groceries, hand us nails and tools, carry packages, rake, or sweep if we let them. They need most of the time to walk down the street (not be carried or pushed in a stroller), climb the stairs, bathe and dress themselves, even if they aren't too quick or efficient—so be patient. At the same time, they are still babies in many ways. Children grow up so fast these days that we may tend to deprive them of part of their babyhood. Just because he can walk and talk and even recite nursery rhymes, we must not expect that he can behave as an adult, sitting at the table, sharing, or listening to reason.

• *Give him ways to work out indirectly his internal struggles, express his independence, and locate his place in the world.* Remember that "play" is not simply recreation to a child. To our infant, play was a way of stimulating his mind and senses. To our two-year-old, it has become a way of expressing himself and sorting out his environment. He can use action toys—tricycle, swing, tools, balls—to work off his boundless energy. He can use dolls to help him learn how to deal with himself. He can use sand and blocks to build and rearrange his world to his liking. He will enjoy books because he is learning the magic of spoken words and likes to see them in the visible form of print. He can begin to use art to express all the new feelings he can't explain in words. With our help and interest, he can dig into nontoxic, washable clay, finger paint, and liquid paint that he can apply with brush or sponge in an easily cleanable setting.

• *Encourage him to express his anger, fears, and conflicts directly.* He has words now, and if he understands that we are willing to listen to them, he can learn to let off a lot of anger and frustration simply by telling us about it. A child who is unable to express his disturbing feelings directly or indirectly in a healthy way may show his conflicts and tension in less healthy ways. A two who has frequent nightmares, who constantly plays with his hair, fingers, or genitals, who bites his nails or bangs his head, stutters severely (though in a two some stuttering is very common, caused by inexperience with speaking) may be suffering from feelings he can't cope with, conflicts he can't resolve. If we notice these or other signs of tension in our child *continually,* we may want to ask if we're demanding too much of him, inhibiting him too much, or giving him too little of the right kind of guidance. He and we may benefit from professional help.

• *Give him plenty of opportunity to socialize, but a lot of time alone with us, too.* In the third year, especially the second half of it, a child can deal with and benefit from a play group, a day-care center, even nursery school, especially if he has no siblings or nearby playmates. There is no need to "send him away to school" at such a tender age if he has one or more children around. In fact, he is probably better off if he can play in a group while Mommy or a familiar neighbor or caretaker is close by in the playground or backyard. Of course, we will want to include him in as much of family life as possible. Important as the social world is to a two-year-old, however, Mommy and Daddy are still the brightest stars of his universe. It is worth the effort to find time to spend alone with our two: he is baby enough to need it and child enough to enjoy it.

With tolerance and patient management, our two need not be "terrible."

12
Handling The Hard Times

INFANTS AND CHILDREN give joy and trouble of different sorts at every age. Most of the trouble they grow through, with understanding and careful guidance. Some, they do not.

Some children mature physically, socially, intellectually, and emotionally at a steady pace, some in spurts. Most babies encounter problems in the course of their development. When our baby's life is generally progressing, we do well to let him be the judge, with our support, of his competence to undertake new projects, his interest in being independent, his overall way of life. There are, however, times and circumstances in many children's lives when parents need to step in decisively to remedy a bad situation. The range of normal development and behavior is broad, but it is still a good idea to be aware of how things can go wrong.

The Hyperactive Child

Richard had always been a very energetic, extremely unpredictable, and generally unadaptable baby. He was his parents' first child, and living in a rather isolated area, they could only assume that this was the way babies were supposed to be. Richard was like a cartoon character of a fussy infant. The clinic doctor just chuckled and said the baby would improve with age. But as Richard grew into toddlerhood, he became even more active and excitable. He seemed physically almost unable to sit still, he screamed frantically whenever he was thwarted, and he remained almost impossible to put to bed.

When Richard's parents moved into a new area and were able to compare him with other young children, they realized that others were not as difficult as Richard. Other kids chugged around and threatened the bric-a-brac, but they were not so totally wild. Richard's new pediatrician, after examining him, observing his behavior, and talking with his parents, diagnosed "hyperkinesis." This, he explained, meant hyper- or overactivity. Sometimes this condition is caused by very slight brain damage that does not affect the intelligence; sometimes it is the product of emotional or environmental factors. In either case, the condition requires careful guidance from parents, perhaps combined with drug therapy. Most children grow out of hyperactivity, but all hyperactive children need exceptionally firm, calm handling. The earlier that hyperkinesis, like all more-than-passing problems, is detected and treated, the more chance a child has for normal adaptation to life. Not all extreme activity is a symptom of hyperkinesis, but if our baby seems too wound up too much of the time, we might talk to our pediatrician about it.

The Tense Child

Sally had been a tense baby—hypertonic, the doctor called it. "She'll grow out of it," he said. "Most babies do—it's like colic." But she didn't. The older she got, the tenser she got, physically and emotionally. It was as though her whole body were clenched. She seemed to have a chip on her shoulder and to be angry all the time.

Her parents couldn't cope with it. They were having problems of their own—they were fighting a lot and were beginning to talk of divorce. They were lucky to have an intuitive, understanding doctor, who spent most of Sally's second-year checkups talking with her parents. He advised them to seek counseling for their marital troubles and suggested that they find a relaxed mother's helper to give Sally some of the tension-free attention that she needed until family life settled down one way or another. Sally's parents had not realized that the person they thought of as a baby could absorb so much of their troubled life, but once the tension began to ease out of their marriage, Sally became a more relaxed and happier child.

Tense or unhappy children are not the product solely of troubled marriages, nor do such marriages always produce troubled children. But parents who notice signs of continuous nervousness or anxiety in their child should examine the demands his environment and experiences place on him. Toddlers' tender psyches do absorb the emotional atmosphere around them like sponges. Sometimes parents need professional help in uncovering what a tense child is concerned about and helping him deal with it.

The Slow Child

Ronald had been a "good" baby. He rarely cried, rarely fussed when left alone for long periods, and always seemed content to sit or lie and stare at whatever happened to be in his line of sight. He began crawling and walking a little later than average, but not out of the range of normal. He would play with things, idly, when they were brought to him, but even when he was a toddler, he didn't seek out toys and trouble the way others his age did.

It took his mother a while to realize all this, since Ronald was so little bother and she had other children to think about. She finally asked her pediatrician about Ronald's inactivity, in connection with his weight, which was getting excessive. His doctor made a careful, in-depth examination of the boy and found that he had a thyroid deficiency, which could be treated medically. If Ronald's mother had ignored the problem, lasting mental retardation might have resulted.

Ronald's case was rather unusual, since "glands" are blamed for slowness and other problems more frequently than they deserve. Because its source was physical, Ronald's problem was relatively easy to correct, once his mother noticed it and sought help.

Some young children who seem lethargic and lacking in interest in the world may, indeed, be mentally retarded, or "low average." Parents who notice such symptoms in their children are often unwilling, understandably so, to face up to the problem. In some cases they are needlessly anxious; their child's "slowness" reflects only his temperament or lack of appropriate stimulation. But even if slowness has no physical or mental cause, a child like Ronald needs extra encouragement to be active, and the matter should be discussed with the child's doctor.

Sometimes the problem is "incurable" in that retardation is definite and permanent. But even that does not make a child a lost cause. Many mental and physical disabilities can be partially, often substantially, overcome today if treatment is started early and parents know what guidance is called for.

The Late Developer

When the other babies his age in the neighborhood were crawling, Johnny couldn't sit unsupported. When the others were walking, Johnny was still crawling, making no attempt to pull himself to a stand. His parents were concerned and insisted on a complete examination of his muscular and nervous systems. Their doctor found nothing wrong and advised them to let Johnny grow according to his own timetable, since he was progressing, though not keeping up with the Joneses' baby. He urged them to relax, adding that a feeling of pressure or anxiety can slow a child as surely as any physical or mental disability can. He reminded them to let the baby have as much freedom as he needed and suggested games and toys that might interest Johnny in trying to walk.

Although it turned out that Johnny had no physical or mental defect, his parents were wise to discuss their worry with the doctor, if only to reassure themselves. The doctor probably would have noticed any major physiological cause for slow motor development during checkups earlier in Johnny's life. But there could be other causes for the trouble—emotional stress, overinhibition, lack of stimulation, or neurological or biochemical problems not always turned up in a routine physical examination. If parents are concerned about the pace of their child's development, they should talk to their pediatrician. He can probably reassure them and help them give their baby the special, casual, fun attention that he needs. Late developers may "bloom" as early as the preschool years, or not until adolescence. They are an interesting lot, whose potential should never be underestimated.

The Late Talker

Jimmy was three and didn't talk. He seemed intelligent, and he lived in a generally stimulating environment, so his parents were worried. The doctor found him physically normal and guessed the cause of his silence. "You can tell what he wants, and you give it to him, don't you? Well, stop. Make him ask." At home, Jim came to his mother in the kitchen, pointed at the cookie jar and grunted. "Tell me what you want, and you may have it," she said. This went on for a while, Jimmy getting madder and madder. Finally he said, clear as a bell, "You heard what I said. I want a cookie!" From then on he talked.

Not all speech problems are resolved so easily. Three is not outside the normal range for the beginning of speech, but parents of late talkers should make sure they are allowing their child to explore and encouraging him to talk, rather than responding only to his grunts and hand signals.

Anita seemed to be developing normally. She was an alert and active baby and cried and cooed as much as any until she was about six months old. It was not until some months later that her parents realized she still sounded like an infant. Other parents boasted about their little ones' saying "mama," "hot" and "bye-bye," but Anita didn't make any imitative sounds at all. The doctor tested her hearing and found that she was almost completely deaf. In Anita's case the defect was remediable by an easy operation, and she soon began catching up in her talking.

If our infant was born with some vocal problem that keeps him from talking, we would know from the relative absence of crying and other sounds during the early months. Children with hearing defects can make sounds, but they cannot learn to talk, because they cannot hear sounds to imitate. Instead of making more sounds in the second half of his first year, a baby with a hearing problem would make fewer. This is another problem to check on as soon as we have any concern, because a hearing disability can retard our child's cognitive growth.

Many children are late talkers but have no physical abnormality or any real problem at all. If our toddler babbles with the best of them, can imitate the dog, or a bird, or music, but won't say any real words while the neighbors' kids are saying whole sentences—first of all, we must relax. Then, look into the child's environment. Do we talk to him? Do we talk too much to him? Do we, or, as is often the case, his older brothers and sisters, respond to his nonverbal language without making him learn ours? Have we been putting a lot of pressure on him to talk? Once we are sure he is physically normal, we may be better able to deal with some of the questions raised above.

The Picky Eater

Mary had always been a good eater. She enjoyed eating everything her mother fixed for her and was seldom temperamental in her tastes or appetite. Suddenly, when she was about two, she stopped eating everything but toast and an occasional banana. She didn't make a fuss about it; she just quietly refused to eat all the tasty tidbits offered her. After a few days, her mother got frantic. She had the child checked over and found that she was completely healthy.

A week later the doctor got another call from Mary's mother. "Mary is driving me crazy! She just won't eat! What's happening?"

"Is there any reason why Mary might be *trying* to drive you crazy?" the doctor asked.

Her mother could think of none, and finally said, "It's just that it's such an effort to cook all this food that is left uneaten, now that I have a part-time job."

"That job may be why Mary isn't eating. Stay home for a week, or change baby-sitters, and see what happens."

Mary ate like her old self the whole week her mother was home, and the next week when she had a new sitter she seemed to like better, she kept on eating.

Young children have very few ways of getting back at their parents. Refusing to eat is one of them. If our good eater suddenly turns picky, and there is no physical or developmental cause (most children's appetites drop sharply around their first birthday, when their growth slows), we should look at what is going on in his life. He may be giving us a signal that he is unhappy. One the other hand, some kids are always small or picky eaters or go through occasional periods of eating little or eating only one food. The best thing to do with these children is ignore their eating habits. Children will eat what they feel like eating when they're hungry—and they can thrive on a surprisingly limited diet. If we constantly try to tempt our child with special foods, or if we make a fuss about his eating in other ways, he will see that he has a tool for controlling or upsetting us and may get in the habit of using food as a weapon.

The Sickly Child

The "sickly" child may be like the picky eater. He has learned, unconsciously, that he gets the most and the nicest attention from Mommy and Daddy when he is sick. Also, without knowing it, his parents may be trying to keep him in the status of a cuddly, helpless infant. We may know many adults who feel "sick" when they are emotionally upset, whose "nerves" are in their stomachs or their heads. It may be hard to imagine babies and toddlers suffering from such psychosomatic ailments, but when confronted with some problem he can't cope with, even a toddler may learn that a "stomachache" wins sympathy points from his parents.

Sometimes it is obvious what a child is trying to do. At eighteen months Chris took a bad fall from his stroller. He was not seriously hurt, and his wounds healed quickly, but the incident caused a day of excitement. The next week, when he couldn't get the cookie or the attention he wanted, he began taking falls: he would "tumble" harmlessly and on purpose and then look for response from his parents. At first they thought it was cute, but when it kept up, it stopped being so cute. So instead of ignoring the falls completely or taking them seriously, they tried a direct approach: "Chris, you can't have a cookie now, but just because I say 'no' is no reason for you to carry on," or "Chris, if you want Daddy to pick you up, just come and ask—you don't have to fall down to get attention." It worked most of the time, and Chris began to get the idea that he didn't have to be so devious.

Not all "sickliness" is so obviously put on. It is impossible to *know* whether a little child really hurts or not. And, of course, little children often do seem to come down with "one thing after another" in the years before they build up immunities to common virus infections. If we consider our child sickly or "delicate," we should check with the doctor. Some parents are not easily convinced. But if a pediatrician, after checking carefully, can find no physical reason for concern about our child's health, then is the time for us to examine the way in which our own attitudes may be causing his "sickliness."

Parents whose baby was born with a difficulty or has suffered a severe but temporary illness or disability may continue coddling the child long after the problem is solved. The child finds security in his "sickliness" and may use it as an excuse not to meet the world on equal terms. Every child needs to be helped to think of himself as basically healthy, even when—or perhaps especially when—he is temporarily ill.

The Clinger

Sickliness is one way children may seek extra security and comfort. Clinging is another. In most children, clinging is only a passing "phase": it comes and goes at different stages of development. Some children, however, never seem to be able to let their parents go. Well past eighteen months, they are still clutching at their mothers' knees or skirts, happy only in Mommy's lap, constantly begging to be picked up. It is very irritating after a while, to all but the most patient of adults, and it may be an unhealthy emotional sign as well.

Parents need to help the clinging child gain confidence and independence. First, however, they should make sure they are giving as much good, solid, *unasked* attention and affection as their particular baby seems to need, because what the clinger is asking for is love and reassurance. Then, they can gently urge the child to play on his own or to join a group he is shying away from, while they stay close by. It takes time and extra patience to help a clinger gradually let Mommy go.

As with other problems, we will want to look into the circumstances that may prompt our baby to cling. Does it happen in certain situations, with certain people, at certain times? Has his mother gone to work, or has there been a separation for other reasons? We will need to be extra watchful under these conditions, so that the baby gets the reassurance he needs to go off on his own.

When our toddler comes to cling, it is probably best to give him a bit of attention, a pat or a hug before guiding him back to his own activity. He needs to know we care, but he also needs to know we want him to stand on his own. Ignoring him, or getting annoyed, or picking him up and smothering him with affection will probably only compound the problem. If our best efforts don't work, or if we find we can't keep ourself from frequent irritation, then we should talk to our doctor or get other counseling.

The "Cold" Child

At the other extreme from the clinger is the baby who continually rejects his parents' cuddling even when unhappy. Frank's pediatrician called him hypertonic, but he predicted that the child would outgrow his tense, anxious behavior and inability to be consoled through physical contact. Frank didn't change as he grew. He developed normally in many respects, but he got only more forceful in pushing his parents away when they tried to snuggle or comfort him. He would endure being dressed but stood for little other physical contact. He seemed to turn in on himself. This coldness was hard for Frank's parents to cope with. They felt guilt but also resentment, and the distance between them and Frank only increased.

If parents don't get overwhelmed by guilt and are able to keep up their loving attention, some children, with patience and persistence on their parents' part, will gradually open up. Frank didn't. So when he was going on three his parents sought therapy for him and themselves.

This kind of situation, whether it is evident from birth or develops later, is one that parents probably cannot handle on their own. It is important to reach children like Frank as early as possible to give them a chance for normal emotional growth. Frank's parents, with the help of a child psychologist at the local mental health clinic, were able gradually to win Frank's confidence and develop a healthy parent-child relationship.

When Parents Need Help

It takes tremendous stores of understanding and patience to work out some of the difficulties that children may grow through, but it is often even more difficult for parents simply to recognize that a problem exists that calls for professional attention.

The Schmidts' regular baby-sitter noticed that four-month-old Alan's eyes looked "odd," but she assumed that this was simply a new baby's "cockeyed" look. When it persisted, she hesitated to ask Alan's mother about it, feeling that she might be sensitive about this defect in her baby. Finally the sitter did mention Alan's eyes and was surprised to find that his mother had not even noticed what seemed a most obvious problem. What is more, Mrs. Schmidt commented, "Alan's father is nearly blind, you know; maybe this is the same problem he has." To an outsider, it would seem that eye defects would be the first thing that a nearly blind parent would worry about, but that is not the way people often are.

Parents are often unwilling or unable to see defects in their children, especially when they unconsciously fear that some serious problem may exist. Pediatricians should pick up potential difficulties, of course, but pediatricians are busy, are human, and haven't the primary responsibility for our child's growth.

We can watch our child without hovering over him, can be concerned without being overprotective, and can compare his development with other children's without being competitive. It is not always possible to know when to worry and when to accept something as a normal developmental pattern. If we are worried about any aspect of our child's life or growth, we should have it checked. The worry can do as much harm as a real problem might. If we do notice some behavior or physical characteristic that seems out of the ordinary, we can keep an eye on it for a while, look for possible causes, and try common-sense correctives. If the condition continues, even if it seems minor, it is time to ask about it. The earlier we catch any problem, especially in these first few years that lay the basis for future growth and learning, the better off our child will be.

Weathering Temporary Stress

All children and their parents must undergo some stressful situations in the course of day-to-day living. Such stress need not be damaging. In fact, with careful handling it can increase our child's emotional strength, but we need to be aware of the kind of strain we may feel and the reactions we may have to it.

Alice's parents had not had a vacation since they had been married. When Alice was going on two, her parents had a chance to go away for a week, and her grandmother said she would keep Alice. Alice loved her Grandma and had spent many weekends at her house, so her parents took off. While they were gone, Alice came down with a bad case of the measles. She was never in any danger, and Grandma was in control of the situation and wanted her parents to have a good time, so she didn't call them home.

But Alice was miserable. When her parents came home, she refused to have anything to do with them. She wouldn't come to them, look at them, or talk to them. Only reluctantly would she take food from them. After a few days she made up with her father; Daddies, after all, leave home every day and aren't supposed to take care of little girls. Mommies, she must have figured, are always supposed to be there, especially when babies are sick, so she punished her mother by ignoring her for more than a week. Luckily, her parents realized what was happening and were not seriously upset by their daughter's declaration of dependence. They didn't lose their good humor, and they showed that they were still going to love her even though she was mad at them. Soon, things were back to normal.

Alice's reaction was typical of many normal, healthy, happy children who must endure brief separation from their parents. Her mother and father thought they were going to keep the separation from being stressful by leaving her with a loved, familiar person. But this wasn't enough (perhaps because of the measles, though that is by no means certain). Still, Alice came through unscathed, and the experience may have been a maturing one for her in the long run.

Parents who must leave a young child should choose a sitter whom the child knows well and preferably one who can care for the child in his own home. (We should try to avoid leaving our baby if he is going through separation anxiety.) If we make careful preparations and are matter-of-fact about going away, the child won't suffer. But we might be prepared for a bit of the silent treatment, extra clinginess, or other signs that the child noticed our absence and is worried that we might go away again. Patient reassurance should overcome this quickly.

Alice's separation had a special aspect: an uncomfortable illness. Children can cope with almost any situation as long as their parents—especially Mommy—are right with them.

If a child must undergo painful medical treatment or be hospitalized for an illness or operation during his first few years, his mother should do what she can to be with him, especially if he has always tended to be timid or unadaptable. If she can stay calm and sure during treatments, holding her baby herself if possible, the child won't suffer the terror and anxiety that is as bad as the pain. (A doctor may keep parents away during some of the more gruesome medical care a child may undergo, fearing that the parents' reaction to stitching a cut or cleaning an open wound may further alarm the child. If we are not allowed to be with our child, we should part calmly and assure him we'll be "waiting right outside.")

Babies, like most people, forget pain quickly when it is over, but they need Mommy when bad things are happening, so their parents should stay as close as possible. If a child must go into the hospital, the mother should try to be with him nights as well as days. If rooming-in is not available, she may be allowed to sleep in a chair by his bed. If the hospital absolutely does not allow parents to stay with their children except during regular visiting hours, or if the nature or length of the illness makes it impractical, a mother should be with her child as much as is permitted, and she would do well to get to know the nurses who will care for the baby when she is not there. This reassures her and the baby and may help the nurses understand her child better. In this as in all separations, the child will suffer less if the parent seems calm and sure about what is happening—tearful farewells or anxious clinging will only make the baby worry more.

Because young children can withstand almost anything as long as they are with their parents, moving probably will not seriously disturb a little one, who doesn't have the wrench of leaving school and friends that older children must endure.

Still, parents should look out for reactions to such potentially stressful situations. Our child may cling more than usual or have sleeping or eating problems for a while. When anything out of the ordinary routine is going on, we will want to hold off on urging our child to take a new step toward adulthood. Weaning, toilet training, or new disciplinary rules can wait until our child has the change or stress under his belt.

Given patient guidance and loving attention during and after difficult situations, a child can actually benefit from a certain amount of stress. A baby learns that he survives separation, change, physical pain, upheaval, and other trying events, and they aren't so terrifying in retrospect. He discovers that a bad thing can happen and his world doesn't fall apart. With this kind of experience, our child can begin to build the emotional strength that is vital to his ability to cope with the crises, illnesses, and losses that all people must face in life.

13
Sharing Life

SUPPORTING OUR CHILD in times of stress is not the same as adapting our entire lives to him all the time. Too many people seem to feel that once they have a child they must submerge their individual personalities in their new identities as "parents."

Tom Schaffer used to spend his Sundays playing golf and would always take a few days of his vacation to go fishing with his friends. Since the Schaffers had their baby, Tom hasn't golfed or fished once; he spends his Sundays with his toddler in the park and his vacations with his wife and child at Grandma's. He'd *rather* be fishing, at least some of the time, but he stays at home, because that is what he thinks a father is "supposed" to do.

Ethel Walsh managed a travel agency until her baby was born. She enjoyed the job, the people, and the bustle of her office. She would like to start working again, at least part-time. Instead, she stays home, washing, cleaning, cooking, and minding the baby, because that is what she thinks a mother is "supposed" to do.

There is no such thing as an ideal parent. Every parent is different, just as every person is different. When we become parents, we don't stop being ourselves, and we shouldn't feel we have to. If a woman was never calm, serene, and wedded to homemaking, having a baby doesn't mean she has to become a sweet "motherly" type. If a man has always been easy-going, retiring, and unassertive, becoming a father doesn't mean he has to turn into a tough-fisted authority. A couple that has always enjoyed living it up doesn't need to learn to like quiet evenings at home all the time.

We have a right, even a duty to ourselves, to be ourselves first and "parents" second—and we'll probably be better and happier parents for it.

Just as we may have become parents with preconceived notions about what parenthood was supposed to be, so we may have had ideas ahead of time about what babies and children are supposed to be. A major theme of this book has been that every baby is different; each baby has his own personality, abilities, and growth pattern. Our baby is different from other babies, and he is different from each of us. He has special needs, and so do we.

Discovering parenthood—learning to be the kind of parents our children need without losing our own individuality—is similar in many ways to building a marriage. Each is a task that takes—and deserves—a lot of effort.

Being a parent is probably different from what we thought it would be. Marriage was, too. It took us a while before and after we were married to get to know each other. It has taken a while to get to know our baby. Since becoming husband and wife, we have probably made a lot of adjustments to each other. We do the same for our baby, and we expect him to adapt to us in some ways. We may have been sure that marriage would be all bliss, and yet every now and then we have a fight. We probably had a romantic idea of parenthood and have found the strain sometimes more than we can take. We find some things we don't like about the person we married and that we may never be able to change. Neither is there any sin in not thinking our baby is perfect. But as with our spouse, we try to boost the good points and live with the bad ones. We married each other for what we are, not for what we "should" be. Within the context of our marriage we can still allow ourselves and each other the freedom to be ourselves. We need to give our child that privilege, too.

Expectant parents sometimes have a mental image of what they want their children to be, or goals they hope their offspring will achieve. They may hope for a doctor, a lawyer, a redhead, a namesake, an image of her father. When the baby falls short, the parents are disappointed; if he excels in unforeseen areas, the parents are bewildered. How much better to accept our child, even as a baby, for what he is, to come to understand and love him as the unique individual he is.

Reconciling Family Conflicts

Because each member of our family is an individual, our needs may come into conflict. Such differences are normal and to be expected. Handled carefully, they need not cause lasting resentment or guilt.

Parents' needs often conflict with their children's. A baby would like nothing better than to have his parents' full time and attention every moment, but that does not mean his parents need to give it to him. A man like Tom Schaffer need not completely give up the pleasure he gains from golfing or fishing. He should be able to spend some time with his family and some time with himself. A woman like Ethel Walsh need not sacrifice the satisfaction she gains from a job. She and her child would probably both be happier if she worked, at least part time.

Children need a lot of tender loving care, but grown-ups need t.l.c. too, and sometimes the kids can do with a little less of it so that parents can share a little more. If a father has been working extra hard and long hours, there is no reason why a child can't stay out of the way to give him some rest. A mother needs time to herself, too, whether a day off, or a few hours in each day when she can ask that the children keep out of her hair.

Some families may need to make greater compromises than these. Daddy may have a chance for a job that he would love but that would mean a lot of time away from home and children. His children and his wife need him, but he needs the job to fulfill his own life goals. He should be able to take the job without being made to feel guilty, and plans should be made to insure that the time he does have at home will be extra rewarding.

Occasionally, a parent simply does not like his children, or one of them, and the feeling may be mutual. This can lead to the sort of conflict that calls for professional help. First, the problem must be faced up to. It is far better, and in the long run less painful, to admit such a difficulty than to deny its existence and let it snowball.

Sibling Rivalry

Sibling conflict is traditional. No matter how sweet and loving a child is, we can't expect him to be overflowing with affection for a small squealing creature who appears in the household and takes much of the attention he had been getting exclusively. The fact that it is expected does not mean that parents have to take sibling rivalry without a murmur. Parents who recognize the special needs of siblings can help their children live together with a minimum of friction and a maximum of satisfaction.

An older child needs to feel that he is still his parents' baby, even with a new one in the house, so he will need extra love and understanding. Many parents find that they can help their older children over the initial jealousy of a new baby by giving them a sense of being responsibly involved in caring for the newborn and by allowing them special privileges that only "big" boys and girls are given—staying up later, going places alone with Mommy or Daddy. Parents can boost the older child's ego by praising talents, skills, and traits that are uniquely his.

Conflicts will still arise, of course. During our baby's first few years, one of our primary jobs may be physically protecting the young one. An older child may not hurt a baby intentionally, but unconsciously (and understandably) he may want to get rid of the intruder, and unintentional hurts may be just as dangerous as intentional ones.

As our baby grows, his older brothers and sisters have a right to be protected, too, since a toddler can wreak as much havoc on a sibling's room, privacy, or nerves as he can on Mommy's and Daddy's. If we are aware of the universality of sibling conflict, and its roots, we can be more tolerant of behavior that, on its face, may seem simply mean or bad.

If we have a second child before our first is two years old or so, sibling conflict will take as much care, but of a different sort. A younger child is apt to be more direct about his feelings and worries and more easily reassured of our love by snuggling and babying than an older one. He will need extra understanding of possible relapses in weaning, toilet training, and other grown-up behavior when he sees a little one enjoying all the things he has so recently given up.

As in most family relationships, the watchword in sibling rivalry is respect for each individual's personality, needs, and integrity.

Parental Conflict

After a day of sibling battles or whining complaints, a weary mother may feel that there is no more damage her kids could do to her. But there is! Children are often the direct or indirect cause of conflicts between husband and wife, especially during the early years, when they are still learning about being parents.

Bob and Mary had always enjoyed a happy, quiet, and calm married life. They had few disagreements on important matters. Little changed after the baby was born, until she was eight months old and Mary started toilet training. Bob was adamant about wanting to wait until the child was much older, feeling strongly that babies need babying and having an idea that early training would seriously hurt his daughter. Their discussions turned into arguments, and the conflict spread into other areas of child-rearing and their married life. As a result, Bob and Mary spent an unhappy year, and their mutual tension helped delay their baby's training well past the age that even Bob had had in mind.

Roger and Carol never disagreed over the specifics of child-raising, but their small son caused a different kind of rift. As the months passed after his birth, Carol became tense and depressed at being housebound and increasingly irritated and tired from keeping up with her son's activity and crankiness. She didn't think such feelings were right for a mother, and she couldn't talk with her husband about them. As time went on Roger grew worried and then put off by Carol's changed manner. They would have continued to grow apart if the tension had not resulted in a tremendous argument during which the whole problem was finally aired so that it could gradually be resolved.

Sources of Marital Strife

Marital conflicts may also arise if one spouse feels the other is devoting so much attention to the children that there is not enough left over for the marriage partner; or if one or both feels trapped, physically or financially, as a result of parenthood. There can be as many sources of strife as there are parents and children.

Conflicts like these serve to underscore the necessity for a husband and wife to be open and direct with each other. The basic ingredients in all our loving relationships, including the new ones as mommy-wife and daddy-husband, are honesty and trust. Honesty may be even more vital now than it ever was before in our marriage. We are dealing with a lot of challenges that neither of us has ever encountered before. A husband may find that he is jealous of his baby. This is disturbing, not only because it is *his* baby, but also because it seems silly to be jealous of such a tiny little thing. Such feelings are normal. A wife may have heard about them but assumed that her husband was so strong and independent that it wouldn't happen to him. Somehow, a husband needs to let his wife know that he needs her, too.

A woman may suddenly feel that she is not an individual any more. Instead, she seems to be someone on whom a lot of people depend. She is more like "X's wife" and "Y's mother" than herself. She needs to ask, in her own way, that somebody take care of her, too, please. And she needs to stand up for her own integrity and work with her husband toward getting time for herself.

If issues like this—and they differ with every person and family—are not brought into the open, they can end up causing bitterness and resentment that did not have to be.

Parents often will find that they disagree on a major aspect of child-rearing. It is important to talk about these differences honestly, calmly, and privately. If they are not aired, one parent may unfairly hold a child's "failure" against the other for years. When disagreements do arise over basic aspects of child-raising, each needs to try to understand the other's views and to make compromises, realizing that the tension that will build up if one parent's strong views are thwarted may result in more damage than giving ground would.

The beginning years of parenthood are important ones for our marriage. We are laying new foundations, just as we were when we were engaged and newly wed. Talking never hurts as much as silence. And now we have not only our individual happiness and our marital strength to think of, but our children's security as well. Children need a stable home in which to grow—and that is rooted in the individual and mutual happiness of their parents.

When faced with a conflict—between parent and child, child and child, or parent and parent—that is especially intense or prolonged, a family would do well to seek professional advice and counseling. Many private and public agencies offer such services. A trained outsider, looking at a problem objectively, can often help a family resolve its conflicts before they do permanent or severe damage.

The Importance of Compromise

The resolution of family conflicts, large or small, requires compromise. If Mommy is feeling trapped and overworked, Daddy would be wise to help out or take over now and then, even if he doesn't relish changing diapers. If his job is wearing him out, he may need to be protected from the kids sometimes. Children, even young ones, need to compromise, too. They may want to stay up for a favorite TV program every night, to go to the zoo every Saturday, not to be left with a sitter, to roughouse endlessly with Daddy—but for family peace of mind and for their own social well-being they need to learn to accommodate to others by limiting their desires or putting them off until later. Parents sometimes feel guilty about not giving children everything the kids think they need, but that is guilt that is wasted. Parents do need to make sacrifices, of course, small and large, for their children, but not to the point of making martyrs of themselves.

Before we had our baby, maybe we went out a lot; nothing fancy, but a movie when we felt like it, or an evening walk, or a spur-of-the-moment picnic with friends. Now that we have a child, such spontaneous excursions are probably a thing of the past.

We will be spending less money on ourselves now and more on our kids, and trying to save a little extra for emergencies and the children's education. We probably won't think twice about this and the countless other "sacrifices" we'll make for our children as they grow. If we have only as many children as we want, when we want them, and if we preserve our own individuality during parenthood, we'll probably regard what we do for our children not as "sacrifices," but as part of the giving of ourselves that family life is based on.

Overdoing Sacrifice

When parenthood places too much pressure on people, they do resent their role and their children. Have you ever heard someone say, after meeting a new baby, "Oh, he's cute now, but wait! You'll do everything for him, and will he be grateful? No! Kids grow up and never appreciate the sacrifices you made for them." A child, small or grown, should not be expected to be "grateful": he did not ask to be born, and he can reasonably expect that the people who took on responsibility for him will do their best by him. But parents who sacrifice too much of themselves may well be hurt when their sacrifices are not appreciated. They and their children would probably be happier if they had been a bit more selfish.

Some couples, faced with parenthood, make the self-defeating sacrifice of their own marriage. They give their all to their baby and find that they have nothing left for each other. We married each other, not our child. Children will occupy only a part of our life, after all, since our marriage will outlast their time at home. So we need to keep being husband and wife while we are being parents. No matter how much we both adore the little one, it is very important that we find time to be alone together.

Every couple makes its own arrangements for time together. Some make a point of getting the baby to bed early so that they have their evening together. Some put the baby in another room so they can have dinner together. Some have parents close at hand so that they get whole weekends "off." Some make a regular "date" to go out and be adults together.

Because they have less of it, they will want to make the most of their time together. A mother will benefit everyone, for instance, if she finds time late in the afternoon, or whenever the baby sleeps, to lie down herself and take a rest so that she is not dead on her feet by evening.

Fatigue is a factor that new parents often have no realistic idea of ahead of time. Somehow, all that we hear and read about what a job parenthood is passes over our head. We may think to ourself, "That's because they just don't know what they're doing!" When told by a neighbor that it took her half an hour to get herself and her toddler dressed to go out in winter, one expectant mother wondered what could be the matter with the woman. The following winter, she was wondering no longer.

The early demands of parenthood are indeed physically exhausting. In the first few months, we may be up half the night. Later, we may wear ourselves out chasing after a constantly active child. We may not realize how much our depression and extra tension are due to plain tiredness. But we will probably find that if we do our best to get some extra rest, we no longer regret ever getting married at all. As our children leave infancy, though the mental, diplomatic, and emotional challenge may increase, the physical demands will lessen, and the children will start giving us a new kind of pleasure.

This discussion of conflict, sacrifice, tension, and fatigue is not meant to give the impression that parenthood is never-ending drudgery. By now a new mother knows that the fun and excitement of watching her baby grow, the joy of sharing a new life, far outshine the drearier moments of parenthood. A child contributes more than himself to our lives. As he grows and changes, so do we. If we let them, our baby and our new roles will bring out facets of ourself and our marriage that can make our personal lives a great deal richer.

Living Your Own Style

A family is, after all, simply a collection of unique individuals with interlocking needs and gifts. We will spend the first few years of our baby's life getting to know his special characteristics, adapting to fit them, and teaching him to fit in with the other individuals in the family and with the group as a whole. Our baby will spend his first few years getting to know himself, getting to know us and our standards for him, and, through us, getting an introduction to the world he will be leaving us for, to form his own family group.

There is no one right way to raise him for this, just as there is no one right way to live a life. The pediatrician's way may work for the pediatrician. The expert's way may work for the expert. Our parents' way may have worked for them. The neighbors' kids live by the neighbors' ideas.

Our way of raising our children is an expression and an intimate part of our whole style of living. Our style is a product of the interests, needs, and personalities of each individual in our family—ours and our children's. It is by allowing for the individuality of each member of our family that we build a style that is uniquely ours and satisfying for us all. If we get to know and respect our child as a person, while guiding him through the hazards and challenges of these first few years, then we are doing the best that parents can do.

BOOK THREE

Guiding Your Preschooler

By EDITH NEISSER

Introduction

READING ABOUT how small children grow through love and friction with the people around them can be thought-provoking and fun. The presentation in this book of the preschooler's nature, his needs, and his relationships has been arranged so that you may readily turn to a particular topic or problem that concerns your family at the moment, or get a panorama of the development of the years from three through five by reading the entire book.

Chapter 1 gives you an overview of the child's development in size and strength, in ability to reason and to learn, to get along with others, and to express and control feelings in serviceable ways.

The next three chapters trace a youngster's relationships with his brothers and sisters (Chapter 2), his contemporaries (Chapter 3), and with adults who represent authority (Chapter 4). The latter chapter takes up the kind of discipline in the family that tends to keep the inevitable contrariness of these years within bounds.

The next two chapters are related. Chapter 5 is concerned with gratifying and keeping alive your child's curiosity in all directions, as well as answering his questions about the differences between boys and girls and where babies come from. The consideration of those questions leads into the following chapter, which involves the way young children develop pride in their own sex membership and learn to value both sexes.

Chapters 7 and 8 could well be read together, since fears are not always generated by real events. Frequently they are the result of disquieting inner feelings that originate in a newly acquired and too busy conscience.

Independence, the subject of Chapter 9, rests on a child's having sufficient freedom from fear so that he may move toward becoming a self-propelling boy or girl.

Development does not proceed smoothly for every child throughout these years, so minor annoyances and larger worries are taken up in Chapter 10. References to this chapter will be found in earlier ones. These and other cross-references are worth following up, for all a child's experiences and relationships are so interdependent that one cannot isolate a topic.

Preparing your child for school is the subject of the final chapter.

If you look up a subject in the Index, you will probably find several references. Again, no bit of behavior is made out of whole cloth but is part of the patchwork design that is the total personality. You will probably discover, for that reason, that the pages the Index leads you to, when read by themselves, are usually less illuminating than a complete chapter or two.

You will probably choose to read and reread sections of the book from time to time, but we hope you will also read the book as a whole. As you see the different phases of growth in relation to each other, your own understanding of and pleasure in your preschoolers can be increased.

1
The Delightful Age

BETWEEN THEIR THIRD and sixth birthdays children are usually delightful, at least much of the time. Their refreshing naiveté and surprising perceptiveness make them good company. Their outspoken affection and admiration for their parents make them responsive and endearing. Mature enough to be fairly reliable in a number of domestic situations, they are still sufficiently home-centered not to give their parents the causes for concern that they may create a few years later when their whereabouts are harder to keep track of and their performance in school or in the neighborhood may leave something to be desired.

Their swift development on all fronts during these years also makes life with the three- through five-year-old exciting and fascinating – if at times exhausting. The six-year-old, twice as old as he was at three, is in many respects twice as knowledgeable and competent. Not until the big spurt of growth at puberty that ushers in adolescence will so much dramatic change again occur in so brief a period as in these years, which, for want of a better term, we call "preschool."

In some ways, this period foreshadows adolescence and is, in a sense, a rehearsal for it. The young child unwittingly is practicing, on a small scale and in the relatively safe setting of home, the independence and self-assertion, the establishment of himself or herself as a member of his or her own sex that characterize and complicate the teens. The efforts we put into helping the preschooler master the tasks in development, acquire the skills, and form the relationships suitable to this period pay off a decade later as well as in the present. A good life from three through five is a sound foundation for weathering the proverbial storms of adolescence.

What Shall We Expect During These Years?

How, in general, may preschoolers be expected to develop in body, in mind, in feelings, and in ability to get along with others?

Right here, we need to recognize two points. Physical, mental, social, and emotional attributes are so intertwined, and their growth is so integrated, that in separating them for purposes of discussion we may lose an important dimension. One cannot say, "This boy, or this girl, cannot play happily with other children," as if that amply described the whole problem. The child may be suffering from hunger or fatigue, or intense fear, or all-consuming anger, or lack of confidence in himself or in the world around him. Similarly, we cannot assume that a child is failing to grasp an idea or master a skill solely because his mental powers are not equal to doing so. In order to learn, a young child needs to feel at ease with himself and with others and be free from persistent physical discomfort.

The second point to keep in mind is the importance of individual differences. We may suggest a *range* of behavior and attitudes likely to occur during these years and some responses typical of youngsters in this phase of development. Yet, children, even in the same family, differ so greatly that no two will exhibit the same traits or react in the same manner to similar situations.

Each Child Is Unique

These sharp individual differences stem from the infinite combination of physical characteristics and tendencies that may be inherited and from the difference in experience and environment that is each child's lot. The uniqueness of each family unit is obvious, but we tend to lose sight of how dissimilar the surroundings are even for children growing up under the same roof with the same parents. Each has his own position in birth order (which is discussed further in Chapter 2), with all that that entails.

Each benefits from a different degree of experience in his parents and a different measure of enthusiasm for bringing up children. Everything that is happening to those parents forms a part of the child's environment. Their health, their satisfaction or lack of it in their work, their friends, and their relatives will color the background against which a boy or girl develops. Parents' involvement or distress over larger issues in the neighborhood or the nation also has an impact.

The Pressures of Rapid Social Change

One condition affecting everyone in our society today is the overpowering swiftness of change, as Alvin Toffler documents in *Future Shock*. Adults, continually bombarded with unassimilable alterations in many phases of their lives, are less able to cope than they might be in a more stable world. Their inner equilibrium is thrown off balance. Small children feel the impact of the resulting anxious uncertainty in their parents.

Add this acceleration in the outer world to the child's own changes within his vastly expanding mental, social, and emotional boundaries, and one can understand the degree of pressure under which most preschoolers today are growing up.

The "Self-fulfilling Prophecy"

Other influences also contribute to the unique flavor of each personality. One of these has been labeled by Ralph Linton, an anthropologist, the "self-fulfilling prophecy." Parents form different expectations for each of their children. Whether or not they mean to, they push their young toward the fulfillment of those expectations.

"She's been shy since the day she was born," says a father of his four-year-old daughter. Now that the girl and her parents are convinced of her timidity, it is impossible to tell whether she has assumed the shrinking-violet role because it was imposed on her, or whether some inborn sensitivity has impelled her to shrink from new situations and strangers to a degree unusual for her age.

Because of the great individual variation among youngsters, especially during these years, and because so much growing takes place in so many directions, any overview must necessarily convey only a rough and sketchy idea of the changes in behavior and attainments that may occur.

Acquiring Skills

We cannot force growth, as that comes from within the individual, but we can provide a setting congenial to it.

We can take advantage of those periods in a youngster's life when he acquires certain skills quite easily and is ready for the new step. Usually, he gives some signal. He may put his readiness into words: "Can do self." Sometimes, he may simply go ahead and try the new step on his own.

Another indication that a specific kind of learning should not be delayed too long: there is evidence that some children who cannot stay dry during the night at four or five years of age had their toilet training delayed beyond the age of two-and-a-half or even three. Possibly delayed toilet training is partly responsible for bedwetting. (Chapter 9 goes into this question in greater detail.)

Essential Tasks of Growing

Not only are there favorable times for acquiring certain skills, but children also need to accomplish specific social and emotional tasks during stated periods. Mastery of these tasks lays a firm foundation for subsequent development. Otherwise, there may be weak spots in the personality that can be troublesome later.

One of the basic tasks for preschoolers, according to Erik Erikson, is the development of initiative, the discovery that they can safely try out their powers. The exploring, experimenting, and questioning to which the three-, four-, and five-year-olds devote themselves are ways in which they exercise initiative. In providing suitable opportunities for such activity, we are also supplying the setting for healthy growth. (More about this in Chapters 5 and 6.)

Along with initiative goes some guilt at times. The youngster is delighted with his recently acquired ability to run and climb, open and shut doors and drawers, lift and carry objects, put together and take apart whatever comes to hand, mold and shape malleable substances. All these activities are really forms of attack, conquest, and possession. In his imagination he becomes Batman or a ferocious beast and plays at, or daydreams about, all manner of daring exploits.

Deep inside himself, he knows he cannot, and must not, carry out his imaginings. He often becomes frightened and guilty because he has thought about being so powerful. A mild degree of guilt helps him become more "civilized." (See Chapter 7.)

Because preschoolers are ready to exercise some initiative, they are ready for greater independence. They also profit from experiences in which they can employ their newfound competencies. Some of our conflicts with them stem from our underestimating how much they can do for and by themselves. (For examples, see Chapters 4 and 9.)

One more growing job is to discover which sex one belongs to and that being either a boy or a girl is good. (This is the subject of Chapter 6.)

They Learn to Move More Smoothly

Development goes from the simple to the more complex and tends toward specialization in the use of muscles during these years. For instance, as he turns three, a youngster is still satisfied with banging a spoon on a pan or putting small saucepans inside larger ones and carrying them around not too steadily. He clutches objects he handles. As the coordination of the small muscles in his hands improves—and he becomes able to sit still for a few minutes—he enjoys fitting simple puzzles together. He uses a hammer at first just to pound, but soon to make an "airplane" out of two pieces of wood nailed together. He tries drawing with a crayon or pencil, can hold one quite readily and draw a crude figure with it.

Before he is six, he may try copying letters or printing his name. The two sticks nailed together no longer satisfy his desire to make an airplane. Now he can use a small saw or a coping saw. He tries to make more complicated airplanes or boats.

Paintings go from being mere blobs of color to being attempts to portray houses and trees or "scenes" that tell, roughly, a story. Block building, for both boys and girls, goes from a few blocks piled precariously one on the other to the intricate structures that five-year-olds like to leave standing for several days.

Greater specialization in the use of the large muscles of the trunk, legs, and arms also appears. Toddlers really "toddle," but the three-year-old strides along nimbly. By the time he is four or four-and-a-half he no longer puts his hands on the door frame to pull himself around a corner at top speed. Outdoors, the three-and-a-half-year-old becomes adept at climbing to the top of the jungle gym, if he has access to one. Before long, he tries swinging from one of the cross bars. On the swings, he can learn to propel himself by "pumping." For evidence of the physical development during these years, compare the performance of the five-and-a-half-year-old on the trapeze, the slide, the rings, and the climbing apparatus, where he is thoroughly at home and full of new tricks, with his hesitant approach to the playground about two years earlier.

Will They Slow Up?

If his parents are good walkers or climbers, the five-year-old has the stamina he lacked earlier to accompany them on short rambles. At four, he might have wilted on such excursions, and at three perhaps needed to be carried on the way home. Surefooted as he seems to be as he scrambles over rocks or climbs fences adroitly, the five-year-old still needs watching to keep him safe.

The increased coordination of the four-year-old is demonstrated by his ability to spin like a top, to hop, and, by the time he turns five, to skip. To go up and down stairs without putting both feet on a tread at the same time, and—dubious though the achievement may be in the eyes of the parents—to slide down the bannisters are among the typically "fourish" achievements.

Many a four- and five-year-old has both the flexibility and the coordination it takes to sit cross-legged with the foot of one leg on top of the knee of the other. Mothers, if they have been intrigued by yoga exercises, may try in vain to imitate this "lotus position."

Both girls and boys, during these years, like to imitate dance steps they have seen on television. They do so with increasing ease and grace. The fives seem so well able to keep in step that fond relatives are prompted to suggest that dancing lessons are now in order.

The five-year-old, if family finances permit or a hand-me-down is available, can usually graduate from a tricycle to a two-wheeler. Swimming, diving, and roller- or ice-skating in clumsy fashion may be attempted at four and almost mastered at five. Three-year-old swimmers, among those who have the chance to swim all year long, are not rare. L. Joseph Stone and Joseph Church, in *Childhood and Adolescence,* describe the alterations in appearance that accompany the preschooler's physical development:

> His proportions are changing. His legs grow faster than the rest of him. At age two they account for 34% of his length; by age 5, 44%, which approaches the half-and-half proportions of the adult. . . . As his legs lengthen and head growth slows drastically, he loses the top-heavy look of infancy and toddlerhood. As the cartilage and bones of his face develop and the fat pads in his cheeks dwindle, his countenance loses its babyish cast and becomes better defined and more like his adult self.

Understanding and Thinking Expand

Physical and mental growth combine, in the almost-six-year-old, to give him the capacity to grasp the fact that some feats are impossible because of his lack of skill, not because they are forbidden. Youngsters, before they leave the preschool period behind, have gained a degree of self-knowledge. They have learned something of their own limitations. They may have gone through, around four, a spell of braggadocio in which they assert their prowess in exaggerated statements. At five and a half, they may say quite realistically, "I can't do that," or, as one beautifully self-confident little girl put it, "I haven't learned to do that yet."

The five-year-old's sense of being himself, an individual who belongs to a particular family, has blossomed beyond what it was two years earlier. Ask a five-year-old where he lives and he will probably not only give you the street address but proudly add the city and state as well. That their country is composed of fifty states is too involved for most five-year-olds to understand, although they struggle with the concept of towns within states and states within the nation.

Communication Becomes More Fluent

As a conversationalist, the youngster at the end of the preschool years has gone far. At three, he may still have had a baby lisp, been unable to pronounce certain sounds, and had a limited and factual vocabulary. He could name many *things* around him, but the intangible eluded him.

At four he probably took pleasure in making up silly words that sent him and his contemporaries into uproarious laughter. "It's ugly. It's an ugly-pugly," says a four-year-old holding a worm in his hand.

"It's an ugly-pugly-wuggly wormy-squirmy-germy," says his companion, and both are off on a spree of nonsense rhyming.

The "how?" "when?" "why?" "what for?" and "who?" questions reach a peak when a youngster is around four and frequently are a source of exasperation to parents. Asking, and feeling that it is acceptable to ask, facilitates mental growth. (Chapter 5 is concerned with this subject.)

Developing Communication

In both clarity of pronunciation and fluency the advance from three- or four- to five-year-old ability is highlighted by what transpires in "Show and Tell" in kindergarten and nursery school. Kindergartners are eager to bring to school interesting subjects and to communicate facts.

"We haven't named our kittens yet, an' my Dad says we can't keep them all an' their mother borned them yesterday an' when we couldn't find her she was in Mr. Foster's Chevy an' he lives next door to us an' he was mad!" may not be a model of lucid narrative, but it is a more intelligible kindergarten type of account than was given by that narrator's younger sister to her nursery schoolmates. Her version was, "Pansy's babies were in Mr. Foster's back seat and she licked them clean and he told my Daddy a lot of bad words about Pansy. You know what he said? He said to my Daddy. . . ." At this point the nursery school teacher, with a fairly good idea of what the irate Mr. Foster said, broke in to ask how many kittens there were. "Oh, lots and lots, like zillions," was the answer, since to a four-year-old, five is as much as a zillion.

The kindergartner, when asked the same question, answered, "I have to think. Maybe I don't know. They were sort of brown and white, I guess."

Even a bright four-year-old has difficulty in dealing with the fact that an object or a group of objects has color, size, and weight, and that in the case of a group, number, too, is one of its attributes. That the biggest may not be the heaviest, or the oldest, if animals or people are involved, is also confusing. Around the time boys and girls enter first grade, they usually have some notion that a group of objects or people may be alike in one respect but different in others, but they are not yet at home with this concept.

Show a five-and-a-half-year-old a jumble of triangular and square blocks of various sizes and colors and ask him to group together those that are of the same shape, or size, or color, and he may be able to do it. Intricate classification is often beyond him. A year later he will probably have mastered the concept of classification

Reasoning Is Concrete and Personal

The title of the delightful children's book *A Hole Is to Dig,* by Ruth Krauss, is an example of how a three- or four-year-old perceives objects. Asked "What is a hole?" or "What is a cat?" he will probably tell you one thing about it, the thing that is most important to him at the moment. "A hole is to dig," if he likes to dig; "A cat is to pet," or "A cat is to have kittens," if kittens fascinate him (not because he has any feeling for the ongoing quality of life). His thinking is egocentric and centered on the particular and concrete.

The five-year-old might tell you that a cat likes milk, or that cats scratch, or that his cat is named Nipper, but he would not be able to answer that question by saying, "A cat is an animal," nor would the fact that a cat lives in a house with people be significant to him.

The Intricacies of Kinship Can Be Puzzling

Classification of objects and animals is not as perplexing as the relationships of members of the family, which throw the three- and four-year-old completely. The increase in four-generation families has made complications for some children. The fact that great-grandmother is the mother of grandma is incredible, for both women look pretty much the same age to their youngest descendants. Besides, how could grandma ever have been a child with a mother of her own? That a child's father is also the uncle of several children varying greatly in age and size is also hard to understand. The custom of some husbands and wives of calling each other "mother" and "father" does not help the preschool child get relationships straight, either. Youngsters who must cope with the concept of stepparents, stepbrothers, and stepsisters get relationships really tangled.

By the time a child is "going on six," if he has had patient explanations of family relationships and is well acquainted with relatives bearing different labels, kinship patterns tend to become clearer.

Inferences Seem Like Magic

The inferences through which adults arrive at conclusions, see "cause and effect" relationships, seem magical to preschoolers.

"I want to go to Roddy's house," says a four-and-a-half-year-old, as he and his mother start out for the supermarket.

"Roddy won't be home now," says his mother.

"How do *you* know?" says the small skeptic.

Since they will pass Roddy's house anyway, Mother consents to ring the bell, and, as she predicted, nobody is home.

The four-and-a-half-year-old is impressed. "You are a magic-mommy," he says in astonishment.

"No magic. I know Roddy and his mother almost always go to his grandmother's on Wednesday, and this is Wednesday. See?"

Magic Thinking

The preschooler's primitive "magic thinking" also shows in his tendency to endow toys and other objects with feelings. A four-year-old will say, "My dolly was lonesome, so I'm telling her a story," or "That spoon is bad. It keeps falling down on the floor. Spoon, I'm going to spank you if you fall down again."

Imaginary companions who play a large part in the lives of many three-and-a-half- and four-year-olds usually begin to fade out (often with a violent end, like being lost in a sewer) from the thinking of five-and-a-half-year-olds.

Another facet of magic thinking is the tendency of three-, four-, and to some extent five-year-olds to attribute everything that occurs to somebody's arranging it. "Why did they make it snow today?" or "Why do they make leaves fall off trees?" That is about as far as they get with cause and effect in the preschool years, but they are on their way.

As set forth in detail in Chapter 7, preschoolers have an unreal conception of their own responsibility for "bad things" that may happen. They equate thinking about something bad with doing something bad. The fives are still troubled by the fear that they have brought about catastrophe, if it strikes them even indirectly. Whether any of us gets over this notion completely is an interesting question.

Ideas About Time

Preschool children are "here-and-now" creatures. Three-year-olds distinguish morning, afternoon, and night, but "day after tomorrow" or "next week" are impossible for them to envisage. "At supper time" or "after one more sleep" have more meaning than "six o'clock" or "tomorrow." Five-year-olds can join in the planning for the next day, or a few days ahead, but "next summer" is too distant to be real. They may know the hour they go to bed or the time they get up in the morning, but a more detailed awareness of time is usually not within their scope, though this depends somewhat on how "time-conscious" the household is. For a preschooler to wait an hour for his father to come home is as trying as for his father to wait all day for a cup of coffee.

To look back to a time when he was not alive is difficult, even at five. The boy who asked his grandfather, "What did you watch before there was TV?" could not comprehend a world so different from his own that it offered nothing "to watch." If the kindergartner attempts to consider history, he tends to telescope Washington, Lincoln, and "before there were moon landings" into a mysterious dark age.

Five-year-olds have come far, but they may deceive us by glibly using terms they have picked up from older children on TV and which they do not really understand. Because they pay attention to inconsequential details to which preoccupied adults are oblivious, they may appear to have astonishing memories. Our son or daughter may be able to tell us the color of the automobile of a visitor a week ago or recall that "Mommy had on her pink scarf last time she took me to the dentist." If we try to skip part of a well-loved story, the older preschoolers will probably catch us and insist on the authentic version!

Relations with Others

To gain an idea of how far youngsters have come in their ability to get along with others between age three and the end of age five, contrast the first day of a group of threes in nursery school with opening day in first grade.

The nursery school probably requires that a parent or someone the child knows well remain with him during the first session. Many of the children stay quite close to the adult who brought them. They pay scant attention to the other children, and not much more to the teacher. When one child does approach another, he may touch, pinch, or prod, rather than talk. Communication is likely to be in brief phrases. Exploration of the play materials and the nursery school setup, except on the part of the most self-assured, is likely to be tentative, in spite of encouragement from the teacher and her assistants.

Two or three children may play alongside each other, but cooperative play, in which views are exchanged and each child takes a definite role, is not to be expected in the first weeks of nursery school. (More about this in Chapter 3.)

Snatching toys away from another child or preempting a firetruck or a doll bed and refusing to relinquish it is the play style for the majority of children on the first day. Tears or a show of anger are near the surface for many of the youngsters from time to time and frequently break out.

The Contrasts in First Grade

Now look at the first-grader who is probably left at the door of the classroom by a parent or an older brother or sister. He is likely to be proud of coming to first grade, even if somewhat awed by it.

He understands that his teacher will be the authority and that his parents are not the only adults to whom he listens. He may listen to his teacher eagerly, fearfully, or sullenly, but he listens.

The rather aimless exploration of surroundings that characterized the three-year-old on his first day in nursery school has been replaced, for most first-graders, by a purposeful examination of the classroom.

The boys and girls understand the use of the materials they find, such as books, paper, crayons, chalk boards, and chalk. If there are fish in an aquarium or other kinds of pets or plants, pictures on bulletin boards, or shells, rocks, pumpkins, or autumn leaves on display, the child may comment, often critically, on them.

If the teacher hands our drawing materials and allows a free choice of subjects, most of the children will have an idea of what they want to draw before they begin. The scrawling and scribbling of the three-year-olds has been left behind.

Many first-graders may be shy the first day, but chattiness and an effort to impress others are also present. If members of the class have been together in kindergarten or know one another from neighborhood play, "best friends" may gravitate toward one another. Conversations, establishing where one lives, one's name, and, to some degree, one's competence and sophistication as to TV programs, are struck up between new acquaintances. Cooperative play comes easily to most, although arguments and cries of "No fair," You cheater, you!" and similar complaints abound.

Impulsiveness Decreases

Discussing the changes in his daughter and her friends between their third and sixth birthdays, a father said:

> At three they belonged to the "I want what I want when I want it" school of thought. They couldn't wait. They were entirely creatures of impulse. I wouldn't say they are exactly patient now, but they aren't quite as quick to fly into a rage or panic if they have to wait. They may ask twenty times, "When will my Mommy be here?" but they are not so likely to weep or say Mommy is bad or they don't love her any more.

A mother who was asked what changes she felt were significant in her youngsters' response to their contemporaries during these years, named the development of sympathy as one of the salient advances:

> By the age of five, you could see what was really sympathy showing up. One

youngster would comfort another who had been mistreated, or would come and look for me so I could do something. Of course, that didn't mean that the one who showed sympathy today wouldn't dish out a bit of mistreatment tomorrow.

As Stone and Church point out, sympathy is allied to leadership, another social trait that emerges in many youngsters, in different forms, around the age of five. Both traits come out of a rudimentary understanding of how other children feel and a capacity for responding to their feelings.

Although violent outbursts and tantrums tend to diminish and often disappear in emotionally healthy children during the later preschool years, boys and girls have by no means attained stability or serenity. Their feelings are still changeable, frequently overwhelming. A five-year-old may have more fears than he had at three, as both his understanding of real events and his ability to conjure up imaginary dangers have increased. (Chapters 7 and 8 deal with this.)

More People Included in Their Affections

The five-year-old's capacity for giving affection has expanded. Adults among his relatives and outside the family are included in his affections and fondly talked of when they are absent from his circle. A favorite aunt may be wanted at a birthday party. A friendly neighbor may find our five-year-old on her doorstep at all hours of the day.

The fours and fives have advanced beyond regarding their contemporaries as little more than objects, but they enjoy one another's company for what each can add to an undertaking. There is a strong flavor of opportunism and hardly a trace of loyalty in the "friendships" of five-year-olds. "I miss Tammy awfully," says her neighbor, aged four and a half, but when Tammy returns from her brief stay with a grandparent and goes next door to find this friend who could not wait for her return, the friend may be playing with another child and not inclined to include Tammy in what is going on. Social skills, except in a few children who seem to be positively gifted that way, are not in the repertoire of the four- and five-year-olds.

They Want to Grow Up, But . . .

Fresh attainments bring a preschooler pride and satisfaction. Sometimes the five-year-old seems to be operating on a level so much beyond his usual performance that we may say of him, "He is doing better than he knows how to do."

Yet sometimes, with visible relief, he will slide back to a more babyish form of response or activity. This retreat may be in the service of development. Perhaps he needs a rest, socially and emotionally, so that he can pull himself together and once more forge ahead. Development is not an ever-upward process.

Our children are probably growing more than we are aware of in our day-to-day dealings with them. We can afford, much of the time, to trust the forces of growth and development if we provide a good setting for them.

An old song goes, "Turn around and you're two,/Turn around and you're four,/ Turn around and you're a young man going out of my door." And indeed, our five-year-old, as he turns six, is, in his own fashion and at his own level, as he enters first grade, a young man going out of our door.

---

2 *When There Are Siblings—And When There Are None*

THE CURRENTS OF feeling that flow back and forth between brothers and sisters etch a pattern into the life of the family and into the personality of each of the children. At times, these feelings are predominantly charged with affection and admiration, at other times with anger and envy. They may influence a youngster's attitudes toward other people as he is growing up—even throughout his life.

Both love and resentment toward a brother or sister are likely to exist at the same moment. Contradictory feelings may be so mingled that behavior is inconsistent.

The dilemma of one four-year-old may have a familiar ring. This little girl complained to her mother that an older sister was "a mean old boss."

"Then don't play with her this afternoon. You can play by yourself or with your friend Ruthie," said the mother.

"Oh, no, I won't do *that!* I have more fun with Sis," was the answer.

Here is one condition that cannot be blamed on present-day developments! As legend and folklore attest, conflict between children in the family has existed since the beginning of time and in all known societies in which one mother takes care of several children.

From what sources do these currents of feeling flow? What are some approaches that may prove useful when a new baby is expected?

How Can We Help?

How can parents help a young child handle his feelings of rivalry so that he is not overwhelmed by them?

What steps can parents take to cultivate friendliness between the children?

To what extent does the position of being eldest, in the middle, or youngest color a child's picture of himself and influence his behavior?

What attitudes and what practical measures will tend to help each child enjoy the benefits and reduce the hazards inherent in his position?

Since the first child in a family is for a time an only child, how can the potential handicaps of being an "only," temporarily or permanently, be overcome?

Final answers to these questions are hardly possible, yet increased understanding of the complex relationship of those who share the same parents may help ease feelings all around.

Sources of Conflict Are Universal

Rivalry can be toned down but not prevented entirely, even though we "do all the right things." Indeed, a certain amount of resentment between the children in the family can be the means of their learning how to control and express competitiveness and aggressive feelings in constructive, socially useful ways.

A small child is possessive. He would like nothing better than to have mother and father all to himself. Sharing anything is hard, but sharing one's parents is all but unbearable in the early years. Look at the way the most amiable three-year-old strives for attention when his mother and a neighbor are having a cup of coffee and he is excluded from the conversation. The small child does not comprehend that parental affection expands to meet the demands of several children. Neither do the three to fives like to give. They much prefer being on the receiving end of good things, tangible and intangible. Yet, in countless ways they are required to give to both younger and elder brothers and sisters in the course of any day—a second source of friction.

Learning to Share

Sharing and giving need to be learned through experiences that are not intolerable. Such learning takes place with less pain and greater psychic economy within a friendly, accepting family.

Competition is characteristic of our society. Some students of human behavior say that this reflects the universal early struggles among the young to capture parental affection. Others say that competitiveness is fostered because adults introduce the techniques of the market place into family life, turning it into a rat race. Certainly, "Let's see who can do the best," or "Are you going to let your sister get ahead of you?" as a theme in family life heightens competition. Probably competitiveness stems from both inner and outer pressures, but in either case it is a further source of resentment between children in a family.

A more obvious reason for antagonisms was pointed out by a father after a long weekend at home with a three-year-old and a four-and-a-half-year-old. "No wonder our boys are always grabbing things away from each other and tattling," he said to his wife. "Do you realize how much they are together? Just being with *anybody* that steadily would make you snap at him pretty often. When one of them says to the other 'Go away!' maybe he's suffering from an overdose of brother."

The Wells of Affection Are Deep

Both the human condition and the way our lives are organized make a certain amount of resentment between the children inevitable, but at the same time, powerful bonds of affection also exist. Over and over, one child identifies with the sorrows or disappointments, the achievements or good fortune of another and grows closer to that one in doing so.

When five-year-old Patsy, whose older sister had had a bad fall, said to their mother, "Em needs you tonight. She'd feel better if you slept in my bed and I'll sleep in the living room on the couch," she demonstrated sincere concern for Em's welfare.

Solidarity often is enhanced by the alliances the children form and the conspiracies they hatch against their elders. Because they discover they can rely on one another at times, a mutuality takes root, although it may be a long time blossoming.

No matter how much the children may quarrel among themselves, let a child who is an outsider attack one of them, and the others in the family will rush to aid the victim—at least most of the time. Even an accusation of wrongdoing or a reprimand from an adult directed at one youngster may rally the others to his defense. Of course, that does not happen invariably. One brother or sister may gloat over another's being out of favor today and then take his part against the grown-ups tomorrow. Each time two or more become allies, their loyalty to one another tends to be reinforced.

Unfamiliar Routines Are Upsetting

A third strong force drawing the children together at an early age, although it is not always apparent, is their conviction that the rules and customs of their own home are the "right" and only way for life to be conducted. When a brother and sister went to stay with neighbors for a few days while their parents were away, they were distressed because routines were different from those to which they were accustomed. Still, their shared knowledge that baths should be taken before supper, and not at bedtime as their hostess decreed, or that eggs and bacon were the proper fare for breakfast and not for lunch, sustained them and raised the confidence each had in the other.

An indirect bit of evidence that children are more attached to those with whom they are growing up than one might suppose is cited in *Review of Child Development Research* by Martin L. and Lois W. Hoffman. Children's choice of playmates tends to mirror the setup in their own families. Eldest children are more likely than others to play with younger ones. Considering that at an early age the eldest is often already quick to complain about having to play with or watch out for his juniors, such choice is, indeed, surprising. "Also," say the Hoffmans, "though children generally prefer others of the same sex as playmates, preference for those of the opposite sex was more frequently expressed by those with a sibling of the opposite sex than by those without."

Out of incidents in which children identify themselves with the feelings of one another and provide mutual emotional support and care, brotherly—and sisterly—love grows. It is an emotion parents need to tend, while accepting the inevitability of rivalry. The mere fact that some anger and jealousy are unpreventable does not mean that unlimited quantities of destructive behavior need be tolerated. Since opportunities to build friendliness are frequent, let us examine how we can turn them to good account.

Getting Ready for a New Baby

When the announcement is made to a small child that a brother or sister will be added to the family, how does he view it? If he is the only offspring, he may interpret his parents' reason for "wanting another" as evidence that he himself is less than satisfactory. To a three- or four-year-old, not liking what one has is the obvious reason for wanting another, be it a toy, a pair of shoes, or a friend.

Realizing how dubious the value of this anticipated addition seems to a small child, parents are sometimes tempted to resort to overselling the immediate benefits. The new baby will not be a playmate for a long time, nor will he, for the most part, be "lots of fun to have around" for his elder brother or sister. Parents can save themselves and their eldest some bad moments if they do not put themselves in a position in which their child can say, "You fooled me." One father relates:

> We learned the hard way that tricks backfire. Asking, "Wouldn't you like to have a baby sister?" or saying, "It will be your baby," are really pretty shabby tricks. Much better to let the older one get angry at Mommy and Daddy for having such a foolish idea as having another baby than to pretend the decision was his.

Timing the Announcement

The months of pregnancy are long for everyone, especially the young child to whom a few weeks can seem an eternity. Too early an announcement is unnecessary, but just when he shall be told the news depends, among other things, on how many changes in his life will be taking place because of the new arrival. He needs at least a few weeks or a month or two to become accustomed to the idea. One mother reports:

> The smartest thing I ever did was to let Pete see two or three small babies being fed and bathed and cared for. Seeing those other babies cuddled by their mothers was no threat to Pete, and the firsthand acquaintance with how utterly helpless they were dispelled any illusions about what a newborn baby is like. I told him that he had been a baby and I had taken care of him just that way, so he knew he hadn't lost out on anything.

A nice balance can be maintained between making preparations for the coming event a part of family life and letting those preparations become the central fact in existence. A small child enjoys assisting in washing and sorting baby clothes when they are brought out of storage, helping to rearrange furniture to accommodate the refurbished crib, and similar homely matters. (Answering questions of the "Where is the baby now?" variety is discussed in Chapter 4.)

A youngster usually fares better if the timing of major adjustments such as starting nursery school, or giving up his bed with sides for a full-sized bed, occur well before the baby is on the scene. If he has a chance to become acquainted with the person who will take care of him while his mother is in the hospital, that separation will be less difficult.

A good-bye from mother when she departs for delivery will tend to prevent the feeling that she has just vanished.

When Babyhood Looks Like the Good Life

In spite of all precautions, a baby in the house calls for sharp changes in daily life. The nature, the timing, and the intensity of the protest against these changes on the part of those archconservatives, the preschool youngsters, vary from family to family. For each child, dissatisfaction comes and goes. Each will, at times, take delight in "helping" with the baby's care, admiring minute toes and fingers, exclaiming over a first smile, but each will also at times decide that "being big" is flat, stale, and unprofitable, as three-year-old Sheila did. To her, it seemed that the baby was loved and played with precisely because he was helpless. If demanding a bottle, crying frequently, and wetting and soiling were the way to her parents' heart, she too would be helpless.

Sheila's parents were inclined to hold the little girl sternly to standards they knew she could meet. When this only added to her misery and uncooperativeness, they listened to an older relative who had lived through similar behavior while rearing her own children: "Give Sheila all the comfort you can, is my advice. Tell her, 'O.K. We'll let you be like a baby in some ways for a while, but being three years old is really more fun.' Go along some of the way—like letting her have a bottle occasionally, zipping zippers for her, and that sort of thing, but don't let her beat a complete retreat. And you'd better prove to her that being her age is worth the effort. You know, let her go places with her father on Saturdays or Sundays. And eat dinner with you sometimes instead of having to go to sleep at six o'clock the way a baby does."

Safety Valves for Strong Feelings

Some children will suggest that having had the baby in the house for a few weeks is enough of such nonsense and it's time he was sent back to the hospital or disposed of in some less humanitarian fashion. Some few youngsters attempt such a disposal on their own. Others may deny the baby exists or ignore him entirely. Some may be extravagantly solicitous, literally trying to smother him with love.

A new baby brings a few problems in his wake for parents, too, and being urged to devote more time to playing with, reading to, or just cuddling the other young ones may seem more than can be expected of anyone. Still, the best investment mothers and fathers can make of their time often is to help those members of the family recently out of babyhood feel wanted, approved of, and "special."

A young child is sustained, too, by knowing that the parents accept his anger, and that his resentment against the baby is quite usual. "It's all right if you don't like your new brother sometimes. When I was as big as you are, I got mad at babies too, but after a while I got to like my sister and brother. You can tell me how you feel, but I won't let you do anything to hurt the baby." Statements along such lines offer a small child the protection he needs when his jealousy becomes frighteningly intense. Happily, children frequently find safety valves of their own.

Some Alternatives

Small girls may turn to dolls, and both boys and girls may use stuffed animals or puppets as objects of tender care or as babies who are soundly spanked because "This one is so bad today I can't stand it any more."

Mother or father may be drawn into playing that she (or he) is the baby while the child takes the role of a parent. As a variation on this theme, the small child may want to take the part of the baby. "Let's play I cry all night so you have to hold me," Vera often suggested to her mother. Vera had hit on a device that brought her comfort in several ways. She achieved the consolation of being held and rocked, which helped her to identify with the baby and to have more kindly feelings toward him. At the same time, she was testing her mother, since she was asking, "Would you love me if I were a baby who cried all the time?"

Such safety valves are all useful and frequently resorted to by a child as brothers and sisters are growing up together as well as when new babies complicate life.

Forestalling Trouble

Experienced mothers have discovered that it is usually easier to ward off quarrels than to settle them. When disagreements are worked out peaceably or circumvented, the children learn that there are better ways of solving their problems with one another than resorting to name-calling or blows.

Avoiding troubles calls for a sensitive ear and an eye alert to danger signals. Among those signals are increasingly shrill voices, extreme "silliness," aimless running around at top speed, or laughter that has ceased to be good-humored and is verging on hysteria. When children have reached that stage, they take offense at the slightest word or touch from a brother or sister. Controls have worn thin and they can no longer stop themselves.

Usually children are relieved, deep inside themselves, if an adult stops them when they are too wound up to unwind themselves. Intervening with a suggestion for a quieter kind of play, a few minutes of affectionate attention, a story or a song may ease the tension that has been building up. Television programs, if carefully selected, may be a resource, but some programs for children who are already excited may be overstimulating rather than soothing.

Watch for the trouble spots in the day's routine, when resentment between the children tends to run high. In some households trouble erupts during preparations for breakfast, especially if mother is not her cheeriest before her second cup of coffee, or father is rushing to get off to work. The less avoidable strain the children are under at that time, the less likely they are to tease one another. A minor change in procedures, such as postponing getting dressed until after breakfast, may start the day with less squabbling among the youngsters.

If the half hour before supper is a period when animosity tends to boil over, the reason is likely to be sheer fatigue, or hunger. Sometimes a before-supper glass of fruit juice or a few carrot sticks can improve dispositions. Some mothers find that the meal on the stove can get along with less attention than the children can. This is a good time to introduce a quiet activity the children can enjoy together.

Cultivating Friendliness

The effort to discover some kinds of play our small children can enjoy together pays off, as it heightens their regard for one another as desirable playmates and likeable individuals. It is helpful to have in reserve some activities that will fill an odd moment of waiting or longer stretches of time. Colored pencils and paper, for instance, may be lifesavers for the ten minutes during which an excited three- and four-year-old are waiting to be picked up by Grandma.

In one family the small children get along quite well when they are allowed to dress up and "play wedding" or "going away for a visit" with a few of their parents' old clothes.

In another household, the four- and five-year-old are most agreeable to each other when they are allowed to cut pictures out of magazines and catalogues, albeit rather crudely, and paste them on sheets of wrapping paper saved for that purpose. When the older girl said to her mother one day, "Ginny is so crabby today. If you let us make scrapbooks, maybe she'll feel better," the mother felt that her daughter had taken a giant stride in assuming responsibility for a sister.

One point of contention between small brothers and sisters is that the younger too often loses, destroys, or misappropriates the treasures of the elder. Since these treasures often look like sheer junk, parents, too, tend to overlook their value to their owners. In the interest of promoting good feelings, we can usually arrange for each child to have some shelf, or drawer, or corner where he can keep possessions that are not to be touched without his permission. Some playthings may be for the use of all the youngsters in the family, but a favorite stuffed animal or picture book does not have to be shared.

Sometimes the best means of furthering friendliness is to arrange for occasional separations. If one of the youngsters goes to play at a friend's house, the other may have mother for himself, perhaps do something special with her, which is healing balm for jealousy.

The Value of Separation

"Whole-family activities" are not always the most desirable form of recreation. If one youngster goes on an excursion with father, even though it is only to watch boats on the river or to the playground in the park, while mother takes another for a treat suited to his age and tastes, everyone may be refreshed.

One of the by-products of separations is that they drive home a point we cannot make too emphatically: everyone is different; everyone need not do exactly the same thing. Young children close in age and constantly together may be so concerned lest one get more of whatever is being apportioned than the other does that they lose the satisfaction of being themselves or of developing an individuality of their own.

Separations also have other uses. After Bruce spent the night for the first time at his grandparents' house without his younger brother, he announced on returning home, "Next time Dickie should come along. I didn't have anyone to play with."

"Being Fair" Can Be a Booby Trap

We are so imbued with the need for "fairness" in dealing with our children that we sometimes wrongly equate it with "equal treatment" and sacrifice the opportunity to meet a need of one, lest it deprive his brother or sister of having exactly the same attention. Because of an illness, starting school, or perhaps a birthday, one child may become temporarily the center of attention. When such a situation arises, we need not feel guilty, although the others in the family may be artists at exploiting any tendencies we have in that direction.

"You stayed at the hospital all night with Amy when she broke her leg. I want you to stay with me, 'cause I had a bad dream," Amy's younger brother may complain. Some suitable assurance is surely in order, but *not* on the basis suggested by Amy's brother.

If every situation is not treated as if attention could be weighed and measured, and each child has found out that his special needs are always met, the three- to five-year-olds will less often raise the cry, "It isn't fair." Small children who have seen that "their turn will come" feel more kindly toward those with whom they must share their parents' love.

Half a Loaf Is Often Better Than None

In the interest of promoting congeniality, we can demonstrate the technique and the value of compromising. If two youngsters want different bedtime stories, and time is too short to read both, we could give them abbreviated versions so that each hears part of his favorite tale.

When one must wait his turn while his brother is on the swing, we can try to find something agreeable to occupy the child who is forced to wait. The capacity to give up part of what we want and cheerfully accept what we can get develops through practice and through finding that compromises bring more satisfaction than sulking.

Parents are laying the foundations for friendliness, too, when they build up each child's self-respect. Letting each one know he is loved and accepted as he is, and that he does not have to be a carbon copy of another member of the family to gain approval, also helps him accept his brothers and sisters.

Exhortations such as "Why can't you be like your brother?" or "If you would only try as hard as your sister" damage self-esteem and foment discord.

Not Position, But How It Is Dealt With, Counts

The relationship between children in a family is influenced, too, by the way their position in order of birth is handled. Being the eldest, youngest, or one of those in the middle may turn out to be an advantage, a disadvantage, or a mixture of both, depending on what each position means to the child and to his parents.

A strong bond, not always consciously recognized, may exist between a parent and the son or daughter who occupies the same rank in birth order as that parent did. By sheer law of averages, both parents are not apt to have been in the same position in their respective families. In the usual course of events, a mother who was, for example, a middle child may be partial to her own middle one, but that partiality is offset because the father, who was the youngest in his household, tends to favor his youngest.

In the Grady family, both Mr. and Mrs. Grady had been "youngests." When their sons were three and four and a half years old, the Gradys admitted to each other that every time the elder boy mistreated the younger one, no matter how much of a pest the younger one had been, they saw themselves as they were at an early age in their own families. They recognized their intense identification with their youngest son.

The moral of this incident is that if parents occupied comparable positions as they were growing up, they need to watch themselves lest they shortchange a particular child, or children.

Prestige and Pressure for the Eldest

The eldest has, undeniably, one advantage. His achievements delight and astonish his parents as the attainments of subsequent offspring rarely do. Then, too, his development is not compared to that of those who have preceded him, as is inevitably the case with the others. The magic and the legends surrounding the firstborn from time immemorial attest to how important the eldest is to his parents.

The eldest usually lords it over the younger ones and usually receives from them, much of the time, an admiration that can be a tonic to his spirits. If the eldest is a boy, with younger sisters, he is looked up to as he may never be again in his lifetime.

Yet, a firstborn pays dearly for his prestige. His parents' pride in him is matched by their lack of experience. "We learned more from our first child than he learned from us," parents often say. "When I think of all we expected from our eldest and the responsibilities we gave him, well, I can only marvel that he turned out as well as he did," a mother admits.

The "Only Child" Hangover

A study carried on by J. B. Gilmore and Edward Zigler, to determine how birth order was tied up with a need for approval or reward, found that eldest children were more dependent on encouragement and praise from others when they were under stress than were later children in the families studied. The investigators suggest that perhaps eldests, who were "only children" in their earliest years, became accustomed to emotional support from their parents and are therefore frustrated when such support is absent.

Because so much is expected of him, and because, too, he is likely to have a certain prejudice against babies and their ways, the eldest in a family may be old and serious beyond his years.

"Seniority rights" granted him help to compensate for drawbacks his position brings with it. Staying up later than his juniors, being allowed somewhat more freedom to go about on his own when he is four and a half or five, may seem like small matters, but they are cherished privileges.

At least, the eldest need not be held down to the level of the younger ones because of convenience. "Linda can wait to start nursery school until her brother is old enough to go." "Linda is really too old for a nap, but I make her take one anyway because her brother still needs one." Such treatment over the years, plus having little brother at her heels when she played with other children, made Linda resentful of him. Being kept to routines and activities suited to a child a year and a half her junior also interfered with her development.

Allowing for slight differences in age as well as for diversity of tastes and temperaments may seem to complicate the parents' task for the moment, but the basic difference between a family and an institution is that a family can, most of the time, provide for the special requirements of each of its members. Such provision is a good setting for healthy development.

Being in the Middle

Proverbially, the middle child—or children in the middle—are thought to be at a disadvantage, not sure where they belong, likely to get lost in the shuffle. This widespread notion is far from accurate. Being the one in the middle is what the child and his parents make of it. The mental picture the boy or girl forms of his situation, based on how he is treated and what he hears, makes it favorable or unfavorable. Actually, more latitude is inherent in this position than in being in the better-defined spot of eldest or youngest.

If a middle child feels neglected, as Pauline did, she will strive for attention by fair means or foul. Pauline had more than her share of problems but not more than her share of anything else. That sad state of affairs was not the result of her position in birth order in itself. Her own nature and some unhappy circumstances in the family during her early years were, in combination, stronger influences than being the second of three children.

Burt, another middle child, fairly reveled in the distinction he was given by being the only one who had both an elder and a younger brother. By the time he was five, he had figured out that he could get the privileges of seniority that the eldest enjoyed. At the same time he could join forces with his three-year-old brother when that suited his purpose. He was an aggressive boy with a positive talent for landing on his feet. Perhaps because he was impelled, without being aware of it, to make an extra effort to win affection, or because he was by nature friendly and full of fun, he went out of his way, even at an early age, to be agreeable. None of the legendary burdens of the middle child weighed on him!

Special Privileges

Parents may need to be imaginative in finding ways to let a middle child be special or get recognition. In one family, the middle girl was occasionally permitted to do something that symbolized being "big" before her older brother had done it. She was the first in the family to go to her grandparents' home in another city for a week's visit. Her mother also built up in her a proud feeling of being "special" because she was the only girl in the family.

If need be, distinction can come for the middle child through being the only son or only daughter, "being the only one who has red-gold hair like great-grandmother Flannery had," or "being the one with a smile like her Daddy's." This needs to be handled carefully, however, so that the child does not feel it is his only reason for being loved or his only claim to distinction.

A hazard for the middle one of three is that the oldest and the youngest may ally themselves, which frequently happens. Then the middle one is, at best, left out. At worst, he or she becomes the butt of the teasing of the two others.

Mothers and fathers can take care, too, that in protecting the youngest from the tricks of the elder ones they do not leave the middle one defenseless. One middle child, looking back, says he was always punished if he attacked his small brothers, but his parents did nothing to protect him from his domineering older sister and the havoc his younger brothers too often made of his toys and projects. Although his memories of the wrongs done him were doubtless exaggerated, his parents probably did not guard his rights as carefully as they might have.

Does It Pay to Be Youngest?

The very circumstances that may hamper the older ones in a family often work to the advantage of the youngest. Parents are more relaxed, more experienced, and not in such a hurry to see this youngster grow up. The youngest never suffers displacement and has plenty of time to finish the business of being a baby. He is often given great affection and indulged in a manner the others may never have enjoyed. A father relates:

> When our youngest was born we knew we were capable of being reasonably good parents. Both my wife and I were scared when our first child was small. We were so uptight about everything, from the way we held her to our fear that she wouldn't measure up in some way, that we hardly had any fun with her. Our youngest was a "good baby" and has been easy to live with these three years. Maybe we are easier to live with and so he's more self-confident than his sister ever was.

A mother says:

> The advantage the youngest in our family has had is that we have more perspective on life, a better idea of what's important and what isn't. We don't feel it's the end of the world if we have to cancel an evening's plans because he's sick and we don't want to leave him with the usual teen-age sitter. I've learned that a three-and-a-half-year-old's tall tales aren't "lies," and that if he takes something that isn't his he's not "stealing."

"The best thing that happens to the youngest, from what I've seen," reports another parent, "is that they've got the older ones not just to play with and to defend them in the neighborhood, but to be models for them and to learn from. Youngest children seem to be more mature. Our younger girl is more mature at four than her older sister was at six."

Boons of a Large Family

A final advantage a youngest often benefits from in a large family is that he finds among the older children, perhaps in the eldest, one who forms a special attachment for him and to whom he is especially attached. That one may become his protector, his mentor, and his ideal—almost like another mother or father, but not as remote as a parent is likely to be.

On the debit side for the youngest is the fact that although parents may be wiser than they were, they are also older. If they have had several children, they may be a bit weary of the duties parenthood imposes. Being five or ten years older than they were when the first child was small, engaging in a rousing game of hide-and-seek or roughhousing with a vigorous four-year-old may be less fun than it was. Parents' meetings at nursery school or kindergarten, even the spring picnic for parents and children, may be a too-oft repeated scene to be interesting.

One who is far younger than the other children in the family may be either dragged unwillingly or left behind when vacations or excursions are planned chiefly with the older children in mind. If most of the conversation in the family is over the head of the youngest, and if his efforts to take part in it are continually belittled, he may feel, although he would not phrase it that way, that he is stuck in a backwater and cannot get into the mainstream of family life.

Plaints of "Youngests"

Jane was such a youngster. She had often heard conversation about "the wonderful time we had the summer before Jane was born." Her complaint was, "You had all the fun before you had me, and you used it all up. It isn't fair."

Another accusation some youngest children make is that they have "too many bosses." Indeed, one of the disguises, and a thin one at that, for hostility on the part of the elder brothers or sisters is bossiness toward their juniors.

The parents of a five-year-old girl who was constantly correcting, criticizing, and interfering with her three-year-old brother were worried about her behavior. They were aware that the boy was becoming at once too dependent on his sister and too angry at her for his own good.

"She means well, but about one tenth of her bossiness would be enough," the mother said when she was discussing the problem with her husband.

"Who says she means well?" the father demanded indignantly. He had had an older sister to contend with and on that account was not too charitable toward his daughter. "She's just trying to show us how superior she is to her brother. She's such a newcomer to halfway decent behavior herself that she has to keep proving to herself and to us that she knows what's right. If you ask me, she's getting to be a self-righteous little prig."

When his wife asked him what he proposed to do about their daughter, he said, "If she needs to boss something, we'll get her a kitten. That's what my mother did when my sister was driving me up the wall, and it was a good idea, too. She won't warp the kitten's personality, and maybe she'll let her brother alone for a while."

Children Learn from Each Other

In the daily interchanges between the children in the family, each is constantly learning from the others. Much as the skills and information they acquire in this way contribute toward their development, perhaps what they discover about the feelings of others and about their own feelings is even more valuable.

They can absorb, in small doses, an understanding of the principle that is so essential for emotional well-being: that it is possible to be angry at those one loves and to recover from that anger. They discover, too, that someone else's wrath may descend on you when you are quite innocent, but that you will survive without losing either self-respect or status. They are likely to accept more readily the fact that nobody can have the exclusive love and full-time attention of another human being, if they learn that lesson in the relatively protected setting of the family.

Another enduring truth that is usually instilled through the rough-and-tumble of brotherly and sisterly rivalry, if it exists in a not overwhelmingly intense degree, is that although nobody gives you the complete protection you sometimes would like to have, and everyone at times falls short of the trust you have placed in him, both protection and trustworthiness will probably be available from members of your family when you most need them.

Because moments of mutual affection come and go, in others and within oneself, the part-time absence of affection does not mean a lack of basic regard for those others nor does it weaken the potential for compatibility with them.

These are among the lessons that are taught, without anybody putting them into words, as the children in a family grow up with both love and friction as their daily fare.

"Only" Need Not Equal "Lonely"

The absence of opportunities for that kind of emotional learning is a disadvantage for the only child. The stereotype that he is selfish and spoiled is too often inaccurate as far as selfishness with material things is concerned. The necessity for sharing attention is harder for him to accept. The "spoiling" an only child may suffer from is likely to be an interference with his drive to do for himself. His capacity to be independent may be "spoiled," or at least the development of that capacity may be slowed down. When there is only one child in the family, parents may give him more protection than he needs or can profit from. The mother of an only son says:

> My husband and I magnified everything our boy did, both the good behavior and the bad. We never learned to be casual, and he didn't either. I think he took us too seriously. If there had been other children, he would have discovered that I'm likely to get very impatient when anyone is slow. He wouldn't have felt I was just disappointed in him and that he was "bad." He probably would have figured out, "Mom treats everybody like that."

In discussing the only child in his book *The Child, The Family and the Outside World,* Dr. D. W. Winnicott, a British psychiatrist, says:

> For all children, the big difficulty is the legitimate expression of hate, and the only child's relative lack of opportunity for expressing the aggressive side of his nature is a serious thing. Children who grow up together play games of all kinds, and so have a chance to come to terms with their own aggressiveness, and they have a valuable opportunity for discovering on their own that they mind when they really hurt someone they love.

"Only" Can Be "Different"

Another disadvantage of the only child is that he tends to be so much in the company of adults and is so eager to have their approval that he finds it hard to enter into the play and the conspiracies of his contemporaries. He does not know how to make common cause with them. He is likely to be serious and overconscientious, and as a result of his anxiety over doing wrong he may be somewhat timid.

Looking back on herself at the age of five, one woman relates:

> I only had to open my mouth for the other children to know I was in some way different. I used such big words! I wanted to play with the other children on the block, but at the same time they frightened me. I was so much more dependent on my parents' approval than they were. I couldn't have described the difference between me and my friends who had sisters and brothers, then, but what it amounted to was that if they were out of favor with their parents, they still had each other. If my parents were to get angry with me, which seldom happened, I was absolutely alone.

Many sound reasons for having only one child exist today. The youngster in that position does have the advantage of having his parents for himself. Not being required to share them at an early age gives his world a degree of stability and reinforces his trust in mother and father, who, after all, have not betrayed him by having another baby. That trust in his parents often facilitates his establishing trust in other people, too.

Substitute Siblings

Fortunately, parents can, to a great extent, fill in the lack of relationships with other children. Nursery school and play groups give an "only" a chance to be with others on a close and continuing basis. Cousins are almost a substitute for brothers and sisters for some only children. When family outings are planned, an only child can be encouraged to invite a friend to go along. Visits back and forth in the homes of other children, to spend the day or night, are a treat to the four- and five-year-olds.

These visits can be brief at first. An "only" may need his mother's presence in order to feel comfortable the first time he visits in a home strange to him. Not every visit will be a great success, but the discovery that on some days other children are agreeable and on other days they are less so is a vital one, too.

One of the benefits an only child reaps is that he learns to play by himself and to develop resources for being happily occupied. "Onlies" often have a rich imaginative life and may become more creative as a result.

A youngster may not be the only child in the family and yet be in the position of being "only." One girl in a large family of boys, one boy with a number of sisters, children widely separated in age, or a child who is markedly different from the others in the household may have the same needs for companionship with children outside the family as the one who is without brothers or sisters.

No child encounters all the forms of competition or affection that it is possible for preschoolers to be exposed to. No child experiences all the advantages or disadvantages that can come from his position in the family. Rarely is a youngster steadily drawn to or repelled by any one of his sisters or brothers. The ebb and flow, the variation in direction of those currents of affection and resentment, which exist side by side and often intermingle, give richness and flavor to the daily life of brothers and sisters and stimulate their growth in many directions.

3
Helping Your Child Get Along With Others

AN EARNEST YOUNG father brought his three-year-old to nursery school on opening day and remained to watch him for a few minutes. The boy stayed next to his father for a moment or two and then began tentatively to explore the room. He sat down at a table where puzzles were laid out, looked at the girl sitting next to him, fitted three or four pieces of the puzzle together, and moved on to explore the block corner. Here he stopped again, said something to another child, saw the toy fire engine in the middle of the floor, and made straight for it. He played with that briefly, then left it to watch two children kneading play dough at another table.

One of the volunteer assistants came up to the father and said, "Jeff seems fine. You don't have to stay, though of course you are welcome to."

"I'd like to stay until I see him making friends and cooperating," was the reply.

"In that case you may be around quite a while. The threes aren't up to much cooperation, and we don't hurry them into it. As for making friends, it looks to me as if Jeff is off to a good start."

Developing Sociability

This father is not unusual. Most parents, in their eagerness to have their children make friends and function well in a group, tend to be impatient with the slowness of the process. Sociability is an important facet of development, but it takes years to flower.

How can we expect threes, fours, and fives to behave with one another?

How can we help them learn to balance sharing and standing up for their own rights?

What about those who are too shy or are troublemakers?

How much and what kind of supervision do children need from adults as they play together in their own neighborhood?

Small children need to find out how to get along with grown persons outside the family, too, and that brings up the question of manners. Is there a place for good manners today?

Shall we send our children to nursery school, and if so, when? How shall we choose a nursery school?

Playmates Contribute to Growth

Playing with other children in the neighborhood, going back and forth between homes, contributes in vital ways to a child's development. Playmates are, first of all, fun. They also educate one another, although sometimes it may seem to parents that what their son or daughter learns from other children in the way of vocabulary or manners leaves much to be desired.

Growth in the ability to get along with others is one of the important directions in which children need to reach out during the preschool years. If the skills of cooperation and compromise are acquired before a boy or girl enters first grade, this will make his life in school easier.

As children play together, they gain practice in solving problems, taking in fresh ideas, responding flexibly to unfamiliar situations. They grow in all directions, sharpening their wits on one another's plans and supplementing one another's imaginative flights of fancy. Play is a child's way of learning and is important preparation for formal education. A child who misses out on the companionship of other children during these years is losing the chance to make the most of his potential for learning.

Tolerance Is an Individual Matter

Different children are ready at different ages for varying amounts of the society of their contemporaries. Some preschoolers will be at a more immature level of companionship than their age mates—which suits them. Youngsters will differ, too, in the length of time each can sustain the effort of being peaceably in the company of other children; and it often is an effort, as well as pleasure.

Some children will play with friends for two or three successive days and then want to stay at home and be near Mother for a day or two. Others are always ready for companionship.

When you suggest to another mother that her son or daughter come to play with yours, you need not feel slighted if she says this is one of those days when her child wants to "stay home with Mommy."

Mothers have their own needs for being with others and being alone. Sometimes, too, they are too overwhelmed with other responsibilities to get their child together with another youngster. When that occurs, nobody need feel deficient. "Honestly, I just can't, because . . ." followed by a recital of obligations and tasks is not a brush-off when you hear it from a friend or a woman you would like to have for a friend, nor is it a lame excuse when you resort to it yourself.

Parents may grow weary of being reminded of the tremendous variation in the ability to get along with others that children manifest. Yet it is only human nature to feel, "Why is Tina so quarrelsome when other children seem to play together without fights?" or "What's the use of taking Bobby to play with another little boy? After half an hour he either goes wild or wants to go home. Then the other kid and his mother are disgusted."

The reasons Tina or Bobby or anyone else cannot hold up as well as his or her contemporaries may be unrelated to sociability. Other events in the child's life, or his rapid growth in other directions at this particular time, may be draining off so much energy that extended periods of play with other children may be more than he can handle.

Mothers can save themselves trouble if they accept the needs and tastes of the threes, fours, and fives in companionship. If a child and the son or daughter of the mother's best friend or closest neighbor are at their worst in each other's presence, that is no reflection on the child or the mother. Two months or three years from now these children may get along beautifully if they are not forced to play together now.

Stages in Friendliness

To understand the response of one preschool child to another, it may be useful to glance at the early development of awareness of others the same size. Anna Freud describes several stages in the unfolding of sociability. A baby looks on any other baby who comes between him and his mother as a disturbance. If his mother cuddles another baby, the year-old or eighteen-month-old child expresses his rage in no uncertain terms.

In the next stage, which usually comes about in the second year, one child will be interested in another as he might be attracted by a piece of furniture or a teddy bear. His treatment of the other toddler is about what his treatment of any object would be. He pushes, prods, possibly bites or kisses him, but has no interest in him as a person.

To a two-year-old, another his own size becomes interesting, but usually more for some particular feature than as an entity. A small girl with long, bright red hair came to play with another two-year-old who had never seen hair that color on someone his own size. He wanted to stroke it and gave it a few pulls. These were in the nature of exploration, not an attack.

Two- to three-year-olds play alongside each other but seldom really interact. They may use the same toy, but in different ways. One such toddler was having a lovely time putting empty spools into a basket, and another, seated by his side, was equally preoccupied in taking them out, but this was not a game they were playing together. Children of this age may be playing at opposite sides of a room. If you watch them carefully, you will see that they are observing each other and really have an awareness of being together.

Even three-year-olds often carry on "conversations" in which each pursues his own line of thought, but there seems to be no relation between the two lines, nor do the topics ever merge.

In *The Conditions of Human Growth,* Jane Pearce and Saul Newton say:

> It might be useful for a little cooperation on the part of the child with other children to be enforced—taking turns, sharing, accepting retaliation for injuries inflicted on others. It is a misconception, however, to think that the child will like this. The child cooperates easily with friendly adults, but pushing him too hard to cooperate with contemporaries tends to set up resistance to the natural development of cooperation.

Of course, stages in friendliness overlap and do not occur at a precise age, but somewhere around the age of three and a half, give or take a few months, a youngster will be interested in having the help of another to carry out a project.

"I'm building a spaceship. Want to help, Mike?" says Steve.

"O.K. I'll put this big block back here and it'll be the part we leave on the moon." Mike entered into the spirit of the construction with ideas of his own, but when Steve and Mike lost interest in the spaceship they also lost interest in each other for the remainder of the morning.

Some four-year-olds and most five-year-olds have real friendships at times, as well as still valuing another child solely as one who is useful in furthering a project. In the friendship stage of the fours and fives, other children are liked and disliked, competed with and admired, imitated and hated by turns. Perhaps the test of real regard on the part of one for another is whether one misses the other when they are separated.

New Ideas from Playmates

Whether they be friends, playmates, or just playing side by side, indoors or out, small children in the course of an hour or two are likely to want the same toy, tricycle, or wagon at the same moment. When a group of children were playing in front of the apartment house where most of them lived, Paul grabbed a wagon belonging to one of the group, pulled it around, and declared, "I'm the man selling ice-cream bars. Who wants ice-cream bars?"

Suddenly, the wagon, unused for half an hour, became desirable to everyone. Another child demanded a turn at it, and still another child tried to grab it from Paul.

Such action was not sheer perversity. Children learn from imitating one another as they play. The behavior of one may stimulate similar play in another. He takes over, elaborates, or transforms being an ice-cream-bar man into being, perhaps, the man who brings a load of furniture or a fireman putting out a fire. Imitating a type of activity, but not the exact activity itself, is referred to by child development professionals as "modeling."

Models may precipitate desirable behavior as often as more dubious kinds. Often we speak of the "contagion" of the behavior of a model when one child indulges in wild aggressiveness and others also become truculent, though in different ways.

In the demand of other children for the wagon, one shouted, "Hey, that's not an ice-cream wagon. It's a fire engine, you jerk, you, Paul! Let me have it."

This five-year-old would-be fireman seldom ventured into play that required his taking on the role of an adult. One interesting facet of "modeling" is that an action or type of play not usual for a child may be called forth by what the model does.

Like many disputes, this one was settled without adult interference. Gail, Paul's five-year-old sister, stepped in, somewhat self-righteously. "You can't have that wagon yet. You wait until Paul is through with it. Don't you know about taking turns?"

Gail was a child who identified with the feelings of others. She was able, frequently though not invariably, to put herself in someone else's shoes. She could take on another's feelings, understand his aims, as she was doing now in entering into Paul's pleasure in his role of ice-cream vendor. Human motives are complex. Gail's championing of her younger brother, which the others accepted, also fitted in with her fondness for telling other children what to do. Gail was a leader, but a leader who could both take account of another's needs and derive satisfaction from running things.

Teaching Sharing

Gail had the background that helps children become fairly willing sharers. Her parents were cheerful, warm, friendly people. Gail's mother had not demanded that her children share their most cherished toys. When another child was coming to play with Gail, her mother would suggest that a favorite doll or stuffed kitten "take a rest for this afternoon," and would put these out of sight. This mother also kept in reserve for such occasions one or two "sharing toys" that could be used by two or three children playing together.

Gail's mother was not aware that some rather impressive research studies have pointed out that youngsters who spend their early years in a lenient, loving atmosphere, in which children are treated as individuals likely to do what is expected of them, tend to be more accepting of others and to cooperate with them better than those who grow up in a family in which conformity is sternly enforced and any deviation from strict regulations is a serious misdemeanor. The way the members of a family treat one another carries over in some degree to the way young children treat their playmates.

Learning Takes Time

Children need time and practice to learn generous behavior. If the wait for one's turn is not too long, and if sharing brings outspoken approval from adults and from other children, gradually, although steadily, over months and years, the preschooler discovers that waiting is worth the effort. Some of the face-saving compromises discussed in the previous chapter are equally useful when children are playing with friends.

Four- and five-year-olds tend to respond to such phrases as, "She *needs* the dress-up hat now, but she will be through with it soon," or "He is *using* the car now." The child who has the desired object may relinquish it more readily if the request from an adult who has stepped in is phrased in words that have meaning to him, for instance, "When will you be through with it?" Learning to share is less painful to the young if they have a chance to carry out a line of thought before the toy they need for it has to be relinquished. "It would help if you would let me have the boat now, because he is a fisherman who must catch fish for his dinner," or "You *might* give her a turn on the swing now," are also approaches that make it easier, sometimes, to be generous.

Generosity tends to be contagious. Children who have been watching a child who behaves generously are more likely to be generous themselves afterward. Exposure to an ungenerous model has the effect of producing unwillingness to share, experiments have shown.

No phrase, example, or interpretation works magic, but some approaches do tend to impress on small boys and girls the idea that taking turns and sharing are necessary.

In spite of our best efforts to make clear

to a three-year-old that generosity does not mean, "What's yours is mine, and what's mine remains mine," we may discover a misconception in the mind of our offspring, as Doug's mother did. Doug and a friend were drinking lemonade. Doug, having finished his own, leaned over and began sucking on one of the straws in his friend's glass. In outraged tones, Doug's mother said, "Whatever in the world are you doing, Doug?" "I'm sharing his lemonade," was that young man's bland answer.

Stumbling Blocks to Friendliness

Many children are not as aggressive or as confident as Doug. They are shy and find standing up for their own rights difficult. Overcoming shyness and discovering how and when to assert oneself are also learnings that come about slowly with practice. Almost every child is shy at times. Indeed, the three-year-old who stands, thumb in mouth, at the edge of a noisy group of strange children at a birthday party or in the park, or who refuses to stay without his mother at the home of another child, is not unduly shy. Such behavior is to be expected at three.

A five-year-old who cannot be comfortable with two or three children, even though he has been with them frequently, is exhibiting a different order of shyness and needs help from the adults around him. Perhaps he is one of those persons who will always be somewhat shy and be content to be by themselves for long stretches of time. Being a "loner" is, within limits, perfectly acceptable even in our gregarious society, but our goal for our children is to have them be at ease with others even though they are quite happy without company.

Sometimes a child who has previously been friendly and self-assured will, because of a frightening incident or for some other reason, become unwilling to leave his mother and turn extremely shy. If that happens, we may have to start over again with small doses of companionship. If there is an obvious cause for his uneasiness, such as a new baby in the family, a move to a new neighborhood, the divorce of his parents, or the death or departure of someone close to him, parents may help him if they put his anxiety into words.

"You feel sort of strange since we moved here. That always happens to people in a new place to live. You'll get used to it here. You know what? I'm getting used to it, a little more every day." Such a statement lets him know he is not alone in his trouble, but that a parent whom he relies on is still strong enough to cope.

The Need for Reassurance

One youngster who came home from play and was told by a family friend that his mother had been in an accident and had been rushed to the hospital, was afraid to leave her side when she returned a few days later. Realizing what a shock this four-year-old had undergone, the mother allowed him to stay close to her for a week or so. Then, when he was still unwilling to join his former comrades she said, "You probably think if you go out to play, I won't be here when you come back. I'll be right here. I won't go anywhere unless I tell you about it first." Repeated reassurance in words, plus acceptance of his coming in from play quite frequently to be sure his mother was where she belonged, gradually made him feel safe in joining the other children.

Sometimes the cause of unwillingness to play with other children is not so easily identified. One little girl who was always on the outskirts of a group and rarely became involved with others was discovered to have a slight hearing loss owing to repeated ear infections and enlarged adenoids. When medical procedures restored her hearing, she began to play with other children with enthusiasm. Physical problems are not often so readily resolved, but if a child is persistently unwilling or unable to enjoy the company of his contemporaries, the possibility of a physical impairment of some kind, however slight, should be checked out.

Helping to Foster Sociability

Rather than trusting that a timid boy or girl will outgrow his aversion to sociability, we can aid the forces of development by giving him opportunities to be with one child at a time for a brief interval. Two is often company and three an overwhelming crowd for the very young. A shy child may enjoy playing with another youngster if his mother's presence gives him the support he needs when he is in someone else's home, or he may be happier if a friend comes to him.

Some three- and four-year-olds play outdoors with others for a short while and then need to come in for a few minutes with mother. After a period of following her around, they are ready to venture forth again. Such behavior can be exasperating to a busy mother, especially in winter when putting on boots and snowsuits can be a bother, but this is not a case of the youngster's not knowing what he wants. He knows very well not only what he wants, but what he needs, although he may not have the language to express it: a respite from accommodating himself to company. He may have found a sensible compromise for managing his shyness.

Parents may need to encourage some small ones who do not have the courage to stand up for their own rights: "Ask him if you may have the tricycle now," or "Tell her you need to use the doll carriage."

Suggestions of this sort are preferable to either shaming a timid child or urging him to hit back or strike a child who is not willing to give up a toy. Standing up for one's rights, even in three- to five-year-old circles, need not be synonymous with a willingness to fight.

Some children who live in unusually conflict-free or extremely repressed households may find it difficult to assert themselves. The conviction, born of experience, that one can get angry and get over it, and that making a demand is not dangerous, is necessary before one can believe one has any "rights" whatsoever.

How Skills Can Help

Researchers who have studied children's behavior tell us that boys and girls are more secure with others of their own age if they can do the things that are valued. The five-year-old who can ride a bicycle and/or throw a ball, who is acquainted with the way to manipulate clay and use paints, who is adept at rudimentary hide-and-seek, freeze tag, and similar games loved by fours and fives tends to be wanted by his fellows and therefore enjoys them and feels more confident in playing with them.

One study of nursery-school-age children showed that a boy or girl who has had experiences and possesses information he can translate into dramatic play is more likely to be acceptable to other children. For example, a child who has been to the zoo, who has watched a bulldozer or a crane being operated, who has "helped" his father do a repair job around the house or his mother bake bread, has the raw materials for playing at adult activities.

Children who have grown up in a restrictive, repressive atmosphere are less likely to exhibit imagination, zest, and spontaneity in play. They are apt to be dismissed as "no fun to play with." That is often really a valid pronouncement. The vicious circle of a child's being shy because he is not well liked, being rejected because he offers little, and not being imaginative or full of ideas because he has been repressed at home needs to be broken before he can become more assertive.

Tattling Versus Responsible Reporting

A number of investigators of children's behavior with playmates have found that children who are not dependent on adults are better liked. The child who frequently turns from his play to seek reassurance from grown persons is less in demand. The one who asks a grown person for help in an activity or in something he is making is a different matter. Such requests do not prejudice his peers against him.

The "emotional dependence" that these studies investigated includes behavior that in everyday language would be called tattling. Young children are apt to carry tales for a

number of reasons. Parents need to distinguish between responsible reporting of a dangerous situation and officious tale-bearing. If a five-year-old or a four-year-old comes in the house to tell us breathlessly that another youngster has climbed on the roof of a shed and cannot get down, or that one of the three-year-olds is pedaling his small automobile in the road, that is a sensible and responsible act. Since we never know what we may hear, we should listen to what our son or daughter has to tell before we launch into a tirade against tattling.

If we are treated to an unnecessary and priggish recital of the minor wrongdoings of one of the neighborhood children, as Lynn's parents frequently were, we can always say something like "Now really, that isn't any of our business, is it?"

Lynn's mother was aware that a desire to get another child into trouble was not the motive for her daughter's tales. Lynn had so recently, and so waveringly, established her own resistance to the very temptations she related others as having succumbed to, that she needed to reassure herself and her mother that she knew better than to fall into such ways!

Being an informer is so distasteful a role to most of us that we are likely to feel disgraced if our own child seems eager to make trouble for someone else. Yet, for the three- to five-year-old, tale-bearing is more a way of reinforcing his own controls than of acting maliciously, as an older child might be doing by tattling.

An instructive contrast between our values and those taught Russian children comes out in *Two Worlds of Childhood: U.S. and U.S.S.R.* by Urie Bronfenbrenner. From the time they enter any group, children in the Soviet Union are taught to "evaluate" the behavior of their friends and dispense criticism or praise as their judgment may dictate. To us, who are steeped in the "mind your own business" tradition, this procedure would seem to encourage exactly what we discourage as "tale-bearing."

Bullies Need Help

Some children seek to display their power and attain their own ends by threatening or coercing weaker playmates. Even bullies aged three, four, and five sense whom they can dominate and whom it is useless to threaten. Usually the bully is an unhappy, insecure child who uses his blustering to cover up his own fear. George was such a four-and-a-half-year-old. All that he had seen in the behavior of his brothers and his parents had led him to conclude that bullying was just about the only way of communicating with others. George saw the world as full of danger and regarded himself as unprotected and not worthy of protection.

The father of a boy whom George had been threatening and pushing around was a man of exceptional sympathy and humanity. Instead of scolding George or sending him home when he appeared, he tried being kind to him and showing an interest in him. When this man took his two boys on an after-supper bicycle ride on a summer evening, he would invite George, who was standing sullenly in his own doorway, to join them.

When another neighbor praised this man for his altruism, his answer was, "If we're going to live on this street, it'd better be a place where my children can play without being scared to death. The most constructive thing I can do is to try to get to George. I think there's hope for him if we don't all expect him to live up to his reputation of being a terror."

Adults outside a child's family can often help a small bully toward better ways of dealing with others and toward a better opinion of himself, too.

The child who habitually bites, hits, kicks, or pulls hair may need more than a kindly adult to trust before he can handle his feelings acceptably. In the one- or two-year-old, hitting, hair-pulling, and biting can be expected to occur occasionally. If the three- to five-year-old child habitually resorts to such acts and has no other means of solving his problems, professional counseling may be needed, but various kinds of "emotional first aid" are worth trying first.

Helping Ease Hidden Fears

Such a child is afraid of many things, but perhaps most of all his own impulses to violence. Deep inside himself he wants to be stopped when he attacks someone. He needs protection from himself, not punishment, by removing him from other children. As a seasoned nursery school teacher said, "When you hurt other people, you need to be by yourself for a bit, until you can manage not to hurt others. I don't let anyone hurt you, and I won't let you hurt anyone. People don't like to be hurt. Next time you can find a better way to get what you want."

Pointing out some better ways, such as asking for what he wants or seeking help from an adult, may be helpful to him.

When a child neds to be restrained from going after another, you can hold him, as gently as it is possible to hold an angry youngster, and say as calmly as you can, "I can't let you do that. I take good care of you."

Building up a child's own picture of himself as someone capable of "finding better ways" is useful, too, but if such emotional first-aid steps are ineffective, then his trouble may go deeper. Help from a child guidance clinic or family counselor may be called for. Seeking such help is not an admission of failure on the part of a parent, and securing it promptly may save the child and his family, not to mention the victims of his attacks, from suffering.

The family doctor or clinic, the minister, priest, or rabbi, the Family Service Society, Mental Health Association, or Child Care Society are among the resources available to locate the guidance clinic, social agency, or child therapist in private practice who can help a child. In a metropolitan area, the telephone listings may be under "Community Referral Service" or "Welfare Council." These agencies know the qualified professional municipal or state clinics as well as the private organizations in the area.

Finding Playmates

For some families, the question is not whether a young child plays well with others, but how to find others near his age for him to play with. If parents are newcomers in the neighborhood or for some reason hesitate to make advances, playmates may be harder to come by.

The happiest situation usually exists when neighborhood children have only to go outdoors and other youngsters appear on the sidewalk or in the backyard. Not all the neighborhood companions may be equally desirable. In friendships between the very young there are sure to be low points. Feelings will be hurt, from time to time, but availability makes up for a multitude of shortcomings.

Mothers enjoy sociability, too, and taking a small child to play with a son or daughter of a friend who may live several miles away provides company for both generations. When this is done, the mother should keep in mind that the host-guest relationship between small children need not duplicate that which good manners dictates for those who are twenty years older.

If a family is new to the neighborhood and no playmates seem to be visible, taking the children to the nearest park or playground may produce at least "playground friends" for them. Overtures to other mothers, if the children seem congenial, may lead to an exchange of home visits, too.

Parents often find, in a new community, that membership in a church, attendance at P-TA meetings (if there are older children in the family), or participation in some activity with like-minded neighbors leads to finding playmates for the preschoolers.

Nursery School or Alternatives

Enrolling a three- or four-year-old in a good nursery school, of course, assures him companionship. If that is not practicable, an arrangement such as made by Mrs. Anson and two of her friends might be suitable. The three families lived a mile or two apart in an area where preschool company was all but nonexistent. Each of them took the three children for one morning a week. One mother would pick up one child and deposit him, along with her own, at the home of the woman who was caretaker for the day. This was a firm commitment. The children became accustomed to one another as playmates and to the mothers as reliable and kindly overseers of their play. Each mother agreed to have some materials ready for the children to use or some activity planned for at least part of the morning, and to take the time to read a story or play a record or two for the children. In pleasant weather the children played outdoors or went for a walk with the supervising mother. It was agreed that the children would not watch television nor be dragged around on a mother's shopping trips. The plan worked well for the winter before these four-year-olds entered kindergarten. Sometimes, if one child was sick, only two would be together.

Children who play together without undue quarreling, who do not frequently overexcite, overtire, or threaten one another, can be "desirable" playmates no matter what their background. Young children tend to absorb their parents' views and values as to what makes somebody "nice to play with" or not nice to play with." The more kinds of children a boy or a girl gets to know and feel comfortable with, provided they are agreeable companions and play constructively most of the time, the richer his experiences will be and the more easily he will fit into the larger society as he grows up.

Supervising Play

Whenever the three- to five-year-olds play together, a grown person or a responsible older child needs to keep an eye on them. A delicate balance between supervision and interference is called for.

The danger signals of mounting tension and some ways of coping with them were described in the preceding chapter.

Mothers should know what research on children's play has revealed. When play space is restricted, conflicts tend to be more numerous. Some play materials and equipment tend to promote cooperation, among them wagons, tricycles, swings, and housekeeping materials. Clay tends to produce friendliness, but that old standby, sand, tends to induce quarreling. Children's tastes change rapidly. What appeared to be an almost ideal occupation for twos, threes, or fours last month may lead to disputes a few months later.

Some children behave in more mature fashion when they are not in their own homes; others, who still need a parent's visible presence to keep their consciences in working order, are more likely to go out of bounds away from home, especially when fatigue sets in. A responsible person needs to keep an ear to the ground for "early warning" that trouble is brewing and step in with a suggestion for a switch in activities.

For sheer safety, young children who are playing outdoors need to be checked on frequently. We never know when a three-year-old will be exhilarated by sitting in a puddle of water on a chill November day. Four-year-olds may decide it would be a good joke to hide under a pile of neatly raked leaves at the curb. No driver could possibly suspect their presence under such a mound, and the outcome could be fatal.

The way mothers, grandmothers, older boys and girls, and others in the household treat the child and his playmates may influence his standing with his friends. If a mother is welcoming, even though she is quietly and consistently firm, visiting preschoolers are apt to be comfortable. If adults are clearly annoyed at the presence of an extra child or two in the house, are capricious, yell at the children, or reprimand their own offspring severely in front of his friends, young visitors may not return or even wish to play with the son or daughter of such a house.

Supervising the play of the three-to-fives also includes protecting them and their guests when necessary from the teasing of older brothers and sisters.

Do It My Way—Nicely

The example of hospitality we set lets our children know how one should treat visitors, but hospitality can be tried beyond all reasonable limits. When those limits are exceeded by small guests, supervising mothers can enforce restrictions without being angry. Four- and five-year-old children of neighbors who arrive at breakfast time, or who ring the doorbell a dozen times a day to know if our youngster is home after having been told he is gone for the day, can be pests.

Yet, if the pests are good companions for our children and are available playmates, they may be worth tolerating. Definite rules such as, "Trudie isn't ready to go out and play before nine o'clock in the morning, so don't come over before then," or "In this house you wait until I tell you it's snack time before you go exploring in the cookie jar," can protect you and still not jeopardize friendships. Mothers need not be imposed upon by the repeated suggestion that "I *could* stay for lunch. My Mom wouldn't care."

Every neighborhood has a few children who try the patience of their playmates' mothers. When we must send such a child home, we should try to do it with tact and good nature, for congenial comrades for our children are an asset not to be disposed of lightly.

Enjoyment of Playing Alone Is Valuable

The ability to be contentedly and constructively occupied when alone is also worth cultivating. A person who does not need constant company and/or entertainment will be saved from boredom and loneliness many times in the course of his life.

Mothers can foster the capacity to play alone by keeping on hand for their children some materials that can be enjoyed without playmates. Simple puzzles, paper and crayons, blunt scissors and old magazines or catalogues to cut up, together with large sheets of paper and paste, peg boards of all varieties, fit-together toys, and of course dolls, stuffed animals, and building equipment are among the items that lend themselves to solitary play. Not to be overlooked are albums of family snapshots or a broken clock or camera the five-year-old can take apart. Of course, no household needs to have all these resources.

Mothers may need to make suggestions and bring out materials to get a small child started playing. Until a youngster grows accustomed to playing alone, we should be satisfied if he is busy and happy for a short while. A family room, where a child can play while his mother sews or irons or his father repairs fishing tackle or reads, is a boon; playing independently need not be synonymous with being banished from human contact. It may be useful to say to a young child, "I'm going to be busy for a while, so you give your doll a bath (or whatever the suggestion may be) and then you and I will go to the store." If intervals of playing alone are followed by an enjoyable activity that a child can anticipate, he is more likely to be content, even though he may ask a few times, "Are we going to the store soon?"

It is often tempting to let the television set substitute for creative play when a child is alone. If a suitable program is to be found and the preschooler's viewing is sensibly rationed, TV may tide everyone over a drab half hour. But in the development of personality, TV-viewing does not take the place of the preschooler's ability to play imaginatively and happily by himself.

Parental example also plays a part in developing a nice blend of sociability and self-sufficiency. A mother who can be agreeably occupied by herself, who has her own resources, is telling her children something important.

Manners in Today's World

Preschoolers need to be able to get along with adults outside the family as well. Knowing how to talk to grown-ups makes a child's life easier. Good manners help. They are a way of expressing consideration for the needs and feelings of others and of conveying friendliness.

A child who hears "please" and "thank you," "good morning" and "good night," said cheerfully, will usually enjoy using those phrases; models have a strong influence on manners. One mother, who has always been careful to introduce her daughter to anyone she meets when the little girl is with her, was both surprised and delighted to hear the girl say, when she brought a playmate into the house and her grandmother was present, "Grandma, here is Penny. We're friends. Penny, that's my gran." Afterward the mother told the little girl how pleased Grandma was to have been introduced to Penny.

Small children feel more comfortable if they have something to do when they are presented to strangers. Knowing how to shake hands and look at the person they are talking to with a smile can diminish a tendency to shyness.

Four- and five-year-olds can learn to let adults precede them through a door, or, if they cannot avoid going first, to say, "Excuse me."

Three-year-olds may have difficulty in sitting through an adult meal without leaving the table on some pretext. Letting them help clear the table often makes a virtue out of what might be a breach of good manners. When young children are learning to keep their mouths closed while chewing food, not to lean on their elbows, and whatever else is emphasized in their homes, they are likely to be loudly critical of any adult who does not observe such decorum. We may find it necessary to stress that a cardinal principle of acceptable manners is not to correct others who may not follow our way of doing things —a hard bit of mannerliness to absorb!

Nursery Schools

Any discussion of how a three- to five-year-old grows in sociability necessarily includes what the nursery school experience can contribute to some children. A good nursery school is not a place where everyone is expected to engage in the same activity at the same time. Dr. D. W. Winnicott, in his book *The Child, The Family and The Outside World,* nicely defines it as "an extension upward from the family, not downward from school."

The answer to the question, "Shall I send my child to nursery school?" is, "That depends on the child and the school." A youngster who has four or five friends nearby with whom he plays regularly and fairly contentedly, whose parents have the time to read to him and let him hear music and can provide him with play materials that encourage creativity, may have no need for nursery school. Nursery school usually does offer experiences the child would not have at home, including being away from his mother for a few hours a day. Some nursery schools offer a two- or three-day-a-week program that may be a gentler introduction for the three-year-old.

A parent will want to be clear about who is responsible for running any school in which a child is to be enrolled. Many good schools are managed, owned, and directed by a well-trained nursery school teacher who makes a livelihood in that way. Since hers is a private enterprise, with no board of directors or other body to aid her in setting policy, one would want to be sure of her goals for the children and what she sees her school as offering them.

Some nursery schools are cooperatives, which means that the mothers must spend a certain number of hours working in the school under the direction of a head teacher who is a professional. Parents usually make up the board of directors.

Many nursery schools are church-connected, but some that use church buildings do not have any religious program. These, like nursery schools maintained in connection with a community center, settlement house, or similar social agency, have a professional staff and possibly volunteer aid and a policy-making board.

Other Kinds of Nursery School

Universities, colleges, and high schools may maintain a nursery school as a laboratory or training center for their child-care, psychology, or domestic science students. Public school systems in some cities have a kindergarten program for four-year-olds that is quite similar to nursery school, and some schools are under the auspices of a government agency. Fees will vary depending on the sponsorship of the school, and parents are the best judges of what they can afford. One should spend a morning visiting one or more nursery schools before deciding to enroll a child. One should also find out whether a school is licensed by the local Board of Health and approved by the state agency that licenses day-care centers and nursery schools. If it is, one may be reasonably sure that it is clean, well heated, and safe, and has adequate light, ventilation, and play space, indoors and out.

Fay Bauling, who has been Chairman of the Advisory Committee for Head Start in Chicago and was for many years Licensing Representative for Day Care Centers for the State of Illinois, says this about evaluating the merits of nursery schools:

> A well-planned program offers the children a wide variety of options. Both active and quiet play, opportunities to do things alone or with other children should be available throughout the session. A competent teacher sets the stage so that each child gets a chance to try out a number of activities each day, to listen and to talk, and to use different kinds of materials. One of the criteria for judging a nursery school is the amount of interaction between the children and the teachers. Are teachers warm, interested and available? Do they seem to care more

about the process the children go through in their play, or creative work, than about having a product that is creditable? If that is the case, never mind if the furniture is a bit battered or the toys not the newest. Nursery school should be one place free from competition and pressure.

Drill in skills or emphasis on intricate handwork is not part of the program in a good nursery school, but that does not mean that the children are not growing through their play.

Judging a School

When a parent visits, she should watch how the teachers respond if one child hits another, overturns a jar of paint, spills a glass of juice, or disrupts the story time. Is the incident handled calmly, but immediately, in a matter-of-fact way?

Those observations will give clues as to whether a particular school will provide the kind of experiences a child needs. The comments of other parents, whose judgment can be trusted and whose children have attended the school, are also helpful.

Some youngsters seem so adept at getting along with other children and being on their own that it is a surprise to find that nursery school is a strain for them. The strain may show up in fatigue before the school session is over, in unusual irritability when the youngster returns home, or in repeated requests to be allowed to stay home. Often, allowing a child to stay home for a period of time with the understanding that he may return to school whenever he feels ready to go every day, results in his showing quite plainly when he is ready. Of course, such a plan assumes that a place for him will be available when he is ready to return.

Teachers and parents need to watch for and confer about how a youngster is getting on at home and at school before deciding how to handle problems of this sort. A parent should not decide too quickly that "nursery school is not for my child," but also should not be inflexible about his going every day if matters are getting worse instead of better.

Many three- and four-year-olds enjoy nursery school but have all the companionship they can handle in the half day there. They may want to stay near mother and not play with other children the remainder of the day. That does not mean a child is not benefiting from nursery school.

Probably one of the most conspicuous ways a child changes between his third and sixth birthdays is in his ability to get along with other children, but his development in sociability will hardly be smooth, nor will it always be "onward and upward." He needs to try out his capacity for friendliness over and over again in a variety of settings. If he discovers that playing with others calls for accommodation and compromise, but that the fun of companionship outweighs whatever one gives up to gain it, his parents can be satisfied with his development.

4 *Contrariness, And All That*

ONE OF THE tasks life sets for the young child is becoming domesticated: learning the rules of his world and the special regulations within his own family; finding out when and where self-assertion is good and when it is taboo; discovering at what times, in what places, and with whom compliance and conformity will be demanded, and when greater freedom of action is permissible. Such teaching is done explicitly and implicitly by parents and is often summed up in the word "discipline." Discipline covers many kinds of parental behavior, but one that it does not cover is punishment. Punishment enters the picture only when the usual ways of living together and teaching, in other words the customary discipline, seem to have become ineffective.

Given the need to become domesticated, and the contradictory feelings of the preschooler, we need to consider how we can balance freedom and controls in teaching our children.

How can discipline be consistent, yet flexible, firm but still kindly?

How can we keep our teaching and the relationships of everyday living in line with those long-range goals: independence, self-esteem, and self-control?

Discipline for the Young

That youngsters want to grow up and be like the adults they admire and love cannot be stressed too often. Much of the teaching, or discipline, parents instill is absorbed by the young through the example their parents set. What parents *are* may teach more than what they say, or do to, for, or with a child.

Children's desire to imitate and identify with their parents is a mother's and father's greatest ally in guiding their young. Yet at the same time that a boy or girl wants to be like mother and father, he wants to be himself. A young child's push for independence, to be a separate individual, to try out his powers and use initiative is strong and essential for healthy development. Some of our demands may go against the grain with him. Growing up is hard and calls for compromises, spoken and unspoken, on the part of the learning generation and the generation that teaches.

Not only his feelings, but also his imperfect understanding of what we are trying to impart, make for confusion in the young child's mind as we teach him an orderly way of living. Anna Freud, in *Research at the Hampstead Child Therapy Clinic and Other Papers,* points out:

> Misunderstandings arise between parents and children because kindly, well-intentioned, sensible arrangements, based on external circumstances, . . . reason and logic, are seen by the child in terms of his wishes, fantasies and fears and come out altogether differently.

To the four-year-old, the rain does not fall on the just and the unjust. If he wants to play outside, the rain is a personal insult, or he may interpret it as the result of his having done "something bad." His father's toothache becomes, "Father is cross with me. I have done something wrong."

During the preschool years, a youngster should, and most of them do, begin to outgrow this unreal view of events.

Yet during most of this period, for most children, the logical, external reasons behind their parents' teaching filters through to them blurred by their imaginings and distorted by their immaturity.

Variety in Discipline

Every family has its own style in teaching its children the conformity necessary and in showing them how to use the freedom that is permissible. Regulations and techniques of implementing them that might appear too brusque in one household might, in another, give the children the unspoken feeling, "We know where we stand and what's expected of us."

Indeed, within a family each child will probably respond differently to the same instructions. One three-year-old may be a self-starter who needs few cues to get him involved in the day's routines, whereas his brother or sister, a year older, needs to be eased into bathtime, bedtime, and even mealtime because making transitions is still hard for him.

The regulations a family emphasizes depend, too, on the available space in their home, the parents' hours of work and leisure, the safeness of the neighborhood, the size of the family, and the closeness in age of the children. One research study of the relationship of space in the home to parental strictness found that the more rooms in the living quarters of the family, the more freedom was permitted to the children.

The testimony of the father of twelve children, three of whom were preschoolers at the time, bears this out. When a friend commented on how stringent were the rules and how submissive the children in this house, the father's reply was, "With so many of us in a house that's about three rooms too small for us, we just have to run a tight ship. There isn't any room for a kid to throw his weight around, or throw anything else around either!"

When to Discard Old Rules

Another force shaping the discipline in any family is the human tendency to bring up our children much as we were brought up, whether we intend to or not. Under some circumstances this becomes a useful handing down of customs, but sometimes old rules do not make sense under present conditions. "I didn't have a two-wheel bike until I was eight. Five-year-olds aren't old enough for two-wheelers," says a mother. Five-year-olds may not have changed in the last twenty-five years, but bicycles have, and if the cost of the bicycle or the safety of the streets is not a factor, this mother's insistence on repeating her own experience is a poor reason for denying her child a two-wheeler.

Although discipline that furthers self-reliance and self-esteem may take a variety of forms, research studies, as reported by Martin and Lois Hoffman, in *Child Development Research*, agree: reason and praise influence children toward taking responsibility for their own behavior and being cooperative in their dealings with other people. That discipline relying chiefly on love and reasonableness furthers outgoing friendliness and self-confidence in adult life is borne out by a study of college students conducted by Marvin Siegelman. His aim was to discover if there was a relationship between the personality of these students and the discipline under which they lived as young children. He found that:

> The college students who indicated a high degree of anxiety tended to recall their parents as rejecting, while those who indicated a low degree of anxiety tended to describe their parents as loving.

We are not stretching this interpretation if we infer that individuals who are continually anxious are also lacking in confidence both in themselves and in others.

Fostering Cooperation

Reasoning with a young child does not mean becoming embroiled in a long and devious argument. "I can't take you to play with Gloria. I'm too busy," is sufficient. We need not let a three-and-a-half-year-old seduce us into trying to answer such questions as "Why must you be busy?" "When will you stop being busy?" and on and on.

We may find it useful to keep certain points in mind in giving a small child directions. A simple clear-cut statement of what we want the child to do and allowing sufficient time for him to do it increases our chances of getting his cooperation. We must be sure he understands what we are telling him. Too often instructions are over a child's head.

If we watch a nursery school teacher when she is talking to children, particularly when she is trying to put a point across to an individual youngster, we will see how frequently she sits on the floor or on a low chair, faces the child, puts an arm around him, and then, when she has his attention, explains what he is to do. Mothers and fathers can hardly do that fifty times a day, but if we want to be certain to get a point across, particularly to a boy or girl who is excited or angry, it is worth taking the time to be sure he is listening. It may save everyone the wear and tear of shouting or being shouted at later.

"No" Does Not Always Mean "No"

Preschoolers, especially those at the younger end of the age scale, are often contrary. They say "No" more often than "Yes" to requests or directions. Their "No" usually reflects their struggle to become a separate entity capable of controlling themselves and their environment, rather than sheer stubbornness or "orneriness."

A group of neighbors were bemoaning, over coffee, their preschoolers' predilection for giving a negative response.

"I've learned that 'No' may mean 'Yes,' so I just ignore it, and about half the time Babs does what I have asked her to. She seems to have to say 'No,' and once she's said it, her protest is over," said one mother.

" 'No' from my three-year-old pretty often turns out to mean 'I'd do it myself, if you'd just let me alone.' When the 'No's' get too numerous some days, I start listening to myself, and I realize that I'm giving a lot more directions than are really necessary. If I ease up, cut out some of the 'Do this,' 'Stop that,' there's less for him to say 'No' to, and I don't get so annoyed."

A third woman, who had no children of her own, dared to raise her voice. "If anyone wants to know what I think, it's my guess that the small fry come up with all these 'No's' because that's the word they hear most."

The mother of a large family spoke up: "But you can't get away from the fact that sometimes when they say 'No' they mean it, and when you have five youngsters in the house all under the age of eight, sometimes you have to meet those 'No's' head on. I belong to the school that once in a while says, 'You're going to do as I say right now.' And believe me, it works, at least in my house, it does."

"I'm sure it does work for you, but I'm not as gutsy as you are," said a quiet young woman with a conciliatory manner. "I deal with my little girl's negativism by making a game out of the whole thing and letting her get the 'No's' out of her system. If I want her to get ready to go outdoors, I say to her 'Is your Woolly Kitty going outdoors?' and she says, 'No.' Then I go through a few more ridiculous things that aren't going out, like 'Is the table going outdoors?' and she keeps on saying 'No' and laughing about it. When I finally get around to 'Is Molly going outdoors?' she says 'Yes'—almost always."

"You'd never go through all that Mickey-Mouse if you had five to deal with," said the mother of the big family.

Stability Is Reassuring

Although we have to find our own approach to discipline, some general principles do hold true. A reasonable degree of stability in the household tends to make a youngster more comfortable. His expanding horizons, increasing independence, and freedom to get around can make his world a bewildering as well as a fascinating place. Along with his growing feeling of power is an underlying, continuing feeling of being helpless and needing protection.

A pattern to the major events of the day, such as meals and bedtime, reasonable boundaries both physical and social, as well as fairly consistent responses from the important adults in his life can supply a needed stabilizing atmosphere. Such stability and predictability differ from overprotectiveness, which implies that danger lurks everywhere. They lay the foundation for the growth of a well-organized personality.

The most disturbed children are those who feel unprotected from unknown (and usually nonexistent) dangers, from temptation, and from their own frightening impulses. This point is discussed more fully in Chapter 8.

Removing Temptation

We may be able to cut down on the number of prohibitions we have to enforce by not leaving temptation in our child's way. Some objects around the house, of course, are off limits. If those are not present in abundance, a five-year-old, and even a four or a three, can learn to stay away from them. The mother who leaves a newly made strawberry meringue pie on a kitchen counter where a three-and-a-half-year-old can pull up a chair, climb up, and sink a grimy hand into it is making trouble for herself as well as her youngster.

In protecting a child from his own impulses, we can tell him we will always stop him when he cannot stop himself. It is sometimes a surprise to parents that if we have faith in ourselves, we can usually bring a child to his senses this way. Many years ago, Dr. Lawrence Kubie described in an article in *Child Study* how a father stopped a wildly excited little girl who seemed, at the moment, intent on breaking up everything in sight. This father sat down where he could look her in the eye, held her gently but firmly, and said, "There are some things I can't let you do. I won't let you hurt yourself or hurt anyone else, and I won't let you destroy things." The little girl looked at her father in surprise and quieted down, almost gratefully.

Reminded recently in a personal conversation of this anecdote, Dr. Kubie recalled that it was his own daughter whom he had quieted that way, and he added, "Letting her know you will prevent her from getting completely out of control is still a good way of handling an out-of-bounds four-year-old."

Indirectly, when we protect a child from himself by stopping overexcited behavior, we are telling him, "You are worth protecting. I care about you." This, too, furthers that long-range aim of discipline—enhancing self-esteem.

Knowing What Is Expected Helps

Parents who follow through on enforcing the reasonable limits they have set also facilitate a child's establishing his sense of self. He learns more about who he is. He gradually acquires the feeling, though it may remain unexpressed, "I am a person who can . . . ," "I am a person who wouldn't . . . ," "I am a person who is expected to . . . and I will do it." Along with these reassuring feelings go some warning ones that can be healthy, too. "I'm not big enough yet to . . . ," or "I'd better not try to . . ." Such attitudes, when a child is faced with a challenge he could not possibly meet, are the better part of wisdom. Parents have strengthened his understanding of his real capacities through the stable structure their discipline has set up.

Freedom Within a Safe Framework

Parents in discussion groups frequently ask, "It's all very well to talk about 'reasonable limits,' but how do you decide when you are holding your children down too much and when you are letting them do as they please too much?"

Steering a safe course between the two extremes involves knowing one's child and his environment. Both restriction and freedom have a place in discipline. Every child needs to learn to accommodate himself to both. Without appropriate freedom of action, a child might be so overprotected that he would not be able to use, or to develop, the capacity to take care of himself, which takes practice. Given too much freedom, he courts obvious dangers, physical or emotional.

Mrs. Rabbit, the mother of Flopsy, Mopsy, Cottontail, and Peter, in Beatrix Potter's *Tale of Peter Rabbit,* knows this. "Now my dears," said Old Mrs. Rabbit to her brood, "you may go into the fields or down the lane, but don't go into Mr. McGregor's garden. Your father had an accident there. He was put into a pie by Mrs. McGregor."

Here we have a model of balance between restriction and permissiveness. There is a suggestion of what to do, with room for choice ("into the fields or down the lane"). Mrs. Rabbit had an eye to future independence. We have the unequivocal prohibition, with a cogent reason for it. No room for argument or wheedling there!

Mrs. Rabbit's discipline was effective, as three out of her four children followed her instructions that day. Only Peter went into Mr. McGregor's garden, where, after painful experiences and panic, he barely escaped with his life.

Taking the Consequences

We must give Mrs. Rabbit credit for her handling of Peter when he limped home, later that day, after his horrendous fright in Mr. McGregor's garden, minus his new shoes and his jacket with the brass buttons. Sick at heart and with a bad stomachache, Peter was put to bed by his mother and nursed tenderly with camomile tea. She refrained from lecturing him. Although she did not let him have the blackberries and currant buns that Flopsy, Mopsy, and Cottontail, who had been good little bunnies, had for their supper, she wisely let her son's physical and emotional distress point up the sad consequences of flagrant disobedience.

When the consequences of going against a parent's instructions are not overwhelming or too hazardous, taking these consequences is usually educational. One may need to point out certain connections between cause and effect, but without lecturing or adding insult to injury with an "I told you so."

The statement of a five-year-old, once quoted in *The New Yorker,* "I don't like it here, 'cause everything I do they blame on me," illustrates the viewpoint of the young. The connection between what one does that one has been told not to do and its consequences in the attitudes of others or one's own physical and emotional discomfort is hard to accept.

Adults can point out calmly, and in a manner that is not punishing, the connection between what a youngster has done and the way people respond to his action or the results that have inevitably followed his behavior. That one answers for one's behavior is an idea that takes root gradually through the years. Taking responsibility for one's actions in small ways furthers the development of self-control, too. We need not be discouraged if our children at the age of four or five are full of fanciful alibis to establish their innocence. "I didn't do anything to break that dumb ol' bowl. It just came apart," typifies the logic of a four-year-old who had put the bowl on his head, pretending it was a helmet. "Bowls are to put things in, not to wear as hats. It's better not to play with things that break easily and weren't meant to be played with," is a statement that may help him view such situations more realistically in the future.

Although the results may not be immediately evident, the effect of living with adults who take the consequences of their behavior is an education in emotional honesty. "I got a ticket for parking too long, and I'll have to pay it. I took a chance when I parked so long in the fifteen-minute zone," tells even a youngster with a hazy idea about parking tickets and parking zones that one acknowledges one's mistakes and pays for them in one way or another.

Consistency and Flexibility

Another component of good discipline is consistency, but consistency needs to be tempered with flexibility or it can become rigidity of a harmful kind.

We might roughly define consistency in discipline as holding certain goals or practices as desirable day after day and certain others as undesirable. Yet certain goals or practices that may be desirable under some conditions would not be under others. This is where flexibility comes in.

Melissa wanted a peanut-butter-and-jelly sandwich half an hour before supper time. Her mother said, "No, but here's a piece of carrot you may have." The next day, arriving home from the afternoon kindergarten session she attended, Melissa asked for a peanut-butter-and-jelly sandwich, and her mother cheerfully made one for her. Melissa's mother, when she could say "Yes," liked to say it wholeheartedly, and that is a part of good discipline, too. No inconsistency was involved, for peanut-butter-and-jelly sandwiches are taboo only immediately before a family meal in Melissa's house, and eating between meals is permissible, depending on what and when you eat.

Destructive Inconsistency

The kind of inconsistency that is confusing and even destructive to a small child is, for instance, being rewarded with laughter and praise for trying to imitate a grown-up dance seen on television one day, and then the next day, when adult company is present, having the same performance greeted with, "Cut it out. I don't want to see you show off that way ever again."

A child could understand being told, "Daddy and I like to see you dance for us, but when we have company of our own, they want to talk to us," but an apparently arbitrary change in his parents' attitude would give him no clues for future behavior.

Unexplained reversal of the permissible and the unacceptable, if it occurs frequently in many different situations, can be damaging. If a mother and father have markedly divergent ideas about what constitutes "good behavior," that, too, can cause difficulties. A study of personality characteristics in nursery school children found that when the parents were usually in agreement in the discipline they believed in, the children were more friendly, spontaneous, and had a firmer sense of belonging in the family. The more widely parents differed in their conceptions and their administration of discipline, the less the children demonstrated those qualities.

In their book *Child Development Research,* Martin and Lois Hoffman say:

> Inconsistent discipline apparently contributes to maladjustment, conflict and aggression in the child. . . . Studies have repeatedly shown a higher degree of erratic or inconsistent discipline, both within and between parents, to contribute to anti-social behavior. The concept of consistency in discipline is multifaceted and quite poorly understood, although everyone is quite ready to agree that inconsistency is *bad* for children. It is reasonable to assume that consistent behavior by the parent will increase the degree of predictability of the child's environment, and lead to more stable behavior patterns.

If this is the conclusion of the most careful analysis of the research on the subject, parents may justifiably decide that in the "consistency with flexibility" department, you often have to play it by ear!

When Adults Need to Be Firm

When firmness is called for, it is well to keep in mind that one can be immovable and impervious to wheedling and to such accusations as "You are a mean, mean Mommy and I won't love you any more" without becoming harsh or angry. We can be firm, too, without being belittling or tearing down a child's decent opinion of himself. We can make a good, clear "No" stick without adding, "You're always trying to get away with something. You'll end up in trouble when you grow up." Good discipline tells a child, "Even when Daddy and I have to say 'No' to you, we love you and think you are O.K."

The more secure we are in our own strength as parents, and the more we realize how big and powerful we look to the three- through five-year-olds, the more readily we can keep our enforcement of necessary prohibitions good-humored, or at least calm. Anger or threats of punishment are not good teaching tools.

"I'm going over to Tommy's to play," says four-and-a-half-year-old Roy on a Sunday morning.

Roy's parents know that in Tommy's house visitors are not welcome on Sunday in the early hours. Tommy's parents have made it clear to Roy's mother that, much as they like having Roy at other times, the hustle and bustle of getting their five children off to Sunday school after a late breakfast makes one more small boy underfoot just what they do not need.

"Never on Sunday, in the morning, at Tommy's, Roy. You know that. You may go over this afternoon," says Roy's mother. The "not now, but later" substitute is one that small children often accept, but in this instance it proves fruitless.

Roy continues to tease. "Why can't I go? I won't stay much. I'll just be there a tiny second of a minute."

"No, this isn't the time they like company. Sis will read you the comics, if you ask her to." Roy's mother tries, in vain, the time-honored and useful gambit of diverting the boy's attention from what he wants and cannot have to what is permissible.

"Tommy's my friend. He likes me to come over. How do you know they don't want company?"

"Roy, you may *not* go now, and that's that, so you might as well settle down to playing here," his father tells him.

Roy has now worked himself up to such a pitch that he can't stop himself. He makes a rush for the door, and his father catches him. "Roy, you are staying here. We've told you you are not going to Tommy's, and we will not let you go." His father is firm, but still friendly. He keeps to the point at issue and does not say, "Furthermore, sucking your thumb when you don't get what you want is disgraceful in a boy your age."

"If you don't let me go, I'll break everything in this house," declares the boy, standing woefully in the middle of the room and not looking as if he were about to break anything. Silence from his parents.

With one eye on his mother and father, Roy drifts off to his room, where he sulks and sobs for a few minutes. Then he emerges and sheepishly approaches his older sister, who is reading the comics in the Sunday paper. "Wanna read 'em to me?" he asks.

"Don't care if I do," she says nonchalantly.

Parents and Security

A recent study examined the effect on the behavior of preschool children of various parental styles of discipline. The children were divided into three groups.

Group I consisted of boys and girls described as being "self-reliant, self-controlled, interested in exploring their surroundings, and generally contented."

The children in Group II were described as being withdrawn, discontented, and suspicious.

A third group consisted of children who showed little self-control or self-reliance and who tended to retreat from unfamiliar experiences.

The parents of the children in the first group were found to be "markedly more consistent, more loving, more secure in the handling of their children, and more likely to accompany a directive with reason." The parents in this group also tended to be more sympathetic and encouraging to their child and to talk more freely to him than did the parents in the other groups. They usually followed through on seeing that the children did as they were told. These mothers and fathers were able to say "No" when that was necessary and to stay with that "No," yet they were not overprotective, nor did they restrict the children unnecessarily.

From these facts, the researchers concluded that firm controls in the preschool years, if parents are warm, are not likely to make children either fearful or overdependent.

The parents of the children who had poorer self-control tended to be uncertain about their own ability to control their children. Instead of using reason, the mothers of the less self-reliant and confident children were found to be inclined to use ridicule or the "I won't love you any more if you act that way" approach as techniques to control their sons and daughters. Fathers of the less-confident children more often did not follow through on directions they had given.

A Time and Place for Rewards

A disappointed, angry, or frustrated child is entitled to a substitute activity when he must be denied the one he wants. Giving a substitute is, in such cases, good mental health practice and to be encouraged. We are not "rewarding" the boy or girl who has had a temper tantrum, who has been involved in some mischief, or who has persisted in asking for what he may not have, if, when it is all over, we let him know he is forgiven and back in our good graces. We can afford, both for his well-being and our own, to be affectionate and friendly rather than distant.

When are rewards in order? How do we make the distinction between a reward and a bribe? A reward for achievement or for good behavior under trying circumstances becomes a bribe when a parent puts himself in a bargaining position. Offering some privilege or a tangible advantage to a youngster for giving up what he wants, or would be inclined to do, in favor of what his parents are asking of him may create such a bargaining situation. The difference between offering a substitute activity, a bribe, and a reward is sometimes a matter of phrasing and attitude; but the bribery attitude can color the parent-child relationship if it becomes habitual. A bribe implies buying off a child.

When there is a clear connection between what is offered and what a mother or father is asking the boy or girl to do, bribery is less likely to enter the picture. For example, "If you play by yourself while I finish what I'm doing, I'll get done faster and we can go to the store sooner. Maybe there we can find some of those cookies you like best," is a reasonable handling of a four-year-old's restless demands to know, "When are we going?" To say, "If you play by yourself for fifteen minutes, I'll give you a penny," would put the whole matter on the footing of bribery.

Bribes are usually offered ahead of time, and rewards come after an achievement. If the reward comes as a surprise, so much the better. Indeed, so many of the accomplishments of the preschooler bring him so much satisfaction in themselves that he needs far less of the "carrot in front of the donkey" type of reward that often seems to spur on his older brothers and sisters. A hug and word of praise may be sufficient for the three- or four-year-old in many situations where a material reward might be of dubious value.

The Delayed Reward

Certainly, for small children rewards should never be offered for anything that involves a long stretch of time, a vague attainment, or more self-control than may be possible. In this class would be "If you are good all week. . . ." A week is too long, and besides, what is "good" and who can maintain "goodness" indefinitely? "If you don't wet your bed for a week (or a month) . . ." sets a goal that may be beyond a child's conscious control. "If you don't cry when the doctor gives you a shot . . ." puts a high value on now showing one's feelings and may, as a result, make a youngster anxious.

One trouble with rewards announced in advance, even if they are only in the form of marking achievement with stars pasted on a chart, is that not getting the reward means failure. In our success-oriented society, failure is almost a form of punishment. The atmosphere in which we live inevitably underscores success and failure sufficiently so that parents do not need to go out of their way to emphasize it further.

If one of our long-range goals is that our children become cooperative and learn that achievement for its own sake brings satisfaction, then we will use rewards sparingly with young children. Of course a "celebration," in which the entire family joins when one of its members has made a new step forward, and which comes as a surprise, is always in order. "Incentive rewards" may be useful in a factory, but factory methods are not desirable in the discipline of the young. If we rely on rewards in teaching cooperation, we may find we have developed in our child a sad case of "What is there in it for me?" before he reaches school age.

Punishment: A Last Resort

If rewards are not to play a major role in discipline, what about punishment? If punishment is really necessary, then let it be immediate, swiftly over, and, if possible, related to the behavior it seeks to deter. The old principle that no punishment should last beyond sundown is still valid. Nor should punishment be deferred. "You can't go on the picnic next Saturday" is undesirable, for when Saturday rolls around the child may have forgotten what he did to cause the deprivation, and his parents may even have forgotten that he was to be deprived.

If a five-year-old who has been told repeatedly to bring his bicycle, or wagon, or whatever into the garage or into the entryway continually neglects to do so, depriving him of the use of the bike for the rest of the day is only just. "If you can't remember to take care of it, you aren't big enough to use it this afternoon," is a train of thought a five-year-old can comprehend.

If a three-year-old has been hitting his playmates, brief isolation may be necessary. A small child can understand that "People don't like to be hit. Until you can manage for yourself, you'll have to stay in your room. When you think you are ready to play with them and be friendly, you come and tell me." Here is an opportunity for taking responsibility for one's own behavior, plus the hint that "You can do better."

If punishment should be swift, then spanking would seem to qualify as acceptable, but that it is soon over is about all that can be said in favor of this method of correction. We can assume that some kind of aggressive behavior landed the boy or girl in the situation that led to his being spanked. Physical punishment is demeaning, frustrating, and painful. It stirs up more anger and feelings of hostility and bears no ethically instructive relation to the child's misdeed. It cannot be interpreted by the youngster as "taking the consequences of his wrongdoing." Numerous and extensive studies have shown that physical punishment tends to breed, rather than curtail, aggressiveness. What is more, the parent who spanks gives his child the model of an adult who hits when he is angry, and models are potent teachers.

Spankings tend to reinforce the child's tendency to strike out by way of retaliation. Spankings, from a long-term view, are self-defeating, since they hinder rather than advance independence, self-confidence, and self-control. In fact, one study showed that the daughters of mothers who used physical punishment and were severely restrictive tended to be extremely dependent as they were growing up.

When we deprive a child of something as a punishment, we are telling him that we consider it valuable. For many reasons, some families impose fines on even the young children for any infraction of the rules. But to a four- or five-year-old, a fine is apt either to be meaningless or to convey the impression that one can make anything all right by a money payment.

A metropolitan paper recently printed an article by one of its columnists headed, "You Can Go Broke at Our House at the Age of Four." The columnist went on to explain how an elaborate system of fines was used to keep the children's behavior in line. What that writer either did not see, or did not regard as important, was that the four- or five-year-olds in his family were being given a set of values that might haunt the parents later. If we are trying to teach, for example, consideration for the needs and feelings of others, but then allow the payment of a fine to take the place of such consideration, what are we really teaching?

Punishment of any kind, to be effective, needs to be infrequent, or the children become inured to it. If we find it necessary to punish a four- or five-year-old, not just redirect or correct him, several times a day, then it is time to examine the roots of his disobedience.

Chronic Disobedience

Sometimes standards that are so high that a child is always falling short of them may cause him to appear "disobedient" when he is merely acting in a manner quite usual for one at his stage of development. Or, discouraged by his failure to meet his parents' demands and win their approval, he may give up trying and go his own—and decidedly disobedient—way.

Living in crowded quarters with no space in which to be active may make a child so tense and restless that he is constantly getting rid of energy in unacceptable ways.

The child who feels unloved and pushed aside because his parents pay scant attention to him, aside from giving routine care, may be among the conspicuously unruly ones. More time alone with his mother and/or father, just for enjoyment and praise instead of criticism, may bring about a greater degree of cooperativeness on the part of the small child.

Some children are always in trouble because they do not have sufficient legitimate outlets for their energy in play, both alone and with other children. If nobody provides them with or helps them use play materials, and if all the activities they attempt turn out to be in the forbidden category, they despair of finding ways of playing that are satisfactory both to themselves and their parents.

Trying to Communicate

Disobedience, particularly if it occurs over and over again in a particular situation, may be a signal that we are holding a child down to a level of behavior that he has outgrown. Five-and-a-half-year-old Morton was using the only means at his disposal to try to tell his parents that his three-year-old brother's seven o'clock bedtime was too early for him. From the point of view of getting sufficient sleep and of getting the seniority right of staying up later than the younger boy, Morton needed to be allowed at least half an hour more of play or of the company of his parents.

After he had been put to bed, Morton would, night after night, get up and come into the kitchen where his parents were watching TV or chatting. He would find excuses to get up two or three or four times between bedtime and eight o'clock. This disturbed his younger brother, with whom he shared a room, far more than if he had been tucked in bed quietly after the three-year-old was asleep. Usually, he ended up being punished for not staying in bed, as well.

When his parents finally decided that perhaps letting him stay up longer would do away with the nightly impasse and told him they considered him old enough now to have a later bedtime, the jumping out of bed grew less frequent and finally disappeared.

The child who seems to be continually disobeying the rules of the household, like the child who seems unable to understand caution (described in Chapter 8), may be anxious. If his parents are having difficulties in their marriage, are worried about problems with their own aging parents, are under tension in their work lives, or feel discriminated against on account of the racial, ethnic, or religious group to which they belong, their anxiety, though never discussed in the youngster's presence, may create uneasiness in him. Then, not really aware of what he is doing, he is driven to forbidden and irrational behavior. Sometimes he may be helped by a simplified explanation that he can understand about the nature of his parents' troubles, with the assurance that they will find some way out.

Finally, the chronically disobedient preschooler may have some undetected physical disorder that makes him uncomfortable. Discomfort, like anxiety, may impel him to bizarre behavior in the hope that something will relieve the nagging malady.

Balancing Controls

If, as we have stressed before, one of our long-term goals is to have our children during these years begin to take responsibility for their own behavior, we need to look at the effect of various kinds of control. A recent study has shown that when power in the family is exercised entirely by the parents, children tend to feel that responsibility for their behavior rests in some force outside themselves.

In families in which youngsters are rarely restricted, wheedle their parents, and the parents are apathetic or see themselves as helpless or are extremely immature, the youngsters are likely to grow up self-centered and insensitive to the feelings and needs of other people. They are apt to be concerned chiefly with what they themselves need or want.

When parents share the power in the family in appropriate ways by letting children make choices that they are actually capable of making and by helping them understand the reasons for restrictions and rules, boys and girls have a good chance of growing up with the feeling that they are responsible for their own actions. At the same time, the young in such families develop some concern for what other people need.

Respecting the Child

When we look for the causes of behavior, when we adapt the discipline in the family to long-range goals as well as to immediate convenience, we are respecting our children. Part of respecting a child is keeping in mind his needs and his limitations. That also means taking account of his unique personality as well as the phase of development in which he happens to be at the moment.

Of course, as he is becoming domesticated, we expect the youngster to accommodate himself to the rules of the world and the customs of the family, but at times the family can also accommodate itself to its individual members. One way of saying that discipline, ideally, respects each member of the family is to suggest that we try not to treat anyone in the family in such a way as to work a hardship on any other member or on the family as a whole. At the same time, our discipline can be so planned that regulations for the family as a whole do not deprive anyone of what he needs in the way of emotional support, attention or recognition, or consideration for his physical limitations.

Respecting a child also means accepting him as he is and helping him to make the most of his potentialities rather than trying to turn him into the "dream" youngster we may have hoped for. A family can be enriched, both at the moment and on a long-term basis, by differences between its members.

If we can tailor our discipline to respect our children, to regard their desire to grow up as well as their need to be cared for and to be childlike, we can more readily make discipline serve both immediate needs and long-term goals.

---

5 *Questions Need Honest Answers*

RUDYARD KIPLING, IN his oft-quoted poem, wrote:

> I keep six honest serving-men
> (They taught me all I knew);
> Their Names are What and Why and When
> And How and Where and Who.

The honest serving-men are not unfailingly popular with mothers and fathers; preschoolers seem to work them overtime and sometimes bring up topics difficult for parents to handle. Nevertheless, the young child's questions are his best tools for learning about the world around him, the people in it, and the way they interact with one another.

Questions are usually a sign of a lively curiosity. Such curiosity is basic to learning and to reaching out mentally, emotionally, and socially. Preschool youngsters take little for granted. Naive enough to believe that a simple explanation must exist or that some person is responsible for all events and phenomena, they demand to know, "Who made the sky?" and "Why can't cats talk?" and "What is 'dead'?" as if they were asking nothing more complicated than "What is ice cream made of?" Their faith in their parents' knowledge is boundless, another aspect of their charming naiveté, and impels them to believe we can supply satisfying answers to any inquiry.

Because questioning is so essential to development, it is worth considering the meaning of different varieties of questions to the children, and to us, as well as some effective means of dealing with questions as they come up in daily life.

Questions Serve Numerous Purposes

Not all of a small child's inquires are by any means merely requests for information. Listening carefully, we will usually be able to detect what lies behind the question as well as the feelings prompting it. How we answer will depend, not on any formula, for none has ever been devised, but on what we sense to be the youngster's need at the moment. We can estimate the amount of understanding he has in the particular field he is asking about and how much he can grasp by way of an answer. The same question at five calls for a fuller explanation than it did at three—and may have a quite different meaning.

Our answer will hinge, too, on our own feelings. At the end of a long day filled with irritations, we might be tempted to meet so innocent an inquiry as "Why does the soap get littler in the water?" with "Can't you see I'm busy? DON'T bother me any more!"

A question may arouse such strong feelings in us that a reply is difficult. "Why doesn't Billy's mother like me?" "Why don't we go to church on Sunday like Grandma does?" "If I'm very, very good, couldn't I have a baby sister for Christmas?" or some other query that hits us in a sensitive spot may tempt us to cut off the questioner.

The way his mother or father receives an inquiry may teach a youngster much more than any facts offered in reply. If he or she discovers that asking is acceptable, the way is kept open for the satisfying of curiosity in other areas, another day.

Conversation Starters

Preschoolers often use a question when they want to start a conversation, as Keith did. This three-year-old came out of the house, observed his father absorbed in changing the spark plugs on his automobile, and said, "Whatcha doing that for?"

"So the car will run better," his father told him. Although Keith may not have been aware of it, the question behind his spoken one was, "Are you too busy to talk with me? Is that car more important to you than I am?"

His father's prompt, willing, and factual response told him something about his father as well as why men tinker with cars. Keith's feeling that his father would not be angry or tell him to go away if he talked to him, even when he was busy, was reinforced. The man-to-man, comprehensible reply also conveyed the impression to the little boy, "You are worthy of a sensible answer."

Had his father made a habit of saying something like, "I'm putting the thingummies on the whosis," which even a three-year-old could recognize as being talked down to, Keith's self-esteem might have been lowered a notch or two. A teasing reply, such as, "There's a troll living under the hood and I'm taking his tonsils out because he had a sore throat," might, for some children, under some circumstances, give the feeling, "You and I know when a joke is a joke." However, Keith's father felt intuitively that a fanciful answer was not what his son was looking for at that moment.

As conversation openers, or for that matter, as attention getters, questions surely have a legitimate place. Consider how much more socially sophisticated was Keith's "Whatcha doing that for?" than his behavior might have been only a few short months ago. Then, he might have stood behind his father and given him a playful swat or called loudly "Boo!" The question demonstrated Keith's interest in somebody else's activity and a desire to interact with him.

When a Question Is Not THE Question

When Melinda Ryan, four and a half years old, pestered her mother with a torrent of empty questions, one following another without waiting" for a reply—"What's this?" "What's it for?" "Where did you get it?" "How does it work?" "Can I work it?"—her mother knew that not just Melinda's inquiring mind, but restlessness and boredom were at the root of these inquiries. An interesting occupation, not reproof for the stream of questions nor answers to them, was Melinda's need.

Mrs. Ryan would say, "Melinda, how about getting out some colored paper and your scissors? I'll fix you some paste and you make me a cutout picture I can put up here in the kitchen. Make one to surprise Daddy when he comes home, too." This and similar pursuits that Mrs. Ryan reserved for just such times tended to alter what the mother called Melinda's "pestiferous moods."

Various kinds of unmet needs may contribute to a youngster's being restless and bored. Insufficient companionship with those his own age is a possible cause. How to provide that is discussed in Chapter 3. He may need more opportunities to practice independence, the topic of Chapter 9. More opportunities for vigorous or noisy play may answer the need of other youngsters; this topic is taken up in Chapter 10.

Sometimes questions stem from a basic, indefinable uneasiness. These cannot be dismissed as "just to get attention." Substitute "reassurance" for "attention" in that statement, and you may have a more accurate diagnosis. A youngster may, for some reason, feel pushed aside. Perhaps a new baby or a visitor in the family seems to him to have displaced him in his parents' affections. Perhaps he has been scolded too frequently for misbehaving. Possibly a parent, under pressure and harried, has not been able to pay as much attention to him as usual. His questions, often utterly inane, are a plea for recognition.

Wanting reassurance when one is troubled is hardly an offense. If the disheartened boy or girl pelts us with a barrage of "Why do I have to play outside? Why do I have to wear a jacket? Why can't I go across the street? Why do you have to go to the store?" and so on, we can try an extra bit of affectionate attention. It may be more effective than either reasonable answers or attempts to stem the tide of "Why's?" Such affection would not be "rewarding" the nagging, whining questions; it would merely be having the good sense to see beneath them to the real difficulty.

Questions About Family Crises

When parents are disturbed about such troubles as an impending move to another city, a sharp decline in the family's finances, the loss of a father's or a mother's job, the threat of a serious illness, physical or mental, to some member of the family, even young children seem to sense it. At such times we may get a barrage of questions from our preschooler about everything except the one question to which he wants an answer. He wants to know what is wrong and why we are worried, but he cannot, or dare not, put that into words.

Young children deserve a simple explanation. If they do not feel shut out, and if their parents are not overwhelmed by the event, the children often show relief and surprising stamina. The assurance that "Daddy and Mommy will take care of you, no matter what happens," and that, "We know what to do," can relieve them greatly and perhaps make it possible for their real and justified fears to come out in questions.

Discussing family crises with children is the subject of *What to Tell Your Child about Birth, Death, Divorce and Other Family Crises,* by Helen S. Arnstein. This book deals with explaining these circumstances in more detail than is possible here, and it can be extremely helpful.

The Stalling Device

Questions play a major part in the gentle art of stalling at which many preschoolers are adept. Although five-year-olds tend to be less prone to this delaying tactic at bedtime than threes or fours, they often return to it as the best method of postponing separation from their parents' company. Ned was a quite competent five-year-old, but when his father or mother would tuck him in for the night, he could come up with queries that would keep one of his parents talking to him for ten minutes to half an hour, or more.

Ned did have lively and wide-ranging interests. To give him his due, he undoubtedly was eager to know the answers when he inquired, "Are fishes unhappy sometimes?" "What is an earthquake?" "Who makes them?" "What if all the daddies didn't go to work ever again?" "What's being rich?" "Do we know anybody who is rich?" "Are rich people bad?"

Ned's astuteness was proved not only by the originality of what he sought to know, but also by his canny observation of the subjects that would keep his father or mother talking. Praiseworthy as were their efforts to give their son explanations in language he could understand, they were allowing themselves to be exploited. They might have done better to say, "That's something to talk about tomorrow, Ned. It's too long a story for tonight." Then, if they remembered to bring up the subject the next day, the boy would not have felt his questions were unwelcome, though in broad daylight he might have been less interested in what his parents had to say on these abstract and knotty points.

Sometimes a youngster will ask a question when the adult is obviously busy with other matters or is hurrying him to do something he is not pleased about having to do.

"Why do you always pick the worst time to ask the biggest question?" his mother said in despair one day. The boy's nine-year-old sister happened to be in the room, and, as older sisters will, she answered for him. "He knows you won't have time for a long, long story, and he just doesn't want to hear too much," she told their mother. Since both the boy's parents enjoyed talking at length, the girl was probably onto part of the truth.

Information-seeking Questions

Compared to questions that have their origin chiefly in a need to relieve feelings, inquiries prompted by genuine intellectual curiosity seem relatively simple to handle. No matter how well informed we may be, we cannot hope to have a ready explanation for all that a preschooler from time to time wants to know about. Nor can we breathe a sigh of relief and think, "At least we've disposed of *that*," when we have answered a question once. The same request for information will probably crop up again, perhaps phrased differently, and require a fuller explanation next time.

Parents are not diminishing their son's or daughter's faith in them if they say, "I don't know, but let's find out together." Libraries and librarians, especially in the children's section, are in the business of helping people find answers by directing them to materials that can be useful. Three or four is not too early an age for being taken to the neighborhood public library and discovering that books, even though one cannot read them oneself, often hold interesting answers. Many libraries also have pictures, films, and other visual aids to information.

Often, we may not find answers designed for the three- or four-year-old. We will need to interpret material intended for an older child and translate it into words and concepts our preschooler can understand. Too much information can turn off a preschooler's interest. The important point is to let him see that finding answers is possible and pleasant, and that we are willing to cooperate in doing so.

Clearing Up Confusion

Small children have frequently been mulling over a subject before they put their interest into a spoken question. They may have evolved an explanation of their own that is far removed from the facts. Their notion of how airplanes fly, or what elephants like to eat, or how the world began, or whatever, may be utterly confused. We may get an inkling of misconceptions that had best be cleared up if we turn the question back, with "You tell me what you think." The reply may also give us a clue as to what the youngster really wants to know. We may have trouble not laughing out loud when we hear what the three- or four-year-old has to say, but since being made to feel foolish is a question-stopper, let us refrain from showing our amusement.

Questions seeking information not only deserve honest answers but deserve to be treated with respect. If a four-year-old's notion of why the moon is in the sky during the day or what makes the sun come up in the morning is so charmingly whimsical that we cannot resist telling it to all our friends, at least we should know better than to relate it in his presence.

Jerome Bruner, a respected psychologist and educator, in *On Knowing, Essays for the Left Hand,* says this about how children learn:

> The opposite of understanding is not merely ignorance or "not knowing." To understand something is, first, to give up some other way of conceiving of it. . . . The development of the general idea comes from the first round of experience with concrete embodiments of ideas that are close to a child's life.

If our answers to his questions are to expand a small child's real understanding, then those explanations need to be in terms that are familiar to him. "Did the first people in the world live in very old houses like Mrs. Page lives in?" asks a four-year-old to whom the rambling, turn-of-the-century frame house of an elderly neighbor seems absolutely ancient. The answer to that inquiry may lead us to tell about how people lived in caves. If he has never seen a cave, and it is more than likely that he has not, we may say, "A cave is a big hole in the side of a hill. Some caves are quite small, so small that it would be hard to sit down in them. The caves that people lived in were usually big enough so that a man as big as Daddy could stand up in them, although the cave people weren't as tall as Daddy. There might be room in a cave for five or six or even more people to lie down and sleep. Of course they didn't have beds to sleep on, or tables or chairs. There are no windows in caves, either, and it was often cold and wet and, we would think, terribly uncomfortable, and full of bugs, and of smoke from the fire they built inside the cave."

Such homely details out of his own experience give a youngster facts he can understand, yet do not picture primitive life as a perpetual "cook-out" with contemporary zippered, waterproof equipment.

"Any subject can be taught to anybody at any age in some form that is honest," Bruner says, but he cautions against the pitfall of oversimplifying and prettifying a complicated subject to the point that it becomes not at all an honest portrayal.

Questions About Conduct

This caution about explanations is especially applicable to those most difficult questions that touch on justice and law, war and peace, life and death, and similar topics on which neat, clear-cut explanations cannot be furnished.

If a five-year-old has heard, as Sylvie had, that some children do not have enough to eat or a place to live, the child may demand, "Why don't they just make everybody in the whole world share everything and then everyone would have enough? Can't the supermarket man give all the hungry people all that peanut butter and jelly and oranges he has in the store?"

Sylvie's father, when his miniature political economist posed this question to him, told her that "sharing" was difficult enough when it involved only Sylvie and her sisters sharing their collected candy on Trick-or-Treat night. Even then, he reminded her, there had been arguments and tears because nobody was satisfied that the division was "fair."

> How could you divide things up "fairly" among all the millions of people in the world who need and who want different things? Who would decide what was "enough" or "right" for each one? Maybe when you grow up, Sylvie, you'll help people who are hungry or who haven't a place that's nice to live in. There are lots of ways you can be a helper to other people.

Inadequate as he knew his explanation was, Sylvie's father felt he had at least let her know that it was all right for little girls to think about such questions. He had not painted either an entirely dark or an entirely rosy picture, but he had tried to show her that solutions to some human problems are hard to find.

We can take care in discussing human relations not to encourage a sharp separation between the "good guys" and the "bad guys," or to give the impression that if a person has one quality we do not like, we then want nothing to do with him. Three- and four-year-olds who are coming to terms with their own consciences tend to see right and wrong as at opposite poles, with no blending at the edges. (This is discussed further in Chapter 7.)

That we like different people for different qualities they may possess needs to be emphasized over and over. Young children tend to be rigid in their thinking and harsh in their judgments, because their own controls are still not in the best working order.

"Don't you like Aunt Fran any more? You told Daddy she talked too much," demands four-year-old Freddy, who finds his great-aunt Fran fun. "Won't she come here again? I like her a lot."

Freddy's mother resisted the temptation to lecture about eavesdropping and explained that she, too, loved Aunt Fran, but that everybody has some faults and sometimes we may get a little angry at someone, although we still like them and we get over being angry.

"You mean like when you tell me you love me even when I do something bad?" Freddy asked, taking a giant stride in understanding personal relationships.

When to Tell the Truth About Myths

Young children's questions may also be hard to deal with because they hit at one or another of the myths we enjoy. We do not want to destroy children's pleasure in Santa Claus, the Easter Bunny, and so on, yet we are safest if we do not put ourselves in a position that allows them to accuse us of deliberately fooling them. If we avoid telling a child anything that we will later have to "untell" him, we are in a better position to retain his confidence and to spare him the confusion of disillusionment. We can be truthful without being cynical or spoiling the pleasure of pretending, but at the same time we can be clear about what is a fact and what is pretense. The children may elect to cling to the myth, but at least they know *we* know the difference.

The Easter Rabbit is such a myth. We may, quite justifiably and unconsciously, enjoy the illusion ourselves. Surely it is entertaining to watch the children's delight in a basket of prettily colored eggs the Easter Rabbit has presumably left at the door. Without acknowledging it, perhaps we would sometimes like to believe in a bit of magic ourselves.

In one family, the four-and-a-half-year-old was perplexed and resentful. She had heard rumors from a playmate that "The Easter Bunny is just for babies and is a lie." Still, in nursery school the talk had been about the coming arrival of Easter baskets purveyed by the miraculous rabbit. These stories had the support of the teacher herself. The mother in this family, annoyed at both her child's playmates and the teacher, was at a loss in trying to resolve her daughter's demand to know whether the Easter Rabbit was "true." She waited for her husband to come home and help her pick up the pieces, emotionally and intellectually, for the girl.

This youngster had a favorite stuffed dog with whom she carried on long conversations. "Doggie" was a comfort to her when she was lonely or discouraged. Doggie had a personality of his own, and the little girl frequently reported what Doggie liked and did not like and what he had been doing while she was out. Doggie was playing a useful part in her growing up, and at this point he came in handily to assist the father in giving an honest answer to the searching question, "Is the Easter Bunny true?"

"The Easter Bunny," he told his daughter, "is something like your friend Doggie. You know a real, live dog couldn't talk or play the way Doggie does, but you like to pretend he can, don't you?

"When you are tired or have to play by yourself, Doggie is good company, isn't he? He makes you feel good, even though you know he isn't a real dog like Spot over at your cousin's house."

The little girl nodded solemnly, apparently quite able to go along with such reasoning. "Doggie loves me and I love him," she declared.

Her father took a deep breath and hoped she would be able to follow the jump from Doggie's being pretend to the Easter Bunny's being pretend. "Pretending about Easter Bunnies is fun, just the way talking to Doggie is fun for you. Lots of stories we like are pretend. As long as you know they are pretend, it's O.K. We don't have to spoil anybody's fun who likes to pretend."

His daughter looked a bit sad. "Will I still get a basket from the Easter Bunny?" she asked plaintively. Alas, the belief in myths often has a materialistic basis!

"Of course, there'll be an Easter basket for you on the breakfast table on Sunday, and then Mommy and I'll hide the eggs in it for you and you can hunt for them. It will be a nice pretending, won't it?" The girl agreed it would be. She snuggled up on her father's lap, satisfied that he was not fooling her, and pleased, though she could not have told why, that she was allowed to keep her cherished imaginary creatures.

A youngster who has bridged the gap between fact and fancy in one context can usually do so more readily in a comparable situation, without feeling cheated or losing his trust in his parents' veracity.

"Where Do Babies Come From?"

Answering the questions we hope the children will ask during their preschool years about the difference between the sexes and where babies come from is not far removed from answering the other types of questions seeking information that we have been discussing. Our answers give our sons and daughters sex information, but that is only one facet of the broader experience described as "sex education." The following chapter is concerned with that far larger aspect of a child's development.

Our feelings about questions touching on sex are likely to be different from our attitude toward other questions. Even in these days of outspokenness about sexual relations on the screen, in print, and in the conversation of many adults, it is still the most intimate of topics. Sex may be surrounded by feelings left over from our own childhood. Few grown persons can honestly say that they can answer their children's questions on this aspect of human relations as matter-of-factly as they can answer those about, say, electricity or why leaves are green, no matter how casually they may talk about sex with their contemporaries.

The story is told of a small girl who asked her mother how babies "get borned." Her mother said, "Come and sit down here next to me and I'll tell you." She gave her daughter an explanation and then asked her if she wanted to know anything else.

"Uh huh. I want to know why I had to come and sit next to you for you to tell me all that." This illustrates how special the imparting of sex information is even to those of us who feel able to dispense facts clearly.

Yet, many of the principles that prevail in answering other kinds of questions hold true in this field. The same question, for example, "Where was I before I was born?" calls for a somewhat fuller answer when a five-year-old propounds it than might have been appropriate when that child was two years younger. Children tend to forget the answers to their questions about reproduction just as they do explanations of other phenomena. They may also ask the same question a week, a month, or a year later just to be sure that asking is acceptable or to discover whether our reply will contain the same information. We should not be discouraged if, in spite of the most careful explanation, our son or daughter clings to his own ideas and rejects the more accurate ones we have tried to instill. Learning takes time, especially when the material to be assimilated may be less clear or palatable than his fantasies.

Understand the Question

Just as in answering other kinds of questions, before giving a reply we must be sure we are clear as to what it is the youngster wants to know. An oft-repeated and probably fictitious anecdote tells of a parent who gave his child a complete story of the reproductive process in response to the question "Where did I come from?" only to be told, "That's O.K., but there's a new boy in kindergarten and he comes from New York, and I wanted to know where I come from." That story has a moral for all of us. We need not give a child more information than he is asking for, as too much can turn him off as readily as does too little.

We can be more helpful if we first determine what notions he already has. We may be amazed at the distorted explanation he has concocted out of his imagination and half-understood remarks made by us and others.

Questions about anatomical differences and reproduction are part of a youngster's healthy curiosity. We want to let him feel that asking these questions is acceptable and that we are ready to answer, or, if we cannot answer right at that moment, we will talk over his questions just as soon as we can. Initiating such discussion then becomes our responsibility. Children frequently ask their questions relating to sex, just as they ask other complicated ones, at inopportune moments, because they sense that we are preoccupied and will need to make our answer brief. A long explanation may be more than they are seeking.

A parent does well to leave the way open for more questions as a youngster is ready to ask them. Our willingness to answer, whether we are fluent with all the facts or hesitant, is the foundation of sound sex education.

As for what to say to those most frequent of the preschoolers' questions, about where babies come from and how boys and girls differ, the precise words and phrases have to be our own. If we feel, in looking back at what we said afterward, that we did not include a fact that might have been called for, we must remember that we will have other chances. Dr. Fritz Redl, who has been an authority on discussing children's sex perplexities for many years, has said that if he felt he had made no more than twenty-five mistakes in talking to a boy for half an hour, he congratulated himself.

For the child under six, the occasion for asking questions concerning where babies are before they are born and how they "get born" is usually either his own mother's pregnancy or that of a relative or a neighbor.

Using Correct Terms

Some children's erroneous ideas about birth involve mothers becoming pregnant by eating something. The same idea occurred to some primitive tribes. If we talk about the baby being "in its Mommy's tummy," we reinforce that misconception. It is better to emphasize that a baby grows in a "special place" inside its mother. That place is called the uterus or the womb. Never mind if the listener pays scant attention to that term. Giving the special place a name makes it clearer that the baby is not mixed up with the food his mother eats.

We can go on to say that the baby is warm and comfortable and safe in that special place until it is big enough to be born.

Then will probably come the question, "How does it get out?" Children, aware of the openings through which they have bowel movements and through which they urinate, may conclude that babies exit through one of these apertures. Again, we can explain that mothers have a special place, called the vagina, that stretches to be big enough to let the baby out when the time comes.

We may get the question, "Does that hurt?" A "natural childbirth" mother's answer will be special. But whatever her experiences during delivery, she can afford to say something to the effect that it may hurt, and mothers go to the hospital to have babies so the doctors and nurses can help the baby come out. We can go easy on the pains of childbirth and talk about the fact that "Mommies are so glad to have the baby that they forget if it hurts a little."

If a child asks to see the place the baby comes out, we can tell him it is between a mother's thighs and draw a simple diagram to illustrate. Using one's own body to demonstrate is not recommended, as this is likely to be more sexually stimulating than factually informative.

Little girls may be delighted to know that they can be mothers when they grow up, but for little boys the news that only girls grow up to be mommies can be discouraging. They are usually reassured if they are told that it takes both a mother and a father to have a baby, and that boys grow up to be daddies.

Usually, the "What do daddies do to make

a baby?" or "How does the baby get started?" type of question is not asked immediately. A youngster has enough to think over in knowing that a baby grows inside its mother.

Just Give the Facts

The question about how a baby gets started, from a four- or five-year-old, is not a request for a description of sexual intercourse but for biological facts. "A baby is started when a tiny cell from the father's body joins a tiny cell in the mother's body. Cells are too small to see, but the baby grows from these cells coming together," is a better explanation than talking about a father's "planting a seed in the mother." The "planting" notion may add to any confusions a small child already has. Discussing fertilization in flowers, fish, or other animals has proved to be far more helpful in straightening out a youngster's perplexities.

More details about how the union of cells occurs are infrequently asked for until after the age of six. But we may as well be prepared to repeat the other explanations we have already made. Many children are not sure they want to believe that babies grow inside their mothers. They may cling to their fantasies.

One mother was shocked to hear her four-year-old tell a neighbor that her baby sister had been bought at the store. "You remember, I told you that a baby is inside its mother before it is born," she said to her daughter. "Yes, I know you told me that, but I was afraid Mrs. Peters would laugh at me if I said that," was the answer.

Just what combination of feelings produced this state of mind would be impossible to say. Perhaps it was the youngster's own disbelief, or distaste for the idea, or an intuitive doubt about the propriety of talking about so delicate a subject, or more likely a combination of all those. Each child interprets and assimilates information in his own way, whether it be about reproduction or any other subject.

Different but Equal

The difference between boys and girls is another concern of preschoolers and is almost sure to precipitate questions. If a child has no siblings, he or she has probably been, or may profitably be, provided with opportunities of seeing both boys and girls of his or her own age without clothes on. Seeing children of the same sex nude is as informative as seeing those of the opposite sex, since one of a child's unspoken questions may be, "Am I all right the way I am?" Observing that there are others who are essentially the same is reassuring. It takes the three- or four-year-old a while to absorb the fact that there are two, and only two, sexes. For all he knows there might be half a dozen!

In answering a little girl's question, "What's he got there hanging down?" when she first takes notice of the boy's penis, a mother can tell her that boys have a penis just as their fathers do. Girls have a vagina and womb like their mother's. If you are born a boy you always stay a boy and grow up to be a man, "like Daddy." If you are born a girl, you always stay a girl and grow up to be a woman, with breasts, "like Mommy." She may want to add that since boys urinate (or make wee-wee, or whatever household term is used) through their penis, it is easier for them to stand up when doing so, whereas girls are more comfortable sitting down.

Being absolutely definite about boys remaining boys and girls remaining girls, and about the desirableness of belonging to either sex helps clear up any worries about losing or having lost that dramatic male organ. We can also take care to phrase our answers to questions about the difference between boys and girls so that boys do not seem to be "the haves" and girls "the have-nots."

The question of why observing other children their own age undressed sets doubts at rest but observing adult nudity may arouse anxiety in some children is discussed in Chapter 6.

When a Child Asks No Questions

That a youngster nearing six has never asked any questions about reproduction or differences between the sexes does not necessarily mean he is disinterested or unconcerned. Since these years are the time when confusions are quite readily cleared up, we may want to make it easy for our son or daughter to bring up the subject. The arrival of a baby either in his own home or in the home of a relative or a friend is often a convenient occasion for bringing up the subject with the child who has asked no questions. If a parent can arrange to take the nonquestioner to see the baby, and it is of the opposite sex, she might casually point out the difference. If the youngster sees the mother nursing the baby, that may be an introduction to the topic of "where babies come from."

If we do not have access to a new baby, we may help a youngster ask a question that is on his mind by saying something like, "When I was little I used to think that babies were ordered from a store. Where did you think they came from when you were little?" Knowing that a parent was once in doubt or had made wrong conjectures may help a child express his confusion.

Another approach to the nonquestioner is to read him one of the excellent books for young children about babies. *The Wonderful Story of How You Were Born,* by Sidonie M. Gruenberg, or *I'm Going to Have a Baby,* by Laura Z. Hobson, are among the good ones for four-and-a-half- and five-year-olds.

Learning from Questioning

The ever-amazing flow of questions in all fields often reveals what is on a youngster's mind, but it can also wear down parental patience. If we are aware of what different types of questions may be telling us, as explained here, and if we recognize how questioning contributes to mental and social development, our tolerance for a child's curiosity may expand. Responding appropriately and not shutting off queries may make the difference between a child's keeping and cultivating the spirit of inquiry and the desire to know, and his becoming indifferent or resistant to learning now and when he goes to school. Giving him the conviction that "It is all right to ask" is a sound foundation for his learning throughout life, for good questioners tend to make good learners.

6 *Masculinity . . . Femininity*

IN ORDER TO grow into a reasonably healthy, happy personality, a small person needs to feel he is "all right" and likable. Basic to that self-esteem is the conviction that it is good to be a boy or to be a girl. A child needs to feel that both sexes are loved and valued. Out of such attitudes come the boy's desire to grow into a man and take on the "manly" characteristics our culture demands, and the girl's wish to become appropriately feminine.

The cultivation of masculinity and femininity is neither direct nor entirely obvious. We shall consider what we mean by these terms, and how parents can create an atmosphere that fosters the qualities involved. Related to this is a preschooler's attitude toward his own body. How do we further healthy attitudes in this area?

Expectations and Behavior

Each society, anthropologists tell us, prescribes certain propensities and activities for its men and for its women. In raising children, parents around the world try to instill the behavior that conforms to the standard of masculinity and femininity in their culture or their own segment of that society. Martin and Lois Hoffman, in *Review of Child Development Research,* describe the standards a society sets for manliness and womanliness as two separate clusters of wishes, feelings, and external attributes —one cluster for the males and another for the females. Once such a cluster has been acquired by an individual, it acts as an internal judge or monitor, approving or disapproving of his or her sentiments or actions. That cluster becomes a part of conscience, as will be discussed in Chapter 7.

By the age of six, and in some respects far earlier, a youngster usually has a fairly good grasp of those qualities associated with "What mommies do" and "What daddies do" in many aspects of daily living, although all their concepts may not be entirely clear.

What Makes the Difference?

Is behavior we call masculine or feminine rooted in the biological makeup of each sex, or does it stem from external pressures? Some students of human behavior attribute the differences in the aptitudes of each sex to the action of hormones, although that hormonal difference is generally agreed not to be present in children of preschool age. Other authorities assert that sex roles are acquired in early childhood. A boy or girl learns to act in ways his or her family considers appropriate for each sex. He (or she) comes to believe that he (or she) possesses some of the characteristics of the parent of the same sex and identifies with that parent. A boy or girl models himself, often without realizing it, on the example set by that parent.

In identifying with a model, a youngster behaves as if events happening to that model were also happening to him. Four-year-old Lola had often heard that she looked like her pretty mother. When her mother dressed up to go out, the small girl took on her mother's pleasure in looking well groomed and attractive. Like most young children, Lola believed that inner resemblance accompanied outward similarity, although she could not have put that belief into words. If she looked like her mother, then she must be like her mother, Lola reasoned.

Another source of learning the behavior typical of one's sex is the tendency of human beings to take on the behavior they perceive as being expected of them. This is part of that "self-fulfilling prophecy" explained in Chapter 1. One becomes, to a great extent, what one is repeatedly told one will become.

A third road that leads to masculine and feminine characteristics is that children discover that they will win acceptance and approval more readily when they conform to the standards held for members of their own sex. A four-year-old boy in a nursery school was part of a group playing they were spacemen. "Now I'm going to be a spaceman painting a picture," he declared, stopping in his play in front of the easels set up in a corner of the room.

"Spacemen don't paint pictures, you dope!" his companions jeered at him, although in this school both boys and girls enjoyed painting and it was not held to be the prerogative of one sex. At the same time, a girl who wanted to be a "spacelady" was rudely told, "Girls aren't in space capsules. You get away from us."

Stereotypes Get in Our Way

In a magazine article, Florence Howe stated:

> Though there is no evidence that their early physical needs are different from or less than boys', girls are offered fewer activities even in kindergarten. They may sit and watch while boys, at the request of the female teacher, change the seating arrangement in the room. Of course, it's not simply a matter of physical exercise or ability: Boys are learning how to behave as men, and girls to be "ladies" who enjoy "being waited on."

This quotation is not from a periodical published in 1910, 1930, or even 1950. It is cited as evidence that "Sexual Stereotypes Start Early," the title of the article, which appeared in the *Saturday Review* of October 16, 1971. The article is an adaptation of an address Professor Howe gave, at the invitation of Columbia's Women's Liberation, to the Superintendents' Work Conference. The author contends that our schools, in spite of a preponderance of women teachers, prepare girls to be second-class citizens, always "assisting," but rarely leading.

Labeling some attitudes and behavior as masculine and others as feminine has unfortunate consequences, since it leads us, and the children, to think in stereotypes. The small girl who is not sure whether she wants a chocolate or a vanilla ice-cream bar and wavers in making her choice, may hear from her father, "Just like a woman to keep changing her mind. None of them know what they want." Again, she may hear, over and over, that certain tasks are "women's work," and that "men are better at using tools," or keeping account of money, or thinking straight. Small boys, if they cry over a minor bump, or betray their disappointment, or have their feelings hurt easily, are likely to be told, "Men don't act that way. Boys have to be able to take it."

Forcing Responsibility

One father, in saying good-bye to his three-year-old son each morning, would say, in a joking manner, "Now you be the man in the family and look after your mother and your sisters today." To the boy, this was no joke, and manliness seemed to be a burden. He knew he needed his mother to take care of him. The insistence on the stereotype became a threat of responsibility he found overwhelming. More than the Women's Liberation movement has made it necessary for us to reexamine some of our cherished myths about "the right behavior" for each sex.

Research on the behavior of preschoolers has demonstrated that belligerence, perhaps because the stereotype has become familiar to them, is more frequent among small males than among females. One way the three- to five-year-old boys exhibit that aggressiveness is in their play with dolls, which take far more of a beating from the boys who play with them than from the girls. Even when little girls are pretending that the dolls have been "very bad," they do not get as violent in pretending to punish them as do the boys. Perhaps a healthy move away from the myths about appropriate sex behavior is the fact that in most nursery schools the boys are allowed to play, in their own way, with dolls. According to a study in one kindergarten, the more masculine boys, when playing with the dolls, showed that they perceived the feminine role both as a caretaking and a powerful one.

How Children See Their Parents

Results of tests to determine how small children view each parent reveal that father is seen as "more aggressive, punitive, and even dangerous than mother." In many households, father is also perceived as the one who is more skilled in using his hands, repairing household appliances, and the one who is looked to for decisions regarding expenditures.

Bearing out the results of such research, while four-year-old Noah was visiting his grandmother one day, she attempted, none too skillfully, to replace a broken plug at the end of a lamp cord. Noah observed her efforts for a minute or two, and then advised her, "You better wait til Grandpa gets home and he'll fix it. My Daddy is the fixer at my house. He says ladies aren't good at that."

Since his grandmother knew that Noah's grandfather did not conform to the image of being "a good fixer," she determined to make short work both of the repair job and of Noah's stereotype. "Girls and women can fix things just as well as men can, Noah. And you know what? Some men don't like being 'fixers' even though they like being men, and your grandpa is like that."

Whether or not the introduction of this point of view widened Noah's conception of what is proper for men and women, his faith in his father's competence is a far healthier attitude than the one seen too often in films, TV comedies, and comic strips. The mass media, in portraying men as blustering, but bungling, and women as achieving their goals through manipulation, indirection, and, too often, duplicity, are not giving the young a picture of either sex calculated to build mutual respect or trust, even when the satire is amusing to adults.

Children tend to "catch" their parents' feelings about the sex each belongs to as well as about the opposite sex. An unhappily married woman, or one who has no husband, may voice the opinion, all too frequently, that men are not to be relied on. She may, too, show by her actions that she considers them untrustworthy. Such an attitude tends to rub off on her daughters and to make her sons feel that manliness is not safe.

A mother who is angry because she is a woman, or who looks down on all activities labeled as feminine, may prejudice her children against the rightness of being female. Comparable attitudes on the part of a father have, of course, a similar detrimental effect.

Are We Unfair to Our Girls?

Alice Rossi, a sociologist concerned with the position of women and a reasonably moderate leader of Women's Lib, has long maintained that in raising girls to conform to the picture of a docile, helpful, somewhat dependent, caretaking person, we are supplying society with the stuff of which are made good assistants to men in laboratories, factories, offices, or health and educational institutions. We are not, even today, raising our girls to become leaders in their own right in many occupations. Our girls tend to grow up believing they are less important, less competent, less courageous than boys are.

So far, young children whose mothers have paid jobs and whose parents share household and child-caring responsibilities still seem to absorb from the general atmosphere the older idea of "men's work" and "women's work," even though the pattern in their own home does not tally with it. With the increasing number of families in which the wife's continuing education and/or her satisfaction and success in her work influence the plans of the entire family as much as does the husband's need for training, a good job, and gratifying leisure pursuits, we might speculate whether the trend will give small boys and girls a more up-to-date impression of the expanding boundaries of masculine and feminine behavior.

Do Boys Pay a Price for Privilege?

Research as well as observation confirms the belief that greater freedom, power, and value are still attached to the part the man plays in our society. Yet life is not entirely full of extra privileges for males. In the great majority of homes, however enlightened they may be, boys are taught, from the time they sally forth to join the other children in the neighborhood on the sidewalk, to keep their affectionate, gentler tendencies bottled up. Demonstrating such sentiments is considered more appropriate for girls.

Boys are expected to prepare themselves to be less dependent on the attitudes and opinions of others, studies have concluded. If a small boy is shut out by his playmates and is, as a result, uneasy and apprehensive, he tends to get less sympathy at home than a girl would under similar circumstances.

A small boy who busies himself with building blocks or construction toys, in preference to playing with other children, may be approved for his self-reliance. His sisters are expected to be friendly and make themselves agreeable to others to a greater extent than he.

How Does Sexual Identity Develop?

Everyone, consciously or unconsciously, has some ideas about himself as a member of his own sex. Everyone regards himself, or herself, as having some traits that are owing to a part of sex membership. The degree to which an individual thinks of himself or herself as masculine or feminine is described by Martin and Lois Hoffman in *A Review of Child Development Research* as his or her sexual identity. This attitude toward himself is only one of a set of interlocking beliefs, which, taken together, make up a child's total self-concept.

Just how sexual identity is established, psychologists and members of other disciplines concerned with human behavior are not in agreement, but in general one's picture of oneself as masculine or feminine comes from several sources.

First is an awareness of being like the parent of one's own sex and different from the parent of the opposite sex. Then, too, a youngster gets a sense of sex identity from the degree to which he or she is interested in and able to master the skills, scaled down to size, appropriate for that sex.

As an illustration, look at Mrs. Chase's experience with her three-and-a-half-year-old daughter, Elaine, who wanted to "help" bake a cake. Mrs. Chase baked in the old-fashioned manner, without a mix. All the dry ingredients had to be carefully sifted and measured. She had been through the assistance to be had from the young with Elaine's two elder brothers, both of whom would invariably lose interest after a minute or two of sifting sugar or flour. Not so Elaine. Mrs. Chase remembers:

> It was uncanny. Elaine stuck with the flour, sifting even though her little hands must have gotten tired. She was entirely different from what the boys had been like. She stayed with it, right next to me, doing what I told her to until the batter went into the pans and we put some in

> a little pan for a cake of her own. Baking was her bag, and no mistake. Then she said in a sort of prissy tone I'd never heard before, "Now I'm just like Mommy. I'm a good baker."

Not all girls are more domestic than their brothers at an early age, but those who do derive satisfaction from pursuits traditionally regarded as feminine have their sense of sex identity reinforced.

Elaine's greater persistence in staying with the baking probably stemmed in part from a feeling that she was expected to enjoy it. That enjoyment, in turn, was enhanced as Mrs. Chase took trouble to find spots in which Elaine could participate. She identified with the girl's interest in helping. Identification is a two-way street. A youngster's sense of sex membership deepens as the parent of the same sex takes on that son's or daughter's feelings.

A third manner in which a boy or girl acquires his feeling of identity as masculine or feminine before school age is through a perception of what each of his parents does or does not do because of being a man or a woman.

We have pointed out that young children have quite definite ideas about the responsibilities and preferences of their fathers and mothers and are eager to fit in with the appropriate pattern. Households differ, of course. Each child will see the customs of his own home as "right," although he may tolerate different arrangements that he observes in the families of his playmates as being exceptions to the rule.

For example, in the Olins' household, the mother easily became discouraged and gloomy. She depended on her husband's more cheerful, buoyant approach to keep her on an even keel. Without realizing it, the Olin children early in life assumed that one facet of masculinity was a courageous, "every cloud has a silver lining," view of the world. How firm this impression had become was brought home to Mrs. Olin when she overheard her four-year-old daughter directing a playmate: "You can be the daddy, and you must cheer me up, because I'm the mommy and everything is going wrong, and I'm going to cry."

In another family, the role of soother and encourager might fall to the wife, resulting in quite a different perception of sex roles on the part of a young child. Still, the essential idea would be conveyed that mutual emotional support is part of a good relationship between a man and a woman.

Parental Behavior and the Identification Process

Let us push back a step further into the parental behavior that shapes masculinity and femininity. The child whose parent of the same sex tends to respond to situations in a manner considered typical for that sex gains in two ways, according to some studies. In observing typical masculine or feminine behavior much of the time, the youngster acquires, through identification, the confidence that he or she can master the necessary behavior. Then, when he or she goes to school and sees that his or her own actions and attitudes match quite well with the preferred behavior of his or her sex, a sense of being "all right" is strengthened.

If a mother or father does not display, or only rarely displays, characteristics typical for his or her sex, his son or daughter may have less markedly typical characteristics. That may lead to the child's having doubts about his masculinity (or her femininity) as he or she encounters the more generally accepted behavior in contemporaries. Yet, in many families, the wife makes numerous important decisions without losing her essential femininity, without being an overpowering figure to her children or a threat to her husband. A working wife may still like being a woman and convey her satisfaction to her daughters, even when they are three, four, or five years old.

A husband need not be blustering and

concerned watching the ball game on TV or proving that he is in command in order to give his children the feeling of having the protection of a strong, responsible male. A gentle, mild-mannered father who has confidence in his manliness may be an excellent model for his sons. In other words, stereotyped behavior is not called for. Gratification in his or her sex membership on the part of a parent is as keenly felt, and as easily identified with, and probably more important than, outward behavior.

The Family Romance

Another vital phase of a small child's development toward manhood or womanhood comes about through an attachment to the parent of the opposite sex during the preschool years. In Chapter 1 these years were described as a "rehearsal for adolescence." Nowhere is this rehearsal more apparent than in the way the small girl cuts her emotional teeth by trying out her feminine charms on Daddy, or the manner that little boys adopt toward their mothers, about whom they tend to be possessive and sometimes protective.

This special attachment to the parent of the opposite sex during these years is a step in the process of growing up. Like other steps, it is a healthy sign of an expanding personality. Also, like other steps or stages, this one needs to be worked through and then left behind. Usually around the age of six, if all has gone well, the boy who has been declaring, "I'm going to marry my Mommy when I get bigger," or the girl who has been attempting to outmaneuver her mother in taking first place with daddy, decides that winning the parent of the opposite sex is a lost cause.

"Mommy and Daddy belong to each other," may have been only an unspoken precept, but it needs to, and usually does, get through to the preschooler. On an "If you can't beat 'em, join 'em" basis, boys ally themselves with their fathers and girls become closer to their mothers, about the time that they begin to shed their baby teeth. Unconsciously, or sometimes quite openly, they choose to be as much like the parent who did succeed in winning the desired object (that is, mother or father) as possible.

We may facilitate a youngster's progress through this phase of development if we accept it in a "Doesn't everybody?" manner. This is sometimes easier said than done. A little girl of three or four is so utterly endearing that her father may be tempted to want to keep her at just that convenient stage of adoration. He may even go along with her in pretending that she will replace her mother. He would do better to assure her that "*Now* you are my little girl, and Mommy is my wife. When you grow up, you'll be somebody's wife, too." A mother can hold out a similar hope to her son: "Boys like to think they want only their Mommies. When you grow up you won't need me, and you'll find a wife for yourself, but we'll still be good friends."

A nice balance can be maintained, and is in most families, between undue encouragement of fantasies about getting rid of the parent of the same sex in order to obtain the one of the opposite sex for oneself, and making a child feel that his greater fondness for his mother, or for her father, is "bad" or a subject for ridicule. As in other situations, the best incentive a parent can offer a son or daughter is the viewpoint, "Growing up may mean giving up some things, but you'll find plenty of rewards to make up for what you leave behind as you grow." We can let a boy or girl know that others—perhaps we, too—once felt that only a father (or mother) would be the one we would love and want to spend all our time with, but that when we get older, we change our minds.

Parents Feel It, Too

Parents tend to feel especially drawn toward their three- to six-year-old offspring of the opposite sex, too. An interesting research study was carried on by Rothbart and Eleanor Maccoby (Maccoby is among the most respected of research designers):

> The parents were asked to react to a child's voice in a hypothetical situation. The recorded voice of a single child, which could not readily be identified as to sex, provided the stimulus material.

Some of the parents were informed that it was a boy's voice, others that it was a girl's voice, and differences in the parents' reactions were then investigated. The results indicated that mothers tended to respond more permissively toward the boy's voice and fathers responded more permissively toward the girl's voice. An unexpected finding of this study was that mothers were more accepting of comfort-seeking in their sons than in their daughters.

For a woman dissatisfied in her own marriage, or for a man overly eager that his son be a "boy who can take it," this period of attachment to the parent of the opposite sex may hold a threat. Considerable security plus a robust sense of humor are called for to survive with unruffled temper when a three-year-old mischief-maker bedevils us all day and turns into an angel when her father walks through the door. Husbands can keep in mind that a weary, out-of-sorts wife can be reassured in countless ways. She may like to hear that a three-year-old has distinct limitations as a companion and that a wife really does come first.

It is only natural to be hurt and feel superfluous if a small daughter or son seems to be usurping the affections that are properly ours, especially if she or he is at the same time making heavy demands on us. If we see the situation in perspective and realize that it is only temporary, we will be far less likely to be resentful.

One-parent Families and Sexual Identity

With all the emphasis on the need for a parent of each sex at various times in the development of a youngster's confidence in himself or herself as a boy or as a girl, a parent who must bring up a son or a daughter without the presence of a mate may be discouraged about giving that child the opportunity for well-rounded development. A one-parent family is not necessarily an obstacle to a child's establishing adequate masculine or feminine identity. Single parents can still provide some companionship and models of the sex of the missing parent, but it may take extra thought and planning.

Those parents who have lived through the experience say that it is better to settle for being a good mother or an adequate father rather than feeling impelled to fill both roles. One will do better, too, by keeping in mind that thousands and thousands of competent, feminine women and masculine men grew up with only one parent in their childhood homes.

Grandparents are a "first line of support." A middle-aged grandfather can be an excellent masculine figure and model for a small boy or the man in a three- or four-year-old girl's life, even though Saturday afternoons with Grandpa are less frequent than we might wish. Uncles, older cousins, the fathers of playmates, or middle-aged to elderly neighbors, far away from their own grandchildren, can also prove valuable in this capacity. A summer play-group for five-year-old boys run by older boys or men with teaching or camping experience can prove a good investment. Small girls without fathers need male companionship, too, and similar resources may be useful.

A woman keeping house alone for her children or sharing a home with another woman may need to make an effort to accept a certain amount of roughness and toughness from a son. One divorcee spoke bitterly of the "atmosphere of daintiness around here since there isn't a man in the house." Overvaluing quietness and good manners at the expense of more typically boyish behavior can work a hardship on young males.

A father left with small children to fend for needs a motherly person for both his girls and his boys, but out of sheer practical necessity, he is likely to have that in the person of a housekeeper. A woman with a young child of her own who lives in the house or brings her child to work with her can go a long way toward solving that problem. Housekeeping skills are far less important than warmth and patience with young children.

Usually, a man finds it easier to enlist another mother who will frequently include his child in excursions, peanut-butter-sandwich lunches, or rainy-day indoor play. Widowers are, in general, more fortunate than widows in that if they seek assistance from neighbors, wives of friends, or relatives they are not likely to be eyed with suspicion or rebuffed as intruders as a young woman might be.

Worries About Psychosexual Development

For most parents, helping young children feel that both sexes are equally important and guiding them through the emotional and sexual development of these years is a far less pressing concern than working through situations involving nudity in the family, masturbation, or sex play between the children.

To adults who have become almost inured to seeing unclothed men and women on the screen and in the theater, modesty in the home might seem unnecessary. Then, too, many of us are still reacting strongly against the prudishness of an earlier day, which may have shadowed our own childhood. As was pointed out in the previous chapter, young children benefit by seeing other children of both sexes, who have not reached puberty, completely undressed. To observe that two, and only two, sexes exist, to have questions answered and doubts allayed is reassuring.

However, the sight of the adult nude body of one's own or of the opposite sex can have a different effect on the preschooler. The small girl who complained on seeing her mother without any clothes, "I'm so plain and you're so fancy," was voicing the discouragement about her own body that young children may feel on seeing adults unclad.

Such experiences may also be sexually stimulating, which can be even more disturbing to a preschooler. Three-, four- and five-year-olds are capable of sexual excitation. Although that *capacity* is a part of healthy development, habitual exposure to the sight of the nude adult body, or the practice of regularly taking baths or showers with a parent, may stir up more intense feeling than a youngster can deal with. This can make it difficult for the child to proceed comfortably to the next stage of development, which lasts from about six to the onset of puberty. During that stage, sexual feelings are far less prominent than in the preschool years, and energies, if all has gone well, are freed for becoming more reasonable, less demanding, and for achieving along many lines.

Certainly, parents are sometimes unnecessarily modest, too. Observing that adults use the toilet is one of the ways two- or two-and-a-half-year-olds learn about using it themselves. Once they have learned that lesson, they can learn that grown-ups sometimes like privacy and that even small children are entitled to it, too. If a youngster does burst in on a parent when he or she is undressed, no harm is done and surely no issue need be made of it. Yet continual parental nudity, for the sake of nudity, is hardly advisable even in today's world.

How Shall We Deal with Masturbation?

We need to take care that a boy or girl does not get the impression that parts of the body are not exposed because they are "not nice" or "shameful" or "dirty." That may be the preschooler's impression if too much, and too intense, stress is placed on modesty, especially if it is accompanied by disapproval of a young child's masturbating.

As a small person explores the world around him, he also explores his own body. Both boys and girls have been doing so since babyhood, as every parent has observed. Mothers and fathers are not likely to be upset by these explorations unless their own upbringing generated a high degree of guilt. Indeed, most parents today accept the fact that a preschool boy or girl may stroke his or her genital area when in need of comfort not immediately available in other ways.

Maria Piers, a noted child therapist and educator, says in her book *Growing Up with Children:*

> Masturbation is a sign of development, just like cutting teeth, acquiring speech, or realizing how puzzles fit together. Like all these necessary steps, masturbation should be neither artificially rushed, nor stimulated, nor greatly discouraged when it does occur. After all, what a child should learn is not that relief of sexual tensions is evil, but that it should not

take place in public. The capacity for adult sexual enjoyment does not emerge all of a sudden in early adulthood. Like all human capacities, it develops step by step. Masturbation is the first step.

Excessive guilt over masturbation can be damaging. The preschool child, for reasons that will be explained in the following chapter, often feels guilty in many situations, out of all proportion to what he has done or to the reproof his parents have given him. Children sense that anything related to sexuality, although they may never have heard the word, has a special meaning for adults. If we need to say to a child who has been embarrassing us by masturbating in front of strangers, as a shy, uneasy youngster is likely to do, "You may do that when you are alone, but not when other people are around," we can take care to keep the tone as casual as possible.

If masturbation seems excessive—that is, a youngster appears to be driven to it frequently throughout the day—it may be a sign that he or she is lonely, unhappy, or troubled by feelings of guilt and/or of being unloved and unlovable. If a new baby has come into the family or some other sharp change in a three- or four-year-old's surroundings has occurred, he may need extra reassurance and comfort. The question to be resolved is not how to put a stop to masturbation, but rather how to meet the child's needs more effectively so that his energies can be freed for other activities.

Perhaps such a child needs more affectionate attention and approval from his parents, more companionship with others his age, standards that are not so high that living up to them is a strain. Some thought about and experimenting with the arrangements of his daily life may be necessary to discover the cause of his being troubled.

If a parent is not aware whether his three- or four-year-old is masturbating after he has been tucked in bed, he should not feel he must find out in order to be a good parent.

Sex Play Among Young Children

One other manifestation of a young child's sexuality that disturbs parents is sex play among children. Almost every preschooler at some time takes part in explorations with other children that might be considered "sex play." If such activities are persistent, we may need to deal with the situation directly in ways that will be discussed. Threats or punishments are no solution. The most helpful attitude on the part of parents is to keep calm and avoid appearing shocked or devastated. To declare that such play is "dirty," "bad," or "shameful" serves no purpose.

A frequent occurrence among the three-year-olds is episodes of undressing. A youngster who is worried about the difference between boys and girls, or not sure whether all boys and all girls have the same genital equipment, may persuade his or her playmates to take off their clothes. If we find our son or daughter involved in such incidents, we will need to make sure he feels he can bring any questions he has to us, even though we may have believed we had already cleared up his or her doubts. To stop the play we might say something like, "We undress when we go to bed or when we take a bath or change our clothes. Other times we keep our clothes on. Taking them off when you are playing is sort of babyish. Lots of children try it once, but you are big enough to know that we don't get undressed outdoors or take off our clothes while we're playing."

The delicate question of whether to report such incidents to the mothers of the other children involved depends somewhat on how we think they will react and how friendly we are with them. One woman found her five-year-old and his two four-year-old friends undressed and playing "going to bed together." She had dealt with the situation calmly by firmly announcing, "We always keep our clothes on when we're playing, in the house or outside, and we'll find something that is a better game than that."

Afterward, she and her husband discussed reporting the incident to the parents of the other children. They decided that one set of parents would probably be extremely upset, or else blame the episode entirely on the five-year-old and forbid their child to see him any more, so that saying nothing would be wisest. As for the other set of parents, with whom they were on good terms and who they felt would undoubtedly take a reasonable view of the children's behavior, they agreed to give that couple an account of what had occurred and how it had been handled.

Some perfectly "nice" children experiment with mutual masturbation once or twice. It is not always the bad influence of "the other children" that is responsible, nor are boys rather than girls, or the slightly older rather than the younger of the children, necessarily the initiators. Keeping that fact in mind may help us refrain from fixing blame on a particular child or predicting a dire future for the suspected instigator.

If we find two or three children involved in sexual activities, we may need to supervise them and keep them supplied with materials and ideas that are sufficiently challenging and enjoyable so that sex play will not be their chief attraction for one another. "Supervision" does not mean that we need be suspicious every time those youngsters are playing together quietly, or that we question a son or daughter about exactly what the two have been doing.

If one boy's or girl's playmates really do seem to be preoccupied with sexual exploration, we may need to provide other playmates. If a child has a number of interests, he or she may be relieved to have us say, "Let's get Dave and his sister over here this afternoon. I think you and Herbie are getting tired of just being together with each other all the time." If we can discourage rather than forbid association with the offending Herbie, we avoid making him attractive just because his company is taboo. We also thus give the child the support he may require to remove himself from Herbie, for whose company he may have no desire.

Unless a youngster is experiencing an overwhelming conflict over feelings about the difference between males and females, or allied questions, he will usually respond to other kinds of play and other playmates. If parents believe their youngster has a deeper problem, they may want to consult a child-guidance clinic or child therapist.

Looking Toward the Youngster's Adulthood

If our goal is to guide our child toward a firm conviction that his own sex and his feelings about it are acceptable, and that the opposite one is also equally "all right," we are giving him good support in his efforts to grow up. We can work toward that goal through our presentation of the roles of men and of women in many facets of daily life and through the way we respond to a youngster's attachment to the parent of the opposite sex during these years. Then we may reasonably look forward to our boy or girl becoming an adult with a capacity to enjoy a full and satisfactory sexual relationship—no slight achievement.

7 *Toward A Healthy Conscience*

"CONSCIENCE DOTH MAKE cowards of us all," said Hamlet. We would all agree that conscience makes us cautious and prudent in many circumstances, and often conforming. Yet it is more than the regulator of "middle-class morality," as Hamlet implies. If the foundations for responsible behavior have been laid down in the early years, conscience may also impel the more mature individual to stand up for his beliefs even when that might entail risking discomfort or unpopularity.

How does a healthy conscience develop? What pulls and tensions undergird it, and what causes it to become troublesomely overactive? What attitudes and teaching on the part of parents make for a useful, working conscience?

Although the actions of the three- through five-year-old do not continually evidence, in conventional ways, how busy his conscience is, an understanding of its operations and its limitations is often the key to his behavior, both the desirable and the less desirable variety.

How Does Conscience Grow?

A boy or girl develops a serviceable conscience as he makes the customs and values of his family, his neighborhood, and his culture part of his own inner monitor. The serviceable preschool conscience is one that asserts itself when actions, forbidden or dangerous, need to be stopped but does not exert such intense pressures or impose such severe restrictions that it interferes with the enjoyment of daily living.

The inner monitor develops through a youngster's relationships with other people whom he loves, depends on, and takes as models. Their approval or disapproval, in words and actions, cultivates it and its accompanying sense of guilt. Some capacity to feel guilt is essential to acquiring the restraints necessary to becoming a socialized human being, as emphasized earlier in this volume.

When a preschooler experiences appropriate guilt over wrongdoing, his feelings range from uncomfortable to miserable. Those feelings are one of the forces deterring him from repeating unacceptable behavior.

Through the growth of conscience come those ethical values of honesty, respect, and concern for the rights of others, including their possessions, and an understanding of why rules and laws are necessary and why we obey them even when it is inconvenient to do so.

Parents instill such values through the manner in which they handle situations in their own lives, which small children observe, often unwittingly. Values are also brought home to the young by the approval or disapproval they receive for their own behavior. If a high value is set on spontaneous helpfulness and consideration, on behaving honorably even when "nobody is looking," on generosity, on the observance of the spirit, not simply the letter, of the law, a child tends to develop a social conscience. That is more to be aimed at as a goal than mere obedience.

Conscience Takes on a "Local Color"

Clearly, different societies, different groups within each society, and different periods in history have labeled various actions as "good" or "bad." As a result, children grow up with inner monitors that make widely differing demands on them. An extreme example of such a variation is the legend of the Spartan boy who stole a fox and let it gnaw his flesh away as he carried it stoically under his cloak. Stealing and suffering pain in silence were, in the ethics of military Sparta, 2,500 years ago, exemplary conduct. A child who did either, or both at once, could live at peace with his conscience. We may assume that some Spartan children were often troubled because they were failing to live up to the painful and unchildlike standards held up for them.

Most children in the late twentieth-century United States are taught a set of values of another kind. Not only stealing, but concealing a serious wound, would result in disapproval from responsible adults.

Conscience Grows Step by Step

Let us see how the values we are trying to establish come, eventually, to take hold. One of the first prohibitions a child comes up against when he can get around under his own power is that he must not tamper with certain objects under any circumstances, nor with some others unless he has been given permission to touch them. In the first category might be the jars and colored sticks in his mother's makeup box, matches, his father's razor, or the earth in the flower pot on the windowsill. Among objects that may be handled or taken with permission might be the occasional piece of candy in a candy dish, the switches and buttons on the TV, the radio, the telephone, or an older brother's or sister's favorite toy.

Long before she was three, Jean had learned to stay away from certain "No-no's" if and when one of her parents or her older sister was within sight and gave a warning, "Not for Jean." That was an advance over having to be separated from the forbidden object in spite of verbal reminders. After a few more months, Jean would stay away from a forbidden object as long as someone representing authority was present; she no longer required an admonition in words.

Between her third and fourth birthdays, Jean went through a stage of walking up to the candy box, or the control buttons on the TV set, or her mother's makeup box,

looking around to see if anyone could observe her, and then solemnly saying, "Not for Jeanie," but succumbing to temptation anyway. She had a budding but unreliable conscience. After she had gained a bit more control, her own warning to herself was usually effective.

A year or so later her conscience was operating automatically, at least in the matter of decorating her face with lipstick. Stuffing it with licorice drops was another story. That temptation took longer for her conscience to conquer.

Different children attain a reliable conscience at different ages. One that is reliable in one situation may still be shaky or nonexistent in many others. For Jean, keeping away from her mother's lipstick seemed to become easier as she began to enjoy using crayons and paper, but it still consumed so much of her reservoir of resistance that, when confronted with other "No-no's," she needed the support of the sight, if not the voice, of one of her elders.

Vacillation is to be expected. The preschooler's conscience is similar to one of those microscopic forms of life that after bulging in one direction tend to shrink in another.

Encouraging a Realistic Inner Monitor

Jean's parents had aided the development of their daughter's inner controls through reasonably consistent discipline (discussed in Chapter 4). For example, if the little girl was spoken to sternly on one occasion for smearing her mother's eye shadow all over her face, she was not applauded as "the cutest thing in the world" the next time she tried it. They had also geared their teaching to Jean's level of understanding and temperament.

Her parents had been generous with encouragement when Jean demonstrated that she could take responsibility for observing the regulations prevailing in the household and when she played outdoors with other children or went to their homes. From her earliest days, most of the adults with whom she came in contact let her know that they had faith in her ability to take a new step and to become more grown-up in her behavior. Mistakes she made along the way were not interpreted as a sign that she was clumsy, uncooperative, or willful. "You are the kind who can do it," "Jean is a girl who does her best," were attitudes that prevailed in her home generally. Even when her mother's or father's patience wore thin, the warmth she usually received tided her over.

Such an atmosphere clearly sets up the boundaries of acceptable behavior. It also lessens the burden of uneasy guilt some children carry because they do not know where they stand or because they lack the satisfaction of believing they can please the adults they love.

Conscience Can Prompt Considerate Behavior

The development of a healthy conscience is facilitated, too, by the example of adults who, without preaching about doing so, carry out their responsibilities and are not in the habit of "trying to get away with something."

An inner monitor that demands consideration for the feelings and needs of others most of the time, as well as prompting observance of the rules, grows out of seeing and identifying with the considerate behavior of a parent or another adult the child loves.

For instance, a father preparing supper for his four-year-old, in a wife's absence, breaks her favorite dish or burns her most useful cooking pan. When his wife returns, he tells her he is sorry about the damage and then carefully glues together the dish or painstakingly scours the pan. A small child witnessing this and other kinds of considerate behavior gets the idea that hurting, offending, or disappointing someone is as much to be deplored as breaking a definite rule. Gradually, as he absorbs the meaning of consideration, his inner monitor will prompt him to help when someone needs assistance.

Right and Wrong Appear Differently with Age

Not all manifestations of a child's conscience coincide with adult values. Small children, in their efforts to cope with a confusing world and their own feelings, often have a "bad conscience" over trivial or nonexistent misdemeanors. Indeed, they may be vocally hypercritical of the behavior of anyone who errs by doing what they themselves have only recently acquired sufficient control not to do (discussed in the section on "Tattling" in Chapter 3).

A four- or five-year-old can be tiresomely self-righteous over details and oblivious to the larger issues his parents have been trying to teach.

An extreme example of such confusion of values is depicted in Richard Hughes's *A High Wind in Jamaica,* that bizarre tale of mid-nineteenth-century children. The ship on which their parents have placed them to return to England from their remote island home is captured by pirates. The children live for several months with the pirates in the midst of lawlessness, seduction, piracy, and murder. "Grown-ups never *do* tell us things," they say to one another when events become incomprehensible. They quickly accommodate themselves to life on the pirate ship, delighted with being permissively treated.

Eventually they are reunited with their parents in England and the pirates are captured and brought to trial. The children are taken to the office of the family solicitor to give their testimony. There this conversation takes place:

> The solicitor asked, "When you were with these men, did they ever do anything you didn't like? You know what I mean, something *nasty?"*
>
> "Yes!" cried Rachel. . . . "He talked abour drawers," she said in a shocked voice.
>
> "What did he say?"
>
> "He told us once not to toboggan down the deck on them. . . ." That comment came from Emily, who was ten, but her five-year-old sister, Rachel, added, "He shouldn't have talked about drawers."

Granted these were children of the Victorian era, but the basic paradox is much the same today. Conscience, in its early phases, tends to fasten on trivialities and fails to comprehend broader issues of right and wrong, honesty and dishonesty.

Parents Can Side with Conscience

When a boy or girl, with disproportionate guilt and anxiety, tells us that he has called someone a "bad name," or walked across the neighbor's grass, or broken a cup that was already cracked, we may be so relieved that nothing worse took place that we laugh and take a "think nothing of it" attitude.

We help a youngster most if we can diminish his guilt yet take the side of conscience. Something to the effect that, "I know you feel sorry, and it's O.K. Everyone forgets (or makes a mistake, or drops things) sometimes. Now that you've told me about it, you'll feel better," is a statement that supports conscience. Punctuated with a hug and a kiss, such a statement does not add to a youngster's troubles by asking him to feel he has been hopelessly foolish.

"True" and "False" Sometimes Blur

For a small child to separate the "real" from the "pretend" is often all but impossible. Take the difficult plight of Tony, an intensely imaginative three-and-a-half-year-old who lived in a home where pets were talked to and treated almost as if they were human. Oscar was a highly intelligent German shepherd dog, who, to dog lovers, appeared to comprehend and respond to anything that was said to him. Oscar had been Tony's companion and guardian since babyhood. One day Tony was not to be found for several hours. His frantic mother had just summoned his father home from work when a nonchalant Tony walked in. He had gone to the home of a new friend several blocks away to play. When his mother reminded him, in the course of a stern rebuke, that he had often been told never to go farther than the corner without asking permission, he replied, "But I asked Oscar, and he knew where I was all the time."

Tony suffered no pangs of conscience as a result of this escapade, since in his limited understanding of the distinction between the real and the imaginary, Oscar, the dog, was as qualified to give permission as any human being. Tony was neither alibiing nor pretending. This was a case of faulty comprehension. Even patient explanations on the part of his parents of the limitations of a dog's understanding made scant impression on him. Tony's vivid imagination made it more difficult to help him separate his make-believe world from the real one in many instances.

"But I do *so* know what Oscar means when he talks to me, and he knows what I say to him, too. You're always telling people how smart Oscar is, but you don't understand him yourself," was Tony's position.

Often a preschooler's statement that appears to adults or even to older children to be a falsehood merely reflects a lack of vocabulary. Four-year-olds who can count to six or even to ten may not take the trouble to do so and will therefore report an incident in exaggerated form. Three fire engines in front of the apartment house on the corner may be parlayed into "millions" or "lots and lots of fire engines, all the way down the street."

Even, "I only took two weeny, tiny, baby cookies," does not always indicate an absence of conscience or a dangerous tendency to prevarication, when the supply of cookies in the jar has clearly been diminished by half a dozen or more.

Helping a Youngster Toward Truthfulness

When a three- or four- or five-year-old has committed some offense that seems to him likely to bring him into parental disfavor, he may construct an elaborate but flimsy tale of why he "just had to do that," or deny altogether that he was involved in the affair, or put the blame for it on another person. Such conduct is quite typical of preschoolers and not to be regarded as a serious lack of feeling for right and wrong, as one might judge it to be in an older boy or girl.

We help a child become more truthful in owning up to a misdeed by not making it seem that he is hopelessly disgraced or by not meting out too severe a punishment when he tells us about it. "Next time you'll find a better way. I don't think you'll want to do that again," or "It would have been better to . . . ," or "I know you feel bad over what happened, and you'll get along better if you don't try that again," are attitudes that accomplish several important aims.

Such an approach lets a child know that telling a parent about his wrongdoing will not make him an outcast. It also lets him know how to avoid similar mishaps in the future and affirms our faith that he *can* do better. That in itself encourages both acceptable conduct and the ability to own up to slips. Since confession is good for the soul and tends to relieve painful guilt, the child who is able to report his peccadilloes without being made to feel worthless is having a healthy experience.

"Chris seemed to feel so guilty and so sure he would be severely punished," said a father in discussing some childish mischief his son had been involved in, "that we really thought we ought to give him the severe punishment he expected."

Although confession need not guarantee immunity from any penalty, the line of reasoning taken by Chris's father can make a young conscience too sensitive, if it is followed habitually. A parent knows better than a four- or five-year-old just how serious a misdeed is and how it should be handled.

In the interest of developing a realistic, not a rigid, inner monitor, parents can certainly trust their own judgment, not the youngster's estimate of the enormity of his "badness."

Avoiding Impasses

We can often avoid an impasse over truthfulness by preventing situations in which untruthfulness would be all too easy. Children tend to give the answer they think we would like to hear, or one that would let them off of some disagreeable task.

If a four-year-old is sent to wash her hands and she comes back seemingly as grimy as ever, the answer to "Did you really wash carefully?" will undoubtedly be affirmative. Maybe she did wash, in sketchy fashion. Maybe she did not even make the attempt because the hot water is so hot, or the faucet is so hard to reach, or she is afraid she will miss something if she stays away long enough to do a thorough job. She then compounds her carelessness with a falsehood. Better not put the question! We know the answer, anyway.

We have the choice of sending her back to do the job satisfactorily or accepting her performance, but to ask for an honest answer, when truthfulness would result in inconvenience, is putting too great a temptation in a small child's path.

The Wish Is Sometimes Father to the Falsehood

Children deviate from the facts for a variety of other reasons. One who feels deprived of affection or companionship, who craves recognition, or longs for a certain toy, may reveal that desire in "tall tales" told to his playmates or the neighbors. In his stories, the absent or totally inadequate father becomes the generous or powerful figure who grants every wish and can do "just about anything." The pet a boy or girl daydreams about owning, or the baby sister a five-year-old girl fantasies would be company for her, are represented as already being members of the household, often to the great embarrassment of parents.

One small boy, whose family lived in an apartment house where pets were prohibited, was so factual in his description of the big, white "Lassie-dog" he owned that the landlord threatened his parents with eviction. "Either you are liars or your kid is," this irate gentleman insisted. "If it's the kid, he should be walloped, and if it's you, out you go. That kid has made trouble for me with the other tenants with his stories about the dog you keep locked in the bathroom."

The parents explained to their son that when he talked about his "Lassie-dog," he should be sure to say it was a "pretend dog." The interest with which the neighbors had listened to his account of the details of keeping his dog in the apartment had been so gratifying to the boy that he was loath to relinquish the attention that ownership of a dog had brought him.

When a small boy or girl is quite obviously weaving a story that is pure fabrication, we can help him by saying, "That's a good 'pretend story,' but you and I know it's just for pretending, don't we?" In that way we anchor the youngster to reality, yet do not brand his imaginings as "lies." We can point out frequently, in various contexts, the difference between make-believe and fact without branding a four-year-old as untrustworthy. This question is discussed from other angles in Chapter 5.

When Conscience Generates Fantasy

Especially hard for parents to handle is a child's report of an event that might be a figment of his imagination invented to secure an end of his own, or might be true—and serious. That was the dilemma in which Claire's parents found themselves. Claire was an imaginative four-and-a-half-year-old. Like many youngsters her age, she was afraid of the dark and would go to almost any lengths to get one of her parents to stay with her if she woke during the night.

One morning she told a most convincing tale of "the Honey Man, an extra big man, carrying a real big bag, all blue all over with a funny thing over his face," who had entered her room during the night, walked around, and then departed by the window through which he had come. Since the family lived on the first floor of a two-story building, the idea that the ground-level windows were an invitation to prowlers had often crossed the parents' minds. Had they, they wondered, said anything in their daughter's hearing to suggest that?

When Claire was asked if she had seen this man put anything in his bag, she replied, "No. He just hunted around. The bag was for honey."

"Why didn't you call us if somebody was in your room? You call often enough for nothing at all," said her father, trying to be casual.

"The Honey Man didn't need you. He said he'd come back later if he wanted to see you." Whatever else she might be, the little girl was not at a loss for answers.

Her perplexed parents settled for telling Claire she had probably dreamed that the Honey Man had been in her room, since nothing in the house had been taken. On the off chance that a potential burglar or molester had been in the girl's room, it seemed unfair to accuse her of fabrication. Yet accepting her story and acceding to her wish to have either mother or father sleep with her, or to be permitted to sleep with them, would make it clear that her parents were worried about her safety, and it was not advisable for other reasons.

Magical Thinking

Another and deeper cause for Claire's fantasy, for fantasy it probably was, may have been an overactive conscience. To children, thinking about doing something "bad" seems as dangerous and as likely to bring punishment as carrying out the deed. They do not distinguish, for instance, between wanting to get rid of baby brother and actually throwing him out of the window.

As has been pointed out, children (like most primitive peoples) attribute magical powers to their thoughts. If an illness or a mishap occurs to a person for whom they wished "something bad" or with whom they are temporarily angry, they may hold themselves accountable for the misfortune and suffer keenly.

Sometimes an explanation of the difference between wishing or thinking something "bad" and doing something "bad" reassures a child and eases his primitive conscience. Such an explanation may need to be made more than once.

As a result of his wishes or his thoughts, a child may anticipate that punishment will descend on him, perhaps in the shape of a witch or an ogre, a large animal, or a strange person like Claire's Honey Man, who comes at night when a small boy or girl is alone and defenseless. Such is the genesis of many unreal fears during the years from three to six, and for that matter, in later childhood. In an unconscious effort to get rid of the fears caused by his overactive—or misguided—conscience, the child often resorts to elaborate and restrictive rituals, which may become so all-pervasive as to interfere with play, with undertaking new experiences or finding much relish in daily living.

Ritual Routines Allay Fear

One four-year-old had instituted bedtime routines including a story, a good-night song from his father, putting on pajamas, and then slippers and robe—always in that order—collecting five toys to take to bed, which must be arranged in a particular way, plus further ceremonies that became a burden to his parents. Following the exact pattern every night at bedtime gave him some relief from his fears that a monster would come up from the basement and devour him.

No matter how kind and gentle the adults around him may be, a youngster may develop a troublesome conscience. He is alarmed by his own impulses to strike out or be violent. These he is learning to deal with during his preschool years, or at least not to act on. Yet even as his actions come under control, the wish to hit out aggressively, the frightening anger, persist within him. Daydreams of glory through aggressions, if they do not take over completely, may be a safety valve. Imaginary companions who take on either human or animal guise, or a doll or stuffed animal, may be a means of displacing or enforcing, as circumstances require, the restrictions that conscience sets up.

Miss Beibler was the imaginary friend of four-year-old Alicia. Miss Beibler needed to be constantly reproved, reformed, and redirected. "You don't know how bad Miss Beibler'd be if I didn't scold her real hard.

Sometimes I even have to spank her and make her stay home when we are going somewhere, 'cause she does such naughty things," Alicia would tell her mother. Through the wicked Miss Beibler, Alicia was getting rid of, or "displacing," some of the guilt her conscience imposed on her, although she had no idea Miss B. was serving so complicated a purpose. In rebuking Miss B., Alicia was also taming her own tendencies toward wildness.

Such a means of disposing of uncomfortable guilt over fancied wrongdoings is a step on the path toward a healthy conscience, a conscience that will in time make itself felt in more useful ways.

Conscience Can Create Worries Over Sex

In the previous chapter, the desire of the preschooler to have the parent of the opposite sex for himself was explained as a part of normal emotional development. Yet this wish, too, can result in distressing pangs of conscience. In a small girl, conflict often arises over her wish to get the better of her mother, since this is at odds with her conviction that mother is far from expendable. Small boys who would like to have their mother's entire attention are often disturbed because they still admire and want to be like those rivals for mother's affection, their fathers. Conscience may then become acutely bothersome in some children.

A small child who has engaged in sex play or even thought about doing so, or who has been severely reprimanded for masturbating, may have a guilty conscience that threatens him with all manner of dreadful punishments. A boy may fear that his penis will fall off or be cut off as punishment. A girl may imagine that she once had a penis but lost it because she was "bad."

Such troublesome consciences are less likely to beset youngsters whose questions about sex differences and about human reproduction have been answered. One who knows he may bring his worries to his parents without either being rebuffed or having to listen to an incomprehensible lecture on biology may be spared unnecessary worries arising from guilt.

Almost all children suffer some guilt over worries related to sex, whether or not their parents give them any basis for such worries. A parent has not failed a son or daughter if such worries come to light. See the previous two chapters and the following one for further discussion of these questions.

"Mine" and "Yours" Are Difficult Concepts

A conscience that deters a youngster from taking things that do not belong to him develops slowly, and again through example. Here we may need to do some soul-searching about our own ethics. To take an object belonging to another is not countenanced by most parents if that "other" is an individual. But what about reminding the bus driver that he has not collected our fare? Or getting a thirteen-year-old into the movies at half-price when twelve is the age for paying adult admission? Or taking an ashtray, a spoon, or a towel from a motel? Family morals may veer to a double standard. Some children get the feeling from their parents' behavior that it would be wrong to cheat Mr. Grimozzi who owns the grocery store on the corner, yet cheating a faceless corporation of a few cents or a few furnishings is all right. "They will never miss it anyway," or "At the rate they charge you, they expect it."

Unless we stay with the doctrine that under no circumstances does one take what is not his, no matter whom it belongs to, we can hardly be surprised if the younger members of the family bring home in their pockets assorted crayons, doll dishes, or small cars from nursery school or from the homes of playmates.

One expects a certain amount of this from three- and four-year-olds. They are often as unaware of the implications of taking what is not theirs as they are of the difference between fact and fantasy in the stories they relate. Conscience expands and becomes increasingly serviceable as we help them, gently, to distinguish between honesty and dishonesty.

Willy was a five-year-old who constantly brought home small treasures such as colored pencils, pieces of candy, crayons, and trinkets. When questioned as to where he got them, he replied that he had "found" them. At first his parents paid scant attention to his peculiar luck. They did not want to accuse him of "swiping" these items, and they dismissed his behavior as "just a phase." Willy had often heard his older brothers say, "Finders keepers, losers weepers," about objects left around the house. This misleading catchword may have contributed to Willy's easygoing conscience.

Taking Corrective Measures

Willy's father, unable to close his eyes any longer to his son's taking ways, said to him, "Willy, everything belongs to someone. At kindergarten I know there is a lost-and-found box. Anything you find on the playground or in your kindergarten room or on the way to school belongs in that box in the school office, so the person it belongs to can get it. When you are at a friend's house you never, never ask to have or help yourself to a toy or picture book or anything else that is theirs."

"Well, sometimes kids give me things because they like me. That's how I got those crayons, even if you don't think I did," Willy asserted stoutly.

"People may like you a lot, Willy, and I'm sure they do like you, but they don't give you their toys and other possessions. You've gotten a little mixed up, I'm afraid," his father told him.

"Well," said Willy, thoughtfully, "those old picture books I just borrowed from some of my friends. I can tell them tomorrow I borrowed them."

"You don't 'borrow' something without asking your friend's mother if you may borrow it, and then you take it back real soon. I think what you and I better do right now is to take those picture books back to the boys you borrowed them from and say you want them to have them back."

Willy reluctantly made the rounds of the homes of the three friends from whom he had "borrowed" the picture books without asking permission to do so. His father made it easier for him by going along and doing some of the explaining.

Willy's parents also kept a close watch on what Willy brought home. If he came home with a miniature car or two that he claimed he had found, they refrained from asking "Where did you get it?," as that might have only opened the way to further falsehoods. They just saw to it that the toy was returned, without shaming or punishing Willy.

His father might say, "Willy, I believe you forgot about not picking up a friend's toys and putting them in your pocket. Until you can remember for yourself, your mother and I will help you by reminding you that you take those cars back to the friend they belong to. You can't take things that aren't yours. People don't like it if you do. We have to be able to trust the people around us, to be sure that they won't take things away from us that are ours. And you know something, Willy? I think you'll feel a lot better after those cars have been returned." Since Willy's conscience was still so shaky, his parents acted for that dormant conscience, although they never spoke of their watchfulness in such terms.

Had Willy been three rather than five, his parents might justifiably have been less insistent on his making restitution. Had he been three or four years older than he was, they might, also with good reason, have felt Willy needed help from a child-guidance clinic. Most children around the age of five or six do some "swiping." That, in itself, is not a sign that they will continue to steal or become delinquents, but it is a sign that until conscience becomes stronger, they need firm reminders.

Indirect Support for the Chronic "Swiper"

If parents have a youngster like Willy, they can help him, in addition to acting as a monitor until his inner one can take over, by not regarding him as a thief. As with any other behavior lapse, a child is helped most by feeling that those around him, especially his parents, have confidence that he can overcome his problem.

Some older children steal because they feel unloved. They are, in effect, not stealing an object they want as much as they are trying to get, by hook or by crook, the love they feel they have been denied. This kind of stealing is usually confined to older children, but it may enter also into the chronic "swiping" of the five-year-old. The child who has a tendency to take what belongs to someone else needs plenty of affection and a life with satisfactions in it. Parents need to take care not to let their unavoidable concern, embarrassment, or worry over stealing color their entire relationship with a youngster.

Such a youngster is also helped to understand property rights if his own belongings are protected from the depredations of other members of the family. Mothers may need to think twice before, in an excess of zeal for neatness, they throw out a four- or five-year-old's "junk." Nor do we allow a younger brother or sister to wreak havoc on an older one's carefully constructed, if crude, skyscraper, or the bits of knotted cloth a girl calls her "babies."

Probably no one measure in itself can expand conscience during these years to the point at which it will always be strong enough to resist the temptation to appropriate another's possessions, especially when no one is looking. Occasional lapses will most likely occur. A combination of example, building up self-respect, and supplying sufficient affection and adventure so that the preschooler does not fall into the habit of "swiping" out of sheer boredom—plus a firm insistence on the return of any articles mysteriously "found"—will usually, in time and with patience, yield a reliable conscience. When conscience becomes active enough, and a boy or girl is uncomfortable over having made off with goods to which he or she has no right, the tendency to "find" or "swipe" or "just borrow" with no intention of returning will gradually fade out in most cases.

Parents may be encouraged when they realize that conscience does not flower through severity or solemn pronouncements on their part. Their youngster's unfolding confidence in himself as a worthwhile person, one who can take the right action and one who has their love and approval, is a basic ingredient for progress toward a healthy conscience. Consistent guidance, attainable standards, and protection from overwhelming and frequent temptations will also aid the development of an inner monitor, which, although faltering at times, over the long haul steadily steers the growing boy or girl into more responsible and responsive behavior.

8
Fears

ALL YOUNG CHILDREN at some times know fear, and each finds his own style of dealing with it. A wide range of feelings and behavior are included in the term fear. The child who stays behind the railing bordering the tiger's cage at the zoo and does not put his hand through the bars because he is afraid of being bitten is showing sensible caution. If he were so afraid of the tiger that he refused to look at him, he would be suffering from a groundless fear, sometimes called a phobia. If any mention of a family excursion sent the youngster into a state of panic lest the outing involve going to the zoo, he would be suffering from acute anxiety, or disabling anticipation of danger or misfortune.

Helen Ross, in her pamphlet *Fears of Children,* says:

> Both fear and courage are a part of each of us, both are ways of feeling, both belong to our efforts to master a situation. But fear is probably harder to understand than courage.

Our consideration of the fears of the preschooler covers three areas: the sources of worry and terror; the children's ways of defending themselves against those feelings; and some steps parents can take that may help their offspring to cope with their fears, be they real or imagined, present or in the future.

Some Fear Is Inevitable

Conscientious fathers and mothers have sometimes tried to create a "fear-proof" existence for their children. Yet, in spite of their preparing a youngster in advance for unsettling events, in spite of their pooh-poohing those villains of fairy tale and legend, the witches and ogres, their children in their preschool years have been subject to unwarranted fears, such as fear of going down the drain with the bath water, or of encountering monsters who spring out of doorways.

The most loving parents cannot completely protect a child from apprehension about unreal dangers as well as actual ones. Although disquietude sometimes comes from outside pressures, some of it also comes from inner turmoil and has no visible or perceptible source. A child's well-being depends, as Selma Fraiberg points out in *The Magic Years:*

> . . . not on the presence or absence of ogres in his fantasy life, or on such fine points as the diet of ogres. *It depends upon the child's solution to the ogre problem.*
>
> It is the way in which a child manages his irrational fears that determines their effect upon his personality development. . . . Normally the child overcomes his irrational fears. . . . If we understand the nature of the developing child and those parts of his personality that work for solution and resolution toward mental health, we are in the best position to assist him in developing his inner resources for dealing with fears.

To understand the genesis of fear, we need to go back to the first year of life. When an infant is uncomfortable because he is hungry, cold, or soaking wet, because he hears a loud noise, or too strong a light is shining in his eyes, he responds with his entire body. If he is hungry, he is hungry "all over." He screams, he waves his arms and legs around and behaves as someone might in a state of utter panic. His discomfort is so disagreeable that after he has felt it a number of times, at its first sign he anticipates with dread what will follow. He has learned fear. If the disagreeable experience occurs too often, he will have learned anxiety as well.

Fear, depending on its degree and the personality of the child involved, may be a help or a hindrance to growth and survival. Caution, a mild and essential by-product of fear, seems to be acquired spontaneously by some children.

Yet, not all youngsters understand the need for caution. "The burned child fears the fire" is a glib proverb that does not always hold true. The three-year-old often has too hazy a notion of cause and effect to connect his behavior logically with its painful results. To understand that whatever has hurt him is an impersonal agent, neither malevolent in its attack on him nor punitive, takes a certain amount of maturity.

Too Fearless for His Own Good

A three-year-old, who had paid no heed to any teaching about safety in crossing streets, was hit by a car. He was not badly hurt, miraculously, but he did have to spend a few days in the hospital. His father explained to him that the car had hit him because he had run into its path and the driver could not stop in time to avoid him. Now, maybe he would remember why people must watch out for automobiles, cross only at street corners, etc., etc. To the father's amazement, the boy had no memory of having run into the street, but insisted he was on the sidewalk when "that automobile came after me." Probably the shock had been so great that the actual circumstances had been erased from the child's mind, but in any case, his experience was not a useful lesson.

A bad experience with real danger will not necessarily teach caution. At best, having been frightened is only one side of learning discretion. A child acquires a sensible attitude toward danger as he becomes sufficiently mature to see the relationship, for instance, between leaning over the windowsill and losing his balance and falling out, or putting an object in an electric socket and getting a shock. He acquires caution, also, as he makes his parents' admonitions a part of himself, a process discussed in the previous chapter.

Those youngsters who repeatedly jump from heights too great for a safe landing, who will not keep away from fire, who are reckless about running into the street, who seemingly disregard parental instruction about safety altogether when they are three and a half or four, may be testing their own power to make everything come out all right. They may indulge in an undue amount of magic thinking about their own or their parents' omnipotence.

The four-and-a-half-year-old girl who declared, "I can climb the highest tree in the world and I won't get hurt if I fall out of it, because my father is a doctor," was bemused by her own wish for, or perhaps fear of, a father who was extremely protective or powerful. Perhaps, too, she was testing his as well as her own ability to control events by climbing higher than prudence would dictate.

A Mask for Anxiety

The three-year-old who, time after time, gets himself into offbeat and dangerous situations is not as likely to be without fear as to be driven by anxiety about some disturbing situation in his life. His anxiety may arise from tension in the atmosphere of his home. He may have been alarmed by arguments he has heard between his parents that he could not understand, questions that he hesitated to ask or that his parents did not answer. These or other causes may push him to explore and experiment in bizarre or forbidden ways.

Then there is the three- or three-and-a-half-year-old who shows no signs of fear of events or phenomena that usually alarm others his age. Thunder, the dark, frisky, barking dogs, or separation from adults who are important to him seem to make no impression on him. If, in addition, such a child is rather listless, lacking in the usual child-like zest for play, if his emotional life seems flat and toneless, or his development is out of line in another direction, we may conclude that he is afraid to show any signs of fear. He may be a child who feels completely unprotected by adults and tries to protect himself by avoiding feelings. Perhaps any show of emotion, any tears or hanging back are so frowned upon in his home that, to him, the greatest of all dangers appears to be displaying fear.

Such children may be headed for trouble and may need, in addition to more affection and understanding from their parents, the help of a child-guidance clinic or family counseling before they can deal with their anxieties in a more rational or constructive manner.

Whereas intense fear may produce panic or paralysis, a moderate degree of fear, when a person of any age is in real danger, heightens certain bodily processes. This, in turn, as adrenalin is poured into the bloodstream, speeds up the pulse rate, quickens responses, and adds strength and stamina. The surplus energy that often comes to the rescue of the person in time of danger or crisis is triggered by fear. Fear is therefore a protective device in some instances.

Dr. Allan S. Berger, writing in *Young Children,* says:

> Anxiety itself is necessary for survival, for it stimulates the development of ways, defenses if you will, of dealing with life's dangers, both the real ones of the outer world and the make-believe ones of our inner world. It is the flashing yellow caution light on life's interminable road. . . . Anxiety is as inevitable a part of our life as our breathing and our heartbeat. Anxiety may be thought of as nature's stimulus to protect oneself.

Dr. Berger goes on to compare anxiety to the tears that form in the eyes and are often a protection to vision, although a great flow of tears interferes with seeing clearly. "What counts with anxiety," he emphasizes, "is how much of it there is and what we do with it.

Outer Pressures: Source of Some Fears

In the three-through-five age span, the children, more on their own, inevitably encounter some threatening experiences. At the age of three, in many neighborhoods, and surely at four or five, a youngster is out on the sidewalk, in somebody's yard, or at the local playground, playing with other children. Often, he will have no more supervision than that afforded by the presence of an older brother or sister engrossed in his or her own play, or an occasional checking-up-on from a mother.

Being persecuted by another child who is a bully, being chased by a frolicsome pup, or seeing a passerby whose clothes, gait, or general appearance are odd, may all seem to constitute danger to a three- or four-year-old and cause anxiety. He has not had sufficient experience to distinguish what might be unpleasant but temporary from what will plague him forever. What is merely unfamiliar gets mixed up with what is threatening.

Today, when witnessing automobile accidents can scarcely be escaped, when many children are exposed to scenes of brutality, and when television brings violence into everyone's living room, children may be anxious because of what they have seen around them. The feeling, "I may be the next one to be smashed up in a car crash" (or beaten, or even shot) is not utterly without basis.

Going to nursery school at four and kindergarten at five means separation from Mother. That, too, may be a source of anxiety. How will he get home again? What if the bus driver or the car-pool mother can't find his house? Will his mother be there when he arrives home? Inexperience and lack of understanding lead to many such painful anxieties.

Misunderstanding May Engender Fear

Coupled with more exposure to the world beyond his own home is the preschooler's active imagination. He is capable of thinking up more possibilities to worry about than he could have concocted earlier.

The four- and five-year-old listen to adult conversation and, instead of letting it flow over their heads, try to make some sense out of it. When Terry heard a visiting uncle say to her father, "So I thought it was time to nail this big shot down and make him talk turkey," she had a mental picture of that uncle nailing someone (a dangerous enemy?) to the floor and forcing him to make noises like a turkey gobbler. A pretty scary world if one's favorite uncle treats people that way!

Adults look like giants to the three- or four-year-old. He often feels frustrated and helpless because he cannot cope with doors or water faucets, steps or spoons scaled for hands that are far larger, or arms and legs that are far longer than his. When help is not forthcoming, anxiety may wash over him.

When Fears Are Generated from Within

Small children cannot always separate what has actually happened, or might happen, from their own fantasies. To a four-year-old, the witch she believes is under her bed is frighteningly real.

Along with this confounding of fact and fancy goes an exaggerated and totally unreal estimate of his own power on the part of the young child. When he gets angry, he feels that his anger is so strong that it might blow up the whole house, or destroy grown-ups.

Related to this is his mistaken notion about the potency of his wishes. A preschooler is often anxious because he has thought about doing "something bad." His parents might stop loving him and taking care of him if they knew how "bad" he was! Wishing the new baby sister would be collected with the rest of the household garbage, or that an irritable and stern visiting grandfather would go back home, seems as wicked as taking action on the wish. Then if the baby becomes mildly ill or grandfather has a fall, the hapless youngster believes his evil wishes caused the misfortune. He worries about what appears to him to be his own power for evil and about the punishment that may descend on him as a result. This point was discussed in detail in the previous chapter.

"Will I Still Be Me?"

Three-year-olds and even five-year-olds have a rather shaky sense of self. The conviction that they are separate, intact beings is still not well established. Here is another important source of anxiety that comes from within. Small children frequently are afraid they may lose a part of their bodies. Something might fall off or they might be injured. Sometimes they hint at these concerns, and sometimes they talk about them openly. Some youngsters may never display any such anxiety because they experience it only mildly or because it is thoroughly repressed from the conscious part of their personalities.

The sight of a maimed or crippled person may bring out questions: "What happened to him?" "Will that happen to me?" Perhaps no open questions are asked, but concerns may be triggered. In small boys, anxiety about bodily injury may center about the loss of their sex organ. This is dicussed in Chapter 5. However, fears of losing a part of oneself are not confined to boys, or to sexual worries.

Usually this particular anxiety disappears about the time a child loses his first baby tooth. That loss demonstrates vividly that one may lose something valuable, yet not be damaged. One is still the same self. This connection between shedding a tooth and ceasing to be concerned about remaining "in one piece" was suggested by the late Dr. Harvey A. Lewis.

The Dark Is an Unknown Quantity

One of the common fears small children usually do not hesitate to show openly is their uncertainty about what the dark may hold. This fear has a nunber of components. Underlying it is more than merely the confusion resulting from not being able to see what is around them.

Darkness usually means the approach of bedtime, and bedtime for most children means being separated from older members of the family, who go on having a good time (or so it seems to the youngster).

Whether small children fear darkness because it brings separation and an increased sense of helplessness, or whether they fear separation because it often occurs, with its attendant loneliness, when darkness falls is a moot question. Both fears probably reinforce each other. A three- or four-year-old may find it easier to talk about the "awful monsters who come after me in the dark" than about those vague feelings of loneliness and being deserted that descend on him.

A further unpleasant aspect of lying in bed in total darkness is that all his misdeeds of the day and the reprimands that followed arise to haunt him.

Fears by Association

Utterly illogical fear may come about through the association of ideas. A three-year-old had been subjected in the course of a few weeks to a number of elderly female sitters with whom she did not enjoy staying. After that, she shrank back and often wept whenever an older woman came to her parents' home, assuming the person would be a sitter. Since her grandmother was visiting at the time, a number of elderly strangers were showing up, each of whom aroused anxiety in the small girl.

A parent who is apprehensive about his small son's or daughter's health, or about the youngster's ability to handle many everyday situations, may find his young children becoming "worry-warts."

"Gladys has inherited her mother's timidity. Her mother has always been afraid of everything. My wife, Gladys' grandmother, was always the same way. Being afraid seems to run in my wife's family," says Gladys' grandfather, who has no patience with fears of any kind.

Gladys has not *inherited* her anxious nature, but she has caught it from the way she has seen her mother respond to situations. Adults who expect the worst and are overprotective of their children convey the feeling that danger may be lurking everywhere.

Some Youngsters Are Anxiety-prone

A final, and to adults most puzzling, origin of fear in some preschool children is *the child's interpretation* of the way their parents treat them.

Nell was an extremely sensitive little girl. The slightest reproof or the gentlest teasing brought on a flood of tears. She was sure her parents preferred either the curly-haired baby sister or the boisterous older brother, both of whom appeared to her to be a threat to her own good standing. Nell soaked up affection and praise like a sponge. Nell was full of fears, chief among them that she was not pleasing her parents.

"You'd think we beat her, the way she acts if anybody corrects her the slightest bit," her father often said.

Nell was unusually susceptible to having her feelings hurt and, as a result, becoming anxious. Children of this sort are a specially demanding challenge for parents.

Fortunately, no child suffers from all these causes of fear, nor are all his fears present all the time. On some days or in some seasons, for reasons we cannot always fathom—perhaps because of tensions within himself or in his surroundings—a youngster may be especially prone to fear. Again, for weeks or months on end, probably because conditions are favorable, manifestations of anxiety may be slight.

Built-in Devices for Defense Against Fear

In addition to the automatic physiological response to a fearsome situation, described earlier, human beings have certain mental mechanisms with which they often defend themselves against fear and make anxiety bearable. Again, no child probably employs all these devices. Some boys and girls may seem to go along without using any. Piglet, the Very Small Animal in A. A. Milne's stories about Christopher Robin and his imaginary friends, is a vehicle onto which Christopher projects his own fears. Piglet invests most of his time and energy in fussing over what might be going to happen. Since Piglet turns to Christopher for comfort, the little boy is reassuring himself when he tells Piglet that everything will be all right or laughs at his small friend's troubles.

Defending himself from fear by insisting that someone else is afraid and in need of reassurance, even though that "someone else" is an imaginary creature, is a useful device for a small child.

Denying Fear May Be a Defense Against It

An emotion that makes one too uncomfortable may be denied. Denial is somewhat different from projecting, or asserting that someone else is suffering from your fear. A five-year-old to whom the annual Fourth of July fireworks in the neighborhood park were a torment, not a treat, declared emphatically, "I'm not afraid of fireworks. I just don't like them one bit." Here was a neat bit of face-saving quite permissible in a five-year-old.

Imaginary companions, human or animal, may help a child handle his fears in several ways. In *The Magic Years,* Selma Fraiberg explains how Jan, a three-and-a-half-year-old, came to terms with her fear of animals "who could bite and might even eat a little girl up," through the invention of Laughing Tiger, an imaginary beast who came to live at her house:

> There is one place where you can meet a ferocious beast on your own terms and leave victorious. That place is the imagination. It is a matter of individual taste whether the beast should be slain, maimed, banished or reformed. Jan chose reform as her approach to the problem of ferocious animals. . . . All the dangerous attributes of tigers underwent a transformation in this new creature. This tiger doesn't bare his teeth in a savage snarl. . . . *He* is the one who is scared. . . . We suspect a parallel development here. The transformation of a tiger into an obedient and quiescent beast is probably a caricature of the civilizing process which the little girl is undergoing. . . . Jan's imaginary tiger gives her a kind of control over a danger which earlier had left her helpless and anxious.

That danger was her own impulse to be wilder or more violent than she felt it was safe to be.

Laughing Tiger was also useful in helping Jan get over her fear of animals, Mrs. Fraiberg tells us, since he vanished at about the same time her terror of large beasts disappeared.

We are all familiar with one of the most useful means that children use to recover from a fear-inspiring incident. A youngster who has been hospitalized, lived through a hurricane, became separated from a parent in a crowd, or even had an exciting but confusing experience such as being taken to a three-ring circus, will reenact it in his play for days or perhaps weeks. As he plays it out, he gets control of it, often through playing the part of the controlling figures. It becomes more manageable, and therefore less threatening.

Being in Control Eases Fear

Rearranging a situation, figuratively or literally, so that it is no longer alarming but something of one's own creation is another constructive solution for a frightened child. Lois B. Murphy, in *The Widening World of Childhood,* tells how one small boy, Martin, dealt with his sense of being overwhelmed at a children's party. Martin became absorbed in building high, narrow structures out of big cardboard bricks. He paid no attention to the other children or the people coming into the room. In doing so, he was proving to himself that his building, not the party, was the important matter for him. He had altered the situation to suit his own taste by isolating himself from it, so that the party as such hardly existed for him.

Four-year-old Delia "rearranged a situation" when she moved, with her parents and her younger sister, to a new home in another city. Her parents had rented a furnished apartment belonging to a woman who also had two small daughters, so Delia walked into a room equipped for girls her own age. Still, she was uneasy and anxious. She took one look around. Then she began tugging at the two small chairs and the low table. She pushed and tugged until chairs and table were where she wanted them. She changed the position of the two mats on the floor.

"Now," she declared to her admiring younger sister, "it's how we like it best, isn't it?"

Marshaling One's Forces

Another device for coping with anxiety described in Dr. Murphy's book is "surveying the situation." Another boy, at the party referred to earlier, came in, stood with his hands in his pockets, and looked over the scene. "This surveying," says Dr. Murphy, "often implies 'defining a safe area,' since in order to survey a situation one must first have secured an observation point."

Mr. Brand, whose five-year-old son was addicted to "defining a safe area" when he was in a situation threatening to him, felt the boy was "hanging back and acting like a baby." Mr. Brand refused to understand that the boy, by getting his bearings when he was under stress, was frequently able to turn a threat into a challenge, but a challenge cut down to a size he could handle. By pushing the boy, the father too often interfered with his son's style of dealing with fear, and by disapproving of it, deprived the little boy of an important, healthy prop.

The Unfamiliar Is Alarming

Protecting oneself against anxiety by being sure everything is in its accustomed place, that no detail of one's surroundings is altered, is a device that is useful in moderation. For a two- or two-and-a-half-year-old, insisting on the precise repetition of routines is quite natural. A five-year-old can be expected to be more flexible. Breakfast cereal served in a different bowl, or the announcement that a favorite blanket will be unavailable for a night because it is being washed, is less devastating at five than at two. Even in an emotionally healthy five-year-old, however, there may still be some protest.

The necessity for keeping objects in the same place and events in exactly the same sequence to ward off panic is usually a sign, in children of five or older, that they are afraid that if one detail is altered the whole fabric of their lives will fall apart. Children who have been subjected to frequent upheavals in their lives, such as sudden, unpredictable, prolonged absences of a mother or father, or losing a parent and being moved from one foster home to another, may take refuge from their anxiety in elaborate rituals to be sure neither objects nor events are getting out of control.

Displacing Fear onto Another

Admitting, even to themselves, that they are sometimes afraid of an adult they love and on whom they are dependent is painful for young children. This was the case with Harry, who found his father an intimidating person, more because he was such a big man than because he ever threatened or hurt the boy. Harry, when he was three, was terrified of bears. Pictures of bears, let alone the real thing in the zoo, sent him into spells of near hysteria.

Harry had displaced his trepidation about his father onto bears, real and imaginary. That was a fear more easily borne. Like many large men, Harry's father was quite gentle in his manner, but what came on strong for Harry was his bulk.

The unwarranted fear of large animals can have such a variety of implications in the emotional economy of the young that considering it, as we have, from several points of view may be instructive.

When Attack Becomes a Defense

Children who grow up in surroundings that seem to present constant danger may come to believe that the best way to reduce the fear of attack is to become the attacker. Their suspicions that their contemporaries are about to strike out at them or snatch a toy away and their anxiety about the possible scoldings or even blows adults may deal them are usually exaggerated, if not completely false. Even when no threat exists, when they are with children or grown-ups who are obviously friendly, such youngsters are poised for an angry response. Clearly, this is among the destructive defenses.

Once more, an excellent example is to be found in Milne's *The House at Pooh Corner,* this time in the person of the bouncy animal, Tigger, who attacks without provocation. This creature arrived at the house of the amiable Pooh in the small hours of the morning. He had not been there long when he said:

> "Excuse me a moment, but there's something climbing up your table," and with one loud *worraworraworra* he jumped at the end of the tablecloth, pulled it to the ground, wrapped himself up in it three times . . . and after a terrible struggle, got his head into the daylight again and said cheerfully: "Have I won?"
>
> "That's my tablecloth," said Pooh and he began to unwind Tigger.
>
> "I wondered what it was," said Tigger.
>
> "It goes on the table and you put things on it."
>
> "Then why did it try to bite me when I wasn't looking?"
>
> "I don't *think* it did," said Pooh.
>
> "It tried," said Tigger, "but I was too quick for it."

Frequently, children who have not had loving parents, who have not known the security of consistent treatment in a stable home, express their mistrust of their surroundings by becoming quick to strike out. Such children, five or ten years later, are the ones described as "hard to reach." They have built a wall of angry pugnaciousness around themselves as protection from an all-consuming fear.

Looking for Reassurance

A defense against fear resorted to by almost every child who has a kindly adult available is to seek reassurance frequently and emphatically. Nina, when she was three, was afraid of the whirring vacuum cleaner, the whining of a siren, the buzzing of a telephone left off its hook. When she heard such noises she ran to her mother and insisted on being held. For an hour or more afterward she would follow her mother around, clinging to her and demanding, "Noise gone? More noise coming?"

Like many of the means children employ to come to terms with fear and anxiety, this one is useful in moderation. Only when a youngster tries to solve his problems by rigidly overdoing some defense to the exclusion of any other kind of behavior do we need to feel the situation is a potentially serious one. We may expect to have three-, four-, and five-year-olds try out inappropriate means of dealing with fears.

We cannot hope to eradicate the fears of the preschool period, but we can often help children manage them. A first step in this direction is to set an example of buoyancy, hopefulness, and a reasonable degree of control. In wartime, in disasters such as floods or earthquakes, as well as in less cataclysmic domestic crises, children with adults who do not panic tend to be less disturbed. That does not mean that parents need always suppress their own doubts and difficulties. But if a mother and father can stay calm when, for example, on a family automobile trip Father takes the wrong road and they are momentarily "lost," or when one parent is unaccountably late in arriving home, the children are less apt to develop the habit of being anxious. If every mishap is the signal for extreme worry and dire forebodings, let alone recriminations, a child naturally comes to believe that is the way to meet uncertainty or mishaps.

Fortunately, today we are not so likely to insist that a young child, particularly a boy, keep "a stiff upper lip" when he is frightened. In many families but, alas, not all, small boys are permitted to own up to being afraid at times without being ashamed, ridiculed, or made to feel unworthy. We know now that feelings are more easily dealt with if they are out in the open. To add disgrace for betraying certain feelings to the burden of being anxious only compounds a child's troubles.

Reassurance in words is not guaranteed to alleviate fears, but it often helps. "We will take good care of you." "We'll all be (or "We all are) together." "I know this seems sort of scary, but Daddy is right here with you." "When I was as big as you are now, I was afraid sometimes, too, but it got better.

After a while you won't feel so frightened." Phrases like these can give more support, as a rule, than denying that any cause for fear exists. "There's nothing to be scared of," makes a youngster feel he is foolish as well as anxious.

When a child has lived through an alarming incident such as being hurt or seeing someone badly injured, being separated from his parents in a crowd, or being bullied by a bigger child, he can be allowed to talk about it. The incident need not become the central fact in life, nor should he be encouraged to rehearse it for everyone he meets. Yet he will probably recover more readily if he can ask questions, receive reassurance, and not feel the subject is taboo within the family.

Introducing New Situations Gradually

The unknown usually arouses some measure of anxiety. A sensible amount of preparation when a child must face a strange set of circumstances assists him in coping more effectively.

For example, a preparatory visit to the dentist when an older brother or sister or a parent is the patient, talking over what the dentist will do and will not do, as well as some explanation of why going to the dentist is necessary, may reduce anxiety about the first dental examination.

Preparation for an event that might be intimidating can frequently take the form of playing out with one's youngster the part he and others will take in the untried situation. This kind of play-acting is described in detail in Chapter 9.

Unfamiliar experiences in small doses, when that is possible, often prevent the unknown from being so taxing that the boy or girl ends up exhausted and therefore more prone to be anxious.

Reexposure Tends to Make Matters Worse

Philip, when he was three, was afraid of the merry-go-round on the playground where he spent some time each day, in good weather, with his mother. She felt that Philip found more than enough to do without being forced to go on the merry-go-round. His father believed that avoiding a showdown over merry-go-rounds was coddling the boy. He coerced Philip into getting on the merry-go-round. The boy fell off—his father said "on purpose." Although he was not badly hurt, his prejudice against this whirling device was reinforced. The next day his father insisted he must go back and try again, or "He'll be afraid the rest of his life."

The second attempt left Phil in a state bordering on panic. Not only, thereafter, was he more afraid than ever of rapidly revolving, dizzying machines, even revolving doors, but he was also afraid to go to the playground. And *that* created an impasse for his mother, as it was his main contact with other children and the neighborhood's best resource for outdoor play.

Action Brings Courage

Giving children something to do to meet a potential danger tends to reduce their sense of helplessness. A family who lived in an area where tornado warnings were frequent developed a useful plan. When warnings on radio or TV indicated that their own neighborhood might be in the direct path of a storm, each one, including the four-year-old, undertook certain assigned duties. As a result, both of taking action and of feeling "I know what to do," anxiety was diminished.

Another family effectively reduced the children's fear of the house burning down, the electric power going off, and other remote, but possible, contingencies that the children had heard about or seen on televison by talking over what each one was to do in case any such emergency arose. The mother and father stressed to the children the protection the community provided and how to summon help or use the materials and resources on hand. The emphasis on constructive action, the fact that "Something can be done about it if . . . ," rather than "How awful it would be if . . . ," helped the children remain calmer when emergencies did arise and less anxious about dangers in general.

In a one-parent family, if no relatives live nearby, both the children and the parent may feel especially vulnerable. "What would we do if some night you didn't come home from work?" Lois, aged four, often demanded of her mother. Her mother finally decided to tell her that if anything like that ever happened, and it was unlikely that it would, and if the woman who looked after Lois could not stay on with her, Lois should go to their friends the Thompsons, who lived downstairs. Lois' mother was careful to tell Mrs. Thompson what she had told Lois. The mother also made sure that Lois knew the full name and address of her grandparents, who lived in a nearby city, and that the Thompsons also had that information and the telephone number of the firm where Lois' mother worked. These arrangements were a great relief to this little girl.

Night Terrors

During the preschool years many children go through a period when they wake up screaming because of a bad dream. Even if they don't cry out, they may be so anxious that they go into their parents' bedroom and beg to be taken into the parents' bed. Here firmness is needed from mothers and fathers. "Children sleep in their own beds, not with grown-ups," is a doctrine that may need to be repeated again and again. A frightened child needs to be comforted and taken back to his own bed. Difficult as it is to get up, patiently return the child to bed, and sit beside him until he is quiet or has fallen asleep, the unfortunate long-term results and complications that parents avoid by not letting a small son or daughter share their bed even in a one-parent family, "just this once," are worth the effort.

Some parents have tried to eradicate fear of the dark and night terrors by taking the small child by the hand as darkness falls and sitting with him in the shadows. They have talked about how the furniture, the doors and windows change their appearance, but nothing is in the room that isn't present when it is well lighted. Making a game of going into a darkened room, holding the youngster's hand, and "exploring"—trying to recognize familiar objects by touching them—is another device that has been tried. These techniques may reduce the fears of some children and are surely worth a trial, but night terrors come, not so much from the absence of light, as from within the child's own, often unconscious, feelings. Rational explanations do not drive out irrational fears. (Chapter 7 discusses this question further.)

If we suspect that our three- or four- or five-year-old awakens during the night "just to get attention," we might try giving him more pleasant, affectionate attention during the day. Everything that we can do to build up his conviction that we approve of him will tend to make him less prone to unwarranted anxieties and will probably help him more than logical explanations or experiments with light, shadows, and darkness.

Leaving doors open or nightlights burning may bring an anxious child comfort, and are not to be considered appeasement or coddling. They will not ruin his independence, but may strengthen it. A favorite blanket or a cuddly stuffed animal may also decrease his loneliness and fears. If the demand for stuffed animals gets so voracious that a youngster wants all seven of his favorites each night, we may need to specify that one or two are sufficient.

Unfortunately, there is no neat formula for banishing nighttime fears. A parent, weary from sitting up during the night with a panicky child, can only be assured that groundless anxieties tend to diminish as a youngster's understanding of what is real and what is "pretend" becomes clearer. As he is better able to distinguish between events that are beyond his control and those for which he is held responsible, his fears will usually become less intense. Experiences that tell him that the unfamiliar may be pleasant and that the new is not necessarily painful also decrease overall apprehension. We can foster such maturity, but we cannot expect it to be full-blown in the years before six.

9
Encouraging Independence

GROWTH IN INDEPENDENCE in preschoolers comes in two flavors. The "sweet" kind, for both parents and children, includes such practical progress as dressing without assistance, being out-of-doors without direct supervision, fetching and carrying in the house, and running errands or taking a message to a neighbor. Parents usually welcome and make an effort to provide practice in these forms of independence.

A youngster's ability to accept brief separations from his parents with equanimity; to solve problems that arise in his play without more than a hint from an adult; to figure out the relationship between events, occasionally; and to brush off, rather than seek, hugs, kisses, and cuddling are among the forms of independence we might call "semisweet" or "bittersweet." Mothers and fathers may find it more difficult to create opportunities for the children to practice this variety. They may also respond with less obvious enthusiasm to their son's or daughter's self-reliance in thinking and feeling. Then, the youngsters, since they seem to be receiving less approval, tend to get less satisfaction from the "semisweet" behavior. The two flavors come in a double package. Both are vital in a child's total development. Each is closely tied to the other.

As a boy or girl moves toward more independent behavior of all kinds, he or she changes in ways that bring mixed emotions to both generations. Pride in a child's advance is often laced with parental regret when, for instance, a five-year-old shows signs of preferring the company of a playmate to that of his parents or his grandparents. Or when, at four and a half or five and a half, he counters adults' rather flimsy reasons for prohibiting some scheme of his own with arguments that make fairly good sense. If his proposals are couched in language suggesting that the grown-ups are not quite as bright as they might be, independent thinking will hardly be regarded as an asset by those grown-ups.

"It is *too* warm enough to take off my sweater. Don't you think I know when I'm cold or not? You ought to have your head examined." Such statements may show a burgeoning capacity to make judgments, for all their lack of diplomacy.

Our youngster also experiences a two-way pull about assuming independent behavior. Healthy children want to grow up, yet when things go wrong—when they are tired, or ill, or distressed—they will slide back to wanting more help, more affection, and more reassurance. As a result of both our conflicting feelings and his own, a child will probably acquire self-reliance in a "two steps forward, one step backward" fashion. Letting go of babyish behavior, even in small ways, carries a threat for him of losing us completely.

Independence Has Deep Roots

Many of the characteristics that are strands in a well-knit personality are components of self-sufficiency. Confidence in oneself and faith in the predictability of one's surroundings, a sense of being a separate individual who can make good things happen, a degree of resiliency and resourcefulness, as well as courage and imagination, underlie self-reliance.

Independence has its beginnings long before the age of three (as explained in the book *Your Child's First Three Years*). In the strictest sense, it starts when a baby takes his first breath. Developing initiative, trying out his powers to explore and experiment has been labeled by Erik Erikson as a central need for the child in the years from three through five. Such initiative forms the basis of independent action, though it is often of the "semisweet" brand. No student of the preschool years, including Erikson, would attempt to sum up the ramifications of development of this period in one neat phrase. Too much is going on, especially in the fluctuations between "I can do it," and "I can't do it. I don't know how." (The question of initiative is also discussed in Chapters 1 and 11 of this book.)

Home Atmosphere Affects Independence

Families communicate to their young, without putting anything into words, what degree of self-determination and how wide a choice are permitted by their own ethnic or religious traditions, the customs of the neighborhood, and their individual aspirations and fears. Parents who see life as offering a number of options in such matters as where one lives, how one spends one's leisure time, and what kind of work one does tend to convey to their children a feeling of flexibility and range in the possibilities open to them. Their youngsters are allowed the pleasure of planning their lives in small ways. "Shall we go to the zoo or do you want to go to the playground next Sunday?" Here is a simple choice, but it offers a degree of flexibility and independence. Opportunities to make selections imply that more than one way can be good. They engender the feeling in the child that decision-making and planning are worth some mental effort because they can lead to getting what he wants.

Contrast this with the feeling that a child absorbs in a home where the parental mood varies between vague uneasiness and seething fury because, "*They* won't let us do what we want to anyway"; "*They* will be down on our necks if we want to try anything." The unspecified "they" might be dominating parents, demanding, among other forms of deference, that married sons and daughters and their offspring assemble weekly and meekly for a "family night" whose warmth has cooled and whose usefulness has been outgrown. Or the oft-invoked and forbidding "they" might be a landlord, employer, or some group who are seen as being, or actually are, an acute menace. In such a family, children are not encouraged to make thoughtful plans or see independent thinking or acting as a means of attaining one's ends. Parents sunk in futility convey the message "What's the use?" to even the smallest children.

In discussing the significance to preschoolers of opportunities for independent thinking, Robert Hess and Virginia Shipman report, as a result of their research:

> Possibilities for alternative ways of action and thought encourage children to consider [those] alternatives, to select, to develop criteria for choice and to learn the basic elements of decision-making and anticipating the future consequences of present action.

Decision-making: Ages Three Through Five

Appropriate opportunities to make choices in everyday living enhance young children's feeling that they have a part in making good things happen through effort and foresight. One point to remember is that when we say, "It's up to you. You decide which you want," we need to offer alternatives among which a child may safely and realistically make a selection. Many decisions are beyond a child's capacity to make, and being told they are his to make puts a frightening and false burden on him. We don't, for instance, allow him to choose whether or not to eat breakfast. But whether breakfast should begin with fruit or cereal, or even include a cheese sandwich, might well be a matter of individual taste, provided a mother, father, or older brother or sister in charge of preparing breakfast has time to cater to a four-year-old's preference.

If a child has to take what comes at family meals, snack time might give scope to his selective powers. Again, the choice would need to be confined to available, sensible items. "Jelly sandwich? Apple? Raisins?" would make more sense than "What do you want for a snack?" The latter might lead to a demand for forbidden foods or ones not on hand.

A youngster can be allowed to choose, within reason, which of his clothes he will wear. If an unharmonious combination of colors seems to be his heart's desire, what's so terrible about that? But if it is a question of shorts versus slacks in frigid weather, or if wearing new shoes when playing in the mud is on the agenda, then parental wisdom needs to take precedence.

If finding playmates is not a spontaneous matter and involves some arranging by a mother, a child's own choice deserves to be listened to. Of course, his choice may not coincide with his parents', but he may have sounder reasons for it than are immediately apparent.

Family Relationships and Independence

Self-reliance is influenced, too, by the tone of the interaction between a child and his parents. One study has shown that in a home where relationships are warm, where mothers and fathers say "Yes" whenever they reasonably can rather than saying "No" as a matter of course to requests, questioning, or spontaneity of any kind, the child tends to show more independence, or "ease in assuming responsibility for his own behavior." Even when parents were warm and loving, but rules were numerous and restrictive, the children did not easily become "self-starters" who could take responsibility for themselves, the study showed.

Backsliding May Precede Advancement

Independence, then, has its roots both in the child's own drive to be an individual and exercise initiative and in the way the family and the neighborhood view attempts to be innovative.

Recognizing the conflicting feelings both parents and children have about advances in self-reliance, we can see why a five-year-old or three-year-old cannot do today what he did with ease yesterday.

How can we give youngsters the feeling that though we welcome their increasing self-sufficiency, we still love and accept them when they need more help than usual, but that we will protect them from too much backsliding by setting limits below which regression shall not go?

Mr. and Mrs. Rand handled Chuck's frequent returns to helplessness in a more effective manner than did a sister and brother-in-law who also had a four-year-old. When Chuck insisted he could not get his socks on, or that he had "forgotten" how to put knives and forks on the supper table, or balked at assuming some small responsibility that usually gave him satisfaction, his mother would try encouragement first. If that brought no results, she would say something such as, "Oh, well, I guess we all have days when we can't do our 'first best.' I'll help you with one sock, and tomorrow I know you'll be able to put both on by yourself."

If Chuck's father was around when one of the "I can't do it" moods hit the little boy, he would take the line, "You're teasing me! I'll bet you can do it before I look at you again." If that approach was ineffective, he might say, "O.K. Let's do it together *this time*." Letting Chuck know he was expected to resume his usual degree of independence in time was a face-saving device for the boy and also put a floor under his return to babyishness.

Sometimes the fluctuation in self-sufficiency took other forms. Chuck might hold tightly to his mother's hand while they were at the supermarket or ask to ride in the cart in which she put her purchases, both of which were customs he had long ago relinquished. Sometimes his temporarily diminished independence took the form of not wanting to leave home to play at another child's house.

Mrs. Rand's sister-in-law held the view that any outpost in independence once won must be maintained or the entire struggle for self-reliance would be lost. When her son had one of those days when he seemed more like two and a half than four and a half, she would say, "Aren't you ashamed of yourself, a big boy like you, not wanting to . . ." etc., etc. By the end of her tirade he *was* ashamed. He was also afraid his unexpendable mother would abandon him as a hopeless case, although those were hardly the phrases he could have used to express his abysmal feeling of disgrace.

This boy tended to have less resilience, as a small child, and later on, than did his cousin Chuck. Although the more Spartan sister-in-law criticized Mrs. Rand's "permissiveness" as coddling and predicted dire results for Chuck, nothing of the sort occurred.

The "I Can Do It" Feelings

Self-reliance may, for equally unfathomable reasons, take a sudden leap forward. Each of us has occasionally arisen on a bright morning feeling equal to anything, or almost anything. That day we breeze through tasks, amazed at how much we accomplish with so little effort.

Some children are subject to the same heightened abilities from time to time. Then, independent behavior gets a boost. Each time this occurs and a youngster discovers that he really can enjoy putting his outdoor boots on by himself, carrying a pitcher of milk from the refrigerator to the table without spilling it, or whatever may be the fresh achievement, he gains an inch more self-reliance, a bit more of the feeling, "I can do it myself."

In discussing the "I can do it" feelings in *The Widening World of Childhood,* a study of how children cope with their environment, Lois B. Murphy says:

> Each experience of mastery is not only a momentary conquest, but a promise of more to come, a reassurance of the capacity to grow up. The sense of mastery is also closely related to a sense of worth, importance and ability to gain respect from others and maintain one's own self-respect . . . we may infer that mastery and coping ability are closely involved with the sense of identity. Through his coping experiences the child discovers and measures himself, and develops his own perception of who and what he is and, in time, may become.

These components of the "I can do it" feelings serve to undergird independence and prevent momentary lapses in self-reliance from becoming complete collapse. The sudden and often unaccountable spurts in "I can do it" behavior are like money in the savings bank. This surplus confidence, like money earning interest, accumulates and can be drawn on in the event of an emotional "rainy day," when self-doubt and discouragement need a corrective.

Here, again, we see the importance of the child's own picture of himself as "the kind who can do it," which he derives from what his parents say and the way they treat him. The stronger his sense that his parents approve of him and that "he is all right as he is," the more readily will he achieve a self-sufficiency appropriate to his age.

Eve, a five-year-old who was small for her age, had frequently been praised for being independent in a family in which that trait was highly valued. Eve was asked by a visiting aunt to go upstairs to the aunt's bedroom, find a package, and return with it to the backyard where the family was assembled. Her aunt explained exactly where it was and then said, somewhat condescendingly, "Do you think you can do that, Evie?"

"Oh, yes, I can, Aunt Kate. I'm *very* independent, even though I'm not exactly a great, big giant of a girl."

Eve's firm conviction that her small size was no barrier to her being competent did credit to the feelings her parents had instilled.

Managing Buttons and Bows

The "I can do it" feelings find expression in a pride in mastering dressing and undressing, washing, bathing, taking responsibility for toileting, and helping around the house. Mothers and fathers can facilitate the accomplishment of such tasks by providing clothing and equipment that the threes, fours, and fives can handle.

Children's clothes today can be blessedly simple to get into and out of, and getting out of them is usually the skill acquired first. Nobody has raised a statue to the inventor of the zipper and inscribed it, "Benefactor of Children," but he merits such recognition!

Whenever possible, outdoor clothing for children should have good-sized zippers that do not present a problem to muscles not yet perfectly coordinated. The easiest way for a child to put on a sweater, jacket, or any garment opening down the front is to spread it out on the floor with the open side uppermost. The youngster stands in back of the top of the garment, leans over, and puts his arms through the sleeves. Then he can swing it over his head, straighten up, and to his delight, he has put it on by himself. A three-year-old can easily do this and also learn to spread his garment out quite easily.

Laying pants out on the floor makes it easy for the youngster to wriggle into them. Clothing that is big enough to get into and out of easily may be less trim than tight-fitting slacks and "T" shirts or turtleneck sweaters with small openings at the neck; but if our goal is an independent, comfortably dressed boy or girl rather than a fashion plate, we should see that clothes fit loosely without being so large that they are droopy.

In a climate that makes snow boots and mittens a necessity, the boots should be big enough to get into readily. The old-fashioned device of sewing mittens to each end of a tape that goes around the back of the neck and through the sleeves of a coat cuts down on wasted time and temper expended in searching for a lost mitten.

One skill in dressing that usually is not acquired until around the age of six is the tying of shoelaces into firm knotted bows.

What Some Mothers Have Done

Experienced mothers have their own bits of wisdom on increasing proficiency in the dressing, washing, and bathing department. Some say that their three- and four-year-olds can manage to get into their clothes in the morning if they are allowed to dress in the kitchen where their mothers are preparing breakfast. One mother relates:

> We have a two-story house. If I had insisted that Hank dress himself before he came downstairs, he'd have been left on the second floor alone, because his father is at breakfast by the time I get Hank up, and I'm giving the baby her cereal. My mother considers letting a child dress in the kitchen and trail around with one sock in his hand while he's drinking his orange juice "bad training," but it works. Hank does get dressed, and pretty well for a three-and-a-half-year-old.

Another mother, who has four children, says that the two older ones are each assigned a younger brother or sister whose dressing, toothbrushing, and hand and face washing he supervises in the morning. That means that the supervisors of the three- and four-and-a-half-year-old are themselves barely six and seven, but everybody grows in independence in this arrangement. "The two older ones actually expect more from the younger ones than I would, and they get better results, too," this mother reports.

For some four- and five-year-olds, the only necessary cues for dressing are to have clothes selected and laid out the night before. Having underwear, pants, shirt, and socks out in plain sight avoids demands for help on the grounds that "I can't find it."

Is Cleanliness Next to Impossible?

Another mother's recipe for independent grooming is a sturdy footstool or wooden box or step just high enough for the boy or girl to reach the faucets in the washbasin and the supplies he needs. "Once the youngsters can understand how to mix the hot water with the cold so they aren't half scalded, they can manage to get themselves reasonably clean. What we lose in spic-and-span grooming, we make up for in pride in being on one's own," the father in this family says.

One young child brought up on this principle expressed his feelings about it interestingly. He had been sent to clean up before supper when his parents had a guest. He reappeared so quickly that he could hardly have done a thorough job. His mother looked at his still-grimy hands, but said nothing. When she was tucking him in bed that evening, her son said to her, "I'm glad you didn't send me back to wash over again. I'd have been embarrassed."

His mother told him she understood that, and that next time he would, she was sure, do better. Be it said, he did.

At bathtime, soaping knees and elbows and scrubbing arms and legs with a soft brush are tasks after a preschooler's own heart. The question is more often how to get him out of the tub than to interest him in washing. For the three-year-old, and even the four-year-old, supervision on a safety basis is still wise. The threes can all too easily become frisky, slip, and have a serious accident if left alone for long.

Other Ways to Help

Independence is also fostered, some parents attest, by having low hooks within easy reach in the bathroom on which the children can hang towels and/or nightclothes. Hooks they can reach in closets and entryways point up the lesson that clothes are hung up. "My very own place" to put clothes and other possessions means a great deal to a small child.

One father made a set of cubbyholes to stand near the back door, so that outdoor boots could be stashed away and found again without appealing to the adults for help.

By age three, children have usually learned to go to the toilet alone, but they may still require reminders before leaving the house or when they are absorbed in play. Threes and fours may still need assistance in wiping themselves clean after a bowel movement, but the fives can usually take care of themselves. An increasing desire for privacy in the bathroom, if it is respected, also adds to independence.

Some three-year-olds go through the night without being taken to the toilet; others will wake and ask to go to the bathroom. Picking up a soundly sleeping youngster, placing him on the toilet, and encouraging him to urinate while he is only half awake does not usually contribute to his taking responsibility for staying dry through the night. Parents may hesitate to put an end to that practice, lest he either wet his bed or awaken his parents later in the night. Experimenting with not waking the youngster sometimes proves he no longer needs the prop of nighttime toileting.

Many four- and five-year olds who still need to get up during the night can take care of their own needs if they are given a flashlight or if their route to the bathroom is lighted with the small bulbs that fit into floor sockets and cast a sufficient glow to dispel complete darkness.

Meantime independence usually makes strides during these years. From clutching a small fork or spoon at three, a youngster progresses to using fork and spoon quite neatly, even helping himself to vegetables or potatoes from a serving dish, if it is held for him. Spreading peanut butter or jelly with a knife is within the powers of many fives. Judgment about what size portions to take, or to request, is still lacking.

Three-year-olds may dawdle over a meal, but five-year-olds infrequently need to be told to finish up. The pace may still be slow, especially if they are engaged in conversation, but they are usually steady eaters. Cutting their meat, or even cutting something as soft as a pancake or a waffle, helping themselves to gravy or a sauce, unless it can be poured from a pitcher, may still be beyond them. "Finger foods," such as raw carrot, celery, or zucchini sticks, hard-cooked egg wedges, and sandwiches make independent eating easier.

Preschoolers enjoy "clearing" and by the age of four are good at taking plates or glasses, one at a time, from kitchen table to sink, or from the family's dining area to the kitchen. This can be a real help, but it also gives small children a legitimate reason for leaving the table and moving around between the main course and dessert when prolonged sitting still becomes tedious.

If the family has a meal at a restaurant or lunch counter, the preschoolers enjoy choosing and announcing their choice of food. (Is it ever anything except hamburger, hot dog, or the peanut-butter sandwich they would eat at home?) Independence can be as growth-promoting when it is a treat as when it is a task, and encouraging youngsters to state what they want, briefly but politely, affords them practice in making a choice and in looking after themselves.

Household Chores Come in All Sizes

One form of independence mothers and fathers would like to instill, but that the young do not always respond to, is the putting away of toys and play equipment. First aid for implementing this worthy custom is to provide a place that is accessible for storing playthings. The time-honored "toy chest," which can be anything from a fiberboard box to a sturdy wooden one, has in its favor that toys can be quickly tossed in, but playthings do get broken and unaccountably "lost" in such a receptacle. If space is available, low shelves are often the most desirable arrangement.

Picking up can be aided, too, by judicious timing. One mother recommends:

> Don't wait until the kids are all tired out to tell them to put their gear away, and don't make it a grim deal. I sing something silly, like "Heigh-ho, heigh-ho, it's cleanup time, you know," and then I improvise some lines to go with the rest of the jingle, and we're on our way. I stick around to give them some hints and lend

a hand from time to time. The important thing is that they learn that toys are put away and that an orderly room is pleasanter to live in than a messy one. If they've built some really terrific bridge, or what not, or have some "work in progress" they want to come back to, that we leave standing.

In another family, a different plan has been found effective. The father describes it this way:

When our three-year-old and five-and-a-half-year-old are through playing, they're tired. So before my wife or I tell them it's time to put things away, one of us sits down for a few minutes and tells them a story, or we just look at a picture book, or have a game of "hide the thimble" or "I see something blue" or whatever. Then we tell them, "Now everybody's had a rest, you can put your stuff away." Usually—mind you, not always, because there is no magic to these things—they get the room in fairly good shape without more than one or two complaints about each other. Sometimes we put on a record or get some music on the radio to help them keep going.

Young children usually enjoy helping in other ways far more than they relish picking up in their own quarters or their assigned play space. Fours and fives can, after their own fashion, make their beds. The result may be a bit lumpy, but they get "A" for effort, and we can take the will for the deed. One small girl delighted in being "beauty operator" for her mother and taking out the rollers from her mother's hair.

Feeding the family pets is another responsibility they enjoy but need to be reminded about. The consequences of neglect are far too serious to allow a small boy or girl to have a starved turtle or even a hungry puppy on his conscience.

Drying dishes, particularly the nonbreakable ones; putting away small items that have been laundered; storing groceries brought home from the store are not beyond four- and five-year-old competence. Fetching the morning newspaper, bringing in supplies the milkman has left at the door, emptying wastebaskets are traditionally the jobs of the youngest. Some fives can water house plants if they are given a small pitcher for the water. Table-setting is not beyond the scope of the three-year-old. A toy floor mop and broom may make it possible for four- and five-year-olds to "help" with floor care, but their zeal flags quickly. They are interested only in manipulating the broom or mop for a minute or two rather than in getting any given floor space clean. The same principle applies to dusting low tables or shelves that they can negotiate but usually won't stay with long enough to be useful.

Other Aids Toward Independence

In the cooking department, convenience foods give the smallest cooks a chance to try their hand at gelatin desserts and prepared pudding mixes. Mothers need to stand by if boiling water or scalded milk are to be handled. Muffin and cookie mixes, with a little supervision, may turn out to be edible products that give five-year-olds a gratifying sense of competence.

"Being a messenger" made one three-and-a-half-year-old feel extremely important. Her father would ask her to find out from her mother whether he had time before supper to get the car filled with gas, or her mother would say, "Daddy was looking for the newspaper. Here it is. Will you take it to him?" When this young messenger was a bit older, her services expanded to her parents' friends in the apartment building. "You could go downstairs and tell Mrs. Cable that you and I bought a new kind of bun at the bakery and if she'd like to come up and join us, we'll have a coffee party." Other instructions of a no more complex nature, carefully carried through, added to her feeling that she could handle a situation by herself.

Even fairly self-reliant five-year-olds may not relish being sent upstairs after dark to get Grandma's glasses for her or to find Mother's lipstick.

Carrying out household tasks, according to his own ability to persevere and to use his hands deftly, and being praised for his helpfulness, tend to reinforce a child's picture of himself as one who can achieve independence. But studies carried out at the University of Minnesota by Dale Harris and his associates showed that doing routine tasks did not carry over and enhance a real sense of responsibility during the later years of childhood and adolescence.

The World Beyond Home

Independence has so many facets that sometimes we lose sight of that useful tool for building it: being in another home for brief or more extended visits unaccompanied by a parent. Some children are fortunate in that they grow up in a friendly neighborhood and/or near relatives. Then, being in and out of other people's homes is just an agreeable part of everyday life. No planning for it is necessary. Four-year-old Jimmy feels at home in three or four households in the apartment complex where he lives. Five-year-old Shirley wanders in and out of the Schmidts' house next door to her own, and of the O'Malley's a few houses down the block, to inquire if her contemporaries are available, and possibly settles down for a visit with Mr. O'Malley or the grandmother who shares the Schmidt home. Nobody thinks of this as "training for independence." When we contrast the lot of the child who has no opportunities, such as Jimmy and Shirley have, to be on his own away from home, informally and spontaneously, we see how much such a boy or girl is losing.

Enough self-reliance to make visits at least tolerable, and hopefully pleasant, comes with practice. Visiting is also discussed in Chapter 3.

Says the father of a rather clinging small girl:

> We fed Marcia chances to be away from home in the tiniest portions. We had no relatives within a hundred miles, so Marcie missed out on that fine old custom of "spending the day with Grandma," which had been a part of my childhood. You can't expect casual acquaintances to take a lot of trouble with a weepy visitor, so before we let Marcie stay somewhere without her mother or me, we made sure she knew the people and the house well, could find the bathroom, and all that sort of thing. Then, we worked up gradually to letting her stay for a meal, and finally, when she liked the idea, overnight. It was a slow business, but it worked. Before she entered first grade, Marcie had several friends with whom she liked to "sleep over." She had even spent a weekend with an aunt in another city.

Since independence feeds on itself, these gratifying experiences of Marcie's also made other steps in self-sufficiency easier.

One resourceful mother played out with her young children just what kinds of things would be likely to happen and what they might be expected to do when they went visiting or "slept over." First she would let the youngster take the part of the adult hostess or host. "What do you think Karen's mother will say to you when you get there with your suitcase?," etc. The mother would take the part of the young host or the visitor. She and her four- or five-year-old would go through playtime, mealtime, bedtime conversations, changing the roles around so that the about-to-be visitor absorbed the feeling of each role and felt more at ease about what he or she would need to do in this new situation.

The grandfather of a four-year-old who was packing up to "sleep over" at a neighbor's house looked askance at the excited preparations. "I'll bet those two monkeys stay up until after midnight and are up at the crack of dawn again. You'll have one tired and crabby boy on your hands when he comes home tomorrow. Is it worth it?"

"You may be right, Pops, but Buddy's so

proud of being able to go all by himself, and it's such a big step forward for him to deal with being away from home, that a little crabbiness will be a small price to pay," Buddy's mother told her father-in-law.

Nursery School and Independence

Nursery schools as an aid to sociability were discussed in Chapter 3. Any thoughts about encouraging independence must also include the contribution a nursery school or neighborhood play group can make to a child's growth in self-reliance.

Good nursery schools offer a child-paced world in which a youngster can use initiative, follow up on ideas of his own, experiment with materials, and be independent in a setting that is at once safe, stimulating, and sociable.

Greta Mayer and Mary Hoover, in the booklet *Learning to Love and to Let Go,* say:

> It rarely makes sense to enroll a child in nursery school unless he says, after visiting it and being told what goes on there, that he wants to go. Of course it may not always work even then. . . . If you decide to send your child to nursery school, or enroll him in any formal group activity, be prepared to stick around for the first few sessions. . . . Don't feel you've made a terrible mistake if Johnny clings to you at first. . . . Also don't appear especially anxious to leave. . . . It should be made clear to him that you and his teacher expect him to manage in time to get along without his mother. Be sure that the clinging is all on his part, not yours. Don't hover over him or try to tell him what to do. . . . If you can make your child feel that your love for him includes confidence in his ability to adjust to this new experience, you strengthen his wish to do so.

A youngster will be able to be on his own in nursery school more comfortably if he has already grown accustomed to getting along without us from time to time and if he has had some experience in playing with other children. He may gain the courage to stay there without a parent with less anxiety if we assure him in words that we will come to get him at the end of the session. If someone else is to bring him home, we must be clear about who and how and tell him we will be at home waiting for him. If someone else is to be at home, we tell him who it will be, where we will be, and when we will see him again. The unknowns in the situation tend to make it more threatening. Sometimes mothers have found that leaving a scarf or a glove of theirs as a token that "I shall return" helps a forlorn three-year-old weather a morning without his mother.

The methods of fostering independence discussed in this chapter will contribute to a child's ability to use the facilities of nursery school, and that, in turn, increases his ability to act on his own in other situations.

How Much Independence Can He Take?

Various children are capable of varying degrees of independence at different ages. As we have seen, the cluster of traits and abilities we group together as "independent behavior" rests on how well a child can use his hands, how quickly or slowly he grasps a new idea and acts on it, how safe he feels in venturing on untried experiences, and how much trust he has in others and in himself. These abilities are rooted in his constitutional makeup, as well as the relationships and experiences he has known in his short life.

We can hardly decide arbitrarily how much independence to encourage or expect. We need to feed experiences to a three-, four-, or five-year-old bit by bit, giving him opportunity to experiment with self-reliance as we sense that he is ready to assume more.

Sometimes a boy or girl tells us in words, "I can do it myself," or "Let me do it myself," or "Don't hold me so tight." The latter phrase may literally refer to his hand being held as he walks on a walking beam, climbs a slide, or crosses the street, but it may also carry the hint that we can let go emotionally as well.

Sometimes boredom, restlessness, or even misbehavior is an indication that a youngster can handle situations calling for greater self-sufficiency or skill. If, for instance, three-and-a-half-year-old Nicky "runs away" time after time, take a look at where he runs to. If his running away takes him to the group of children playing with obvious enjoyment down the block or across the street, he may be telling us that he is ready for more companionship and does not need to stay so close to home.

Sometimes the ease with which a child performs one act gives us a clue to a more complicated one he is ready to take on. For example, a three-year-old who has no trouble getting his clothes off is probably ready to learn how to put them on.

In offering opportunities for a youngster to attain the "I can do" feelings in an increasing number and variety of situations, we need to be alert to the cues he gives us. We can put some effort into being inventive in concocting ways for him to feel at once safe and independent, and be patient when he shows us that we have overestimated what he can do.

10
Minor Annoyances And Larger Worries

MORE PEOPLE, BOTH parents and professionals, are paying more attention to children and how they grow today than ever before in history. We may justifiably believe that we do better for the young than did earlier generations, in which small boys and girls were regarded as miniature adults or as being full of evil that had to be beaten out of them. At least we recognize that the world appears to three-, four-, and five-year-olds far different from the way it appears to adults, and that many of the minor annoyances in bringing up our sons and daughters stem from their misconceptions of the world around them.

Life in an industrialized society, especially in cities, is ill adapted to the needs of preschoolers. Our pattern of living and our values, as well as the lack of adequate health services, the lack of sufficient space, and the lack of enough adults who will take time to listen to youngsters deprive many of them of the opportunity to develop their potential for becoming creative, responsible, and responsive human beings. Many of our larger worries have their roots in these conditions.

Yet urban living may not be the only source of our vexations. On an unfrequented beach on the remote Pacific island of Bora Bora, this writer came upon a young mother, native to the island, and her two small daughters. The mother was braiding palm fronds into a lovely pattern to make a new wall for the thatched hut in which she and her husband lived in a clearing at the edge of the lagoon. She was trying to teach the elder of the girls how to hold the palm fronds and plait them without cutting her hands on the sharp edges. Her husband's fishing nets were drying nearby in the sun.

The scene seemed almost ideal for rearing happy children. No traffic hazards, plenty of sun, play space, sand and water, and no danger of disturbing the neighbors if the children's voices grew exuberantly noisy. Yet this young mother had as many complaints, and surprisingly familiar ones, as her counterparts in an apartment complex in a metropolitan area might have. She said that plaiting the palm fronds was rough and tedious work. Her daughter was clumsy and not interested in learning how to do it. Left alone with the two children while her husband fished on other beaches where the catch was better, she never got to the village, and she tired of having no one to talk to except the children. Our exchange of views took place in French, a language in which neither of us was exactly proficient, but there was no mistaking her meaning.

The aggravations that arise between parents and three- through five-year-olds are due, perhaps, as much to the human condition as to the pressures of our particular society. From Boston to Bakersfield to Bora Bora, the activities of the very young, if they are a parent's sole social diet, can be by turns wearing, threatening, and boring, although the children are at the same time endearing, amusing, and challenging. The demands that three-, four-, and five-year-olds make, early and late, not out of willfulness or lack of consideration, but out of their helplessness and immaturity, are often difficult to meet.

Not What You Do, but How You Do It, Counts

A degree of accommodation of one generation to another is called for, no matter where or how young children and their parents live together. What accommodations shall be made, and when and how, are questions that each family answers for itself according to its own tastes and tolerances. Strict or lenient styles in living may work out equally satisfactorily. How we feel about the restrictions we enforce or the freedom we encourage and what those regulations and privileges mean to the children influence the pattern and tone of family life more than do the rules or liberties themselves.

Children need to have their capacities taken into consideration, but mothers and fathers need not constantly make all the concessions. If, for instance, privacy and quiet are important to parents, they are not being rejecting or cold if they arrange some times when they are not to be disturbed, short of actual emergencies.

Small children can usually understand, if we take the trouble to explain the situation, that grown people sometimes are tired, or do not feel well, or have work to do, and cannot always be ready to do what the children would like. A postponement of father's company will not be unbearable if a youngster has learned from experience that father says "Yes" to a request for his company or his help more often than he says "No." If father says, "Can't do it now, but we'll do it after supper," and remembers that commitment, his refusals in the future are easier to take.

When Piping Voices Become a Burden

"I wish I'd been a mother in the days when the rule was, 'Children should be seen and not heard,' " remarked a young mother with three boys under the age of six.

To this young woman, the reverberation of small feet tramping up and down the hall, the shouts of brotherly arguments, or the slamming of doors all came under the head of "making a racket" and were acutely painful to her. Fortunately, she realized that if she was implacable about the level of clamor she permitted, she would have to be more elastic in other directions. Although it was sometimes difficult for her to do so, she shut her eyes to a certain amount of disorder and overlooked sketchily washed hands as a small price to pay for achieving the relative quiet that was necessary to her comfort.

One of the lessons preschoolers need to learn is that different occasions call for different kinds of behavior. Being noisy may be permissible outdoors, but not in the house. Indoors, talking or playing in the usual way may be approved from breakfast time on; but before the family's rising hour, although threes and fours may be wide awake, they are expected to keep quiet.

If two youngsters share a room and one of them habitually wakes early, it can be hard.

Ione, a lively three-year-old, was an early riser. Except in winter, when daylight came late, Ione was ready to begin the day before six in the morning. Her five-year-old sister, on the other hand, could sleep until almost half past seven, when their mother called them to get ready for breakfast. Ione seemed unable to remember what "being quiet" entailed. Singing or talking to herself as softly as she was able, pattering around the room to see if her favorite doll was where she left it the night before, opening drawers and cupboards, or standing at the side of her sister's bed and giving her an ever-so-gentle prod "to see if she is really sleeping or just pretending" were to Ione ways of being "very, very still." If Ione woke her sister, which happened about five days out of seven, the older girl would be grumpy. Then the two engaged in a noisy quarrel, which woke their parents, or became conspirators in mischief, which usually had the same effect.

Neither punishment nor reward served to keep Ione sufficiently quiet. Then her parents tried a new tack. At bedtime, Ione chose two or three toys that lent themselves to quiet play. These were put within easy reach so that she would not need to get out of bed to search for something to do when she woke up. Before her parents went to bed, they put a bread-and-butter sandwich on Ione's nightstand so that she could have "an all-by-herself picnic" if she was hungry when she awoke. This routine did not work magic, but it did alleviate the situation. It kept Ione quieter, and because she stayed in her bed, she sometimes dozed off again.

Making a Game of Keeping Quiet

A game one mother found useful when banging and shouting became too much for her, or when she feared the din was disturbing her neighbors, was an invention she called "Mousy-quietness." The game might take the form of tiptoe, finger-on-lips follow-the-leader. Or it might be seeing if toys could be put away, with mother participating, without anyone making a sound. Again, the tiptoe routine supplied the fun. Sometimes she would have one youngster pantomime some activity, and anyone who recognized it could whisper his answer to the actor. Of course, the game usually ended with someone breaking out in giggles, but it did serve to lower the noise level for a time.

Children can be encouraged to keep their voices down by the example of parents who do not customarily shout. Small boys and girls tend to be better able to control their noise if at some time during the day they can be as unrestrainedly clamorous as young children occasionally need to be.

A small child *can* be taught to move quietly and keep his voice down, but the price of that teaching may be high. A divorced mother lived with her four-year-old son, Lawrence, on the third floor of a rambling old house owned by two elderly sisters, who were the only other occupants. Since one of the conditions on which the mother and her son became tenants was that the boy should not disturb the owners, quietness became the cardinal virtue for him.

Coming in from play (and even in the backyard, shouting was taboo), Lawrence would creep up the stairs and say proudly to his mother, "You couldn't hear me one bit, could you?" She would praise him for his good behavior and tell him that people liked a boy who didn't get in the way. (Hardly good mental hygiene, but pardonable under the circumstances.) Lawrence had few of the satisfactions that properly should be a four-year-old's lot, but he did derive a sense of achievement and power from being able to move so silently that nobody knew he was in the room.

The elderly ladies, encountering him in the kitchen, which his mother had the privilege of using, would say, "Larry is a good boy. He's never noisy." Then they might invite him to sit with them and watch television or surprise him with a treat of candy. Being quiet was the accomplishment that brought approval, and the message that came through to Lawrence was, "As long as you don't make a sound, people will like you." This led him to believe that to sit, undetected, behind a sofa or under a bed, listening to adult conversation, should be acceptable behavior. The old house had marvelous alcoves and walk-in closets where he could hide. When he did so in the rooms he and his mother occupied, she would laugh and tell him he was "a good hider," but if one of the elderly ladies found him, she would declare he was "a bad, sneaky boy."

The day he hid in the sisters' automobile and remained undiscovered until the two women reached their destination an hour from home, the less gentle of the two gave him a spanking. His mother also punished him for "being sneaky."

The moral of this story is that we can "overteach" a way of behaving so that a youngster believes that observing one rule is all that counts. At what point being quiet becomes being sneaky may seem clear enough to adults. To a small child who has no idea of the implications of not making one's presence known and who has had silence stressed, the situation becomes confusing.

"When kids make a noise, at least you know where they are, and that's worth a lot," an older woman frequently told her younger friends who complained of the din their children made.

A Time for Messiness

A time and place for legitimate use of sticky, gooey materials helps to keep messiness from spilling over and becoming more predominant than most adults find endurable. Small children love to handle moist, pliable substances. Adults, to whom such materials may be distasteful, tend to forget how children enjoy them. Clay and dough, mud and water, sand and finger paints are among the materials that offer threes and fours the chance to mess to their hearts' content. Some nursery school teachers would include tea leaves and coffee grounds among the materials that give variety to these tactile experiences, but only a few tolerant parents can encourage such experimentation.

With smock, apron, or bath towel to protect their clothes and several thicknesses of newspaper to cover the surface on which they work, youngsters can have their fill of squashing, pounding, shaping, and manipulating dough, clay, soapsuds, and the like. Finger paints and large sheets of brown wrapping paper or newsprint offer an excellent means of indulging the inclination to use spreadable substances and a gratifyingly wild mixture of colors.

"You may not put your hands in the mashed potatoes and mix them with the beets, but after lunch you can make something much prettier with finger paints (or paste and colored paper)," may be a kind of substitution acceptable to both four-year-olds and their parents.

A Time for Cleanliness

The avoidance of messiness, like the avoidance of noise, can be overemphasized, but some restrictions on continual slovenliness are wholesome. Hands can be washed before meals and after toileting. For those who enjoy going barefoot, a pail of water and a towel at the door, or just inside, to get feet reasonably clean before coming in the house, may be useful.

Preschoolers are sufficiently intrigued with lathering soap all over themselves to find baths acceptable, but routine handwashing may be tedious. The stock answer to the directive, "Wash-up time, we're going to eat soon" is usually "I did wash." That may mean that washing took place half an hour or four hours ago, and whatever its efficacy at that time, a repeat performance is in order. We cannot expect young boys or girls to wash or comb their hair without reminders. When they do wash their hands and faces, threes and fours may become so involved in playing with soap and water or get their clothes so thoroughly splashed that supervision is needed to prevent undue messiness. Older children in the family can be effective supervisors.

Toothbrushing may be so fascinating that, once reminded to embark on it, a small person may prolong the squeezing out of toothpaste, putting it on the brush, allowing it to fall off, and then starting the whole process over again without ever getting the brush in contact with his teeth. Such messiness needs to be stopped by saying, "You can squish your clay or your dough, but toothpaste is not to play with."

Cleanliness routines may become such a source of conflict at three or four that it may seem better, for the peace of the household, to keep them to a minimum for a time rather than endure the struggles and tears they produce. Five-year-olds can usually, with a few reminders, handle essential cleanliness measures fairly smoothly. These routines are also discussed in Chapter 9.

Cleanliness, a praiseworthy quality at the right time and place, can also be overdone. Some few children—and girls are more likely to be victims of this misfortune than are boys—learn all too well the lesson of not getting clothes dirty and of staying away from anything messy. Even sandbox play with wet sand becomes an activity from which the overclean shrink if they have found neatness and cleanliness the only way to a mother's heart.

The business of childhood is vigorous play. In these days of drip-dry clothes and sturdy fabrics meant to withstand grass stains, mud, and even grease, emphasis on spotlessness seems unnecessary and often works a hardship on a lively boy or girl.

One mother, who valued appearance above everything and took pride in seeing her attractive little girl look appetizingly fresh, would exclaim in disgust, "How did you manage to get *that* dirty so fast! Half an hour ago you were all nice and clean. What am I going to do with you?" Such statements, made time after time in a tone of stern disapproval, made her already timid daughter afraid of risking her mother's displeasure. So she stood on the sidelines, rarely joining in play and becoming more timid than ever.

Without spoiling a small child's zest for living or making him too conscious of dirt and germs, we can teach him not to pick up a piece of candy from the sidewalk and put it in his mouth, or accept the offer of a half-consumed lollypop. Small children touch everything and often taste it, too. Substances that we do not want them to taste or that are poisonous need to be kept out of reach, out of sight, and, in the case of medicines, under lock and key. Threes and fours do not understand the difference between, for example, not eating sugar out of the sugar bowl or drinking maple syrup and not tasting the powder that looks much like sugar or the liquid that has the appearance of maple syrup but is used to scrub the floor.

We need to make a distinction between what is prohibited on the grounds that it is sticky and messy and what is taboo because it is dangerous—and, for the sake of our child's future trust in us, we must be honest about which is which.

Perspective on the Amenities

In the same category as noise and dirt in many homes is "bad language." Words that not long ago were banned have now become so common in print, in motion pictures, and in the conversation of many adults and older children that we can hardly be shocked if four-year-olds' vocabularies also include them. Yet four-year-olds have epithets of their own invention that still outrage many parents. To hear them saying, "You're a poo-poo," or "I'm going to put doo-doos all over you," or "I'm going to flush you down the toilet because you're a wee-wee" may not be shocking, but it can be tiresome to adults.

A certain amount of occupational deafness to such conversation may assist us in surviving until our youngster outgrows his flair for bathroom language and may hasten the day when he will relinquish it. One father's antidote for objectionable language was to suggest, "Wouldn't it be funnier to call your friend a broken old stove than to use the words you use?" The father was aware that this brand of banter would not have the appeal to the small child, who is still interested in the products of his own body, that "bathroom talk" had, but it was in the long run a more serviceable way of attacking the problem than implying that the youngster's chosen vocabulary was "dirty." The child got the message that his father was not shocked by "bathroom words" but preferred that they not be used in his presence or that of other adults.

In dealing with objectionable language, too much noise, lack of neatness, or similar aggravations of preschool behavior, we should keep in mind that these are quite usual problems of development. Almost every child will for a time be less clean, less well-spoken and mannerly than his parents might find convenient. But look at the whole child in the context of everything else he does. Is he usually happy and able to play with enthusiasm? Does he go fairly smoothly through most of the day's routines? Does he communicate with others freely and readily? If the answer to at least some of these questions is affimative, we can afford to overlook, within the limits of our own tolerance, such typical preschool deviations from decorum as we have been discussing.

What Is the Whiner Trying to Tell Us?

On the borderline between a "minor annoyance" and a "larger worry" is the whining voice of a youngster who is usually discontented, frustrated, and provocative. Adults are often out of patience with him and as a result answer him curtly, insist that he repeat his statement in a more agreeable tone of voice, and generally add to his emotional discomfort.

Whining is usually a symptom, not the malady itself, and as such needs to be attacked indirectly. If we are confronted with a boy or girl whose customary tone is whining and complaining, we might ask ourself whether this youngster is receiving recognition and encouragement enough to convince him that he is a lovable, worthwhile individual? Does he have opportunities to make appropriate choices from time to time? Are the adults around him consistent in the limits they set for him? Do his parents take time to listen to him, play with him, enjoy his company and let him enjoy theirs? These questions may possibly uncover emotional needs that are not being adequately met and that are the source of his discontent.

Another thing to remember in trying to help a child whose frustration shows up in a whining tone of voice is that it undoubtedly took a long time for him to develop the whine (it is a mannerism that sneaks up on one), and it will not go away overnight.

Worries About Health

Emotional and physical well-being are so closely intertwined as to be inseparable. Feelings and bodily processes both respond to pressure. When a youngster's appearance or behavior seem to have gone askew, we must consider whether the cause of the trouble may be some infection or organic problem before we decide that "He is just stubborn," or trying to get attention, or scared, or whatever. At the same time, before we decide that the medicine cabinet is our best ally, we might look at the events in his life that may have upset both feelings and physical functioning.

Feelings can no more be overlooked, if they are at the root of the trouble, than can a high fever or a painful sore throat. Like physical symptoms, disturbed feelings, which show up in many ways discussed in this book, may need treatment from a qualified professional, a counselor in a family service agency, or a child therapist in private practice or in a child-guidance clinic.

A few boys and girls seem to go through the years of early childhood with such good health that their parents say, airily, "That one never gets sick." That state of affairs is less common than are occasional, perhaps slight, but worrisome and sometimes puzzling problems of physical well-being.

The "Picky Eater"

One such problem is the disinterest in eating that besets many three- and four-year-olds. During these years, children often go through quite long spells when their appetites lag and eating seems a bore and a burden. They may have periods when they want raw vegetables and little else, or when bologna sandwiches are the only food they will touch. A youngster may eat ravenously for a few days and then have no appetite for a week.

Eating is not a moral issue, nor is a poor eater being defiant. We can accept the fact that appetite may be capricious. If its variations are not seen in terms of uncooperativeness and resistance, it tends to stabilize by the time a youngster is five or six.

Struggles over how much a child shall eat are useless, although in some families encouraging a child to "take a little taste of everything" seems to make for a more cosmopolitan palate. For one who is a slow eater, it is discouraging to have older members of the family finish eating and leave the table while he is still trying to plow through the food in front of him. Rather than be left to complete his meal alone, he may give up entirely and say he has had enough. It is possible that such a child is being served discouragingly large portions.

Breakfast may be by far the poorest meal of the day. The stand that "Everyone must have juice, a bowl of hot cereal, and egg and bacon to start the day" does not assist in cultivating the appetite of the three-year-old; and it is appetite, not will power or cooperation, that we are aiming for. Appetites tend to improve when mealtimes are pleasant and when the child does not get a mental picture of himself as someone who will not or cannot eat a large number of foods.

When Bowel and Bladder Control Lapse

Another difficulty during these years may be that the child who was apparently dependable about using the toilet and staying dry at night slips back into wetting and/or soiling. The occasional accidents in toileting that happen to many small boys and girls, because they put off toileting or are in an unfamiliar place and hesitate to ask where the bathroom is, are different from a complete breakdown in control. Sometimes a temporary lapse occurs because of a cold or other slight illness, but that, too, usually corrects itself if the youngster—and his parents—do not panic over it.

If the return to wetting or soiling has no medical basis—and the child's doctor is the one to make that decision—and if it is persistent, parents should consider the possible outside pressures that might be the source of the trouble.

A new baby in the family, arrivals or departures of other people important to the boy or girl, starting nursery school, or merely some event over which he or she is pleasantly excited may be the cause of a loss of nighttime bladder control and, less frequently, daytime control. The change in the household or in what is expected of him may be upsetting to the youngster because he must now be more "grown-up" than he feels capable of being. Loss of bladder control, especially at night, may be his unconscious protest against having to relinquish the privilege of being cared for.

"I know you don't want to wet your bed at night. Sometimes that happens to children when they are worried about something. If you talk about what is bothering you, you may feel better and be able to stay dry at night again," is an approach that may help. If a parent has a good idea of what is worrying a child, it might be mentioned as having caused other children to lose control for a time.

Some youngsters "forget" to use the toilet, and not simply because they are absorbed in play. Cliff was one who had never become quite reliable in the matter of going to the toilet when he needed to urinate, although he was nearly four. Cliff had been so hemmed in by prohibitions since babyhood that in desperation he usually resisted the signals from his own body that his bladder needed emptying, as well as commands from his parents. In Cliff's case, sessions at a child-guidance clinic, for him and for his parents, finally helped to change the attitudes in the family. Then Cliff no longer needed to defend himself from overwhelming demands by constantly resisting.

When the cause of not acquiring or not maintaining control of elimination is deep-seated resistance, other unacceptable behavior is usually also present. Here, again, we need to put in focus everything that is happening to the youngster and try to meet the problem as a whole, rather than resorting to a gimmick that attacks only part of the difficulty. Some of the suggested remedies for lack of complete control may be far too hard on the child. For example, denying him fluids from late afternoon until bedtime in the hope that it will cut down nighttime wetting may make a child miserably thirsty. Punishment or shaming only add to his discouragement, which is probably already acute. Expressing confidence that he can and will do better, occasionally reminding, but not nagging, are aids to a youngster's own inner controls.

If a really disheartening situation has developed, either because control has not been established or because it has broken down completely, psychological help may be needed.

The subject of toileting is also considered in Chapter 9. Teaching the child to use the toilet is discussed in the book, *Your Child's First Three Years.*

Will Poor Speech Be Outgrown?

Among other babyish kinds of behavior that often persist is poor enunciation. Three-year-olds are not likely to have perfect pronunciation, but the five- or five-and-a-half-year-old usually is readily understandable. If a child is developing well in most directions, is alert and interested in his play and in trying to use language, the inability to pronounce one or two sounds clearly at the age of three or even four and a half is not serious. The substitution of the sound "w" for the sound "l," resulting in such confusing statements as "We had wiver for wunch," will probably correct itself if a youngster hears the correct sound.

Parents and older brothers and sisters should avoid falling into the trap of adopting the three-year-old's mispronunciation in fun. Children learn from good models in speech as in other matters. The small one's style of talking may be ever so endearing, but his family help him most by using correct speech sounds.

Many three-year-olds, when they are excited, may not be able to get their words out smoothly. They hesitate over the initial sounds, and their parents may believe they have a stutterer on their hands. That type of stutter we can afford to ignore, as it usually disappears before a child is old enough to go to school.

Persistent inability in a child of four and a half or five to start a word without repeating the initial sounds, or spasmodic repetition of sounds whenever he speaks, is usually a sign of anxiety, if no physical impediment in his vocal apparatus is present. Trying to find and ease the source of that anxiety is what is needed, not making a child repeat what he has said or calling attention in any way to his defective speech.

Some children stutter or stammer only when they are in new situations or with strangers. In a study of children who stutter, researchers found that parents of stutterers were less realistic in what they expected of their children (in other words, set standards too high) than were the parents of nonstutterers. Another study, comparing a group of young boys who stuttered with a group that did not, found that the mothers of stutterers tended to "reject their children more often than they accepted them, while the mothers of a similar group of boys who did not stutter accepted their children more often than they rejected them."

Many schools, hospitals, and clinics have speech therapists on their staffs who can help children who have marked and continual difficulty in speaking.

Size and Weight as Signs of Healthy Growth

Parents are often concerned because they are not sure how much a child should be growing during these years. Obviously, if growth did not slow down after the first six months of a baby's life, we would be a race of giants. Individual rates of growth vary tremendously. Two preschoolers of the same age may differ by as much as five inches in height or fifteen pounds in weight and yet both be within the range of normal and be perfectly healthy.

A gain of three to six pounds and two to four inches in a year is evidence that a youngster is growing satisfactorily. It may be interesting and useful to keep a semiannual record of a child's weight and height as documentary proof of progress. If a change of doctor or clinic becomes necessary, such a record also may be appreciated by the new medical adviser.

"Bigger" does not necessarily mean "healthier" or "stronger." Indeed, the conspicuously overweight child is at a disadvantage on several counts. He is likely to be awkward and to be the butt of his playmates' ridicule. From a health point of view, overweight, even at an early age, is generally regarded by the medical profession as a potential hazard.

Healthy Attitudes Toward Health

By the time a child is three, parents have usually discovered the tempo and general behavior that signify that a particular youngster is well or that he may be "coming down with something."

The mother of a lively brood says, "When one of our children walks when he could run or sits when he could stand, I can be pretty sure he'll have a fever by evening. In this house, who needs a thermometer?"

She may be exaggerating the validity of her hunches, but a sharp change in a child's level of energy or in his color or general bearing is not to be overlooked.

For reasons we cannot always understand, some children are more susceptible than others to colds, sore throats, stomach upsets, or elevations in temperature. Such susceptibility is worth reporting to the doctor when we take that child for a checkup, but not in the child's hearing. We should avoid letting the youngster get the impression that he is fated to be ill frequently, or letting it be said in the family or among the neighbors that "He (or she) always gets everything. Poor kid just has no resistance." The doctor may have recommendations about diet or routines or some special measures that will help to give the susceptible child a better chance of fighting off slight but bothersome illnesses.

If a child seems likely to contract minor illnesses, we may need to protect him from becoming overtired or from whatever seems to put a strain on him. If he is allergic to certain foods or other substances, we should try to help him avoid them without letting him become unduly concerned about his health.

"Everybody has something he can't do," a father with an asthmatic daughter told her. "You can't eat eggs and white bread. O.K. Brother can't see to read in school if he forgets his glasses. When I was little I had to wear special shoes that laced up when the other kids were wearing sneakers. Everybody has to take care sometimes." Such an attitude helps a child feel he is not odd because he must observe a few restrictions.

Children have a strong drive toward health. They tend to respond to sound medical treatment and also to bounce back from an illness quickly. We can cooperate with their tendency to be well by using all the means at our disposal to prevent or remedy any impairments. We can give our children the point of view that most youngsters usually feel well, but if they do get sick, something can be done about it.

When to Consult the Doctor?

When a child is sick, there is no substitute for professional skill and diagnosis. Medical science may not always have a ready and complete answer, but intelligent parents realize how infinitely superior it is to the counsel of even an experienced relative or neighbor. When a child runs a high fever, vomits repeatedly, complains of a severe pain, coughs hard and continually, or acts in a manner so unlike his usual self that common sense tells us he is sick, we want medical help and we want it as promptly as possible. Even a mild illness that lasts more than two or three days is not to be ignored.

Keeping a sick child quiet, warm, and on a bland diet until we can get in touch with the doctor or clinic is sensible. Unless the doctor has given specific directions about medication to be given when certain symptoms appear in a particular child, it should be a rule not to do amateur prescribing.

Another aspect of the question of when to consult the doctor concerns the time of day chosen for getting in touch with him. Many pediatricians instruct the parents of their patients that they prefer to be called on the telephone during certain hours.

A mother may tend to wait until her husband comes homes in the evening so that they can decide together about phoning their pediatrician or taking the youngster to his office or to the clinic. From the standpoint of family solidarity, that is fine; but from the practical point of view of both the child's well-being and the doctor's convenience, a mother might do better to report the condition while the doctor is still at his office.

The decision to take a child to the doctor may need to be made because of some persistent and increasing sign of poor health. Perhaps we suspect that a boy's or girl's hearing is not what it should be, even allowing for children's inattention to what they don't want to hear. Perhaps a cough has hung on far too long to be attributed to the damp weather and the fact that "colds are harder to shake off this year." Listlessness and vague pains, a sharp decrease in appetite, and a willingness to stay in bed cannot be overlooked in a five-year-old who, up to a few weeks ago, was full of energy. In these and similar instances, the doctor will appreciate having the youngster brought to his office promptly. The sooner steps are taken to correct whatever the condition may be, the more effective treatment can be.

When Keeping Records Pays

No matter how casual we may be about writing most things down, it is well worthwhile to keep careful records of the dates of the inoculations our children have had and who administered them. In Sara Gilbert's *Your Child's First Three Years* is a chart of the childhood diseases that confer immunity, the inoculations a child should have, and the times at which such immunization needs to be given. This chart can help to avoid omitting any of the available and proven preventive measures for protecting a child.

Parents may say, "We all had measles (or scarlet fever, or whatever it may be) in our family when we were kids, and we survived just fine. I can't believe all those shots are necessary." But this is a shortsighted line of reasoning. A light case of a childhood disease that is now preventable may have been survived (if survival is all one is concerned about) by millions of children in the past, but there is no sense in risking the complications and/or damage to vital organs that may come in the wake of those illnesses.

We may be sure we will never forget the contagious illnesses or the immunizations our children have had, but we may not be available when that information is needed. Such data had best be recorded.

How Much Television for Young Children?

Television-viewing in some families becomes a facet of daily life that qualifies as "a worry"—and no wonder, when, according to a careful study, the average American child between the ages of three and sixteen spends one sixth of his waking hours in front of the television set.

Television is a source of information and entertainment that enriches life in many directions, but we need to learn to use it with discrimination. Keeping a television set going all day long without regard for what program is on the screen wastes time that might be spent more constructively.

Almost every TV station provides some programs that are suitable for the young. Television-viewing can be a pleasant treat for a youngster if he watches two or three programs in the course of a day. But such viewing tends to lose its flavor if it is his only way of spending his time. As for permitting preschoolers to watch adult programs indiscriminately, is there any logic in allowing the emotional strain of seeing a procession of incomprehensible and often disturbing situations?

"I keep the TV on, but our youngsters don't just sit and watch it. They are playing and talking and really don't pay much attention to it," say some parents. Then why, if no one is really watching it, should it be turned on? We are subjected to sufficient noise in the course of the day without the jangle and jabber of unwatched programs.

A research study has documented some effects of TV on young children. The hours they spend in viewing must be taken from other activities. Some are taken from sleep and some from what the study described as "casual play." We may interpret casual play as the ability to fill in an odd quarter of an hour with enjoyable, reasonably constructive, perhaps creative activity on their own. It is this cultivation of one's own resources that tends to wither when television is omnipresent. Some mothers insist, "But it keeps them out of mischief and they don't make all kinds of a mess getting out toys that they play with ten minutes and then leave. Whatever else it does, TV saves me a lot of work." There is no denying that argument, but without being hard on busy mothers we might suggest that a toy-strewn room may mean "Children growing here," whereas one in perfect order with a three- and five-year-old glued to the TV set may indicate a sterile life for the youngsters.

Several studies have indicated that viewing an aggressive film on TV does not drain off and reduce aggression in a youngster as effectively as does channeling angry feelings through direct and legitimate action. Such an active outlet might be punching an inflated plastic figure or engaging in games that involve running, climbing, and jumping.

What Is "Too Much" TV?

When a youngster becomes so addicted to television that it is the only activity he enjoys, when he rarely, if ever, turns to any kind of spontaneous play, then we may suspect that he is escaping from an existence that holds no other gratifications. The five-year-old who, when asked what he likes to do, replies, "Watch TV. What else?," has probably been permitted an overdose. Perhaps too many restrictions or lack of parental ingenuity have made him hesitate to spend his time in other pursuits that children this age can find satisfactory.

For such young TV addicts, limiting the hours of viewing is usually only a partial solution and less effective than examining the total picture of the boy's or girl's relationships and surroundings. Perhaps what is needed is more opportunities to play with other children, in an organized group or nursery school, or in his home or theirs. More time with his parents or more recognition and encouragement might generate incentive to try other activities.

It is probably easier to wean a three-year-old or a five-year-old from TV addiction than an older child. "He will outgrow spending hours watching," is usually an unfounded hope. If parents believe their son's or daughter's TV-watching pattern needs to be modified, they can make the change gradually. They may need to start by modifying their own watching pattern, turning the set on only for a program they really want to see.

Just how many programs a three-, four-, or five-year-old may watch without becoming an "addict" depends less on the quality of the programs, or even the actual time devoted to viewing, than on what he does when he is not parked in front of the television set. If TV is only one of a number of his interests, then one cartoon more or less is not critical.

Inevitably, in addition to watching the programs that are suitable for him, the preschooler will often be in the room when other members of the household are watching their favorites or listening to news reports. At such times it can help to get the youngster started on some kind of play he particularly likes.

TV Versus Being Read To

Television as a force in the lives of our children is here to stay, but it is no substitute for the warmth and closeness of human relationships. One of the ways in which such warmth comes through to small children is cuddling up to a friendly grown-up and listening to the reading or telling of a well-loved story or verse. The most aesthetic and delightful TV program cannot take the place of those homely, plotless, highly personalized tales made up for the benefit of the three- or four-year-old and featuring him as the principal character. The story usually begins: "Once there was a little girl named Beverly." At this point the child interrupts to say, "Just like my name!" The tale goes on to reveal where Beverly lived and what she and the other members of the family did each hour of the day. The real Beverly listens more entranced than by a well-plotted, beautifully written masterpiece. She is likely to prompt the storyteller if he is so careless as to omit detailing what Beverly had for supper or what color her bedroom slippers were.

Children who have the kind of relationship with parents or grandparents fostered by such moments together, and for whom being read to is a frequent and happy experience, will be less prone to TV addiction. They will probably still enjoy television, but being read to and hearing stories will be a good balance to the time spent at the TV set.

Worries and Annoyances in Perspective

Vexations and anxieties over children's development, their health, or the way they spend their time are neither new nor confined to the United States. In spite of the study that has been devoted to children's behavior in the past half century, we still cannot set down a blueprint for the optimum development of the preschooler. But this much we do know: the crucial question is not "Do I have annoyances and worries over my youngsters?" but rather, "How am I doing with the inevitable problems that crop up?" As has been emphasized throughout this chapter, we must try to see the whole child, rather than a specific problem. If problems are to be kept to manageable proportions, we must try to balance, sometimes to juggle, the children's needs with our own. At some points, adult needs will take priority, but in other circumstances the youngster's requirements will come first. Our goal is not to get rid of all conflicts and aggravations, but to accept, live with, and try to work through problems without letting them seriously interefere with either our enjoyment of the children or the satisfactions the children find in life.

11
Preparing Your Child For School

PREPARATION FOR SCHOOL goes on throughout the first five or six years of a child's life. Sometimes parents take explicit steps to provide experiences or information to further this preparation. More often it is woven into the fabric of daily life without anyone's being aware of what is taking place.

Whether a child is "well prepared" or "ill prepared" depends on intangible attitudes and relationships as well as on what parents may say or do. A child's own unique constitution and all the events in his brief past influence how he will assimilate the preparation his parents provide.

Starting "real school," which usually means first grade, is a milestone, despite the fact that a six-year-old may already have had a year of kindergarten and have attended nursery school as well. The child who lives in a school district that has no kindergarten may enter first grade having had no previous contact with anything resembling a scheduled school day.

A population survey quoted recently in *The New York Times* found that one in every five children of three and four years of age was enrolled in some kind of established nursery school. Still, the difference between a neighborhood nursery school, conducted in a casual manner, and a large, rather formal kindergarten in a public school is often more marked than the difference between kindergarten and first grade. Whether the big change in a child's life comes when he goes to kindergarten or starts first grade, attending a school that houses, in the same building, classes for the "big kids" is a great event.

Parents are not immune to the excitement, tinged with apprehension, that pervades the atmosphere as opening day approaches. The chill some of them feel in the air that September morning is not owing entirely to a seasonal drop in temperature. Now their youngster will be on his own as he never has been before. Parents sense the challenge to their offspring, and indirectly to them. They will be judged by how this child performs.

Most mothers, and some fathers, are poignantly aware that early childhood, when parents are the unrivaled models and arbiters, tends to end at the classroom door. From here on, increasingly, "what my teacher says" and "what the other kids do" will compete with the wisdom mother and father dispense. The values and standards of home will remain strong in the primary grades and usually will win out in the long pull, but questioned they will often be. That is a sobering thought when "Get ready for school" advertisements fill the newspapers.

What Does "Getting Ready for School" Mean?

When we think of getting our son or daughter ready for school, our first thought may be of new shoes and alterations on "hand-me-down" skirts or pants. Then there are visits to the family doctor or a clinic or specialists to have sight and hearing checked. Discovering any defects and correcting them before a child enters school can prevent unnecessary confusion and frustration for him as he is required to use his eyes and ears in unaccustomed ways.

Parents may eagerly drill their young in writing their names, recognizing letters, reciting the alphabet, counting. Some schools discourage this. Many educators insist that although some boys and girls learn to read almost spontaneously and holding them back would be foolish, the pushing of sheer memorizing is at best a waste of effort and may even prejudice a boy or girl against learning.

What, then, are the attitudes and the skills, the abilities and the facts that can be absorbed at home in the years before five and six that will make a child a better "learner" and lay the foundation for his profiting from and enjoying his formal education? How do parents create a setting for learning?

In their concern with making sure their children learn certain facts or skills, parents may overlook important facets of the youngster's education in the years from three to six. Both learning and education go on in and out of school at any age, and it may be useful to define and distinguish between them.

Dr. René Spitz, in a recent paper, *Fundamental Education,* explains that "Education, by changing the person himself, becomes a permanent part of the personality." Learning is an important branch of education, but it is not the whole story. What one learns is stored, through a complicated process, in a "memory bank." To preserve what one has learned, one must use it, for without the reinforcement of practice and use, a skill or a body of information will, as Dr. Spitz puts it, "be subject to the wear and tear of life . . . deteriorate and disappear."

Education Is Not Just School

In this broader sense, "education" is not just having gone to school. It is the effect that all one's experiences and relationships—all the learning one has done in school and out—have had on the way one tackles a problem, responds to other people, forms judgments, or expresses feelings. Education affects what we are. Learning affects what we know.

As an example of this distinction, consider what takes place when a child first recognizes letters. He may be delighted and amazed that all the road signs having the letters "s-t-o-p" have the same meaning. Picking out the word "stop" becomes a fascinating game. A wider world begins to open up. Yet, let us suppose an impossible situation. If this child were to have no more experience with reading, never see another written word, he would, in all likelihood, forget the combination of lines and curves that signify the word he has learned to read.

Now consider a youngster who has had scant acquaintance with picture or story books. Then, at school, at the home of a friend, or in his own home, he is read to by someone he cares for. This person is also fond of him and likes reading to children. Through being read to, he discovers the joy of imagining, along with the author, delightfully impossible creatures, landscapes, or events; of hearing about children like himself or those quite different; of reveling in nonsense or the rhythms of verse. He is attracted at first to being read to because someone whom he admires is paying attention to him. Clearly, that person likes reading. Right here is a motive for his becoming involved with stories and books.

Being read to usually, but not invariably, seems preferable to watching television, listening to the radio, or going to a movie, because when he is read to, he has not only the story but also the person reading it to interest him. Books have entered his life as a source of pleasure. Gradually, sometimes quite suddenly, being read to becomes a resource to rescue him from the sulks or doldrums. His personality has expanded. He will hardly be the same again!

Such an experience is "education," since while the material he learns through being read to may or may not stay with him, the taste for listening to poems and stories, and later for reading on his own, is permanent and is, incidentally, excellent preparation for school. If books have been a source of pleasure at home, then using them in school will tend to be gratifying.

What Does It Take to Learn?

Social and emotional well-being and readiness to learn are vital aspects of being prepared for first grade.

In recent years, attention has been paid to the fact that whereas some children come to school eager to learn, others are so blocked, so unable to grasp or disinterested in grasping subject matter as to be judged mentally deficient by their teachers. Further study of some of these children revealed that, long before they reached first grade, events in their lives, rather than their lack of native endowment, had dulled their ability to assimilate information and make it a part of themselves.

Given a boy or girl who is not indeed mentally handicapped, how he will respond to his teachers and their teaching is largely determined by his attitude toward himself and other people, particularly those in authority, his feeling about trying anything new, and his parents' attitudes about schools and learning.

The basic ingredients of the "mix" for learning and for absorbing education are a part of that sequence in development that has been described in earlier chapters. Against the background of being prepared for school, these developmental steps may take on added significance. They are worth reviewing in this light.

Learning takes confidence and courage. The foundation for these qualities is laid down in infancy. The baby who feels comfortable much of the time, whose mother is generally reliable about feeding him when he is hungry and satisfying his need for affection, develops trust in that good mother. His feeling, long before he understands language, is, "She is good. She is good to me. Therefore I am good."

Giving Baby the Right Start

Babies who develop trust in the person who takes care of them in their first year have a start toward liking themselves and trusting others. Five or six years later they will be likely to regard teachers as persons potentially friendly who will be helpers, not capricious tyrants. Trust, of course, will need to be seasoned with judgment as a child grows, because utter, blind trust would make no sense in many situations.

Out of trust in themselves comes enough confidence for babies to reach out, use their senses, and become acquainted with their world. Learning at any age and in many situations calls for reaching our boldly with one's mind and with one's senses. Good mothering in early life is basic for good learning later on.

Also necessary for learning is a nice blend of the ability to move about independently, to control oneself in some degree, and at the same time to accept a measure of control from others. Maintaining self-regulation and acquiescing to regulation from outside is one of the directions in which a child grows during his second year. If his development is proceeding in healthy fashion, he is keenly aware that he is a self-propelling individual.

Three- and four-year-olds, as every parent knows, are full of curiosity. They take the initiative, as has been explained earlier, in making discoveries. They speak out frequently—sometimes, it seems, continually. Exploring and speaking up are excellent ways to learn in many situations, but *only* using initiative and expressing feelings would hardly be an appropriate approach for every situation. Initiative will, from time to time, in even a single day, run afoul of necessary adult restrictions and need to be curbed and redirected. When that happens, a small child feels guilty. We have seen earlier in this book that guilt in small doses can temper curiosity and make for a healthy conscience. (See also Chapters 1, 7, and 9 on this subject.)

These same ingredients, *if they are in a proper balance,* are also an aid to learning. To what degree too much guilt can impede experimentation and learning is illustrated by an answer a three-and-a-half-year-old in nursery school gave. The little girl was painting with blue and yellow paint. Her teacher noticed that the girl was mixing the two colors. Since this child was extremely timid and seldom ventured to try anything she had not explicitly been told to do, the teacher, in a much encouraging manner, said, "Cindy, what do you get when you mix blue and yellow?"

"You get a whipping," was Cindy's answer, distilled out of three years of harsh repression that had made her all but inaccessible to the warmth the teacher offered.

Children who have not been mistreated as Cindy had, but have been able to work successfully through each step in development, have gone a long way in "learning how to learn." Their energies are not frittered away in anxiety but can be mobilized to master a subject and grapple with an unfamiliar problem, be it sounding out a word or following directions when the class goes on a field trip. These children have gained approval for making a bold attempt in the past. They feel "it is safe to learn." That which is new is not bound to be painful, but can be pleasant. The opposite of Cindy's plight was the happy approach of a five-year-old boy whose usual response to suggestions made by his teacher was, "O.K. That'll be great. I'll try it."

Parents may resent being told, when they are looking for a means of instilling those concrete abilities that will help their sons and daughters become good students, that confidence, the capacity to move about independently, to control bodily functions, and accept directions, together with a willingness to risk taking the initiative in exploring surroundings, are the foundations for effective learning in school. Indeed, it would be easier were there an exercise, a sort of "intellectual push-up," that could be practiced daily and that would guarantee the mastery of reading and writing in first grade!

Parents need to recognize that because they play such a vital part in the development of their children's feelings and ability to live with others, they are usually too involved with their offspring to make the best teachers of reading and writing.

In a paper entitled *Parents and Teachers—Who Does What?* Dr. Rudolph Eckstein points out:

> There must be bringing up that is based on [parental] love . . . and there must also be bringing up in terms of a love which allows for distance. For this reason parents, even if they are good teachers, don't

make good teachers [of school subjects] of their own children. . . . Every one of us, even if he is a fine teacher otherwise and has all the patience in the world for learning processes, finds that it breaks down at home. . . . If it didn't break down, it would only function because one would be so distant from the children that one relates to them as if they were students. . . . Parents and teachers . . . have two different functions: the teaching that comes out of intimacy, of closeness, . . . and the kind of distant love and distant teaching that is typical of the school system.

A Child Needs to Like Himself in Order to Learn

The hard fact is that children who have self-respect, who believe in their own worth, whose curiosity has not been brutally squelched, have a head start in school over those who are afraid to try out their abilities or to trust anyone because the results of doing either have only been more hurts, as was the case with Albert.

Albert's mother had died when he was an infant. He had been cared for, or more often not cared for, by a succession of relatives who found the droopy, whining boy unappealing and burdensome. When his father remarried, the stepmother took a dim view of the boy and gave him as little attention as possible.

If Albert, when he was four or five, asked a question or asked for help, which he seldom dared do, the response was usually a flat "Shut up. Get our of my way," or perhaps a less quotable admonition. If he had the bad luck to irritate his stepmother, she locked him in a dark closet. The father found the new wife no more likable than did the boy, but the father could—and did—walk out on the situation.

When her husband left, the stepmother lost no time in placing Albert in a foster home. That was the last he saw of her. By the time he was of an age for first grade (to say he was "ready" would be too optimistic), Albert had known three foster homes of varying quality, besides having had two stays in the county institution for dependent and neglected children.

A few months before he turned six, he had been placed with patient and kindly foster parents, but the damage done to him had been so great that it was not to be repaired quickly, if at all. He was destructive, suspicious, unwilling to talk or to cooperate. Everything that had happened had told him he was a worthless nuisance.

Going to school meant to him encountering one more set of persons who would make demands he could not meet. He could not have put those feelings into words, but they were, nonetheless, his response to the classroom.

Albert, and thousands of children like him, have trouble in school and fail to learn, not because they have learned nothing before they entered first grade, *but because they have learned the wrong things too well,* as Robert Hess points out in a study on learning. The lessons of their lives have instilled apathy, fear, and defiance.

Learning blocks also occur in children whose experiences have not been harsh, but who are, for some reason less easily detected, short on self-confidence.

This discussion of what interferes with learning may serve to highlight the self-esteem, the faith in others, and the zest for living that are a sound foundation for the early grades.

Telling It Like It Is

A parent's own feelings about schools and teachers influence his child's attitude toward learning. Few parents today would use school as a threat, although in a moment of exasperation with an uncooperative five-year-old they might, as one mother did, exclaim, "Just you wait until you get to school. Your teacher won't let you get away with acting like that." Of course, picturing schools as institutions specializing in punishment sours the young on them immediately.

Often, the tendency of well-intentioned parents is to go too far in the opposite direction: "School will be fun. You'll have friends your own age to play with. You'll learn to read and write and do all sorts of interesting things. Isn't it exciting to be a big boy and go to a real school?"

Yet such a rosy view hardly squares with the real state of affairs. If we put ourselves in our youngster's place and recall how we felt on the momentous day when we entered first grade, we will probably remember that we had some misgivings. Perhaps we were afraid of making some mistake that would betray our bewilderment. We may have imagined everyone else knew exactly what to do and we alone were worried about finding our way home at noon, finding the toilet room, or remembering to bring a dime tomorrow, although we did not understand why we were to bring it.

If we thought about our younger brothers and sisters safely at home with mother, having a midmorning snack in the familiar kitchen, tears of loneliness may have filled our eyes. The teacher may have talked too fast for us to understand what she was saying. All these and many other circumstances may have made our first days at school less than pleasant.

Even if we can bear to summon up memories that may have been long buried, we may elect not to discuss our own childhood feelings with our first-grader-to-be, lest we create anxiety where it need not exist. Yet, does anyone really escape having some bad moments? In discussing the desirability of being honest, rather than overselling school, Dr. Norman Paul, writing on "Parental Empathy" in *Parenthood—Its Psychology and Psychopathology,* says:

> The child finds school terrifying or restrictive or both, and concludes that he must somehow be inadequate. Didn't his parents imply it would be exciting and pleasant? Is there something wrong with him because he dreads the ringing of the school bell, finds the teacher a big, threatening person, and distrusts all the children who sit around him? Although he is experiencing the very feelings that many others have experienced, he is left with an impression of aloneness in his trouble. Ashamed of his inadequacy, he pretends at home that all is well. The parents are relieved that he has already adjusted to school. And the whole painful process of getting used to the new life is submerged in silence. . . . And so each child is left to traverse life's problems alone, as though his responses were so unique and uncharacteristic that they must be kept private.

Perhaps parents, in presenting what school will be like, might take the line Mrs. Hansen followed:

> You'll have lots of different feelings about school; at least I know I did, and your Daddy says he did, too. Sometimes it will be fun, but other days maybe you won't like it so much. Right at first, you may not have many friends, or even know the other children. The boys and girls on our block whom you play with may not be in the same classroom you are. The funny thing is that probably all the other children feel the same way you do. They want to make friends, but they feel strange, too. We can always talk about it if something at school bothers you or you don't understand what your teacher wants you to do. You go to school to learn lots of interesting things, but that takes a long time. You'll be a good learner.

Can Children Understand the "Dailiness" of School?

If we are to be realistic in talking about first grade, two points probably need to be made clear. That many children have misconceptions about these two points is demonstrated by two anecdotes that have become folklore. The first concerns the child who returned home at the end of his first day at school in a rage: "That old dump of a school is no good. You said I'd learn to read and I was there all day and I didn't learn anything. I'm never going back again."

The other story concerns a six-year-old who had looked forward to going to school for months and had gone with enthusiasm on the first day; but, when her mother told her it was time to get up and dress for school the next morning, she said, "What? Not again! I went to school yesterday!"

We need to emphasize to the children the gradualness of learning to read, to write, to add, or to do the other things one learns in first grade. We can prevent keen disappointment if we explain this carefully along with the statement that one goes to school for a long time.

Mothers Interpret the Teacher's Role

In addition to giving children a candid but encouraging view of school, parents need to think carefully about how they explain what a teacher does. A teacher is neither another mother or father nor a policeman. He or she is a giver of information and the ultimate authority in the classroom. Without making teachers seem a stern and forbidding breed, this can be put in words a six-year-old can understand:

> In school you do what the teacher tells you to, just the way Daddy and I expect you to do what we ask you to do at home. You can always ask your teacher if you don't know what to do or don't know what she means when she tells you something.

Such an attitude reassures a child that he will have a source of help when he is a stranger in a strange place, and also lets him know there will be limits on what is permitted.

For a variety of reasons, not all parents offer an encouraging picture of first grade. Some are more concerned that their children behave than that they have a satisfying learning experience. Sometimes, in metropolitan neighborhoods, real hazards exist for the small child who goes back and forth to school on streets where older children may threaten him or do him physical harm. Some families may feel that their children will not be given a fair chance by teachers or other children. If the schools have become a pawn in a struggle for power in the community, parents may fear their child will have only mediocre instruction. When such conditions exist, parents find it difficult, if not impossible, to reassure their children that going to school will be, on the whole, interesting, safe, or rewarding. Perhaps the best one can do under such circumstances is to stress that "Lots of people are trying to make things better, and some teachers are going to be friendly to you."

Various Approaches Taken by Parents

How different parents present school to their children has been brought out in a study carried on at the University of Chicago by Robert Hess, Ph.D., and Virginia Shipman. Mothers from various neighborhoods were asked what they would tell their six-year-olds before they went to school for the first time.

Some mothers stressed obedience to the teacher and the need "to be nice and quiet, and listen." Others stressed safety in crossing the streets on the way to and from school. Still others said they would talk about what the child would learn in school. Some, probably themselves frightened by the entire idea of school, said they would reassure the youngster that he could come home again and that mother would pick him up when school was out.

Clearly, the concerns and anxieties of these mothers colored their children's ideas of what might go on in school. The emphasis in many of the replies was on what a child would need to beware of, with no mention of the satisfactions that might also exist.

Reading what these mothers said, one realizes that the human tendency is to present only one facet of schools and teachers, which can give a child a lopsided view of what he will do in school.

Few mothers gave as well-rounded a picture as the one who said:

> First of all, I would take him to see his new school. We would talk about the building, and after seeing the school I would tell him he would meet new children who would be his friends and that he would work and play with them. I would explain that the teacher would be his friend, would help him and guide him in school, and that he should do as she tells him to.

Seeing Is Believing, So Take a Look

A visit to the school is certainly desirable. Some schools do arrange for parents to have a conference with their child's teacher before opening day. Mothers bring their children along, giving teachers and pupils a chance to have a look at one another. The child who has seen the classroom, the corridors, and—not to be overlooked—the washroom will feel less strange when he enters as a pupil.

Some suburban schools and schools in small communities plan for first-grade teachers to make home visits, if classes are not so large as to make this impracticable. A few parents object to these visits as "prying," but usually the teachers are welcomed. It is one way to avoid having meetings with the teacher come about only when something has gone wrong.

Any plan that offers an opportunity for the pupil and his mother to come to the school and discover how the day is spent and who will be in charge is a definite advantage for everyone involved. One father relates:

> The best thing my father did for me before I started school was to walk with me, not once but lots of times, over the route I'd take to and from school each day. That gave me a thread for finding my way back, in every sense of the word, and being sure I knew how to get home again kept me on solid ground for the first few days when I might have panicked, as I was small and scared and, I suppose, overprotected.

Separation Takes Practice

One form of overprotection that may make going to school harder for a six-year-old is not having become accustomed to being away from his mother for a day, or part of a day. This happened to Bea, and it resulted in her spending the first few weeks in school either crying quietly or sitting in a tense and depressed state, unable to take in what was going on around her. Bea's parents had moved many times from one city to another and from one neighborhood to another since she had been born. Neither her mother nor father was quick to make friends. They were far from relatives and were too proud or too shy to ask favors from casual acquaintances. As a result, they had no one to whom they could say, "Will you take our children for an afternoon?" When the mother went to the hospital for the birth of Bea's two younger sisters, her father took his vacation time and stayed home. Bea had never learned, through pleasant times with adults other than her parents, that others would and could take good care of her. The message that came through from her mother's constant presence was, "You could not get along without me, so I will not leave you even for a day." Although leaving her children with someone else occasionally might not have been easy to arrange, the obstacles to doing so were not as insuperable as Bea's mother believed them to be.

Independence develops as preschool children have the opportunity to practice it. Separations, in small doses, can prove it is safe, even enjoyable.

"The World Is So Full of a Number of Things"

When we take our children on excursions to the zoo or the airport; to see a farm or for a ride on a bus (or, if we can find one, a train); to a museum if one is nearby; to the fire station or to the library to select a book; to watch a house being built or a sidewalk repaired, we may not think of it as preparation for school. Yet such experiences, in digestible portions, give children a background of information and assurance. They tie in with topics that will be talked about in first grade. What is more, on such excursions a youngster acquires the manners needed for enjoying oneself without infringing on the rights of others in public places.

He usually can learn through these experiences whom to ask for information if it is needed; what to do if he is separated from the adults in charge of him; what it means to wait one's turn in line and why that is necessary sometimes; how one buys a ticket, whom one gives it to, and what it means to "get change," even though the arithmetic of getting change may be beyond him. The four- or five-year-old whose mother encourages him to tell the bus driver, even though she is right there, "We want to get off at Second Street," not "I want to get off at Grandma's house," is being helped to take a big step in abstract thinking.

If his family has a telephone, learning to answer it competently and summon the person being called promptly develops poise and the ability to think on one's feet.

Four- and five-year-olds can usually handle such matters with a bit of practice. These, and other challenges that teach them how to deal with the red tape that is involved in the simplest undertakings in our complex society, contribute to children's knowing their way around and tend to make the experience of going to "the big school" less overwhelming.

What Can Parents Teach the Preschooler?

Although mere memorizing that has little or no meaning to the child is not beneficial, encouraging him to think, to be curious, to inquire is highly desirable. Parents have countless opportunities every day to encourage their children to think for themselves. When we turn a question back to a youngster with a friendly "What do *you* think about it?" or "Let's see how much we do know about that" or "Let's find out together," we give him the courage to search for an answer on his own.

Every child does not invariably respond to opportunities we offer him for learning, but we can at least expose him to the opportunities. We can let a youngster set the pace in learning to count, to recognize and name colors, to discover certain fundamental principles about size, weight, shape, roughness or smoothness, wetness or dryness. Differences and correspondences between one object and another also interest him. The four- and five-year-old who has been an eager watcher of some of the children's programs on educational television stations will probably have accumulated a backlog of information of that kind and have become interested in learning to read numbers and letters as well.

The meaning of "more" and "less," "thicker" and "thinner," "heavier" and "lighter," and similar comparisons can be woven into play with the young child or into household tasks he does alongside his mother or father. The discovery that an object has a number of properties is a breakthrough. "This cup is not only red; it is little, it is light, and you can put things in it. Here is a big, green, wooden box that is heavy, but, like the cup, it is made so you can put things in it, too. Now how about that?" Such discoveries are exciting.

The revelation that two small blocks can fit into the same space as one big one expands the possibilities for using the blocks and also for understanding the relation of the whole to its parts. Adults do this in so many situations every day that we forget how surprising it is to a four- or five-year-old. Jean Piaget, the Swiss psychologist who has contributed so much to our knowledge

of how children learn, says that at this age, size, shape, and arrangement of objects confuse a child's comprehension of "how many" and "how much." (Chapter 1 discusses the understanding of the preschooler.) When the child works out for himself the unchangeable fact that whether he has five toy cars in a parking lot he has constructed, or three in the lot and two on the road he has built, he still has five cars, a youngster has had to do some hard thinking.

"How many forks do we need on the table if four of us are eating supper?" The four- or five-year-old is learning more about mathematics if he figures out that four people will need four forks than if he parrots "One and one are two," or even "Ten and ten are twenty" to impress a visiting grandfather.

Kitchens are good science laboratories. For instance, "Here is a nest of cups (or cookie cutters). The little one fits inside the big one. You can't get the big one inside the little one." Obvious? Not to a three-and-a-half-year-old or even to a child a year older.

"Here is a one-quart milk bottle and here is a one-quart mixing bowl, and here is a pitcher with a quart of water in it. If the water in the pitcher fills the bowl, will it fill the bottle?" To most four- and five-year-olds, a tall, narrow receptable seems "bigger" than a low, wide one. It is incomprehensible to them that the same amount of water will fill each. A year or two later that profound truth will be easily grasped. So we do not push for "learning"; we make the experiment a game.

We can also make a game of "I see something blue" (or yellow, or round or square, or three-sided or four-sided), or suggest that children walk around the room and point to as many objects of a certain shape or color as they can find.

Playing with Words

New words can be fun for the small child to try out, and a good vocabulary is an advantage to a first-grader, although the number of words is less important than enjoyment in using them. The discovery that several separate words can describe much the same thing adds range and flexibility to expression. He who can talk about a newly planted tree, for instance, as "small," "tiny," and "low" as well as "little" or "not tall yet" may be experiencing the tree more fully. Whatever points up various ways of saying or doing something tends to widen a child's horizons and make him a bit more at home in the world.

Parents can encourage imaginativeness in using words by asking, "Tell me how this feels" or "How does this look to you?" "What does that sound like?" "How do you feel about it?" These and similar inquiries that stimulate formulation of comparisons or descriptions of objects, sights, sounds, tastes, and smells sharpen budding powers of observation. We may be surprised at how fresh and fluent the children become in their use of language.

Different meanings of the same sounds intrigue the five-year-olds, too. "A pair of shoes" and "a pear that you eat," "a traffic jam" and "strawberry jam" illustrate the variety in language and stretch his mental processes.

We can hardly emphasize often enough in a variety of connections that "There is more than one good way to say things; isn't it more fun that everyone chooses his own way of saying them?" Such emphasis tends to broaden the narrow view a four- or five-year-old has of life and help him make associations more readily.

Classifying Things That Belong Together

Children are bombarded with a welter of information today. Parents can give them some guidelines for sorting out experiences and facts. Just getting the feeling that objects, animals, and sensations can be sorted into appropriate groups is a kind of education that makes learning easier.

We take it for granted, for instance, that beads, cars, or birds can be of various shapes, sizes, or colors and still belong to their respective categories. We lose sight of how puzzling and fascinating this can be to a five-year-old. A robin is one kind of bird and a blue jay is another, but both are birds, because both fly, have feathers, wings, and two legs, and lay eggs. This explanation failed to satisfy one five-year-old, who insisted, "I want to see a bird-bird, not just a robin bird or a black bird. Why isn't there a plain *bird?"* Here is a question that has puzzled philosophers for centuries. What do we mean by the general term, if only particular kinds exist? Young minds need a long time to digest this concept!

The ability to see that what applies to one object or animal or sensation also applies to other slightly different ones in the same general class—in other words, the ability to generalize from a particular instance—is a complicated mental process. A start on using the mind this way will be an invaluable aid to youngsters in school.

Directions Can Be Specific

Since mothers do a great deal of teaching in informal ways, it may be instructive to look at what ways appear to be effective. In another study made by Robert Hess and his associates, the mothers in the experiment were given specific tasks to teach their four-year-olds. First they were to teach the children some simple sorting procedures with blocks. They were then to show the youngsters how to use a toy called "Etch-a-Sketch" to make a simple design. With this toy, lines are made by turning knobs.

After a mother was satisfied that her child could do each task, she left the room, and one of the research staff took over. He asked the child to do the task he had just done with his mother. The conversation between mother and child had been recorded on tape.

The children who performed the tasks well with the research worker were the ones whose mothers had given them specific instructions: "The long block with the X on top goes in the middle" was more effective than vaguer directions, such as, "Fit that one in over there." Also, it was more effective for a mother to praise a correct response than to scold a child for making an incorrect move. In addition, if a mother asked questions or made comments that encouraged the youngster to talk about what he was doing so that she could be sure he understood what was wanted, his learning went along better. "Show me which block has the X on it" or "Can you show me which block is the longest?" impelled the children to function better.

Children's efforts were more successful, too, when their mothers explained the game or the task in words the children could understand. In the "Etch-a-Sketch" knob-turning task, a mother who said, "Use the same hand you use to draw with when you turn the knob" was giving her child a direction that had meaning for him. Merely saying "turn the knob" was less effective, especially if she gave no explanation of the fact that turning the knob produced lines and that making lines to "fit together" (or some other phrase that would convey the idea of a design) was "what we want to do."

The desirable teaching methods were not complicated. They would come naturally to many mothers, yet such teaching is sound preparation for following directions in school.

Useful Information for Five-year-olds

Along with the closely intertwined mental, social, and emotional preparation, which has been discussed, a youngster about to enter first grade will need certain practical information.

Most important for any boy or girl venturing beyond his own front door by himself is knowing his full name, not merely that he is called "Brother" or "Fuzzy." His address and telephone number, if the family has a phone, can also be part of his informational baggage.

Many youngsters, when asked their mother's or father's name, answer "Mommy" or "Daddy." They can be taught that other people call them "Mr. and Mrs. James Brown." As an extra precaution, a child may also be taught the name of a relative or close friend of the family who might be called in an emergency if his parents could not be reached. This is especially important if his mother is employed and not readily available during the day.

When a boy or girl uses a pencil or a crayon to draw, or merely to scribble, we can show him how to hold it properly. That will be a help when he starts to print his name. He may already have learned how to print his name in kindergarten or nursery school, or as a result of watching some educational television program. In any case, being able to do this gives him a good start in first grade. One advantage of being able to read his name is that if we mark his clothes plainly, he can then identify them. That may cut down on losses of caps, mittens, rubbers, sweaters, and such.

Children have usually learned to count at least to ten by the time they enter first grade. Actually, one who is thoroughly at home with the numbers through five has an adequate foundation for being at ease with number work in first grade.

When parents read to a son or daughter, they can point out that the story begins at the top of the page and goes down to the bottom, and that we begin to read at the left and go on to the right. This he will discover for himself if read to often enough, from watching the way our eyes move across the page and noticing the position of the pictures in the book when it is right side up. No harm in explaining it anyway.

Five-year-olds are usually able to dress themselves with no effort, but tying shoe laces may be a bit difficult. In case a boy or girl has not caught on to the knack of tying a bow with a firm knot, we will save him embarrassment if we give him some extra practice in doing so.

A Good Feeling About School

Each child will react to starting school in his own style. Some are slow to adapt to the new routines and demands but accommodate gradually and steadily. Others appear initially to be taking school in stride but some weeks or months later rebel, invent excuses not to go to school, or show in other ways that they are under real strain.

Some boys and girls do well in the classroom, learn enthusiastically, behave quite cooperatively but at home are irritable, anxious, or more boisterous or quarrelsome than usual. Extra affectionate attention and reassurance to offset the pressures of school are called for when this happens. Since the special virtue of home is that it is a place where one may be "bad" as well as "good," it may, within limits, be more economical emotionally to let off steam at home.

Many first-graders refuse to discuss what goes on at school. They give only the annoying answer, "Nothing," to the daily interrogation, "What happened today at school?" Parents who have seen several children through first grade have discovered it is better not to expect an accounting of what took place each day. "The fewer questions we asked, the more the kids were usually willing to talk," a mother says.

The school and the teachers need parental support. At least the teacher can be given the benefit of the doubt. If we are told she is "mean" or "unfair," we must try to find out what it is the child thinks she does that is "bad." Often it is a misunderstanding or misinterpretation of what she actually said that has caused a young child to become outraged. If we listen to our son's or daughter's retelling of what transpired, we may be able to read between the lines and help our child acquire a better perspective on what actually took place.

Parents need to maintain a delicate balance between upholding their youngster and upholding his teacher. "I won't hear a word against your teacher. She's the boss in school," is as unwise as immediately jumping to our child's defense when he says he has been wronged.

A calm, honest approach to a youngster's complaints is most likely to help him. We can accept the fact that he finds some parts of the school day difficult, some aspects of it threatening—and teachers sometimes unfair. But "It will get better. New things are often hard" is a line that tends to sustain him.

In one family, a timid first-grader began to find school tolerable when her parents proudly displayed on the kitchen wall her paintings and "writing" done at school. Their pride and genuine interest in what she brought home made leaving mother and submitting to the restrictions of the classroom seem worth the effort.

Another mother confesses a mistake she made with her eldest but corrected with the younger ones:

> When our eldest started school, I often said to her, "Now that you are big enough to go to school, you are big enough to go upstairs to bed at night alone," or "Now that you are in school, you are big enough to help me more," and so on. I kept expecting all sorts of new steps forward, when what she needed was a chance to slide back and have a bit more support from us at home. She was putting all she had into getting along at school and didn't have the energy, physically or emotionally, to meet more demands at home.

Taking it for granted that every child goes to school—on time, every day (mostly)—that what one learns there is important, and being matter-of-fact but firm about this helps a boy or girl accommodate in time to what is expected of him in his new life. Most of all, reassurance that this first-grader will be able to be "a good learner," will like school, and that his parents are pleased with him and standing by him, supports him through this major transition.

BOOK FOUR

The Early School Years

By DORIS P. MOGOL

THIS BOOK HAS *been so long in the process of being born that I owe much to some of my teachers who have helped me in the past—Dr. Geneva Goodrich, Mrs. Sidonie Gruenberg, and Dr. Mordecai M. Kaplan.*

I am also indebted to my editor, Mrs. Mary Hoover, for her guidance and help in the writing process; and to Dr. Ralph Moloshok, Dr. J. M. Malamut, Miss Eleanor Hester, and Miss Francine Foley for information and assistance. Last, but not least, my thanks to Mrs. Liba Frescia, librarian of the Child Study Association of America.

Introduction

THE OLDER I get, the more I realize that it takes a lot of courage to be a good parent! Children have a way of forcing their parents to confront their own feelings even when those feelings are uncomfortable and hard to accept.

That is what this book is about. It is intended to help parents hear themselves as clearly as they wish to hear their children—and to help them to recognize that the reality that adults sometimes try to hide from themselves is almost never as frightening as they imagine it to be.

As a matter of fact, it is only when adults can find this kind of compassion for themselves, and when they can have an enduring faith in their own ability to grow, that they can have such feelings for their children. Children need the comfort of having parents like this—parents who can accept their own reality as it is, without feeling that this is the way it always will be.

This takes courage, for nothing in life is certain! But if every day of every year is a new "jumping-off place" for the future—then who knows what we can do.

1 The Special Years

THE YEARS FROM six to ten are special years for parents and children in a very particular way. It is during these years that they will confront in the world outside the home what they have done together in the way of growing and maturing in infancy and and in early childhood. Now they will find out how the patterns of living that they have evolved together work in the school and in the community, how well they can cope with new challenges, and finally, how well they are prepared for the period of adolescence that lies ahead.

It is important to remember that these are still growing years for parents as well as for children, and that the changes in each affect the other. First let us take a brief look at what happens to most children in this age group in terms of their physical and emotional development, and then we will talk a bit about how the interaction ensues.

These years are what some psychologists call the "latency period." This means that the struggle for sexual identification that occupied the child so intensely between the ages of two and five is for the time being relegated to the background. The latency period lasts for boys until the age of about twelve and for girls until about ten. Then latency gives way to a few years of preadolescence, when children move turbulently toward puberty. Of course, there is great variation in these spans; some youngsters achieve puberty and sexual maturation earlier than others, and some achieve it later; but most of them adhere more or less to this pattern.

As adolescence approaches, youngsters begin again the struggle to find out who they are in terms of their maleness and femaleness. This is not to say, however, that the process of learning sexual identification does not go on at all during the middle years before adolescence. It certainly does; but in other terms. Through learning what are considered male skills or female skills, participating in male-oriented play and female-oriented play, cultivating modes of dress and behavior special to his or her sex, this kind of redefinition of a child's feelings about himself as a man or a woman occurs throughout latency and extends into adulthood.

Still, during the six-to-ten years, it is a little less pressing for boys and girls to discover themselves in their sexual roles than it is at other periods of growth. These years are devoted to discovering who they are otherwise, and what they can do. At six the child acquires both new freedom and new responsibilities. In going off to school, he is on his own for the first time in his life. Unlike nursery school, first grade is truly the upward step; it is a job he is *required* to do not only by his family but even by law. Things are asked of him in first grade that he must perform whether he wants to or not. He is no longer regarded as a baby, even by his parents; and for the first time he feels he is being judged by a parent figure, his teacher, and not only being guided by her (or him).

A Matter of Self-image

How the child will tolerate this kind of judgment by his teacher and by his peers—and even by us—will depend, of course, largely on the picture of himself that he brings to school—inside himself. According to Erik Erikson, a child begins to develop these opinions about himself very early in infancy. It is then that he first absorbs the attitudes that his parents have toward him and starts to make them his own. As time goes on, this picture fills out, and by the time he reaches school age, his self-concept has been fairly well established as a combination of what he thinks his parents feel about him and what he feels about himself.

For example, Tommy, aged six, was a charming, intelligent child, the youngest in a family where his siblings were already fourteen and seventeen. Everyone in the family treated Tommy with gentleness and respect. They enjoyed him and encouraged him in every way. Nevertheless, because he was so much younger than his brother and sister he was unable to share many of their activities, and he came to see himself as he thought everyone else in the family saw him, as "low man on the totem pole." When he got to school, although he was friendly and outgoing, he was fiercely competitive, wanting always to be best at everything and quick to resent a slight from anyone, including his teacher. He was a fighter. Fortunately, a sensitive teacher, recognizing Tommy's capacities as well as his emotional difficulties, challenged him along lines where he could do well and created situations in which he could become a real helper in class. As time went on, Tommy no longer felt quite so low on the totem pole. He began to stop measuring himself against his siblings and began to compare himself with his classmates, which was, of course, more appropriate and less frustrating. What is even better, as he became more and more confident, he became less competitive altogether, and when we last saw Tommy, he was learning to control his temper.

Development of Judgment

At this age the child is making the transition between what Jerome Bruner calls the "pre-operational" behavior of the nursery school and the "operational" behavior of the elementary school child. Before the age of six, a child can learn only—or largely—by testing out what he wants to do in real life situations. As he grows older, however, he begins to develop the ability to do some of this in his imagination. He can imagine "what it would be like if. . . ." He can do trial and error without externalizing it. As he grows, he continues to store the result of his experiences in his cerebral storehouse—his memory; and finally later on he can call it forth—"remember it"—to serve as a guide for the options open to him at that time. This process is what we call the development of judgment.

Girls and boys in the first and second grades are beginning to make real friendships as part of discovering who they are. They are more discriminating than they were in the past about whom they play with, but they make their choices on the basis of who is "fun"; they still do not make sharp distinctions between their male and female friends. Boys and girls still mix together freely in groups as they did in the preschool years.

Although in these days there is less difference between their play than in former generations, nonetheless, when girls are alone with girls they will still tend to play with dolls and other "girlish" toys, whereas boys will tend to play with cars and soldiers, blocks and trains. We do not know to what extent this is innate or due to upbringing.

In the third and fourth grades, children begin to stick together with friends of their own sex. Each group flaunts an ostentatious contempt for the other, which is a kind of taunting that presages the flirting of preadolescence. At this age some children are beginning to be seriously interested in the world around them. Boys are concerned about the draft and about fighting in a war, although they still continue to play soldier without recognizing the inherent contradiction between their rational fears and their dreams. Girls are beginning to be interested in fashion, although like boys, they will often be sloppy and messy about their appearance without apparent concern.

"Toys" are no longer interesting to this age group. Beginning with the third grade, youngsters are usually more interested in playing competitive games, games of skill, or in participating in creative activities. Clubs and groups are beginning to be formed with special projects in mind that usually don't get finished. Boys tend to roughhouse with each other at ten, becoming increasingly physical, while girls tend to prefer activities that allow them to keep their bodies to themselves.

"I Must Be Me"

As both sexes approach preadolescence in the fifth grade, we can notice that the insistence on expressing an individuality that includes sexual differences and focuses on "self-expression" has filtered downward from the adolescents to this preadolescent group. At this time, although some of the girls are beginning to mature, boys are much slower. While girls compare their budding shapes, boys will search in vain for hair under their arms or on their chests and chins. But no matter what their stage of physical development may be, both girls and boys are saying to their parents, "I must be me!"

This, in brief, is an outline of the developmental changes in our children from six to ten. But what about us as parents during these years? How do these years differ for parents from the earlier years of childhood?

Until now the child has been little more than a baby. Now suddenly he is off to school, and he seems both more grown-up and more vulnerable than ever before. This is an important time for both parents, but especially for a child's mother. For the first time in several years, mother is automatically gifted with a block of "free" time! She will have a choice to make, where there may have been no choice before, about what she will do. It is both confusing and exciting because such choices are usually not easy. It is especially hard for some women to accept the fact that they may not be needed at home full-time any more. They can no longer evade the confrontation with themselves. Now that they can no longer hide behind the apron or the baby carriage, they must decide where their personal interests lie—at home or elsewhere. Like her child, the mother is also being pushed out of the nest and into the world to discover who she is.

In any case, beginning with the school years, new demands will be made upon parents as well as upon their children. When the six-year-old returns home from school, there will be a change in his relationship to his parents. He will need new kinds of guidance and reinforcement rather than the protectiveness of babyhood. For the first time, he will need help in facing experiences in which we as parents will have no part. We will be his models and his teachers in learning how to cope with other children and in making some of the childhood decisions that we all remember having had to make at one time or another.

These are the years when he will begin to establish attitudes toward himself and his world that will support him in later years or that will leave him at the mercy of the crowd. As the child begins school, he will be confronted by problems that may still remain unresolved in our own lives as adults, and yet as his parents we will be asked to guide him.

This kind of learning is painful, but painful change is part of all growth. When any organism grows, whether it is a flower pushing aside the dirt to reach the sun, or a butterfly shedding its chrysalis to fly away, or a baby becoming a child, there is a corresponding break in the pattern of things around it. When children grow, like their counterparts in nature, their environments too must change to accommodate their growth. We are an important part of our child's environment, and the changes we will be asked to make in ourselves will not be easy. Although we may think we are being motivated by an interest in our child to inquire what we believe and what the world is about, this growth will really be for us. For it is a paradox of parenthood that it is only when we as parents find our own fulfillment that we may teach our children how to live.

2
Coping With School

There was a child went forth every day;
And the first object he looked upon,
that object he became.

And that object became part of him for the day, or a certain part of the day, or for many years, or stretching cycles of years:
The early lilacs became part of this this child. . . .
And the apple-trees covered with blossoms, and the fruit afterward, and the wood-berries, and the commonest weeds by the road;
And the school mistress that passed on her way to school.

"There Was a Child Went Forth" — Walt Whitman

EVEN THOUGH Walt Whitman lived before the age of psychology, he knew with his poet's heart that this is the way children learn. In the years of early childhood they absorb the world in which they live through their very pores. They look at it and feel it, mostly without going through all the conscious mental processes that we as adults have come to associate with learning.

Have you ever noticed how a blade of grass grows even in the city? How it will suddenly appear through a crack in the sidewalk in its natural push to reach for sunshine and rain? That's how it is with children. Learning is as natural as breathing. A child learns in order to live. When he is a baby, he must learn what his family is like by discovering what kind of behavior will help him get the kind of satisfactions he needs. Later on, he will need to learn about other people and other places, about nature and about ideas, so that he can locate himself in the larger world outside.

For a child, learning is something like map-making. The more clearly the map-maker can see the terrain, the hills and the valleys, the pitfalls and the horizons, the more accurate the map — and the easier the trip will be for the traveler. The trick in helping our children is to realize that every one of us sees the world differently according to our own individual capacities, and that the map for none of us, parents or children, can be identically the same.

Learning from the Home Environment

For example, even for children within the same family, the world is not the same. Besides the fact that each of the children was born intrinsically different, with different physical and emotional characteristics, and perhaps of different sex, the place of each in the family is different. One is younger; one is older. One has a sister and no brother; the other, a brother and no sister. They were born to their parents at different ages so that when Jenny was six, her parents were twenty-seven and thirty; now that John is six, his parents are thirty-one and thirty-four; John has a ten-year-old sister and Jenny has a six-year-old younger brother. John's parents have learned a lot about children since Jenny was six; and what is more, when John was six they had achieved a financial stability that they did not have when Jenny was the same age. When Jenny was six, her mother still stayed home most of the day to care for John, who was still a baby, but when John went off to school, his mother took a part-time job.

Thus, the environment for all of us is different. And there are, alas, no easy prescriptions for how to bring up our children. The best guide for healthy child-rearing is to know ourselves as best we are able and to understand what our child is living through at every stage of his growth.

By the time a child is six, he has already learned a lot. His learning certainly does not *begin* in the first grade. He will take to school what he has already learned at home. We as parents are teachers whether we like it or not. In their early years, children learn almost everything from their parents. In fact, recent studies have shown that babies learn more and learn earlier from their environment than we had ever thought. We have known for a long time that babies are sensitive to their parents' emotions, to the way in which they are held, to the tone of voice they hear. What we did not know is that the intellectual development of infants can be nurtured by stimulating the child with colors, sounds, and textures. In fact, it has been shown that practice in intellectual learning of this kind in infancy can help children learn more readily in later years. This means that at six our child has already learned a lot from us. He has learned without being told how we feel about life and how we feel about him. He has learned, from watching, hearing, and sensing, about marriage, sex, children, money, work and play, and a thousand other things that we were not aware of teaching him. In short, he has already drawn himself a map of his own of how to travel in his world.

What Do They Learn?

It often comes as a surprise to parents when they find what their growing children learn at home is sometimes not precisely what they intended to teach. How can it be, if parents are such influential factors in a child's learning process, that children sometimes hold different values from those of their parents and seem to feel differently about so many things from the way their parents do? How can this happen? Why may children "hear" different messages from the ones their parents believe they are sending?

Partly it is because few of us *see* and *hear* what we ourselves do, and what we say, as clearly as we might. We are unaware of the ambiguous nature of some of the messages we send. The source of that ambiguity is worth examining closely.

By the time we are adults, we have developed habits of looking at life in a certain way and ways of doing things that have become "second nature" to us. (In fact, we may find some of these ways of behaving so "natural" that we begin to think of them as "right" or "normal" for everyone.) We tend to forget that much of our present behavior reflects the way we learned to live in our own childhood as a result of pressures of that time. When we were children ourselves, we coped with our lives as best we could, just as our own children are doing today. We developed ways of dealing with problems, as our children are doing now, that were "right" for us at the time or enabled us to survive. These responses were not always the most "healthy" ways to behave in the long run, and today, *consciously,* we may disapprove of them; but even so, some have become part of the fabric of our lives.

Our ways of coping with the most extreme stresses in our early environment are especially likely to leave an imprint on our behavior thereafter. For example, it is a frequent complaint of schoolteachers that many children from the ghetto "tune out" in class. They don't seem to listen or hear. Although this behavior is certainly inappropriate in school, it is the only way in which children of poverty can live with the dehumanizing noise and brutality with which they are frequently surrounded in their daily lives at home. This is called "blocking out" and is a healthy response to stress. In order to cope with certain situations, we all occasionally "block out" what we are not equipped to handle; trouble arises only when this becomes such a habit that it is an unconscious and nonselective response to life.

We all have such response-patterns that we are unaware of. This can make our behavior in some areas ambiguous and confusing to our children.

Let us look at Betty and John King. Originally from homes where money was always scarce, they now live on the outskirts of an affluent suburban community with their two children, Danny, twelve, and Judy, nine. Both of them work in a bookshop in town, from which they draw a modest income. Through stringent saving and self-denial, Betty manages to stretch their budget to include all kinds of extras for the children, despite the fact that she and John have not had a holiday away from home since Danny was born. Every year both Danny and Judy go to a private camp for the summer. They each have their own TV and plenty of new clothes. Judy takes music lessons and goes to dancing school, and Danny just got a brand-new steel tennis racket with carrying case for his birthday. In fact, Betty and John spare no effort to help both children become part of the affluent world in which they live.

The paradox is that Betty and John are both "intellectuals" and active liberals in local politics. In talking about the community, they refer with some contempt to those with money and power. They insist that for themselves, they prefer a different kind of life.

How confusing for the children! What values are they being taught to absorb as they are pushed by their parents into the very group that the parents profess to despise? Is it any wonder that Judy is a poor student but a solid member of the "in" clique? Is it any surprise that Danny is an aggressive and competitive boy with only one interest in life—to win!

Betty and John can't understand how their children "got that way." "How can they be so different from us?" they ask each other. Neither of them realizes that they themselves are ambivalent, unsure of what values they really believe in. They don't see that Danny and Judy are responding to an aspect of their parents' feelings and behavior that the parents are unaware of.

Erik Erikson speaks of the need for parents to be healthy "models" for their children. Betty and John are ambiguous models because of their own unresolved conflicts. When parents themselves are torn between conflicting values—professing one thing but in their behavior subtly supporting another—this leaves the children in virtual limbo. Which shall they choose? It is a Hobson's choice—they will feel somewhat cheated and "guilty" either way.

Developing a Positive Self-concept

The behavior of Bob Green, father of seven-year-old Richie, is an illustration of a conflict that expresses itself in a different way. Bob appears almost rejecting of his son, although he really loves him deeply. Coming himself from a rigid and authoritarian parental home, Bob is essentially a very dependent person who covers up his feelings of dependency by a noisy display of "masculine" aggressiveness. Because he regards feelings of dependence as unmanly, Bob consistently denied them to himself while he was growing up and is determined that *his* child shall not be "pampered." In an effort to make him "independent and free," Richie has therefore been plunged since babyhood into one situation after another that has been too tough for him to handle. At his father's insistence, he was weaned from the bottle at nine months. Toilet training started in earnest when he was a year old. As a result, Richie wasn't completely "trained" until he was almost four. His earliest experiences with other children in the park were embarrassing and demeaning for him because he still wet his pants long after they had graduated to grown-up zippers and dungarees. Richie is also a finicky eater, but no one in the family sees any relation between that and the painfully premature weaning experience.

At four, as a reward for learning the secret of bladder control, Richie was given a "two-wheeler"—but without training wheels, so that once again he was confronted by failure.

The sad history of Richie shows us how a parent's preoccupation with denying his own problem can prevent him from distinguishing his child's needs from his own. In an attempt to make his child competent, Bob mistakenly defeats his own purpose by leading his child into the very failure that he seeks to spare him.

This involves what Erikson calls "reinforcing self-concept." A child who is given a chance to work at something he *can* do develops a positive self-concept, real self-confidence that will help him to tackle increasingly harder tasks with some assurance of success. On the other hand, a child like Richie, who has known only failure in the past because he has been exposed to impossible tasks, will approach every new situation with a habitual expectation of defeat. His "I can't" will no longer bear any realistic relation to the difficulty of the job at hand; and as his self-confidence diminishes, his negative self-concept becomes reinforced, and his own prophecy becomes self-fulfilling. Failure breeds failure—and success begets success.

Thus we can see that learning to want to learn begins at home. If a child feels uncomfortable with what he is being "taught" at home, he will be receptive to what is taught at school. If a child senses at home that his parents are seeking to know him as a separate person and to help him be himself, he will develop a trust in adults and a confidence in himself that will transfer itself to school. Parents cannot lie to a child about how they feel about themselves or about what is important to them. Above all, they cannot conceal how they feel about him.

The secret of helping a child to become all that he can be is to appreciate each child for what he is. Some parents who appear to accept the fact that everyone is born with different capacities and different inclinations find it hard to live with these differences in their own children. Although it is absolutely logical that a parent may prefer being with one child rather than another because somehow they "operate on the same wavelength," this does not mean that the child who is different cannot also be loved and enjoyed and encouraged to be himself.

On Schools

We have all heard much talk in recent years about what kind of schools we want for our children. What do we want our schools to do? What purpose should they serve in our communities? Are they teaching our children what they really need to know?

Traditionally, schools were intended to teach children the skills that were necessary for their survival. In earlier days, these were rather fundamental skills—the "3 R's," we used to call them. That, together with learning about housekeeping for girls and farming, hunting, or an artisan's craft for boys, sufficed to enable young men and women to find their places in society. Today, this simplicity of curriculum is no longer enough.

In the past hundred years, the world has changed more rapidly and more radically than ever before in the history of man. The body of knowledge that has been accumulated in the twentieth century alone would stagger the imagination of the Victorian scholar. Science has expanded our horizons in every direction, and the youngest nursery school child is familiar with the challenges of space. Television has made a war that takes place half way around the world part of everyone's daily experience, and technology has made neighbors of people in lands that were previously only the stuff of fairy tales.

Thus, whereas in the past it was possible to give children some facts about their world and to send them out into it with confidence, today this is no longer so. Even if schools were to attempt it, it would be impossible to cram into our children all that they would need to become "experts" in even *one* subject! What are schools to do?

In addition to having *more* to learn than in previous generations, our children will also have new kinds of problems to face as adults. They can look forward to living in a world in which they will spend less and less time in making a livelihood and more time in leisure pursuits. Automation will deprive many of them of a creative interest in their jobs and will force them to find satisfactions and fulfillment in other ways. Their life expectancy will be even more extended than ours, and the problem of a fruitful old age will be even more pressing than it is today. What is more, as the world population increases by 70,000,000 people a year, our children can look forward to living in an overcrowded world, where space will be at a premium, and where natural resources will be seriously overtaxed. Health problems will also multiply. Even as medical science grows increasingly competent, the mounting effects of pollution can be expected to take their toll.

How can schools equip our children to live in a world like this? What will our children need to survive?

What Can Schools Do?

We, who grew up in a simpler age, may be unused to thinking about schools in a critical way. Many of us are still convinced that the school curriculum should confine itself to the hard stuff of books, and that it is not the business of the school to offer any "frills." Some parents even reject those "frills" in the curriculum that have already met with broad general acceptance, such as art, gym, music, guidance, etc. But is it possible that, in fact, we do not have enough "frills"?

Educators all over the world are beginning to reevaluate what schools are all about in terms of how they prepare their students for life. Initially, these concerns were focused principally on "disadvantaged" children. Head Start programs were developed as teachers became aware of the fact that some children had different educational needs from middle-class children and that the traditional academic methods and materials were not meaningful or effective for them. Today, however, school people are thinking in these terms for *all* children, as they are beginning to recognize that "miseducation" is prevalent everywhere and that middle-class children, rich children, slow children, and bright children are all being given much outmoded subject matter in outmoded ways.

Today, therefore, the emphasis in education appears to be swinging more and more

toward educating the *whole* child (as John Dewey urged in the twenties and thirties) in a school environment that will contribute as much as possible to his full development as a human being. Teachers are beginning to realize that competence in the world of tomorrow will include the cultivation of personal characteristics and kinds of intellectual skills that were seldom considered before as part of the educator's job. To cope with the mounting accumulation of knowledge, the child today needs to know how to find out for himself what he wants to learn; he needs to be able to plan for himself what he wants to do; and he needs training in using resources—both books and people—to discover what he needs to know. In other words, he needs to develop a self-reliance that will enable him to sharpen his skills of communication and discrimination in order to survive.

Schools today cannot continue to function as isolated institutions apart from the community. Schools cannot truly educate children if they remain apart from life, teaching factual matter alone and concerned with the standard "graded" child. For such a child is a statistical myth, as parents probably discovered long ago. Teaching must concern itself with individual children, taking into account the growing capacities and changing needs of each developing child. Because we know that each child is intrinsically different, and that each develops at his own natural rate, there is no other way to educate the child as a person.

What Can Parents Do?

Thus, it becomes obvious that parents can no longer stand apart from their school, as if to hand over their children for so many hours a day without questioning what goes on within its walls. True, teachers have been professionally trained; but we as parents have much to contribute that is equally as important as academic learning. Will we be content to remain, as so many parents are, mere "suppliers of children" and "supporters of bond issues . . . incapable of participating directly in the education of [our] children or in decision-making about the community's children?"

Dr. Ira Gordon of the University of Florida, who raised that question, uses the term "parent power" in outlining some ways in which parents can contribute to creating a meaningful education for their children. Parents can no longer afford to relegate that power to others. Those feelings of alienation that our children often express in the turmoil of adolescence frequently have their birth in these early years when they feel that their parents are simply not interested enough to do anything about matters that are of real concern to them. Our children need to feel early in life that we are their partners in this and other important undertakings. They need to know that we are aware of their needs and that we are doing our best to see that they are met.

This certainly does not mean that respect and appreciation for what most teachers are trying to do should give way to an overconcern for classroom trivia; then parents become only an interfering nuisance to the school. It means only that parents have an obligation to see that their schools become truly a part of life, reflecting the values and goals that they feel are important for their children. That is why it is important for us to work with the school and to help the business of education to become a genuinely cooperative and realistic enterprise.

The first hurdle to overcome will be to recognize that all schools have problems with change. As in other institutions everywhere, school personnel are burdened with administrative details and with traditional ways of doing things that are hard to modify. But it is our job as citizens, as well as parents, to see that our school is doing its job as best it can within the framework of what is available to it within our community.

If we do not have the time to spend away from home, or from work, to become active in the P.-T.A. or to help out at school in other ways, there are still things we can do to indicate our interest and concern. We can become actively involved by phone or mail in community issues that affect our school. We can support appropriate candidates for the school board and for other public offices affecting education. We can get to know the child's principal and the problems of the school; and, above all, we can make his teacher feel that we are working *with* her to help our child.

Preparing Your Child for School

The first day of school—every first day—is a very special day for the whole family. It means a change for everyone, and especially for a child.

In the first grade, he will be stepping forth into a new world where everything is strange for him. Even though we may have taken him to school earlier in the year to show him around or to meet his teacher, that was only a trial run. This is the "real thing"!

Handling Feelings

He will probably have all kinds of feelings about leaving home, and he will look to us as parents to help him handle them. It is natural for all of us to have confusing feelings, and how we handle our own at this point will give him some indication about how to handle his.

For a mother, it is an ambiguous business. She is joyous and sad at the same time. It's exciting, and it's frightening. Will he be able to handle it? How good a job did she do? What will happen to her? It is a milestone in the life of a woman when she is no longer needed full-time at home. Even if she has another younger child, she will have a new block of free time to do with as she will. What will she make of it? This is also the beginning of a new stage of growth for her, requiring a decision as to what kind of woman she really is.

For a father it is also a time of ambivalent feelings. All his youthful feelings about himself and other children come again into play as *his* child goes off to school for the first time. His expectations for his child—as his fledgling leaves the nest—may be colored by what he demands of himself.

For all children, it is important to go off to school with the knowledge deep inside that their parents have confidence in them and that they will not demand what cannot be given. This is something we can't really *say*. It is in the way we look at a child and the way he knows that we are looking at *him* . . . and not at a reflection of ourselves. He will need to know that we will be waiting for him when he returns from school to hear all about it; and he will want to know what went on at home while he was away, as if to have been there too a bit himself.

Feeling comfortable and special about going to school on the first day may include, for a child, the chance to wear the clothes he picks out for the occasion. It may include anticipation of a favorite lunch when he comes home. It may include an extra nap after lunch with a new book or a story to quiet down excited spirits. The child may test us to see if we still love him by "acting out," or behaving in ways that will tempt us to say: "Now that you're a schoolchild, I don't expect that from *you!*" But DON'T SAY IT! That's what he's afraid of, that things have changed too quickly and too soon. A part of him still wants things to stay the same as they always were, at least at home, until he is sure he can manage the things that are different at school.

How a child feels about his first days will

have a lot to do with how he feels about school after that. And we mustn't forget that all this is not limited to the first day in first grade—it happens every year!

Each new grade is a new challenge, a new and exciting upward step. After the first year, we have learned a bit as parents what kind of reaction to expect from our child in response to this kind of challenge. Each year we may find that the same patterns are repeated, with variations as he grows older, until in adolescence he either becomes genuinely confident in himself or he wants to deal with these feelings alone without us.

In any case, it is important to let the child know that we respect his feelings, and perhaps that we feel like that a little bit, too. If we are honest with him in this way, he will be able to acknowledge his uncomfortable feelings more freely to himself, if not to us. He won't be forced to deny them because he senses that they are unacceptable to us. It is only when such feelings are known to the child that they can be dealt with.

Different children react differently to new situations. One child may express his fears openly. He may show how frightened he is at leaving home and facing this new world alone by constantly questioning us about what will happen at school. He may return for a while to some of his more infantile ways. We can help him by not being impatient and by letting him know that we understand how frightening it is to do something new for the first time, but at the same time reassuring him that he will probably have fun.

On the other hand, another child may hide his concerns under a show of eagerness to get going. He may be impatient with us because we haven't got his things ready just the way he wants them and, as if to jump the gun, say something such as, "Boy, will I be glad to get out of here!"

One little girl may spend what seems like hours in indecision about what to wear, and she may burst into tears for "no reason at all" when we don't enter into the decision exactly as she would like us to. What she may be needing is some reassurance from us that we think she is fine just the way she is. Although we need to make her feel that we know she will be pretty whatever she wears, perhaps it might be a good idea to choose for her at first or to make the decision together the night before.

No matter how a child reacts, it is often good for children to take something along to school on that first day—whether it is *the* first day, or just another first day—something from the summer holiday, or perhaps a drawing or arts-and-crafts object the child has made himself.

The important thing is to make the transition as easy as possible without denying the special quality of this special day. A child will absorb how parents feel about it, too. If we can make him feel that this is a happy part of growing up—but scary, too—then we have gone a long way toward helping him on the road to maturity.

Getting Along in School

We have considered at some length how to nurture attitudes and feelings that will help the learning process at school. Still, the fact of the matter remains that there are many ingredients of the school situation itself that can cause problems for a child.

What shall we do, for instance, if a child comes home unhappy because he doesn't get along with his teacher? How about homework—shall we help or not? What if he doesn't seem to be doing as well in school as we know he is capable of? These are questions that parents face in the course of their child's development, and they are not always easy to handle. Let's talk about them now.

Getting Along with the Teacher

It's hard when a child comes home from school almost every day in a grumpy mood. We all know how disturbing it is when he slams the front door as he comes in and begins to pick a fight with anyone who happens to be around. Something obviously went wrong at school. But what do we do when are are told that the teacher is "mean" or that "she always picks on *me*"?

The first thing to do is to remember that there are two sides to every story. We can make an appointment with the teacher to speak to her about our child. When we go to see her, we should remember that she is as interested as we are in doing a good job and that she will most probably welcome any help we can give her. We might ask her first if she is aware of how unhappy the child is in school and whether she has any ideas about why this is so. Then we should try to listen to what she has to tell us as openly as we can without showing the defensiveness that we all feel when we are anxious about our children. Perhaps we can contribute some information about our child that the teacher doesn't know; that will help the situation.

For example, Evan was a smart and charming little boy who seemed to be the terror of the second grade. His mother was at her wits' end to know what to do about it, and the teacher was threatening to fail him in class because he never "listened" to what she was saying. At a conference between them, Evan's teacher learned from his mother that he had been quite ill as a baby, and she suggested that he be given a thorough medical checkup. It turned out that he had only partial hearing in one ear, a disability of which even he had not been aware. When he sat in his regular assigned seat in the back of the room, he couldn't hear the teacher, and he misbehaved out of frustration and boredom. Evan's seat was changed—and so was Evan! He became quieter and happier and began to enjoy school in a way that he never had before. The teacher treated him with a new kindness and understanding, and he was able to make a greater effort to concentrate and to learn now that he too knew the real reason for his past restlessness.

The impairment of any physical faculty, if it is relatively minor, often goes unnoticed by the child who suffers from it as well as by the adults in his life. Children learn early to "compensate" for their disabilities in various ways. They often disguise a problem without even knowing what they are doing. A child who is slightly deaf like Evan may cock his head to one side to hear better—or if that doesn't work, he may just decide to forget about the whole thing, concluding that it's too much effort to try to hear people when they don't talk loud enough.

Similar behavior is typical of children with vision impairment. Sometimes children compensate so well for diminished or impaired eyesight that until they are tested even they are not aware of not seeing properly. Often such children run into all kinds of trouble at school, just as Even did.

A regular checkup at the pediatrician's should include all the usual items of concern plus measurement of hearing and vision. Even a child's mode of walking should be checked, since his feet or legs may be troublesome in a way that may hinder his athletic activities, even though he does not recognize what is amiss.

Not all school problems are as fundamental as this. Sometimes misbehavior in class reflects a real clash of personalities between the teacher and the child. A teacher, being human, may have preferences and biases about boys or girls, or quiet children or noisy children, curious children, black children or white children. Teachers carry their own preferences with them as we all do, even though they may try very hard not to acknowledge them even to themselves. If a child seems to be suffering in such a situation, it may be wise to consult the principal after a meeting with the teacher, and perhaps arrange to change the child to another class. If this is done with tact, the teacher can be helped to recognize that it is not a defeat, and that no teacher can be expected to be equally effective with *all* kinds of children.

Anything that disrupts normal daily family life as he knows it can also disturb a child at school. A new baby, a death in the family, divorce, moving to a new house, or just a big row between his parents can trouble a child so much that it affects his whole behavior. It is sometimes helpful for parents to alert their child's teacher to what is going on at home so that she may be prepared for such a change in behavior and cope with it accordingly.

In short, the secret of getting along with the teacher is to regard her or him as our partner in this job of educating our child. Too often there are feelings of antagonism between parents and teachers that prevent them from working together; each blames the other for not doing a good job. The effect upon the child who is caught in the middle is the same as in a family where parents disagree about their children and pull in opposite directions. For the child's well-being it is important for us to keep regularly informed as to what is going on in his class and to participate in parent activities on the class level as much as we are able.

Homework

Homework is a ticklish subject for most parents and many schools. Originally homework was taken for granted and expected as part of the overall program of every school. Now, however, some schools are beginning to question whether or not a six-hour day isn't enough for youngsters in grades 1 to 5. Many schools that are small enough to give their students the individual attention they need in class are reconsidering whether homework assignments are necessary at this age, or whether they deprive children of opportunities to use themselves at home in a different and more creative way.

However, homework is still an established practice in most school systems from about second grade on, and it serves several purposes. It fosters good work habits; it offers an opportunity to do individual projects outside the classroom involving techniques of research that will be needed for independent work in later grades; and, at its most fundamental level, it gives a child practice in areas where his skills are weak.

All these are valid reasons for homework and for encouraging a child to do it by himself. How can we do this? When should we give him a hand? These are questions that trouble most of us at one time or another.

First of all, we can encourage a child to do his homework by establishing a schedule with him that allows a regular time to be set aside for homework every day. It is usually best to set this time just before dinner or after dinner, allowing him to have a play period to blow off steam immediately after his return from school. It is also important to provide him with the tools that are needed to do homework: a quiet, private corner with a desk or table of convenient height, a comfortable chair, a good light, paper, pencils, pencil-sharpener, a dictionary, and whatever else he might need. If it is possible, it will be helpful to get a set of good reference books for him like one of the *Time-Life Informational Series,* the *How and Why* series, *The World Book,* or another set. The child's teacher or the school librarian can often make helpful recommendations.

Our attitude as parents will also help or hinder the willingness with which he will sit down to do his work. He will be much more amenable to it if we are conscientious about our own obligations and if we show him that we regard his work with respect.

Now comes the question of whether or not to help. There are no hard and fast rules, but there are some guidelines to help us to decide. First of all, it is important to know *why* he is being assigned the work so that we can work out with him how we can be of most help. For example, if he needs practice in arithmetic because he tends to be careless and sloppy at school, then a "hands-off" policy may be in order, with some explanation to him of our expectation that doing it alone will help him to assume responsibility for his own successes and failures. However, if he really does not fully understand the concepts and methods involved, we should help him by all means.

No matter how competent a child may be, all boys and girls like some help with homework every once in a while. For example, we can help our child with his arithmetic tables or spelling words by making "flash cards" together (or buying them) and using them like a game. We can participate in a research project by helping him to collect magazines and by showing him how to find pictures or articles relevant to what he is doing. We can take him to a museum that has an exhibition on a subject he is interested in, to a factory, or to a different neighborhood. There are many ways to help a child with homework that will indicate our interest in what he is doing but won't deprive him of the satisfaction of doing it himself.

Last, but not least, we can make sure he has a library card from the local public library and that he uses it. We should go with him the first time, introduce him to the librarian, and ask her to explain the lending system to him so that he can go by himself with confidence later on.

All this will help to give the child a sense of continuity between his school and his home that will enrich both experiences for him.

What to Expect of Your Child

One of the most troublesome aspects of being a parent is to know what to expect of our child. This is especially true in the area of schoolwork, because so much of the child's future seems to depend upon how well he does in school.

As short a time as fifty years ago, both children and parents knew very early in life what was expected of them. They knew exactly what roles they had to fulfill and what learning would be required along the way. School was a preparation for a clearly defined way of life.

Today, however, things are different. Standards for behavior are not as narrowly defined as they once were, and the "future" – the world that the child will have to function in and cope with as an adult – is difficult to foresee. As a result, both children and parents are confronted with confusing choices that did not exist before. What shall a parent expect and demand of his child under these circumstances? What shall a child demand of himself?

It is much harder to grow up – and to "bring a child up" – in a society where both parents and children have choices as to how they shall behave and what the child will "be," than it was in the simpler world of the past where tradition and custom more or less decided these matters for everyone.

All this is reflected in a child's attitudes toward school. He no longer enters school with a blueprint for the future. From his earliest school years he will be required to make choices and decisions on his own about what is important to him. It takes a good deal of confidence and self-definition on the part of the parents to be able to equip a child to make such decisions and to accept whatever those decisions might be.

Competition

If a child goes off to school knowing that his parents need him to be a winner, he will feel the pressure whether we express this to him verbally or not. But if he goes off knowing that we are eager for him to enjoy school and expect him to look upon the challenges of learning as a worthy experience for himself, he will feel very differently. The kind of self-assurance that is necessary to enable a child to reach out for learning and test himself against others can come only with the firm conviction that what he is doing is worthwhile to himself and that his achievements are not being "used" to satisfy somebody else.

Let's look for a moment at Stevie Michaels. Despite a high intelligence, Stevie is known as an "underachiever." He has done poorly in school ever since first grade, and now in the fourth grade he is beginning to be a real concern to his parents, especially his father. Stevie's father was the son of immigrant parents, and he has spent much of his life establishing himself as a typical

American "success." A rigid disciplinarian, he pushes his children the way he pushes himself to make up for feelings of worthlessness that have plagued him since childhood. Mr. Michaels is so afraid that his children will not be a credit to him that he has made them both afraid. As a result Stevie's manners are perfect, and it is hard to imagine that turbulent feelings lie behind his charming little face. But Stevie is filled with such feelings. His anger and frustration find expression in his stuttering as he tries to repress the angry words that are bottled up inside; he lies and cheats at games to feel less inadequate; and he provokes other children into misbehaving so that he can look like the "good boy" to his father or any other adult who happens to be around.

What has happened here is that Stevie senses that he is being used to reinforce his father's own self-esteem. So much of his energy is being expended in protecting himself from this manipulation that he has nothing left over to help himself grow. Stevie is certainly not aware of this unconscious process. But at all costs he must preserve the tiny nucleus of "self" that is left within him.

Overprotection

On the other hand, there are parents who consistently discourage their children from competition and achievement. These may be parents who suffer from such extensive feelings of inferiority themselves that they need their children's dependence as evidence to themselves of their own worth. We all know parents who won't let their Bobby go on Cub Scout hikes overnight "because he catches cold so easily." We know Margie, aged eleven, who goes everywhere with her mother and never seems to have any friends of her own. Such children are often the "I can't" children—"Mary is just like me; she can't do arithmetic any more than I can!" But in truth, if these children were left alone to explore their own potentials, they *could*. What has defeated them is their parents' need to keep them as they are.

The hardest thing for parents to do is to realize that their children are separate people, with their own needs and their own goals. Until parents are able to acquire such a perspective, their children will not be able to do it either; and it is only through an awareness of "separateness" from parents that children can become responsible for themselves.

Nurturing Autonomy

The nurturing of such autonomy begins long before school age. During his early childhood years, caring for our child occupied most of our time, and he was probably never very far from our thoughts. But it is easy to confuse the time we spend with our children with "seeing" them and "knowing" them as people, and often it comes as a shock to us that perhaps we don't really "know" our own child at all. Sometimes a stranger will have a view of him that we have never seen. He is often a different child with his teachers, his classmates, or even with the school bus driver.

It happens to all of us: this sudden shock of recognition that in some ways we haven't been really "seeing" or "hearing" our children. Our dreams, our hopes, and our fears all get in the way. Most parents put so much of themselves into their children that they can't contemplate the possibility of "failure," and so the danger lies in the fact that too often they see their children not as they are, but as they must see them.

What we expect of a child is thus often determined by what we need him to be. In a thousand ways we tell this to our child every day. By our tone of voice and by our expressions and gestures, we tell him what we think he can do and what we think he is. And for the most part he believes us. A child's picture of himself comes very largely from what his parents tell him that he is, and often this prophecy becomes self-fulfilling.

All of us as parents would like to have some Olympian vision that would permit us to see each of our children equally clearly; but alas, that is not the way it is. We all know that we feel more confortable with one child than with another and that we can "understand" one better than another. There are certainly many reasons for this; but the extent to which a child resembles a parent nearly always enters into it. If a child's way of responding to life is the same as ours, we usually can feel comfortable with him. If not, we all know the friction that comes between parents and the child they can't "understand." On the other hand, if parent and child are too much alike, there can also be trouble between them. It may happen that when such a child is working through a problem or conflict that the parent has not yet resolved for himself, he may be a painful reminder of the parent's own earlier turmoil; whereas the sibling who operates differently (in an emotional sense) may prove less threatening.

The beginning of every new school year is a wonderful opportunity to start afresh and to encourage the kind of autonomy and self-motivation that we have been talking about. It may be helpful to remember that whatever negative feelings a child has about going off to school, he also has many positive feelings that can help *us* to help *him* enjoy school in a fulfilling way. Every child has a reservoir of energy and enthusiasm within him that pushes him to grow if he is permitted to. From six through ten his physical growth includes the gradual mastering of the large-muscle coordination needed in games, etc., and of the small-muscle coordination needed in reading, writing, drawing, weaving, cooking, or playing musical instruments. His natural curiosity expands together with his ability to comprehend distance in time and space and with his increasing ability to conceptualize. He begins to exercise his imagination in many creative ways, if he is emotionally free to do so, and to become concerned with the broader questions of truth and justice. With his growing awareness of the world, he is beginning to recognize differences among people, and along with this, he is awakening to the presence of the opposite sex. First this awakening takes place in a negative way, but toward the ages of ten to twelve there is a positive, but tentative, reaching out.

We can encourage all these growth factors by recognizing them for what they are and by realizing that a child is constantly changing as he grows. We can help him over the hard times by enabling him to recognize this, too, and by helping him to feel that life can become richer for him as he is increasingly able to do more and to learn more about his world.

None of this is possible unless parents themselves still feel some of that same sense of growth within themselves, no matter what their age. No child will pay attention to what his parents *say* about the joys of learning unless he sees some of this in action at home. The parent who remains glued to the TV himself has no right to expect more from his child. The parent who never reads cannot expect his child to love books.

When a parent gets excited over a bird or a flower or a beautiful sunset, the child is impressed by what he sees his parent really feels. It is also true that concern for the community at large cannot be taught in a home where conversation is limited to gossip, and family talk is mostly about personal matters.

Although parents can expect of their children ultimately neither more nor less than they expect of themselves, this does not mean that they can demand it from their children indiscriminately. Each child is different, as we have said before; and as a result, the urge to grow will be expressed at different rates and in different ways. Sometimes we as parents get so "hung up" on our own ways that we need help to see what is truly going on in our child.

There are several persons in the community who can help us to see our child more clearly. The pediatrician can obviously give us guidance and advice about the child's physical growth and some information about how this is related to his emotional development. A child's teacher can tell us a good deal about what the child is like away from home; and working together with her, telling her what he is like at home, can give us both a pretty whole picture of him. The Scout leader, the mother of a playmate, a neighbor—all these have perspectives on children that might add something to our own. Sometimes it is hard to listen to someone else telling us something about our child that we have not been aware of and that we really don't want to hear. But if we can divorce ourself from the kind of involvement with him that makes any comment about him sound to us like criticism, we can receive valuable insights that we can acquire in no other way.

3
What Friends Mean

"For what is your friend that you should seek him with hours to kill? Seek him always with hours to live."
The Prophet—Kahlil Gibran

THESE ARE THE years in which friends become increasingly important to children and in which they will become more and more selective about them. Until the age of six, boys and girls play together without much concern for differences in sex, but in the first grade we see the beginnings of change. By the time a child is in the second grade, boys stick pretty close to boys and girls are beginning to play only with girls. In third grade, boys and girls make tentative forays into enemy territory, sometimes expressing affection for one another, but mostly teasing and taunting—not relating at all. This keeps up, gaining in intensity, through the fourth grade, until in the fifth grade, some youngsters are beginning to have a fairly mature awareness of the opposite sex.

This kind of cohesiveness with one's own sex helps the members of both groups to anchor more firmly their own sense of who and what they are. Boys reaffirm their boy-ness and girls their girl-ness by sticking together. Boys are only now beginning to identify securely with their fathers, and the painful process of loosening the ties to mother is reinforced by this kind of social behavior outside the home. It also reinforces the girl's identification with her mother.

One of the major functions of friendship in these years is to discover who one is. By comparing and measuring himself (or herself) against others, the child begins to learn about the differences between people, and about himself. Until he is about seven, he plays mostly with children who live in the neighborhood. Boys and girls usually play together freely in the pre-seven years, and groups are formed largely according to geography and chance. Children are not yet very selective about their friends, and except for the very aggressive child—or perhaps the very shy child—almost everyone in the neighborhood is included in the "gang."

From seven on, children tend to choose their friends more carefully. As they begin to see themselves more clearly, they also begin to see other people more discriminatingly and to choose their friends for reasons other than availability. At this point, children learn a lot about what makes relationships tick by testing out on their age-mates some of their own ways of behaving at home. They begin to find out what works and what doesn't work, and to recognize the need to modify their behavior somewhat away from home.

For example, Johnny, aged eight, can usually get what he wants from his parents by being stubborn and cajoling by turns. But this does not work with his friends. At home, Mary's parents encourage her quiet ways, convinced that this is the way a "lady" should behave; but at school Mary is usually left out of the games the rest of the class plays at recess because she is too timid about running around, afraid to tear her dress.

Children are also beginning to test out more than behavior among friends. They now begin, on their own level, to test the truth of what their parents have taught them over the years about morality. They need to find out for themselves about lying and stealing, about bullying and kindness, and about sharing and selfishness, to name a few of the moral dilemmas of most concern to children this age. Sometimes they find that what they have been told at home is not always entirely so in the outside world. There, a child very likely learns that the bully *can* get to be the club leader, which he so desperately wishes to be himself; or that the cheater in class will *not* necessarily be found out and, what is more, that he will get a higher mark in the math test *without* having worked for it; or that the selfish boy, who doesn't share at all, still has lots of friends.

Such situations raise one of the most perplexing issues of parenthood. How can we help our children to cope with such contradictions and retain their integrity? Perhaps the answer lies not in "reason" but in "feelings." How we *feel* about ourselves dictates the standards we set for our behavior. Does it make us *feel* good to be kind? or *bad* to be cruel? Our inner feelings —or "conscience"—usually tell us what is right for us. Virtue in this world is not always rewarded in kind, and children cannot be shielded from the recognition of this painful reality. They must be helped to realize that the "rewards" they can expect from "moral" behavior will come principally from within themselves and from the respect and love of those whom they in turn respect.

Parental values are more important to a child than parents often realize. A child will make them his own if his parents have truly done so themselves; but moralizing and preaching won't do much good unless he sees that his parents really live by what they are telling him.

Who Are Your Child's Friends?

As noted already, children first form friendships among neighborhood children. Since people who live in the same neighborhood tend to be similar in many ways, it is unlikely that in the early years our child will have much intimate contact with children of other races or from sharply different backgrounds.

When the child becomes nine or ten, however, his horizon broadens through school, scouting, and other community activities, and he may want to exchange visits with children who live in other parts of town. At this age the child has begun to select his friends according to what kind of people they are, with less emphasis on accessibility and proximity to home base. How will we feel about friendships that will take our child out from under our wing, away from what is familiar to him and into neighborhoods that are different from his? How will our feelings as parents affect our child?

Let's look for a moment at George. He is nine years old, Caucasian, and Protestant. His parents appear to be open and welcoming to all his schoolmates without regard to differences in skin color or religious faith. One day after school, George went home with David. While they were drinking hot chocolate in the kitchen, David's mother reminded him that he was due at Hebrew school at 5 o'clock. George stopped sipping his drink. Suddenly he turned to David and, looking at him carefully, said: "I *thought* you looked Jewish, David. Your hair is so black." The irony of the matter is that David's hair is *not* black! In fact, George and David both have light-brown hair and resemble each other so much that they have sometimes been mistaken for one another at school.

What made George see his friend so differently all of a sudden? What was it that distorted his perception so that he suddenly saw David with black hair instead of with the light-brown hair that he actually has?

This is a dramatic illustration of the way in which children absorb what their parents *really* feel about people who are not like themselves. It demonstrates how children will unconsciously translate that reality, without regard for truth, into terms that will make them more comfortable with their feelings at the time. Because George suddenly felt uncomfortable with his friend, he had to assign some characteristic to him that could explain this discomfort and relieve his feelings. Such self-deception can be dangerous. When a child is not free to see people as they really are, it can lead to serious trouble, especially later on in adolescence.

Protecting Your Child

Sometimes it is hard to realize that the child is growing up and must be given the freedom to make many choices on his own. If we try to control everything including the friends he chooses, we will be depriving him of the opportunity to learn how to make good choices—a skill that comes only through practice. This means, of course, that sometimes he will make bad choices, too; and it is important that we have enough confidence in ourselves and in him to allow him to find his own way of overcoming these when the time comes.

But how about when the child forms friendships or gets into situations that we feel could be dangerous or possibly damaging in some other way? What do we do about that without "getting his back up"? For example, what do we do if our daughter likes to go after school to her friend's house, where an alcoholic mother is the only one at home all day? How about the boy next door who always gets into fights with our son but whom for some reason our child adores? Or the boy who is full of destructive mischief and gets our child into trouble? How about the girl who is our daughter's age but is already giving boy-girl parties?

These are commonplace situations in the lives of all parents and children. How we handle them can be crucial to our child's friendship choices later on in life. It is important that we set limits that will protect our child from problems that he is not yet able to handle on his own. We can talk with our child about his friends. We need not run them down or impugn our youngster's judgment, but at the same time we can make it perfectly clear that we feel there are certain situations he cannot yet handle all by himself. We can insist that after-school visits with certain friends take place only at our own home. Or we can explain our reasons for discouraging a particular friendship, stating our objections openly, and at the same time planning for our child to be constructively occupied in some other way.

Most children appreciate the firmness with which their parents protect them from situations that they may be too "proud" to admit are beyond them. They appreciate being valued—and being told that they are valued by the limits we set for them.

Setting Limits for Play

The same principle applies to parental supervision at home. No child likes to feel spied upon or confined by rules that he considers unreasonable and that his friends reject. But we are doing him a favor as well as ourselves if we set rules for play at home that *both of us agree to beforehand.* For example, whenever it is possible, we should give our child a place of his own to play, with no holds barred—where he can make a mess without getting us upset, where he and his friends can "build a house" without ruining our favorite chair, and where we can look in every once in a while to see that no one is being hurt. On the other hand, throwing balls is for OUT OF THE HOUSE! Closed doors are sometimes a problem; but they are not necessary at this age if children can feel sure that their parents will protect them from intrusions by younger (or older) sisters and brothers and that their privacy will be respected.

As far as a child's cooking inclinations are concerned, we can let safety, rather than fear of mess, dictate our limits, on the whole. Almost all girls and many boys enjoy making cakes and cookies on a rainy day. This should be encouraged, by all means—it is a great way to spend an afternoon. But it must be an activity that is carefully supervised; stoves and some cooking equipment are not safe toys, no matter how competent the child. With a little encouragement, children can and usually will clean up fairly well afterward.

Making and Keeping Friends

Some children seem to attract other children as naturally as bees are drawn to flowers. Their telephones are always ringing and the front door bangs to and fro as the neighborhood troops in and out. What is it about such children that is so appealing to others? Why is it that other children who appear to be equally attractive in adult eyes always seem to be alone?

Children's needs differ just as adults' do, and the child who prefers often to be alone may be just as healthy as the child who is the most popular one on the block. Although all children need friends, some need them more than others. At this age the popular child is usually a healthy, energetic youngster who can give and take easily and who goes along pretty much with the conventional interests of his age group.

The child who is especially creative or talented or who has superior intellectual capacities very often finds himself on the outskirts of the group, and what is more important, not really minding the fact that he is. The problem of popularity is not a matter of concern to such children. Their sense of self is already well developed for the most part, and their interests in other children is more a matter of sharing interests than of just wanting company.

The shy child, however, does present a problem both to himself and to his parents. Many children are naturally, but superficially, reserved and find it hard to be immediately open to new acquaintances. Parents can help the child like this, who *wants* friends but can't seem to go about making them, by creating an atmosphere and environment at home that will be appealing to children of this age. For example, it might be good to have plenty of play equipment around, where and as we can, and provide plenty of good snacks when the child has guests. Food has a way of making things easier between friends. Being prepared to suggest interesting things to do can help, too.

It is also a good idea to become friendly with neighbors and take an active part in school activities so that we can get to know people with children the same age as ours. If we invite them over as a family, our child will not feel that we are pushing him into a situation that is awkward for him, but that this is a family activity in which he is naturally expected to participate.

When a child doesn't seem to *want* friends, however, shyness or loneliness can be an indication of something more serious, which may demand professional help.

Being "Popular"

Parents are often more concerned than is necessary about their child's popularity. As pointed out earlier, every child needs friends his own age, some more, some less; but it is the child's comfort with himself that should indicate to us how much he needs to be with others. Needing to be with people all the time can be just as damaging to his growth as constant solitude. Like adults, children also need to be alone some of the time. They need to be alone to think, to read, and to create an inner harmony—to sort out the turbulent feelings of growing up. They also need the physical rest afforded by a certain amount of respite from being with others.

When parents do not recognize these needs, they deprive their children of nurture as surely as if they were to deprive them of food. In addition, if parents push for popularity beyond their child's tolerance, they do him the disservice of setting up false standards for judging his own worth.

4
Coping With Prejudice

> "Well, are they? are they? of course they are! they're just like me? but are you sure?"
>
> *Killer of the Dream*—Lillian Smith

IT WOULD BE unrealistic to say that all our children's problems will disappear if we are good parents. This is obviously not true. There are many conditions in society that work against the good feelings that parents create at home. Special strengths are often needed to combat them. One of the worst of these is prejudice. Although at this point in our history, almost everyone is tragically familiar with the prejudices that affect black children, Puerto Rican, Mexican, Catholic, or Jewish children, to name just a few, some adults would be shocked to think that they apply similar prejudices to their own children.

Any kind of stereotyped thinking is prejudice. For example, if we say that we don't like people with red hair, that is prejudice. However, if we dissociate the red hair from the person and say that we don't like *red hair*—instead of saying that we don't like *people* with red hair—then this would be a personal opinion, to which we are entitled.

Without realizing it, all parents sometimes tend to make stereotyped judgments about their own children or their children's friends. At one time or another we have all made "snap judgments" about a child, without dissociating certain characteristics from the child himself. For example, how many parents tend to feel that a boy is a "sissy" if he is artistically inclined instead of being interested in sports? But who is to say that athletics are better than art? Or more manly? The little girl who buries her nose in a book as soon as she learns to read may be looked upon as "odd" by other children and sometimes even by her parents. The child who doesn't do well in school but is marvelously dexterous with her hands is still "dumb." Fat children are "lazy," and so it goes.

Whenever we make judgments at all about another person—child or adult—without really seeing or hearing HIM, we are acting unrealistically, from prejudice. A Columbia Broadcasting System drama called *The People Next Door* illustrated this very well. In the play, two families living next door to each other in a middle-class suburb were friends. The older adolescent son in one of these families looked like a fine, upstanding American boy. He was clean-shaven and open-faced, talented at the piano and charming to everyone. The other family had a long-haired son about the same age who played the guitar and dressed like a "hippie." His parents had disowned him some time ago because his appearance and apparent indolence upset them so much. Some months later, his fifteen-year-old sister was discovered to be a heroin addict, and although her parents had no evidence at all, they immediately accused their "hippie" son of introducing his sister to drugs. It turned out that the "fine young boy" next door had been trading in drugs at school for years and was responsible for an epidemic of addiction among his neighbors and classmates.

How many times have our own preoccupations with stereotypes led us to approve of children who "look nice"? How many times have we assumed that a child from "a good family" must be all right for our own children to play with? How many times have we heard someone say, "You wouldn't want to be friends with a child from a family like *that*"? It can be very uncomfortable to realize how deeply such prejudices can corrupt our judgment. We must face this possibility in ourselves if we are to equip our children to do likewise.

As parents, our job is thus extended to discovering where our own prejudices lie. Until we are aware of what they are, we will not even be able to see our own children clearly and certainly will not be able to help them to evaluate their friends realistically.

No parent can protect his own child from the prejudices of others, no matter how hard he tries. But we can *help* the child to cope with prejudices if we teach him that it is a reflection only on those who practice it, and that the rejections he may suffer because of it have nothing whatsoever to do with him. If we can get these ideas across to him, we will be helping him to direct his anger where it belongs: at those who do the hurting, rather than at himself.

On Being of the "Wrong" Color, Religion, or National Background

Being part of a racial or religious minority makes a child feel special. It doesn't matter what minority a child is part of; all children from minority groups feel "different." Among white children, the differences don't inevitably "show"; and this sometimes makes it harder for them to come to terms with their differences. Italian children, Polish children, Catholic and Jewish children, all look pretty much alike even though prejudices may keep them apart. The dark-skinned child, however, cannot escape his blackness. He is never faced with the choice of whether

or not to admit to being black. He grows up knowing from his earliest years that he is a black child in a white world and that he will have to learn to live with the battles that will have to be fought.

Some white children, on the other hand, don't learn about their special status until they get to school. Then it can come as a terrible shock to learn that to others they are faceless "kikes" or "wops" or "hunkies."

How to Help

For all children, white or black, the answer is the same. A child's pride in himself begins with pride in his heritage and in respect for his family. No one can rob a child of his self-respect if he is equipped to do what he must by his parents' conviction that he *can* do it. Every child is part of yesterday through his genes and part of tomorrow in what he can do to make the most of himself.

Although these feelings are important for *all* children, they are especially important for "minority" children. We should be sure our own child is familiar with the history of his race and his people. We can help him to become comfortable with himself so that he will have a positive self-image. We can encourage him to have some friends with backgrounds similar to his own, but also to mix with others. He will learn that the similarities between children of different backgrounds often transcend their differences.

Although it does no good to dwell on the fact that life is hard and people are often cruel, we should not gloss it over either. It will help the child to cope with prejudice if he knows that we can do it and that we share his anguish and his frustration. The hardest thing will be to help the child not to become so bitter about the injustices he experiences that he himself becomes prejudiced against others as unjustly as others sometimes are against him.

On Being Nonathletic

In our society, with all its emphasis on competitive sports, the child who is not good at physical games may also suffer from feelings of rejection and "difference." Even though he may qualify for membership in the group in every other way, if he is a dud in baseball, football, or basketball, he is often O-U-T!

This rejection is usually not limited only to the ballfield; it often means that if he is not a good athlete, he is not part of the "gang" either—that he has few friends and needs constant reassurance that he is okay anyway.

All boys and girls need to be able to feel that they are good at something physical even if they are nonathletic. There is no feeling in the world like the feeling that comes from having mastered a physical skill and having our body obey our commands. Such control of the body confers a sense of being whole, of being alive.

Individual sports can be especially appealing to nonathletic children. They often do well at swimming, judo, skating (ice and roller), skiing, bicycling, and hiking. Girls who fall into this category may also enjoy dancing.

Creative Activities and Hobbies

Sometimes a child who has difficulty in expressing himself in physical activity will find a release in creative activities or in hobbies that can help to compensate for a disinterest in sports. Activities such as sculpture, music, dramatics, woodworking, general arts and crafts, rock-collecting or mineralogy, stamp-collecting, or model-building are only a few of the programs offered by some local Y's, scouting groups, or after-school clubs. In a large city, the museums and libraries may also offer interesting opportunities of this kind.

If none of these facilities is available, perhaps we can help the child on our own. Although it will require some time and effort, we can find books at the public library that will help us to start him off—and once he is interested, he'll soon get to know "how" better than we do.

On Being Nonacademic

Some happy, well-adjusted boys and girls seem unable to do well in school. Some parents feel so hurt about this that they are unable to admit, even to themselves, that they have a nonachieving child. Some may even go so far as to deny it. They may blame the teacher, or they may blame the child. They may say he is not TRYING hard enough, and that "if only he would try harder . . . ." They reject any suggestion that implies that the work may be too much for him or that he may need special help.

Why is it that parents who rush to the doctor when their child is sick are reluctant to admit that he needs help in other areas? Part of the reason is that when a child does not measure up academically, both parents and teachers often feel that *they* have somehow failed. His nonachievement makes *them* feel less. They cannot accept it, even if he can. In a world where competition is the measure of success, it is hard to face the fact that for some the race is too swift.

Parents who can enjoy their child for what he is will also enjoy the things their child *can* do, and they will not make him compete in areas where he cannot. All children learn more and can learn better if they are relaxed and free from excessive pressure.

A child will respond if his parents encourage him to pursue interests that he can enjoy. This enjoyment may even be reflected in improved work at school.

Helping Him with Schoolwork

If we have the patience and the skill to help the child with schoolwork, we should by all means do so. Sometimes, however, parents find it easier to have their child tutored by someone else. Some schools and community centers offer programs of student-tutoring in which older boys and girls help younger ones with schoolwork. This can be especially helpful for the nonachieving child, who may find it hard to relate comfortably to adults in situations where he is expected to achieve. In fact, these very same children who are being tutored by older children sometimes also enjoy—and benefit from—tutoring younger children in subjects they know well.

A child's school can probably recommend a teacher who would be happy to tutor the child after school hours. Many retired teachers also enjoy doing this on a part-time basis. We should keep in mind that tutoring is unlikely to accomplish much unless the child relates well to the tutor.

Reading

Parents can help their children become better readers by encouraging them to read whatever interests them.

Children who have a special interest, whether it is sports, movies, rock music, or various hobbies, will usually try very hard to read whatever is available on the subject. Even though their reading ability is quite limited to start with, they will often improve their skills markedly without being aware of it as they work to gain information on what intrigues them. When a child has a great deal of difficulty with reading, however, it would probably be helpful to consult a person trained in remedial reading.

Games

Many popular children's games can also help children to sharpen their skills. Puzzles, for example, increase their abilities to perceive relationships. Scrabble for Juniors, Spill and Spell, or other simpler games can help with spelling and conceptualization. Monopoly, checkers, and other games can help to develop powers of reasoning. Whatever the child enjoys, whether it is doll houses, cooking sets, trains, models, or games, all children's play can be a happy learning experience if parents use their energies and imaginations to make it so.

5
Are They Really As Irresponsible As They Sometimes Seem?

> I meant to do my work today—
> But a brown bird sang in the apple tree,
> And a butterfly flitted across the field,
> And all the leaves were calling me.
>
> And the wind went sighing over the land
> Tossing the grasses to and fro,
> And a rainbow held out its shining hand—
> So what could I do but laugh and go?
> "I Meant to Do My Work Today"
> —Richard Le Gallienne

THE SPIRIT OF discovery that Richard Le Gallienne is talking about in this poem is something that many of us adults have forgotten. Although it is unlikely that today's child would be so enraptured by the song of a bird, or a butterfly, there are other wonders and distractions in life to divert him from his responsibilities. What *are* our child's responsibilities, and what should they be? How about the distractions? What do they contribute to his life?

Much of what parents consider distractions may really be part of a major task of children this age: the discovery of what life itself is all about. In order to discover what his ultimate responsibilities are, a child must learn about the world and all it has to offer, and find his place in it.

How are we going to teach the child what life is all about? What are we going to say to him about self-fulfillment and responsibilities and all those other words that have come to have such negative meanings in our time? Much of what we say to our children about the purpose of life—and in particular the purpose of *their* lives—we say without being aware of it, by how we lead our own. If our approach to life is to retreat from it rather than to embrace it with all its pains and ambiguities, then we cannot expect our children to look very far in their own search for self-fulfillment. If the idle life is our ideal, our future goal, we must realize that our children will translate this dream into their own terms, whether we like it or not.

Finding self-fulfillment is probably the hardest task any of us has to do during his time on this earth; and the worst part of it is that no one can chart the course for anyone else. But the one thing we do know is that genuine self-fulfillment is unlikely to be attained unless a child learns early in life to *enjoy* using himself well in the pursuit of his own goals.

Handling Responsibilities

During the ages from six through ten years the child is exploring a new world. Before this time, he has been tied to his parents. Now he is a schoolboy with a life of his own, and for the first time he will be responsible for himself for a good part of the day. We can help him to manage this with confidence by encouraging him slowly to take on increasingly difficult tasks from his earliest years. He can begin in the first grade to lay out his clothes at night for the next day, along with any books and other equipment he will take to school; and he can work up gradually from there to assuming full responsibility for himself in his later adolescence. Step by step we lead him up the ladder. Although each task may be progressively more difficult than the last, the view from each ascending step of the ladder is much broader, too.

It sometimes helps in the beginning if we share new tasks with the child. Plunging him into a new situation of any kind with a sink-or-swim attitude can lead to failure and discouragement. It is best to be prepared to spend some time helping him assume a new responsibility, once we have decided he is ready for it.

Children often tend to respond unrealistically in the face of a new challenge if they have not been well prepared all along to take it in their stride. Some children will deny their fear by boasting and bravado; others may retreat into the familiar world of "I can't," and still others may resort to the psychosomatic cold or stomach ache that will permit them to avoid the situation entirely.

For example, Gary was entering first grade. When he walked into the classroom for the first time, he proudly announced to his new teacher that he already knew how to read because "they had taught him how" in kindergarten. The teacher didn't really know if this was true or not, but she hugged him and said she was so glad to have him in her class, but would he mind doing the exercises the rest of the class was doing anyway, and maybe it would also help him brush up on some of the things he might have forgotten over the summer? It turned out that Gary had not known how to read at all. But by going along with his little face-saving fiction and not confronting him with it directly, his teacher permitted him to accept the fact that he couldn't yet read and that no one really expected him to. This was his first step in approaching his new responsibilities with more comfort and in developing a more realistic way of handling problems.

This does not mean that the child should be "babied." It is one thing to recognize his limits and help him to admit them, and quite another to deny him the opportunity to be as competent as he is able. For example, when he is old enough to go off to school, he is old enough to be expected to help a bit around the house. When he is old enough to go outside by himself to play with the other children in the street, he is also old enough to be expected to come home when he is told. Certainly some leeway can be permitted on occasion for the forgotten glance at the clock or the absorption in a game. But as a rule, if the child is of an age to be at all independent, he also has the responsibility—for his own safety and for his parents' peace of mind—to observe the rules of the house.

It sometimes helps children to develop this kind of self-discipline if parents emphasize that all privileges carry responsibilities with them, and that as they grow older and are able to do more, more will be expected of them. Children soon come to recognize that these are not arbitrary rules, but that there is a "quid pro quo" about life—in other words, a fair exchange.

Schoolwork is of course the major responsibility for all children during these years and for some time to come. In an earlier chapter, we spoke of how we can facilitate the child's attention to his work and encourage his productivity. It would be unfair and unwise, however, to permit schoolwork to serve as a convenient excuse for the child to "get out of" whatever else he is required to do around the house or within the family. If he complains constantly that he has too much work, then there is something seriously wrong somewhere. Either his school schedule is unreasonable or he is having problems in understanding his work that require our attention. Perhaps we are asking too much of him; a child at this age often requires help from us to program his time so that there is enough for everything—for schoolwork, for household jobs, and for play.

Chores

That brings us to the subject of chores. It is generally accepted by most child psychologists that participating in family chores is as important to a child's healthy development as sharing family fun. Whether it is in the house or in the yard, most parents welcome a helping hand from their children. Sometimes, however, just because they are children, parents tend to delegate all the more distasteful chores to them without regard for their preferences. Assignments should be varied so that no one in the family has to do the one thing he hates to do all the time. Even a child of six can do a variety of things in the home, such as set the table, vacuum, empty trash pails, sort laundry, etc.

As a matter of fact, children respond very well to being genuinely needed. Provided it is not "make work" that they are doing, they enjoy knowing that they are really contributing to the family well-being. They appreciate the thanks they get (and we must be sure to give it to them!), and they are proud of doing their jobs well.

However, it is not always as easy as this,

as all parents well know. Very often, out of the blue it seems, a ten-year-old will balk at the simplest request. He may "go on strike," complaining that "John's family doesn't make him do all that work—what do you think I am?" The answer is that this is not John's family. Every family is different. Perhaps John's parents have other help around the house and his help is not really needed. Or perhaps his parents have given up assigning jobs to him, preferring to do the work themselves rather than listen to the complaints they get if they insist that John do it.

Although it is sometimes easier for parents to do jobs themselves than to insist that the children do them, this is really what the youngsters call "copping out." Even though it requires enormous self-discipline not to blow our stack completely when dealing with a reluctant child, we are not really doing him a favor by depriving him of the right—yes, the right—to work and to have the satisfaction of doing something worthwhile. It is often harder to work along with our child than it is to do the job alone. But spending time in teaching him how to do well something that has to be done is helping him to grow; it develops attitudes of cooperation that will stand both child and parents in good stead later on. Also, taking over from him with impatience and disgust may make him feel guilty and inadequate, no matter how joyous he may appear to have gotten out of the work. It will deprive us both of growing together and will give him the idea that he can weasel out of other jobs later on in the same way.

Neatness in the Child's Room

As the child grows older, the most pressing housekeeping problem often becomes the care of his room. Often he will insist on leaving it sloppy and messy because it is HIS room! When we find half the clothes our daughter possesses dumped in a pile on the floor, what do we do? Do we just close the door and say to ourselves that what we don't see doesn't bother us? Or do we brave the storm and insist that she pick up the mess? Perhaps we do a little bit of both from time to time. If urging her to pick up never works, it is certainly in order to say, the next time she wants a new dress or a new sweater or a new pair of shoes, that we're sorry, but until she can take better care of her things than she does, we can't see giving her something that will be so abused later. Again, "quid pro quo"—a fair exchange.

On the other hand, children's concepts of neatness are almost always different from their parents'. Most parents (women especially) are concerned with their own appearance and with the appearance of their home, not only for themselves, but also because of what friends and neighbors might think. Children have a much more utilitarian attitude toward themselves and the place where they live. If they are clean enough to satisfy health requirements and orderly enough to find what they want when they want it, that is usually enough for them.

However, these differences need not necessarily be a source of trouble between us. We can try not to nag at Johnny for his long hair or at Susie for her shabby dungarees. We need not judge the condition of their rooms by the same standards that we set for our own. And we should remember that it is this kind of "give" that helps children to accept our suggestions and criticisms in other more important areas and to become increasingly responsible for themselves later on.

Responsibility to Themselves

Earlier in this chapter we alluded to parents' responsibilities to themselves—to continue even as parents to nurture their own growth. For example, Janet was a young widow of 36. Her husband had died two years previously, leaving her with two children who were nine and eleven. During the day, Janet worked at a part-time job that allowed her to be home when the children returned from school; but three evenings a week she went off to art classes, which she enjoyed very much. Her mother was horrified at what she called her daughter's "neglect" of her responsibilities, and this troubled Janet. Where did her real responsibilities lie? To herself or to her children? And was there a difference anyway? It took a long time for Janet to work it out so that she felt entirely comfortable about what she was doing. But after several years had gone by, and her children were old enough to express their feelings about the kind of mother they had, they told her that the best thing she ever did for them was to pass on to them the love of life that had sustained *her* throughout all those trying years.

Teaching about responsibility means first being responsible to ourselves in the way we want our child to be. It does not mean that a woman should be tied down to her children and her home without relief, or a man so burdened by his efforts to earn a good living for his family that he cannot spend time on other things. It means seeing our home and our family as a major responsibility, but nonetheless not everything. Most men still have it easier than women in this regard; most women still feel a conflict in what they see as opposing needs. It is important to the whole family, however, to recognize that everyone has needs as an individual and that children are greatly impoverished if both their parents don't set some personal goals for themselves apart from their love for other members of the family.

Building a Bridge

Losing sweaters, coming home late, leaving messy rooms and jobs undone, and a million other annoying habits plague the parents of every child—and we call this behavior "irresponsible," which, of course, it is. For the most part, it happens because the outside world is so tempting that children are often inclined to forget what they have to do—or even willfully not do it—in order to get out there faster.

But sometimes there are more complex reasons for a child's irresponsible behavior. By not doing as his parents ask, or expect, he may be trying to get back at them for some injustice he feels is being done to him. He may accidentally break a parent's favorite vase or forget to give an important telephone message because he is angry inside; he may forget his homework book because he can't cope with the assignment and feels resentful and inadequate; he may hurt himself by stumbling on a roller skate carelessly left lying around, thus drawing attention to himself at the very moment his sister is displaying a poem she wrote.

There may be any number of reasons behind irresponsible behavior. But we can be sure that if the child does behave this way consistently, things are troubling him of which he is perhaps not even aware.

In any case, there is no sense in nagging the child about it. Nothing ever gets done just through nagging. Even if it should appear to solve an immediate problem, the hostility that nagging arouses will defeat any chance at all for learning why the problem arose in the first place. If this behavior continues despite all our efforts, perhaps it would be wise to talk it over with the child's teacher or with the school guidance counselor, or even to seek other professional help if it is a source of serious parent-child conflict.

The habit of responsibility develops gradually in all of us. Only as children begin to understand the real meaning of cause and effect, and to feel a give and take, can they understand that for the most part irresponsibility just doesn't fill the bill.

6
Everybody Else Does!

This above all: to thine own self be true,
And it must follow, as the night the day,
Thou canst not then be false to any man.
Hamlet—William Shakespeare

HOW DO *we* answer the familiar complaint, "Everybody else does"? It is hard to know just what to do. How far do we go along with "everybody else"—and when do we stop? Will our child suffer too much if we don't let him do what the others are doing? Are we being too old-fashioned? Or are we really just being "sensible"? Whatever our inclinations, the danger is that such decisions will be made on the basis of wanting a respite from our child's badgering and pestering, rather than with the firm conviction that what we are doing is right.

Sometimes parents are so eager for their child to be part of the group that they will go along with whatever the others are doing without considering whether or not this is right for *their* child. Then there are other parents who are so determined to maintain what they call their own "standards" that they tend to say "No" to whatever their child suggests without really weighing the merits of the issue. It would be a lot easier for all of us if these dilemmas could be resolved simply; but it is much more complicated than that.

Values and Customs

Perhaps the best advice anyone can give to parents looking for guidance in this area is to read what Polonius had to say to his son Laertes, as quoted at the beginning of this chapter. When we talk about deciding what we will permit our children to do, we must first look at what we really believe in—our own values. The trouble is that we often haven't bothered to think through what our values really are. Many of us may have adopted unquestioningly the values handed down to us by our parents or by the church, without bothering to do what some young people are beginning to do—reexamine those values in terms of today's needs.

Unless we take the time to sort out our values carefully, we may allow many of the customs by which we live to be confused with what we call "values." If we are to guide our children sensibly, we must recognize the difference.

For example, let's look at our habits of saying "please" and "thank you," of giving special courtesy to older folk, of eating in ways that will not offend other people at the table. These are *customs* that have developed over the years to express a value most of us hold dear: *respect for other people.* We call these customs "manners." Manners, though not in themselves sacrosanct, are worthwhile customs to preserve because the value they represent is still important to our way of life.

There are other customs, however, that may not be worth preserving in our child's lifetime because the values they express will no longer have meaning for him or for his world. For example, customs of dress and appearance have changed a great deal in recent years in accordance with changing values revealed in new definitions of "masculinity" and "femininity."

Today we no longer value toughness and business acumen as purely masculine traits, nor do we consider gentleness and sensitivity solely female attributes. We recognize that a boy can enjoy cooking and drawing as well as a girl, and that some girls prefer baseball to dolls. These changing values are reflected in the way our children dress, and it would be as inappropriate for us to insist upon preserving the old ways as it would be for us to travel in a horse and carriage.

What has all this to do with the child at six or ten? Just this: he is growing up in a world where many young people are reexamining old values and asking their parents to do the same. Although he is still too young to be involved in this as a conscious process, the atmosphere of questioning pervades the climate in which he lives, and it won't be too long before he, too, will be asking questions. It is important for us as his parents to start thinking about our own values now, before he confronts us with the questions, so that when he does, we will know where we stand.

In the early school years, the child will be exposed, probably for the first time, to other children whose values are different from ours and whose families will hold different truths to be just as valid as we hold ours to be. Unless we can give our child some firm reassurance that we have thought through what we say, he will be lost in a sea of confusion.

Making Decisions

It is only when parents keep abreast of what is going on in the world, keep aware of what is changing and what is constant, that they can help their children make healthy decisions about living.

Training in making these decisions starts early. From the beginning, children need reinforcement for their healthy instincts and their positive feelings. They need our help in establishing distinctions between healthy ways of behaving and ways that violate basic human values. For example, at first it may mean helping our child to see the difference between taking a dare from his friend to climb to the top of the jungle gym, as against taking a dare to steal a pencil from the 5 & 10. Later on it may mean having to choose between being a member of a gang that is involved in all kinds of neighborhood mischief, or being left out of the "fun" altogether. Whatever the choices may be, and although they change as he grows older, the basis upon which he must learn to make his decisions will remain the same. The values that we teach him must be interpreted and reinterpreted at each stage of his development, so that he can learn to make these choices and decisions by himself—and for himself—knowing that he does so with our confidence and support.

In an attempt to establish an identity of his own, a child will often look indiscriminately to his friends for cues as to what he should do and how he should behave. It is our job as his parents to clarify the differences for him between healthy and unhealthy responses to today's realities. Because he is still a very small child, he will

need us to protect him as much from himself as from others. On the other hand, we cannot do all his deciding for him.

When there is a discussion about whether or not to allow a certain privilege or activity, we should always hear the child out. When he is talking to us, listen! His point of view, though different from ours, is worth knowing about, and we may not have realized how important it is to him. Sometimes, in fact, where basic values are not involved, it is a good idea to permit him to do something that he wants to do even though we may feel he is not ready to do it. Perhaps he is more mature than we think. Perhaps not. But even if we are right, it is important to let him make his own mistakes and take the consequences—provided that we know in advance that the consequences will not be too severe. If we deprive our child of this right (and it *is* a right), we will be sheltering him from the opportunity to strengthen his decision-making faculties by testing them against reality. This is the only way any of us really learns what life is all about.

Let's take Kevin, age nine, for instance. Many of Kevin's friends traveled to school on the public bus from outlying areas. Kevin wanted to try going somewhere on his own by bus, too, even though—living close to school—he had never before been on one by himself. He wanted to visit his father at work. Knowing that Kevin was essentially a responsible child, his mother yielded to his insistence, although with some reluctance, for Kevin would have to change buses. She warned him to telephone if he was lost and to be careful. No one heard from Kevin for more than an hour after school, and both his parents were beginning to be worried about him when he walked into his father's store. He was exhausted but also proud. As his parents had predicted, he had gotten mixed up about the bus change, so rather than risk riding miles out of his way, he had walked the three miles to his father's store in the heart of town—and now his feet were sore. Both Kevin and his parents had increased respect for one another after that. Kevin realized that his parents had known what they were talking about when they told him they felt he wasn't ready to go traveling around the city by himself on a complicated bus system. His parents realized that Kevin was more resourceful than they had imagined. They didn't rub it in about the sore feet, but they didn't baby him about them either. These were the consequences of his misjudgment, and that was the important thing for everybody to remember.

Setting Limits

Since each child has different needs at different times and develops at his own rate and in his own ways, his particular limits and rules must be tailored especially for him. What is more, they must change as he grows. An appropriate bedtime for Johnny at nine years of age must be determined by how much sleep he needs, not by the bedtime hour observed by his friends. At ten, however, the limits need to be reviewed again, by parents and their child together, with consideration for his increasing maturity and responsibilities.

One of the most helpful contributions we make as parents can be to aid our child in feeling comfortable with our decisions about what we permit and what we do not permit. All children will exert great pressure on their parents at one time or another to let them do what "everyone else" is doing. Sometimes we will even feel a little guilty about being a "hold-out" and making things so difficult for him. But he will accept the limits we set more comfortably than we think if we have talked them over together first and if he knows that we have taken his real feelings into account.

Even if the child protests loudly—slams the door, or swears at us, or hits his little sister—under it all he appreciates the protection we give him and the sense of individuality we encourage if we don't always go along with the crowd. It is far easier for him to blame us for not giving him permission to do something that deep down he is not quite sure he really wants to do anyway, than to find a way out all by himself. If it is a matter of watching television, for example, even if everyone else in the class watches "The Horror Hour," it won't make the child less popular if he lets his friends know that his parents "think it's terrible junk" and that they "won't let me watch it ever." In fact, even though he won't admit it, he will appreciate that we stick by our guns, and he will never tell us that the program gave him nightmares when he sneaked a look at it one night while we were out.

What it all boils down to is that we must know our own child and must honor our own inner convictions before we set the rules. Only then can we evaluate "what everybody else does" sensibly, in the light of our own standards, and stick with the decision. Despite the arguments and battles that will inevitably occur, this is the only way to give our child a sense of direction that will enable him to make his own healthy decisions later on when he will be faced with the difficult problems of adolescence.

7
Sex Education In The Early School Years

> ". . . the most wonderful story in the world—the REAL TRUE story of how you were born."
>
> *The Wonderful Story of How You Were Born*—
> Sidonie Matsner Gruenberg

WHY IS IT that parents who feel entirely comfortable talking to their children about God and the mysteries of life find it difficult to tell them about their own bodies and about the relations between the sexes? Why is it that parents who are meticulous in teaching children not to play with matches, or to cross streets against the light, or to talk to strangers, do not equip them with knowledge of sex and hygiene in the same sensible way? What is it about this subject that sets up such strange barriers between parents and children and blocks communication between them? Current statistics indicate that a large proportion of children and adolescents are incredibly ignorant about the fundamental facts of reproduction and related matters, and that even a preponderance of college students don't know as much as they should. All this is borne out by the dangerously rising incidence of venereal disease and by the increasing number of illegitimate pregnancies among adolescents.

Even in the face of these alarming facts, many parent groups all over the country continue to resist the establishment of courses in their schools on sex education and family life. Although such courses have found considerable acceptance at the high school level and in colleges, much misunderstanding persists about the necessity for providing suitable information in the earliest grades.

Dr. Ronald J. Pion, of the School of Public Health of the University of Hawaii, advocates giving youngsters elementary instruction in the basic concepts of human reproduction, medicine, and health care in early childhood, preferably beginning at the preschool level. "Just like arithmetic, family education can begin with the simplest forms in kindergarten and follow the same sequential development up to calculus," says Dr. Pion. Dr. Takey Crist of the University of North Carolina adds that, "College is just not the place for young people to have to learn where babies come from."

The fact is that no matter how we look at it, sex with all its pleasures and its pitfalls is here to stay. If we are to be realistic about our children's education, we will have to include sex in our curriculum.

The difference between animals and humans lies not so much in our reproductive functioning as in the way we feel about it. Unlike animals, men and women are not driven solely by instinctual needs, but also by feelings that lead them to be mutually selective when they choose to have sexual intercourse. These feelings bind a man and a woman together for more than the satisfaction of physical desire and the perpetuation of the human race. Families continue to be important to all their members long after the children have become self-sufficient.

Preparing to Talk About Sex

Before parents talk to their children about sex, it's best to get their own feelings straight. It does little good to give "book" explanations about the birds and the bees if underneath it all we still feel uncomfortable talking about such things.

One reason we may feel ill at ease lies in the strictures that probably were imposed upon us in our formative years by our religious and cultural heritage. But perhaps an even more important reason can be found in our discomfort about our sexual identity. Because being male or female is such an important part of who we are and determines so much of what happens to us in life, we often incorrectly blame all kinds of problems on the "burdens" of our sex. It is easier to attribute our disappointments with ourselves to the role our sex forces us to play in life and in our families. It is easier to say, "Men are like that" or "That's women for you!" than to recognize that other more personal emotional factors may be at work that it is within our power to change.

Thus, adults who are mature accept the fact of their sexual identification and put it in its place among other facts about themselves, like their height, their coloring, or their race. Being male or female is just another fact.

If we can accept all the facts about what we are with comfort, if not always with pleasure, our easiness with our sexuality and our sex role will be rather generally apparent. How we feel about this will come across to our children long before we begin to think in terms of "sex education" – in fact, long before they are old enough to speak.

Of one thing we can be sure, whether or

not we choose to provide our children with some kind of sex education at home and to encourage it at school, they will get it anyway. If we leave it to chance, they will probably acquire a lot of misconceptions from friends that will not be pleasing to us and certainly not helpful to them. It is part of good common sense to heed the old saying: "An ounce of prevention is worth a pound of cure!"

Beginnings

Our child's sex education started when he was an infant and we held him in our arms for the first time. The tenderness we felt and showed told him more than words could tell about our feelings for him as the product of our own sexuality and love. The way in which we responded to him in his early years when we fed him (whether or not he was nursed at the breast), when we cared for him, when we bathed him and played with him, told him volumes about our feelings about the human body—and especially about *his* body.

As he grew older and became more observant, his questions about sex differences and how babies are born were probably simple, or perhaps he didn't even ask much at all. But he saw how his parents felt about each other as a man and a woman, and as he became gradually more and more aware of his own sexual identification he began to identify with the parent of the same sex and to make some of that parent's feelings his own.

In many families today, a child's questions about reproduction are asked, and responded to, as unselfconsciously as questions about what makes thunder and why does Susie go to mass instead of to temple.

Yet parents who feel entirely at ease explaining how babies grow in a "special place" in their mothers, how the baby gets out of that place, or is "born," and how every baby develops from the union of a sperm from the father and an ovum from the mother, may be uncomfortable when their child finally asks—usually not before six—how the sperm gets to the ovum. It may help them feel more relaxed with this question if they recognize that the child is only asking for some simple scientific information, and not for a description of all that sexual intercourse means to adults in general.

We can tell the child that the father puts his penis in the mother's vagina, and that is how the sperm gets from the father's body into the mother's body. Children usually accept this as off-handedly as they accept the news that thunder may not be heard until a second or so after the lightning flash is seen because sound travels more slowly than light. If a child asks, "Does it hurt?" we can assure him that it doesn't.

Once we have got over this hurdle, we may be surprised to discover with what naturalness the child comes to us with his questions. If a question leaves us uncertain as to what or how much information he wants, our saying, "Well, what do *you* think?" will ordinarily clue us in to any misconceptions he may have and to the facts he is really trying to find out. In this way we give the child the information he needs without offering more than he is ready for and can handle.

If the child has not started asking some questions about reproduction by the time he is six, it may be an indication that he feels reluctant to talk to us about the subject. Perhaps some of this reluctance stems from his sensing that *we* are reluctant, too—not quite sure of what he is ready to know, or hesitant to talk about such matters. That is why books have been written about sex for parents to read with their younger children, books like *The Wonderful Story of How You Were Born* by Sidonie Matsner Gruenberg. This is a beginning book that explains conception and birth in simple, unaffected terms. Although Mrs. Gruenberg uses accurate terminology in speaking of the parts of the body and the process of insemination, she gives it the warmth and glory that properly belong to the miracle of birth.

Calling a Spade a Spade

During our child's earlier years, perhaps we were not as comfortable with the realities of the body as we are today. Perhaps we used terms such as "poo-poo" for bowel movement or "privates" for penis or vagina, because we were embarrassed to call them by their right names. Perhaps we even gave our child some misinformation about where babies come from in the belief that he was too young to understand the truth. In any case, even if we did evade the issues a bit when he was younger, now that he is going to school is a good time to rectify these mistakes and get him started off on the right foot. It is time to begin identifying parts of the body by the right names, if we did not do it before.

At school other children will probably introduce him to names for parts of the body and especially for the genital organs that we find distasteful and derogatory. This is quite usual. We can counteract the fascination that these words may have for our child by not making a fuss and by indicating our own feelings that it is too bad that some children have to use terms like that about their own bodies and about human reproduction. If we forbid our child to use such words at home, we should simply say that they offend us and many other adults—without using moralistic terms. He will outgrow this phase if we don't make "gutter" language seem so important that he can use it as a weapon long after its early shock-value has passed.

As our child grows older, he will need to know more and more specifics about his own body and sexual functions. Even though we may have told him before that babies come from sperm which Daddy's body produces and which unites with Mother's ovum to fertilize an egg, he will want to know this over and over again in progressively more sophisticated terms. He may want to know all about reproduction in household pets, other animals, and plants. We should be sure our own information is correct when we answer; we might even suggest that we track down the answers together. Books are listed in the Bibliography that can help parents with the fundamentals and with explanations if they feel they need such assistance.

When he gets to be about eight or nine, the child will begin to compare his physical development with that of his friends. The locker room at school is a new experience for both boys and girls; there they have the opportunity to see the difference between themselves and their older schoolmates. A boy may become aware of the fact that some boys take pride in a large penis, and he may be troubled that his is small. He will need reassurance from us that his penis is the right size for him and that it will grow as he grows, to whatever size it was meant to be. Or, a girl may suddenly become aware that some of her friends are beginning to grow breasts; and she too will have to be consoled about her flat chest with the assurance that every girl develops differently and at her own rate, and that her time will surely come.

Explaining Puberty to Girls and Boys

Children of both sexes need to be prepared ahead of time for the pubertal changes that signify that their bodies have attained sexual maturity: menstruation in girls, and in boys the capacity for seminal emissions. Considering the fact that some children mature very early these days, girls had best be acquainted with the facts by the time they are nine or ten and boys no later than eleven. Children are interested in the subject by these ages and not as likely to be self-conscious in discussing it with their parents as they may be after the first signs of approaching puberty have appeared.

A girl should know that when she becomes sexually mature one of her two ovaries will release an ovum each month. The ovum will travel through the adjacent one of her two Fallopian tubes into her uterus, or womb. If it is not fertilized by sperm during this journey—that is, if conception does not take place—it will continue journeying through the cervical opening into the vagina and pass out of her body. At the same time her uterus, which for several weeks prior to ovulation has been building up a rich lining to nourish the ovum in case it is fertilized, gets the message, through her body's hormonal system, that insemination did not occur; the uterine lining is sloughed off, resulting in the monthly menstrual flow. When a girl understands the cause of the menstrual flow, and how miraculously intricate her monthly cycle is, she is not only protected against being frightened by the "bleeding" of menstruation, but she also tends to place greater value on her reproductive role.

It is wise to talk to the daughter about how she will care for herself during her period and to give her a supply of pads and a belt, so that she won't be at a loss if we don't happen to be around when she first menstruates.

A boy should know that when his two testes, or testicles, located in his scrotum, begin producing semen, he may have nocturnal emissions, or "wet dreams": ejaculations while he is asleep. This is a normal reflex action that many boys experience. It may be accompanied by erotic dreams, which are normal, too. However, not all boys have wet dreams indicating (and perhaps reassuring them) that their bodies are producing semen. The onset of sexual maturity in the male is not as plainly signaled as in the female. Boys may need help with understanding this.

Masturbation

This is the age when children begin to masturbate as part of the process of sexual self-discovery. More often they will do this alone, but sometimes in the company of other children. Such sex play is to be expected. Accepting it without surprise is not the same as encouraging it. It is best not to make a fuss if we should happen to come upon our child in the midst of such play, whether alone or with a friend. If the child is alone, we can just leave him alone. If he is with others, we can calmly inform the group that we will help them find something else to do. Reacting with shock or indignation lends far too much importance to an activity that is universally experienced by all children and will in all probability be a passing phase if it is not overemphasized.

Masturbation in itself is not physically dangerous in any way, despite all the old wives' tales to the contrary. It is natural for a child to find pleasure in the manipulation of his genitals once he discovers that this is possible. The practice of masturbation might well be viewed in the way informed parents look upon the thumb-sucking of infancy. It should not cause parental concern unless it becomes such a preoccupation that a child has no other pleasures and lacks interest in other pursuits that children this age engage in. Even then, preoccupation with masturbation should be seen as a *symptom* that something is troubling the child—not as the problem itself. It would be wise for parents to look closely at the child's whole life structure and, perhaps with professional help, try to discover the underlying source of the trouble.

Generally speaking, sex play between children can be kept at a minimum by the ordinary rules of the house regarding play and by providing our children with plenty of wholesome play opportunities. Certainly, sensible adult supervision is in order. As we said in an earlier chapter, this does not mean hovering anxiously over the child; it means only that we should be aware of where he is and what he is doing most of the time during these years.

The best protection against unhealthy involvement with sex play (or masturbation) is our continuing interest in our child's daily life and our awareness of all his various needs. Our willingness to anticipate questions related to sex in the early years and to answer what he asks on his own level all along the way will make him feel free to come to us when he is perplexed and to ask us what he wants to know as he gets older, rather than to rely on the information he receives from his friends, which is apt to be inaccurate. Both parents can contribute to the sex education of their children. But as the child grows older, it may be better for him—and easier for him—to discuss these matters with the parent of the same sex or with some other adult of his sex whom he knows well and trusts.

Approaching Puberty

As was said before, every child matures at his own rate; but by the time the child is in the fifth grade, some members of the class will already have begun to show signs of puberty. A few of the boys will have some heavier fuzz on their arms and legs, and the search for underarm and pubic hair will begin. Some girls will begin to have curvy shapes, and there even may be one or two who have begun to menstruate.

The onset of puberty is especially hard on girls who mature so rapidly. Boys rarely begin to show dramatically that they are approaching puberty until they are about twelve or thirteen, but girls face the problem earlier. Whether or not actual puberty is the question, however, it is important for all children of this age to be aware of the fact that physical maturity in itself will not auto-

matically equip them to handle sexually oriented relationships. Prepuberty is the time to lay the groundwork for self-imposed restraints later on, during what may be one of the most difficult times of the child's life.

In essence, the skills for coping with the sex-related problems of adolescence are no different from the skills we have taught him for managing other aspects of his development. When he was two or three years old, for example, we didn't let him run around wherever he pleased without supervision just because he had learned to run. We waited until he had developed some degree of judgment and maturity before we allowed him to go outside by himself. When he learned to read fluently in the third grade or so, we didn't buy him just any junk comic or magazine that may have tempted him in the candy store; we helped him find other, more appropriate reading matter that interested him, expecting that in time, given a fair chance, his tastes would become more mature.

Now that our boys and girls are facing puberty—or perhaps have reached it—the same kind of attention must be paid to protecting them from using their newly acquired sexuality in a damaging way. They must be well prepared to recognize that sexual relationships involve responsibility to both parties, as well as joy; that having information about physical hygiene, contraception, and venereal disease is as important as acquiring a driver's license before they drive a car, and that a good relationship is not to be achieved without preparation and effort.

In other words, it all comes back to helping children to know themselves well. It means helping them to recognize their own limits and their own potentials, as we have helped them to do so many times before in other aspects of their growing up.

Being What You Are

These are the years when the child lays important foundations for responsible and satisfying sexual functioning later on and acquires the stability to carry him through the turbulence of adolescence.

A major part of this stability will lie in the achievement of a secure sense of sexual identification. This lessens the need for too-early or inappropriate experimentation. We have spoken about how a child acquires this sense of his own maleness or femaleness by means of identifying with the parent of the same sex, but we have not yet emphasized how important it is for all children to get an appropriate kind of echo from the parent of the opposite sex.

Most of us would agree that in daily life a man tends to feel most truly male when a woman makes him aware of how his maleness affects her; and conversely, a woman tends to feel most truly female when a man responds to her in that way. The messages that growing boys and girls get from their mothers and fathers about their developing sexuality must not be seductive, but nonetheless there should be a certain indefinable something that makes a child feel proud of his sex. A father responds differently to his daughter than to his son, and the same is true of mothers and their sons. All this is not only healthy and natural, but it is actually essential to a child's development. Although the primary male-female exchanges are, of course, between the parents themselves, children must be permitted to be aware of their special appeal to their parent of the other sex in a healthy, open way, as a reinforcing echo to tell them again who they are.

8 *Communicating About Drugs And Similar Dangers*

> "Good moring," said the little prince.
> "Good morning," said the merchant.
> This was the merchant who sold pills that had been invented to quench thirst. You need only swallow one pill a week, and you would feel no need of anything to drink.
> "Why are you selling those?" asked the little prince.
> "Because they save a tremendous amount of time," said the merchant. "Computations have been made by experts. With these pills you save 53 minutes in every week."
> "And what do I do with those 53 minutes?"
> "Anything you like. . . ."
> "As for me," said the little prince to himself, "if I had 53 minutes to spend as I like, I would walk at my leisure toward a spring of fresh water."
> *The Little Prince*—Antoine St. Exupéry

A FEW YEARS ago, although drugs had already become a way of life for some children in ghettos, the epidemic had not yet reached other parts of town. Today it is a different matter. Drugs are everywhere. Newspapers, magazines, television, movies, and books, books, books—all warn us about the horrors of drugs until parents are confused and bewildered. Many of them feel helpless and afraid. It is particularly troubling when they see that even children from some of the "best homes" are involved with drugs. What are they to do?

The excerpt at the beginning of this chapter tells us better than volumes of talk what "drug education" is really all about. When the little prince chooses to walk toward a spring of fresh water, he is choosing Life. He is choosing the joy of experience, and he is accepting the pain of effort. Boys and girls will not turn to drugs if, like the little prince, they can enjoy the challenge of life. They will turn to drugs only if they don't know the facts about drugs or if the alternatives are worse than the drugs themselves. The best way to fortify our children against the temptations of drugs is to give them the facts and to help them value themselves and life itself.

How Does It Start?

The difficulties that lead to a child's involvement with drugs start long before he is ever exposed to the temptations of the drugs themselves. Almost universally, youngsters who are now "deep into drugs" tell us that it was a sense of restlessness and loneliness that led them to seek relief in drugs. True, some of them started out of curiosity; but even if this was their initial motivation, underneath it all was that pervasive feeling of emptiness that led them to keep it up after the true experimenters had stopped. They say they liked the feeling of being one of the gang, and they liked what the drug experience did to them.

At first glance, there seems to be no common denominator among these young addicts. They come from every geographic, social, and economic milieu. But whether from the streets of the city or the shelter of the suburbs, nearly all of them seem to have grown up with a sense of deprivation, of facelessness, and of isolation. Most of them have no meaningful relationships with any important adults in their lives; and almost all of them complain that no one in their family was really in tune with what they were thinking or feeling while they were growing up.

While the child is still very young, it is important for him to know that we are on the same wavelength that he is. He needs us to help him understand himself. Right now, while he is still small, we as his parents have to take the initiative in guiding him firmly and in helping him to learn what life is about and what it has to offer. Later on, he will have insights into himself of which we will not then be a part. But he must first learn from us how to confront reality before he is able to do this on his own. The young addicts we are talking about have not been able to do this. Coming from families in which they felt isolated and alone, they have always been out of touch with others, alienated from themselves.

Let's look at Janet Baker, for example. Janet is now eighteen and she has used drugs since she was twelve. Her story is important to parents because her problems began when she was very young, long before she became a drug addict. Janet's family lives in a fashionable suburb of Los Angeles. Her father is a successful physician, and her mother is a busy housewife and an active member of the community. The past two years of Janet's life have been spent "on the road," away from home, and yet before that her parents had no idea that she was using drugs.

Janet looked then like a poster picture of a real American girl. Until the ninth grade, she was an outstanding student, and at one time she had even been elected to the Student Council, the youngest member ever to serve. What went wrong?

According to Janet herself, ever since she was a little girl, her parents had never had any time for her—that is, time that was really for her on *her* terms. Either they were busy "improving" her with lessons or other activities, or they were so tired that they didn't have the energy to just sit around and talk. At her house, nobody was ever expected to BE—everybody was expected to DO.

When Janet came home from school in the afternoon, her mother was always on the phone, Janet says, or working in the kitchen, so that she was glad when Janet and her friends disappeared downstairs into the playroom. "I always knew where she was," her mother said, "and I always wanted her to bring her friends home."

Both parents were very proud of Janet. She remembers that guests were always shown the paintings she made in first grade—or later on they were captive audiences for the latest piece she learned on the piano. Her parents always boasted about her marks, and Janet says it made her sick to hear them talk about her that way. She felt that her parents cared more about how successful she made *them* feel than about her. She is very bitter about it. She says nobody ever just hugged her and told her that they loved her for no reason at all.

So when Janet was in the seventh grade, she "had had it." Not that she didn't still work hard at school or enter into after-school programs; she did. But in between times, she "turned on" with grass. "It made things easier," she said. She wasn't so aware of the hypocrisy of it all if she was "high," and she "really dug" the feeling of closeness she got from smoking secretly with her friends.

By the time Janet entered high school, she had already experimented with pills and an occasional dose of speed, so that at fifteen she was ready for heroin, which she quickly found as available to her as everything else had been.

The next three years were a nightmare. Things kept going from bad to worse until Janet left home. Now at eighteen, after three years of lying, stealing, cheating, and worse, Janet is in a residential center, and she is determined to begin again.

Janet's story is not meant to be frightening. It is told because it is important for parents to realize that they must be at least as concerned about what is going on *inside* their children as they are about what is happening *outside*. They must know as much about *what* their children are as they do about *where* they are.

Setting Limits

Curiosity is an inseparable part of growing up. It is a healthy and natural impulse that we want to nurture. But we also know that "curiosity killed the cat." How can parents protect their children from being curious about things that can harm them, like drugs?

Here we go back again to the principle of setting limits. Protecting the child against drugs is all part and parcel of the process that begins when we teach him about the fundamentals of safety and health care, like not getting into medicine cabinets or household cleaners, or not crossing the street against the light. Over the years we have built a relationship with our child, and a sense of trust, that will enable him to accept our rules because he has found out that "mother and father know best." This trust will carry over into the more complicated do's and don'ts, even when it is difficult for him to obey us, and even, perhaps, when he thinks we are being a bit unreasonable.

But setting limits is not enough. Rules must also be accompanied by explanations that will make sense to the child. Even in the beginning, it is not enough just to warn the child not to accept gifts of food or candy (or anything at all) from strangers or older children at school. The warning must be accompanied by an explanation. It may be simple at first. For example, we can explan that some people are "sick" people who do mean things to children. One can't always tell if they are "sick" by how they look, but even if they don't look "sick," they may still be dangerous.

As our children grow older, the explanations can become more sophisticated. We can tell them in simple terms about the sickness of drug addiction and about the addicts' terrible need for money, which leads them to steal and lie and cheat and, what is even worse, to get other children to use drugs.

Sometimes, however, there will be no way at all for us to explain the limits we set for our child—no way that he will be old enough to understand. In those instances, an arbitrary "No" is enough.

It is not an easy task to strike the right balance between keeping in touch with what the child is thinking and being intrusive and dominating. But if we follow our natural instincts about him, if we show him that we are open to him but that we don't want to "push," he will usually respond by telling us what we need to know about himself. For example, when he comes home from school and is grumpy, we need not just pass it off. We can ask him what's wrong. If he doesn't want to talk about it at first, we let it alone and try again later on. If the mood keeps up, we can ask him what we can do to help him feel better. If the mood passes, perhaps we can find out what was troubling him so a few minutes ago.

In other words, we can let our child know that we hear him. Whether he is talking or not, he is telling us about himself. The best help we can give him is for him to know that we are waiting to listen.

Confronting Reality

In these early years, the child will learn more about how to handle his uncomfortable feelings from watching how we deal with ours than by all the preaching in the world. If he sees his parents "popping pills" or drinking heavily to help them function in their daily lives, this will say a great deal to him about how to confront reality. How will we protect him then from being at the mercy of anyone who comes along with a similar quick and easy remedy for trouble?

It is up to us to counteract the misconceptions that he is exposed to daily in advertisements everywhere that prescribe easy remedies for everything from fallen arches to broken hearts. Unless he learns from us how to confront his problems seriously, he will be an easy mark for dream merchants as he grows older.

The implication today, however, often is that it is old-fashioned and stupid to suffer when chemical "remedies" are so readily available. The more thoughtful among us know that this is not true. No serious problem (other than a strictly medical one) was ever solved by anything other than hard work. Suffering, pain, and indecision cannot be avoided. Our child must learn from us in his earliest years how to face his problems squarely. This teaching must begin as soon as he is old enough to understand what we say and to make himself understood.

One of the hardest lessons in the world is to learn to face oneself and to accept one's own mistakes. Although all children sometimes take the easy way out of uncomfortable situations, they must be shown that it doesn't help to blame someone else, or to pretend that problems don't exist, or to think up all kinds of excuses to avoid a confrontation with oneself. That is not the way to solve problems. We can help our child best by teaching him during these years—in kindly ways that do not undermine his self-esteem—how to be honest with himself. This will serve him well when he is faced with more serious problems later on.

What Drugs Do They Use?

Although many youngsters living in poverty areas have already begun to use drugs of all kinds before they reach their teens, this is not usually true for children in areas where there are fewer economic and social pressures. For these more fortunate children, the motivation is often less a matter of escape from reality than a desire for novelty or a need to be part of the gang at any cost.

The drugs abused by middle-class children of this age are generally the solvents, the ordinary, everyday substances that can be found around almost every house or garage: plastic cement, nail polish remover, lighter fluid, cleaning fluids, gasoline, and benzene are only a few of the popular solvents used for "sniffing."

The procedure for getting "high" is to soak a piece of material in the solvent and to put it into a paper or plastic bag. The bag is then held close to the face, and the fumes are inhaled directly through the nose and mouth. At first, there may be a powerful rush of good feeling called a "jag." However, this lasts only a short time, and the sniffing may then be resumed in an attempt to prolong it.

Coughing, sneezing, and pains in the chest may then ensue, followed by headaches and other bodily symptoms. In fact, if the child has used a plastic bag, rather than a paper one, he may even suffocate in the very process of inhaling. Other common effects of a sniffing "high" include: a staggering walk, a slurring of speech, hallucinations, distortions of the senses such as double vision or a buzzing in the ears, or a persistent drowsiness possibly leading to coma and even death. Less visible long-term dangers of persistent sniffing may be internal damage to the liver, the kidneys, the bone marrow, and the brain.

Persistent sniffing can lead to a psychic dependence. However, before this comes about, children are already so debilitated from frequent use that dependence is not common.

Another common method of obtaining a "high" for children of this age is to dilute a Coke or a 7-Up with aspirin or some other pill that will bring on the feeling of pleasure that they seek.

Thus we can see that there is no way to protect our child from drug abuse except by building a protective system into the child himself. Since the substances available to abusers are present in *every* house, and since there is no way at all of preventing our child from having access to them, the only prevention lies in his being able to say "No!"

I Dare You!

Who responds to dares? Children. It is a common everyday challenge—"I dare you!" But what happens when those dares include sniffing glue or aerosol or taking pills? How will our child react to being called "chicken" or to being less of a hero? Or to being left out of the gang because he won't go along?

It is a hard business, this matter of helping our child acquire enough inner strength to resist a harmful dare. The training for it has to begin early in his life and, like everything else in growing up, depends upon our ability to nurture his self-esteem and to help him recognize a situation for what it is.

The reality of the matter is that glue-sniffing, aerosol-sniffing, and pill-popping are extremely dangerous activities. They can inflict irreparable physical damage. A child will be able to realize the danger of these activities and to recognize that all this could happen to him *only* if he is comfortable with himself and free from the need to prove his own worth to himself and to his friends at all costs. It is a neurotic need to defy known danger, to test themselves again and again against the most hazardous odds, that leads children to this kind of self-destructive behavior.

If our child has faith in himself and faith that his parents are on his side, it is unlikely that he will "dare" his life away.

Informing Your Child: At Home

Some parents are reluctant to talk to their children about drugs because they feel that they would only be "putting ideas into their heads" if they did so. But no child in these days can escape learning about drugs in one way or another. He will hear about them wherever he goes as soon as he is old enough to leave his parents' side. He will hear about drugs from the news media, from radio and TV, from magazines, and especially from other children. If we don't tell him first what we feel he should know, and in the way that we feel he should know it, we will leave him to the not-so-tender mercies of misinformation that he will pick up elsewhere.

Recognizing this, parents often try to warn their children away from drugs with lurid tales and exaggerated stories about the dangers of drug use, without knowing very much about it themselves. This is probably as destructive as telling the children nothing at all. If we are carried away by our own fear and try to frighten our child by telling him things that are not true, he will not believe us even when we tell him what is indeed the truth. That is why it is important always to be sure of one's facts. If we destroy our credibility by giving him unsubstantiated horror tales, we will lead him to assume that everything else we tell him about the dangers of drugs is also exaggerated. This can have serious consequences.

The only way that we can help the child to acquire a wholesome fear of dangerous drugs is to begin talking about the subject as soon as we feel that he is old enough to understand. In the beginning, we can help him make clear distinctions between "medicines" prescribed by doctors and "drugs" that people take on their own initiative just because they think they will feel better if they do. The latter includes patent medicines that can be bought in the drugstore without a prescription. It is important for our child to realize that all chemical compounds are designed to serve specific purposes and that they can be dangerous if used carelessly. We can point out the analogy between what we are telling him about drugs now, and the way we talked to him when he was a baby and warned him not to touch household cleaners in the kitchen or to go into the medicine cabinet. In the Bibliography is a list of books and pamphlets that tell us what he needs to know and can help us get the facts straight.

At School

The term "Drug Education Program" is often misunderstood by the very people who are most afraid of drug abuse. Too often it means to them no more than a few P-TA meetings with speakers and panels and a few "lectures to the kids." Then the matter is comfortably forgotten for the rest of the school year.

The substance of a good program is more than that. What is worse, inadequate "programs" give everyone a false sense of security; they think they have come to grips with the problem, when it really remains as much a threat as ever.

A good program of drug education in the schools involves everyone—the staff, the students, and the parents—in an intensive search to know more about the reasons for drug abuse, the nature of various drugs, and ways of finding satisfactions in life that will lessen the temptation to turn to drugs. It becomes a group learning experience that provides its participants with opportunities for personal growth as well as information.

The emphasis in such discussions will differ according to the different needs of the participants and their different capacities to understand. For example, in one New York school parents and teachers separately take part in discussion groups in which each group airs their common problems and new light is thrown on old hang-ups. The school curriculum itself includes discussions about drugs from the earliest grades on. Beginning with simple talks about health, medicine, and the use of herbs by the early Indians, it goes on to include a historical survey of drug use in ancient times and in the East, where drug abuse appears to be one reason for the decay of flourishing civilizations. In the upper grades students discuss current news items about events related to drugs or to the value systems of modern youth.

Although such comprehensive programs are rare, this is the goal that parents must strive to reach in their own schools if they are to defend their children successfully against the ravages of drug abuse. It is only when a child grows up with full awareness of what drugs are *really* about that he is protected against seduction by users who need new recruits.

9 *Teaching About Money*

"What is this life, if full of care,
We have no time to stand and stare . . ."
Leisure—W. H. Davies

WHY IS MONEY such an emotionally loaded topic? How realistic are our attitudes about money? Does it sometimes have other meanings for us than the ones we recognize? There is no question about the fact that before we can begin to teach our children the "value" of money, we must first be honest with ourselves about how we really feel about it and why we use it as we do.

Money as a Symbol

In the beginning, money was invented simply as a convenient medium of exchange. When someone helped his neighbor out, he received as payment not a horse or a cow, but a small token that indicated that the favor would be returned another time, upon demand. But as time went on, money came to have a "value" of its own. People began to forget what money was really *for.* They began to "collect" money. Even if they didn't need the goods and services money would buy, they spent their time and energy working for more.

Of course, this is an oversimplification of the history of money; but it explains why many young people today feel that their parents misuse it in dangerous ways, and why as adolescents their rebellion often takes the form of rejecting what their parents worked so hard to acquire.

Let's look at some of the ways we use money at home. Our children learn more about what we consider the "value" of money from what we do with it than from what we say about it. Even if we ourselves are unaware of what money means to us, our children are not. For example, Harry sees that his father drives a Cadillac, while they have barely enough money to cover essential household expenses. This tells him a good deal about what his parents think money is for, and how important they feel it is to impress the neighbors.

On the other hand, Tony gets a different view of money as he watches the piggy bank in the kitchen slowly getting fuller and fuller and knows that this is money his parents are saving to send him to college. No one has to tell either Harry or Tony what their parents really value.

At one time or another most of us have used money in an effort to get something that really cannot be bought in a store—and we didn't even know we were doing it! We have given gifts to buy affection. We have tried to buy status or power in the community. Or we have withheld money to exert our influence. Perhaps we gave ourselves all kinds of reasons for doing these things, but were they the real reasons?

For example, why do Johnny's parents "spoil" him so? They make it hard for all the other parents in the neighborhood—Johnny gets from them anything he wants. Is this because they love him more? Or because they are richer? Chances are that these are not the reasons that their "generosity" has very little to do with Johnny at all. Very often parents overindulge their children because they want to make up for the deprivations of their own childhood by showering their children with all the things *they* dreamed of but never received. "Generosity" can also be an expression of guilt for neglecting a child in other ways. Sometimes it is just a matter of "showing off."

Whatever the reason, the child like Johnny, who is being smothered with material possessions, is usually not getting what he really wants. He feels little love behind the giving. He senses that it is really not for him that all this is happening, and he resents it. Sometimes he tries to fight this uncomfortable feeling that he can't put his finger on, and can't name, by demanding more and more and more. So parents and children become each other's unhappy victims.

Frugality can be just as deceiving. As much as we tell ourselves that times are hard and we should draw in the purse strings, is it really necessary to eliminate that 25¢ allowance? Is it really true that making our children earn everything they get will make them appreciate it more in the end? Isn't there a happy compromise somewhere along the line?

It is hard to give our children an appropriate perspective on money and how to use it when we so often have trouble with it ourselves. Let's not forget that money is for *living*—not just for today, but also for tomorrow—and that's what it's all about.

Allowances

Allowances are important because they give boys and girls a sense of independence and help teach them the basic principles of budgeting. When a child has money of his own, he learns how to spend it through trial and error. If we can stand watching him "waste" it, he will soon find out that the quarter spent on candy will not be there to be spent on a comic book, and he will learn to make good choices on his own.

No child should get such a large allowance that he is able to buy whatever he wants. Parents who give their children that much money are depriving them of the real joy of wanting something so badly that they are willing to work and save for it. No pleasure in getting things easily compares to the thrill of having done it yourself!

But at any age, whatever a child gets should be his to spend as he chooses. We let him make his own choices about spending even if they don't appear to us the best ones. We let him take the consequences of his decisions. If he spends his school bus money on a movie ticket, he walks home from school, even if it's raining—or we give him the opportunity to earn extra money by paying him to do a chore that would otherwise not be required of him. In other words, in friendly fashion, we help him to face the realities of life.

When and How Much?

The child probably should be old enough to have mastered some simple principles of arithmetic, adding and subtracting, before he gets a weekly allowance. This usually happens at about the first grade, though some children seem to understand what coins add up to a dime or a quarter before they can write numbers and do "school" arithmetic.

At first it is better to limit the allowance to a very small sum. It is asking too much of a child of six or seven to plan for the use of a sizable amount of money. We should give him just enough for an extra treat that he can buy for himself. This will give him a chance to go into a store, to choose what he wants to buy, and to learn how to make a purchase by himself, including making change. He may even decide on his own to "save" for a toy he wants, but this should be his decision, not ours.

Later on, in the third and fourth grade, a child is ready to handle larger sums of money. At this stage, we will need to help him plan what "essentials" he will become responsible for and decide together what "extras" his money will be expected to cover. For example, his allowance might include money for carfare, school supplies, lunch, and scouting or club dues, in addition to the extras we have agreed upon together.

The amount of money the child is given should be determined with several factors in mind. First and foremost are what he really needs and what we can afford. Over and above that, although the decisions cannot and must not be made primarily on the basis of what other children in the neighborhood get, this is also an important consideration. If we live in a neighborhood where all the kids go bowling every Saturday morning, it is important for our child to be able to go, too, and to pay for this himself. On the other hand, if the neighbors' children are receiving more money than we can afford to give our child, or if we feel that they are getting more money for their age than we are *willing* to give our child even though we can afford it, we will be doing our child a favor to discuss these matters with him openly and to explain to him how we have arrived at our decisions.

Chores

A dilemma in most families is when to pay for chores and when not to pay. How much should we expect of our child as his share of the family's workload, and when should he be asked to contribute only with the recognition that this is above and beyond the call of duty?

Where the family situation is such that the parents do all the work around the house and there is no one else to give a hand, then children can certainly be expected to pitch in without pay most of the time. But even here, there are occasions where it might be in order to pay a child for something that he is asked to do. Pay "pays off," if for no other reason than that it relieves the pressure and generates some enthusiasm for what might otherwise be drudgery.

In households where some outside help is available and a child's required chores are more limited, there are still jobs to be done for which he can be paid without having it look like "made work."

Although these decisions must be made on the basis of individual family needs, in nearly all situations there are more jobs to be done than people to do them. A child can help out in many ways that are within his competence. The six-year-old can wash a linoleum or tile floor; the ten-year-old can run a variety of errands; and almost anyone can rake leaves, polish shoes, polish silver, wash the car, or do any number of other jobs that are needed around the house.

Whatever jobs we pay for, the rate of pay should be somewhat commensurate with the going rate outside the home; and the job and what will be paid for it should be clearly defined in advance. Some allowance in terms of pay may be made for the fact that it is all in the family. But in any case, if we have assigned the job properly, with our child's level of competence in mind, we should certainly insist that the job be done well—children need to learn that we earn our pay. They also need the joy that comes from seeing "finished" work.

Generosity and Thrift

These two qualities have been respected in our society since Biblical times, and most of us would like our children to be both generous and thrifty. Are these "natural" virtues, or can we teach them to our children?

In their early years all children are what we call "selfish." They grab, they demand, and they do not willingly share their toys. Until the age of six or seven, children cannot quite grasp the concept of empathic give and take, and it is no coincidence that it is at six or seven, when this awareness is beginning to sprout, that our child is off to "real" school. Before that, even if he went to nursery school, his horizon was more or less limited to what he wanted for himself, and he did not yet have the ability to become aware of his companions as people with feelings like his own.

Sharing as a result of empathizing with others is hard for children to learn, and some people grow up without ever learning it. It is, in its finest sense, unselfish behavior that requires great maturity and nobility of spirit. However, although most of us are not constantly so noble, even if we would like to think we are, we have learned in life that there is no getting without giving. We have learned that generosity is a way of making other people like us, as well as being rewarding in itself, and that it gives us a certain status to be known as a generous person.

There is nothing wrong with seeing this practical aspect of giving, provided we also know that too much giving of one's means, or even of oneself, can be destructive, and provided we can also *take.* We have all known people who insist on giving so much in every relationship that the other fellow begins to feel uncomfortable about taking. Such compulsive givers can't accept from others because it makes *them* feel somehow less. They call it "pride," but in reality it is quite the contrary. Whereas true pride involves a strong sense of self and self-respect, compulsive givers suffer from a crippling absence of these very qualities. Giving becomes a way of putting others in their debt in order to reinforce their own fragile self-esteem.

Young children often seesaw between these two extremes of selfishness and giving. Both are part of how they really feel, and they need help with reconciling the conflicting impulses.

There is an old French saying: *"Les extremes se touchent,"* which means that opposites have much in common. This is true of the impulses we are talking about here. One child will be standoffish and will hoard his toys as a way of reasssuring himself and bolstering his self-confidence, while his friend tries to accomplish the same thing by an exaggerated display of affection and by giving all his best toys away. The child can be helped to strike a happy balance between these two extremes if he knows that his parents' primary concern is for him, and yet they have room in their hearts to care for others, too. Then he will feel secure and loved, and he will want and learn how to contribute to these feelings in others.

"Waste not, want not!" Although this proverb dominated much of early American life, it has long since been denied by the consumption-oriented credit economy in which we live. How confusing to a child who is being taught at home to spend his money carefully to see the seduction of advertisements all around him. This year's model is bigger and better; "buy now, pay later."

A respect for the value of money is hard to develop in a society in which last year's model of almost everything, from refrigerators and cars to dresses and pop tunes, is discounted only months after it appears. What do such attitudes say to a child about people? About the value of relationships? Are they as transient as "things"? What is the value of work and craftsmanship if only a short time later an item is to be discarded for something new?

Thrift has many meanings. Thrifty parents who shop carefully at the supermarket and the department store, and prudently repair the family's possessions, are not only saving money; they are also showing respect for the effort that went into acquiring the money they are spending. By budgeting our funds, we teach the value of making careful choices, of planning expenditures ahead of time instead of deciding impulsively on purchases that might upset the budget and deprive the family. Not that there isn't room for "impulse buying," too. The spontaneous decision to buy something extravagant is part of the fun of life! But it is the exception, not the rule.

Our child sees and absorbs all this. Whether we know it or not, our attitudes will influence how he spends his money and how he lives his life. We can help him to realize that although life is lived *now,* there is a time ahead that also needs attention today. It is in this larger area of life-planning that realistic attitudes toward saving and spending will later have their major effect.

Handling Differences

Children often have feelings of guilt or jealousy about having more or less than their friends. Because many of us, as parents, are still busy denying that we have these same feelings ourselves, it is hard to deal with them in our children.

By and large, our child's attitudes toward these issues will reflect our own. If we enjoy our life and recognize that finances are only one part of it, then our child will be able to accept his lot more easily. What this means is that although his envy will not automatically disappear, we can help him to realize that his feelings are natural, and eventually the positive values in his own life will help him to come to terms with these differences.

Children who are more affluent than their friends also have problems in handling differences. They may feel unjustifiably guilty, or superior—or both. The same principles apply in helping them to accept their good fortune more realistically. The added element here is that children of affluence must be helped to recognize that it is not only "fair" to share with others but in their case may require special sensitivity to the feelings of others.

If pride in oneself can be dissociated from what one has, a wholesome attitude toward these differences can be achieved. Although almost everyone will admit that what one *is* is more important than what one *has,* this attitude is often difficult to maintain in the face of the emphasis on things that we find in everyday life. However, parents can help by discussing this with their children and by recognizing that the entire range of human emotions is part of life. Life is on the whole too full of joy to allow the avoidable uncomfortable feelings about money to deprive us of happiness.

10
A Sensible Approach To TV And Movies

> Quinquireme of Nineveh, from distant Ophir
> Rowing home to haven in sunny Palestine,
> With a cargo of ivory,
> And apes and peacocks,
> Sandalwood, cedarwood, and sweet white wine.
>
> • • • •
>
> Dirty British coaster with a salt-caked smoke stack
> Butting through the Channel in the mad March days,
> With a cargo of Tyne coal,
> Road-rail, pig-lead,
> Firewood, iron-ware, and cheap tin trays.
>
> *Cargoes*—John Masefield

NOW THAT THE whole world can be brought into view with only the flick of a wrist, most children no longer find their dreams in poems or between the covers of a book. Television has become for them the magic carpet to carry them wherever they want to go—and even, perhaps, to less comfortable places.

Some parents are troubled by this turning away from the enjoyment of books that was so important to them in their own childhood. Many are passionately involved in a battle over the vices and virtues of television. Although there is a lot of pro and con about it in many areas, we must all recognize that television is an important influence on our children and that it is likely to become even more so. Whether it will help or hinder their development will depend upon how realistically we make use of it in our own homes.

Expanding Horizons

Thanks in part to television, children grow up faster these days than they used to. They learn to read at an earlier age as they memorize commercials, and as there are increasing numbers of programs specifically designed to teach reading. The world has opened up for children in an entirely new way; they are becoming more aware of what the adult world is doing than ever before in our history.

Because of TV, children of all ages are already on familiar terms with space. They have been with the astronauts on the surface of the moon. They have seen rice paddies in China, and the Eiffel tower. They have seen wars, famines, weddings, and births. They can tell you all about the latest in everything from cars to cleansers. In fact, television bombards our children with so much information that none of them can fail to absorb some of it.

What does this kind of sophistication do to traditional parent-child relationships? What kind of influence can parents have in the lives of children who no longer regard their parents as infallible or as the source of all wisdom? How can parents deal with this new spirit of inquiry and still function securely as heads of the family?

Obviously, the arbitrary attitudes of past generations of parents toward their children are being severely challenged by this new explosion of knowledge and experience. Children can no longer be made to accept parental opinions without question. Today more than ever they must be listened to and heard by their parents; and parents are being forced as never before to give sound reasons for what they say and do.

Television and Aggressiveness

One of the principal arguments against TV is that it teaches children aggressive behavior. Violence seems to be everywhere on TV. Even the cartoons are full of it. Bugs Bunny clobbers and gets clobbered, the Flintstones survive one hazardous incident after another, and Batman is always the good guy who beats the villain at his own game.

Some psychologists say that such violence is good for children because it relieves their aggressive impulses vicariously. By watching his favorite television show, they say, a child sees someone else doing what he would like to do himself, and this diminishes his own need to express himself violently in real life. His own feelings become more manageable and his anger more acceptable when it all gets worked out on TV.

Besides, say some students of human behavior, violence is part of the reality of life. We cannot shelter our children from it. The expression of violence on TV is a good way of introducing children to the possibilities for violence that exist around them, without having them become personally involved with it.

Although all this may be true, there are some who propound equally valid reasons against children's watching violent programs. Dr. Albert Bandura of Stanford University has conducted studies indicating that children tend to imitate the aggressive behavior that they observe and that they will reproduce a display of violence in real life after they have watched it on TV. Although his studies are open to some question, there is certainly a good deal of merit to both arguments from the "common sense" point of view, and the answer probably lies somewhere in between.

No matter how we feel about it, however, we should always be selective about our child's television-viewing. The kind of programs that we permit the child to watch should be determined by our feelings about what is appropriate and what is not appropriate for him at his age, and by his sensitivity and susceptibility to what he sees. Sensitive children are sometimes very much upset by what they see on the television screen. It is sometimes better to forbid them to watch any frightening programs at all until they are old enough to handle them more comfortably.

In any case, the matter of program selection can never be left entirely up to the child. No child is equipped to evaluate what he sees on TV without parental assistance. Since violence of some sort is inevitable on most programs, even if we restrict and censor his viewing, our child will have to come to some understanding of what he sees. Our job as parents is to be supportive and comforting interpreters. We can let him know that although violence exists and aggressive feelings are just as natural as loving ones, violent behavior is not the most effective way of solving problems in the long run. The child can be helped to see alternatives to violence and to understand that although we all get angry from time to time, it is a destructive way of dealing with important issues if we permit angry feelings to mask the underlying reasons for our discontent.

Television and Passivity

Many educators oppose TV because they believe it encourages mental and emotional passivity in children and diminishes their initiative for constructive activity. In pre-television days, they say, books and radio left something to the imagination. When a child read a story or listened to the radio, he had to fill in missing parts himself with his own imagination. Television makes spectators out of our children. They cease to participate in what is going on even to that limited degree.

Although this criticism is certainly true, it is perhaps too harsh a condemnation of TV. There is room in every child's life for the kind of fun and entertainment that makes no demand. The pressures of our modern world are felt even by our children: there is more to learn and more to be done today than ever before. The opportunity to unwind in front of the television set is as important for them as for adults.

Nevertheless, let's look again at this question of passivity. What is really going on in our child as he watches TV? Many students of TV and its effects on children deplore the notion that just because a child is sitting immobile in front of the TV screen he is being passive. Changes may be taking place inside him that will take effect only after the set is turned off. He may be stimulated to read the newspaper after watching a news program on television. He may want to learn more about other things he has seen on TV and try to find out about them in books. He may acquire new ideas and new attitudes toward people and social issues that he will later discuss with us at the dinner table. Is this passivity?

Of course when television-watching is abused, then all the arguments against it are true. But this would apply to anything—overeating, oversleeping, overexercising, and even overstudying. No excess is healthy.

We have all known children, and also adults, who are "TV addicts." They sit for hours before the television set, perhaps even having their meals there. Their eyes seldom leave the screen, and they are hardly aware of what is going on around them. Television addicts are so preoccupied with TV that they really don't care much about any other activity.

In this sense, TV addiction is the same as any other addiction. The addict is concerned only with getting what he feels he needs, and it is only when he is indulging in his addiction that his tensions seem to be relieved. As with drugs or alcohol, TV-viewing can become a way of escaping reality, of avoiding the necessity to cope with the pressures of life.

Our obligation as parents is to keep in touch with what is going on inside our growing child as much as we can, so that we can help him confront reality every day without the need to run away to the comfort of a Never-never land of TV. It is up to us to see that television will not be his only outlet from boredom. This will require effort on our part, and the strength not to succumb to the habit of using TV as a convenient baby-sitter. Later on in this chapter we will discuss some ways in which parents can control their children's television-viewing.

Fantasy and Reality

Does television enhance a child's concept of reality? Or does it blur it? Probably a bit of both. There is no question that, thanks to TV, modern children have a broader and more realistic view of what life is about than ever before. They know about aspects of human behavior that previously were only talked about behind closed doors. They are politically better informed, and they are aware of differences in race and economic circumstances even though there is no exposure to such differences in their daily lives.

This is not the whole picture, however. There are other aspects of TV that may tend to confuse children and to blur their conceptions of reality. For example, how real is a war that can be turned on every evening with the 6 o'clock news? How real is a TV family whose members always seem to get along and parents never shriek at their children? What misconceptions does a child acquire about death when a favorite TV hero dies on a program at 5 o'clock only to reappear in another role at 6?

Most children are too immature and too inexperienced to grasp the full meaning of

much that they see on the television screen. For the most part, they tend to accept what they see without questioning. Recognizing this, programs like *Sesame Street* or *Mister Rogers' Neighborhood* root their fantasy in reality and thus nurture both without confusion. Perhaps this is one reason that both programs are so popular with children—besides the fact that they are fun!

However, fantasy is not always so clearly defined. Sometimes parents have to intervene with explanations and comforting remarks to help their child place what he is seeing within the framework of his own grasp of reality—and that, only parents can do.

But what does TV mean to children whose own real lives are filled with all kinds of problems for which there appear to be no solutions? They watch television, too! Children whose parents are alcoholic, children whose parents are neglectful, children who themselves have a disability that makes them different from other children—they, too, enjoy TV. What is TV doing to help these children to cope with their problems realistically? Since almost every story on TV has a happy ending, how do these children feel about themselves when they cannot solve their own problems? Isn't it natural that if *their* stories do not have a happy ending they should feel somehow inadequate? How realistically does TV prepare *all* children for the sad fact that some sadness is here to stay?

The goal of TV, as far as children are concerned, should be to encourage fantasy as the delight that it is to old and to young—and to make sure that the realities it portrays are real.

Television and Values

There has also been much controversy about what values television is really teaching our children. What does it say to them? What messages do our children carry away about the way to live their lives?

The aim of a commercial TV show is to sell its sponsors' products. No sponsor—off the air! Programs are constantly being interrupted by advertisements, all of them persuasive and many of them misleading. Children are urged to buy things all the time. Not only are they encouraged to ask their parents for expensive toys, but they are also pushed to tell us about household products and to urge us to buy them.

Not only is the emphasis on "buying" to bring happiness a dangerous concept, but it also triggers real problems in many families. Some parents who can well afford to do so refuse to buy most of the toys and games advertised on TV because they do not believe these are the kind that will bring real enjoyment to their children. This is hard for children to understand, and parents and children often battle about it. Later on perhaps they will appreciate their parents' point of view, as they themselves become more selective. But how about the child whose parents are poor? However his parents feel about the products advertised on TV, they cannot afford to buy them. What does this do to the parents' and the child's feelings? It is frightening to contemplate what is being taught about values. Children are being told that happiness and prestige can be bought at the store—now, with a new doll, a truck, or a game. How will these joys be bought later in his life? With a pill? With a "shot"?

Much of the advertising on adult TV is also destructive. Ads for sleeping pills, beauty creams, washing compounds, and hair oils tell us and our children that health, youth, beauty, and success can be bought, that it's all just a question of making the right purchase. Where are we being told anything true about wisdom, work, or love?

Although programming itself has improved enormously in some ways, especially in terms of "social consciousness," most programs are still unaware of the image they project to children about "heroes" and "heroines." Most of us are not exceptional people. Where in TV is the everyday face and the everyday life? What kind of unrealistic goals does TV set for our children, and what kind of self-concept does it give them when on television the exception becomes the rule?

What Can Parents Do at Home?

Each of us must decide for ourselves what role TV is to play in the entertainment and education of our children. There are very few absolutes about TV-watching, but there are some guidelines that can apply to all of us:

• *Location of the TV set.* The TV set should be placed in a room where our child can sit comfortably, preferably no closer than 3 or 4 feet from the screen. There is no truth to the rumor that TV hurts the eyes, any more than reading does. A dimly lit room (with the light in a position that will not reflect in the screen) is more comfortable than a totally dark room, because there will then be no after-image when the set is turned off. However, also contrary to popular notion, there is no damaging physiological effect on the eyes from watching in total darkness.

• *Amount of time spent watching TV.* If a child sees his parents watching TV every evening and part of the day as well, they won't have much success in restricting his television-viewing. However, if we set limits for our own use of TV, he will accept his restrictions more gracefully. No child should be permitted to watch TV during all his spare time. If possible, he should not have his meals in front of the set except on special occasions for special programs. Ordinarily, he should not be allowed to watch TV until his homework and his chores have been completed; and if the weather is nice, he should be encouraged to play outside during the daylight hours.

Sometimes it is fun to play a game with the child before bedtime, or to read a new book together. He may protest and say he prefers TV, and we may feel hurt that he is rejecting our offer of companionship. We needn't worry about it. If it isn't his favorite program he's missing, he will soon forget his protests and become engrossed in whatever we're doing together. But we should be sure he knows that this hour together is also for *our* pleasure; we should not make him feel that we're doing him a favor.

Nighttime watching should be carefully limited and supervised so that the child can get the sleep he needs. Too much TV, or the wrong kind, can bring on nightmares and restlessness, especially for high-strung children.

It is certainly in order to use the TV as a baby-sitter sometimes when we are too busy to be with our child. But most of the time it is better for all of us to let the work slide a bit and play with him rather than to put him in front of the TV.

• *Censoring the child's TV fare.* Parents should always be aware of what their children are watching on TV, just as they keep track of where their children are in the neighborhood. Before we next say, "Go and turn on the TV," we should be sure that there is something on television that is appropriate for him to watch, or find something else for him to do.

We should be familiar, too, with the content of the programs that our child sees, taking a look at his favorites not just once, but every once in a while, to be sure that they maintain the quality we approve of. Too often parents will ask, "Well, what's *that* program about?"—and the child, being human, will answer evasively even though he knows that the show is really not for him.

Although we worry about our children's seeing things that will corrupt them on TV or at the movies, if we are reasonably careful with our supervision, chances that the occasional blooper that slips through our net will not have much effect. The detrimental effect of bad TV and movie fare is largely cumulative, so we need not worry about an occasional mistake. We shouldn't worry, either, if we get that "Everybody else does." Underneath, our child will like being protected from disturbing programs, just as he appreciates sensible limits about everything else in his life.

• *Watching Together.* Television-viewing can be a very pleasant pastime for the whole family. If we keep an eye on the daily program as it is published in the newspaper or a television guide, we can select programs that will be fun for everybody. It's almost like an outing to plan the meal so that we will all be through before the program begins, or perhaps to have a picnic together in front of the TV. Such occasions derive their value from their specialness. If this is done all the time, "togetherness" becomes a bore, and we will have lost the opportunity to share TV with our children in a warm, easy way.

What Can Parents Do in the Community?

Instead of just complaining about current TV fare, we can "*do* something!" The public is helpless against poor television programming only if it permits itself to be.

Television stations are very vulnerable to public opinion, as are individual programs. We can write to stations encouraging them when we like something, or expressing our dislike. Above all, we can support our public TV stations, which usually try quite consistently to provide good adult entertainment and wholesome children's programs. We can support the Public Broadcasting System with money and/or time. If we can give neither of these, we can at least write to indicate our feelings.

No citizen has a right to complain about anything unless he is also willing to take action. Our children will look at TV with a more critical eye and develop a more selective taste if we lead the way at home and abroad.

Movies

For the most part with children this age, television has replaced the movies as a source of entertainment and preoccupation. In the first place, TV is more available; and second, it's a lot cheaper.

Although children still enjoy movies, they are no longer the thrilling experiences that they used to be. Nevertheless, movies offer an opportunity for a family outing that can be enjoyed by all. It is always important, however, to be selective about the films our child will see. The guidelines offered by the film industry itself are not always appropriate, and it is the better part of wisdom to make careful inquiries on our own.

Until a child is about ten years old, he should not go to the movies alone or even with another child unless an adult is with him. Of course, there are always exceptions to this rule. Small community movie houses are usually safe enough, but this is not always true in large cities, and there is no sense in asking for trouble.

11
Vacations: Together Or Separately?

The things that haven't been done before,
Those are the things to try;
Columbus dreamed of an unknown shore
At the rim of the far-flung sky.

The Things That Haven't Been Done Before—Edgar Albert Guest

VACATION! WHAT A glamorous word. It conjures up exciting new vistas, or the prospect of long, lazy hours of relaxing idleness, depending upon our tastes and our pocketbook. However, this is not the whole picture for parents. There is always the question of whether or not to take the children. Since this is not something that anyone can decide for anyone else, let's look at some of the pro's and con's of family vacations and vacations for parents alone. Certainly, both have their good points.

Parents Without Children

Although vacation with children can be a marvelous experience for the whole family, it does not offer parents a chance to be alone together in that special way that comes only with the absence of responsibility. For children *are* a responsibility. No matter how much fun we are having together, we are still concerned with their safety and well-being, and with seeing that they are having a good time. No family vacation can free us to concentrate only on ourselves and each other.

Every once in a while most parents need a refresher course in being married to each other just as much as children need to be away from their parents. Under the pressures of daily living, many couples tend to forget about the enjoyment that can be found in just being together. Children need their parents to get away together, too. Not only do they need to be reminded that Mother and Daddy have a life of their own in which children do not share, but also a brief separation like this can give them a

new awareness of themselves and an appreciation of the joy of family life.

So we need not feel guilty about leaving our children. Even if they complain that we are deserting them, at this age they can probably spare us easily for a few weeks. If we feel that they can't, then perhaps *we* are too tied to *them,* rather than the other way around. It is healthy for children to have to learn to cope with new situations and to test out their own abilities without our help. Real separation problems arise only if parents leave their children too frequently, or for too long a period of time. At this age, a few weeks is long enough.

The big question is, of course, whom to leave our children with. Should we leave them with their grandparents? A sitter? A friend? The answer depends on what these people are like. If any one of them is a person who is "good with children," who likes our children and whom our children like, then that is our answer. It is always best not to leave them with someone who is "just doing us a favor," or with someone who is being paid to "sit" but who is inexperienced or has no feeling for children.

If possible, we should arrange for the children to live at home while we are gone rather than send them elsewhere. There is really no substitute for the comfort of familiar surroundings, no matter how often they have gone visiting at someone else's house.

On the other hand, if there is no way to do this, then a visit to Grandma or an exchange of sitting services with a friendly neighbor is a good way to handle it. If our children feel comfortable where we send them, they can be helped to look upon their visit as a special treat; but we must be sure not to leave them so long as to wear out their welcome.

Some wrap-up tips for vacationing parents:

- Always leave your address and phone number or itinerary together with the pediatrician's telephone number in a prominent place where everyone in the family can see it.
- Also the name and number of someone to call in case of emergency.
- Sometimes it helps to leave the telephone number and/or address of the child's best friend so that whoever is taking care of him can help him to arrange dates.
- Arrange to have the child's favorite foods in the refrigerator or the freezer, and perhaps pin up in the kitchen a few sample menus that include the things he likes best to eat.
- Let his teacher know when you expect to be away and who will be caring for him, so that if there are any problems in school she will be able to handle them appropriately.

Our children will enjoy receiving postcards and mail from us, especially if they are not at home. It will give them a feeling of being in touch with us and a sense of importance to receive their very own mail. The gifts we bring back for them can be mementos of our holiday, so that they can share it with us. Elaborate presents may only reinforce their suspicion that we feel guilty about having left them, and that is not the feeling we want to promote.

Family Vacations

Family vacations are a wonderful way of being together without the usual responsibility of home. The only problem is, "Where shall we go?" Mother wants the mountains; Dad, the seashore; the children, a ranch in the West. The solution is to compromise. There are many years ahead, and each one of us can have his turn.

The important thing to remember about a family vacation is that no matter what we choose to do, it should have something in it for everyone. A child of six cannot be expected to enjoy a holiday when most of the time is spent sightseeing and in one-night stands at hotels or motels along the way. Nor can his parents be expected to enjoy a holiday that is devoted solely to his entertainment without consideration of their needs for change and relaxation. There are many things to do that will give all of us some of what we want.

The possibilities for vacations are endless. Some suggestions are listed below, and at the end of the chapter are listings of resources for further information.

Farm Vacations

This is an especially nice way for a city or a suburban family to spend their holiday together. Farm vacations are usually relatively inexpensive, and so they may be a possibility for families with limited budgets and a taste for country life. However, whatever the family pocketbook, it is always a thrilling experience for city children to see the cycle of the seasons at first hand and witness the miracles of nature at work as they become acquainted with farm animals. Many farm families invite their guests to participate fully in the daily chores that are part of farm life, and many offer swimming pools and other more sophisticated activities that have little to do with the farm itself. In either case, after a farm holiday, children will never again take for granted the food they eat and the milk they drink every day. Above all, they will have become aware, in a way that nothing in the city can show them, of the direct relation between man and nature.

Long and Short Trips

Long sightseeing trips are fine for children of eight through ten and older if they are interested in what is going on around them, but it is not the most relaxing holiday to take with younger children. As a matter of fact, children, like adults, get a lot more out of traveling if they stay in one place for at least a few days so that they can absorb what they see more comfortably.

Sightseeing can be an exciting occupation if parents plan what to see ahead of time and include the children in the planning sessions. Good preparation for any trip makes it come alive with meaning for everyone. Maps, guidebooks, history books, and pictures can be obtained in libraries and bookshops. Preparation pays off when a child exclaims with the joy of recognition, "That's where. . . . ! We read about that back home!" It also saves time on the trip, when there are other things to do than to read books.

Sightseeing should be interspersed with things for the children to do that will appeal especially to them. For example, a visit to a local amusement park or zoo, a boat ride, a swimming or ice-skating expedition. If decisions are made in a family conclave, the prospect of looking forward to "his" treat will help a child to tolerate, if not enjoy, some of the "museum-ing" that is often just not his "thing."

A weekend sightseeing trip to a nearby point of historic interest or a visit to a large neighboring city can be an exciting refresher for the whole family. For even a small child, the novelty doesn't have a chance to wear off until it's time to go home again. Not too much should be crowded into a short period of time, however. It is still best to take it all in small doses and not wear everyone out in the process of trying to see all there is to see; no one can ever really accomplish that, anyway.

Resorts

In the old days, resorts were places where middle-aged people went on holidays to get away from the children, and old people sat on the porches and rocked. Today, an increasing number of resorts cater to families and have special programs and provisions for children of all ages. When selecting a resort for the family, parents should be sure that it offers the facilities best suited to their needs.

With young children it is usually advisable not to go to a formal resort where they must always be on their best behavior, but to look for a comfortable place that has plenty for children to do and perhaps provides individual cottages or cabins. Some such places have simple cooking facilities, so that at least the children's meals can be prepared. Children may like to "go out" to eat; but for the most part, they don't really enjoy restaurant food, and it is better and less expensive to feed them "at home."

A resort that caters to families usually has sitters available. If parents have been with the children all day long, they deserve some nights to themselves if they want them. On a vacation, children have to learn to share their fun, especially when parents keep their needs in mind during the days.

Some resorts have day-camps for children, or other child-care facilities. It is purely a matter of taste whether or not parents prefer to spend the daytime hours with the children on vacations, but if they choose a resort that has a day-camp, it is important to look into the competence of the camp personnel. No child likes to be shoved aside just so that his parents can have a good time without him. If this is to be a *real* family vacation, it is the parents' responsibility to choose a resort where the day-camp is equipped to give their child the fun that they, themselves, expect.

Camping

Camping has become increasingly popular in recent years as a way of spending a family holiday. With the increased interest in ecology all over the world, there has been a rebirth in appreciation of the joys of nature, and hundreds of families have taken to the road to explore the beauties of America. National and State Parks all over the United States, the Virgin Islands, and Puerto Rico have facilities for camping; and many families are even discovering the excitement of camping in Europe, where hiking and hosteling began.

There are as many ways to go camping as there are places to go. A family can go camping in a car with a tent strapped on the roof or travel in a "camper." They can stay in cabins along the route or visit a ranch camp, which provides a base for short camping trips or other adventures for its guests. The advantages of such vacations are obvious. It is a thrilling experience to confront or rediscover nature's wonders with the children. It is a way of being together in which even the younger members of the family can help with providing the necessities for living. It stretches children's horizons in a natural, healthful way and teaches them "new" skills, some of which are as old as history. On the whole, camping is an inexpensive way to spend a vacation, and wherever a family decide to go, they will find other families with children, even babies and pets.

The disadvantages are that small children need a good deal of supervision to keep them out of the way of natural hazards. It is best to select a site where they can wander fairly freely without parents having to be too concerned about their safety.

On a camping trip, the children should be briefed clearly as to the location of their campsite and the license number of their car. It might be a good idea to put name tags on them with their camp address.

The books on camping listed at the end of this chapter tell in detail what needs to be taken along. In addition, however, it's always helpful to take some inexpensive paperback nature books, so that the whole family can learn to identify the wildlife and the flowers and trees that they will see along the way.

Ranch Camps

From coast to coast and border to border there are ranch camps in every state and for every taste. Some "dude ranches" are as sophisticated as hotels and offer their guests a variety of entertainment opportunities as well as the simpler pleasures of riding and exploring nature trails. For those who prefer a more authentic experience, however, there are ranches that offer no more than simple fare, clean and attractive accommodations, and an opportunity to participate in the life of a real working ranch. The host families of such ranches are usually available to act as guides for adventure trips in the surrounding countryside. Although these pack trips, float trips, or hiking trips are thrilling experiences, participation is usually limited to children of ten or older, for obvious reasons.

Homes Away from Home

Some families prefer to rent rather than to travel. Rental homes are available for the summer or even for a few weeks during other school holidays. This is a wonderful way for children to become part of the life of a new community and to discover in depth what it is like to live somewhere else. There is an agency, described at the end of the chapter, that specializes in vacation exchanges, listing homes in all parts of the world that are available for exchange, so that costs can be relatively low depending upon the kind of house and the location.

Another agency provides homes abroad for reasonable fees and in out-of-the-way places. Again, the cost depends upon the season and the vacationers' pocketbook and tastes.

Some city families prefer to rent a summer cottage near the seashore or in the woods not too far from home, so that Father can commute to work daily. Others prefer to spend their summer in a cabin in a remote wilderness or in a foreign country.

No matter where a family chooses to go, however, it will probably be a healthier holiday for all if all members can be together a considerable part of the time. On the whole, the business of having a weekend father throughout the summer is not the most wholesome practice for growing children, or for the parents themselves.

Mini-vacations

Have you ever said, "I feel as if we'd been away for a week!" when you only spent the day in the country? This kind of mini-vacation can be a memorable event for all concerned.

The whole family will enjoy an unexpected outing all the more if they take time off every once in a while to spend the day together in some special way. "Time off" does not necessarily mean going away overnight or even taking the children out of school (although sometimes even this can be done with the consent of the school). It can mean just leaving the usual weekend chores and running away for a day of fun.

Although we all want to instill a sense of responsibility in our children, we also want to help them to become spontaneous and flexible enough to meet life at the flood. We want to give them the ability to make compromises and adjustments with routine so that they can learn to have fun while still fulfilling their responsibilities. This is at the heart of bringing up children.

Children must learn from us while they are young that it is as important to set limits for work as it is to set them for pleasure. Young people can grow up to accept their obligations only when they see that they also have an option to put their burdens aside every once in a while to enjoy themselves at other pursuits. Otherwise routine becomes so oppressive that the ultimate purpose gets lost in the shuffle.

Children Without Parents

Sending a child to camp is a big decision. It means that he is growing up and getting ready for a life of his own and that someone else will be taking care of him. The empty bed, the empty room, will be either a promise to parents of a new freedom and a new life together, or a difficult reminder of the fact that children and parents are always destined to part.

Parents often have so many unconscious feelings at a time like this that the decision about whether or not to send a child to camp is sometimes made without any consideration of what is best for the child. For example, parents sometimes push their children off to camp before they are ready to go because the parents are eager for them to have the opportunities that they never had. Or they may keep their children at home and say that they "don't believe in camp" even though the children are eager to go, because of their inability to face the problem of the empty nest.

In other words, there are as many reasons pro and con camp as there are combinations of children and parents. For most children and most parents, however, camp can be a rewarding and important experience. If the camp is the right one for the child, he can have a happy time that will give him a new sense of independence and a new awareness of comradeship with his peers. He can learn new skills, and he may be helped to find new strengths within himself that he never knew he had. Last but not least, he will be exposed to all the beauties of nature that surround almost every campsite and that cannot fail to impress him and awaken new sensibilities.

When is he ready to go to camp? A child is ready when both he and his parents recognize that this is what *he* wants (whether he *says* so or not)—and when his parents feel comfortable about sending him away from home. The age can vary from six through ten depending on the child and on his family situation. If a six-year-old is the youngest of several children who are already going to camp, he may be able to cope with a camp experience at a much earlier age than his friend who is an only child and perhaps less at ease with other children.

To make camping a happy experience, it is as important to send a child to the "right" camp as it is to send him at the "right" age. Here again, parents' feelings sometimes get in the way of selecting a camp that is most suitable for their child. The important thing to remember is that camping should be fun. A camp should not be chosen just because it is nearby, or because it is where all his friends go. And it probably won't be fun for him at all if parents choose a camp that specializes in his weaknesses rather than his strengths because they want camp to bring about that miraculous change in him that they were unable to bring off at home. A child will enjoy camp only if he feels comfortable there. If there is a wide enough range of activity for him to shine where he is able—and accept the fact that there are other things he is not so good at—then camp can be fun and contribute to his overall growth.

Choosing the Right Camp

All camps that are listed in the directories of the American Camping Association and the Association of Private Camps are qualified in the sense that they meet certain minimum standards for safety and health, for the size and quality of the staff, and for the ways in which their programs fulfill their stated purpose. If parents send a child to a camp listed in one of these directories, they have some assurance ahead of time that the camp will be what it purports to be and that the child will be well cared for.

But parents want more from a camp than that. They want to know that their child will have a happy summer and that he will grow in skill and maturity. The camp must be right for *him*. No one can dictate which camp to choose, but there are certain guidelines to follow.

The first and most important essential in selecting a good camp is to like *the director*. A director is responsible for everything about a camp: the program, the staff, and the overall feeling that one gets when entering the camp. An experienced director will have a philosophy of camping that he has evolved over the years, and it is important to learn something about him and how he thinks and feels before making a decision.

If possible, it is wise to have a visit with the director. Chances are that if both parents and child like him, the summer will be off to a good start. During the visit, they can see how he responds to the child and how the child responds to him. The child should be encouraged to ask questions and to participate in the conversation; after all, it's *his* summer that is under discussion. But if some of the child's problems need to be discussed, parents can find a tactful way to get the child to leave the room, so that he won't feel his privacy is being violated by such a sharing of confidences with a stranger.

Distance from home is a factor to be considered only if there will be problems getting there for visiting days. Otherwise, it really doesn't matter very much whether the camp is 50 or 200 miles away. Once the child leaves home, camp will be another world for him, no matter how near or how far.

The *physical accommodations* of a camp should be hygienic and safe, but a child does not need all the comforts of home. One of the reasons for sending him to camp is to give him new experiences and to help him to test his skills in new areas. If he is lodged in hotel-like quarters and swims in a country-club atmosphere, he may be deprived of the opportunity to learn to cope with nature and to see how full of wonders a lake can be.

The *costs* of camps vary from $400 a season to more than $1,000. Camps run by nonprofit institutions are, of course, less expensive because they are partially subsidized; but it would be wrong to assume that because one camp costs more than another, it is necessarily better. A camp is only as good as its director and its staff, and these are the major factors to be considered. Magnificent facilities must not automatically be equated with a "good camp." It may be. But it ain't necessarily so!

Specialized Camp?

Despite the fact that during the past few years there has been an enormous growth in the number of specialized camps (riding, music, tennis, foreign language, etc.), unless children have special problems, authorities do not recommend such camps for children until the age of ten or older. Before that time, no matter how strong a child's inclinations may be in certain directions, they feel that he will benefit more from a well-rounded experience than from specialization.

"Every parent wants the best for his child," says Francine Foley of the Camp Advisory Service. Some want the best in the sense of physical comfort, others in the sense of athletic or intellectual opportunity. But the fact remains that no matter what camp is chosen, parents should bear in mind that camping should be an experience that is different from his daily life and offers him opportunities to grow that he can get in no other way.

What Size Camp?

It is always confusing to decide whether to send a child to a large camp (150 to 200 campers) or a small one (anywhere from 25 to 100 campers). There are advantages and disadvantages in both.

A large camp often has more facilities than a small camp because it operates on a larger budget. This means that a child might have more elegant accommodations and/or a broader variety of activities to choose from. It also means that he would have a wider choice of friends than he might at a small camp, where there would be fewer campers in his age group.

On the other hand, small camps can give a child a feeling of intimacy and of being part of a large family that is not available in a larger group. In a small camp every camper has a chance to play an important part in the life of the camp as a whole, and this is most appealing to some children. A shy or timid child might feel more comfortable starting out in a small camp. It is also true, however, that if the ratio of campers to counselors is low (that is, fewer campers to each counselor), the overall size of the camp doesn't matter so much.

Full- or Part-time?

Most camps do not take campers for less than the full season. This is not true, of course, of Scout camps or others of that kind. But generally speaking, most experts feel that it takes children a full summer to develop their relationships with their fellow-campers and to consolidate their skills. On the other hand, if there is a special reason for splitting a child's summer—either because it is a financial strain to send him to camp full-time, or because of other plans—then it is best to send him to camp for the first half of the season so that he will be in on the beginning of things, making friends and getting started with others.

A Few Tips

• When you get the camp list of what your child is required to bring to camp, don't elaborate on it and send too many extras. The director knows what the child will need, and no child likes to be too different.

• Once your child is off and away, write to him regularly—chatty letters about what is going on at home. Don't stress how much you miss him, and don't give him detailed accounts of what you are doing with his brothers and sisters. Write to him about what will interest *him; his* concerns and his friends are much more interesting to him than anything else.

• Above all, when he writes at first that he is homesick and wants to come home, don't put too much stock in that. By the time the letter is mailed, he has probably forgotten all about it. If you *must* telephone, call the director and ask him what you want to know. Phoning the child will only encourage him to feel sorry for himself and make the adjustment harder for him than it needs to be. It will be easier for everyone to leave the child alone as much as possible to work things out in his own way, with his counselor's help.

Day-camps

Although sending a child to day-camp for the first time is not quite as big a break as sending him away to camp, it is still a large step and an important occasion for the whole family. Because the child is younger, his feelings about leaving home for the entire day will be somewhat the same as his older siblings' about going away to a resident camp for the first time.

If a child has not gone to some kind of day-camp by the time he is six, it is time to start thinking about it. Children need other children and the kind of learning that every good day-camp provides. In fact, even if he lives in the country or in the suburbs, at day-camp he will enjoy learning how to swim, how to work with craft materials, and how to compete at games in a different way than if he spends his time at the local swimming area or playground. Day-camp will provide him with an opportunity to learn how to play in a group and to develop new skills that should help him during the rest of the year.

There are few special do's or don'ts about when to send a child to day-camp, or where. All that has been said about choosing resident camps applies to day-camps, except for the qualification about distance. A day-camp should not be too far from home, since the child will have to make the trip there and back every day. It should not be more than 45 minutes away, at the most, so that he will not be overtired and can enjoy his time at home with his family and friends at the end of the day.

Farm Vacations

Farm and Ranch Vacation Guide ($2.50), with Adventure Trip Supplement. Farm and Ranch Vacations, Inc., 36 East 57th Street, New York, N.Y. 10022.

This guide covers the United States and Canada; lists fly-in vacations accessible only by small plane; and indicates where children are welcome, with or without families.

Dude Ranch Vacations. Dude Ranchers Association, Billings, Montana 59101.

Country Inns and Back Roads ($2.95). Berkshire Traveler Press, Stockbridge, Massachusetts 01262.
Covers all parts of the United States.

Long and Short Trips

Mobil Guides ($1.95 each). Simon & Schuster, Inc., 630 Fifth Avenue, New York, N.Y. 10020.
Northeast, Northwest, Great Plains States, Southeast, Great Lakes area, California and the West. Includes what to do, where to stay, where to eat, what to see.

AAA Publications. 1712 G Street, N.W., Washington, D.C. 20006.
Available free to members. *Tour Guides:* Northeast, Northwest, Southeast, Middle Eastern States, Florida, North Central States, South Central States, Great Lakes, California and Nevada. *Travel Guide to the Caribbean. Traveling with Pets.*

Off the Beaten Path by Norman D. Ford ($2.50). Harian Publications, Stony Hollow Road, Greenlawn, N.Y. 11740.
United States and Canada – inexpensive vacations undiscovered by most tourists in beautiful surroundings and/or places of historic interest.

Auto-Europe, Trip Planner Atlas and Guide by Bert W. Lief ($2.95). French and European Publications, 610 Fifth Avenue, New York, N.Y. 10020.
Includes roads, time and distance calculator, ferries, border information, permits, rules of the road, currency conversion tables, telephone information.

Ski, Annual Ski Guide ($2.95). Rand-McNally, Inc., P.O. Box 7600, Chicago, Illinois 60680.

Family Travel Fun ($1.95). Rand-McNally, Inc., P.O. Box 7600, Chicago, Illinois 60680.

Camping

Trailering Parks and Camp Grounds ($5.95). Woodall's Publishing Company, 500 Hyacinth Place, Highland Park, Illinois 60035.
Outstanding book of its kind. Describes facilities, costs, where to rent trailers, etc. Identifies special character of each campsite and activities available in each area. Covers the United States, Canada, Mexico, Central America.

Campground and Trailer Park Guide ($4.95). Rand-McNally, Inc., P.O. Box 7600, Chicago, Illinois 60680.
Similar to Woodall, but not as exhaustive and easier to read. Covers the United States and Canada.

Campgrounds in Virgin Islands National Park (St. John). Virgin Islands Government Tourist Office, 16 West 49th Street, New York, N.Y. 10020.

Campgrounds of the Caribbean (Jamaica). 54 West 56th Street, New York, N.Y. 10019.

Eastern Camp Grounds and *Western Camp Grounds.* American Automobile Association, 1712 G Street, N.W., Washington, D.C. 20006.
Available free of charge to members.

Camping and Caravanning in France, Michelin Guide ($3.00). French and European Publications, 610 Fifth Avenue, New York, N.Y. 10020.

The Campers' Bible by Bill Riviere ($1.95). Doubleday, Inc., 277 Park Avenue, New York, N.Y. 10017.
Truly a bible for beginning campers, and helpful to everyone. Information about tents, utensils, campfires, safety, food, etc.

Food for Knapsackers by Hasse Bunnelle ($1.95). Sierra Club, 1050 Mills Tower, San Francisco, California 94104.

Green Mountain Club. 108 Merchants Row, Rutland, Vermont 05701.

Appalachian Trail Conference. 1916 Sunderland Place, N.W., Washington, D.C. 20036.

Appalachian Mountain Club. 5 Jay Street, Boston, Massachusetts 02108.

Homes Away from Home

Home Exchange Directory ($8.50). Vacation Exchange Club, 663 Fifth Avenue, New York, N.Y. 10022.
This directory may also be obtained through a local Pan American Airways agent. To make a home exchange, write for a subscription form to list it; you will receive a directory listing homeowners all over the world who want to

exchange their homes for varying periods of time.

At Home Abroad. 136 East 57th Street, New York, N.Y. 10022. Fee, $15.
An agency that arranges rentals from cottages to villas for a week or a year in any part of Europe, Israel, and the Caribbean area. Fee is applicable to rental.

Resident Camps

National Directory of Accredited Camps. American Camping Association. Bradford Woods, Martinsville, Indiana 46151.
Includes listings of specialized camps by category. Parents of children with special needs or preferences should indicate these when sending in their request, and they will receive special reference notations along with the directory. The ACA also publishes seven regional directories and will provide information on day-camps.

An Accredited Private Camp for Your Child. Association of Private Camps, 55 West 42nd Street, New York, N.Y. 10036.
Covers the Eastern Seaboard only.

Advisory Council for Camps (a subsidiary of School and College Advisory Center). 366 Madison Avenue, New York, N.Y. 10017.

Advisory Service on Private Schools and Camps. 500 Fifth Avenue, New York, N.Y. 10036.

New York Times Camp Advisory Service. *The New York Times,* Times Square, New York, N.Y. 10036.

The Easter Seal Directory of Resident Camps for Persons with Special Health Needs. National Easter Seal Association for Crippled Children and Adults, 2023 West Ogden Avenue, Chicago, Illinois 60612.
Includes information on camps for children with emotional and mental impairments, as well as children with physical disabilities.

Directory of Resident Summer Camps Under the Auspices of Jewish Communal Organizations. National Jewish Welfare Board, 15 East 26th Street, New York, N.Y. 10010.
Covers all of the United States and Canada; many of these camps will take campers of other faiths.

Directory of Jewish-Sponsored Camps. Jewish Camp Information Services, Dept. D-71, Box 572 FDR Station, New York, N.Y. 10022.
List of all camps supported by Federation of Jewish Philanthropies of New York and some other Jewish organizations. Identify age and sex of child when requesting directory. Also serves disabled children.

Scout Camps, Boys. Consult nearest Scout office or Troop Leader. *Girls.* Girl Scouts of America National Headquarters, 830 Third Avenue, New York, N.Y. 10022; your local troop, or the nearest National Branch Office in: Boston, Massachusetts; Washington, D.C.; Atlanta, Georgia; Chicago, Illinois; Kansas City, Missouri; or Burlingame, California.

Day Camps

Directory of Day Camps Conducted by Jewish Community Centers. National Jewish Welfare Board, 15 East 26th Street, New York, N.Y. 10010.
Covers United States and Canada.

12
Health: Your Concern And Your Child's

"My soul lives in my body's house . . ."
Doubt—Sara Teasdale

CHILDREN TAKE HEALTH for granted—but their parents don't! It takes a certain degree of maturity and experience to realize that good health is something to be treasured—and has to be nurtured. High spirits, wonder, and excitement are commonplace to the healthy child, but parents know all too well how painfully absent these feelings are when a child is sick. Most parents don't spend much time worrying about those sick days. They know that colds, headaches, stomachaches, and the like are all a part of growing up, and they take such minor ills in their stride. There are some parents, however, who feel that every day brings a new threat to their children's health. They worry about illness before it happens, and when their children are sick, they hover over them anxiously.

Parents' attitudes toward health affect their children's. Just as in every other aspect of living, parents are the interpreters; children respond to sickness largely in terms of how their parents do.

Children of parents who are realistic about health have positive attitudes about the prevention of illness. They have been taught good health habits since their earliest years, and they expect good health—not illness. When these children do get sick, they have the advantage of optimism to help them get well, and that is half the cure. Children of anxious parents don't fare quite so well. They often adopt their parents' anxieties about illness, and they tend to become sick more frequently than other children, perhaps because this is what they expect.

Parents who worry and fuss excessively make their children uncomfortable about their bodies and about themselves. For example, many a young girl has grown into adulthood to discover to her surprise that she is pretty and slim, although for years she had seen herself as fat because of her parents' constant concern with weight and diet. Many a child has gone off to camp for the summer to find that he enjoys everything that is put before him and that his digestion is not as fragile as his parents had led him to believe.

A parent's first job in guarding a child's health is thus to give him a realistic perspective on himself and his environment. This is hard to do; but it all goes back to principles we have discussed before, the need to help children to confront reality as best we are able.

Unless a child learns when there is real cause for concern and when there is not, he will not be able to recognize genuine dangers or to set sensible limits for himself. He will not be able to anticipate rationally what will happen when he crosses a street, when he climbs a tree, when he stays up late, or when he eats too much. As he gets older, the list gets longer; but no list can be long enough to forewarn a child of all the dangers he may confront in life; he has to become able to see them for himself.

The best foundation for health that a parent can supply is healthy habits, sound information about what a child needs to know, and above all, a feeling of confidence in himself.

Teaching Good Health Habits

The first steps in teaching a child the rudiments of health care should already have been taken before he reaches the age of six. From the beginning, a child must be helped to feel that he shares the responsibility for the care of his own health, and that he cannot push this responsibility onto his parents as if it were solely *their* job to care for him.

He must be taught habits of cleanliness and safety right from the start. He must learn to wash his hands after play, after he goes to the bathroom, and before meals. He must learn to bathe regularly, to brush or comb his hair, to clean his nails (and later to see that they are trimmed), to brush his teeth, and to change his clothes regularly.

He must learn to do all these things because he *wants* to. This will not come about all at once. At first, most children "don't have time" for such routines unless they are reminded (pestered, sometimes) by their parents. But gradually they will become more cooperative as they begin to understand the logic behind what we are asking them to do.

The important thing is to see that our child does these things himself—for himself—as he becomes increasingly more able. Even though he does not clean his own nails as well as we could clean them, it is far more important that he learn to do it alone. The more we can equip our child to be self-sufficient along these line, the healthier he will be.

Diet

All children need a well-balanced diet to grow on. Certain foods contain vitamins and other nutrients that are important to help their bodies do the work they must do in these developing years. Some doctors believe in supplementing a child's diet with vitamin pills or drops; others do not. In any case, the fact that our friends give vitamins to their children, or that the advertisements all say it is the thing to do, is not reason enough to put our child on a regimen of vitamins without first consulting our doctor.

Milk is an essential in every child's diet (unless he is allergic to it). If we can't get our child to drink it, maybe he will eat it in the form of custards, ice cream, or cheese. In addition to milk, our child should have foods every day in each of these categories:

• Fruits and vegetables – children often like an assortment of raw vegetables for a snack (raw string beans, peas, carrots, celery, radishes, cauliflower)
• Meat, fish, or eggs
• Potatoes, rice, cereals, bread, noodles, or spaghetti
• Margarine or butter
• Sugar

Sample Menu

Breakfast:	Citrus fruit (high in vitamin C), juice, berries, or melon Cereal, bread or muffins, or pancakes, etc. (preferably whole grain or enriched grain) Egg (one or two depending on appetite) Toast Milk
Midmorning Snack:	Juice
Lunch:	Soup or vegetable (can be raw vegetable) Salad or sandwich Milk
After-school or Midafternoon Snack:	Juice, fruit, raw vegetables, cold cereal and milk, or cheese and crackers
Supper:	Meat, fish, poultry, cheese, or eggs Vegetables, varied Salad Milk or fruit dessert Milk
Bedtime Snack:	Milk, cookies

(These foods may be combined in stews, casseroles, etc. Substitutes can be made in one meal for another; for example, instead of bread for breakfast, spaghetti for supper; instead of egg for breakfast, meat or fish for lunch.)

Sodas and candies should be avoided as much as possible, but they can still be used as treats for special occasions.

Sleep

Although the amount of sleep needed varies from child to child, most children need less sleep as they get older. At the age of six, a child probably needs from ten to twelve hours of sleep a day. Some children continue to need that much until they are nine or ten, but after that age many begin to manage with nine hours and still be bright-eyed when they get up in the morning.

The amount of sleep a child needs depends upon his general health, how much and how fast his energy is consumed during the day, and how fast he is growing. His state of mind also influences his need for sleep. When a child is happy, he usually requires less sleep than when he is not. When a child is troubled, he finds it harder to get up in the morning to face a new day, and he is exhausted at night just from trying to cope.

The temperature of a child's room should not be too high for comfortable sleep. His bed should be made the way he likes it, and even until the age of ten, he should be allowed a favorite toy to sleep with if he wants it. A private talk with a parent before he goes to sleep can put him at ease and prepare him for a quiet night.

Exercise

Although some children require more exercise than others to bring about a feeling of health and well-being, all children need some physical activity. Growing boys and girls need to develop muscles strong enough to support their increasing size and to promote good posture.

Children should be encouraged to be active either in group sports or individually, not only because it's "good for them," but also – and just as important – because it's fun. While they are involved in hitting a ball, running a race, or climbing a tree, they don't have time to think about their problems. A child should have some physical activity every day, outdoors, if possible.

Posture

Good posture distributes the weight of the body evenly so that there is no undue strain to create pains and fatigue. It encourages the muscles to do their proper jobs, and it prevents distortions of the body that may be difficult to correct later on.

What's more, good posture is a major element in good looks and beauty. Try it yourself and see how good it feels.

Some Factors Affecting Growth

The "average child" is only a statistic. That is why modern height and weight charts are no longer calculated in precise figures. Instead, the figures for a child's normal growth are stated in ranges that allow for a wide variety of differences. For example, according to a chart of weight and height issued by the Children's Medical Center of Boston, Massachusetts, a boy of nine is within the normal range if his height is anywhere from 47 to 57 inches and his weight from 50 to 60 pounds. The permissible variation is similar for girls. Thus, it is clear that children the same age can vary enormously in both dimensions. Since all children undergo a growth spurt in the years just before puberty, variations become even more marked then.

Through his genes, a child inherits his tendency to grow rapidly or slowly, to be small or tall, stocky or slender. These characteristics are passed down from generation to generation, and although children may look very different from their parents, their size has still been predetermined by their ancestors. Although environmental factors decide whether or not a child achieves his full potential growth, nothing can extend or diminish that potential, which was determined before he was born.

Boys and girls differ in their growth patterns. Boys are generally bigger at birth, and when they reach puberty they usually grow larger than girls in all dimensions, including height. During the years from one to nine, however, the rate of growth for girls and boys remains more or less the same. After that age, girls will be taller for several years, since they mature earlier; boys will begin to catch up and usually even surpass the girls as they approach puberty, a few years later.

Other Factors Influencing Growth

Experts have long known that a child's economic and social environment influences growth: children from middle and upper classes tend to be taller and sturdier than others. This is because they are generally in better health. They eat regular well-balanced meals, get the proper amount of sleep, get more outdoor exercise, and receive better medical care. Generally speaking, the healthier the child's environment, the better he will grow.

The influence of race and climate on growth has not yet been fully evaluated. Experts presently feel that the influence of these factors are negligible except as they are related to a child's socioeconomic status. Although children, especially girls, mature earlier in warm climates, this does not mean after maturation they will be any taller than their counterparts in the temperate zones. The correlation between Negro, white, and Japanese children remains the same when children from the same social and economic levels are compared.

The Small Child

Despite the fact that there is a wide range within which a child's height can be considered normal, both the very small child and the very tall child suffer disadvantages that can be troubling.

Parents and teachers often forget that although a child is much smaller than his classmates, in most areas he is capable of the same achievements as the others. They tend to "baby" such children and to be surprised when they perform well. Such underexpectation can be damaging.

If a child is not expected to "keep up," the chances are that he won't. If his parents are continually urging him to eat in order to grow, or to exercise in order to stretch, his feelings about himself will not be happy ones. As we know all too well, unhappy children rarely make the most of themselves, and the short child who suffers from feelings of inferiority because of his size is no exception.

If our child is very short for his age, it is up to us to help him know that size is no measure of worth. We can steer him away from activities that might bring failure because of his size and help him to develop self-confidence in what he can do well.

The Tall Child

Tall children also have problems. Their parents and teachers often expect more of them than they can deliver. A tall child of seven is no better coordinated or more intellecually capable than his classmates just because he is taller.

A tall child needs the same degree of protective concern as any other child his age. No matter what a child's size, short or tall, he must be helped to like himself as he is. In order to do that, we must show him first how much we like him just that way.

Illness

Outside of the usual diseases of childhood, children are generally quite healthy during the years from six through ten. Respiratory infections account for most of their absences from school, and they rarely suffer from serious illness.

Children do vary in their susceptibility to illness. Some seem to be sick all the time, whereas others are rarely sick. Whatever their health pattern may be, however, all children are more vulnerable to illness at some times than at others.

For example, a child is more likely to become sick when he is tense and tired than when he is in good spirits. His whole physical condition is often affected by his mood, and his "You make me sick" or "It gives me a headache" may be perfectly true.

Psychosomatic Illness

Illnesses that are the result of bodily changes brought about by feelings are called "psychosomatic" illnesses. Contrary to popular notion, they are *not* imaginary; they are very real. For example, when a child is tense or severely troubled, his muscles may tighten, his teeth may clench, and his glands may respond to the extra demands put upon them by producing more or less of whatever they are supposed to produce. All this is a normal response to stress that is experienced by animals and humans alike.

Even teeth can be affected by our feelings. Clenching the teeth can loosen or even break them. The extra acid that the body produces to cope with tension can erode the enamel, causing cavities and possible damage to the gums.

Colds and allergies are often the result of infections in mucous membranes of the nose and throat that have become dried out because of emotional strain. Most of us have had the experience of being so frightened that our mouth and throat felt dry (those mucous membranes again!), or so scared that we began to sweat in the cold (sweat glands overreacting), or so emotionally upset that we felt nauseated (stomach muscles overreacting).

The list of psychosomatic illnesses is long, and children suffer from many of them: asthma, chronic fatigue, persistently recurring colds, constipation, diarrhea, colitis, hives, stomach cramps, chronic allergies and headaches, to name only a few. These conditions often disappear for a while, only to reappear when life becomes too much.

Signs of Trouble

Parents are usually able to handle most of a child's small crises. The banged finger, the bruised knee, the sniffly nose, the upset stomach, and even a high fever all seem pretty much routine by the time their child is six. Parents get to know their children's idiosyncrasies, like the fact that Josh needs lots of sleep whereas Amy doesn't, that David breaks out in hives from strawberries, and that when Karen gets a cold it always goes to her sinuses. They don't have to call the doctor very often about symptoms they are familiar with. It is the unfamiliar ones that are troublesome.

Any sudden change in behavior can be a sign of trouble. For example, when a child who has always been "a good sleeper" suddenly becomes sleepless and restless at night, when a lively child suddenly becomes lethargic, or when schoolwork takes a downward plunge, it is time to take a good look at what's going on.

Although such fluctuations in behavior are to be expected in the normal course of growing up, they should not be neglected; and if they persist over a long period of time, they should be taken seriously enough to be called to the attention of a professional.

This also applies to changes in bowel habits (persistent constipation or diarrhea), changes in eating habits (loss of appetite or a sudden voracious hunger), and any pain that is unusual and continues for any length of time. Children this age often feel pains in their legs and arms—what used to be called "growing pains." Now that it has been discovered that such pains can have a variety of causes, it is best to draw them to the doctor's attention if they persist.

Recurrent colds, allergies, sweating, fainting, frequent vomiting, tremors or shortness of breath, all are symptoms that the doctor should be told about.

In other words, parents must be able to strike a balance between being vigilant and taking it easy. This is not simple, and most of us occasionally seesaw between the two extremes.

The important thing to remember is to make every effort to really *see* our child every day, just as we try to *hear* what he is telling us in one way or another. Health care is no different from all the rest of child care. It demands the same willingness to open ourselves to reality and to teach our child to do the same.

The Pediatrician

Annual visits to the pediatrician are essential to good health care. But giving checkups and prescribing medicines are only part of what the modern pediatrician sees as his job. He sees his job as having as much to do with reassuring parents and preventing illness as with curing it. It is important to look upon our child's pediatrician as a source of advice whenever we are troubled about our child, but it is equally important to know that we can take care of a lot of minor concerns.

Most pediatricians are busy people, and they don't have time to spend on issues that are a matter of common sense. We can free our doctor to spend more time with us when we really need his advice if we remember that he cares for many children, of whom ours is only one.

Eyes

When we visit the pediatrician for our child's annual checkup, he will probably examine the child from top to toe. We shall discuss in detail here only one of the items in the examination, one that has special relevance now that our child is in school. Eye examinations are a routine part of every checkup. Even before a child can read, he is tested with a special eye chart that has shapes instead of letters. Later on he graduates to an adult chart. Most pediatricians feel that this examination, together with an inspection of the child's eyes with a specially lighted instrument, is enough to help them detect any visual disabilities in most children.

If our child is referred to a specialist for glasses, however, we should be sure that he is made to feel comfortable about them. Most children, as a matter of fact, *wish* for glasses; they are objects of envy for many children who don't wear them. The problem in acceptance of glasses most often lies with parents.

Parents need to watch themselves for signs of eye trouble, as children may not realize that they have a problem. The book *How to Protect Your Child* by Gene Accas and John H. Eckstein gives a list of warning signs that may alert parents to incipient eye troubles.

Teeth

A child's teeth are no less important to his health than the rest of his body. Modern dentists have long recognized that teeth can influence—and be influenced by—a child's overall physical and emotional condition. So it is important to teach our child to respect and preserve his teeth.

When he is about six years old, a child begins to get his permanent teeth, the ones he will have for the rest of his life. His "six-year molars" will appear behind the "baby teeth" already in his mouth. Between the ages of six and ten he will lose most of his first teeth, beginning usually at six or seven with the lower central incisors (two lower front teeth), then the upper central incisors (two upper front teeth), and at eight or nine the upper and lower lateral incisors (side "eye" teeth). The first and second bicuspids (the double-pointed teeth next to the "eye" teeth) appear between the ages of ten and twelve, and the "twelve-year molars" complete the mouth until the "wisdom teeth" appear in the late teens or early twenties.

Every child should visit the dentist twice a year to have his teeth cleaned and examined for possible cavities. Some parents worry about a child's exposure to the X rays that many dentists use to discover hidden spots of decay in teeth. Experts tell us, however, that the procedure is now so refined that a child is exposed to the X rays very briefly and locally (only the mouth itself is exposed), and that this eliminates the possibility of any danger to the child.

At home, the child should brush his teeth twice daily and rinse his mouth with lukewarm water to dislodge any particles of food. Some children enjoy selecting their own flavored mouthwash, and it may help them to remember to brush their teeth because they enjoy using it. It may also help to buy the child a special bathroom cup or install a container of disposable paper cups; this can sometimes ease the tedium of brushing and help in establishing a healthy habit.

"Braces," or Orthodontia

The purpose of "braces" (corrective dental appliances) is to direct the growth of the jaws and the positioning of permanent teeth in order to make room for teeth where they belong. Although a child's mouth and jaws continue to grow along with his body until he reaches his full growth, his permanent teeth are the same size when they begin to emerge at age six as they will be for the rest of his life. This means that sometimes a child's permanent teeth are too big for the spaces allotted to them in his small mouth, and they come in crooked and may cause a distortion of his occlusion (sometimes called "articulation"), or "bite."

Unless a child's occlusion is seriously out of line, most orthodontists prefer to wait until a child is about twelve years old to fit him with corrective dental appliances. As the twelve-year molars take their places in the mouth, they may again change the alignment of a child's teeth or his occlusion, so that corrective work done before these molars appear may have to be done again. Of course, if the teeth do not meet sufficiently well for him to chew properly, or if the alignment is so crooked that it disfigures the child, braces are necessary at an earlier age.

As with every other part of a child's body, the mouth has its own regenerative powers. A minor malocclusion or minor crookedness may correct itself by the time a child is twelve or so. As the mouth grows to make room for new teeth, earlier arrivals may be pushed into their proper place and nature will have done its own work again.

Some dentists also believe that corrective applicances are a psychological intrusion in the mouth that children under twelve can tolerate less comfortably than older ones. In addition, the care of these appliances, the job of keeping them clean, is more burdensome to a young child, who does not really appreciate the end result of orthodontia anyway, than to an older child, who is more competent and more realistically concerned with his appearance and health.

When a Child Is Sick

Every once in a while a child may say he feels sick and wants to stay home from school. Even though he has no fever and there seems not to be anything really wrong,

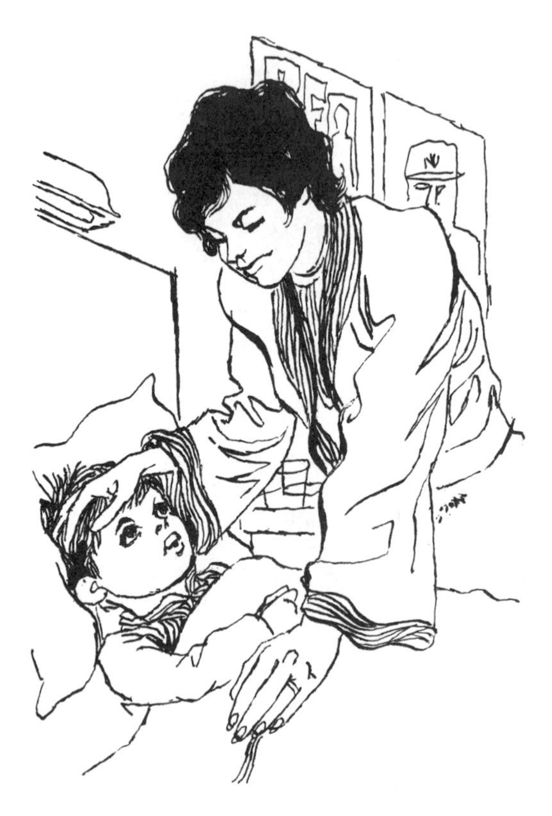

why not give him a day off? Everyone needs a day off now and then, to get some relief from the pressures of living and to gain a new perspective. If the child knows that we recognize this as a valid reason for staying home, he won't have to pretend to himself and to us that he is sick when things get too much for him.

That day at home can be better than tonics or medicine. He will need us to baby him, to make him rest in bed, to leave him alone to think things through for himself, and perhaps to be available to talk things over with him later on. We would not want, of course, to reward such behavior with special treats or trips. Besides, he needs a quiet day for collecting himself and putting things together.

There are other times, however, when our child really is sick. He wakes up in the morning with a fever, or with vomiting or a cough, and has to stay home whether he wants to or not. How he takes it depends largely on our attitude toward illness in general and toward him in particular.

If we can take illness in our stride, with all its discomforts and inconveniences, our child will feel that way about it, too, after a while. A child whose parents feel like that, who give him all the sympathy and attention he needs when he is sick without making a fuss about it, is usually able to accept his uncomfortable feelings without complaining too much and to cooperate in what is being done to help him.

Of course, if we have been up half the night with him, or have had to miss a party we had been looking forward to, it is pretty hard to be sympathetic and casual. There is no way to pretend that we aren't tired or disappointed, or to be cheerful about bedpans or inhalers. As long as parents don't make the child feel guilty about it, or responsible, there is no reason to hide their true feelings from him. Our honesty about our feelings can help him come to terms with his own. After all, his illness is just another shared family experience. Even parents are ill at one time or another and need other members of the family to help out. That's what families are for.

Unfortunately, not all parents are able to look upon illness so philosophically. They view being sick as a calamity, a punishment, or a curse. They feel as if fate has played an unkind trick on them—and their children feel the same. A child who absorbs attitudes like this will react to being sick with feelings of anger and fear. At the very time that he needs most to be comforted, he will feel guilty, as if he had done something wrong.

Guilt is fostered by comments such as, "If you had put your sweater on yesterday, as I told you, you wouldn't be sick today," or "See, I told you not to eat so much candy." Such reproaches don't help; they only make things worse. In addition to guilt, the child builds up a defiance toward his parents that can lead to his using illness as a weapon against them.

Your Doctor and Medication

More and more physicians are moving away from giving medication to children for minor illnesses. Unless a child really needs an antibiotic or other drug, unless he can get well in no other way, the cautious pediatrician will prescribe only aspirin to relieve fever and discomfort. He feels that the body has such regenerative and curative powers that it can do the job better than any medicine, even if it takes a little longer.

But too many parents don't want to wait for the body to do its own work. Since the discovery of antibiotics, many parents try to push their pediatricians into prescribing such medication to hurry up the process of getting well. This is neither good medicine nor common sense. Not only does the indiscriminate use of antibiotics build up a resistance to drugs that a child may need to fight a more serious illness, but it may inculcate attitudes toward drug use that can be dangerous later on.

When Your Child Is Seriously Ill

When a child is seriously ill, all other issues become secondary. At a time like that, every parent is naturally worried, and it is hard not to hover anxiously over the child. This is a time when we need to be strong. It is not the time to share our anxieties with our child or reveal our own doubts and fears.

When a child is very sick, anxious behavior will only frighten him. However, we must impress the seriousness of the situation upon him, without showing anxiety, in order to obtain his cooperation in the task of getting well. We must be as firm with him in illness as in health. We can help him to be optimistic by encouraging him and by being optimistic ourselves. Determination to get well is a large part of any cure.

Preventing Accidents

The statistics on childhood accidents are frightening. About 15,000 children die each year from accidents that could have been prevented, and the largest percentage of these occur in the home. Thousands more children suffer from some physical injury that requires a doctor's attention. Accidents are the foremost health problem for children.

Although much progress has been made in discovering medicines to prevent and cure most of the illnesses of childhood, the same cannot be said about accident prevention. However, there are certain precautions that help to prevent accidents:

• *Train his body.* Helping a child to develop a sense of control over his body will help him to avoid accidents. Children who are at home with their physical selves are less likely to feel awkward and ill at ease and thus less likely to have falls and bumps and other accidents of this nature.

• *Avoid fatigue.* Studies have shown that children are much more susceptible to accidents when they are tired. In fact, statistics show that the largest proportion of accidents among school-age children occurs in the late afternoon and early evening.

• *Be alert to troubled feelings.* When children are under stress, they are more likely to have accidents than at other times. If the child appears to be disturbed about something, we should try to help him talk his feelings out. All children are more vulnerable when they are feeling angry or preoccupied with a problem.

Teaching Safety at Home

Even a schoolchild will not always remember all the safety rules that we taught him when he was younger. Children of six through ten still need to be reminded about knives, gas stoves, matches, and other household hazards. It is still the best policy to keep medicines in a locked cupboard or, if that is not possible, on a high shelf of the medicine cabinet. Even though the child can now climb, why not get them out of temptation's way?

Since the child is no longer a baby, the best safety education lies not in keeping him away from all potentially hazardous equipment and objects, but in teaching him about their use. If we gradually let him help us more and more in the kitchen with using knives and other sharp instruments, he will be less likely to want to try them out on his own. If we teach him how to cut safely, he will not be as susceptible to accidents of this kind. We can teach him what plastic bags are for and what they are *not* for. We can show him how to put pot handles toward the back of the stove so that no one will get scalded by accidentally knocking over a boiling pot.

The same applies to gas stoves and electric burners. Girls and boys love to cook. If they are given the opportunity to light the stove once in a while under adult supervision, they will not be so tempted to do it when no one is around. We can also let the child light a match when we need one every now and then, and explain how easily he can burn his fingers and how matches cause fires if they are not properly extinguished.

Although at this age the child is not likely to confuse medicine with candy, as he might have when he was a baby, there is still danger in leaving medicine lying around the house. The dangers now lie in the possibility that our child might try to "cure" himself by himself if he doesn't feel well when we are not at home, or that, if he is a bit older, he might experiment with a pill because a friend has told him about the "high" one can get from pills.

The best protection against these possibilities is to impress upon our child that medicines are to be used only when the doctor tells us to. We should explain that medicines are chemicals; each causes special reactions in the body, and each thus has a very specific purpose. If medicines are used for purposes other than the ones for which they were intended, they can cause serious trouble.

Again, we must be good models for our children. By showing respect for what medicine can do and by not using it indiscriminately ourselves, we will help him to absorb these same attitudes.

Toys are often another source of preventable accidents. When we buy a toy for the child, we should be sure that it has no sharp edges, that it won't spring in his face, that it won't burn him if it is electrical or has an explosive cap, and that it contains no poisonous substances. The child should be taught to put his toys away so that people, including himself, won't fall over them.

Teaching Safety in the World Outside

Parents cannot be with their children every minute of every day, nor would they want to be. The safety habits our children learn are the best protection we can give them.

• *On the streets.* When our child first starts off to school, we should accompany him to the bus stop if he goes by school bus, or to school if he walks. Depending on the traffic in the neighborhood, we will have to decide when he will be allowed to go alone. But in any case, we should continue to impress upon him the importance of looking both ways at every street crossing, of watching out for driveways, and of observing all traffic signals. Most important, we must observe these precautions ourself.

• *Bicycles, etc.* When children are on their bicycles or skates, they tend to get carried away by the speed and pleasure of the sport. We must impress upon our child that a bicycle is more than a toy and that he must observe certain rules of the road. Some communities require bicycle licensing, but even if ours does not, the child should learn certain elementary precautions. For example, if he rides on the sidewalk, he must watch out for others for his own sake as well as for theirs. If he rides in the street, he must obey local regulations about bicycle riding and keep his eyes and ears open.

• *Water safety.* The child should be taught to swim as early as possible. Many schools demand a certain proficiency in swimming in the upper grades, but while he is young is the best time to learn. The ability to swim is also the best water-safety precaution in the world. Even if a child can swim, and certainly if he cannot, it is important to impress upon him that he is *never* to go near a lake or pond or swimming pool when adults are not around. No child should ever be in a boat without a life preserver. As far as ocean bathing is concerned, he should understand that the ability to swim is sometimes no protection for either adult or child against strong waves or undertow.

Most of the time parents can handle everyday accidents themselves. Cold water, peroxide, and an adhesive bandage can take care of most of the common mishaps of childhood.

The Medicine Chest

Every home medicine cabinet should contain the following supplies:

adhesive tape
adhesive bandages
gauze
absorbent cotton
rubbing alcohol

- boric acid
- calamine lotion
- eyecup
- hydrogen peroxide
- iodine or tincture of merthiolate
- petroleum jelly (Vaseline)
- aspirin (baby or adult, depending upon what the doctor recommends)
- talcum powder
- thermometer (rectal preferred for children)
- tweezers

Special Equipment

- hand basin for bathing in bed or in case of nausea
- rubber sheeting
- inhalator
- hand bell (for a sick child to call assistance)
- quiet-time playthings (puzzles, clay, coloring books, models, etc.)

Telephone Numbers on the Wall

- pediatrician
- parent's office
- pharmacy
- hospital
- police
- neighbor or relative
- school

Animal Bites

If an animal bite does not break the skin, there may be discoloration in the immediate area of the bite, but this is not serious. If the skin is broken, first treat it like any other cut, washing it out with soap and water and applying peroxide to disinfect it. If the animal is known, all that is necessary is to check with the doctor to see if he recommends a tetanus booster shot. If the animal is not known, it is important to have it checked for rabies. Chances are that the animal is not rabid, but it is always better to err on the side of safety.

Insect Bites

First, if the stinger is still in the skin, remove it with tweezers. Then, if no symptoms occur other than a mild redness and swelling, wash the area with cold water and apply a bit of household ammonia or bicarbonate of soda paste to the inflammation. Sometimes calamine lotion helps later on. If the child feels itchy all over after the bite, if there is a great deal of swelling, if he seems to be short of breath, or if his tongue and throat feel swollen, rush him to a hospital *immediately*. He will need medication to counteract an allergic reaction that can be extremely severe, even fatal, if not treated promptly.

Burns and Scalds

Although burns are caused by exposure to dry heat and scalds by steam, boiling water, or hot oil, the effects are the same. Quickly wash all minor burns in cold water. If there are no blisters, apply Vaseline and cover with gauze. If there are blisters, cover only with dry sterile gauze, allowing the area to breathe. *Do not* prick blisters. Major burns of all kinds, of course, require professional attention.

Cuts and Bleeding

Wash minor cuts with soap and water, rinse with peroxide to disinfect the wound, and cover with a sterile bandage. If the wound is in an area that will be exposed to dirt or come in contact with clothing, it is best to paint it with tincture of merthiolate. If the wound was caused by a dirty or rusty object, call the pediatrician about a possible tetanus booster.

In case of major injuries, follow the same procedure. If the bleeding continues, apply a dry sterile dressing and press on the wound to staunch the bleeding. If the cut is on an arm or a leg, elevate it to help make the blood flow less freely. Continue to apply pressure until you can get medical attention.

Nosebleeds

Nosebleeds can be caused by picking scabs in the nose, by broken capillaries (tiny veins), or by a blow on the nose. The child should sit still and breathe through his mouth. Apply ice wrapped in a towel or handkerchief to the bridge of his nose or to the area under his nose and above his mouth. He can lie down with his head *lower* than his body. He should *never* lie with his head up or at the same level as the rest of the body, because the blood flowing from the nose can clog the throat and cause choking. If the bleeding doesn't stop after a short while, the doctor should be called.

Broken Bones and Sprains

If a child appears to have a broken bone, he should not be allowed to move or put weight or pressure on the suspected break. Although a fracture is usually indicated by swelling and extreme pain, these symptoms do not always occur, and it may be hard to distinguish between a sprained joint and a break. If in doubt, see the doctor.

Sprained joints should be wrapped in cold compresses to reduce swelling. Later on the limb may need to be put in a sling, or strapped, depending upon what the doctor orders.

Head Injuries

If a child appears to have no ill effects other than discomfort after a head injury, probably nothing serious is wrong. *But,* if he faints, vomits, is extremely irritable and appears pale, or has a severe headache after such an injury, take him to a doctor or a hospital *immediately.* If the child is unconscious, keep him still and warm (not hot) until an ambulance comes, and *do not* leave him unattended.

Eye Injuries

To remove specks of dust or other *foreign objects* from the eye, pull the child's upper eyelid over the lower one. This will cause tearing, which may wash out the offending particle. If that doesn't work, use lukewarm water in an eyecup to wash out the eye. If the particle is visible on the white of the eye, use a *clean* handkerchief to remove it.

A *cut on the eye* requires professional attention.

If a child's eye is *splashed by chemicals* (household cleaners, etc.), wash out the eye by pouring *lots* of lukewarm water over it. Pull up the eyelid to see that the water gets all over the eyeball. Then place a sterile gauze pad over the eye and take the child to a doctor.

Poisons

If a child has swallowed a poisonous substance, the usual procedure is to make him vomit by tickling the back of his throat. However, vomiting *should not* be induced if he has swallowed oily substances, strong alkalis, or acids. *Never* make a child vomit when he is unconscious; call an ambulance or take him to the nearest hospital.

See the Bibliography for books on coping with accidents and other emergencies while awaiting medical assistance.

BOOK FIVE

Growing Into Adolescence

By LYNN MINTON

The author is grateful to Dr. Donald Gribetz, Clinical Professor of Pediatrics, Mt. Sinai School of Medicine, for his valuable assistance with sections of Chapter 7; and to Dr. Avrum H. Ben-Avi, Adjunct Professor of Psychology, New York University Graduate School of Arts and Sciences, and Dr. Robert T. Porter, Associate Clinical Professor of Psychiatry, Mt. Sinai School of Medicine, for insights into the relationship between parents and children.

Special thanks to my husband, my parents, and my children, who were the source of many of the ideas in this book.

Introduction

WHEN WE WERE in school, we were often told that these were "the best years of our lives." But most of us didn't believe it. When our children were babies, elderly ladies on the street would remonstrate with us not to look so harried because these were the best years of our lives. But there were too many diapers to change and too many eating schedules, there was too little time to read, and we were tired, and we didn't believe it then, either. But now that our children are growing into adolescence, life is more interesting. Now, *now* we can believe that these are the best years of our lives.

Only nobody says it any more, because everybody knows that living with children this age can be harrowing. It is, of course, but it can be immensely satisfying at the same time if we don't let the problems wear us down. That, in essence, is what this book is all about. As we gain insight into what children of eleven to fourteen are experiencing, we become more able to perceive opportunities for mutual understanding and closeness, to forge during these years a rapport with our children that will form the basis of a rewarding lifelong relationship.

There will be ideas in these pages that simply do not fit your life or your child or that go against your grain. If a suggestion is not your style, ignore it. Use what you can, build on it, shape it to fit you exactly. The Bibliography can direct you to further reading in those areas of particular interest to you. The book is arranged so that one gets an idea of the physical and emotional changes that are typical of this age before moving on to the specific problems they can create. After reading the first two chapters, there is no strong reason not to skip around, dipping first into areas that intrigue you most or that are the most pressing, if you like to read that way.

If the use of "she" for parent and "he" for child grates, please accent that "he" for parent and "she" for child would be no more accurate, and saying "he or she" in every sentence would have driven you up the wall. So, if you and your husband (or you and your wife) are lucky enough to share equally in bringing up your children, we hope you and she (or you and he) will share this book, too. It is for both of you.

everything is to-
ings went on just
een changed in the
I the same when I
almost think I can
le different. But if I'm
xt question is, Who in
am I? Ah, *that's* the great puzzle!" said Alice.

"Explain yourself!" said the caterpillar.

"I can't explain *myself,* I'm afraid, sir," said Alice, "because I'm not myself, you see."

With overwhelming suddenness, Lewis Carroll's heroine of *Alice's Adventures in Wonderland* is propelled far from the warm and comfortable shores of her childhood. She finds herself in a strange land where nothing is familiar. Most frightening of all, she finds that she *isn't* any more, but exists only in an ephemeral state of *becoming.*

Surely that is a story of this time in the lives of our children when strong and inexorable forces inside them thrust them toward adulthood. Their bodies change and grow faster than at any other time in their lives, except for their first year. But becoming an adult is not just a question of growing bigger. It involves a disruption of the entire functioning, physical, emotional, intellectual, of the child so that he can, in effect, create himself anew. The metamorphosis from child to adult takes about eight or ten years. This book is concerned only with its beginning, the years from eleven to fourteen, a critical time whose most significant happening is the crisis we call puberty and its aftermath, adolescence.

As every parent knows, no child can fit neatly into someone's stereotype of a particular age group, and least of all, the child growing into adolescence. Nevertheless, this chapter will offer a brief survey of how children in general develop during these years, to provide a rough idea of what to expect and to serve as a general introduction to the rest of the book.

Growth Toward Puberty

The coming of puberty is heralded about two years before its appearance by a sudden spurt of growth. In girls, the spurt occurs at about ten or eleven, and in boys an average of two years later, although there is a wide variation within the normal range. During a time of relative stability and peace, just when a child had learned how to be a satisfactory child—how to function at home and at school, how to cope with his parents—he is suddenly jolted from within. Perhaps he has been gaining four to five pounds a year. Now a boy will gain thirteen to fourteen pounds and shoot up four to five inches, and a girl will acquire eleven pounds and three to four inches in a year. The growth in height and weight is accompanied by other changes. The girl's breasts begin to bud and then bloom, her hips to widen. She becomes softer and rounder. The boy's shoulders broaden, down grows on his upper lip and chin, and he becomes more muscular and angular. Pubic and underarm hair grows. The voice becomes deeper and fuller. Limbs stretch out faster than the trunk, producing the typical "all arms and legs" appearance. And, of course, the genital organs and the reproductive system begin to develop and soon will be ready to function.

Emotional Pressure

In addition, the glandular functioning has its effect upon his emotions as well as his contours. He becomes moody and restless. He has to be moving, to be on the go. His hands cannot be still. He fiddles with knives and forks and knocks over ketchup bottles, twists his hair while he reads, picks his nose and his nails, cracks his knuckles, worries the hole in the elbow of his sweater, sometimes has a facial tic or other nervous mannerism, and bounces balls off the floor, wall, and ceiling until they resound inside his mother's head. Living with him can be nerve-racking.

Incredibly sensitive, he can pick a fight out of the air. "You made beef stew for supper because you *know* I hate it." Sometimes he seems to be raw to every possibility of hurt. We ask what is the matter and are told, "I don't know; I just feel rotten, that's all." Or, "Can't you leave me alone for once?"

Outbursts of anger may be followed by

elation, crying spells by a spurt of constructive activity; he is enormously resilient. The same child who said on Sunday, "Sure I'll help," retorts on Monday, "Whaddya think I am, your slave or something?" Warm and friendly at times, stubborn, disobedient, and unruly at others, the child of this age can be definitely characterized as unpredictable.

We comment, "Your hair looks lovely pulled back like that."

And she jumps on us, "It does not. It looks awful and you know it."

We suggest, "Wouldn't it be a good idea to do your homework now and play later?"

And he retorts, "Wouldn't it be a good idea to let a person do his own thinking?"

As they approach puberty, children become ever more curious and eager for sexual knowledge, buying *Playboy* magazine like international spies at newsstands far from home and giggling and trading misinformation with friends. A boy is interested in the sensations and size of his penis and anxiously makes comparisons. Girls who have not yet begun to develop find their early-maturing friends drawing away from them toward other interests, and they wonder when it will be their turn. Both sexes are still likely to be uneasy with each other. A boy will tease a girl he likes and be generally unbearable to her. A girl will tend to be aggressive, not very feminine, and perhaps rude to the boys, and she will whisper and giggle about them with her girl friends.

Sooner or later, whether it is wished for or dreaded, puberty arrives. The girl begins to menstruate; the boy becomes capable of ejaculation. The time of this occurrence varies considerably. The average age of menarche in girls is about twelve or thirteen, and the average age of first ejaculation in boys is about fifteen, but the normal range extends for several years before and after.

Social Maturation

The difference in social maturation is especially apparent in seventh grade. At parties one can see some boys and girls gyrating sensuously opposite each other to the insistent beat of the music, while others cluster in groups of the same sex and still others play tag, or (boys, mostly) indulge in target practice with peanuts, or play "fountain" with shaken-up bottles of ginger ale. The seventh-grade classroom has little girls in the front row, while squeezed behind their desks in the rear, tall as their mothers and fully blossoming, sit young women of the same age. As a group, the girls tend to tower over the boys in the class at this point and to find most of them babyish and silly.

But the variations are enormous, and development is often uneven. A girl may menstruate and have the contours of a fourteen-year-old and yet behave like an eleven-year-old and cling to the ways of childhood. Or she may behave like a young woman, menstruate, and yet have a preadolescent shape. The various parts of the body grow at different rates of speed, so that at any given time the whole may be out of proportion, disharmonious. That is why youngsters of this age are often awkward, tripping over their own feet, unable to predict the distance between their elbows and lamps and vases. A young person at puberty may fluctuate between childhood and adolescence, sometimes touching both shores within minutes, belonging nowhere, out of step with his own body, and finding no place in his world that truly fits him.

Of course, size and weight, body shape, hairiness, muscularity, breast development, and size of genitals vary not only because of a child's stage of development but also because of his inheritance. Normal variations from the prevailing ideals of femininity and masculinity can make a young person utterly miserable. Frail stature in a boy or a flat chest in a girl—"God just forgot me, that's all," cried one fourteen-year-old—can initiate an all-consuming preoccupation with repairing the "defect." A boy will do push-ups and lift weights every morning and night. A girl will perform breast-developing exercises, followed by daily measurement and the studying of herself in the bathroom mirror—front view, left side, right side. A large nose may lead a child to beg for plastic surgery and set off an endless quest in magazine advertisements for products that will make it appear less noticeable.

Subjective View of Self

The young person's view of himself is, of course, highly subjective. A beautiful girl may focus narrowly on a birthmark on her arm. A homely boy may take enormous pride in his new muscles. A youngster may accept the new odors of his body or find them disgusting, ignore pimples or feel completely blemished by them. Mirrors are indispensable, and the child will search in them endlessly for the secret of who he is and how he looks to others.

A girl may suddenly find the sound of her own name detestable. Karen is a baby name, Karen is for uglies. Karen wants to know if she can change her name legally—immediately, this afternoon, so that she can inform the teachers tomorrow that they must start calling her—what? It's a problem. How to choose a new name that really embodies her new image? Ah . . . Martha! She rolls it off her tongue, writes it in script, letters it carefully, simply at first and then in ornate letters with a grand "Miss" before it. She plays with her new initials, calls up her best friends and tries "Martha" out on them. Then her little brother gets word of it and calls after her, "Marthamallow! Marthed potatoes! Marthapartha needs a bartha!" And it's all ruined! She vows to murder him, slams a door in his face—and is back to Karen again.

As the youngster begins to look more grown-up, people tend to expect more from him, and often he is not ready for that. He does not know how to behave. He may adopt a kind of protective coloration, an interim disguise, that will mask his vulnerability until he is ready to meet the world as a new person. Eccentric dress, sloppiness and dirtiness, different hair styles and manners of talking or moving—all are ways of covering up as well as trying on new images for size. A pony tail may have been right last month, but the girl must search for the right style to go with her picture of herself today. On the other hand, he may be afraid of making changes, too. We suggest a different frame for his eyeglasses, and he refuses because "everybody is used to seeing me like this."

Exaggeration is one of the keynotes of the stage. The child never just feels good, he feels *marvelous.* He is not blue, he is completely and utterly *miserable.* Her friend Jill has not been a little inconsiderate, she has been *disgusting* and will never be spoken to again.

The French writer Simone de Beauvoir, in *Memories of a Dutiful Daughter,* writes of herself shortly after her first menstrual period:

> I looked awful; my nose was turning red; on my face and the back of my neck there were pimples which I kept picking at nervously. . . . Embarrassed by my body, I developed phobias: for example, I couldn't bear to drink from a glass I had already drunk from. I had nervous tics: I couldn't stop shrugging my shoulder and twitching my nose. "Don't scratch your pimples; don't twitch your nose," my father kept telling me. Not ill-naturedly, but with complete absence of tact, he would pass remarks about my complexion, my acne, my clumsiness which only made my misery worse and aggravated my bad habits. . . . I was hovering . . . between girlhood and womanhood.

New Scope of Understanding

Before he is eleven or twelve, a child's understanding is limited greatly by what he can experience. The concept of burning, for example, is associated with the odor of smoke, the sight of blackened toast, the sensations of a burned finger, the crackle of flames. The idea of justice he can appreciate in terms of being fair, giving everyone his turn, not cheating, getting what is coming to him. But he cannot go much further. Time has to do merely with the clock and when you wake up or go somewhere, and being early or late.

Now, however, he begins to develop a new scope in his intellectual functioning. A qualitative change occurs, which is not just a question of being more intelligent or learning more. He becomes able to reason more logically, to conceptualize, to think abstractly and move from one abstraction to another. He can speculate about the many possible effects of something he wants to do. He can keep a lot of "ifs" in his head at the same time and come down to earth with an answer.

Unfortunately, the pressures of discovering his new self and striving to cope with the changes of puberty often prevent the early adolescent from fully utilizing his burgeoning intellect immediately.

Boys seem to experience urgency about sex sooner than girls and become sexually

stimulated by the nearness of a girl or the merest suggestion of a part of the female anatomy. They indulge in fantasies, daydreams, and masturbation as a normal release for this tension. They find an outlet in sports, roughhousing, and other activities for which they have enormous energy. But since their emotional equilibrium is upset, they expend much of their energy just trying to maintain control of themselves. Often this control is shaky; outbursts "for no reason" and other turbulent behavior are common, as well as intense fatigue. The inner demands on their energy may be reflected in seventh- and eighth-grade slumps in schoolwork.

Feeling of Uniqueness

A child will claim that he is not moody, that the rest of the family keeps "bugging" him. If a parent says, "Don't worry, it's just adolescence," he will bark back, "It's *not* just adolescence." He is sure that nobody ever felt this way before. If we say we know how it feels, that only shows that we don't really understand. Needing to feel unique, he nevertheless sees no contradiction in trying to be like all his friends. They are very important to him now, and his moods are often precipitated by the breaking of an old relationship or the making of a new one. Because he feels out of step, it helps to be with others who are going through the same changes. And, indeed, his main aim is to differentiate himself from his parents and their generation. The typically long telephone conversations are part of the continual dialogues that reassure him that his desires and feelings are normal.

Before puberty and just afterward, most children cling to friends of the same sex. Girls often have crushes on other girls or on female teachers or popular singers who personify their ideal or have qualities that they admire. They will often affect the mannerisms and style of such a person, with an eye more for surface detail than for substance.

Warm and sometimes intense friendships with young people of the same sex are characteristic. Girls who see each other every day may exchange letters several times a week, often addressing them in a flowing hand that would do justice to a royal calligrapher and sealing them with wax, for effect and to insure privacy. These associations help to prepare them for the intimacy and gratification of later heterosexual relationships.

Until they are ready, they tend to draw back from any close attachment to one member of the opposite sex. Wanting love, they nevertheless want to avoid stimulation that they recognize they are not yet up to handling. But in time they become well acquainted with their new bodies and feelings. They come to understand and adapt to the changes, in their parlance, to "put it all together." Girls begin to accept their femininity, to become softer, more receptive to boys; and boys, in their turn, accept their masculinity, yearn to become men.

Self-absorption Is Typical

Growing up, becoming a self-sufficient person with thoughts of one's own, ideas of one's own, values of one's own—an identity—is a slow, gradual process that receives special impetus at the onset of adolescence and does not relent for many years. Parents often feel intense disappointment because it seems that their child has become selfish, and in truth he is now self-absorbed. This need not be a lasting character trait, but simply the normal narcissism of the time. Self-discovery requires a certain amount of introspection and concentration on personal thoughts, feelings, and goals.

Although a child of thirteen or fourteen is still family-centered, still needs his parents' guidance, limits, support, and protection, he is reaching out. He is beginning to feel the need to loosen family ties. He weighs and tests values that he has previously accepted without question. Because his parents' influence is so powerful and their identities are so strong, he must get out from under their shadow if he is to shape himself to his own measure. Often he finds fault, picks fights, rebels, condescends; he can be cruel and hurting. He may sometimes define himself as in opposition to his parents. Their ideas are not worth listening to; they don't understand "where it's at" today, how things should be, *anything.* Childlike obedience to parental wishes and standards is simply not conducive to finding out what *he* really thinks, who *he* really is. He wants to walk to his own rhythm.

Yet this pressure to loosen the emotional bond with his parents is often countered in early adolescence by the temptation to solve all his problems by returning home to the warmth and comfort of the nest. Often he is "just like his old self," warm, seeking advice and the old rapport, helpful to sisters or brothers, trying to please, a pleasure to talk to, to have around.

This is a time of life when a child's emotional growth may be slowed if parents look upon his rebellious behavior as a complete repudiation of themselves and everything they have tried to do for him. It is true that some young people do seem to glide through adolescence with enviable grace and a minimum of confusion. Mothers and fathers may point them out as models of comportment who never cause their parents "a moment's worry." The implication seems to be that this period could be tranquil if only one knew the formula. Undoubtedly, adolescence is easier for some youngsters than for others. However, some "easy" adolescents simply have excessively controlling parents who, without realizing it, offer the child less leeway for the normal experimentation of adolescence, show less tolerance for its swings in temperament, its disorder, its challenge. In such households, the young person may not experience the constructive changes that normally occur during this time; his growth toward emotional maturity may be delayed.

Understanding Helps Parent and Child Alike

It does not always do much good to read in a book that a certain period of life produces problems, that parents should accept this as natural and not become upset or alarmed. It is a rare parent who can, at the moment a problem arises, think to herself or himself, "Aha! The terrible two's!" or "So *this* is early adolescence!" But still, if we know fully why children of a certain age behave the way they do, we can sometimes, upon reflection, understand, feel better, and think more clearly how to help them—and ourselves.

Then, too, when we understand that these problems are not evidences of our failures, that our child's rebelliousness and criticisms are necessary to him and not necessarily a reflection of where we have gone wrong as parents and human beings (no matter what the child may say!), we can usually cope better with what comes along.

Parents who understand the pressures on a young person are better able to absorb his provocations without being crushed by them. They can manage not to respond continually with anger or counterpressure, but to provide the support he needs. Gradually, they let go, as he is ready, avoiding a rending power struggle. No amount of intellectual acceptance can prepare parents emotionally for this experience. But as their child becomes a person in his own right, they, too, can become ready to give his season its time.

2
Communicating About Puberty

BY THE TIME our children are eleven or so, most of us have had quite a few conversations with them about how they were born and the physical differences between boys and girls. Probably we have managed better than Sigmund Freud himself, whose son, Martin Freud, recalls in *Man and Father:*

> There had been a discussion in the family about cattle when it had become clear to father that none of his children knew the difference between a bullock and a bull. "You must be told these things," father had exclaimed; but like the majority of fathers, he had done nothing whatever about it.

Probably, we have also prepared our children for the physical changes of puberty, so that they are not left to wonder or be afraid or put together snatches of misinformation as their bodies begin to mature. Many parents even today feel that further discussion of sex and sexuality is not needed until young people are ready to marry.

This feeling is understandable. Even with society far more open about sex than it used to be, the topic still generates powerful emotions, and it is hard to talk about it with our young. *Seventeen* magazine took note of parental reluctance in this area recently when it printed an article by Oscar Rabinowitz with Myron Brenton explaining to its young readers "How to Talk to Your Parents About Sex."

Acceptance of Sexuality

But parents need to be aware that their children are intensely concerned and frequently anxious about their maturing bodies. They worry about whether they are developing normally and whether they will be attractive to the opposite sex. We want to give them the information they need and to reassure them. We want them to accept the sexual part of themselves as natural and right and to begin to develop their own values about sexual behavior.

The appearance of a single pubic hair or the beginning of a curve of the breast may raise questions in a child's mind. Does this mean that something else should be happening? Comparison with friends may reveal wide variations in which part of the body begins to develop first and how long it takes. The child wonders which is the "right" way

and needs to be reassured that the maturing is progressing normally.

A girl may accept her first menstrual period as a normal occurrence and then be terribly worried because three months pass without another. She needs to know that this is normal, that periods are often not regular during the first year. Slight spotting between periods is normal also, although intermittent bleeding should be discussed with her physician.

A girl's acceptance of the changes in her physique depends greatly upon her feelings about herself as a female. Some girls welcome what is happening with immense satisfaction; others are frightened by what it implies. Some are upset by menstruation; others take it in stride or are proud that they are now able to bear children. The psychiatrist Theodore Lidz says, in *The Person: His Development Through the Life Cycle:*

> During early adolescence, when a girl is learning to feel at home with her woman's body and with woman's role in society, the parents' attitudes are particularly important—their attitudes toward their daughter but also toward one another. When a mother not only accepts her life as a woman but finds fulfillment in it, and when a father admires and appreciates his wife, a girl can welcome the signs that she has become a woman and feel secure that she will be loved and desired as a woman.

The Importance of "Normality"

When a woman gives birth to a child, she wants to know immediately, "Is he normal? Has he got all his fingers and toes, everything he's supposed to have?" Similarly, as our youngsters begin to mature, they worry, "Am I O.K.? Am I attractive? Will boys (or girls) like me?" Breasts have been such an enormous preoccupation in our society, becoming almost synonymous with sex appeal, that it is not surprising that girls with small breasts often fear the boys will not like them. Girls become anxious, too, if one breast grows faster than the other, if they feel they are growing too bosomy, if any hair grows on the breast—indeed, if anything about their faces or bodies seems to them "abnormal" or unattractive.

Boys are generally eager for their shoulders to broaden, their voices to become more manly, and their sexual organs to mature. They will study each other in the showers and lavatories at school to see how they measure up, and they often envy the fellow with the most muscular frame or the largest penis. A boy with a small penis may fear that he will not be man enough for sexual relations. He needs to be told that the size of a penis has no influence on male or female pleasure in intercourse, and also that one cannot judge the size of an erect penis from observing it in its limp state. A smaller penis tends to undergo greater enlargement during erection.

Sometimes a boy becomes alarmed because of a soreness or slight swelling around the nipples. He thinks he may be developing breasts, fears that perhaps he is not "all boy." He needs to be reassured that this is not uncommon in boys his age and usually disappears after a short time.

If a boy or girl continues to be concerned about his anatomy, perhaps he would like to discuss it with a pediatrician, who can make it clear to him that he is normal and answer his questions from a medical view.

Excessive Emphasis on the Physical

With their bodies changing and developing as children grow into adolescence, there is much unavoidable emphasis on physical looks. Young people often come to feel that outward appearances are more important in life than they really are.

The fulfillment of a man or woman in life has very little to do with the size of the breasts or the penis or whether the woman has a pretty face or the man is tall or muscular. It may have a great deal to do with how a man or woman *feels* about his body and himself, whether he feels proud or inferior, lovable or ugly, because this feeling strongly affects the way he expects to be treated and the way he acts toward others. Parents can help a child to feel good about himself, to accept his body and to look forward to what he will become. A parent should not put extra emphasis on the physical by frequent comments about how good-looking or skinny or tall or bosomy a child's friends are. A mother who only asks about a boy's date, "Is she pretty?" conveys a value judgment about what she considers important. On the other hand, opportunities abound to illustrate the fact that very good-looking people may be involved in empty marriages and that people who at first glance seem less physically attractive can and do have relationships with wife, husband, children, family, and friends that are warm and loving, supportive and satisfying.

Our efforts should further a youngster's appreciation of himself as he is, not center on experiments to "correct" what we may consider his less attractive features. Such attempts can backfire, as when a mother buys a padded bra for a daughter who had not felt lacking until that moment; or when a girl is reminded continually not to wear her hair pulled back a certain way because "it makes your nose look longer," or urged to choose a certain dress because "it makes you look slimmer." Parents tend to do this more to girls than to boys, but boys are frequently urged to participate more in sports to "put a little muscle on you," or hounded about their eating habits until their few pounds of extra fat or few pimples become far more damaging to their self-esteem than need be.

On the other hand, if a child is obviously concerned about a physical problem, we want to do whatever we can to help him overcome it. Doctors can do more today for acne (see Chapter 7) than when we were adolescent. Medical advice should be sought if the child considers himself too thin or too fat. If a youngster has crooked teeth or another correctable physical problem, a specialist should be consulted. If a family cannot afford the treatment he recommends, perhaps the doctor knows of a clinic where appropriate care can be obtained.

Sometimes a girl feels that having her hair straightened is important, or a boy wants to wear lifts in his shoes. A parent who truly accepts the child as he is and makes this very clear may still decide to go along with such needs at a particular time. We might say, "I think your curly hair looks fine; it's just right for your face. But I can see you hate it, and that's reason enough for us to do something about it right now. I hope that later on you will like your hair as much as we do."

Very often, after an approach like this, a child will hold off from taking the step. But if she does go ahead, she is less likely to perceive her parent's acquiescence as further proof of her deficiency.

Fathers and Daughters

A father can be particularly helpful to his daughter in this regard. "What! You want to buy cream to cover up your freckles? Why, I fell in love with your mother because of her freckles!" A father's reactions to a daughter are particularly significant now. Dr. Lidz says:

> To a very large degree the girl, despite her careful attention to what she sees in the mirror, and despite her constant comparisons of her own physique with those of her friends and movie starlets, does not achieve an estimate of her charms by what she sees as much as through how she perceives others regard her. The father is very likely to draw away from a daughter entering her teens, feeling that he should no longer be as physically close as previously, and he is often withdrawing from the sexual feelings she induces in him. The daughter often feels that her father now finds her unattractive or is actually repelled by something about her. It requires considerable tact on the part of a father to convey somehow that he considers that his daughter has become attractive and likes the way she looks and yet assume a proper distance.

Boys' Early Sexuality

Some boys become alarmed because they have erections at the slightest sexual stimulus, perhaps just looking at a particular girl or seeing a sexy picture in a magazine. They may be afraid they are oversexed and might lose control of themselves. Boys become embarrassed, too, by spontaneous erections that occur in nonsexual situations, such as while sitting at a desk studying or riding in a bus. They are convinced that everyone is noticing them, which is not true. The presence of an erection upon awakening, although a universal male experience, may cause anxiety. Boys who understand that these reactions are normal, that they are simply another aspect of becoming an adolescent male and are neither surprising nor shocking to adults, do not need to agonize privately or feel guilty or upset.

Who should talk to a boy about these matters? It is usually the father who talks to his son and the mother who talks to her daughter, but if one parent finds it too difficult (or if it is a one-parent family), the other can often fill in and do a good job if he or she is able to be relaxed and matter-of-fact. Perhaps a parent could confess, "Look, things were different when I was younger, and it's hard for me to talk about this, but I think it's important, so let's try."

Frequently, it is the child who is embarrassed in this situation and not the parents! Adolescent boys and girls can be positively allergic to the slightest mention of their anatomy or sex-related subjects by a mother or a father. If this is true and we feel our youngster might be stewing about something, there are several other possibilities. Books, pamphlets, and articles are impersonal and private and can serve a useful purpose if a child is willing to read one. Sometimes after reading, the child becomes relaxed enough to discuss his concerns with his parents. It is always a good idea to peruse a book before offering it to a child. No matter how highly recommended it may be, we should know what is in it. We may consider the tone too folksy or too technical for the individual child, or the point of view may be too "modern" or too old-fashioned for our home. Some parents prefer to ask their religious counselor to suggest a book that is appropriate for young people of their faith.

Sex education classes at school can be helpful. Question-and-answer sessions afterward perform an extra service in revealing that all the other kids have the same concerns, even if the questions have been written down and submitted anonymously. If a child has an understanding, intelligent older person he can talk to—an uncle or aunt, a guidance counselor at school, a youth leader at church or community center, or simply a family friend or older brother or sister—that can be enormously helpful. We should make a special effort to utilize such resources fully.

Erotic Dreams

A boy should be prepared well ahead of time for the possibility of having nocturnal emissions. He may already have learned from his friends that "wet dreams" occur, but all sorts of myths abound. He may have been told that they are weakening or that he is losing irreplaceable masculine fluids from his body. He is likely to become embarrassed by the stains on his sheets, not realizing that his parents expect and accept this occurrence. He needs to be told in advance that nocturnal emission is a normal process, that it is the result of sexual excitement caused by dreaming, which reaches a climax with the emission of semen, and that the seminal fluid rapidly replenishes itself.

Such a thoughtful discussion with a child can also deal with the vivid erotic dreams that accompany nocturnal emissions and may occur at other times, and can produce great anxiety. Most of us understand the difference between dreams, fantasies, thoughts, and feelings on the one hand and acts on the other. We can forgive ourselves for having "forbidden" feelings because we are aware that everyone has them. We understand that we are accountable only for what we actually do, not what we think or dream of doing. Being a basically normal person does not mean that one will not have some pretty wild notions sometimes. Young people need to be helped to understand this.

Unbidden Sexual Thoughts

As youngsters are maturing, sexual thoughts come unbidden into their minds and can be as frightening as their dreams and fantasies. A child may imagine having intercourse with a teacher, with his mother, father, brother, or sister. He may imagine being raped or raping someone. He needs to know that others experience these fantasies, and they are nothing to be ashamed of or worry about. They do not mean that he is abnormal or likely to carry out such fantasies.

Homosexual fantasies and dreams are particularly disturbing. Psychologist Wardell B. Pomeroy says:

> It is a common experience to be stirred by a sexual feeling toward someone of the same sex through a fantasy, a dream or in some other way. Most people are horrified by such thoughts and feel intensely guilty about having "perverted" feelings. But most of these people will never take part in a homosexual act and those fleeting thoughts will never interfere with their heterosexual lives unless they carry guilt and fear into them.[1]

What can a parent do to help a child who may be bothered by such fantasies? "If you wait for him to broach the subject himself," warns Dr. Pomeroy, "you will wait forever," because most youngsters would rather admit almost anything than even the most fleeting homosexual thought. Newspaper articles, books, plays, and motion pictures can serve as a springboard for a discussion during which a parent can see that the child understands that his fears are groundless.

Burden of Needless Guilt

A great many adults today were burdened with guilt about childhood feelings and experiences that were, had they but known, common and normal. Today, virtually all physicians and psychiatrists agree, for example, that masturbation is harmless, and most religious groups are reexamining their attitudes on this subject. It is something that most people do in private at one time or another during their lives as a way of releasing sexual tension. The physical effects of masturbation are not significantly different from those of any other sexual activity. Yet, many of our children remain in the dark ages about this form of self-

[1] Wardell B. Pomeroy, Ph.D., *Boys and Sex: A Long-needed Modern Sexual Guide for Boys* (New York: Delacorte Press, 1968) p. 72.

gratification, feeling themselves wicked and dirty and perhaps fearing that they are in some way damaging themselves. Modern parents can spare their youngsters the anguish that earlier generations went through on this account.

Masturbation can become excessive, but so can any other activity. Television-watching, for example, is not bad in itself, but if a child sits glued to the set for hours upon end, one wonders why he cannot find other satisfactions. The problem, then, is not the television-watching but the pressures in his life and the lack of other satisfactions or ways to relieve his tension.

Early Maturers

Young people who begin to mature considerably earlier or later than their peers can have a hard time of it. Eleven-year-old boys who become strongly attracted to girls, while all their friends still hate them, tend to feel out of step and to worry that they must in some way be peculiar. Reluctance to admit a growing attraction to the opposite sex is expressed in a comment by a seventh-grader who had just watched a female classmate saunter by. "If I ever stop hating girls," he remarked to a friend, "she's the one I'll stop hating first!"

But boys who begin to grow tall and mature early usually flex their muscles, admire themselves in the mirror, and feel pleased with themselves.

Girls who shoot up and begin to develop before their classmates are more likely to feel awkward and self-conscious. Of course, some girls are eager to grow up and welcome every sign that they are doing so.

Late Maturers

Late maturers seem to suffer more. They feel left behind as, one by one, friends begin to spurt up and have intriguing new interests. A lot of teasing can go on in the locker room, making the child who is slow in maturing feel absolutely miserable. The more physically mature youngsters tend to draw away from the others. Among boys there is talk of "wet dreams," of sex and girls. Among girls there are whispers about boys and romance and love stories. The late starters are apt to feel left out, possibly abnormal, and with a gnawing fear that it may never happen to them.

They need to be reassured, to be told that their time will come. If a mother or father or an admired uncle or aunt has been a late developer, the photograph album can be brought out to illustrate that this runs in the family. Parents should make it clear that every child grows at his own pace. Some grow rapidly and reach their full height as early as thirteen; others begin their growth spurt later but inch up little by little until they may—as with the tortoise and the hare—outstrip the early starters. Each person has a growth rate that is right for him, with wide variations from the "average."

Nevertheless, the late starter may very well feel left out *now*. We might hear, "Why do they keep lining us up by size? I never see grown-ups lined up according to how tall they are," or "Jill has got so stuck-up, she goes around with this bunch of girls who think they're so *big* and spend every Saturday *shopping!*" It is a wrench for parents to see a child in low spirits and not be able to do the one thing the child really wants—speed up the maturation process. But reassuring the boy that he *will* be a man, the girl that she *will* be a woman, that this is one of those things that have to be waited out, may at least relieve their most pressing concern.

It is helpful, too, if a child can become involved in group activities that are not composed only of boys and girls of the same age. A chamber-music group or a chess club, or sewing, woodworking, or typing classes, for example, sometimes include persons of varying ages and take for granted differences in size. Joining such a group affords a good chance, also, to make new friends when some old ones may be drifting away. Also, if a child can, through taking lessons, become proficient in an activity that interests him, it can give a helpful boost to his self-esteem.

Sexual Curiosity

We are likely to find our youngsters again intensely curious about sexual relations, but this time with emphasis on the specific details of intercourse. Although they may have learned what is involved, they cannot quite picture how it happens. As one youngster put it, "Do you just take off all your clothes or what?" Lovemaking and its meaning to a man and woman are a mystery to them. They are more apt to consult each other and whatever books and magazines they can get their hands on—or R-rated motion pictures they can get in to see—than ask us. And, of course, they imagine much.

One twelve-year-old girl, on a vacation trip with her parents, rushed in to impart the information that two "teen-agers," a boy and a girl, had just checked into the hotel and taken only one room. "I'm sure they're not married. . . ." Giggles. "Isn't it against the law? Do you think they have two beds or one in the room?" We are free to gloss over the subject or to try to find out what else she wants to know and help her. Youngsters put out these feelers from time to time as circumstances move them to. If we draw back, they quickly withdraw, too. At this age, they usually do not push for information as they may have done earlier. They are reluctant to admit their ignorance and may be embarrassed about discussing adult sexuality with parents.

We need to pay close attention when children bring themselves to ask questions, because the expressed question often is only part of the child's concern. For example, a girl who has developed early and at thirteen has a woman's breasts, a woman's curves, may ask, "Is it normal for me to grow this much this early?" The mother may respond, "Yes, certainly." But there may be more behind the question. The child may have received stares, remarks about her figure; she may have been noticed by older boys who are responding to her physically. But she herself may be far from ready emotionally for this interest and may be frightened by it. She is not prepared to cope with her new sexual attractiveness, and she needs a chance to express some of her concerns and to be guided and reassured.

There is a wonderful cartoon showing two preteenage boys coming away from a sex-education lecture, one saying to the other, "I know what they do and I know how they do it—but I don't know *why* they do it." As our youngsters mature, their own physical, glandular, and emotional changes begin to give them an inkling of that "why." And these increased sexual feelings may bother them. They sense that their inner stirrings have something to do with sexual relations, and they may find this frightening or, like the thirteen-year-old just mentioned, feel threatened by possibilities for which they are not yet ready. Some children try to deny the existence of their burgeoning sexuality by clinging to childhood, perhaps refusing to wear more grown-up clothes and avoiding any sort of activity with the opposite sex.

Sometimes parents overlook telling a boy about menstruation and its connection with reproduction or a girl about ejaculation and the changes boys are undergoing. Most women can remember from their adolescent days how some boys seemed to understand immediately why a girl might not feel like swimming on certain days, while others would pester and pester her to go in the water, obviously *ignorant!* It is good for girls and boys to know that the other sex is also undergoing physical changes, with their attendant worries.

The Importance of Early Information

Some parents may be surprised to read in a book that eleven- to fourteen-year-olds should be informed about both contraception and venereal disease. Perhaps we might digress for a moment and tell a true story about a devoted father who took a week's vacation in order to be with his 18-month-old son while his wife was in the hospital giving birth to their second child. The father lovingly ate with his son, played with him, bathed him, and tucked him into bed each night for five days while his wife was away. He never talked to Jess about his mother or even mentioned her name; the boy seemed so happy and preoccupied that it seemed best not to "remind" him that Mommy was missing. Why upset him and raise questions that would be difficult to discuss with a child that young?

This father loved his son enough to give up a week of his vacation time to be with him. He was intelligent enough and aware enough of his child's emotional needs to understand how much a father's presence would mean to Jess while his mother was away. Yet he assumed that the child, who had spent practically every waking hour with his mother for eighteen months, would not even notice that she was missing unless someone else brought up the subject. When Jess's mother returned home, he screamed when she went to pick him up and pushed her away roughly. He refused to let her come near him until evening, when he finally acknowledged her. Whatever thoughts he had had about her absence, one fact emerged clearly: he had noticed it.

Many parents are like that father when it comes to talking to their children about sex-related subjects. They seem to feel that if they don't bring the subjects up, their child will not be concerned with them. They argue that talking about these matters may upset the child, make him overly curious, overstimulate him, or encourage experimentation. In fact, as psychologist Isadore Rubin points out:

> The issue is really not one of ignorance versus information but one of getting information given carefully by responsible sources as opposed to getting it from poorly informed friends or irresponsible sources. Who has not heard stories of young boys who have used plastic wrap as contraceptive, or girls who have douched with soda pop and of others who have taken a few of their mothers' birth control pills? Today, when so many bits of information or misinformation are available in one way or another, it makes sense to provide young persons with a thorough knowledge of contraception in order to counter the dangers of any smattering of incomplete or incorrect knowledge that they may pick up.

Since not many parents are happy about the idea of their children's having sexual relations at this age, why provide this information *now?* Won't it seem as if we sanction such behavior? Psychiatric thinking, says Dr. Rubin, "suggests that the best time for a child to receive factual information about such subjects is *before* he has reached the age where he must begin to make decisions about it, when his emotions in respect to that information are dormant or less involved.

Sexual Relations

What do we say to an eleven- or twelve-year-old child about birth control? Perhaps something like this (not necessarily all at once in a big speech, but over a period of time in one's own way): "You're not ready to date yet, and there's no hurry. But the time will come when you're going to be dating, falling in love, considering having sexual relations, and you ought to know how we feel about it."

Then, if we feel that sexual fulfillment can be achieved only in a long-term relationship between two people who respect each other and care about each other, we would say so. Or, if it is our belief that sex outside of marriage is wrong, we would tell him that, even though he probably already knows how we feel from things we have said all along. But then we could add, "Our hope is that you will feel as we do about sexual relations, but whatever you decide, we want you to know how to behave responsibly." Children should know the ineffectiveness of homemade improvisations. Young people should understand that there is no reliable "safe" period during the month when a girl cannot conceive. Many parents also see that their daughters have the name of a doctor from whom they can obtain more information if they wish.

An emotionally healthy, sensible young person who has respect for himself is not likely to become promiscuous just because he knows how to prevent pregnancy or is knowledgeable about venereal disease. The young person who engages in irresponsible or self-destructive sexual behavior usually has other, deeper problems, and his sexual activities—or it could be drug-taking or stealing or truancy—are a *symptom* of these difficulties. Knowing how to use contraceptives does not make such a child promiscuous, but it may prevent his behavior from having tragic consequences.

Venereal disease is a major health problem among young people of all social classes in this country today. We need to inform ourselves and our youngsters about it.

When we were this age, nobody talked to us about gonorrhea and syphilis because our parents took it for granted that "nice" people did not get such diseases. But, as gynecologist James L. Breen puts it,

> Even the nicest person having intercourse with an equally nice person runs the risk of venereal infection and is, therefore, a possible infector of another nice person.

Families need to know the symptoms of venereal disease and that early treatment can bring cure. Many persons are not aware that venereal infection will not disappear without treatment. Thus, because the symptoms often disappear after a time, a person may believe he is cured, whereas the infection is still in his body and later can cause great damage, including sterility, blindness, and death. Books and pamphlets giving detailed information about venereal diseases are available from state and federal departments of health, local health clinics, and many community centers and schools.

Sexual values, of course, go beyond how one feels about the question of premarital intercourse for boys and girls. They involve concern about the other person, an unwillingness to exploit someone else or to hurt someone else (or oneself), or to pressure someone else into a relationship that he does not want or for which he is not emotionally prepared.

Instilling Sexual Values

When we talk to our children about the importance of surrounding a sexual relationship with the deep concern and love of marriage, do they see these values expressed at home? If their parents' relationship is a good one, it will be more difficult for someone to tempt them to accept a sham. Our children are going to make the choices that affect their future, and they may emulate us or they may not. We cannot determine or control their behavior; we can only influence it. And all the indications are that children who are trusted and well informed tend to behave more responsibly.

Our children are living in a society that provides an incredible amount of sexual stimulation—motion pictures, jokes, books, women's clothing, advertising, and so on—and yet frowns on adolescents' being sexually active. We expect them to wait perhaps ten years after they become sexually mature before seeking sexual fulfillment in marriage. Traditionally, daughters have been especially protected, while parents often looked the other way or even smiled approvingly as their sons "sowed their wild oats" with someone else's child. Many husbands and wives today are determined not to make their own children as tense and apprehensive and *warned* as they were.

Complete silence about sex communicates its own message, of course, and leaves our children to the media. One mother was upset to find her fourteen-year-old son reading *The Anderson Tapes,* a detective story heavily spiced with masochistic and sadistic sex. "Most people," she told the boy, "don't need to hurt each other or be hurt in order to enjoy sex." "Oh, I know *that,*" he responded impatiently. "I just finished reading *Airport*" (a novel in which all the sex is between married men and women not their wives). Today, inexpensive paperback books, sold at stores where a child buys his ice cream and soda, tell stories of every imaginable kind of sex act. People are writing out their kinkiest sexual fantasies, publishers are printing them, and motion picture companies are filming them. And if our child is not personally exposed to these films or books or magazines—which would be a feat indeed—there is some child at school who is, who sees all, knows all, and tells all, or what he thinks is "all."

If we are not going to pack up and move away from civilization, we must somehow impart to our children healthier ideas about what sex can be.

3
Boy-Girl Relationships

IN SIXTH GRADE, when the children are about eleven, the boy-girl parties usually begin. In some communities this happens a bit earlier, in others a bit later, but the manifestations are the same. While most boys are still inviting their friends to football and baseball and bowling parties and the like, and most girls are giggling with other girls at pajama parties, *some* girls and *some* mothers of girls – and a very few boys – are ready for something else. And the other children in the grade are alerted that something new is beginning.

After a while, as more and more parties are given that include both sexes, more youngsters are drawn into the scene, many reluctantly, not yet ready, joining in the swim only to get a cautious toe wet and then pulling back. Sixth-grade boys are undomesticated creatures, not lending themselves particularly to the social graces. They enjoy the party food, all right, but their elbows knock over glasses of punch onto the furniture and the prized outfits of eleven-year-old girls. In general, they are unsatisfactory party companions. And some of them flatly refuse to put in an appearance at a function where girls are to be present: "Me go to Bill's? Are you kidding? He's having girls!"

A boy will often develop close friendship with another boy at this point, or a group of boys will gang together. Frequently the talk is about sex, but the affection and loyalty are still for a boy's buddies. Boys may ignore girls even though they have begun to be attracted to them, because they need time to get used to these feelings, time to become ready.

Girls also have intense relationships with members of their own sex. Two girls like to be together all the time; they hold hands as they walk along or throw their arms around each other. They call each other on the phone the minute they reach home. They have frequent sleep-over dates and so on. Both boys and girls may find it safer right now to be with members of their own sex. Parents – and children – need not become alarmed if such an attachment has occasional overtones. This is not uncommon around the time of puberty, and youngsters, by and large, eventually move on to interest in the opposite sex. As a matter of fact, such close friendships are absent from the case histories of adult homosexuals. They appear to be a normal step on the way to heterosexual attachments.

Boys and Girls Together

Little by little, boys and girls – some beginning at eleven, others at twelve or thirteen or fourteen or sometimes later – begin to come together for companionship. They see each other in class if they go to a coeducational school. They work and play together at school, in community clubs, and in other activities, and they gab and kid around together at the local "hangouts" where everyone goes for pizza or sandwiches or soda and ice cream. Or they meet "on the block," in the neighborhood. Although interest in each other has heightened and seeing each other matters now, which it didn't a year or two ago, for a while that is all there is to it.

Then, gradually, certain boys and girls may fall into the habit of leaving school together and going for a snack, or perhaps one boy waits for a particular girl. Or maybe they meet every day walking to school or on the bus, and they talk. Or they fall into step after church, or they take music lessons at the same school. There are any number of possibilities. These are not dates, exactly, but the boy and girl are getting to know each other in a casual, comfortable way.

The informality of these early encounters helps youngsters feel more at ease. Nobody has to make conversation for a whole afternoon or evening. There is no set beginning or ending, and the boy does not have the responsibility of "taking out" the girl or of paying her way. This kind of informal meeting can lead to a group of boys and girls going to a movie or the beach or the skating rink, or arranging to meet at a certain point before going on to the football game together. Such casual associations and group activities are healthy learning experiences in boy-girl relationships during which young people find out what members of the opposite sex are like and how to talk to them.

Most youngsters of thirteen or so are not ready for more than that, although, under social pressure, they may decide they are. One mother whose thirteen-year-old daughter asked permission to go on a single date with a boy from school responded, "Do you really want to have to talk to – and listen to – Freddy for one whole evening?"

The girl had not thought of it that way at all. "Ugh, no!" she said.

What about these first boy-girl parties? One mother who waited up for her thirteen-year-old son to return home from a party asked him, "What did you do?"

"The same thing they did at parties when you were my age," he told her.

"It was so long ago, I can't remember," his mother persisted.

"Try," he came back—and was out of the room.

Boys in particular have a passion for privacy and an incredible resistance to anything they regard as poking into their affairs. The only way some parents can find out what the kids do at parties is to have one or help chaperone one!

Developing a Social Code

A great deal of trouble and worry in connection with parties can be avoided if parents in a community or the Parent-Teacher Association can get together and agree on a social code. (The Parents League of New York, Inc., at 22 East 60th Street, New York, N.Y. 10022, has published a booklet containing a Suggested Social Code for Teenagers and Their Parents.) In some areas this is natural and easy, but often in big cities, where a child's friends may be drawn from diverse groups, it is difficult. An agreement concerning youngsters in this age range generally includes such points as no parties without at least one parent at home as a chaperone, no drugs or liquor or smoking permitted, and whatever other rules the parents in the community believe are important for their children's well-being. In this way, no child or parent is pressured into undesirable situations because "everybody else is doing it," and parents are more able to relax, feeling that other parents will take the same kind of precautions they would. Of course, there are always parents who do not go along, but such an arrangement is still better than just keeping one's fingers crossed.

Some parents feel free to call up the home where a party will be held and ask the host's parents about the arrangements, but this is difficult for many people, and their children usually resent it. Occasionally there is a really considerate mother who calls up each parent whose child is invited to her youngster's party and says, "I just want you to know that my husband and I will be home all evening and that the party will be over at ten."

Good parties for young people of eleven, twelve, and perhaps thirteen need as much planning as parties for very young children, and for much the same reason. The youngsters generate a lot of excitement and energy, and it needs channeling. The boys and girls are not yet ready just to talk to each other or to spend the entire afternoon or evening dancing—or smooching. They will be hungry, and the hostess who wishes to have happy guests is well advised to provide plenty of their favorite foods, keeping in mind that greasy fingers will probably not be wiped on napkins and that olives and pickles are terribly handy to throw. Party activities can be organized in advance by the child, perhaps with a friend or two or perhaps with a parent.

Sometimes parents are less welcoming to their child's friends than they realize. Perhaps the furniture in the living room is "too good." The child just knows that his friends will spill something or knock something over, and that his parents will be annoyed and show it. Or he has to serve fruit punch because his parents are against soda—but all of his friends want soda. Some marvelously secure young people of this age can dare to be different and let the rest of the gang follow along—but not many. Or a parent will treat a boy "like a kid" in front of his friends or embarrass him in other ways. It just becomes easier not to bring anyone home.

When parents are truly hospitable, youngsters may even use their homes as a base for dating. One well-organized young man brought his first date home for lunch; then they went out to play tennis, returned home to change, went off to a television studio to see a show being taped, then back home again to get bicycles for a ride in the park. The date cost him money only for transportation, and he and his girl were too busy to be awkward with each other or to have to depend on conversation for long stretches of time.

Avoiding Social Pressure

Gradually, one's child swings into all this social activity—or he does not. Says Thelma Purtell in *The Intelligent Parents' Guide to Teenagers:*

> Strange as it may seem to extroverted fathers and gregarious mothers, there is the occasional child who honestly does not want a social life. These parents suffer much more than their children, feeling that their offspring are afflicted with the agonies they themselves would experience if they were left out of the group. They should realize that there is the possibility that the child is perfectly contented, listening to records, experimenting with chemicals or curled up with a book.

When parents become concerned because their child has not become involved in boy-girl activity, they may begin to exert pressure on him. Sometimes a child is pushed to be more social, to go to a party or participate in another kind of activity. Parents may feel justified if the youngster later says that he had a good time. He may even say he is glad his parents urged him to go. But what is lost if we let a child wait until he himself feels ready? And what is gained when we give a child the feeling that we always know better than he what is good for him? How is he encouraged to develop his own critical faculties, his own judgment about what is best for him to do and how to act in a particular situation? He has to have a sense, as educator John Holt says in *What Do I Do Monday?,* "of being in charge of his life." He has to know that if he were in charge it would not necessarily turn out badly.

Many young people are avid for boy-girl activities at an early age. They are precocious, or eager to get a head start, or simply curious to see what all the talk is about. For such youngsters, parents sometimes need to revise their ideas about how early to permit certain activities if a child is truly ready.

The First Dance

Do you remember your first dance? Many people, particularly women, do. And many bear deep scars from that night and other first boy-girl encounters. A woman recalls:

> I had been hoping and hoping this one boy would ask me to the school dance. He was the only fellow in the grade taller than I was, and we had been sitting in the back of the classroom next to each other for two years. He did ask me, finally, and I remember that my mother and I had a big hassle over lipstick and whether I should wear my glasses—I was blind without them, but I hated them. And then the boy ditched me the minute we got there! He spent the entire evening with a short, cute girl named Dolores who was wearing a crimson dress with a skirt that flared when she danced. None of the other boys came near me. I felt like a big lump. I managed to get through the evening making trips between the food table and the record table and the ladies' room, trying hard not to look at *them.* After that miserable night nobody could convince me it was "lovely to be so nice and tall," and I walked hunched over for years.

And a thirteen-year-old girl of the 1970's told it all in one short sentence when she arrived home after her *second* dance. "Oh, Mommy," she exclaimed, beaming, "I wasn't a wallflower tonight!"

Boys need not worry that nobody will ask them to dance, but they are nervous, too. They are afraid they won't know what to do or will do something dumb and embarrass themselves. And it would be humiliating if they asked a girl to dance and she said no. "I guess I took a lot of time checking it all out, you know, seeing who was there and all," said one young blade of thirteen, rather coolly, after his first dance. "There was a lot of good stuff to eat, too. . . . Did I dance with anyone? Well, not exactly."

Of course, if a boy is turned down, he can work up his courage and ask another girl to dance. He does not have to put in waiting time. So dances are, in the end, not the potential torture for boys that they are for girls. A lot of this can be avoided if the youngsters can be won over to an afternoon or evening of some party games and some dancing, with planned, relaxed ways to help them come together with a partner —from catching a balloon with a partner's name in it to choosing a pair of shoes from a pile and searching, Cinderella-style, for their owner.

Helping a Child Belong

It is hard to know who suffers more, the child who is having social trouble, feels shy, ugly, left out, painfully self-conscious, or her parents. Most youngsters want very much to belong. The suffering of adolescents drawing toward their first encounters with the opposite sex is often real and deep, and its impact may affect the person's thinking and feeling for a long time.

How can we help a child move more easily in the social world? We need to know first what his trouble is, why he is having difficulty. It is vital to try to look at the problem through the child's eyes. A lovely young person may, for some reason, consider herself unattractive and be extremely self-conscious because of this. Her problem is not her looks, but how she feels about them.

Sometimes when a child does not begin to date or go to school dances or parties, it is the parent and not the child who begins to get frantic (although the child catches the parent's mood soon enough). Parents may try berating a child into sociability—if you didn't slouch, act so bossy, look so sloppy, twiddle your hair, or wherever the problem is pinned, you would get along better. A child who is already humiliated by her wallflower status at dances may be told, "You just stand there; you don't even try." Sometimes these admonitions help; often not. But even if they help, the cost may be too high in terms of what it does to the child to achieve his measure of success.

Overemphasis on Popularity

Some parents put a destructive emphasis on popularity, implying or even saying outright, if you do this, you'll be popular; or, if you behave that way, you'll never be popular. A child can come to feel that the be-all and end-all is popularity, rather than the true development of his own personality and individuality, his identity. How much of himself will he betray in the fevered search for a multitude of friends, preferably, perhaps, of a socially desirable type? Would he prefer not to talk so much, smile so much? Is it more natural for him to be a more private person? The tragedy in this kind of betrayal of self is that it attracts friends who are drawn toward his disguise, forcing him to continue in it, while the kind of youngsters to whom he is naturally inclined turn elsewhere for friends.

Sometimes a child lacks confidence because his parents are too hard on him in one way or another. Perhaps they have too-high standards, are rarely satisfied with his performance or his friends or his activities. With the child who lacks self-confidence, we should ease up as much as we can. If a child has a rather serious personality difficulty—is often unkind, rude, sarcastic to his contemporaries, has many fears, feels that others make fun of him, or has some other problem that interferes with his relationships with the children in school and in the neighborhood—we need to know what is causing his feelings and his behavior.

Some children are simply late bloomers. They make their way slowly and blossom in their own good time at fifteen or even at seventeen. What they need from us is confidence and support—and patience—until they are ready to come into their own.

Some girls—and boys—will never shine at the big dance, never be relaxed at parties, but they do just fine when they are with girls and boys working at a school activity or sharing any mutual interest. We should encourage this type of child to become involved in the kinds of activities that are her strong point and help her to avoid dances and other affairs that become situations of humiliation and misery and may indeed convince her that she is inferior or "unpopular."

Build on the Child's Assets

What are her assets? Can she play an instrument, cook, sew, garden or grow house plants from seed, swim, type, repair things, paint, sculpt, play chess, collect stamps or coins, take marvelous pictures; is she a crackerjack skater or tennis player, or does she love to watch baseball or football? The list is endless. A youngster can be helped to develop her interests and skills. Then she will tend naturally to get to know others who are similarly inclined. Of course, the interest must be genuine. Young people themselves always advise against phoniness. As one girl put it, "It's no good pretending she likes something she doesn't; she won't have any fun. So what's the good of it?"

A young person who is interested in others will often find that they return the interest. But it is hard for anyone, child or adult, to care about others if he is unhappy and has a low opinion of himself. Here again, we need to know why he feels that way in order to help him.

Social poise at a party, the ability to make light chitchat, to fit in and be part of a gay crowd, come easy to only a fortunate few. Most young people are awkward in social situations until they have had enough experience and success to help them develop confidence. They may be so anxious that they clam up; they may want so badly to be interesting that they cannot think of anything to say.

A youngster will envy those children who seem to "have it all together"—who seem, at an early age, to know who they are, where they are going, and how to handle themselves with both boys and girls. These lucky ones just don't seem to have the same worries he has, he thinks. A child knows that *he* tries to hide his uncertainty, but often fails to realize that many others shiver under their poise, that bragging is usually an attempt to cover up feelings of inferiority, that a great many young people his age are actually in the same boat he is, just—only just—pushing off from shore.

Sometimes it helps to explain that early success does not necessarily mean that a young person will always be ahead. What charms the girls at thirteen, for example, may bore them at sixteen; and a thirteen-year-old boy's idea of feminine charm will probably change and develop as he gets older. But this kind of philosophizing may not help much, partly because the young people do not really believe it and partly because it is this minute that is important anyway.

Striking a Balance

If young people can be supported through these early occasions, they will probably begin to take hold themselves as time goes on. Parents need to strike a balance between sharing their knowledge and overwhelming the child with advice and suggestions. Some parents have a knack for passing on their social know-how, giving a child a needed hint in a constructive way that he can accept. Others only make a child more self-conscious and angry at what he construes as criticism.

Youngsters can be cliquish and cruel, and the child who is left out may suffer deeply. Contrary to popular myth, such suffering rarely ennobles. When a child begins to feel himself or herself a failure at social encounters, he becomes even more self-conscious and uneasy. The problem compounds itself. Then others tend to find him or her more difficult to be with, and it becomes harder and harder to break the cycle. Whatever can be done to help is worth it. Sometimes a parent can chaperone frequent excursions to the skating rink, the bowling alley, the public pool, or wherever the young people in the community like to go. Gathering together our child and a few other young people for an afternoon's fun is an excellent way to encourage wholesome relationships with others—if our child likes the idea. It offers a youngster a chance to get to know and be known by others his own age, to gain experience talking, learn how to be a good listener, empathize with others' thoughts, hopes, joys, sorrows, pains.

The First Date

When they begin to date, both boys and girls should understand that the other sex worries, too, about how they look and what to say and do. A boy may be attracted to a girl but afraid of her at the same time; she may laugh at him or not take him seriously. A girl worries that he may find her dull or uninteresting or may talk about her with his friends. Neither one has ever thought about it before, but what do girls (boys) like to talk about? He has not given much thought to manners before, either, but now he is hesitant—will he know how to do the "right" thing at the right time? He has a moment of panic when he notices his dirty fingernails and remembers how many times his mother warned him that girls find this revolting; he wonders what else about him may be revolting.

Girls worry that they will not be asked out; boys are anxious that they may be turned down—the same kind of situation that prevailed at the dances and will continue, more or less, for a while. If a boy is rejected by a girl, we can try to help him to see her "No, thank you" in its proper perspective and not feel diminished by it.

He needs to understand that he is not crazy about every girl he meets, nice though many of them may be, so he cannot expect that every girl will want to be with him. If he is turned down, perhaps it is because she is too shy, or her mother is very protective, or she only likes brunettes—none of which ought to affect his self-esteem, disappointing though it may be. Of course, the same thing goes for girls. Our aim should be not to prevent all hurt, which is not possible, but to try to see that the hurts of today do not really injure the child's opinion of himself and that he learns from them as much as he can.

We should get across to our children how inevitable and natural it is to make mistakes at the beginning, to say the wrong thing to a girl, to offend a boy in some way, to be so nervous that one forgets a name and so cannot make an expected introduction—the possibilities for humiliation are infinite. Parents have to try to help youngsters recognize that self-consciousness is par for the course and that the best cure for it is to be considerate of the person one is with.

Boy-Girl Behavior Differences

Boys and girls also should be made aware of a basic difference between them that affects their behavior. Even though changes occur in girls' bodies at puberty as they do in boys', most girls do not suddenly become interested in sex as the average boy does. Girls are interested in boys in a new way, but it is more in terms of dating and romance than in sexual relations. Says Eric W. Johnson in *How to Live Through Junior High School:*

> The early adolescent sexual feelings of boys are commonly satisfied not by contacts with girls, but by private activities: nocturnal emissions and, much more frequently, masturbation. But while this male sexual activity is going on, many boys are socially very anti-girl, whereas the girls, although not erotically aroused, are socially greatly interested in association with the other sex.

When dating does begin, girls may flirt and act enticingly without realizing that they are exciting boys sexually. They may be genuinely surprised at the boys' reactions. A boy may think that this is his fault, that he has made a mistake. But the problem arises because of the difference in outlook between boys and girls at this point. It is possible, however, that if the double standard disappears and women and men become equally free *and equally responsible* sexually, we will find that girls experience stronger sexual pressure at an earlier age.

If at the start a child is frequently rebuffed in his or her desire for dates, he may want to retreat for a while.

We may wish he would not "give up." We may want to talk about it in an effort to help, but he may not want to think about it, much less talk with us about it. And he probably does not think of himself as "giving up" but merely as sitting out the situation for the present. The average child will test the water again after a time. Meanwhile, his wishes should be respected. If other things are going well at school and at home, and if he has some social contact with boys and girls in clubs or other activities, there should be no pressure on him to do anything more. Of course, if a child has no friends or is unhappy for a long period of time, help is obviously needed.

Is the Child Ready for Dating?

Perhaps he is not really ready for dating. He is not yet grown up enough, and it was actually group or parental pressure, not his own wishes, that impelled him toward dating. It has been observed that mothers tend to be content when boys take time to be interested in dating but are more apt to press a girl to test her wings. One of the most important things we can do for a child this age is to help him cope with pressures to begin dating before he is ready and to support him in moving toward it at his own pace. Being ready to date implies a certain maturity, a desire to spend time with someone of the opposite sex, being secure and relaxed enough and skilled enough socially to go on a single date without its being more strain than pleasure. Young people are better off if they do not push themselves or feel pushed by their parents. They can learn to get along with the opposite sex in various other social settings.

We need to judge a child's readiness; we should not be influenced by the fact that his peers are dating, or by the child's insistence if we sense that he really is not ready. Some children are ready at an earlier age than others. Physical development is not the only guide. A young person may be intensely curious about the other sex but not interested in actually dating for a while. We may push a child into dating before he is ready by giving him the feeling that we expect it or consider it desirable.

We can help our child and ourselves by giving some thought to how we really feel about his dating. One mother confessed that she felt somewhat depressed when her son went on his first date. She is not unusual—or sick. A young person's dating presages the time when someone else will be as close to him as we are now, when he will be ready to leave home and start a family of his own. If we recognize such feelings in ourselves, we are better able to prevent them from affecting our behavior with our child and his friends. Unrecognized feelings like this give rise to situations in which a daughter can never find a boy whom her father considers "good enough" for her, or a mother is critical of every girl her son takes out.

Masculine and Feminine Roles

We do have, and need to accept responsibility for, a strong influence on the way our children feel about femininity and masculinity. The way a husband and wife treat each other and the way they feel about themselves is part of the everyday experience of their children's lives. Is a mother admiring of her husband; does she respect his judgment and his decisions? Does she enjoy being a wife and mother? Or is she hostile, cold, competitive? Is she submissive, domineering, or an equal? Does she like being a woman? Is she affectionate and loving? Both sons and daughters receive daily doses of her prescription of what men and women are and ought to be and how they stand in relation to each other. Similar influence is exerted by their father's behavior. What does he think of women, of his wife? Does he treat her with warmth, kindness, consideration? Or is he insensitive or sarcastic or indifferent?

What does masculine mean in our society? Traditionally, we think of strength, of dominance, of a defender of the home. What does feminine mean? Traditionally, soft, submissive, gentle, nurturant. But not everyone agrees any more what little girls are made of, and what they ought to be doing with their lives. It seems certain that women will have more choice in the future; more possibilities will be open to them and more arrangements available to them to continue their careers after their children are born if that is what they want. And more girls will be seeking husbands who are willing to accept a new kind of equality in marriage. A magazine article published recently told of a contractual agreement between a young man and his wife to take equal responsibility for all the jobs in the household, child care included. Under this arrangement, each can pursue his career equally. The wife does not have to feel that she can work only if she can juggle the job, children, cooking, and cleaning. Some men are deciding that they, too, have been cheated by the traditional division of labor in the home. They want to see more of their children and are willing for their wives to help them support the family.

Today's youth seem to be blurring the distinction between masculinity and femininity in their dress, appearance, and interests. Perhaps certain things should have no gender. In the past, girls have been brought up to love ballet, boys to care about baseball. Boys were given the idea that music and art were somehow girlish, and girls that these were suitable feminine pursuits. Then boys and girls married and often complained that they did not have common interests. No one—least of all women—has ever denied that gentleness and tenderness are important in a husband and father; but it was rarely listed under the qualities labeled male, and many men in our society have felt they had to be tender on the sly so as not to be caught at it. Surely boys ought to be able to cry and girls to climb trees without being thought of as, respectively, sissies and tomboys. What is left of being a man or a woman if these cultural attitudes are changed? Only physical differences? Maybe not. Maybe we are moving not toward a unisex, but toward new definitions of the masculine and feminine roles. These roles have been differently defined in other cultures, and in other eras, so that they need not be considered sacrosanct.

Of course, many men—and women—are uncomfortable about the idea of more freedom for women and prefer the traditional outlook. The important point for parents is that whatever our own inclinations, it is clear that times are changing, and we should not assume limitations on women that may not exist for our daughters. And perhaps we ought to prepare our sons for new kinds of relationships, in which it is not necessarily assumed that women will submerge their interests to those of their husbands.

Helping the Child Perceive His Role

The way a father behaves toward his daughter influences the way she thinks about herself and her femaleness. If a father shows that he feels his daughter is developing well, is lovely, this gives her confidence in herself. Does she have to prove herself to win his approval, or does he value her for what she is? Is he loving or cold? Whatever kind of man he is, he is her first and most important model of what men are and should be. His treatment of her conditions her expectations for the future.

A daughter is also helped immeasurably by a close relationship with a mother who accepts herself as a woman, who is emotionally available as needed, who can delight in all her daughter's strengths without becoming competitive, and who knows how to cherish a budding rose, thorns and all.

Similarly, a son needs the feeling that he is his father's idea of what a boy should be, that his father respects him as a fellow male. Does he feel that his father cares about him, is interested in him, and is proud of how he is maturing? All of this is conveyed in actions as well as, sometimes more than, in words. A father who says he is pleased with his son's woodworking or bowling score, for example, but finds fault with him continually as they work or play, negates his words. A father who is considerate and supportive of his son gives his boy the feeling that he is a worthwhile person. Is the father authoritative but flexible, firm but reasonable? Can he be gentle as well as strong? This is going to be the son's deepest image of what a man should be.

In a home where there is no father, a mother needs to be careful not to lean too much on her son, particularly as he is maturing. A son should be treated as a son, not expected to take a man's place in the home. Wherever possible, other men should be brought into his life. Can he often visit or be visited by an uncle or grandfather or a close family friend? Some mothers engage a "boy-sitter" one afternoon a week when their children are small, but a boy this age begins to outgrow such an arrangement. Sometimes it is possible to have a live-in male student who functions as a kind of big brother to a boy. This can become complicated, however, if there is a teen-age daughter in the home as well. When a mother takes her son on trips, it is good if another boy can go along as well. Each family will fashion its own ways of meeting the problem. But a boy needs masculine figures in his life, should not grow up in too feminine a world.

What kind of mother does a boy want and need? "A motherly one," said one boy. But motherly means different things at different ages. Right now, it means being somewhat less protective than before and neither domineering nor too permissive. As with father and daughter, a mother who shows her son that she has pride in his ability and accomplishments and confidence in him, treats him with warmth, affection, and respect, helps him to become a man.

The influence upon children of their parents' marriage cannot be overestimated. Do parents appreciate each other and respect each other? This strongly influences the child's feelings about relationships between men and women. If parents have frequent bitter quarrels, this can cause young people more anguish than is always understood. Unfortunately, however, a great many homes are not as happy as both partners would wish. Although they may be resigned to their relationship or working to improve it, both need to help their children get along in the situation as it exists. Such parents can try not to let the bitterness of the marital situation spill over into hostility toward the children. It is important, too, to guard against letting a child fill the emotional place of a husband or wife. Where it is humanly possible, parents should try not to let the children witness or overhear marital discord. Beyond that, and as the children grow older, ways might be found to show them that not all marriages are like this and that relationships between men and women can be close and good.

4
The Struggle Over Limits

TWELVE-YEAR-OLD RON WOKE up Monday morning feeling exhausted and not much like getting out of bed. "Why did you let me watch that movie until 11:30?" he berated his mother. "You knew I'd be tired in the morning!" Needless to say, Ron had insisted the night before that he would be just fine in the morning, that he was quite old enough to decide for himself how much sleep he needed. He had pressured his mother until she finally gave in, more from fatigue than conviction.

Now, this morning, he is telling her in effect that *she* is supposed to be the responsible one, that she has no right to let him do anything he wants. What he means, really, is that he is counting on his parents to provide wise and firm limits for him. How else, after all, can he safely push? And push he must, because he is on the final lap of his journey toward independence. Unfortunately, there is a time lag between his desire to be on his own and his ability to control his impulses and regulate himself. And deep down he knows it. This is where his parents come in. They must be able to say "No" to him even when he pleads or fights, and to say "Yes" even when they are still fearful, to let him go when they still want to hold him safely and warmly to them.

Perhaps the most difficult thing we must do as parents is to help our children become independent of us. We nurture them from the day of their birth, we guide them through difficult times, we comfort them when they are miserable, and we share their delights and their triumphs. We are part of all the days of their lives. All this time we are deriving the deepest satisfaction from giving of ourselves, from the feeling of being important to our children, of being needed, necessary to their very existence.

The Beginning of Independence

Then a time comes in their lives—adolescence—whose natural end is their independence of us. Their freedom. It is difficult to face because, for one thing, we cannot really envision what kind of relationship we will have with our children when they, too, are adults. So we know only what we are losing—our children as children. The irony is that the better we have done our job, the more independent of us they will truly be. Still, independence can mean many things.

Do you remember how exhausted and uncertain you felt during your first weeks at home with your new baby? How the continual round of feeding and diapering and responding to cries made you feel that you might never again have a moment to yourself?

One harried new mother phoned her pediatrician after a particularly wearing night spent more by the crib than in bed. "When will he become less demanding?" she implored.

"Never!" responded the doctor. What he neglected to mention, of course, was that her baby would be demanding in a very different way at four months than he was at four weeks and than he would be at four years. And that the mother, who would gain in knowledge and experience, might well find subsequent demands upon her easier to bear, and surely more interesting, than the current strain upon her weary body.

Just so, in our relationship with our grown children, independence need not mean emotional separation. Strong bonds of warmth and love can coexist with independence. The situation between our children and us will change, but if things go well, we can look forward to many years of being part of each other's lives in a way that all of us will find rewarding.

Letting Our Children Go

How do we move toward this time? How do we let go? Not in a burst at sixteen or eighteen or twenty-one, but gradually, little by little as the children push in this direction or that and we bend and give and hold back, often not knowing if we have let them go too far or held on too tight.

And our children do not make things any easier for us. In order to find themselves, they must begin to separate themselves from us; indeed, they must push us away. In early adolescence they do this with a vengeance, all the while holding on for dear life because they are not yet ready to stand alone. The thirteen-year-old daughter who presses to go out on a date with a boy may be terrified if we actually permit it. She will feel unloved unless we restrict her actions to protect her from venturing beyond her depth.

In order to become free of us, they must attack our way of doing things. In order to find out what they think, they must challenge our thinking. Like the writer who said, "How do I know what I think until I see what I write," our children often seem to say, "How can I know what I *don't* think until I hear what *you* say."

Sometimes parents are so controlling that they insist that children accept their way under all circumstances. On the beach one hot summer day, a mother pressed her daughter, "Wear your sandals until you reach the water, or you'll burn your feet." The girl, who was at least thirteen, resisted: "If the sand burns my feet, I'll come back and get my sandals." But her mother continued to press, unable to permit the child, even in this very limited instance, the experience of finding out for herself, of possibly getting burned.

How much toleration do we have for our children's experimentation? It is not easy to watch a child set out in the wrong direction and not call out "Stop!" When our children were small, we would stop them if we thought they might be risking a broken leg, but we would tend to stand aside if the worst possibility was only a bad scrape. This is the kind of thinking we have to update to meet today's problems. Needless to say, they are far more sophisticated, but our basic dilemma is the same. Overprotection may give parents peace of mind and extend their control, but it is not in the best interests of the child. Suzanne Strait Fremon writes, in *Children and Their Parents Toward Maturity:*

> A child who is too protected will never develop his sense of danger, his judgment of people, his evaluation of circumstances, his knowledge of his own possibilities and limitations, and his ability to organize himself and his actions.

We try to protect our children from all

kinds of things while gradually letting them take over. Again, that is very much the trick of being a parent, sensing when they are ready to take over and neither hovering too long nor not long enough.

Freedom to Come and Go

By the time a child reaches eleven, he has already spread his wings in the neighborhood. He goes to school alone, he can travel on the bus and go to the grocery store, the shoe repairer, and the bakery if they are fairly near. The schedule, of course, varies depending on the community. Where public transportation is available, he can usually go to his piano lesson alone, or to have his braces adjusted or his hair cut. But now he begins to want to venture farther afield, to go to a movie or concert alone or with friends, to go rowing in the park, to go to an amusement park on the other side of town, to come home alone from a friend's house at night. How can we tell when he is ready?

Very much as we have been doing all along—by knowing our own child. How capable is he really? How much self-confidence does he have? Does he tend to be cautious or reckless? How comfortable is he with people? In case of emergency, would he go to someone for help? How does he react when he is frightened? Does he panic, or would he think clearly enough to call home? What are the realistic dangers in a particular situation; for example, if a hundred twelve-year-old boys were to go off to that amusement park, what might happen to one or all of them? We have to balance the dangers of children not experiencing freedom enough for healthy growth with the dangers of their being frightened or hurt. If we are too permissive, a child can get into serious difficulty because of lack of experience, or he may feel that we don't care.

Sometimes we have to say "No." Even though he sounds and looks as though we are forbidding him what he wants most in the whole world, we decide that the responsibility is too much for him just yet. Occasionally a child who is very much afraid of something will push for it as a way of denying his fear to himself. But a child should not have to be so brave or so daring in a situation that has real dangers.

We must judge each request on its individual merits. Perhaps he asks to go on an all-day outing to the beach with some friends. We say we feel this is too dangerous for him this year. He replies that he is quite capable of looking out for himself; why can't we have faith in him? Although he is pressing hard—we never want him to have any fun, we spoil everything, and so on—we sense that underneath he is nervous about the whole idea. He very much needs us to say "No" and to help him get out of the situation gracefully without losing face with his friends.

When he has cooled off, we can discuss with him trips to places he might enjoy that are not quite so far afield and would help him gain experience and confidence. We can talk about next year or the year after and try to help him understand that we will let him go when we think he is ready. He may angrily reject this faraway possibility now, but he will begin to look toward it and it will help—the door is not closed forever.

We may feel more comfortable with a child who admits fear, who says, for example, "I'd like to go on the train alone to visit Grandma, but I'm a little nervous about it." With him, we can discuss the pros and cons, decide when to encourage and when to hold back, learn how he feels about various experiences. A child who will not admit he is frightened, who boasts with bravado, "Of course I can do it," is generally harder to help.

The Need for Guidance

A youngster develops over the years a sense of his environment, where it is sensible to go and where it is not. He learns to answer such questions as: Should I come home from there by myself after dark? Is that a good place for a girl to go alone? Would I get into trouble there? But meanwhile we need to guide them.

We need not go along with the crowd. We have the responsibility to protect our child, and we cannot delegate it to those generous and devil-may-care parents all his friends seem to have. But it is true that the only child who cannot—when it happens too often—does become stigmatized, left out. So we need to balance his need to be part of his group against the importance in our eyes of a particular restriction.

In order to justify their restrictions, parents may be tempted to exaggerate the dangers in a situation. But we cannot expect a child to trust what we tell him about heroin, for example, if we have lied to him all along about other things. If he wants to come home alone at night from a party, we can talk over with him the real possibilities of danger. Then, even if he does not come around entirely to our view, we expect him to comply with our wishes. We should not feel that we have to frighten him in order to get him to obey. If there is an honest relationship between parents and child, the child will respect the parents and be more apt to be swayed by their opinions. Remember that, as times goes on, he will increasingly tend to make his own decisions, with or without our counsel. His trust in us is important to both of us.

Some parents hesitate to take a strong position lest they be considered dictatorial or punitive, or alienate their youngster. They mistake a child's rebelliousness and criticisms as evidence of their failure or of the child's lack of respect and love for them. It is very hard to feel otherwise. We know that beefing is par for the course—a kind of background music to adolescence—but each confrontation hits us afresh. It is *our* child criticizing *us*. It really is hard to feel sure of ourselves and secure in our opinions. Think of it sometimes as if he and we were playing parts in a play. His role is to push us, and our role is to stand firm. If we were to give in, to change our role, it would throw everything off—most of all him.

The Child's Room

Not only do we limit our child's freedom outside the home, but also inside it. And nowhere are our rules more apt to be questioned or ignored than in the area of his room. "This is MY room. These are MY belongings. Why can't I live in a mess if that's what I like?" If some social scientist made a study, he would probably find that every ten minutes, at least, somewhere in the United States, a twelve-year-old girl was saying this to her mother. Most of us these days find it rather difficult to come back with, "Cleanliness is next to godliness." All right then, why *does* her room have to be in order?

Are we saying to ourself that banana peels on the floor, muddy shoes on the bedspread are unhealthy, unsafe, and revolting? No doubt we can reasonably look upon decaying fruit skins and things of that ilk as hazardous, but the bedspread is not that clear-cut, particularly if it can be thrown into the washing machine once a week (possibly by her) and needs no ironing. And revolting? To whom?

Well, we cannot believe that she can work well amid that junkheap. She is not learning good habits and will gradually descend into sloth, there perhaps to remain. But most of us know capable adults who work well, thrive even, in comparable disorganization. Of course, it does seem as if a person could work more efficiently if she did not have to spend time looking for objects long since buried under other objects. But some children seem to possess built-in divining rods: they know exactly where under that mountain lies that red ballpoint pen.

At this point we may have to face the fact that we want her room in order because *we* just cannot stand living with that mess. Could we keep her door closed all day and pretend we have one less room in the house? No? It still drives us crazy?

Presumably by the time our child is eleven or twelve we have taught her everything we know about organizing belongings and placing soiled clothes in the laundry hamper, so what we are dealing with here is not a failure of intellect on her part. Still, we could offer to devote some time to helping her arrange her things, and it is possible that she does not have enough shelf space or whatever. But the chances are, quite frankly, that her room is messy because she likes it that way.

Rethinking the Problem

We will want to think carefully about how much rearrangement of her surroundings we feel justified in demanding. How much cleanliness and neatness do we have in mind, and how often would we expect her to put her room into that condition? She is right in considering her room a special preserve, a part of her, really. At the moment it reflects her feelings, for reasons that we—and possibly she—cannot fathom. She is comfortable with it this way. So it is not a good idea to push her any further than is absolutely necessary. Would a once-a-week, or when-company-is-coming, pick-up and put-away be enough if she agrees to make her bed and empty her wastebasket every day and not leave food or drink lying around indiscriminately? Would we be able to agree to close our eyes to the clutter at other times?

We can discuss our feelings and ideas with our child. We can try to limit ourself in time and space—that is, to this room and the present; try not to torture ourself with visions of our daughter as a wife and mother with cockroaches in the cupboard and potato chips crackling underfoot, all because she never learned (and we failed to teach her) to keep her room clean. She still has some growing up to do, so it is not sensible for us to think of her or label her as a slob for life.

Most of us feel we have to convince our children that clean is better than dirty, that order is more esthetically pleasing than mess. We want them to *care* whether their rooms are neat or not. This caring may come in time or it may not, but it must come from within the child.

When children share a room and one likes order and the other likes clutter, it is sometimes possible to divide the room so that each has an area to live in as she likes. We may hang a movable curtain, or install a sliding, accordion-pleated room divider. In any case, each child must agree to respect the other's private domain and know who is responsible for doing what cleaning and when. The more clear-cut and understood that can be, the better.

How He Looks

The way a child dresses, the way he combs his hair, the way he arranges himself, is also of deep importance to him. Whether he is sloppy or neat, whether he looks like everyone of his friends or has his own particular style, it is what he wants for himself. Parents need to encourage cleanliness and to offer guidance about dress and grooming, but it is a sensitive area. If a boy's hair is always standing up in back, his father might invite him in for a conversation one Saturday morning while he is shaving and then casually offer him some of his hair cream while he is using it. If a girl wears her hair in an unflattering way, a mother might point out hairdos in a magazine that she thinks would look well on her daughter.

The trouble, though, is that this sort of hinting often turns into pushing, or the manner in which a suggestion is made belittles the way the child is now. We don't want our child to become dissatisfied with his appearance or more self-conscious. He cannot accept our guidance if he sees it as a put-down of his taste, or of him. Wherever possible, we should permit him to reject our advice and do things his way. Youngsters of this age tend to be sloppy. Sometimes they wish they could throw a big blanket over those disturbing bodies of theirs. Some of them do! Dirtiness seems to be more fashionable than ever among some children today, but most of us are still unhappy and embarrassed by a sloppy, dirty child. Some days it may seem that all we talk about is his appearance. We decide that his messy habits are ruining our relationship.

How much can we bear? We must bear what we can, keep reminding ourself that he will probably outgrow this phase sooner or later. Sooner, if we can avoid making it an issue, making him feel that his rights and his manhood are at stake. If we look around, we will notice that many of his friends also look as if their parents had neither bathtub nor mirror. It is important also not to comment upon his appearance in front of other people.

When we are exasperated because he cannot seem to wash—in fact, he smells—it is not helpful to call him a slob or a pig. We can remember how we feel when he calls us selfish or a mean mother. It happens to most parents, and yet it can make us feel awful—and angry, too. And it does not particularly make us feel like doing what he wants. It is this way with our children, also. The worst thing about a label like slob or stupid or lazy is that after a while a child gets to believe it himself. Most of us know a grown woman who seems to be always on the go and yet refers to herself as lazy.

It is good sometimes to think back to our own adolescence, to the ways our own parents enforced limits that helped us to learn and grow. Memories of being embarrassed in front of friends or members of the family, or of being made to feel incompetent or hopeless, are also useful. They can help us to understand how our children feel if we do this to them.

Often it helps with a child to agree to a kind of performance contract. Together we discuss the various points at issue. We consider his ideas; he considers ours. We come up with a compromise that we are both willing to live with. Neither of us may be completely satisfied, and yet it seems a way of meeting our mutual needs. This does not imply total equality between parent and child, nor does it mean that we are giving up our parental authority. We remain free to exercise control as necessary. But when a child is able to participate in regulating himself, he moves closer to self-control, which is the ultimate aim of all discipline.

The Telephone

Unfortunately, the telephone problem is going to get worse before it gets better. Children this age need to talk on the phone. What they do, really, is to have extended visits with one another this way, relieved of the anxiety and inhibitions that often accompany face-to-face talks. They gossip, they chatter, they giggle, they whisper. They discuss in endless detail all the happenings of the day they have just lived through. They make dates and break dates. They compare homework. They call to remind one another to watch a television show or to bring colored pencils to school tomorrow or to wear their matching purple jeans. They recount in excruciating detail the movie they saw last Saturday. They make loving noises and hating noises, ecstatic noises and revolting noises. Sometimes they eat while they talk, or listen to records, or even do exercises. They talk lying down or standing up or in any one of a variety of contorted positions on a chair, a bed, or the floor. They complain about their parents, their teachers, their brothers and sisters, their other friends. The telephone for them is an escape from the family, a release from tension, a tool for developing social skills, a joy. They can talk on it for a very, very long time.

Needless to say, there is nothing inherently harmful in all this, and they never seem to get sore throats from it. Unfortunately for them, other people in the household want to be able to make and receive calls. If the family can afford a second phone during these years, the situation does become easier. But if not, we can try setting a firm time limit on calls and a firm limit on the number of calls per day or per week. In addition to the inconvenience, youngsters this age can often run up astronomical phone bills. When this money is needed elsewhere in the family budget, a definite limit on the number of calls per child must be set for financial reasons. This means that every call above the agreed-upon number must be paid for out of the child's own money; we can hang a checklist and collection box on the wall next to the phone, if necessary.

Sometimes, however, phone bills upset parents who would not object to the same money being spent on other, equally nonessential, activities. It is a way of looking at things. Such a parent might feel guilty calling a dear friend in another town once in a while and running up a two-dollar phone bill. But she would feel perfectly comfortable spending that sum on round-trip bus fare to visit the friend, or spending even more to have lunch with her at a restaurant. If we have this difficulty, we might want to reconsider our attitude toward telephone bills in view of the genuine importance of the telephone to an adolescent.

Verbal Hostility

We have to be willing to accept a certain amount of outspoken resentment and hostility from our youngsters. The child has to test himself, his opinions and values, against us. He should not have to deny his feelings or hide them; he cannot learn to handle them that way. But at the same time, he is greatly in need of our continuing support. In the past, parents often felt it was wrong, disloyal, for children to express anger or hatred toward them. Children were made to feel guilty for those feelings. But today we know that our children cannot feel love for us all the time, that it is normal for them to feel positively murderous toward us some of the time. These feelings, if we accept them philosophically, do not last, and they do not damage the good basic relationship we have with our children.

This does not mean that we have to tolerate continual verbal abuse. The child has a right to complain, but not endlessly. Neither does he want us to lecture him continually. He is entitled to bring up the subject again for review, but not every minute or at any hour of the day or night. He cannot throw things, use language that offends us, or become more abusive than we can bear.

Remember, too, that he does not have to agree with our restrictions; he just has to abide by them. It is not helpful to keep at him in an effort to prove that we are right and he is wrong. This causes a great deal of wear and tear on both of us and gets nowhere. He has to do it, but he does not have to like it.

We must not expect our son to feel warmly toward us when he has to come home earlier than he wanted, or our daughter to be gracious every night when she is clearing the table. Remember that this is a stage of life when a child may become annoyed with us even when we think we are being lovely. One mother tells of exclaiming "Oh, how cute you look!" when her twelve-year-old daughter appeared in a new pants outfit one morning. To which the girl replied rudely, "If everyone's going to be saying that to me all day, I might as well go right in and take it off!"

Setting Bedtime

When we say, "You must be in bed by 9:30," is this because our child happens to need ten hours of sleep each night, or because we think children of twelve should have a 9:30 bedtime, or because we need the peace and quiet and privacy? It is helpful to know the "why" of the rules when our child protests: "Nobody in the whole class has to be in bed as early as I do!" "I'm not tired. Why do I have to go to bed?" "I'm old enough to decide how late I should stay up."

Some children seem able to regulate themselves at a fairly early age. They wash when they are dirty, they do their homework before it piles up, and they actually go to sleep when they are sleepy. If a girl like this stays up late one night reading or watching television or gabbing on the phone with a friend, she will probably decide on her own to get to bed early the next night. If we regulate this child's bedtime arbitrarily or fuss on the rare evenings when she stays up too late, we are interfering with her growth. She is learning more when the natural consequences of her actions continue to influence her: she stays up late, she is sleepy the next day, she goes to bed early that night. The other way—she stays up late, mother is grumpy—may get her to bed at a set time for as long as she lives at home, but it is not helpful to her in the long run.

What about the child who knows he is exhausted when he stays up beyond a certain time but just cannot seem to take that fact into account when he is involved in a hot game of gin rummy with his brother? He needs us to control him for a while yet. Bedtime is at 9:30 (or whenever); he can gripe, he can plead, but bedtime is at 9:30. We are not angry with him, because we know that nobody likes to have to go to bed when they are enjoying themselves, and we are not asking him to be delighted. We are only asking him to do what experience has shown is best for him. Exceptions? "I have just this one more chapter of *Tom Sawyer* to read" or ". . . just these three more math problems to do." If this is a regular nightly story, we need to be firm. We might suggest that he set his alarm for an hour earlier and finish the next morning if he absolutely must. Some youngsters work better this way. On the other hand, if he is usually willing to abide by the rules, we will want to make an exception from time to time, making clear that it *is* an exception.

Changing the Rules

Perhaps "everybody" really is allowed to stay up later than he is. He feels like a baby with so early a bedtime. He is ashamed when his friends call at 9:45 and are told that he is in bed. Or he lacks the time to get his work done and have some fun, too. Maybe we need to renegotiate the contract. What bedtime would he feel was sensible? What does he do with his time? Is he so loaded with schoolwork and chores and practicing the trumpet that he honestly has no time to take it easy? Does he play around a lot after he comes home from school? Every child needs a chance to unwind after the school day, but perhaps he could be starting the things he has to do a little earlier? Is there anything he would give up that could provide him with more time for the things he feels he is missing? How much sleep does he actually need each night in order to function well? Would we be willing to experiment for a week with a bedtime an hour later and see how he feels? It is a good idea, when we have agreed to something like this, to let the week go by without day-to-day comments such as, "You look a little sleepy this morning," or "You had the extra time and I see you still didn't get your closet cleaned out." We should make it a fair chance, meaning that both of us have an opportunity to evaluate how it is working without bias. If we have a complaint about his closet or something else he is supposed to do, it is worth talking to him about these things separately and not letting our feelings about them complicate the bedtime arrangements.

As a youngster becomes able to get along with less sleep, his staying up late may infringe upon his parents' leisure, their time to relax and talk alone together. It is tempting, then, to insist upon an unreasonably early bedtime. And since we feel a little guilty about pushing him to bed just to get him out of the way, we are apt to camouflage our needs with talk about "his own good." The issue of bedtime then gets cluttered up with odds and ends—our guilt, his anger—that really need not be there and that just add unnecessary complications.

Why should we feel guilty about wanting a little relaxation? Our needs are legitimate. But why should he go to bed just because we do not want him around? When the situation is reexamined as a problem in logistics, it often can be worked out reasonably well. If he has a room of his own or there is a family room, he could be asked to retire to it after a certain time, without boisterous play or clamorous comings and goings. If children share a room and one goes to sleep earlier than the other, space needs to be found for the older one to work or enjoy himself without disturbing us. Will the kitchen do? Some arrangements can be worked out if a family puts their heads together. If there is one thing that adolescent children recognize, it is the need for privacy. If they feel welcome to come and go as they choose most of the time, they are likely to accept restrictions that ensure everyone's rights after a certain hour in the evening.

On the other hand, some children do feel like second-class citizens living in their parents' home. Perhaps they are constantly asked to remove themselves and their belongings from the place where their parents are together. Or, perhaps their parents express their demands in such a way as to reinforce that feeling: "As long as you're living in *my* house you must . . ." wipe your feet or be polite or whatever. It is much better to place the emphasis on mutual respect and concern for the feelings and needs of everyone in the household. After all, we really want our children to think of it as their home, too. And often we will want to balance our need for adult conversation (or quiet!) with their need to feel part of the family group, one of us.

Household Chores

Sometimes a mother hesitates to insist that children help with household chores lest she be considered unkind or unreasonable. She may feel, for example, that her children should help her after dinner. But they have made it clear that they have their own work to do and think it is unfair that they should have to help with hers. So she does not press, but she is angry each night as everyone gets up and leaves her to clean up after them. In one way or another, her children will feel her resentment, and it is not good for them or for her.

When a child's help is needed, he should be expected to give it—and sometimes to beef about it. But certain things can be done to make it more palatable.

We should not expect a perfect job. We probably will not get it, and he will dread helping if he can never do the job well enough to suit us.

We should try not to wait until we must have the milk immediately before asking him to go to the store. If he has some leeway in choosing when to perform a particular task, he is more likely to perform it graciously.

We should not interrupt his homework to ask him to do a job. His work deserves to be respected also.

It is not undermining his sense of responsibility if we give him a day off occasionally. It is good for him to feel that when he is overtired, or overburdened with work, or feeling low, someone cares and makes allowances.

We know that life is easier for us because he helps. We know that it is nicer for us in the kitchen when he is setting the table or peeling the potatoes while we put the roast on. Let him know it, too. "Well, you finally remembered to put the salt and pepper on the table" is not praise!

Needless to say, it is better to give him a job he likes than one he hates. Few grownups rush to do jobs they dislike.

When two children dislike working alone, can they get along well enough to share jobs?

When he comes in to help with a chip on his shoulder, we should try to overlook it. He is thinking, "Okay, I'll help, but don't expect me to be nice about it." This is a compromise of sorts; we are getting the help; he is getting the satisfaction of showing how he feels. That's fair enough.

Do household jobs teach a child responsibility? It is hard to say. Surely the child whose job it is to feed the dog or the turtle—and who remembers to do it on his own—feels important and necessary to the animal. Then again, if he is always forgetting and feeling guilty about that, or his mother is always reminding him or doing it for him, it is another matter. Most household chores that children are asked to do, such as folding laundry, helping with the dishes, and the like, are deadly dull. In themselves they give a child no feeling of achievement at all. He has to do his share because he is told to. But satisfaction will come only from feeling that he has been important to us. Unfortunately, a job is often robbed of this by our constant criticism of a child's performance or our grumpiness because he is late in doing it. Or his work is discredited by our own general feeling of contempt for housework. Where any of these conditions prevail, a youngster will get little that is positive out of doing his assigned task.

When a child is downright miserable at having to do a certain chore and does it poorly or ungraciously or both, there is no way we can be sincerely appreciative. It is a good idea under such circumstances to offer him the chance to help in some other way, if possible.

Sometimes it is unfuriating to read about being reasonable with our children. We feel like the six-year-old who, when urged to be good, retorted "My good is all run out." For one reason or another we just could not cope all day; when the children misbehaved we charged through the house creating havoc; we screamed at our daughter, exploded at our son. The way we feel now, what we need is a new son, a new daughter, and a new disposition. But we can take heart. It really is impossible to be kind and understanding and reasonable all the time. If we forgive ourself, we will find ourself better able to forgive the children, too.

There may be periods when it seems to a child that a rule holds him back every time he tries to turn around. He will tell us he feels "fenced in." He will fight hard on a tiny matter that we know cannot be that important to him. He will complain that he "can't breathe around here." Sometimes life in general becomes too much for a youngster. He lets down on compliance, and we, understandably, tighten up. But this is the very moment he can stand it least. Then, too, a parent sometimes presses too hard, making too many rules or getting after a child without giving him a chance to follow through on his own, in his own way. Or a child outgrows some of the restrictions that were suitable last year, or only last month. They feel as tight on him as last year's clothes.

If we sense that our child is feeling particularly pressured, we can let up on him for a while and give him the extra breathing space he needs. Leeway given in the right spirit at the right time is just as important as proper limits.

Television Privileges

Joe's mother came home one day from a P-TA meeting and informed her son, "You said that nobody else in your class has to finish his homework before he can watch TV, but Mrs. Schultz told me that Teddy isn't allowed to watch TV on school nights at all!"

When Joe returned from school the next afternoon he told his mother the actual situation. "You're right about the rules at Teddy's house, Mom," he said. "But the thing is, his mother is always going out evenings and Teddy cheats."

We all like to feel that our children will follow our rules whether we are there or not. We take a dim view of "cheating," of complying only when someone is there to see. But there are ways in which parents make such rebellion more likely. Is Teddy's mother inviting defeat by asking too much? Teddy sees his parents go out to enjoy themselves after their working day. If he has done his work, perhaps he thinks he should be able to enjoy himself as well.

Joe, on the other hand, wants to watch a program or two before he settles down to work. Would he do his work conscientiously afterward and would he leave himself sufficient time? If his parents insist that he finish his homework first, will he rush through it in order to get to the TV set? Work before play is a good habit to develop, but it can be overdone. A child often needs to unwind after school. Television provides for some youngsters this age a release from all the cares of the school day or from new and disturbing sexual impulses.

When a child seems to be living in front of the television set to the exclusion of practically everything else, parents would want to find out why—is he bored, unhappy, having trouble with school, friends—and to attempt to deal with the underlying problem.

If parents do decide to limit TV watching, or anything else, they should know why they are restricting their child and what they expect to accomplish by it. Are they restricting TV, for example, because they feel the youngster should be playing outdoors more, or spending time with friends, or reading, or studying, or helping about the house? Or do they disapprove of the programs he chooses to watch?

Perhaps his interest or activity could be stimulated in another area. A positive desire to do something else, perhaps with a parent, would draw him away from TV and be less apt to leave him feeling deprived. It is wise to ask the child how much television he thinks is a fair amount per week. Parents sometimes overlook this step, expecting that the child will make outrageous demands that would only cause more conflict. But when children are approached this way, they generally try to be responsible. Sometimes a child asks for the chance to cut down on his own, rather than have a set ration of hours per day or week imposed on him by his parents. This is worth giving a try.

In a large family, squabbling over who watches what may be reduced if everyone joins in preparing a weekly schedule for watching. Sometimes a father insists upon watching "the game" whenever it is on, or a mother feels that a movie she wants to see deserves priority over a child's regular shows for the evening. Or a child may feel that because he watches a certain show every Tuesday at 7:30 he owns that time slot. The resolving of this kind of conflict depends on the values of the family. In some families it is expected that the hard-working wage-earner deserves priority over the rest of the family, or that the parents do because they are the parents. In others everyone takes a hand in deciding what programs are watched.

The way in which parents announce their preferences to their children is important. There is a world of difference between, "Tonight's game is the playoff, sure to be a great one. I know you'll enjoy it; why don't you watch it with me?" and "I'm watching the game, and that's that!" Still more difficult for a child is, "If you were considerate you'd appreciate how tired I am when I come home from a day's work; you'd want me to watch my show" or "If you had any taste, you wouldn't be watching that junk anyway." When parents make decisions unilaterally, they have to be ready to take the beefing. Attempts to avoid this by making the child feel guilty or witless are unfair, hard for a youngster to handle, and not conducive to good parent-child relationships in the long run.

Limits for Our Sake

Along the same line, there are some things in a family that children should be expected to do, or refrain from doing, for their parents' comfort or peace of mind. There is nothing inherently wrong, for example, with a youngster's listening for hours on end to what a parent considers perfectly dreadful music. But he ought to be willing to turn off or lower the hi-fi when another minute of that particular record will drive the parent up the wall.

Some parents find it difficult to make a request like this without camouflaging it. Instead of asking the child to stop the music because they need to have quiet for a while, they feel that they have to have a "real" reason. So they criticize the music. An argument then ensues about the music, the child's taste, and/or the child's rights as a human being to like what he likes and play what he likes to play. All of this can be avoided simply by asking the child for a kindness. When there is give and take in a family, parents often do things they don't feel like doing because the child needs or wants them. A child will, too, if the request does not imply criticism and he can comply with dignity.

When They Break the Rules

We make certain rules, we are clear on them, the children are clear on them (more or less), but compliance is spotty. One day he comes home on time; the next day he forgets. He is chronically late to school. The phone bill will break the bank. What do we do?

Child psychiatrist Fritz Redl writes, in *Pre-Adolescents: What Makes Them Tick,* that most of the more serious difficulties between children and parents could be avoided. They are not inherent in the actual problems of growth. They are produced by the way in which adults react to them. He does not advocate that parents give up and let children do as they wish. What he suggests is that parents study each situation as it arises and decide what to allow and where to draw the line, or intervene. Inherent in his thinking is that parents need to try to be as flexible as they can, to tolerate rebelliousness within certain limits, during these difficult years. We do want our youngsters to become self-disciplined, to develop "inner controls," but this is not necessarily synonymous with getting them to do what we want them to do.

But suppose limits are being consistently overstepped and our patience is wearing thin? Let us pose an extreme situation. Our child walks in one day and tells us he has robbed a bank. Would we yell at him, punish him? Chances are, our first thought would be what in the world has got into him. In other words, why? Similarly, when a child cannot seem to get to school on time, we need to determine why. Is it because he is afraid of a tough kid on the bus, or is having difficulty with the work, or the other children, or the teacher? Or is he (even at this age) reluctant to leave us? These various possibilities leave us with different avenues of approach to the same behavior. Dr. Redl suggests, "Don't fight the behavior. Interpret the cause of it first, then judge how much and in what way you should interfere." If a child is having serious trouble in school, for example, we won't want to make an issue of his tardiness, but to work with the problem that is causing it.

Reasons Behind the Rules

We must consider, too, just how wholehearted we are about what we ask of our child. Sometimes a parent actually encourages a child's misbehavior without realizing it, because the parent derives subtle satisfaction from it. For example, a father looks at his daughter gabbing away to yet another friend on the telephone and says, "If you're not on the phone with one kid, it's another. Don't they know anyone else's number?" No doubt he is genuinely annoyed that every time he wants to make a call, there is his daughter tying up the line. But deep down, this rather shy man is pleased by his daughter's popularity, and his manner of criticizing her communicates this to her. He is telling her to cut down her use of the phone, but on a deeper level he is really encouraging her to do just the opposite.

Take another situation. An eleven-year-old boy constantly tracks mud into the house from the ballfield and never seems able to wash all the dirt from his face and hands. His mother is always telling him to wipe his feet before entering the house, to use a washcloth and soap, and so on. But something deep inside the impeccably neat woman delights in this muddy-faced ballplayer of hers, and that feeling is communicated to the child. It is not something that he could put into words, but something he senses. So all the while she thinks that he is disobeying her (and so does he!), he is actually responding to what she really desires. If we are not getting compliance from a child, we should give some thoughts to whether it is what we honestly want.

Possibility of Compromise

When there has been a good deal of argument and resistance about an issue, we might try a hands-off policy, no nagging or even hinting for, say, a week. Then, if our child has not made an effort to do better on his own, we can have a talk with him to see how he thinks he could improve his performance or why he feels he cannot. Perhaps he leaves his bed unmade every day when it is supposed to be made before he leaves for school. He says, "I can't help it, Mom. It's the one job around here I just can't stand!" Perhaps he could make an arrangement with his sister, who hates taking her turn at clearing the table. Or perhaps there is something he could do for us in return for our making his bed. Or maybe if he leaves his door closed every day we could decide it was not that important and give in on this issue. If discussion yields no meeting of minds, and we feel it is time to insist, we should state our decision without rancor, tell him what we will expect from him in the future, and then change the subject.

If he still does not comply, we may need to restrict privileges or exert pressure in some other fair way (a child this age is too old for spanking). But we must be ready to ease up as soon as he shows a willingness to comply. Parents who constantly meet rebellion with angry threats and punishments succeed either in thoroughly cowing a child or simply fostering more rebellion, often concealed—a child is less and less at home, for example.

As time goes on, we will be able to supervise less and less of our youngster's life. Mutual respect and affection will be all we have going for us, our only credit in the bank, as it were. We want the kind of relationship that will enhance our influence on him later in all kinds of situations when he is away from us, affect his decisions about how fast he drives a car, what he does about sex, alcohol, cigarettes, or experimenting with drugs.

The child always needs to know why he must do this or may not do that. This is more than ever true as he gets older. It is hard to explain the reason for every little thing we ask, but in general a youngster should understand the reasons behind the rules that regulate his life. He should have a chance to discuss all restrictions with us and to have his thoughts and feelings respected. When we have to overrule him, we will want to do so in a manner that preserves his self-respect. Although they beef, children by and large accept reasonable rules. They need rules. Rules, when they allow adequate room for growth, provide the security that enables a youngster to test and develop his powers in an emotionally healthy fashion.

5
Values

NEWSPAPERS CARRY HEADLINES such as: "Mayor Indicted on Three Counts of Fraud"; "Plot to Fix Criminal Cases Laid to County Prosecutor"; President Accused of Lying to the People." And we must try to give our children acceptable values by which to live. The task gets harder all the time. How can we help our young people to lead worthwhile lives in a society that often does not support their best instincts?

The truth is that nobody really knows precisely how values are passed on from one generation to another. We need to be somewhat suspicious of anyone who says: "This is how to produce a good person." In ancient times Socrates pointed out the many noble Greek leaders who had unworthy sons. We can all find among our acquaintances examples of fine people whose children are no credit to them—or the reverse, children who have become admirable human beings despite rather unprincipled parents.

Virtue, therefore, is not necessarily contagious. A parent who is generous, honest, just, and responsible is not guaranteed children with the same assortment of commendable qualities. Good example is not always sufficient. What is more, children perceive their parents differently from the way the rest of the world does. They see another side of us. For example, a mother who gives generously of her time to the hospital-fund drive may be stingy with her time at home.

Deciding Our Standards

Then, too, how certain are we of the standards we want to impart to our children? A group of New York City parents met one evening to discuss values. They explored such questions as, "Do our children reflect in their actions the way they are treated by their parents? Is it wrong to be manipulative in planning for our children? Do a child's friends have greater influence on him today than they did in the past? Would we honestly be willing to allow our children to live lives that are significantly different from ours, with different values from our own? If today's children are more flagrant in their rebellion against authority, is it because they are more open, more truthful, or more bold? If we as parents do not agree on absolutes, how can our children develop standards?" The group attempted to agree on a single value that all thought was necessary and could not do so. Today social change is rapid. Good people do not all agree on what is most important.

Are we ready for our children to judge us by our own standards? Sometimes parents are not. After all, when our children were younger, they accepted pretty much everything we told them about life, and they believed our judgments about people. Now they are beginning to question our views and to be critical of our behavior. It is healthy, but hard to take. Perhaps we find ourselves saying things like "You think you know better?" or "What makes you the expert all of a sudden?" Yesterday we were ten feet tall, but their eyes reflect a smaller image now.

In order to find their own identity, our children must develop their own values, seek out new experiences, and make their own judgments about them. They will try on for size new attitudes and new behavior, accepting this, rejecting that. Erik Erikson writes, in *Childhood and Society:*

> The adolescent mind is essentially a mind of the moratorium . . . between the morality learned by the child and the ethics to be developed by the adult.

Does that mean we ought to forget about trying to impart to our children the most important thing about ourselves, our values? That it is just a question of potluck what they pick up from us and others? Our common sense tells us this is not true, either. We know as well as we know anything that something of what we are as human beings comes across to our children. We also know that a child is naturally more receptive to his parents' values if he feels they value him. In other words, our relationship with our child will affect what he will accept and make part of himself in the course of developing his own ethic.

Differences in Background

Most of us want our children to work through to their own values—just as long as they end up where we are! This is not as unfair as it may sound. If we are thoughtful people who think seriously about our values, it is natural to want to share our perspective with our children. But how can they think just as we do? We are a generation older. Our experience of life is both greater and different. Some parents, for example, have struggled up from an impoverished background and become able to give their families a way of life and luxuries unknown to them when they were children. Toys, clothes, surroundings that were the parents' childhood dream are their children's birthright. But can these children have the same feelings about work, about money, about possessions that their parents have? If you fly to the top of a mountain by helicopter, can you feel the same about the view from the summit as those who hiked uphill all day to reach it? The values we have developed through our experience of life will not necessarily have the same meaning to someone without that experience.

We often hear of parents who struggle to put their children through college only to have the youngsters drop out before graduation. These young people seem not to value all the hard work and sacrifice that went into earning the money for their education. Why? In some cases it is relevant to ask what value was actually conveyed to the child by the parents' struggle. What else was sacrificed along the way? Did the struggle become more important than the child himself? Sometimes a father takes a second job in order to put aside money for a child's future schooling and because of this is rarely home, often tired and irritable. Perhaps that youngster would benefit more from the presence of a father who is nice to be with and can spend more time at home. But it is hard to know what is best to do. There are no easy answers. It is not wrong to work hard so that children will have more than their parents had. But when children are used to fulfill their parents' own youthful dreams, they may rebel, needing to make their own choices.

Our example *is* a powerful force in educating our children. How do we measure up to what we expect of them? Do we tend to have one set of rules of behavior for our children and another for our friends? Do we ask them to value what we do not? Are we, for example, as polite to them and their friends as we expect them to be to us and other adults? Do we do as we please with our own leisure time but harp at them to use their free time profitably? We teach our children early not to make cutting comments about people in their presence. We don't say, "Mommy, why is that lady so fat?" or "Why does that man have such a funny nose?" while the person is within hearing. But many parents feel free to criticize their children's friends about their appearance: "When are you going to cut your hair?" or "Don't you ever comb it?" or "What kind of getup is that?" Young people are easily hurt. They may hide their hurt behind bravado or even rudeness, but they are vulnerable.

Imparting Our Values

How does a child learn to be honest, to care about others, to be courageous, just, and generous? Given an opportunity to see the answers to a test, what makes one child cheat and another not? What makes one child join the crowd in picking on a weakling and another stand up for the underdog?

Partly it has to do with the way *we* handle ourselves and the people in our lives, the daily ethical judgments *we* make about one thing or another. Our youngsters draw conclusions about our values as they see us practice them. Small children take it for granted that parents will have more privileges than they and can do all kinds of things they tell the kids not to do. But at this age, youngsters begin to inspect parental behavior very closely and to point out mercilessly any discrepancy between what we do and what we expect of them. They also notice how parents treat each other and their own parents.

Some young people feel that their mother and father are fairly happy and lead productive lives. Others perceive spiritual emptiness, loneliness, unhappiness, lack of concern for others. When we think about imparting values to our children, we need to take a careful look at ourselves and ponder what our children can see in us that they will want to emulate.

We all have our weaknesses. Often it is easier for us to detect wrongdoing in another than to face up to it in ourselves. Recently a mother found after a long railroad trip that the conductor had failed to punch about $30 worth of tickets. She was about to cash them in when it occurred to her that this would amount to stealing. Just the week before she had roundly condemned a friend of her son's when she heard he had taken a model plane kit from a local store. Now she had been about to indulge in something she realized was comparable. All of us may not be quite so reflective, but we find that when our youngsters reach this age they develop an annoying habit of noticing this sort of thing, of doing our reflecting for us. When this happens, we can try to rationalize our behavior. Or we can admit our shortcoming and try to change.

Values Are Changing

That parents could preach one set of values to their children and live by another was possibly more acceptable to youth when we were growing up. Certainly, a discrepancy between what people claim to value and what they practice in their lives has never been unusual. Psychologist Kenneth Keniston says in a lecture, "Youth and Violence: The Contexts of Moral Crisis":

> When social change is slow and institutions are powerful and unchanging, there occurs what we might term the "institutionalism of hypocrisy." Children and adolescents routinely learn when it is "reasonable" to expect that the values people profess will be implemented in their behavior and when it is not reasonable. . . . In almost all societies, a "sincere" man who "honestly" believes one set of values is frequently allowed to ignore them completely, for example, in the practice of his business, in many interpersonal relationships . . . in relationships to his children, and so on—all because these areas have been officially defined as exempt from the application of his credal values.

But today values seem to be changing so quickly that "exemptions from them have not yet been defined and the universal gap between principle and practice appears in all its nakedness." This contributes, says Keniston, "to one of the central characteristics of post-modern youth: they insist on taking seriously a great variety of political, personal and social principles which 'no one in his right mind' ever before thought of attempting to extend to dealings with strangers, relations between races or international politics. . . . They frequently come from highly principled families with whose principles they continue to agree; and they have the outrageous temerity to insist that individuals and societies live by the values they preach."

A more compassionate view of this problem is taken by psychiatrist Stanley Lesser, who believes that parents want their children to see an image of themselves as they would like to be, their ideal self. He says, as quoted by Morton Hunt in an article entitled "The Gentle Art of Understanding Your Parents":

> And children want to see their parents as exemplifying that ideal. In adolescence, however, children become even more aware of reality; they interpret the difference between ideal and reality as hypocrisy or duplicity, and become deeply disillusioned. After some years, however, most children realize that what they saw was neither hypocrisy nor duplicity but only the normal gap between one's aims and one's achievements; with this realization, they achieve an adult relationship with their parents. The pity is that so many years are wasted before understanding overcomes disillusionment and replaces it with compassion and deepened love.

Conflicting Principles

It is difficult to live by our high principles. When the clerk at the supermarket makes a mistake in our favor, most of us accept it quietly, rationalizing that this makes up for one of the many times we are sure the clerk has overcharged us. This kind of negotiating with principle allows us to do what we want instead of what we should do. So shame is another reason for hypocrisy, shame that we are not better than we are. We would like to be better and, quite naturally, try some of the time to convince others that we are what we wish we were.

How can we help our children to be better than we are? They, like us, must develop their own moral judgment. Professor Lawrence Kohlberg of Harvard University suggests that one way to help children toward this goal is to form the habit of discussing situations that require moral reasoning. He believes that so-called character-building programs that teach youngsters *rules* of behavior—always be generous, loyal, honest, and so on—do not lead to real moral growth unless the reasoning behind the rules eventually is accepted by the individual. In a lecture, "Education for Justice: A Modern Statement of the Platonic View," he defines moral education as "the asking of questions and the pointing of the way, not the giving of answers, the leading of men upward, not the putting into the mind of knowledge that was not there before."

In a series of experiments, Kohlberg and his associates exposed children to situations in which a moral conflict existed and there was no simple right or wrong answer. For example, they asked, "Before the Civil War, we had laws that allowed slavery. According to the law, if a slave escaped, he had to be returned to his owner like a runaway horse. Some people who didn't believe in slavery disobeyed the law and hid the runaway slaves and helped them to escape. Were they doing right or wrong?" The psychologists drew the children into discussions by asking them further questions as they responded. They found that after a while, with this kind of "practice," children's comprehension of moral situations increased and their moral judgment became more mature. They also found that children usually preferred the highest level of moral reasoning they could understand. Their sense of justice was sharpened.

Talking Out Right and Wrong

Situations in the child's life can be used as springboards for discussion. Our son comes home with this story: He was playing ball with some friends in the park, and despite their polite requests a man walked right across the field, interrupting the game. One of the players, in anger, threw the ball at the man's legs. The man picked up the ball and refused to return it, although it did not belong to the boy who had thrown it and this was going to stop the game for all the other boys. Our son feels strongly that this man had no right to do as he did, but he realizes that the boy who threw the ball was wrong, too. One might get into such questions as: If you do someone an injury, are they justified in getting back at you any way they can, or are there limits? Children can be helped to become more sensitive to the consequences of their actions, can learn that it is often not easy to decide what would be the right or just thing to do.

Children can recognize, also, that one can decide what would be the right thing to do in a particular situation and yet not have the will to do it. One question posed to a group of seventh-grade students in an ethics class in New York City was, "Pretend you are a doctor on your way to treat a group of children who have fallen ill with a serious illness in a neighboring town. You are notified en route that your own child has been stricken with the same illness. Should you turn back to take care of your own child or go on to treat the group?" Some youngsters said the doctor should go back to treat his own child; others said he should go on. But many of the latter group added that if they were in that spot they would go back to treat their child, even though they personally believed it was the wrong thing to do.

Opportunities for similar discussions frequently arise in the home, but parents often do not think to make use of them. We are apt to make a quick moral judgment rather than encourage our children to talk and reach their own conclusions. But children learn best, according to Professor Kohlberg, by working out their own responses. An eleven-year-old sees a thin, poorly dressed boy help himself to a pear from a fruit stand and comments half facetiously that if he were going to steal he would darn well take candy and not a piece of fruit! Then, reflecting on the child's appearance, he asks, "Do you think that kid stole because he was hungry?" This can lead naturally into a discussion: Is it ever right to steal? Do you think a hungry person might have another alternative?

Discussions like this are least useful

when either parent or child is on the defensive; it is hard to learn when what we are really trying to do is prove we are right. On the other hand, if our child has done something we consider particularly kind or helpful, we can praise him and ask him for his reasons. For these talks to be meaningful, the child must be able to give his view without being criticized. Otherwise, he will go silent at the very first sign that we are "into that again." Let him finish. Parents should not show shock if his morality is somewhat primitive and should try not to end discussions with a moral or a point. The child should have a chance to weigh it all afterward. We can let him know how we feel without pressuring him into agreeing. He has to make his own way in his own good time to more sophisticated ethical thinking.

Learning from Mistakes

Our youngsters need to have the same chances we have had to make mistakes and learn from their mistakes. They need to be able to feel and think differently from the way we do, even when we are sure they are wrong! Frequently young people seem so contrary that parents conclude they have no influence at all. But even the most rebellious youngsters care what their parents think. They often become more willing to accept counsel when their parents become able to accept disagreement. And they will learn more from their mistakes if we can refrain from overemphasizing them.

Some parents have what their children consider extremely materialistic values. They are keenly interested in success, possessions, social position. What happens when such parents try to defend this way of life against a child's idealism, try to get him to become more "practical"? Generally, young people become disillusioned at this. As one older adolescent boy put it, "All my life they told me to do right—and now they tell me I have to forget everything they ever taught me if I want to 'get ahead.'" Parents who have sacrificed their own youthful idealism to make their way in the world may need to believe it was necessary. But maybe our children who have absorbed our hopes and our best ideals can find a better way to live. We ought to let them try.

People do not necessarily hate their parents just because they do not share their values. Actually, one often hears a grown man speak lovingly of his father's faults. But it is hard for our children to be relaxed about differences just now. We need to accept a certain amount of self-righteousness on their part.

Sometimes, however, children are seriously and justifiably alienated by their parents' different ways of looking at things. As put by one grown woman:

> I finally realized that my mother would never value me as I longed for her to because she just doesn't value what I value. I'm proud of all the things I can do with my hands. I make my clothes, I refinish old furniture, and I have a green thumb. People are always bringing me forlorn plants they can't grow. But my mother just thinks of things like that as stuff you can get other people to do for you. It's my sister, a biochemist, whom she thinks of as her "smart" daughter.

Some parents have great respect for the son who earns a great deal of money or the daughter who marries a rich man but find it difficult to regard a child as successful where the rewards are not financial. Clearly these parents need to rethink their ideas about what is important. A child who feels "gypped" will not be strongly motivated to give others their due.

Working Toward Change

Our society seems to give less and less support these days to our best impulses. Corruption and selfishness are all around us. But many good people are trying to change things. And our children need to feel that this is possible, that their lives can make a difference, that they are not helpless. As Peter Marin and Allan Y. Cohen write, in *Understanding Drug Use: An Adult's Guide to Drugs and the Young:*

> What the young need now are . . . parents . . . who side with their children against the powerful bureaucracies and myths that paralyze them . . . [who seek] not

> how to adjust them to things but how to find them viable alternatives.

We want our youngsters to feel that what they do matters, that *they* matter, that they can influence their environment. An attitude of "What's the use?" or "What can you expect?" or "You can't fight city hall" is discouraging. We need the energy and idealism of our young people to do battle with our immense social problems. When a young person hears on television or reads in the newspaper about a family displaced by fire or a recreation center that has been vandalized, he may feel the urge to help. And we ought to make time to encourage these efforts. Maybe he would like to look among his belongings for games or books or clothing to give. Perhaps he wants the chance to earn money to contribute. When a child can help like this, he feels that his efforts can make a difference. Parents often complain that children are self-centered, and they frequently are. But they can also be quite the opposite. It is a good idea to be alert to any expression on their part of the values we admire and encourage them.

Outside Influences

The family is not solely responsible for inculcating acceptable values in the young. Parents can expose children to a variety of situations in which values will be reinforced or extended. As Theodore Lidz writes, in *The Person: His Development Throughout the Life Cycle:*

> Society usually provides means of strengthening ethical standards as children approach and pass through puberty. The Scouts mobilize the idealistic strivings of youths and provide a code of ethics while seeking to interest the young adolescent in nature, as well as providing a favorable group setting to offset antisocial gang formation.
>
> Religious feelings become important and churches provide confirmation ceremonies with preparatory classes that reinforce ethical values. The adolescent with his new interest in ideals and ideologies can now find an interest in religion although it may have only bored him previously. He has need for such strengthening of his superego and he is beginning to seek reasons and meanings in life. . . . The youth now often experiences a closeness to God and feels that he has support and guidance in countering the temptations that are besetting him.

A basic moral principle—Do unto others as you would have others do unto you—assumes first that people must be aware of the consequences of their actions. The very young child who grabs a toy from a playmate is not yet able to realize that the other child will be unhappy as a result of what he has done. Later on, understanding this, he can become concerned about the consequences of his act. As a child becomes older, he becomes involved in more sophisticated situations in which the consequences of his actions are not always apparent. Parents need to help children to see all the possible consequences of things they might like to do.

One of the most frightening aspects of modern life is that people can become widely separated from the consequences of some of their actions and may, therefore, contribute unknowingly to terrible events. Professor Charles Reich of Yale University speculates, in an article entitled "The Limits of Duty":

> Let us follow the process of creating an evil more closely. A scientist who is doing his specialized duty to further research and knowledge develops the substance known as napalm. Another specialist makes policy in the field of our nation's foreign affairs. A third is concerned with maintaining the strength of our armed forces with the most modern weaponry. A fourth manufactures what the defense authorities require. A fifth drops napalm from an airplane when he is told to do so. The ultimate evil is the result of carefully segmented acts; the structure itself guarantees an evasion by everyone of responsibility for the full moral act. Indeed, the system, especially when it is combined with advanced technology, makes it unlikely that those who participate in the process will have any real

> awareness of the ultimate consequences. Neither the scientist nor the man in the State Department nor even the pilot actually sees the horrors of burning napalm on human flesh. The basic result of our system of doing things is to destroy awareness, alienate all of us from the consequences of our actions and prevent the formation of that very responsibility which has been at the center of our idea of criminal justice.

Parents often worry about the strong influence of their child's friends upon him at this age. Sometimes it seems as if anything a friend says has more weight than his parents' opinions. Prior to sixth or seventh grade, children look mainly to their parents for advice. But after that time the child's peers tend to have equal or greater influence on him. To some extent, this is an inevitable and healthy part of growing up. But parents may increase a child's vulnerability to pressure from his peers.

Many parents themselves overemphasize the importance of popularity, of being part of a group. Getting along with people, having people like you, paying attention to what other people think is often stressed by parents from the time the child starts school. Later, it is difficult for the same parents to pull back when their child insists something is all right because "everybody's doing it."

Spending Time with the Child

Then, also, parents in this country tend to spend less and less time with their children. In this way, many parents turn their children over to the children's friends. Professor Urie Bronfenbrenner of Cornell University makes the startling statement, in *Two Worlds of Childhood: U.S. and U.S.S.R.*, that children in the United States used to be brought up by their parents, but that this is no longer true.

> While the family still has the primary moral and legal responsibility for the character development of children, it often lacks the power or opportunity to do the job, primarily because parents and children no longer spend enough time together in those situations in which such training is possible.

Something else is sought by our children to fill the void.

In a recent study, 766 sixth-grade children reported spending during the weekend an average of two or three hours a day with their parents. Over the same period, they spent slightly more time than this with groups of friends and an additional two to three hours per day with a single friend. In short, reports Bronfenbrenner, they spent about twice as much time with friends, either singly or in groups, as with their parents. As Bronfenbrenner notes, "It doesn't take children very long to learn the lesson the adult world teaches, 'Don't bug us! Latch on to your peers!' "

Yet another, more disturbing result emerged from the same study. When the characteristics of the predominantly peer-oriented children were compared with those of predominantly adult-oriented children, the peer-oriented children reported engaging in more antisocial behavior, such as "doing something illegal," "playing hooky," lying, teasing other children. Clearly, says Bronfenbrenner,

> The vacuum left by the withdrawal of parents and adults from the lives of children is filled with an undesired—and possibly undesirable—substitute of an age-separated peer-group.

Bronfenbrenner, who refers to us as a "split society"—parents on one side, children on the other—regrets also the gradual disappearance of what is referred to as the "extended family": all the aunts and uncles and other relatives and friends who used to form part of a growing child's environment and his sphere of influence. These days many people settle in urban or suburban surroundings, often at great distances from their parents and other relatives. A study made by Professor Herbert Wright and his colleagues at the University of Kansas showed that children growing up today in small towns still get to know a substantially greater number of adults in different walks of life than do other youngsters and are more likely to be participants in the adult settings into which they enter. The other adults in these children's lives "extend" the family, help reinforce values. Often, too, they fill in for a parent who cannot function well at a particular time.

Of course, the extended family can have its disadvantages. Novelist Ann Richardson Roiphe confessed in a recent article, "The Family Is Out of Fashion," that she

> . . . would rather live in a swamp of stinging mosquitoes and biting crocodiles than spend a month with my very own blood ties. Because of educational differences, because of major value disagreements, because of the peculiar American experience that allows us to develop, peas from the same pod, into a multitude of fruits and vegetables so different from one another they can no longer cling to the same vine, we could no longer live together. We speak as many languages as destroyed the Tower of Babel. . . . It is no longer possible for us to reintegrate into an extended-family unit without violating the development of personality, of free choice, of education, of varied cultural growth that was so dearly won, so bitterly fought for by several generations of uneasy Americans.

There seems to be little doubt, however, that the greater the distance between parents and their children, the more the children will turn to their peers for sustenance and approval.

Friends Are Important

But even where parents and children have a close relationship, a child's friends are important. Some children are not members of a group or gang, either because they cannot find one that suits them or because they are not wanted or have other consuming interests. But for many young people at this age, the need to belong to a group is compelling, and they will make a great effort to achieve and retain a place in it. A young person gains from his group a feeling of strength and power.

People often think their child should be able to resist following the crowd. This is easier for a secure child, but how many are secure at eleven or even at fourteen? A child who has a feeling of his worth and place in the group can dare to be different. According to psychologists L. Joseph Stone and Joseph Church, writing in *Childhood and Adolescence: A Psychology of the Growing Person:*

> It is not enough to say that young people should have sufficient moral character to reduce group pressures; failure to conform [even when the group is doing something one considers wrong] can produce feelings of guilt and inadequacy as severe as going against one's own conscience. Thus the group can place the adolescent in a double bind situation such that either of the courses open to him will lead to painful consequences.

Sometimes parents feel one particular child is a bad influence on their youngster, and this worries them. It is a good idea in a situation like this to give some thought to what the child is really getting from the other child. Sometimes parents misinterpret a relationship or misread a youngster. We may see our own child's good qualities, despite unattractive surface behavior, yet fail to see beneath another child's mask. Then, too, the child who looks "perfect" to us is not always so, as we ought to remember from our own youth. In some situations, a relatively stable child gives support to a "wild" one, and the relationship between them, with all its complexities, may contribute to the growth of each. When we criticize our child's friends, we are attacking his judgment. Accepting his friends tells him that we have faith in his judgment, and children tend to live up to our assumptions about them.

Dangers of Poor Choices

But suppose our child has a friend who steals, for example; what do we do? That depends. First, it is probable that all we know about this child's behavior comes from what our youngster has told us, which means that if, on the basis of information we get from him, we take action that he cannot tolerate, he may be less communicative in the future. Second, how does he feel about what his friend is doing? Perhaps he is disturbed that his friend's controls are that shaky and worries whether he will be able to control himself in this or other areas. Or perhaps he is sounding us out to see how we react. The best course is to state honestly how we feel about his friend's behavior, but not indicate that we feel the child is a candidate for Sing Sing. We have to judge what the friendship means to our child, discuss it with him, and let him decide how much to see of his friend. Antisocial behavior is not necessarily contagious. Psychologist Eda LeShan writes, in *Sex and Your Teenager: A Guide for Parents:*

> There are times when it is a necessary part of growing up to live through a particular relationship. Much growth and learning about oneself can take place, even in some of the most ill-advised friendships.
>
> The only real protection against poor friendship choices is whatever help we can give our children in respecting themselves so much that they are unlikely to choose relationships that will hurt or demean them, and that we help them to understand enough about human motivation and behavior to judge others with insight. . . . Surely if a youngster seems to be making one bad choice after another, we might conclude that his perception of his value as a human being is very poor, indeed, and under such circumstances we and our child need to seek help in taking a look at this pattern.

Although the influence of one friend can be strong, in general it is not as powerful as the pressure of a group, and it leaves the child more latitude to think for himself. If a child belongs to a group, many of whom are experimenting with drugs, for example, it is fairly certain that pressure will be exerted upon all to join in. Today, perhaps more than ever, parents are concerned about group pressures toward drug-taking, violence, and other dangerous behavior. We do not want our children to pay a penalty all their lives for making serious mistakes in adolescence. When a child's friends seem to be clearly destructive, parents will want to know what draws their child toward such a group, what he is getting out of it. Can we help him satisfy his needs in some other way? Are there opportunities at school or in the neighborhood for him to join other groups? Does he have a special interest or hobby that might be encouraged, which would involve him with other young people? We would want to be particularly welcoming to other friends at this point. If we decide we must put our foot down and insist that he stop seeing a particular group, we need to offer alternative possibilities.

When a child refuses to withdraw from a group whose members experiment with drugs or engage in other dangerous activities, the chances are that he is participating in these activities; parents need to face this. Professional counseling can often give helpful insights into such a situation and is worth considering.

Following the crowd is rather common at eleven or twelve, but as a child grows into adolescence it is good if he can learn to be somewhat discriminating, if he can begin to develop as a person who exists apart from, as well as in, a group, if he can begin to evaluate fads in fashion and ideas rather than accepting them whole. A youngster may continue to need the support of his gang for a while, but this need can coexist with a growing identity of his own. Parents help a child to resist the pull of the crowd when they support his struggle to think for himself, encourage his maturing judgment—even when they disagree with his views.

Who are the adults, after all, who do not need to run with the herd? They are mostly those who, over a considerable period of time, have developed faith in their own judgment and achieved the emotional strength needed to go their own way. To be able to stand apart from one's friends, one's neighbors, when one believes they are wrong requires great courage. This takes time to acquire. By sharing our lives with our child and supporting the best that is in him, we give him the best chance we can.

6 *Changing Attitudes Toward School*

CAUGHT IN THE pubertal undertow, many children undergo profound changes in their attitude toward school, their ability to work, their behavior in class, and their relationships with their classmates. It is not surprising that a child's school hours reflect his physical, emotional, and intellectual turmoil. What is going on inside him, after all, does not cease as he walks through the school door. It is probably more remarkable that some youngsters perform as competently as ever during those years, and that others come into their own, doing better work than they have before.

But inner confusion, transient enthusiasms, moodiness, what educator Edward C. Martin refers to as "general twitchiness"[1] take their toll of most children this age in one way or another. Suddenly a child will become uncharacteristically sloppy about his work, or sloppier than ever. He will experience a general slump in performance or in those courses he likes least. Or his work will show the same uneven quality, the same ups and downs as his behavior outside of school. Or a child who has always gotten along well with his teachers and tried to please them will become critical and rebellious: "Why does he make us do this?" or "What is the point to that?"

The parent's role throughout this period is difficult. Even understanding that a bad year at school is not uncommon for this-age child, we cannot just relax and wait for him to settle down again. We are afraid he will become accustomed to working at an inferior level, to poor study habits. We are concerned because marks earned during the last year of junior high school are considered for college entrance and may be important to his future. And we believe there must be something we can do to counteract his apathy or downright antipathy to school. We also perceive that some of his criticisms are right on the mark: this assignment does appear to be inane; that regulation does not seem to consider the students' feelings. But we may not know the school situation well enough to feel sure of ourselves here either.

Understanding the Problem

There are no easy answers to these school problems, and sometimes there are no answers at all. But in order for us to be of any help to our child we need to understand fairly well what is going on, both with him and at the school. Everything we have been discussing up to this point can shed light on the child's outlook. It is clear that the urgency of other needs can distract a child from concentrating on equations and intransitive verbs. This has always been true with youngsters of this age and does not exist because of the current state of American education.

Our child may feel that pleasing a teacher is for babies, that going along with adult authority is demeaning. Certain subjects may be seen as feminine or masculine and consequently a threat to a boy's or girl's efforts to establish sexual identity. Friends

[1] Edward C. Martin, "Reflections on the Early Adolescent in School," *Daedalus* 100 no. 4 (Fall 1971): 1087–1103.

are an important part of school life, and problems in social relationships are also reflected in the child's attitude toward school. In many schools, the atmosphere is anti-intellectual; the popular and respected child is the one who excels in athletics or other extracurricular activities.

It is hard for the best schools to engage a youngster this age productively, and unfortunately, the average junior high school "by almost unanimous agreement, is the wasteland—one is tempted to say cesspool—of American education," according to Charles Silberman, director of a three-and-a-half-year study of American education commissioned by the Carnegie Corporation of New York, in his book *Crisis in the Classroom: The Remaking of American Education.*

Many junior high school children are faced every day with maddening rules, an inflexible administration, and teachers who are wasteful of students' time, who show lack of respect for them, do not trust them, do not allow them a measure of dignity, perhaps do not even like children. A great many junior high school teachers would rather be elsewhere, teaching high school, for example, and they leave when they can. The curriculum is frequently boring, and the sameness—every day every subject, very little variety—is deadening. Silberman says:

> Because adolescents are harder to "control" than younger children, secondary schools tend to be even more authoritarian and repressive than elementary schools; the values they transmit are the values of docility, passivity, conformity, and a lack of trust. . . .

The child's individuality and humanity are repressed.

Sometimes parents tend to look at school complaints as did the father who said, "Look, I went to school, my father went to school, my son goes to school. Once in a while I loved it, lots of times I hated it. But I didn't think to run around complaining about it—or if I did, my parents weren't very sympathetic. My boy needs to do a little more work and a lot less lying around and all his school problems would be over."

Judging the School

It is hard for parents to know how to react to a child's grumbling about school, particularly when it really does look as if his problem is basically his own laziness or refusal to listen to his teachers. Silberman quotes a parent: "When my son was unhappy at Newton High school and doing poorly, I could never decide whether he was the problem or if perhaps he was right when he said that much of the school did not teach him anything." Now in an experimental annex of his old school, this boy has "an incentive which has focused his every bit of energy toward doing better today than yesterday and suddenly a hunger for many tomorrows which will enable him to do more."

This generation of American parents could decide not to tolerate bad schools, to sensitize themselves to what their children are experiencing.

A Visit Is Revealing

Of course, there are good schools and schools that are trying to improve, trying to find new ways to help children learn. Probably the best way to get a feeling for what is going on in our child's school is to go and see for ourself. Surprisingly, parents often resist visiting school, thinking, "What can I see in one morning?" or "They'll be on their best behavior when I'm there anyway." But we can learn a great deal in several hours. We can prepare first by listening to our child talk about school. If he has a particular problem, we can try to get a sense of what is at the heart of it so that we will know what to look for when we visit. If a child's complaints center around a certain area—specific regulations, school lunches, his history teacher—we can sit in on the class, join him at lunch, if possible. If this is not possible, why not?

We can take a walk around, observe the children changing classes. Do they seem at ease and cheerful? What is the relationship between the staff and the students? How do the teachers talk to the students? Are the halls and bathrooms clean? Are the books in the library in good condition? Do the students have a bulletin board for their own announcements? Must they get administrative approval for everything they post?

When we visit the principal, are the people working in the office welcoming? Does the school use parent volunteers as teacher aides, library helpers, tutors? Or are they wary of parents' presence? In classes, how do the children seem: alert and interested, or bored, listless, angry?

With what kind of feeling about the school do we come away? Is it too controlled or too chaotic? Does it seem that learning is taking place? How would we feel about spending six hours a day five days a week in this environment?

Do the teachers seem to see the students as individuals? The best teachers try to find ways to deal with students on a one-to-one basis. Are the children's complaints taken seriously enough by the teachers, by the administration? Are the children themselves taken seriously? One girl who complained about having to work in a group with a particular child was told jokingly that it would turn out all right because the girl she hated today would no doubt be cherished next week. This response made the child furious. She could have accepted being told that it was not practical to rearrange the work groups, but she was sensitive to being laughed at or treated as one of a species with certain defined characteristics—again not as an individual in her own right. A child does not have to find every subject pleasing, does not have to be happy all the time, indeed, will not be. But the impersonality of some schools, the feeling a child gets of being manipulated, pushed around, ordered about, herded, tears from his rights over himself, detracts from his possibilities as a learning, growing person.

Possibilities of Action

After a visit to school, we will know a great deal more about the kind of place where our child spends his days. Talking to other parents and children will broaden the picture further. We may find that our concerns can be divided roughly into two categories: the things we can try to deal with on an individual level with our child, his teacher, perhaps the guidance counselor or class adviser or even the principal; and those things of a broader nature that will require further study and concerted action by a parent group if progress is to be made.

Just how drawn into group activity we eventually become will depend on a number of factors: how bad the situation is, how active and effective the parents' association is, how much time we have to devote and what we feel we could contribute to their efforts, and so on. It is encouraging if other parents are willing and eager to work for change, much more difficult if they are apathetic and cynical about the possibility of making a dent, particularly in a large city school system. But parents' groups have been working with some success to bring about changes in many communities across the country. An organization can contact others for information and can raise money to send representatives to visit schools that are being run in new ways and achieving greater success in educating children.

But in the meantime, no matter what broad changes may be needed in the school, if our child is having trouble we need to deal with it now. Just how bad is it? Is he doing badly in everything, all across the board? Has he lost interest in school, just drags himself there, can't see the point of studying? Or is he having trouble only in one subject? Does he zip through his work, all haste and no head? Or does he spend long periods of time at his desk, staring out the window? How long has this been going on?

If he is achieving somewhere in his life, even at a hobby or music lessons or sports, this needs to be considered in the total picture. Can he concentrate on things he likes to do? What does he think about his work? Why does he feel he is not working up to par? What does *he* think needs to be done? How does he feel about his teachers? What impression does he give about his place among his classmates; does he belong, or is he pushed around or isolated? Children can be terrible to one another, and being "out" may cause serious school problems.

We will want to talk to our youngster's teacher or the school guidance counselor. This can be included in the earlier visit, or we may decide to take time to think about what we observed and discuss it with our child before talking with the appropriate people on the school staff. Either way, they need to be consulted. We can learn their impression of our child's behavior in school, how he gets along with his classmates, whether they feel he is working up to capacity, their estimate of his ability. How well does he read? Does he need special help in a subject? How does his work compare with that of the other youngsters in the grade? This conversation will help in evaluating the problem and may provide several valuable suggestions about helping our child.

A complete medical checkup (see Chapter 7), including hearing and eye examinations, will reveal if there is any medical basis for the trouble. The doctor should be told that the child has been having difficulty in school, so that he can be on the lookout for clues.

Educator Eric W. Johnson suggests, in *How to Live Through Junior High School,* that parents try to make an honest self-evaluation of their own role in their child's school performance:

> What are you doing that might be causing your child to underachieve? Are you too "managing"? Do you apply too much pressure? Do you provide emotional support? Do you respect him as a person? Do you condemn him too much? Are you too punitive? Do you set a good example? Do you provide intellectual stimulation?

Does our child believe in his eventual success; that is, does he feel that if he works hard he can do well in school? Professor Jerome Kagan of Harvard University, in *A Conception of Early Adolescence,* suggests that two thirds of the children in any class have "a barrier to serious involvement in the mission of the school" because of their rank. The top one third, he feels, expects success and is motivated by this expectation. The more competitive the school, the more the point is driven home. Junior high school is often a child's first experience with tracking, the grouping of people according to their ability. Says Professor Kagan:

> This hard event forces each student to scrutinize his intellectual profile in some detail. Tracking often frightens those in the top track, many of whom do not believe they are talented enough to warrant the challenging assignment. It saddens and angers those in the lower track, who resent the invidious categorization and are forced to invent a rationalization against the importance of academic accomplishment. Once that rationalization crystallizes, it becomes incredibly resistant to change.

Do we feel our child lacks confidence in himself? How do we view his abilities? For some parents, doing well means that a child has to get 100 per cent or be the first or at least one of the best. Many bright young people don't *feel* intelligent because when they come home with an 85 on a test they are asked, "What did Johnny get?" or are prodded, "Next time, try for 90."

What kind of response does our child get when he shows us a written report? We do not want to encourage bad work or sloppiness, and if a youngster has obviously just slapped something together, we do him no service to oooh and ah over it. On the other hand, when he has worked hard with only partial success, we need to recognize and appreciate the effort. Most people, and children are no exception, are encouraged by warmhearted praise. And more often than not there are things to speak well of even when an overall effort is not up to par.

With a particularly sensitive child, we might have to go easy on the adverse criticism for him even to *hear* any of the good things we have to say.

Evaluation of the Child

Parents are sometimes so angry at children for not doing better that they allow themselves to confuse honesty with tactlessness, thoughtlessness. Naturally, a child needs to know our standards and values; what is in question is how strongly and how often. And standards cannot be absolute. They need to be standards for this particular child and they need to be realistic and related to what he wants for himself. Every parent and every teacher knows that a barely passing mark may represent as much work and achievement for one child as an A for another. But most schools do not evaluate children on their individual achievement without regard to their standing in the class, or without competitive grades. The valiant effort of a C student to perform at the highest level of his competence is rarely valued as much as it should be. Does this mean that all C's should be valued as much as all A's? It depends on how well a child is using his potential. As a parent, our job is not to get an A out of a C student at any cost, because the cost is invariably too high. It is useful sometimes to ask oneself, "Will my comment be helpful?" Simple, but it is surprising what a stopper that can be for a lot of things one might otherwise say.

If a child disagrees with his placement for a particular subject, he ought to ask his teacher why he feels he belongs there. We may need to discuss this with the teacher as well. If we agree with our child, perhaps we could encourage the teacher to observe him specially for the next few weeks. Sometimes a child wishes to be with friends in another group, or does not want to make the effort to work hard in a subject, or dislikes the teacher of a particular section, or overestimates his ability. In these cases a parent, while being sympathetic, should encourage him to work where he is.

We do not want to denigrate extracurricular activities or successes. They are enjoyable and satisfying, which is important. We tend sometimes to think of our children as creatures in preparation for adulthood, rather than as persons whose lives now need to have meaning for them and be fun as well. In any case, working on a class play, playing on the hockey team, or helping to put out the newspaper require participation in a team effort and give important experience in working with others, in planning and executing a project from start to finish. Sometimes activities like these unleash a child's potential, show what he can do when he is involved in an area that he has chosen. And success in one field—in a school debate, chess match, baseball team, art competition, woodworking exhibit—encourages effort in other areas and builds self-esteem when his accomplishment is valued by people he respects.

When a Child Fails

Sometimes a child has simply not worked enough, and he fails. Failing under certain circumstances is more useful to a child than being pushed to study in order not to fail. He needs to be permitted to experience what happens when he does not work. If we pressure a child enough, we may get him through with a passing grade that he would not have achieved otherwise. But what about next year? What he learns now may keep him from failing in more important situations in the future.

Sometimes a child fails because he has bad luck. He has concentrated his efforts in an area the teacher barely touched on in the examination. It could have gone the other way had the test been arranged differently. We can point this out to the child. Suzanne Strait Fremon, in *Children and Their Parents Toward Maturity,* stresses the importance of helping a child understand all the factors that go into a situation—his ability, how much he has studied, luck, relationships among people. He needs to learn "how to take what happens and build on it." A child who is depressed about a failure—"What's the matter with me?"—can be helped to shift emphasis from himself to the matter at hand—What's the matter with his report or his understanding of algebra? Does he need to pay more attention in class, does he require special tutoring for a while? Can he use some advice about doing research or organizing his material? Mrs. Fremon suggests turning "I'm just not good enough" into "I'm not good enough yet" or "I'm not good enough *for that particular thing."* This kind of support strengthens a child.

Homework and Work Habits

Parents often complain that a child does not spend enough time on his homework. But time is probably used as a criterion too often. A child forced to spend an hour on an assignment often learns to "put in time" rather than to sit down, concentrate, and get the job done as well as possible in as short a time as possible. If he tends to let his homework go until he is too tired or has not enough time to do it thoroughly, he may need some structure imposed upon him. But the kind of regulation depends on why he has fallen into this habit. Are there just too many activities so that school work gets last call on his energies? Does he find it difficult to stop and play and settle down to work? Then perhaps he ought to have a regular time each day for beginning his work.

Some people seem to have no hangups about work. If they have something to do, they are able to sit right down and do it. Others are not so fortunate. They put off work and concoct all kinds of excuses to do something else instead. Or when they do get to it, the slightest thing disturbs their concentration. Many of us vary in our work habits depending upon the job to be done. If we are efficient about the important things in our lives, the small things about which we procrastinate or are sloppy will not interfere too much with our functioning. A housewife who has no difficulty getting her daily chores done but always puts off writing letters is all right, but turn it the other way around and she is in trouble.

Our children will be working all of their lives, of which their early adolescence is only a part. We want to be careful that whatever we do now to encourage work does not do that job at too great a cost, does not compromise their capabilities thereafter. Without a lifetime zest for learning and working, all the information that can be crammed into a child during his school years will be useless by the time he is thirty.

The Problem of Distraction

Young people at this age, good students and indifferent ones, are frequently restless; when they try to concentrate, feelings, emotions, thoughts about other things crowd their minds, pushing out algebra and Spanish verbs. Sometimes parents insist that a child work in his room "away from distractions" when the worst distractions are inside him. A youngster often finds it lonely working off by himself. Can he study where we are ironing, or sewing, or reading? There is no reason why he should not write at the kitchen table while we prepare dinner, or in another part of the house where

there is activity, if he is not bothered by it. Some people can get their work done amid all kinds of goings-on, and this should not be discouraged. To a person like this, what is onerous is banishment to peace and quiet, not the actual work he has to do.

If our child complains about the homework or has difficulty getting it done well on his own, it is possible the teacher's instructions are unclear. One hears the children on the phone many nights: "Did she want us to translate the sentences or just fill in the missing words?" "Were we supposed to read up to page 435 by this Tuesday or next?" Of course, often it is a matter of their not paying serious attention when the assignment is given. According to Eric Johnson, homework for the junior high school child should have four main purposes:

> To give the student a chance to practice and master skills or content taught at school; to encourage or require independent creativity such as writing, doing projects or research; to encourage or require wide independent reading; and to provide time for reading "study" material in courses like history. . . . Homework should generally not be the learning of new concepts, new lessons, or new skills. These should be taught in school and homework used to reinforce them. Unfortunately, there are too many teachers who spend so much time "hearing" children "recite" on the previous night's homework that they haven't enough time left to teach the new material and consequently throw the responsibility for new learning on the

child at home, where, if the child is puzzled, the buck is passed to the parent. If this is happening frequently in your school, a conference with the teacher or principal might be in order so that you may find out how you can help and incidentally, call attention to a condition of which the school may have been unaware.

Homework is not always valuable. A child may be right when he says an assignment is boring or useless. Our recognizing this and being sympathetic may be all he needs to help him through it, but if his time is commanded night after night like this, we will want to ask his teacher what she hopes he will learn from this work.

To Help or Not to Help

We all know well enough that we are not supposed to do our child's homework or write his reports for him, but many parents find it very hard to let their child hand in a less than perfect paper. So their contribution becomes more substantial than it should be. When this happens, a child may be pleased to hand in what he feels must be a better paper, but he cannot help but feel diminished by the situation. One boy reported that his father had "the greatest ideas" and he knew his reports were getting better because of this—"I don't know what I'd do without him." We want to give a child a sense of his own strengths, not ours.

We can discuss concepts in math or physics or history in order to help him think through the problems more clearly. We can listen to his thoughts, ask him questions, read his work, suggest research sources. But the idea is to stimulate his thinking, not substitute our own. Many parents like to correct spelling and grammar errors, feeling that their child learns more if this is done at the moment when he is most involved with the writing. Teachers usually do not like this, believing they can help a child better if they are able to see what he can do on his own. But some are flexible enough to go along with a parent in this area and in others when the child is clearly learning and improving. One guide to how much assistance to offer might be to consider: Will my doing this make my child more or less likely to be able to do the next assignment on his own?

The Teacher

Our child cannot get the hang of the math this year; or he is suffocating under what seems like an interminable list of historical names and dates to memorize, and he has no interest in the period being studied; or he is suddenly unable to create an English composition, feels like a clod, and believes that the teacher so regards him. Is it his fault, or is it the result of poor teaching?

When a child has an inadequate or really bad teacher in a subject that is difficult for him in itself, it is a problem. He may be spending an inordinate amount of time working on or worrying about just this one course. Can the school offer any suggestions? Some schools will work with and advise parents who want to help their children with their work; others are completely hostile to the idea, sometimes with good reason. Parents frequently are able to stimulate their children's interest in certain subjects or to help them grasp new concepts or ideas, but much depends on the parent, the child, the relationship between them, the subject, and the school.

Are ideas and current issues discussed at home? Is our child drawn into talk about the connections between conditions in the past and the present? Between economic theory and how much a bar of chocolate costs? Is his opinion respected in family discussions? One parent said, "But Freddie says the most ridiculous things—if only he'd think it through before he speaks. How can we respect his opinions?" But a child will not join in family conversation if he is constantly made to feel stupid. If his ideas are listened to, he may be stimulated by a discussion to find out more about a subject. Sometimes children are shamed into studying, but in the long run this may detract from love of learning for its own sake.

Motivation to Learn

Motivation is a complex issue. One child told his social studies teacher that he could do better if he were more interested in the work. To which the teacher replied, "Perhaps if you put more effort into your work, your interest would increase."

Our children want to know why they are studying something, why it is necessary. Sometimes teachers skip this step, assuming, as in the case of grammar, for example, that the answer is obvious. Frequently young people are not respected enough to be told why a subject is important. Professor Kagan suggests that "the twelve-year-old is willing to believe that learning is valuable and that certain skills which seem irrelevant now are probably necessary for his role as adult." But he needs adults around him who believe in the importance of what they are offering him and can impart this belief to him.

Now that our children are studying material on a more adult level, we may find it interesting to read a few chapters of their history text or one of the novels they have been assigned, if we can spare the time. Young people are usually pleased at the idea that something they are studying is important enough to interest their parents, and this may heighten their own interest in it. Children generally work better if their parents value academic work. Even during these years, a percentage of youngsters continue to be well motivated to study. These are often young people who strongly identify with their parents' values and wish to please them. Parents who are concerned with intellectual achievements and who encourage academic competence help the school to compete with the distractions of this age.

Once in a while a child complains of a teacher who is cruel, who picks on him and makes his life miserable. We need to investigate, to talk to the teacher and, if necessary, the principal. Sometimes this helps ease things. But sometimes it doesn't, and the best thing we can do for our child, if we feel he is justified in his feelings, is to let him know that we are on his side. We understand. We can listen patiently to his complaints when he comes from school and sympathize with him. We do not like to undermine the authority of teachers, but children can understand the difference between a good teacher and a bad one, and we will not be lessening the effectiveness of his other teachers by upholding him when he is right. Mrs. Fremon believes that when parents lend support to their child in this way, it helps to "immunize" him against a cruel teacher's behavior; the teacher loses much of his or her ability to hurt the child. When a youngster knows that his parents are there and on his side, he experiences situations differently; he feels safer. As one boy put it, "Oh, they wouldn't do that to me—they know you'd be down on them right away."

Young people want a teacher to care about them "as a person," to be fair, and to have the ability to excite them about a subject and create an atmosphere in which they will learn. They want their teacher to know what he is talking about. Children often have an instinct for recognizing power that lacks authority and will puncture it when they can, while respecting true authority, indeed, seeking it out.

Going to school is our child's life for many years. Now, as he begins more and more to question the school's power over him and demand that it justify itself, we want to be listening.

7
Everyday Health Guide

EVERY PARENT KNOWS that for good health a child needs plenty of nutritious food, exercise, fresh air, sunshine, and sufficient rest. But living with a child on a day-to-day basis reveals immediately that carrying out this prescription is not that easy. A child growing into adolescence presents special problems because parents cannot control and supervise his behavior as much as before—particularly as he reaches thirteen and fourteen—and yet the youngsters themselves are not yet able to take full responsibility for their own health care. Certain things need to be insisted upon; others one may let slide. But which is which?

Posture

For example, parents—since the beginning of time, probably—have been urging,

"Stand up straight!" or "Stop slouching!" To get some young people of this age to stop slumping into chairs would require constant reminding, otherwise known as nagging. Is it worth it? What happens to them if they do continue to cruise around jaw forward, neck bent, shoulders hunched over? There is no evidence that this contributes to bad posture or curvature of the spine later in life. If a child's posture begins to cause him back pain *now,* that will probably motivate him toward improvement. Also, bad posture is not very attractive, and if we approach the issue from that angle we might achieve some results—more, perhaps, than if we talk about sitting up tall so that the internal organs have plenty of room, the blood can circulate freely, and the muscles can relax. All true, but it is hard to make this kind of information register with young people. Possibly the child does not realize how his slouched figure looks. He probably stands fairly tall when he checks himself out in the mirror in the morning. If he actually saw himself in a full-length mirror, slouched as he so often is, perhaps he would realize what he was doing to his appearance. On the other hand, this may be exactly the picture of cool sophistication he has been trying to achieve.

Girls who have grown taller faster than anybody else in the class traditionally hunch over until they develop some pride in their height or everyone else catches up with them. But the main thing with both sexes is that, since no functional damage is done, poor posture is not worth nagging about.

Acne

Many of us who were troubled by acne as adolescents used to think that if we ate a piece of chocolate it turned into a pimple. We might not have put it just that way, but if we succumbed to our terrible desire to purchase a chocolate almond bar (a double whammy: chocolate and nuts) on the way home from school, we started peering into the mirror the minute we got home to see if the pimple had popped out yet.

Now, scientists have conducted tests that indicate that neither chocolate nor other fatty foods, fried or otherwise, have any adverse effect upon the skin of adolescents. Of course, young people with acne, like other youngsters, require a well-balanced diet, but they need not forswear chocolate nut sundaes, peanut butter, or brownies until they are old enough to vote.

Acne cannot be blamed on dirt, either, or on masturbation or sexual fantasies, as was sometimes done in the past. It *is* caused by sex hormones, which are produced during adolescence at a suddenly increased rate. The hormones trigger the sebaceous glands to produce an oversupply of sebum or oil, which in turn plugs the ducts leading to the surface of the skin. Bacteria present on the skin enter the ducts and break down the sebum, producing fatty acids. If a person's skin is sensitive to this substance—usually an inherited tendency—acne occurs. It is not contagious. As the body achieves hormonal balance after the turmoil of adolescence, skin eruptions usually cease. Young people with acne should be told that it won't last forever.

Because acne is so commonplace and eventually stops by itself, parents often do not worry much about it. They may advise their children to "Try to forget it" or "Don't worry about it; that only makes it worse." Worry makes everything worse, acne included. Youngsters often break out at examination time, or just before an important party or a dance. But we cannot will ourselves to stop feeling upset. What we can do is take advantage of the many possibilities available today for prevention and cure of acne if a child is having a hard time because of it. Extreme cases may make a person feel so ugly that he hates to leave the house, and even one pimple can make a sensitive child miserable.

Care of the Skin

Whatever is important to general health is important to the skin also. Fatigue, anemia, infections all can cause flare-ups of acne. A well-balanced diet and sufficient rest are particularly important to a child with acne. Long before serious research was conducted into the causes and cure of acne, doctors noted that their patients' skin was always much improved after the summer. The rays of the sun or an ultraviolet lamp (in moderation) dry the skin, reducing oils and causing peeling, and also killing the surface bacteria.

Youngsters should be alerted not to pick at or squeeze pimples, as this increases the chance of scarring and may spread the acne.

If a youngster's scalp is oily, his hair ought to be washed several times a week and, if long, pulled back from the face, perhaps tied back at night, and his (or her) pillowcase changed frequently.

Daily skin care for a young person with acne should include washing *gently* morning and evening with warm water and a hypoallergenic soap. Hard scrubbing is irritating to the skin and tends to spread the infection. Steaming is helpful because it loosens pores. After washing, the child soaks a cloth in hot water, wrings it slightly, and places it over the pimples, repeating several times, then blotting with a clean towel. Facial saunas do the same job. After steaming, doctors recommend a mild astringent, applied with clean cotton, and then one of the medicated creams that help to dry the skin. These creams also do a good job of covering the pimples, camouflaging the redness.

If acne is severe and is not helped by these methods, a dermatologist should be consulted. He may try one of several antibiotics that have been found helpful. He can remove blackheads, and he can drain the pus from pimples to prevent infection from spreading. In extreme cases, there are other possibilities. If a child's face has become pitted or scarred, the dermatologist may recommend dermabrasion, or skin planing. One need not wait until the skin eruptions have stopped before having this procedure done. It is relatively minor and preferable to letting the scars accumulate until the end of adolescence.

Eating Habits

Somewhere around third grade for our children, many of us found that all our magazines began to disappear. Our children were appropriating them to cut out pictures of leafy green vegetables and brimming glasses of milk to paste in their nutrition scrapbooks for school. They were learning about proper diet, about nutrients, the

importance of protein, the basic seven food groups. They started pressuring us to give them carrot sticks and celery stalks stuffed with cottage cheese, and they wanted to tape posters about good eating habits all over the kitchen walls.

What every parent of a teen-ager wants to know is: Where did all those carrot and celery-stalk lovers go? So much for brainwashing in the early years!

At eleven, a child is usually eating at least almost every breakfast and dinner at home, and we see what he is putting into his stomach. But at thirteen or fourteen and thereafter, a child may suddenly be rushing out without breakfast, be at a friend's for dinner, or even snack so much that he eats no dinner at all. There may come a point when a mother who has not wanted to be rigid about food and eating habits realizes that she has slipped from being casual to being lax—her child is really not getting enough of the proper foods.

During this period of rapid growth, a

youngster's food needs are great. His protein and calcium requirements, for example, are almost double those of younger children and adults. He needs at least a quart of milk a day, in one form or another, and plenty of food rich in high-quality protein, such as meat, poultry, fish, cheese, and eggs. Those large appetites are normal and need to be appropriately satisfied.

The average child who does not eat enough of the right foods, however, still may continue to gain in height and weight. Thus, if his parents explain to him the dangers of poor nutrition, he is likely to retort that he doesn't feel his bones melting or his hair falling out just yet. We stress that he is increasing his susceptibility to infection, and he comes back that he has not had a cold in months. We explain that food is energy, fuel to run the body, that if he does not get enough of the right fuel, he may lack energy, feel tired, get headaches. And he acts as if he cannot conprehend the connection. It is truly a rare child of this age who will be impressed by a discussion of nutrition.

Getting Through to the Child

The situation now is not hopeless, though. For one thing, knowledge about nutrition is one of those things children sometimes absorb without being willing to admit it. If they are put in possession of the facts they may decide to eat somewhat differently, but they're darned if they will respond to that "Drink another glass of milk, Freddie" baby stuff. If a child feels low in energy he may—when he understands the relationship between pep and what he eats—start paying more attention to what goes into his stomach. If he knows that insufficient protein or calories may stunt his growth, he may be moved to improve his eating habits. If her hair is not as shiny as she would like, she may think twice about the connection between lustrous hair and what she eats.

Our job, then, is to let our children know what foods they should be eating, and why, without getting their backs up. Perhaps pictures of leafy green vegetables and the rest of the basic seven on the kitchen wall? We tend to nag our youngsters to eat certain foods or not eat other foods, but we rarely think of giving them a short refresher course on nutrition at a receptive moment—or at several appropriate moments over a period of time.

Why does he need to drink milk if he "eats all that ice cream"? A significant percentage of teen-agers suffer from calcium deficiencies. Ice cream and other foods derived from or made with milk are good for a child. But in order to obtain the calcium in one quart of milk he would have to eat two quarts of ice cream, or six cups of cottage cheese, eight servings of pudding, four ounces of cheddar cheese, or about twelve servings of cream soup. These foods are excellent, but it is clear that a youngster needs to drink milk (unless he is allergic to it) if he is to fulfill his daily calcium requirement without resort to medically prescribed calcium pills. If a child dislikes plain milk, keep trying until you find a flavor—chocolate, coffee, strawberry—that will make it palatable to him. Would he drink malteds, hot cocoa, milk shakes?

Our children do not have to worry about cholesterol because their bodies do not store it at this age. That is fortunate, because eggs, in particular, are an all-round food rich in various nutrients.

A daily vitamin pill, while it gives leeway, does not make up for a really inadequate diet. Food has certain values that are not in vitamin pills.

The Importance of Breakfast

Studies of students and workingmen have shown that those who eat no breakfast or a nutritionally poor one tire more rapidly—late-morning slump—and do not think, study, learn, or work as well as they could if they had eaten properly. A good breakfast should include fruit or fruit juice, egg, buttered toast, milk, and cereal, too, if the child is hungry for it.

If a youngster frequently dashes off in the morning—"Sorry, no time for breakfast, gotta run"—perhaps we could help him organize himself so that he has more time.

If a child says he just is not hungry that early in the morning, he should be encouraged gradually to acquire the habit of having a good breakfast. Perhaps he could begin by taking only a piece of fruit or a glass of juice for several days, then add cereal or buttered toast and so on. After a few weeks, he could be eating a full breakfast—if he wants to.

Lunches and Snacks

Lunches are important, too. A midday meal that is low in protein but high in sugar and starches tends to produce quick energy, but when the sugar level of the blood drops later in the afternoon, the child feels tired, perhaps headachy, pepless. If a child takes his lunch from home, we can pack it with an eye to the nutrients he needs. We can add cheese to the luncheon meat in his sandwich, give him nut-raisin cookies instead of vanilla wafers, stick in an apple or a pear or a banana, remember that a chocolate bar with fruit and nuts has more protein and vitamins than a plain one, and so on.

A child need not have every nutrient he needs at every meal, but over the course of several days his diet should work out to be balanced. Ideas other mothers have used to interest their adolescents in nutritious snacks are the following:

• Keep soup in a pot ready to heat when everyone comes home famished from school. Soup and crackers or buttered toast are filling and nutritious, and particularly popular in the winter.

• Put snacks in individual, attractive, covered refrigerator dishes for eating right from the container, and vary them: one day individual custards, one day cut-up raw vegetables (not just the usual, but string beans, peas and pea pods, cauliflower, cherry tomatoes, accompanied by a paper cup of creamy salad dressing to be used as a dip). Don't forget color; serve green, red, orange, white, add a sprig of parsley, dill, watercress. The more attractive nourishing food is, the better it can compete with the empty-calorie foods that youngsters find so tempting.

• Have plenty of fruit and vegetable juices prepared and waiting in colorful pitchers. Never overlook the importance of convenience. Even having to add water to a can of frozen concentrated juice may seem like too much effort to a child after a day at school.

• Keep a supply of mixes and dips—liver pâté, minced sardines sprinkled with lemon, deviled eggs mixed with olives or pickles or pimiento—to be eaten with bread, crackers, or chips; whipped cream cheese for date-and-nut bread, and so on.

Of course, pies, butter cakes, butter cookies, and the like contain nutrients, too, and children love them. They are all right when eaten in moderation and when they don't spoil the appetite for meals. Needless to say, they are high in calories, which is fine for some children, less so for others.

Of the snacks that young people buy on the run outside the home, popcorn, potato chips, and peanuts are better for them than most cookies and candy. And, of course, fruit juices from the vending machines are a better idea than carbonated drinks.

When asked about candy and soda, many physicians advise parents to forbid the use of both, since they have little or no food value, are bad for the teeth, and spoil the appetite for the nutritious foods a child needs for health. But it is extremely difficult to banish candy and soda completely from the diets of young people. Some parents are able to motivate their children to substitute foods containing natural sugars such as those found in fresh fruits, or the synthetic sweeteners found in low-calorie soda or sugarless gum. These are preferable to candy and other products sweetened with sugar containing sucrose, which are harmful to the teeth. When children themselves become interested in preserving their teeth or reducing their weight, they are more apt to want to eliminate such empty calories from their diet.

Overweight

A great many young people between eleven and fourteen are overweight. Sometimes it is just "puppy fat"; a child puts on a little extra weight around ten or eleven and then, often without any particular effort, loses it or "grows into it" by the time he is fifteen or sixteen. Other children become too heavy at about this age because they indulge in too many high-calorie foods and too little physical activity.

Still others become overweight before

puberty and probably will be after it, unless they do something about it. They can lose weight, but the problem has to be approached in a special way. One startling fact has emerged from the most recent studies of this group of adolescents: the great majority of them eat less than the average child of their sex of normal weight. Yes, less!

This is so revolutionary an idea that most people simply do not believe it. Why, then, are these young people overweight? Because they do not move about nearly as much as thin people. Even when playing a sport such as tennis or volleyball, they move slowly and are often standing still. Why this should be so is complicated and not yet fully understood. But it seems clear that their bodies do not utilize fats and carbohydrates as they should. Too much fat is stored and too little energy is provided for the child, which is why he does not feel like being more active. Unfortunately, this lack of physical exertion results in even less fat being burned, and the cycle perpetuates itself.

Exercise Is the Key

The crucial factor, according to Dr. Jean Mayer of Harvard University, who has done pioneering research in the treatment of overweight, is exercise. Since most of this group of overweight adolescents have become that way because they are abnormally inactive, it is vital to get them moving.

Every overweight adolescent would do well to consider how exercise can help him. A 15- to 20-minute walk, for example, burns up about 100 calories, roughly the amount contained in two cups of popcorn.

Most people think of weight only in terms of what we eat, but weight can be lost by increasing the expenditure of energy as well as decreasing the intake of food. There is a belief that exercise is worthless in control of overweight because, it is thought, the more you exercise, the hungrier you get, the more you eat—and there you are, back where you started. But this is not necessarily true. And it is not true for the many overweight adolescents whose activity level is significantly lower than it should be.

It is difficult for any adolescent to find time for a lot of exercise each day, and the overweight teen-ager may find it harder than others to walk, run, do indoor exercises, engage in sports. He needs to push himself, but it will begin to come easier after a while. For those who are willing to undertake an hour of exercise a day, the rewards can be great. An hour of bicycling or fast tennis will cause a weight loss of one pound a week—a good rate of loss—without any change in eating habits. The same is true of an hour and a half of Ping-Pong or three quarters of an hour of swimming (but not just floating or sitting at the edge of the pool!). Dr. Mayer suggests a daily walk of about an hour and a half at the brisk pace of four miles per hour for that one-pound weight loss.

Jogging, bowling, baseball, skating also help—the type of exercise does not matter. What is important is that it be regular. If one or both parents are overweight, and since the tendency to overweight seems to be inherited, this is likely to be true, they can engage in these activities along with their child, especially on weekends. Exercise is good for us all. It makes the body more firm, improves muscle tone, and helps posture, as well as increasing one's feeling of well-being. A great deal of planned exercise may seem laughably impractical for your family, but one important fact should be considered. Exercise is a positive approach to losing weight, difficult, perhaps, but not necessarily unpleasant. Dieting is negative, involving deprivation. Whatever can be done to eliminate or ease the amount of dieting is probably worth trying.

Dieting Safely

Until an overweight child becomes active enough to burn up what he eats, he will need to cut down on foods that are high in calories but low in protein, minerals, and vitamins. These include sugar, candy, soda, cakes, pies, and other rich desserts. A child who is overweight needs a balanced diet and the same nutrients as an average child. But he cannot have as much leeway with high-calorie extras. When a child's doctor has ascertained a need for weight loss, he can recommend a safe caloric minimum and a good daily diet, taking into account the child's rate of growth and development and his energy expenditure.

Crash or fad diets can be harmful. Misguided attempts at reducing are a major cause of anemia in adolescents, and they seldom work in the long run, anyway. All studies show that unless everyday habits are changed, weight lost is gained right back.

Weight loss should not be rushed. A pound a week is a sensible goal. The child needs energy to get through his day. If he diets too strenuously, he will be tired and move even less, which is what we are working against. We need to remember, too, that his bones are growing, his muscles are developing, his teeth are forming just like those of the normal-weight youngster. Serious damage can result if he goes for too long without getting enough of the important nutrients.

A child should never be given diet pills without a doctor's prescription. It is preferable, of course, to help him lose weight without getting him on a routine of pills.

The parent of an overweight child has an even greater need to learn about nutrition. And we need to debunk dietary myths. Toasted bread *is* just as fattening as plain bread; thinly sliced bread is less fattening only because there is less of it; water does not make a person fat; margarine has the same caloric value as natural butter. We need to learn to plan meals and snacks for the most pleasure and the least calories.

Planning the Diet

Library shelves are filled with books and pamphlets offering ideas on meal planning and recipes to make dieting more interesting and less painful. The Bibliography suggests a few that are particularly pertinent for young dieters.

Emphasis always should be on changing eating habits, substituting lower-calorie foods for higher-calorie ones, not simply depriving a child of all sugars and starches. A dieter needs interesting, varied, fully satisfying meals just as everyone else does, perhaps more.

The following are some suggestions to help a child lose weight:

- Having dinner ready at a regular time each night may make a child less likely to snack. On the other hand, it sometimes works out well to give a child five small meals instead of three larger ones each day to reduce hunger and the feeling of deprivation—or three meals and two regular, planned snacks, one after school and one before bedtime.
- Skipping meals is a bad idea. It causes fatigue, and generally a person eats twice as much later on to make up for it.
- Learn how to make tempting low-calorie desserts and snacks. Keep a container filled with low-calorie, ready-to-eat snacks in the refrigerator. For ice cream sodas use low-calorie soda, skimmed milk, and dietetic ice cream and fruit flavorings.
- If the child's doctor has put him on a diet of a certain number of calories each day, and he loves to snack, he could reserve a certain amount of his daily calorie allowance for snacks. Then, if he is going to be in a situation, such as a party, in which he expects to be tempted, he could utilize an idea suggested by *Seventeen* magazine—the "snack bank"—saving some of the calories allowed for snacks for several days or even a week in order to splurge on a special occasion.
- Do not use food as a reward, an expression of affection, or a solace for troubles. Substitute noncaloric treats instead: trips together, activities and sports together, gifts that are not related to food gain or loss. When you are tempted to bring home a cake, bring home a treat from the five and dime instead.
- Give praise when weight is lost but loving support all along that does not depend on weight loss.
- Let the child know that other children have successfully overcome weight problems.
- Explain that there will be times when, although he is continuing his regime faithfully, no weight is lost. If these plateaus are expected, they will be less discouraging.
- Encourage new activities that involve his moving around—taking up a new sport, walking to pick up his kid sister at school, doing some of your marketing, mowing the lawn, vacuuming, or whatever active job you can think of for him to do on a regular

paid basis. Perhaps having a dog that has to be walked would help.

• Boredom increases the temptation to overeat, so it helps to encourage substitute occupations for hands that yearn to pick up a piece of candy. Would the child like to begin organizing a stamp collection, learn to type, build a model, learn to knit, do needlework, hook a rug, paint, model in clay?

• Chart his progress, providing short-term goals. Perhaps the child could set up his own goals, aiming toward a certain loss per month or by the time vacation begins. Other kinds of incentive may also help him to lose weight: saving money he would have spent on sweets to buy something he wants, working toward a specific goal in a sport or in exercises at home.

• Has he an overweight friend who would like to go on a diet and might exercise with him? The buddy system is probably one of the most effective aids to losing weight.

It is helpful when weight reduction can be supervised outside the home, through a reducing club at the Y or at school, a weekly weigh-in at the doctor's, a summer camp program for overweight youngsters. In this way the parent's role can be just that of appreciator of progress, encourager, ardent supporter.

If a parent is overweight, too, he should remember that making fun of himself for being fat demeans the child as well. If the parent feels hopeless about losing weight, this makes the child feel pessimistic about his situation.

Parents of overweight children often act in many ways, usually without realizing it, to sabotage the dieting effort. The child should not be urged to take seconds, to taste a freshly baked cake, or to break his diet "just this once."

The best impetus to reducing is a child's motivation. If he does not really want to diet and exercise, his chances for long-term success are not good. We should not be angry with him for eating or for not exercising, or ridicule or humiliate him for being clumsy or fat or because his clothes do not fit. We should not berate him for sitting around too much or nag him to exercise or be more active or more social. Making an overweight child feel worthless or depressed is not difficult, but it is not a successful dieting technique. And we do not want to give him the impression that our love depends on how big or small he is.

Getting Enough Sleep

A child who cannot drag himself out of bed in the morning is not necessarily a youngster who has not had enough sleep. Some people are never peppy when they first get up, no matter what time they went to bed the night before. It is later on during the day that a parent can judge whether a child is getting enough rest. Young people this age generally require about nine or ten hours of sleep a night. But their needs vary. If a child is getting less sleep yet does not seem tired, perhaps he is able to manage with less rest than most people. It is an enviable ability.

Few children like to go to bed, and adolescents are no exception. Often a child wants to get more rest, plans to get to bed earlier, but cannot seem to settle down. He jumps up to make another phone call, raids the refrigerator for another apple or the cupboard for a cookie. Then he remembers some homework that he decides he should do. Or he settles down early enough but he has so much on his mind that he cannot fall asleep. He "can't stop thinking." He is "trying" to fall asleep but can't. He may worry because everyone else is going to bed and he does not like to be the only one in the house awake.

Limits about bedtime, as discussed in Chapter 4, are important. But when a child has trouble getting enough rest because he is tense or overstimulated, it is little help if all we can think of to do is get tough about his bedtime. Perhaps we can both try to figure out how he can arrange his life to get the rest he needs. We have to start the conversation on the right note, because otherwise he will claim that he is *not* tired, he *is* getting enough sleep, and the conversation is all downhill after that.

Identifying the Problem

Sometimes the problem is complicated by a child's poor sense of time, of how much he can accomplish in any given fifteen minutes or hour. He leaves something to work on between 8:30 and 9 that will take him at least an hour and a half to do. He is probably a person who can never correctly gauge how long it will take him to do an errand or come home from a friend's house. Perhaps we can interest him in doing a time study for a week, keeping a record of important tasks he performs, writing down time started and time stopped. He may learn something that will help him.

If he regularly procrastinates about doing a particular task—his math homework, a certain chore—we want to learn why.

A youngster may be worried about school, friends, home life, himself. These problems become interwoven, too, as when tension makes him feel tired so that he does not sit down to his homework as early as he should and then is not ready for bed until late and is tired again in the morning. Helping a child with his problems, as discussed in Chapter 8, may help him to get more rest as well.

Parents and child share a common interest: the child's health and well-being. In families sometimes this mutuality of concern is forgotten; parents fight with their child to do things "for your own good," and the child angrily tells his parents he is doing something such as drinking milk "for *your* sake, not mine." A young person has to begin to take responsibility for his own health, for doing what is good for him for his own sake. And we need to work *with* him to accomplish this, not, as it sometimes seems, *against* him. In any case, we ought not to let our concern provoke us into nagging him about sleep or about other health matters. Sooner or later, this is self-defeating.

Fatigue or lack of energy may have other causes besides insufficient sleep. Poor diet, rapid growth, lack of exercise, illness, or emotional problems can all make a youngster feel listless. A physician should be consulted if the situation does not improve in a reasonable time.

Sometimes it is helpful if a child can get into the habit of going to bed fifteen minutes or half an hour early and then listening to music or the ball game on the radio, or reading for a while. A regular nightly routine is in itself soothing—laying out clothes and school things for the next day, perhaps having some warm milk or cocoa and crackers.

Cigarettes

Many young people do not seem to be deterred from cigarette smoking by the known risks of cancer and heart disease. While the percentage of adult smokers has been decreasing, the percentage of teen-age smokers has been increasing, and the percentage of twelve-year-old boy smokers has doubled in recent years. Many young people smoke because they are trying to look older; others are responding to pressure from their group; still others find that the aura of danger attracts rather than repels them. Smoking is part of the devil-may-care ambiance they are trying to cultivate. Even if they think seriously about the risks, they mistakenly believe that they can always stop before they are old enough to get into trouble with their smoking.

Recently, however, there has been evidence of lung damage to teen-agers who smoked cigarettes for only a few years. Breathing tests given several hundred Connecticut boys and girls who were regular smokers revealed abnormal lung function. Although some of this damage may be reversible if the youngsters stop smoking, it is possible that there are effects, such as arrest of lung development, that are permanent. Obviously, smoking reduces endurance and breathing capacity and is a risk young people should be encouraged to avoid. The American Heart Association reports that teen-agers are much more likely to smoke if their parents do.

Seeing the Doctor

As our child grows older, he may resist going to his physician for a regular checkup. He feels fine, he says, so why bother? But a friendly, trusting relationship with his doctor cannot be sustained if they see each other only in moments of crisis. At some point he may have a problem he feels he cannot discuss with his parents, or that only a doctor can answer. Then it may make all the difference if he has a doctor with whom he feels comfortable. His physician also will want to keep an eye on how he is doing, to catch problems that need treating, to offer guidance concerning habits that may affect his health now or later on in life.

What Should a Medical Checkup Include?

The doctor will take a comprehensive history of the child and his family. If he is seeing the child for the first time, he will ask a long list of questions about him from birth onward. He will want to know, for example, about past illnesses, operations, accidents. He will ask if there is a history in the family of a specific disease such as diabetes. If a physician has seen the child before, he naturally need only be brought up-to-date.

The doctor will then inquire about the child's general health, his habits, and his way of life. How much sleep does he get? Does he sleep well? Does he have plenty of energy, or does he tire easily? A child this age should be peppy; if he is not, the physician will want to find out why. Does he have a good appetite? Is his elimination regular? Does he take any medication? Has he had allergic reactions to medication in the past? Other allergies? Does he have frequent colds? Sore throats? Headaches? How does he get along at home? At school? Has he been depressed lately? As the doctor talks to the child, he is also studying him.

The physician also gets clues to possible hearing or visual defects. He notices posture, skin, general appearance. He asks about complaints, symptoms, problems.

The physician will also order laboratory tests. In a complete urinalysis, the urine is tested for albumen (to detect abnormalities of the kidney such as nephritis) and sugar (a screening test for diabetes). It is examined under the microscope for abnormal cells that might indicate kidney or urinary-tract infection. Among blood tests, a hemoglobin or hemacrit test is given to screen for anemia. The Tine test screens for tuberculosis. There is a significant increase in active tuberculosis during the prepubertal growth spurt.

When a physician has done a comprehensive history, physical examination, and the above tests, he will detect most of the things that can be detected about a patient in this age range. Other special tests may be ordered if there is some specific indication that they are needed.

Immunization

If a child has already been immunized against polio and measles, the American Academy of Pediatrics makes no further recommendation with regard to those diseases for this period. Many doctors, however, do give a polio booster every four years. If a child has neither had measles nor been previously immunized, he should receive the vaccine now. In addition, a child may need to receive once during these years a combination booster for diphtheria and tetanus. Because diphtheria is not the menace it once was, some parents have become lax about immunization. Serious outbreaks have occurred in recent years, however, because the germ that causes diphtheria has not been eliminated from the United States. The D-T booster should be given ten years after the child received his last one. The American Academy of Pediatrics presently advises revaccination against smallpox every six years, but physicians expect this recommendation to be revised soon because smallpox is so well controlled. Many pediatricians do not routinely give it this often. Because mumps can be very painful if contracted during adolescence and can cause sterility in males, many pediatricians recommend that children who have not yet had the disease be given the mumps vaccine. There is controversy as to whether adolescents should be immunized against rubella (German measles). In earlier childhood, both boys and girls should be immunized, chiefly as a public-health measure to help eradicate the disease from the community. Many physicians feel that teen-age girls who have not previously had the vaccine should be immunized, whether or not they have had a supposed case of the actual disease in childhood. Others do not immunize because of the danger of giving the vaccine to a girl who is pregnant, and because it is not yet known how long the immunity conferred by the vaccine will last. If it wears off after three, five, eight, or even ten years, young women will be unprotected as they leave their teens. Accordingly, it may be recommended in the future that a booster be given at the time of marriage. Immunizing adolescent boys is not so essential, although most authorities feel that they, too, should have the vaccine.

Other immunizations are required only if a child is going into an area where a particular disease is endemic.

The Final Conference

An important part of the checkup, during which the pediatrician discusses his findings with parent and child and makes his recommendations, is the final conference. At this stage of a child's life, a checkup may produce anxiety. The child is more modest, for one thing, and also may be so concerned about his development that he takes a doctor's grimace as an indication that something is dreadfully wrong. A doctor who understands young people will make a point during the conference of saying, "Everything is in order, all according to schedule," or something by way of reassurance. If a young person seems concerned about any aspect of his development, the physician will reassure him, explain what is necessary, and give him an idea of what to expect in his development in the near future. Sometimes the doctor may be able to anticipate difficulties and will then discuss preventive care.

As a child begins to be more mature, a physician usually likes to see him alone for at least part of the checkup. Then, with the reassurance that his questions have no punitive intent, he can ask in a straightforward way about school, drugs, sex, or other matters.

Doctors are particularly concerned today with drug use. Many will begin by asking about cigarette smoking and then go on to inquire about a child's possible use of medicines in general, such as antihistamines, aspirin, tranquilizers. Then, if the child looks drawn, sallow, has lost weight, is jittery, or too talkative or too quiet, he will probably ask directly about other drugs.

If a physician has a good rapport with his young patients, they are likely to ask him direct questions concerning their sexual problems or fears. Or, if a doctor feels that a child is anxious about some aspect of sex, he will draw him out, discussing masturbation, petting, intercourse, the possibility of venereal disease, pregnancy, or whatever he feels is indicated.

A good doctor will encourage a child to talk about himself. Symptoms that the youngster might otherwise be embarrassed or reluctant to mention may be important.

The American Academy of Pediatrics suggests a checkup every year, or at least every two years. Of course, a physician may ask to see a child more often if an aspect of his health requires more frequent supervision.

Years ago, many pediatricians used to stop seeing children when they reached their teens. Today it is becoming more common for the pediatrician to follow youngsters through adolescence, and many now have special hours for seeing adolescents so that the teen-agers need not sit in the waiting room with babies and younger children. Sometimes a child himself asks to change doctors somewhere along the line for one reason or another. A youngster ought to be able to talk easily with his doctor. He should have a doctor of the same sex if that is important to him. When a child does not wish to be cared for by a pediatrician any longer, he usually goes on to an internist or a general practitioner. A girl often consults a gynecologist as well. In recent years, a new possibility has been added: the specialist in adolescent medicine, a physician primarily concerned with the problems of this age group. Many large cities now have adolescent clinics, where pediatricians, surgeons, internists, gynecologists, psychiatrists, psychologists, social workers, and nurses work as a team to provide health care and counseling for young people.

8
Adolescent Misery

DO PARENTS CAUSE adolescent misery? No. But many parents tend to make it worse. And many parents help ease it. What distinguishes between the two?

Not love. Most of us love our children and want them to be happy. We do not like to see them moping around or irritable or downright miserable. We do not *plan* to embarrass or infuriate them or constantly get their backs up.

A saintly disposition is not the answer, either. All parents have their clashes with adolescent children. This time of life, says anthropologist Ruth Benedict in *Patterns of Culture,* is as "definitely characterized by domestic explosions and rebellion as typhoid is marked by fevers."

Nevertheless, there *is* a quality that sets apart the relationship of some parents with their adolescent children—good communication. That quality in the life of the family eases pain, softens hurt, and helps a young person to be more optimistic about his future.

Recently *The New York Times*[1] printed a little exercise for adolescents. The questions went like this:

Do your parents wait until you are through talking before "having their say"?
Do your parents seem to respect your opinion?
Do your parents tend to lecture and preach too much?
Do you discuss personal problems with either of your parents?
Do your parents talk to you as if you were much younger?
Do they show an interest in your interests?
Do your parents trust you?
Do you find it hard to say what you feel at home?
Do your parents have confidence in your abilities?
Do you hesitate to disagree with either of them?
Do you fail to ask your parents for things because you feel they'll deny your requests?
Do they really try to see your side of things?
Do your parents consider your opinion in making decisions that concern you?
Do they try to make you feel better when you're down in the dumps?
Do your parents explain their reason for not letting you do something?
Do you ask them their reasons for the decisions they make concerning you?
Do you help your parents to understand you by telling them how you think and feel?

Obviously, the exercise is designed to gauge the relationship between young people and their parents. If a child feels that his parents lecture him, do not really try to see his side of things, and do not try to make him feel better when he is down, he has little incentive to discuss his problems with them. On the other hand, a child who believes his parents respect his opinion, trust him, and make it possible for him to disagree with them is more likely to let his parents know what he is thinking and feeling and to talk to them about the things that really matter to him.

What is at the heart of a good relationship is, of course, good communication, and in this sense the questions are particularly revealing. Many a parent says, "How I wish my son would tell me what's bothering him," or "I would so like my daughter to confide in me," or "I'm sure I could help him if he

---

[1] Millard J. Bienvenue, Sr., "Why They Can't Talk to Us," *New York Times Magazine,* 14 September 1969, p. 86.

would give me the chance." Such parents need to look at what happens when their child does talk to them.

Suppose a thirteen-year-old comes home from school really downhearted after losing a class election for student-council representative. He lets his parents know how hurt he feels, although he probably put up a cool front at school. How do his parents react? Consider the following possibilities:

• They use the opportunity to give him some advice that they think will he helpful to him in the future. If he has any hope of succeeding in school politics he had better soften his critical attitude toward his schoolmates, an attitude much in evidence at home in his behavior toward his younger sister and brother. They help him to analyze his failure and to see that he is doing wrong so that he will have better luck next time.

• They try to cheer him up by playing down the defeat, saying that the student council does little anyway, and in any case he has to learn not to take things so hard.

• They try to cheer him up by assuring him that it was all for the best since he needs the time to study, having done badly in math this year.

• They say: "You're lucky it wasn't worse. You'll do better next time. You'll get over it; this time next year you won't even remember it. You shouldn't feel so bad. You *can't* really feel so bad. You shouldn't worry."

• They rub in the fact that they have been telling him all year he would never be popular if he kept refusing invitations to parties and other social gatherings.

The poverty of the last possibility is blatantly obvious. Although many parents cannot resist "rubbing it in," most of us do realize that this is not a helpful approach. But the other responses are also lacking. None are altogether helpful; some would be extremely irritating.

What They Want from Us

A parent who tries to make light of a defeat, political or social, or to convince a youngster that it was all for the best, may feel that he is being sympathetic and understanding. But when a person is hurting he needs a soothing balm—not advice, not

criticism, not analysis, and surely not reminders of other failures. He should not be made to feel guilty or unmanly for feeling hurt or pressed to feel better right away. We need to deal with his immediate feelings first. Then, later, the child can look ahead, accept reason. It is important not to gloss over a hurt, writes psychologist Dorothy W. Baruch, in *How to Live with Your Teen-ager,* or to try to pretty it up or turn it, presto, into cheer. And telling a person not to feel what he does never makes the feeling go away.

An approach that recognizes his feelings—"What a shame! You must be disappointed. I know you had your heart set on it"—shows the child we understand. It tells him, also, that it is all right to have the feelings he has. Such an approach helps him to recover.

As a child grows into adolescence, he often becomes more secretive, less confiding. There are things he just does not wish to discuss with his parents. But a child whose relationship with his mother and father is nourishing to his spirit, to his self-esteem, will tend to remain in good communication with them, to let them know when he needs them. If, no matter how sympathetic parents feel, the child does not come home with his problems, they should consider how they respond to him.

The Need to Be Appreciated

Our son shows us a story written for school. It is imaginative, even funny, but all those spelling errors are like red flags in front of our eyes. He is fourteen, for heaven's sake! "Can't you use the dictionary when you're not sure how to spell a word?" we explode. So this bright youngster does not feel like the author of an imaginative and funny story. He thinks of himself as a dud who will never learn to spell.

Suppose the child were in a family that cared not two pins about spelling. He would feel proud of himself after showing them this composition. But, we may say, we *do* care about spelling. Are we supposed to close our eyes to those glaring errors, that carelessness? Perhaps, at least some of the time. We assume, after all, that his teacher points out his mistakes if she thinks they are important. And it is clear which response from us will encourage the child to share his work in the future, indeed, to write at all.

Children, like husbands and wives, need loving appreciation at home, not critics. Advice has its place, of course, but it needs to be sensitively timed and offered only after effort has been appreciated. What is more, advice given too often becomes nagging, advice given in anger arouses hostility, and advice given without respect for the child's feelings can damage self-esteem.

Empathy

Our daughter has been a trial to live with lately, moody and snappish, and not very open to overtures from anyone. Then, one day she comes home miserable. She tells us that she has had a terrible falling out with her best friend, who is now telling mean stories about her to "everyone." She does not think she can face going to school tomorrow. The ups and downs of friendships cause much misery during these years.

Knowing how difficult the child has been lately, we may suspect that the friend has had good cause for her anger. Our daughter is probably "in the wrong." We could begin to ask her questions hinting at that conclusion and try to help her understand how her friend must have felt. Or we could reassure her that there are other girls, that everyone will forget all about it in a day or two. And, after all (as the tears continue to flow), it is not the end of the world. "For heaven's sake, if you get yourself into such a state over something like this, how will you ever handle big disappointments?"

All of these words are familiar to parents, who have themselves been children and been exasperated to hear them from *their* parents. They may be "right," they may be sensible, they may be said with reasonably good intentions, but they don't help much. A child comes to know he will be offered this "routine" and tends to keep even more to himself.

Do we hear how we sound when we go on this way? We ought sometimes to listen to our own words, our own tone of voice. It is a way of putting ourself in our child's shoes and learning how it feels.

Their Suffering Is Real

Perhaps one of the reasons that we lose touch with our children at this age is that we do not really believe they are as unhappy as they frequently seem. How could they be? Most of us, if we think someone is making a fuss over nothing or next to nothing, cannot work up much sympathy. It is a rare person who can feel for someone even though he himself sees the other's troubles as slight, or self-inflicted, or even humorous.

We see our children as having their whole lives ahead of them, with crucial choices as yet unmade, destinies as yet undecided. They are looking forward to romantic love, instead of backward at it, as their parents may be. It is difficult for parents not to feel a little envy of their children, particularly if some of their own choices have turned out badly, if their destinies are less than satisfying, their own sex lives on the wane.

It is hard not be be impatient if we feel they exaggerate their difficulties and dramatize minor aches. One hindrance to communicating well with our child may be an understandable lack of empathy with the troubles of this time of life. It is hard to be supportive when deep down we feel they've got it good! Can we try to feel with them and accept the truth: that their pains are real, their suffering is genuine?

Universal Miseries

Such feelings are shared by adolescents the world over. How they are manifested and directed depends on the culture in which the child is growing up.

Psychologist Norman Kiell writes, in *The Universal Experience of Adolescence* that if we could reach back to the emotions of our own adolescence, we might be more understanding, but most of us cannot. The pain of adolescence is such that most people forget how it was with them. Says educator John A. Rice, in *I Came Out of the Eighteenth Century:*

> . . . but where is one who does not wince at the memory of his adolescence? . . . Women say they cannot remember the pangs of childbirth. Crafty nature blots them out, lest there be no more. So also one does not remember one's second birth . . . from childhood into youth. This second birth . . . becomes in memory a dull pain.

Perhaps everyone else is maturing, but he is not—no signs of growth. Or no one else is maturing yet, but her breasts have become an embarrassing protuberance under her sweaters. No use to tell her that in one year she will be pleased about her body. Right now she is *different.* She is certain people are *staring* at her. And we talk of a year from now; why, we might as well be speaking of an eon!

This does not mean we should not let a child know that it won't always be this way. Tactfully done, it may help a little. Sometimes it helps, too, to arrange an opportunity for an early-maturing daughter to spend some time with a somewhat older cousin who has been through it all recently, or an adult with whom she has rapport.

Reading May Help

Books about young people undergoing similar trials can be reassuring that one is not alone. *The Diary of a Young Girl* by Anne Frank, although written while the thirteen-year-old Dutch girl was in hiding from the Nazis during World War II, offers striking insights into the turmoil of the adolescent spirit. Constantly in conflict with her mother, although her father was "a darling," she wrote one night:

> I'm boiling with rage, and yet I mustn't show it. I'd like to stamp my feet, scream, give Mummy a good shaking, cry, and I don't know what else, because of the horrible words, mocking looks, and accusations which are leveled at me repeatedly every day, and find their mark, like shafts from a tightly strung bow, and which are just as hard to draw from my body.
>
> I would like to shout to Margot, Van Daan, Dussel—and Daddy too—"Leave me in peace, let me sleep one night without my pillows being wet with tears, my eyes burning and my head throbbing. Let me get away from it all, preferably away from the world!" But I can't do that, they mustn't know my despair, . . . I couldn't bear their sympathy and their kindhearted jokes, it would only make me want to scream all the more. If I talk, everyone thinks I'm showing off; when I'm silent they think I'm ridiculous; rude if I answer, sly if I get a good idea, lazy if I'm tired, selfish if I eat a mouthful more than I should, stupid, cowardly, crafty, etc. etc. The whole day long I hear nothing else but that I am an insufferable baby, and although I laugh about it and pretend not to take any notice, I *do* mind. I would like to ask God to give me a different nature, so that I didn't put everyone's back up. But that can't be done. I've got the nature that has been given to me and I'm sure it can't be bad. I do my very best to please everybody, far more than they'd ever guess. . . . [I'd like to] try for *once* to be just as disdainful to them as they are to me. Oh, if only I could!

When parents believe in the pains of their children, this creates a rapport between them that eases the intense loneliness the young person feels. Of course, an adolescent rarely believes his parents can truly understand him; obviously they have never felt what he feels. But he is encouraged by their support and warmed by their concern, although he may not always show it.

Handling Moodiness

Parents do not have to, should not, cannot tolerate all moods, all outbursts. A child needs to be aware that there are limits to what is tolerated in the household. And there must be room, too, for a parent's moods, feelings, and concerns. But we want to offer as much of a haven as we can.

A girl bursts in the door after school. Her mother says, "Boy, you seem full of pep this afternoon."

And she responds, "Do you *have* to talk like that all the time?"

"Like what, for heaven's sake?"

"You just make me sick, that's all."

At which point the mother, if she is in A-one condition, will be alert enough to realize that she has done absolutely nothing to deserve this outburst. Her child has had a hard day at school and obviously needed to explode the minute she reached the safety of the nest. If the mother's sagacity and cool persist, she will not react defensively with the "What did *I* do?" approach, knowing full well that this will only impel her daughter to think of some way to justify her outburst and that the dredged-up complaints may drum up a full-scale battle. She will not comment on the child's irritability, either, because this, too, will make matters worse. The girl will deny indignantly that she is grumpy, it is her mother who is impossible, and so on.

What the mother does say and do naturally depends upon the child, what has helped in the past, and what the mother herself feels capable of at the moment, having perhaps had a rather hard day herself. Sometimes it works just to ignore the words, mention that there is a milkshake freshly made for her in the refrigerator, and retire from the combat zone for a discreet period.

To let a child go too far is not good for either of us. She will feel guilty, and we will begin to feel like a sacrificial lamb. It is a good idea to act before we are so angry that we find ourselves counterattacking, to stop the child firmly while we still remain fairly calm. If we cannot, if we are pretty hot-tempered ourself, then she will have to face our temper, and that is not so terrible. Sometimes parents who remain icy calm throughout any scene drive their child wild; the child may continue to provoke in an effort to force an expression of feeling. But our anger should not be so uncontrolled as a child's. That is, we should not attack a youngster's personality, looks, or ability. We confine ourself, if possible, to the child's behavior at present, which should, in any case, leave us plenty of ground!

"Instant Tradition"

Typical of this age is "You never . . ." or "You always. . . ." Any parent can fill in the blanks. It is called instant tradition. The child cancels out all the ways we have tried to be helpful and understanding in a blanket condemnation not only of our present behavior but also our past actions and past concern for him. (Parents also are sometimes guilty of this, and, needless to say, it is not helpful when we do it either.) It really does little good at a time like this to take him literally. He does not actually think that we never do anything to please him or always make scrambled eggs in the morning when we know he prefers boiled. Such gross exaggerations had best be accepted with equanimity. Of course, the trouble is that an accusation often has a small grain of truth in it. Many of us tend to respond guiltily. "Do I really make scrambled eggs more often than boiled?" we ask, appalled at ourself. However, the issue probably is not scrambled eggs versus boiled, so we need not waste too much time on it. Maybe our son is upset about something totally different; he needs to let off steam at someone, and mothers are, alas, very convenient. Or perhaps he is feeling deprived in relation to his sister (the scrambled-egg lover) or by life in general; he picks on eggs when he has something else in mind.

We need to absorb a certain amount of rudeness and irritability during these years, stopping short of martyrdom, of course, without doing battle.

Probably the most difficult problem for most parents to cope with is unpleasant behavior whose particular target is us. As our children grow into adolescence we, mirrored in their eyes, lose all our charm, our taste in clothes, our tact, our conversational élan, anything we ever thought we knew. For parents who are not secure in their feelings about themselves—and how many of us are?—this is especially painful. We cannot tolerate it with the sense of humor and sunny disposition that we may display toward his other foibles.

His criticisms hurt; they pierce our most vulnerable parts. We feel disliked, even hated. We also feel like failures. We have been told that this is the way all adolescents are, but when *our* child rejects *us* it is intensely personal.

Why They Reject Us

Why does it happen? And can it be avoided or softened? Along with the upsurge of sexual feelings accompanying puberty, explains psychiatrist Theodore Lidz, in *The Person: His Development Throughout the Life Cycle:*

> . . . there is some reawakening of . . . the sensuous and affectional attachments to the parent of the opposite sex. . . . The boy may now begin to idealize his mother and find nothing wrong in commenting on how beautiful she is and seek ways to please her and gain her affection. . . . Then, as the real upsurge of sexual feelings gets under way, the youth begins to turn away from his or her attachment to the parent, unconsciously and sometimes consciously concerned by the sexual aspects of the attraction. He begins to find fault with the parent, criticizing him or her, convincing himself that the parent is not attractive and not an object worth seeking. The criticism also spreads to the parent of the same sex.
>
> The girl is apt to dream of being a woman more capable than her mother, a person more attractive to her father, and may begin to talk to her mother in rather condescending tones, sorry for this "has-been" who has passed her prime.

So it happens that out children sometimes reject the very people they most need and love. For even while they are constantly finding fault with us, they love us, too. And there are moments when they feel guilty because of their feelings about us and miserable because they know they have hurt us.

Accepting Their Attitudes

A parent who likes herself as a woman (or himself as a man) and has a sturdy inner core will manage better during the upheaval. And he or she can offer more support to the child, whose safe passage through adolescence is immeasurably aided by the emotional availability of his parents. It is helpful to the girl and her development, for example, says Dr. Lidz:

> . . . if the mother is not angered by the condescension and can allow her daughter to indulge in . . . fantasies of being a more desirable female and potential sexual partner than her mother. It helps the girl gain self-esteem and enables her to feel capable of relating successfully to boys.

If the father can accept the fact that his son will be better than he is in some fields and not regard his boy's development as a challenge to his position, the boy can be encouraged to develop his strengths without fear.

Our children do envy their parents' position as the decision-makers, holders of the purse strings, heads of the household. And a lot of their rebellion reflects their feelings of helplessness in the face of this power. Then, too, while we are feeling that we can never strike the right note with our child, he may feel the same about us. When he wants to talk, perhaps we are rushed or in a bad mood. When he is busy doing his own work, we want him to stop and help us. When he wants to act grown up, we treat him like a baby. When he acts babyish, we tell him to act his age.

Fostering Better Communication

Sometimes a direct approach is helpful: "We really have been growling at each other lately. Is there something at home that's getting you down?" Or, simply, "Is something the matter?" or, "Is there some way I can help you?" If a youngster does respond, we should be receptive and patient, try to appreciate how things look from his viewpoint. Perhaps there are changes we can make to ease things for him. Young people who will not come clean about what is troubling them, assuming that they can put a finger on it, often complain that it never helps to try to talk to their parents. Nobody ever listens. It just starts a fight; nothing ever changes. A child who is willing to talk it over has not given up. He still believes his parents care about him and hopes to get along better at home.

Adolescents frequently feel that their parents do not like them very much. More often than is realized, a wide gap exists between the way parents feel about a child and the way the child perceives their feelings. "How can he possibly feel unloved?" a parent will ask. But the parent, though truly loving, may on a day-to-day basis criticize, nag, find fault, grump, and rarely express love affectionately.

We should try to make openings for easy talking and be flexible enough sometimes to drop what we are doing when a child wants to be with us alone, without his brothers or sisters around. We can make a habit of dropping into his room to chat at night before he goes to bed, or of taking long walks, or going biking on weekends. Possibilities depend on the family's interests and working schedules. Perhaps we can watch baseball or football on television with him; maybe he can show us how to develop photographs, and when the work is finished we can relax together over a snack in the kitchen. Perhaps we can learn a sport or a game together, or a craft, at home or at a class given locally. Working with him on his stamp collection or another hobby, playing checkers or chess or other games, painting a room or making curtains or knitting scarves for every member of the family are other possibilities for joint activity. Every mother and father can come up with ideas especially suited to themselves and their child. Working or playing together, we and our child get a chance to talk without "making a big deal out of it." We are, in effect, creating unhurried, unpressured, agreeable situations where communication between us is likely to flourish. Some of these ideas take a lot of time, others a little. We do what we can, but most of us can find a half hour every day or an hour several times a week to simply enjoy being with our child.

Other Helpful Approaches

It also works wonders for a child's morale to be pampered and catered to occasionally, especially when life is particularly rough. Gestures of warmth make a difference, an unexpected offer to help him with something he wants to do, for example. We need not wait for a special occasion to give him a present. Candy he loves, a gadget from the five and dime, something attractive to wear, stationery printed with his name, a record of his favorite rock group, a magazine concerned with his special interest, two tickets to a ball game or a concert—all convey warmth, concern, love. A word of warning: We should not give clothes or objects that reflect a taste or interest we wish the child had, but which he has resisted!

Often a relative or friend of the family with whom the young person has a rapport is able to be helpful, and we should encourage such contacts even though it is hard not to be a little envious when our child can unburden himself to someone else, but not to us.

Serious Problems

If people at any other time of life behaved the way these youngsters do, they would be considered abnormal. The extreme shifts in mood, the periods of intense depression followed by elation, the outbursts for no apparent reason, the unreasonableness, are "normal" only in the context of this period.

But not all behavior can be shrugged off as "adolescence." Some behavior, although not uncommon at this point, is nevertheless cause for concern. Dr. Fritz Redl writes, in *Pre-adolescents—What Makes Them Tick?"*:

> After all, there are such things as juvenile delinquents and psychoneurotics, and we shouldn't pretend that everything is bound to come out in the wash.

The idea of a child's "growing out of" difficulties is sound enough when the problems are simply "growing pains." But when serious problems persist over a considerable period of time, we cannot take them lightly. Says Dr. Redl, if a child's disturbing behavior

is too vehement and impulsive, too unapproachable by even the most reasonable techniques, then the chances are that Johnny's antics are symptoms not only of growth but also of something being wrong somewhere and needing repair . . . definitely serious, hangovers from old, never really solved problems, results of wrong handling, wrong environmental situations or other causes.

Some signs of serious trouble are frequent running away from home, chronic truancy, behavior that is too withdrawn or too aggressive, compulsive overeating accompanied by overweight, serious learning difficulties. One should also be concerned about disturbing traits that persist for a long time or seem to go very deep. For example, intermittent cruelty to a brother or sister is not uncommon or abnormal, particularly now when intense, troublesome feuds do tend to develop. But continued, frequent acts of cruelty or acts that actually threaten the safety or emotional well-being of the younger child cannot be shrugged off.

We may become so accustomed to quarrels or lack of civility that we regard a child's behavior as ordinary and are perhaps not alert to the fact that his depression has gone on too long unrelieved, or his demands have become more and more unreasonable, or his bickering has developed a malicious undertone. Very often a child signals that he needs special help by blatant antisocial behavior such as shoplifting; but a youngster who cannot make friends over a period of time or "just can't concentrate" on his schoolwork may need help just as much.

We are closely involved with out children, and sometimes for that reason alone may fail to evaluate the situation clearly. Dr. Redl advises:

> Whenever you are very much in doubt, it is wise to consult expert help for the checkup—just as you would in order to decide whether a heart murmur is due to too fast growth or to an organic disturbance.

9
Money: Earning It And Having It

EVERY NEIGHBORHOOD HAS some children who are resourceful enough, and want money enough, to create jobs and businesses for themselves.

What did you forget at the store today?
Bread for your dinner?
Milk for cereal?
Candy and cookies for your children?
I will go to the store for you. 50¢ for ten items or less. See Joe Gibbs, apt. 7B afternoons after 3:30

Homemade bread fresh from the oven, orange bowknots and spirals, brownies, raspberry sherbert, chocolate fudge cake and other good things to eat. Susie's catering service. Only the best of ingredients are used and no mixes. Ask for my price list. All orders require 24 hours notice. Weekends only.

Unfortunately, many people do not have confidence in youngsters this age. The average eleven- to fourteen-year-old (not without some reason!) is considered less than responsible, less than serious, and less than capable by most of the adult population.

When asked if she would subscribe to Steve's personalized newspaper service, for example, one woman answered, "I'd like to help Steve out, but you know kids. Next week he'll decide it's too hard to get up that early in the morning and I'll have to go back to my old delivery service."

Susie had similar trouble with her catering service. It was difficult at first for people to believe that a thirteen-year-old girl could bake cakes, breads, and cookies that were as good as one could buy at the store. Since Susie had learned to bake from a superb cook, namely her mother, she *was* good, and word-of-mouth soon provided her with many customers. She had underpriced her goods, however, and she had to go out of business after a few months of spending half of her weekends slaving for too little reward.

Eleven-year-old Joe was never able to drum up enough business for himself. Surely there must have been many people in his large-city apartment building who needed last-minute items from the store. But they never called on Joe, perhaps because they had visions of his losing their money, crushing their loaves of bread, or breaking their eggs.

Steve's newspaper business did thrive eventually, earning the fourteen-year-old money for a camera, a tape recorder, a trip to another city, and enough after-school snacks to sink anybody but an adolescent boy.

Their Reasons for Working

Why do children work? That's easy, they would say. We want more money. What do children gain from their work? More than money. The family wage earner is usually endowed with added respect and authority. Success is often measured in terms of earning ability. Being able to earn is a recognized badge of maturity. The youngster who begins to earn money, especially on a regular basis outside the home, has reached a symbolic point on his journey to adulthood. And while children work for the cash, the effect on their self-esteem is, in the end, the more meaningful fruit of their labor.

If we can do a needed job and do it well, every one of us derives satisfaction. When the job has a monetary value to someone else, the satisfaction is enhanced, and all the more so for young people, for whom it is a new experience. They begin to feel more important; they refer to "my job" in front of others. Youngsters who hold a job often have a special cachet among their peers. They are thought of as more grown up.

Youngsters rarely feel that their parents give them enough money. However adequate their allowance may be, being able to add to their income through their own efforts gives them the feeling that they can help themselves, that not everything in their lives depends upon being in their parents' good graces. As we have seen, this is of crucial importance to children who are growing into adolescence.

A boy has an absolutely desperate need for a new racing bike, but his parents feel that his old bicycle should last him through the end of high school. The situation is not hopeless, however. He can work to get his own racer. A girl wants a polo shirt with a cupid design such as all her friends wear. But her mother says, "No, there's not enough drawer space for all the shirts you have already." Nevertheless, she can work to earn it.

The discipline of doing a regular job, on a regular basis, on his own, helps a young person to see himself as a responsible, capable, and reliable person. Although parents want to be available for advice if needed, the more a child can manage on his own, the more satisfaction he will derive from the experience.

When Steve began his newspaper delivery service, his parents could not believe that he would get himself up at 6:15 every morning. But they resolved, nevertheless, not to interfere. They felt that if he lost customers because he could not drag himself out of bed to make deliveries on time, that in itself would be a learning experience. On the other hand, if he had to rely on his parents to push him out the door each morning, he would be robbed of an essential source of satisfaction—doing it on his own.

Values Beyond Money

As it happened, Steve surprised them. The business had been his idea, and he was determined to make it succeed. Although he already had a wind-up alarm clock, he took money from his savings to purchase an electric alarm and set the clocks to ring five minutes apart each morning. He got himself up, he got himself out, and he got the papers to his customers on time every day. Carrying out his own project in his own way, by himself, made him justifiably proud of himself and enhanced his feeling of self-worth. His parents found him more willing to try other new things, unconnected with work, as a result of his increased self-confidence.

What if a child cannot manage on his own like this? Sometimes it is because the job was his parents' idea, not his, or because he did not have a realistic picture of what the job involved or of what he could manage. Helping a young person evaluate a project *is* a parent's job. We need to discuss with him what is involved and listen to his ideas about how it can be done. We should not push a child into something or hold him back because of lack of confidence in him. At the beginning, a child would probably be better off taking on a simple, small job that he obviously can handle, rather than attempting a complicated arrangement where success is questionable. On the other hand, if the child himself has conceived the larger project and his parents have made sure he understands all that is involved, they will probably want to support him. There is such a thing as going into too many "what ifs" and "you'll nevers!"

Because a youngster's job often involves manual labor, such as mowing lawns, washing cars, or assisting with carpentry, he is likely to develop a respect for people who work with their hands, to see that "blue-collar" jobs can be difficult and tiring and can be done well or badly, just like other work. These are no small fringe benefits.

Granted the desirability of paid work, what kinds of jobs can young people of this age get and do? Work around the house is usually easier to find, although parents and children tend to disagree about which jobs should be paid for and which should be considered "chores" or work that the child contributes to the household. A chore, suggests Eric W. Johnson,

> . . . is something a child hasn't the right to refuse to do (like making his bed) and which you would not have to hire someone else to do. On the other hand, a *job* is something he would have the right to refuse (like painting a room) and which you would hire someone else to do. By this definition, chores should not be paid for, and jobs should.

Naturally, in a family where both parents work and money is tight, children of this age, particularly of thirteen and fourteen, will be expected to pitch in with baby-sitting, preparations for dinner, and other household chores that would not be considered part of the child's regular responsibilities in another family.

Jobs that many children do for money in their own homes include baby-sitting, shoveling snow, mowing grass, raking leaves and other yard work, gardening, cleaning the garage, washing and polishing the car, ironing, mending, preparing school lunches for all, preparing dinner one or more times a week, preparing breakfast, taking a younger brother or sister to a weekly music lesson, listening to him practice, cleaning the cellar, cleaning kitchen cabinets, washing the insides of windows, and other odd jobs.

Many of these jobs are also performed for

neighbors. In answer to a questionnaire circulated by Eric Johnson, junior high school students listed the following among their paid jobs: deliveries, wood-chopping, taking inventory in stores, caddying, washing windows, painting, repair work, vegetable picking, delivering prescriptions for a drugstore, tutoring, and taking care of plants or pets while their owners are away. They also mentioned businesses that they had developed either alone or with friends, such as growing and selling plants, selling old paper, selling greeting cards, carpentry, and professional photography.

Should Working Teen-agers Contribute?

If they are earning their own money, should young people have to contribute to the expenses of the home or be given a smaller allowance? If the family needs the child's help, then, of course, he should be expected to contribute a portion of his earnings. This would be particularly true of thirteen- and fourteen-year-olds who have a greater earning capacity. It does not seem right for a child to have a substantial earned income that he can use for entertainment and still receive an allowance if his parents have a difficult time just paying for family necessities.

But most parents in comfortable circumstances do not expect children of this age to contribute money toward family expenses. The big job of these young people is school, and their contribution to the household is usually in the form of regular chores performed without pay—bedmaking, dishwashing, and the like. If they choose to find paid work, they generally are not required to take a reduction in their allowance. When a child cannot enjoy relatively free use of money he earns at this age, his incentive to work is dulled. On the other hand, the few who earn fairly large sums may want to contribute to an unusual expenditure, such as a special vacation, but this should be their own decision. Children ought to be able to work for what they want, just as their parents can.

Should the money a child earns or receives as his allowance be entirely his own, to squander or to save as he sees fit?

To answer this question we need to ask why a parent would want to regulate a child's spending or have him account for what he does with all his money. The responses are generally that a child cannot be left to learn to manage money on his own, that the child who is profligate with what he has does not necessarily learn to spend sensibly through continually practicing the opposite, that parents need to keep track of what their children are doing with their money, that children ought to make charitable contributions, learn to save, be directed toward wise purchases, and so on.

Learning to Handle Money

How do people acquire their ways with money? How did we? From imitating (or rebelling against) a parent? From parental guidance through our childhood and adolescence, or trial and error as adults, or perhaps both? The way some adults deal with their financial affairs makes one question their qualifications for imparting wisdom on the subject! Can a mother who is wildly extravagant teach her child to budget? Maybe. But sticking to a budget requires not only knowledge but also a certain temperament.

We may see in the same family a boy who saves carefully, plans each expenditure, and a boy who buys on impulse the most impractical gadgets or treats all the guys to sodas. But their ways of managing money would not be the only differences between those two brothers. A child's way of handling money reflects his personality just as everything else does.

A parent complains, "That kid can't hold onto money; when he's got it, it burns a hole in his pocket until he blows it all on something worthless." It is very difficult for a parent to watch a child "waste" his money. We work very hard to earn what we have, and we naturally do not like to see money "thrown away." But there are several points here. What is "something worthless"? Is there possibly some value to the child in being able to spend his money "any old way" he likes? How does a child learn to handle money responsibly?

Needless to say, an object may have value to a child that his parents cannot see. It may have value to a child even though he loses interest in it after a short time. Parents tend to think that longevity is all-important in a toy, practicality in clothes, but young people may think differently.

When a child spends all his allowance on the day he receives it and has nothing for the rest of the week, what does he do? Does he ask for an advance, swipe change from the dresser, or offer to do some chores to earn money? Does he moan about his fate, or contentedly accept his paupered condition until allowance day rolls around again? Allowing him to appreciate the consequences of his actions means refusing to advance him money if it is clear that he will only get deeper into debt. But giving him a chance to earn some is an honorable solution.

One idea on squandering money: The urge to spend wildly cannot be indulged by most of us in later life because our tastes become too expensive, our budgets too retrictive, our heads too sensible. Only when they are young can children indulge themselves fully in quite this way, without guilt or worry, unless parents impose it. After a while, they learn that 50¢ spent on a toy car on Monday cannot buy baseball cards on Thursday. And sooner or later, because of their own needs and desires, they *want* to learn how to manage better. Then they become receptive to parental guidance.

One eleven-year-old was referred to as "the last of the big-time spenders" by his family because he always raced over to the shopping center to spend his allowance the minute he got it. When he received a fairly large sum for a birthday or other occasion, he invariably spent it all that very day.

But there came a morning when he soberly informed his parents that he had "saved" his allowance and bought something special with it. Since this was only 24 hours after he had received it, his parents needed a few seconds to realize what their child was saying. He had resisted his usual impulse to spend his money immediately and had waited *a whole day,* considering the expenditure, before making his purchase. He was reporting what was for him a victory. Fortunately, his parents had had a good night's sleep and had their wits about them at that moment, so they were able to value and applaud what was indeed an accomplishment for this particular child. It is with such victories as these that a person moves forward.

The Danger of Overemphasis

A child is likely to learn to be responsible about money if (1) he is allowed to decide how to spend his own money; (2) he is not made to feel guilty or stupid about how he spends it; (3) his parents advise him, but not too often or too critically; and (4) he is intelligent enough to learn from his experiences, which our children are if we allow them the opportunity.

Sometimes parents who talk about their child's not knowing the value of money are guilty of valuing money over other important things in life. Perhaps their child feels that they put too high a premium on materialistic things, and he needs to rebel against that. Or perhaps the parents are using money as a weapon with which to manage the child. People have all sorts of quirks and foibles about money. We will spend a lot on furnishing our home, for example, but feel guilty about leaving a single light bulb burning "unnecessarily." All this is relatively harmless until we try to impose our peculiarities on our children as rules of reason. If a mother grew up with little, she may be tight-fisted with money even though more is available now, or she may be particularly liberal, wanting to give her children things she did not have. In either case, her children will not grow up in the same atmosphere as she did and probably will not feel about money as she does.

When children use money or possessions to compete or show off, or when they talk a great deal about money and who has what, they may be reflecting their parents' attitudes. It is often a good idea for parents to reexamine their behavior in this regard. Is the message they are sending what they really want to communicate to their child?

Of course, the way a child this age spends his money is not entirely his own business. He cannot be allowed to buy things we consider dangerous to his health and safety. We have a right to insist, for example, that he cannot buy a motorcycle, because we think he is too young to ride one, or buy cigarettes, alcohol, or drugs. A family's rules about certain places being off limits, certain movies being forbidden apply no matter whose money is involved. But a child ought to be free to make his own decisions within the protective boundaries the family has set.

How Much Allowance?

It is impossible to say what a typical allowance ought to be for a young person of eleven to fourteen. Family resources differ, as do children's needs, and of course what is typical varies from neighborhood to neighborhood throughout the country. A parent needs to know what other children in the child's class or neighborhood are receiving and also what those allowances cover. Obviously if Billie-down-the-block has to pay his carfare to and from school out of his allowance, the amount does not seem as big as it did at first glance. We always hear that "everybody" gets more money than our child. To hear him tell it, the rest of the gang live like oriental potentates compared to him. There always *are* a few children who seem to have money to throw around, but what do most of the youngsters get? If a child really has less, that is, if he goes to a school or lives in a section where all the youngsters have a great deal more than he has, parents do need to discuss this with him and not ignore the problem or slough it off.

What should an allowance cover? When a small child first begins to receive an allowance, around age five, it is usually a very small sum—a nickel, a dime, seldom more—just enough to give him the feeling of having money of his very own to buy candy, or put in the bubble-gum machine, or purchase a small toy at the five and ten. Very few children are willing or able to save a portion of this first small amount—even for a week—and parents usually do not expect it. It is not at all unusual for the entire sum to be spent the day it is received.

Later on, the amount is increased, but it usually continues to cover only small personal pleasures, that is, candy, games, toys, and such. By the time they reach eleven or twelve, however, many children crave to handle larger sums of money and begin to have more definite opinions about how money spent on them should be used. Parents usually begin gradually to increase the child's allowance to cover other expenses. Movies, concerts, and similar entertainment are usually among the first items included. A child learns to save for such events and, since going to them is optional, he will not be deprived of any necessities of life while he is learning about budgeting his money satisfyingly.

If a child is managing well, parents can begin to include items such as writing paper, school supplies, transportation, hobbies, books, cosmetic and toilet items, gifts, after-school snacks, and minor articles of clothing. He must learn how to put aside the money for these items until he needs to make the purchases.

A girl who has shown good taste and judgment when shopping with her mother for clothes may now be given money to budget for certain items in her wardrobe. Underwear, socks, pajamas or nightgowns, and hair ribbons are a good beginning; mistakes in these are not crucial. Usually a parent does not increase a child's responsibilities in this way unless the child herself is anxious for it and has been or is now given certain preparation.

It is not enough for a parent simply to give

a child a larger allowance and then leave her on her own. Parent and child need to consider how many pairs of socks, underwear, etc., the parents would ordinarily buy for the girl. Starting with a year's supply is often too difficult at the beginning. If it seems feasible, using a three-month period, or a season of the year, perhaps, is a comfortable way to begin. Then parent and child can begin to comparison-shop among stores and brands, go shopping together and get an idea of what these items generally cost, survey quality, size, color, available assortment.

A girl sees that if she splurges on one beautiful nightgown, she will be able to afford only three nightgowns instead of four. A parent's guidance includes pointing out this fact, and which materials shrink, and that the ribbons on the expensive nightgowns will look less lovely after one washing because they need ironing and mother does not iron underwear and nightclothes. The child sees that planning purchases requires thought, time, and effort. After considering the information, she makes her own choice. Over a period of time she will learn to take advantage of sales, to understand what is and is not a bargain, to get the most for her money. With experience, she will become more able and efficient.

Allow a Little Leeway

Including several categories of purchases in her allowance also gives a child a little leeway to be extravagant in one area if she is willing to economize in another. Needless to say, we expect mistakes at the start and do not overemphasize them. Later on we will be pleased as our thirteen-year-old picks up a blouse on a shopping trip, feels the material, and says knowingly, "This material is *cool* but it will look positively *gross* after a few washings." Just because a child has a clothing allowance does not mean that we cannot go along when a child buys. But we go only if wanted after the orientation days; that is the understanding.

With boys a more inclusive allowance usually does not begin with clothes; even the most clothes-conscious of today's Prince Valiants do not want to be bothered shopping for things to wear until they are older. They hate trying on and usually have neither the patience nor the interest for comparison-shopping. But they have other needs: sports equipment, hobbies, gifts for friends, clothing extras such as fancy belts or sporty shoes. The idea is to start with the item with which the child is most likely to succeed. Boys early gain a feeling for what constitutes a good bat, ball, and glove, for example, and are interested enough to learn to make sound judgments about purchasing them.

A child might be given a special sum of money earmarked for certain expenses only; or that sum can be pooled with his regular allowance, with the understanding that he must now pay for certain new expenses. In the first case, one does not run the risk that clothing money will be used for after-school snacks, and it is often a good way to begin. But after a while, one wants to move on to the next arrangement. When mistakes and imperfections are taken for granted in a family as part of the normal order of things, it is assumed that managing money, like everything else, will bring its share of error. Starting with small sums and fairly simple optional items decreases the risk.

We let our child know exactly what his allowance covers. We check with him every so often to see how things are going and to find out if he has some ideas about changes. But we do not hang over his shoulder. It is not unreasonable to ask for a rough accounting for the first few "pay days" after we have enlarged his allowance and responsibilities. But after that, a youngster should be free to keep his own counsel, unless we have reason to believe something is seriously wrong.

A few children are ready by the time they are almost fifteen to receive a "full" allowance that covers all their expenses, but most have not yet the experience or the judgment this requires and do not seek the added responsibility. But beginning at eleven, say, to increase the items covered by a child's allowance and gradually build his ability to manage his affairs over these years can have great advantages for a family.

Responsibility Helps

Parents and children tend to have many arguments about money during the adolescent years, and the more responsibility a child has for his own expenditures, the more reasonable he will be—probably—in his requests. Also, when parents make periodic reevaluations of his income, this cuts down on what can turn into frequent bickering over a multitude of items. If parents are fairly consistent and firm and refuse to be badgered into giving extra money except under extraordinary conditions, they avoid constant nagging, which occurs only if parents encourage it by rewarding it. We need to bend when there is a genuine financial emergency, but when pleading becomes routine we are free to suggest that the child start putting his own money away.

Taking on full reponsibility for his financial affairs decreases a child's feeling of dependence upon his parents, a feeling that becomes increasingly onerous as he gets older. He begins to get the feeling that he can manage his own life, which makes him more optimistic about his future. He feels more important.

In our society we prolong the adolescent period by the lengthy schooling we expect of our young people. We live in an age when people tend to define themselves by the work they do: I'm a lawyer, or I'm an electrician, or whatever. But we have a large pariah group, the young, who are denied the opportunity to support themselves through productive work and must depend upon their parents for the basics of their lives for a very long preparatory period. Many of today's school dropouts reflect a need to begin ordering their own lives.

Giving a child a "full" allowance does not make him less financially dependent on us, but it does change the day-to-day basis on which he lives. He is buying and choosing his own clothes and accessories, his toilet articles, everything that can possibly be arranged under his aegis. As he gets older he will probably be expected to work in his spare time, to contribute toward these expenses. What is asked of him will depend on the working capability of the young person, the job opportunities in his area, and the financial situation of the family, plus his school-work load and other responsibilities such as music lessons or athletic practice. If a child is deeply involved with piano studies, for example, and practices for several hours a day, his family probably will not require a financial contribution from him unless they must.

It is a good idea to have periodic reviews with a child of how he is coming along. If he never has any money and cannot figure out where it has gone (a not uncommon complaint of adults as well as children), he ought to try to keep a record of what he spends. If this seems a terrible burden, he can regard it as a temporary measure only, to be done for several weeks or a month until he gets a clearer picture of his spending. Although a child should be free enough to make mistakes in spending, he ought to know what the mistakes are so that he can learn from them.

Permitting a child to use his own judgment does not mean that a parent withdraws entirely. As with other things, first we do it for them, then with them, then they do it while we watch, then they go it alone with guidance as needed.

10
Drugs And Other Escape Mechanisms

CHILDREN DO NOT, at first, ask sophisticated questions about drugs. They want to know the answer to one very simple question: "Why—if heroin and LSD and drugs like that are so dangerous—do people take them?" A very sensible question. But the answer is not easy. Because if people did not derive certain pleasures from these drugs there would be no problem. Nobody would use them.

The child, searching to unravel the mystery, persists: "Why do people use drugs?" (He is not, of course, talking about drugs prescribed for illness.) It is tempting to make the answer as simple and straightforward as the question. After all, we feel, drugs *are* bad; we do not want our children anywhere near them. So we may respond that anybody who smokes marijuana, shoots heroin, takes pills is sick, or bad, or crazy. "Drugs are poison, you must have nothing to do with them. You can see for yourself in the newspapers that people are dying every day from breaking that rule." Simple, really.

But it isn't. Now that we are some years into the drug scene we should know that if the problem were that easily handled, more and more children would not be involved with drugs of a dozen different descriptions. Why can't we simplify our response? Because any such simplified warning is not true and, because of that, it is not going to send us home free. The very first time our child sees a perfectly normal friend contentedly puffing a joint of marijuana—and offering him one—it is going to be very clear that we lied to him on at least one score. This picture will be so different from the sick scene we painted that he may wonder if any part of our warning against drugs is true. In lumping all drugs and drug users together, we have made it possible that our child will use them also, once he sees the kid next door or the gang at school smoking marijuana with apparent safety; he may assume that the whole drug scene is as harmless as this looks to him. Of course, such an assumption is untrue. Even marijuana smoking is *not* without danger. But we are not in a good position to convince him of the possible dangers if we ourselves have thrown everything into the same bag and colored it an unrelieved, macabre black.

Answering First Questions

What then do we do with that first question? Of course, a single pointed question does not appear out of the blue one fine day to be dealt with honestly and intelligently once and for all. As with imparting information about sex, we give our children the facts about drugs over a long period of time. The drug scene comes to their attention at an early age now. Probably we have already had some discussions about it with our child. But as he gets older he will hear about drugs and see people using them. Chances are he will be approached to try them, probably by a friend. He will need to talk about the various drugs again and again. He will be talking about this with friends. He should also be talking with us. He will need to receive increasingly sophisticated answers with more and more information in response to his questions.

Very few of us are well prepared for this job. Heroin, marijuana, LSD, "speed" (methedrine or methamphetamine), and the rest were probably not in our experience as children or young adults. Now we must learn what dangers—and attractions—they hold for our children. The latter—attractions—is where a lot of us get hung up. We have a bright, curious eleven-year-old boy, alive to life and its possibilities. And he asks that question: "Why?" We find that we have tremendous difficulty admitting to him the very simple, obvious fact that people take drugs to make them feel good, to give them feelings and sensations that are intensely pleasurable, interesting, exciting. Or give freedom from pain, both physical and emotional, relieve tension and anxiety. Or to impart a feeling of being at peace with oneself and one's surroundings.

Says singer (and former speed freak) Johnny Cash:

> I'll tell you why I took amphetamines, because it felt good. There isn't anybody can get a kid off drugs by telling him it doesn't feel good. He knows how it makes him feel. For a while you're so stimulated, your mind is like a high-speed camera clicking away at three hundred and sixty degrees and you see and know everything. There are all those beautiful visions, all right, and those realizations and feelings of love and awareness.

But we dare not tell this to that curious, questing young person. We are frightened that once he knows this secret he will want to experiment for himself. Everything in his environment impels him to seek a good feeling. In the words of one young person, "It's a good thing to feel good, and the sooner you feel gooder the better."

But *we* know the secret and *we* are not seduced into using such drugs. Why? Because we also know the very grave dangers involved, and we are not willing to take the risk. For most of us, in effect, the game is not worth the candle. Says Johnny Cash:

> You go down the other side of that whole thing, and the going down ain't worth the coming up. . . . I still worry that I might have damaged my brain with pills. I don't think so, but I'll tell you, even after three years off drugs, at least once a week I'll have a horrible nightmare. I've got pills in my pocket that I'm trying to hide from somebody, and I'm always falling down and cursing myself, and somebody's chasing me and I'm going to jail, and somebody's beating me. All kinds of horrible things. At least once a week. It was every night at first.

The Need for Trust

But our children do not have our experience, our judgment. Can we trust them? There comes a point in every youngster's life when that question becomes irrelevant; unless we are going to put a 24-hour guard on him, we must trust him. But, we may still protest, at this age wouldn't we be justified in shading the truth a little to protect him a while longer? Why should we open the door?

We must face the fact that the door is already open. If we want to be believed later, we must be honest now. We even have to try not to make mistakes out of ignorance, because children tend to believe that such mistakes are intentional distortions.

We do not, however, just throw a book labeled "drug facts" at our child and let him loose with it, any more than we do with information about sex. We tell him what he asks or needs to know, and along with this we impart our own value judgments and our feelings about how we hope he will act. His protection, then, comes from a combination of his own intelligence and judgment and what he is able to take from us.

As we go along, we will want to tell him the complete truth, offering as much scientific detail as he can handle about what the various drugs are, what they do, how they affect one's thinking, feeling, and behavior, their dangers and their pleasures and the special hazards they present for young users. Our child will seek to understand the differences between the various drugs and, as time passes, will probably begin to ask increasingly complex questions, both philosophical and provocative: Why not get high once in a while? Does marijuana make a person feel sexy? Why do you smoke or drink (if you do) when cigarettes can cause cancer and alcohol can lead to alcoholism? When we know the answer, we should tell him what we know. If we feel unsure of our facts, we ought to say so and try to inform ourselves more adequately. If our child questions our own use of drugs—alcohol, tobacco, sleeping pills, etc.—we need to avoid reacting defensively. Admitting our fallibility is less damaging to our standing with him than arguing the point. The child is usually more interested in communicating honestly than in faulting us.

Here are some of the basic facts about the most common drugs used and abused today.

Heroin

Heroin, also called smack, horse, H, and scag, is not a controversial drug. Derived from opium, it kills the pains of the body, the pains of the mind, and, quite often, the user himself. Why would anyone want to try heroin? When injected into a vein it produces a "rush" of excitement that is sometimes described as akin to sexual orgasm. Within a few minutes, the person begins to feel drowsy; he feels pleasantly warm and at peace with himself and the world; he feels self-confident, like "somebody." For persons who have difficulty experiencing these feelings in everyday living, the drug exerts a powerful attraction.

Unfortunately, when the drug wears off, reality with all its pain returns. In order to continue to escape, the user continues to take the drug. But he must take it in increasing amounts because his body begins quickly to build up a "tolerance" to it; he needs more and more heroin to achieve the same effect. Soon he may need to have it three or four times a day. In a very short time the user's previous worries are replaced by one all-consuming preoccupation—where he is going to get his next "fix." At this point, the main reason for using the drug is to avoid the misery of not having it. The drug experience has become the purpose of his life. He has become "addicted"; that is, he suffers severe "withdrawal" symptoms if his body is deprived of the drug.

Youngsters often begin by sniffing heroin, usually under the mistaken belief that this is not dangerous. However, heroin passes quickly through the nasal membranes into the bloodstream, and one can become addicted, or die, from sniffing as well as from injecting. The progression to injecting heroin under the skin ("skin popping") and finally into a vein ("mainlining") occurs as the user is drawn by his need for a stronger and faster "fix." Becoming listless and apathetic, he is often unable to maintain a regular school schedule at this point or to sustain genuine relationships with others. In addition, large sums of money are required to support a "habit," so that the addict must frequently resort to stealing—sometimes from his family—or other criminal activity.

Heroin addicts suffer from a variety of physical ailments directly related to their habit: abscesses, collapsed veins, and infection from unsterile syringes or needles are common, as is hepatitis, spread through shared needles. Preoccupied with the search for heroin and indifferent to food, users become generally run-down and are easy prey to infections. Tuberculosis and pneumonia are not uncommon. When drugged they are less sensitive to pain; they may injure themselves and not know it. Deaths from overdose ("OD") are reported daily. In New York City, heroin kills more young people than all the contagious diseases combined.

Most youngsters, if fully informed of the dangers of this narcotic, will not experiment with it, understanding that heroin is not a joyride to be taken casually now and then to brighten a dull Sunday. Those who get into heroin are often children with a strong need to flirt with danger, a need to hurt themselves or their parents, or those who find life too hard to bear and cannot resist the temporary escape provided by the drug experience. They often have a greater than average sense of incompetence and do not experience excitement in their daily lives. They assume the future holds only failure for them, and look toward a tomorrow in which things are going to get worse.

LSD

LSD (lysergic acid diethylamide, "acid") is a manmade chemical so powerful that approximately 150,000th of an ounce is a sufficient dose for one person for several hours. Colorless, odorless, and tasteless, it is ordinarily sold either in a sugar cube in which a tiny drop of LSD has been absorbed, in powder form, or in capsules of various colors.

Why do people take LSD? They experience hallucinations (sensory experiences not caused by external stimuli) of sight and sound and, to a lesser extent, of taste, smell, and touch. Walls may appear to move, colors seem more brilliant, unusual patterns appear, music can be "seen" as well as heard, time slows down or seems to go in reverse. Images appear, sometimes realistic, sometimes fantastic. LSD "trips" come on within a half hour or more after taking the drug, are most vivid in about two hours, and continue for varying periods of time up to perhaps 10 to 16 hours, gradually diminishing.

Users often feel more creative (although studies to compare creativity before and after LSD experiences have found no significant changes) and have a sense of oneness with the universe and of gaining insights into their own personalities. The experience is strongly emotional, often visionary and dreamlike.

The Bad Trip

Frequently, however, the dream is a nightmare, a "bad trip," with feelings of dread and horror that may include sensations that one's body is dissolving and that one is losing one's mind. Although LSD is not known to be addictive, there are many cases on record of the development of psychosis and severe and lasting anxiety or depression after an acid trip. Strangely, too, there occur "flashbacks"—a recurrence of the LSD experience days or even months after the drug was last taken. These may be brought on by physical or emotional stress, by smoking marijuana, or by taking certain medications, and they can be intensely frightening.

The kind of experience a person has with LSD can vary greatly depending upon his personality, his mood at the time, the people with him, and the circumstances in which the drug is taken. The same dose may act differently upon the same person at two different times, or it may produce both ecstasy and horror during one trip. Certain personality types find it particularly difficult to tolerate the alterations of feelings that occur under the influence of the drug. Crippling and death by accident are possible also; persons feeling they can float or fly may step out of high windows or, feeling invincible, may walk into a lane of moving traffic.

Some studies have purported to show that women who have taken LSD during early pregnancy or shortly before conception run a higher risk of giving birth to abnormal babies. These studies have now been discredited. There is some indication that repeated use of LSD may cause lasting chromosomal damage to the user, but the evidence is inconclusive. Clearly, however, any substance whose effects are so powerful and unpredictable is dangerous.

Several other substances produce effects similar to LSD, although milder. The two most widely known are mescaline, which comes from the peyote cactus, and psilosybin, which comes from the Mexican "sacred mushroom."

Stimulants and Depressants

Stimulants and depressants come in pills of many colors and are designed to change one's mood upon demand. Want to fly? Take a pretty orange pill. Want to cool it? Take a "red bird" or a "yellow jacket." These "up" and "down" drugs have been with us for a long time. Because of our familiarity with them and because they have legitimate medical uses, many parents tend to be unduly casual about them.

Young people take "up" drugs in order to reduce fatigue, increase their alertness, and achieve a feeling of well-being. Amphetamines such as Benzedrine and Dexedrine ("Bennies" and "Dexies") are used to help them cram for an examination, to have more energy for athletics, or to stay awake in order to drive. Or they may take an "up" because they're feeling down. Because these drugs also suppress the appetite, they are used in dieting as well. "Up" drugs also include cocaine, which is being used more and more frequently, caffeine, and nicotine.

What are the dangers? If you don't *feel* hungry or tired—even though you lack food and sleep—you may push yourself further than is good for you, perhaps going without food or sleep for several days. In addition, when the drug wears off, you will tend to feel the accumulated fatigue and be depressed. The temptation, then, is to take more pills, falling into an insidious cycle that is difficult to break. People who get into the habit of using stimulants to pull them out of the doldrums usually lose weight, become jumpy and irritable, and are often suspicious and hostile. They become run down and are less resistant to infection. Heavy doses may cause a temporary psychosis, involving feelings of terror, confusion, and loss of touch with reality. Abrupt withdrawal of the drug from a heavy user can result in a deep and suicidal depression.

Another "up" drug, Methedrine ("speed"), is injected intravenously in large amounts to produce a "rush," the feeling of exhilaration that comes with injecting heroin. This ebbs within minutes and is followed by a high, a flood of physical and mental energy, a feeling of power. The thoughts of the "speed freak" may run faster than his ability to articulate them, so that his speech is often unintelligible to someone not tuned into his wavelength. When the drug wears off, in two to four hours, the user feels weak, exhausted and, again, down.

The dangers associated with using other stimulants are present with Methedrine, only more so. The user often becomes irrational, impulsive, and sometimes violent. There is a progressive deterioration of his relationships with family and friends and of his normal inhibitions. He becomes run down and is easy prey to infection. He often suffers from abscesses, collapsed veins, and related problems that any person who injects a drug intravenously is subject to. Liver damage may result. Occasionally, death during athletic contests has been blamed on the use of speed or other amphetamines. It is probably more accurate to view the drug as contributing to death from other causes. Young people who are into the drug scene warn that "speed kills."

The pace of life has led many adults to turn to "down" drugs—barbiturates, tranquilizers, and alcohol—in order to relax from the tensions of their existence. Young people often find these drugs first in their own homes and use—and abuse—them for the same purpose their parents do. Barbiturates (Seconal, Nembutal, and phenobarbital) and tranquilizers (Miltown, Equanil, and Librium) calm a person down and help him sleep. When they are used often, tolerance develops—one needs more to produce the same effect—and the user can become addicted to and dependent upon them. With heavy users, withdrawal of the drug requires hospitalization. Deaths from overdose can occur. Combinations of drugs such as barbiturates with alcohol can be especially lethal.

Alcohol

Alcohol (ethyl alcohol) is well known enough not to require extensive discussion here. Roughly 70,000,000 Americans drink with some regularity, ranging from small amounts to overindulgence. They drink seeking relaxation, self-confidence, an escape from unpleasant reality, an aid to sociability, or, simply, pleasure.

Many people believe that alcohol is a stimulant because it does provide an initial lift. But this sense of well-being comes because one's aches and pains and worries are depressed. One's inhibitions and controls are depressed, too, so that people find the "nerve" to do things they would not—and sometimes should not—do if they were not under the influence of alcohol. Most adults who drink are able to enjoy their liquor in moderation and lead perfectly normal lives. But according to the National Institute of Mental Health, an estimated 5,000,000 to 6,000,000 adults in the United States are alcoholics and perhaps 10 per cent of all drinkers cause serious personal problems to themselves and their families by their drinking. In addition, alcohol, because it depresses their reflexes, impairs their ability to drive a car. It does not, however, always discourage people from driving, and half of all fatal crashes involve drinking drivers. There is, in addition, abundant testimony linking excessive drinking with arrests for crime. Alcohol is addictive.

Writing ten years ago in *The Intelligent Parents' Guide to Teen-agers,* Thelma C. Purtell said:

> The use of alcohol is apparently incorporated in our adolescent culture whether we like to face the fact or not. In a society that accepts adult drinking, it is natural that teen-agers, in making demands for adult prerogatives, should include the right to find out for themselves about liquor as well as everything else. Drinking by the teen-ager, beyond the family circle, constitutes another form of experimentation in the business

> of becoming an adult. The amazing thing is that this can occur in a nation which through its laws makes clear that young people are not expected to drink at all.

Mrs. Purtell also said, "Parents will have solved the drinking problem when they have helped their young people to be the sort of individuals who do not need to turn to such a treacherous ally in times of boredom, anxiety, or adversity." Now, a decade later, much the same words of advice are being offered to parents concerned about their children's interest in other drugs, and alcohol continues to be a problem.

Today, Peter Marin and Allan Y. Cohen write, "Drugs (meaning marijuana et al.) have become . . . a normal part of the adolescent world."

Marijuana

Marijuana (pot, tea, grass, or dope) is derived from the common hemp plant, *Cannabis sativa,* and is commonly smoked in pipes or cigarettes called reefers or joints. But it is more than a drug. It has become a symbol of today's youth culture. Feelings about marijuana often serve to distinguish the young from the old, and to alienate the young from the old. There is great controversy about marijuana, and it has become difficult to separate fact from myth. Respected physicians differ in their interpretations of the available data and in their views about the possibilities of danger from prolonged or heavy use. Because of the highly emotional climate that surrounds the drug and because of the variability of its effects on different users and under different circumstances, it is difficult for parents to make a judgment about it.

One fact, though, is clear. Huge numbers of young people are experimenting with marijuana today, and before our children are very much older they will be forced to make a decision about whether or not to try it themselves. We ought to think back and remember how many of us took our first sip of alcohol or first puff of a cigarette—whose taste and effects we may have found unpleasant—because of pressure to do what everyone else was doing or to appear sophisticated to our friends. There is similar pressure on our children today to try marijuana. A child may be curious to see for himself what it is like, or he may want to be able to say he's tried it, or he doesn't want to have to say he hasn't tried it. So we must attempt to understand what it is, what it offers to the young, and what dangers it may hold for them. Then we can decide how to discuss the problem with our children.

Varying Effects

What is it like to smoke marijuana? This question cannot be answered simply. The quality of the drug is not constant; the chemical potency of the hemp plant can vary greatly, and the purity of a particular reefer is always in question because marijuana is distributed illegally—you can't be sure what you're getting. Sometimes it is mixed with other drugs or substances that may be dangerous. In addition, the same amount of marijuana of a particular quality can have different effects upon different persons—and indeed upon the same person at different times. A great deal depends on the "set"—whom you are with, where you are, how you are feeling. Are you relaxed, happy, unpressured? Or are you ill at ease, tired, apprehensive? Are you with friends you like and can trust? Or are you alone or in uncongenial surroundings? Marijuana will tend to accentuate the existing conditions, so that you feel more relaxed, or more anxious, depending upon how you felt to start with.

In ordinary low doses, marijuana usually produces a mild euphoria. Immediate physical effects usually include a reddening of the whites of the eyes, an increased heart rate, dryness of the mouth and throat, and a cough owing to the irritating effect of the smoke on the lungs. At the start of a "high" many smokers giggle as if at a private joke, then become quiet and reflective. Most users report experiencing a heightened perception of their surroundings; their appreciation of people, objects and various activities is enhanced. They say they see colors and shapes more vividly, that listening to music gives more pleasure and yields new sensations. Time is slowed down. One may seem to exist outside the passage of time much as one does while daydreaming. The marijuana smoker tends to focus on himself and his experience and prefers to ponder rather than to act. He feels pleasantly warm, at peace with the world. He rarely becomes aggressive or domineering, in contrast to a person intoxicated with alcohol. Marijuana is not a narcotic and is not addictive. No physical craving develops for it, and it causes no hangover.

Most smokers of marijuana use it occasionally, perhaps a reefer no more (and probably less) than once a week. They continue to function in school and at work. They use it as a means of relaxing, to be employed with discrimination. Sociologist Enrich Goode writes, in *The Marijuana Smokers:*

> The recreational character of pot smoking is possibly its most outstanding feature. A typical intimate, informal (four to ten people) pot party will involve frequently and typically passing the joint from person to person and staring into space for long stretches of time with nothing apparently actually going on. . . . It will appear boring and vacuous to someone who is not high . . . the marijuana experience is typically thought of as *itself* a recreation. Being high is thought of as fun, a state of pleasure. For one who is not high and never has been, understanding its appeal, especially at such a party, would be like sitting in a concert hall and being deaf.

What are the dangers of marijuana smoking? As long as the use of marijuana is illegal, there is a danger of obtaining marijuana that has been contaminated by some other substance. The immediate source may be a friend, but there is no way of knowing the road the marijuana traveled before it reached him. Some young people have had severe reactions to marijuana; hallucinations and short spells of terror and paranoia have been reported. Whether this was because of contamination or the personality of the user is not entirely clear.

We do not yet know enough about the physical and psychological effects of long-term use of marijuana. A large number of studies, by both private and government agencies, are being conducted to determine the answers to these questions. Meanwhile, we cannot say with certainty that even moderate use over a number of years is without risks.

Marijuana can trigger the return of symptoms, including hallucinations, of an earlier LSD trip.

While under the influence of marijuana, the user may have lapses of immediate memory; he may forget what he has just said or done and have difficulty in judging distances. Since marijuana also alters his perception of time, it is clearly a hazard in driving a car. Most smokers, however, have no urge to drive while high on marijuana. Perception returns to normal when the effects of the drug wear off.

Excessive Use of Marijuana

Some young people become heavily involved with marijuana. The marijuana experience becomes the most important thing in their lives and they spend a good deal of time arranging it and discussing it. They tend to lose interest in school, other activities, and "straight" friends. Obviously, for them the drug is a hazard.

Excessive marijuana use, like excessive drinking, is an indication of other adolescent difficulties. Although marijuana is the means the child uses to "tune out," one needs to learn what problems in his life make prolonged escape so appealing.

Most experts are careful to distinguish between the use of marijuana by adolescents and by adults. This is important to keep in mind. Research bears out the fact that all drugs are most potentially dangerous and unpredictable in their effect if the user is of unstable personality. And adolescence is a time when under normal circumstances the personality is unstable. The staff of the Child Study Association writes:

> When marijuana is used as an easy way out of anxiety, restlessness, self-questioning—troubles traditionally associated with adolescence—development may be slowed down or postponed indefinitely. The task of growing up cannot be accomplished without a certain amount of struggle and pain. It is by fighting through his problems as they occur that an adolescent learns who he is and builds strengths to cope with the inevitable stresses of

> later life. Although a young person may argue that drugs are "where it's at," their use can make it impossible for the user to know truly where he's at in his emotional development.

Parents and children need to be concerned with the fact that use or possession of marijuana is still in many states a crime for which young people are being sent to jail, sometimes for long terms. Is this a risk a young person wants to take? A police record is a serious matter.

Marijuana and Sex

Does marijuana increase the pleasures of sex or make a young person sexually promiscuous? Boys in particular are often drawn to drugs by their fears of sexual inadequacy and the hope of finding an aphrodisiac that will give them confidence, courage, or magic powers to heighten their own or a partner's pleasure in sex.

Of course, in this age of relaxed sexual mores, parents (and many adolescents) are frightened by any possibility that standards may be lowered through use of a drug. In *Drugs and Youth,* Dr. Robert Coles, Dr. Joseph H. Brenner, and Dermot Meagher write:

> The use of marijuana does not lead in itself to promiscuity or to sexual liaisons that may be later regretted. The actual effects of marijuana on sexual desire, arousal and performance are usually related quite directly to the sexual maturity and experiential knowledge of the user. Young persons who have not yet had sexual intercourse are not likely to be aroused by marijuana; in fact, if anything, many related that in this respect grass turns them off. On the other hand, some who have enjoyed a steady sexual relationship with one partner have asserted that, after smoking marijuana and often for a day or two afterwards, the act of sexual intercourse becomes much more stimulating and satisfying. They claim to enjoy a fresh excitement and a new delight in their own and their partner's body.

Does marijuana lead invariably to the use of heroin or other such strong drugs? This belief arose because it was found that many heroin addicts had smoked marijuana before trying heroin. However, even more heroin addicts have drunk alcohol before going on to heroin. The kind of person who is drawn to that long road will probably try several drugs along the way. But neither alcohol nor marijuana sets him on a course that heads inevitably (or even usually) to heroin. It has been remarked that the use of marijuana puts a person on the "drug scene" where heroin is also available, at the same time lowering his inhibitions so that he might be drawn into using a drug that he would otherwise resist. Nevertheless, the fact remains that the overwhelming number of marijuana smokers do *not* go on to heroin.

Psychological Dependence

Is marijuana habit-forming (habituating)? Yes, although it is not physically addictive. Like other habits, it can be broken—with more or less difficulty, more or less regret, depending upon the psychological need it fills for the user. However, withdrawal is not accompanied by physical symptoms.

There is often confusion about the terms habituation, dependence, and addiction. Coles, Brenner, and Meagher point out that all of us are creatures of habit; we are habituated to eating at certain times, combing our hair a certain way, and adhering to innumerable other routines in the course of a day. Some habits we think of as good, others as bad.

> The repetitive act of taking a favorite drink every day is a habit . . . to do without it could be felt as deprivation. But when there is no dependence or craving, it is a simple habit, albeit one not willingly given up.
>
> What differentiates dependence from habit? When a person depends on something or someone it is implied that without that support he would suffer a state of disequilibrium. He might or might not be able to take steps to restore his equilibrium by shifting dependence to another direction or by readjusting his needs.

Psychological dependence on drugs can create special problems for adolescents who, as we have noted, are particularly vulnerable to drug use because of their immaturity. Parents are understandably concerned about experimentation with marijuana. They fear that their youngsters might become seduced into smoking on a regular basis. This depends upon the individual. Some young people with serious problems have a greater need to escape from everyday pressures than others. But Dr. Coles and many other professionals say that the excitement of smoking pot is not so seductive to the more solid young people. They can take it or leave it. They find it interesting but not so enticing that they would be likely to become overinvolved with it. It is like alcohol. Of the many individuals who try alcohol, those who become alcoholics are the ones who have other problems.

> Of the great number of adolescents and young adults who smoke marijuana, only a very small percentage become psychologically dependent on it. Admittedly, these few are indeed in trouble. The dependence, however, is determined much more by the particular drabness, pain and ugliness of their lives and of the immediate world in which they live than by the actual smoking of marijuana in whatever quantity.
>
> Psychological dependence is not the same as addiction. Marijuana, unlike heroin and some other drugs, is not addictive. Addiction to a drug takes place when profound changes occur in the chemistry and physiology, or the workings, of the body—profound, but reversible changes. . . . Near normal bodily functions can go on only when a continual supply of the drug is pumped into the system. . . . The person who is addicted suffers painful withdrawal symptoms if the supply of the addictive drug is stopped abruptly. For example, a chronic alcoholic, upon withdrawal, may "go into the DTs" (delirium tremens) with convulsions, hallucinations and feelings of terror; the person addicted to barbiturates . . . will suffer severe irritability and insomnia, possibly accompanied by convulsions seven to ten days after withdrawal. Fortunately, the withdrawal symptoms can be greatly modified and danger diminished with good medical care. It is clear that the chemical system of the body takes an appreciable time to adjust to functioning without the addictive drug.

Our Children and Drugs

Having achieved a certain understanding of the effects of the more commonly used (and abused) drugs, and the differences among them, a parent is better prepared to think clearly about the threat they may possibly pose to his or her own individual child. What are our expectations? Do we expect our child not to experiment with any drugs whatsoever—ever? Or do we view the problem as involving a number of factors, such as the nature of a particular drug, the age and nature of the user, the frequency of use? Are these expectations realistic in terms of the kind of child our youngster is, his friends, his school, his general environment? Where expectations are unrealistic, they deprive a child of useful guidelines.

Many parents in the past tried to make sure their children would never smoke a cigarette or take a drink. They felt they had legitimate reasons for this position. But is it reasonable to expect that a child will never try what his friends try if he feels he is stable, his friends say it's great, and his friends aren't all bad? What happens to parent-child communication when youngsters feel their parents have a closed mind on any subject?

Of course, conditions vary in different sections of the country. However, in many areas today parents should be prepared for the probability that their high school child will try marijuana at least once. Considering the availability of marijuana, its appeal to the young, and the fact that its dangers are often equated by responsible persons with those of alcohol (which many parents drink), a normal child is likely to be highly curious about it. Many factors will affect how he handles his curiosity. Is he very much influenced by what other children do? Does he always have to wear what the others wear, get the same haircut, and so on? Then he will probably be more likely to go along with his peers in experimenting with drugs, also. Is he inclined to be independent, to think things through on his own, to resist group pressure? His reaction may be different.

Keeping the Lines Open

If we accept the possibility that a child might want to try marijuana, we make it possible for him to continue to communicate with us no matter what happens. If we refuse to entertain this possibility the child may try it anyway but then have only his friends to discuss the situation with. How do we make it plain to a child that we are against certain behavior and at the same time create the kind of atmosphere in which our children feel they can come to us with any concerns or problems they may have? This is similar to the way parents convey their values about sex. When we ourselves were growing up, many parents did not want to sanction premarital sex but wished to be available if a girl did get into difficulty. Some parents were able to meet this difficult challenge admirably, but others created such fear that if their child got into trouble she was desperately afraid to go to her parents and thus lost the benefit of their advice and support.

Now, although we may recognize the possibility of our child's wanting to discover for himself what marijuana is like, we are justified in hoping that he will not experiment with it at this age, just as we would feel very differently about his having sexual relations at thirteen than at eighteen or twenty. Parents are on reasonable ground in wanting children to postpone certain experiences until they reach a certain age. A thirteen-year-old cannot handle an altered emotional state comfortably; one would not want a thirteen-year-old to drink a whole highball. In addition, he has not the judgment to make a good decision about whether to repeat the experience.

Parents often let a child have a sip of alcohol or glass of wine as he gets older, so that he can satisfy his curiosity about this drug at home, rather than elsewhere. But marijuana, of course, is illegal. It is foolish for a parent to break the law and smoke pot with a child. That is not the kind of message we want to get across.

At this age, one might say, "You know there are many things, like driving a car, that you have to wait to do until you're old enough. I don't think you are old enough to experiment with any drug right now. I hope you will wait and decide what to do about this when you're more experienced." We give our reasons for believing that age does make a difference in this case. We also assume that, as with limits about other issues, when our child is mature enough, he will make his own decisions.

In communicating our knowledge and values and expectations, the necessity for absolute honesty and avoidance of scare tactics cannot be overstressed. One mother reported watching with her eleven-year-old boy a television documentary that showed a young drug user having his stomach pumped after an overdose of barbiturates. "You can imagine how much it must hurt to have those tubes put down your throat," she remarked.

"No, it doesn't," he came back. "When you have a lot of pills in you, you don't feel the pain." It is unfortunate, but children these days seem to expect their parents not to level with them about drugs. When they catch a parent in a mistake—intentional or not—or even an exaggeration, their cynical expectations are confirmed. Needless to say, it lessens their trust.

How should we set forth our opinions about experimenting with drugs to our child—as hopes, recommendations, flat prohibitions? The way we discuss what we expect of our child in this area ought to be consistent with our way of confronting other issues—it should, in other words, fit into our overall relationship with our child. Parents tend to become very panicky and deal with the issue in a manner that is not characteristic of them. Out of fear, they may close their eyes to the possibility that a problem might exist—thereby seeming to their child to be more permissive than they really are—or they may suddenly become rigidly authoritarian.

Discuss Risk-Taking

At some point we might try to get into a discussion of taking risks in general. This is a topic that nearly always interests children this age, and it is vitally relevant to the drug scene. When a child buys a raffle ticket, for example, he is avid to hear who the winner is; maybe he will be one of the lucky ones, he thinks excitedly. But when that same young person considers the risks involved in experimenting with marijuana he may tend to minimize or dismiss the possibility that he could be one of the unlucky ones.

A child needs to learn to weigh the possible consequences—pro and con—of everything he would like to do. If he wanted to try marijuana, for example, what desirable effects might he expect? What are the chances of his achieving them, and how much does he want or need this? What are the drawbacks—physical, emotional, or if he gets into trouble at school or with the police? Would he be harming anyone else? What would happen if he did not try marijuana? Is the real risk sufficiently large so that the possible gain is just not worth it? When a child and a parent can discuss risk-taking rationally, the chances of a child's acting rashly are diminished. Children need help from their parents in learning how to weigh variables and make good decisions. But they are turned off by parents who tend to turn what starts out as honest discussion into a lecture.

Sooner or later most youngsters ask their parents, "How can you talk about a drug if you haven't had any experience with it?" Or, "Don't knock it if you haven't tried it." One should avoid being drawn into a debate, but we might point out that most of what we know we have not learned from personal experience but from the accumulated experience and study of others—scientific discoveries, historical facts. Unfortunately, young people, although they can appreciate this intellectually, often just are not satisfied by it. They suspect that our reaction to marijuana is partly emotional, caused by our lack of experience and fear of the unknown, more than by the hard facts. It never helps to argue about this. We can make known the real risks entailed. Above all, we need to listen, hear what our child has to say, trying not to interrupt him even if we believe he is mistaken. If we can remain calm and really hear what our child is telling us, we can learn a lot about what is happening

in his group and what he is confronted with—information he might not otherwise share with us. There is nothing to be gained from trying to argue him down.

Family Patterns Are Significant

Other aspects of family life may become involved in parent-child discussions of drugs as a child gets older. For example, what is the family's pattern of using drugs that are "socially acceptable"? Do they pop a pill for the slightest ache? Do they take sleeping pills or diet pills or tranquilizing pills frequently, or to excess? Do they preach about marijuana with a cigarette between their fingers? Do they need coffee to get them moving every morning and a few drinks to relax them every night?

Marin and Cohen write that some of "what appears to parents and the young as rebellion is in part an imitation of adults: a grotesque unconscious mimicking of their patterns of distraction and escape. The young continually see adults treating their own symptoms, changing their own moods.

Adults rarely confront the underlying causes of their discomfort."

A study of 5,900 junior and senior high school students in Canada showed that students whose mothers used tranquilizers were three and a half times as likely to be on marijuana as the children of mothers who did not; five times as likely to be on LSD or amphetamines; seven times as likely to be on tranquilizers; and ten times as likely to be on heroin or other opiates. Similarly a study of 12,000 students at six junior and senior high schools in New Jersey revealed that fathers of students who have injected speed used prescription tranquilizers or stimulants at a rate five and a half times that of the fathers of nonusers. Among mothers the rate was three times as high. Illicit drug use was shown to be two to three times as frequent among students whose parents smoked one or more packs of cigarettes a day as among students whose parents smoked less or not at all. No such relation was found in the case of parents who drank in moderation.

When children ask, "Why do you smoke when cigarettes make you more susceptible to cancer, heart disease, and other illnesses?" our answer may be instructive. Many adults started smoking before these dangers were well known and now find it difficult to stop even though they may want to.

When a young person asks, "Why do you drink when alcohol can lead to alcoholism?" the answer may be instructive to us as well as them. Alcohol was part of our experience as we grew up. Although most of us know at least one problem drinker, we see this as the exception rather than the rule and do not live in fear that drinking in moderation will lead to alcoholism. The Child Study Association of America writes:

> Those who use drugs in moderation do not have to be apologetic to their children and they are in the best position to respond effectively. Parents who depend heavily upon one or several drugs may be in for a harder time. They are likely to feel guilty and defensive and consequently are handicapped in discussing drugs with their children. It does not help in such cases to argue that alcohol, cigarettes and tranquilizers are not illegal. What is important is that our children understand that we do not approve of excessive use of drugs by any age group or any person including ourselves.

When we are honest with our children and admit our fallibility, they respect us. Even parents who have had or still have extremely serious problems with drugs are not necessarily disqualified from providing the guidance their children need. It makes the task more difficult but not impossible. Very few young people are interested in condemning their parents for past errors; they are much more interested in a candid discussion about drugs in which their parents demonstrate their ability to look objectively at their own drug use.

The Allure of "Escape"

Drugs, of course, are not the only way people escape from the tensions of daily living. Nor are young people the only ones who seek escape. The pressures of marriage, child-rearing, unpaid bills, work—being alive—are such that everyone seeks to escape them periodically. We have our "escapist" literature and movies, entertainment that does not ask too much of us and takes our minds off our troubles temporarily. Mothers may escape the chores of the household by taking an afternoon off and doing as they please. If we didn't allow ourselves such releases occasionally, we wouldn't function as well. It isn't escape that's a bad idea. What is?

When a woman leaves a sinkful of dishes at home as she goes off on "an afternoon out," she will find the dishes there when she returns. When we leave our problems behind for a while they don't disappear, either. And we do not expect them to—we face them anew, perhaps refreshed, when we return. When any escape mechanism is used constantly to avoid dealing with problems that could and should be faced and worked through, it becomes destructive.

Young people, of course, particularly need to work through the problems of growing up and not avoid or postpone them. They, too, may use escape mechanisms other than drugs. Some have an overactive social life.

Others, like some adults, load themselves down with too many activities or too much work, so that they "don't have a minute to think." Youngsters who try to escape continually are often those who lack a sense of their own worth and feel unable to cope with their deepest problems. If a parent can own up to his own escape mechanisms, he will be better able to talk about this with his child, to try to discover what pressures are on him and help him deal with them. Such sharing nourishes parent, child, and home.

Coping with Temptation

As our child gets older, there will be practical problems in connection with drugs for which we will want to prepare ourselves. Will we permit him to go to a party where drugs are likely to be used? If our answer to this is no, how do we plan to prevent this? By an inquiry before a party to the host or his parents? A mother may want to phone the parent but her child says, "For heaven's sake, you'll make me look like a baby." Or the mother herself just won't feel comfortable asking a woman she doesn't know well, if at all, questions that may indicate she has no faith in this parent's judgment. It is touchy. When parents have worked out a general code of conduct for parties, as discussed in Chapter 3, presumably the situation would not arise.

If drugs appear unexpectedly at a party, if one youngster pulls a reefer out of his pocket, for example, lights up and begins to pass it around, what do we expect our youngster to do? He may feel under considerable pressure to join in. How can he resist, or leave without embarrassment? Discussing such possibilities, working out possible ways to deal with them, is a way of arming a child in advance.

What do we expect our child to do if he knows that a child in his school is using or passing drugs on the school grounds? Sometimes a child will say, "I'll tell you what's happening if you promise not to tell other parents or the school." How should a parent handle that? This kind of request for secrecy comes up about other things, too. Some parents handle it this way. They say, "If I feel it is absolutely necessary for me to take action, I'll discuss my reasons with you and we'll see what we can agree on. Certainly, I would not do anything without telling you first. I hope you trust my judgment enough to tell me what's on your mind, but that decision is up to you." This opens the door to confidences in a way that respects everybody's rights. There is a good possibility that we and our child together can work out a way to take any action that is really needed.

It is a good idea to know—and to make certain our child knows—his school's policy with regard to children who are suspected of or caught using or passing drugs on school grounds.

Children may ask a young teacher whom they like about drugs. What do the teachers in our child's school answer when asked if they have tried or use various drugs? One child reported that his teacher replied, "No comment." It is clear what this connotes to a child. Teachers, like parents, need help in handling children's questions about drugs, especially questions that put them on the spot. What kind of training is our child's school giving teachers to help them deal with this? Does the school system have an effective drug-education program beginning no later than fourth grade?

Sometimes parents delude themselves that they can protect their child by removing drugs from his environment at home, at school, etc., so that he is never exposed to temptation. But this is not possible. School cannot be a jail, and we cannot follow a child around everywhere he goes. Our only protection, and his, will be sound information about drugs and the quality of our relationship with him.

How to Detect Drug Use

Parents frequently ask, "How could I tell if my child were using drugs?" Needless to say, this depends upon the drug and the extent to which it is being used. Can one tell if a child has experimented with marijuana at a party? Probably about as easily as one could tell if the child had experimented with sex at that party; that is to say, not at all, if the child does not want us to know. If a child wants his parents to know about his drug use, he will either tell them or find a way to let them discover it easily for themselves. But we sometimes hear that a child has been deeply involved with drugs for as long as two years without his parents' being aware of it. How can this be?

First of all, many of the symptoms of drug use—carelessness about appearance, moodiness and irritability, frequent phone calls and comings and goings, locked doors, desire for privacy, loss of interest in school, inability to concentrate—can be caused by other problems or just by adolescence.

Second, parents, for a variety of reasons, sometimes need to hide from themselves the possibility that their child is in serious trouble, so they ignore clues that are obvious. Then, too, as a child gets deeper into the drug scene, he becomes very good at covering his tracks.

Herman V. Land, author of *What You Can Do About Drugs and Your Child,* suggests that parents need to be suspicious if there is even a possibility of drug use and search among a child's belongings for evidence. But Drs. Marvin J. Gersh and Iris F. Litt, specialists in adolescent medicine and authors of *The Handbook of Adolescence: A Medical Guide for Parents and Teenagers,* feel this is a disastrous approach, serving only to "drive a wedge between parents and teenagers. Only the symptom will be uncovered, not the cause for it." "We have found," they report, "that the best way to discover if someone is using drugs is to ask him." Of course, a child who has become dependent upon drugs may not respond with honesty if he feels this will lead his parents to take action he cannot tolerate.

Discovery of drug use is only the first step in helping a child with a drug problem, and the way one goes about it can crucially affect everything that happens after that. If we spy on our child, listen to his conversations, go through his possessions, we break down the trust between us and correspondingly lessen our ability to influence his future behavior.

When there are signs that a child is not functioning well over a period of time in one or more areas, parents should be open about their concern. If they and their child are fortunate enough to communicate well with each other, parents have a good chance of learning what the child feels troubled by. Being in close touch with a child is in itself a good sign. Land reports that "in virtually every case of addiction, there is a breakdown in communication." In families where communication has broken down, new efforts need to be made to restore it (see Chapter 8) and professional help sought if the situation is more than parents can handle alone. If we know our child has become involved with drugs, a safe step would be to consult the family doctor.

If a child is alienated from his parents and their life-style, it will be harder to reach him about drugs and other issues. But if we care about him, we keep trying. He may sometimes reject our advice, as all children occasionally do, yet continue to want and carefully weigh our opinion. We do him a service by answering his questions honestly, telling him how we feel, and listening to him.

11
Planning For When The Children Leave Home

IT MAY SEEM somewhat premature to think about this now. Perhaps our oldest child has only just turned eleven and we have younger children besides. The day when they will all march off, leaving the nest empty, seems far away, its problems hardly pressing. Has the time really come to consider what our lives will be like when they leave us?

Fifty years ago, the average life expectancy of a baby girl was fifty-five years. A mother did not worry about creating a new life for herself after her children were launched because there would presumably be little time left for that. She was considered old at forty. Today, the life expectancy of a baby girl is seventy-four years. It is literally true that child-rearing is only a lovely phase in our lives, and not necessarily the longest one. We may live thirty years or more after our children have essentially left home. That period is too important for us simply to come upon it unawares, unprepared, in a state of emotional crisis. Crisis, because no matter how well we know intellectually that the children will eventually leave home, we are not usually able in imagination to feel what it will be like. For a woman whose main role has been that of "Johnny's mother," it is an identity crisis: Who else am I now when that is not enough?

Right now, the lives of many of us have children at the center. Our children make us feel needed and worthwhile. Our emotions are very much engaged in their concerns. If launching them threatens to create a vacuum nothing else can begin to fill, we will, despite our best intentions, move very slowly to prepare our young birds to fly. The side of us that is afraid of letting them go will hamper the side that nurtures selflessly. We may, although we won't want to, cling. And this will color our children's last years at home and make those years less satisfying than they could be. So, for reasons both selfish and selfless, these next years ought to be a time of getting ready for a new way of life, for us as well as for them, with our preparations muted, not occupying center stage, but conscious, intellectual, emotional, pressing. How?

The Hours of the Day

As our children become more independent, what will fill our hours? New and different possibilities are opening up for women to study and work after they are married and have had children. We need only think in terms of the opportunities of the future instead of the limitations of the past. True, all challenge holds some fear. Writes Anne Morrow Lindbergh in *Gift from the Sea:*

> Who is not afraid of pure space, that breathtaking empty space of an open door?

We all need a focus to our lives besides the children, a serious interest, whether or not we need to earn some of the family income. If earning money is necessary to help with our children's college education or for other reasons, it is even more important to plan so that our efforts will not have to be forever channeled in routine, low-level jobs. But no one should settle for just killing time or keeping busy. Reading all those books we never had the leisure for is not enough. Having endless freedom to be self-indulgent palls when it is endless. A scattered dipping into courses can be a beginning, but it is not a fulfilling occupation.

What are the choices? Someone who already has a serious interest is a step ahead. Others need to think more about it. Is there a field that always held an attraction for us, a skill or talent not yet developed for lack of opportunity or because it used to seem as if women could not do such things? Perhaps a new notion has recently begun to percolate in the back of our head. We can contemplate this and begin to form a design for structuring our life as we have more free time. Then, even if we do not wish to make any major commitments of time or energy now, we can keep a thread going through these next years—the volunteer work we do, the courses we take, some of our reading can be geared toward our purpose. We can maintain membership in a professional society, subscribe to the professional journals in our field, read the new literature, attend conferences, keep abreast of new developments.

If we are thinking about starting our own business, we can begin to learn—from independent reading or courses or friends in business or a part-time job in a similar enterprise—about financing, packaging, pricing, keeping records, insurance, taxes, marketing, distribution, advertising, and so on.

We could begin to learn a new language if that would be helpful in our field. In New York City and many cities in the Southwest with large Spanish-speaking populations, for example, being able to speak this language is an asset in many positions.

In large cities, particularly, courses are available in everything from photography and interior design to such crafts as silversmithing and instrument construction.

Educational Opportunities

If we discover that we need to fill gaps in our education, colleges or universities in forty states and the District of Columbia have continuing education programs with class schedules and accelerated degree programs geared to the needs of the adult woman. Those who want to combine study with homemaking will find that possibilities are proliferating, often with help from federal funds. Tuition varies widely, ranging from very modest to relatively high.

The idea that one has to attend classes on a regular basis or go to school for four consecutive years is being challenged in a number of ways. The State University of New York at Brockport, for example, offers a Bachelor of Liberal Studies degree for completing a program that includes correspondence courses, private reading, and television classes, plus some classroom attendance at Brockport or elsewhere. The only residence requirement is that one attend an annual three-week seminar in Brockport.

Women who cannot enroll in school on regular schedules will benefit from a huge program for part-time students being launched by the University of California. Its emphasis will be on individual study with books and tapes, supplemented by generous counseling in widely scattered "learning centers." There will undoubtedly be more plans involving independent study in the years to come, although not everyone is likely to be enough of a "superego freak" to be able to work consistently and well on his own.

The University of Missouri at Columbia conducts educational programs for adult women on a statewide basis, utilizing facilities of 116 extension centers and branch campuses. They offer seminars, noncredit short courses, credit courses, independent study programs, and interest and aptitude testing.

Granting credit for a mature woman's life experiences is part of the program advanced by Illinois State University, which offers mature students such services as individual counseling, vocational testing, and assistance in locating remedial courses. Older students are permitted to enroll on a part-time unclassified basis without meeting the usual entrance requirements. And registration priority is given to mothers and working women who need to schedule their classes at convenient times. The Continuing Education Association is an undergraduate organization for returning students.

Increasingly we hear the word "paraprofessional," meaning a person trained to work alongside the professional doing skilled tasks for which the professional does not have time. Because social problems such as the needs of the young and the aged, the poor and the sick and the troubled are growing faster than the resources available to meet them, paraprofessional training, often on the job, is being offered at an increasing rate in various parts of the country. The New York School for Social Research in New York City offers several intensive one-year programs leading to jobs as social work assistant, school psychologist assistant, mental health worker, community health intern, counselor assistant, or community planning intern. The programs combine weekly two-hour seminars at the school with two-day-a-week unpaid jobs as assistants in the field under professional supervision. No previous training or experience is required, and upon completion of the program the student should have acquired a base of knowledge and experience that will enable him to function as a paid or volunteer worker in his chosen field.

More than 400 programs are listed in the U.S. Department of Labor compilation, "Continuing Education Programs and Services for Women." This prospectus is in itself an astonishing indication of how opportunities for women have grown in the past few years. In 1968 its offerings took 104 pages, whereas the 1971 edition requires 167 pages to list all the possibilities.

Learning as a Volunteer

Serious volunteer involvement is another way to learn, to gain a skill, test an interest, acquire valuable experience for a paid job. One woman who had organized alumnae clubs for her college in various parts of the country was offered the job of assistant dean of admissions for the college's division of continuing education. She was assigned to recruit and interview adults who were returning to school after a ten- to fifteen-year absence.

Others are rewarded for years of political work at the precinct level by jobs in government, like the mother who now has a high-level administrative post on the mayor's staff in New York City after many years of volunteer political activity. Another woman who had been active in the cultural life of her suburban community became executive director of its new cultural center after a summer in a residence workshop to train administrators of the arts.

In some communities, volunteer jobs are particularly varied. They offer a chance to be in contact with different kinds of people and utilize a wide range of skills. In San Francisco, the Volunteer Bureau has asked for swimming aides to help with classes for retarded children, a bridge teacher for psychiatric outpatients, and an artist to draw brochures, letter signs, and design posters for a social service agency. They also need volunteers to teach patients at a convalescent hospital to grow flowers and vegetables, to teach unwed mothers to cook, teen-agers to knit, children at a day-care center to make handicrafts, and Chinese to speak English. They want a hostess for the blood bank, an assistant at the children's art museum, someone with business knowledge to counsel minority businesses, someone to teach a class in Spanish for a hospital staff, someone to make speeches to various groups explaining the work of a philanthropic agency. And the list goes on. It should give us an idea of a service we could perform or a need in our community that we might fill.

Evaluating Skills

But perhaps we are ready to go back to work full-time or part-time and need to evaluate what we might do and what we have to offer a prospective employer. Most women who have not worked outside their homes for several years, if at all, underestimate their potential, according to professionals at Catalyst, a national nonprofit organization that is trying to help married women broaden their horizons and utilize their abilities more fully. Rearing children and taking care of a home, they remind us, requires more knowledge, ability, skills, common sense, and judgment than most occupations.

A vocational kit developed by Catalyst suggests that a woman ask herself a long list of questions in order to evaluate her interests and abilities. Is she generally efficient and on time? Do friends, neighbors, fellow members of the P-TA or other organizations for which she has worked feel they can depend upon her?

How well does she get along with others? Is she sensitive to other people's concerns? Is she a good listener? Do people frequently ask for her advice and respect her judgment? Can she work well with people even if she does not like them very much? Is she able to get along with persons whose backgrounds differ from hers? In her life as a housewife and mother she comes into contact with many different types of people —the clerk at the supermarket, her child's teacher, the repairman, her neighbors, her family. How pleasant and successful are these relationships?

Women tend to believe that the qualities required in the professional and business world are in a different category from those exercised every day by a woman running her home. But diplomacy is diplomacy, whether it involves exercising tact with a teacher or a business associate of our husband's, or a business associate of our own. If we can see a tedious though necessary household or community job through to the end, if we are willing to consider a new way of doing a task we have done dozens of times, we can think of ourself as hardworking and flexible, and be fairly confident that our attributes will not vanish just because someone is paying us to use them. On the other hand, most people are not equally capable in all areas, and the point of this kind of self-evaluation is to help us find out what our strong and weak points are, so that we can arrange our priorities realistically. By thinking in terms of our own life—the people with whom we relate most satisfyingly, the jobs we do and the kinds of satisfactions we get from various aspects of them—we can get a better idea of our abilities, our readiness to work, and our value to a prospective employer.

One revealing test is to keep a comprehensive minute-by-minute log of our activities for one week, leaving out nothing. We would include the time we spent in front of the bathroom mirror every day, the minutes we spent looking for a child's socks or helping him with his homework, the period we were on the phone working out plans for the P-TA fair, or just gabbing. This way we can judge how much time we really need for ourself, our husband and children, the house, and our other activities. How much of what we do could we give up or delegate to someone else? How much time does that leave us for a paid or volunteer job?

Reasons for Working

What do we want from a job? Is money an immediate and pressing need, or can we enter a field where the compensation is not primarily financial? Could we accept a job with a low starting salary as long as there were good prospects for the future? Or can money be eliminated as a consideration so that we could work as a full- or part-time volunteer? What else is important to us? What do we find stimulating—meeting people, working toward a goal, the exchange of ideas in our field, being of service to others? Says Catalyst:

> Most people have a cluster of experiences, aptitudes and character traits that suit them for more than one occupation. If you worked before, it is natural to think in terms of your past experience, but unless it was substantial and fully satisfying, look closely at what you have done in the intervening years before deciding on your field of work. You may find that you have developed interests and abilities in recent years that have greater significance for the kind of job that is right for you today.

Education, past work experience both paid and unpaid, skills, talents, and general aptitude and ability all need to be weighed and considered.

"We are seeing married women with families returning or starting from scratch to carve out careers in almost every field," writes Jane Schwartz Gould, Director of Placement and Career Planning at Barnard College, in a recent magazine article. Some start out at jobs beneath their ability until they prove themselves, like the woman who began as the secretary to the director of development at a college and one year later became an administrator at the same college.

Many agencies sponsor workshops offering educational and vocational guidance to help women assess their goals and learn of opportunities in work, community service, and education, along with ways and means of achieving them. Back-to-careers programs for mature women are conducted at universities, YWCA's, state employment services, and shopping centers.

Both private and nonprofit personnel organizations are springing up all over the country to help women find part-time jobs and to create more such jobs by doing missionary work among employers. The Distaff Staffers of Washington, D.C., find part-time work for editors, writers, architects, and psychologists among others. New York's Newtime—the new time is a 25-hour workweek, 9:30 to 3:15, five days a week—has found positions for researchers, lawyers, secretaries, fund raisers, and designers and continues to sell business and the professions on the value to them of meeting some women's need for a shorter working day.

Catalyst, in conjunction with the Massachusetts Public Welfare Department, demonstrated the productivity of part-time workers during a two-year pilot project in Boston. Here, fifty college-educated housewives, who had not previously been trained in social work, were hired part-time to take on twenty-five hard-to-fill full-time jobs as caseworkers. Result: They had 89 per cent as many face-to-face contacts with their clients as their full-time counterparts and reduced turnover to one third its usual rate. Although they received some training on the job, their own experience as housewives and mothers contributed toward their understanding of their clients' problems.

The paired job is another way of organizing part-time work that is being tried in pilot projects. On an individual basis, too, some women have been able to convince employers that two people working in tandem can bring more than their share of talent and energy to bear on one full-time position. A partnership arrangement can enrich the classroom when two teachers with complementary skills divide the school day between them. Sometimes paired jobs bring together a senior and junior partner in a position that utilizes their different degrees of skill.

Part-time work is a good solution for many women while the children are still at home, if we can educate more employers to be receptive to the idea. Opportunities are probably best in those fields in which there is a manpower shortage.

Our Marriage

If we are married, we will want at this stage to give thought to nurturing that relationship. As our children need us less and less, will our marriage be able to fill our emotional needs? Marriages are prone to trouble at particular points in time: just after the honeymoon, at the birth of the first child, when the youngest child enters school, and when all of the children leave home. This last is traditionally a time for reassessing the relationship. The marriage changes because its equilibrium is upset. If children have been the main source of mutual interest, the major unifying force, there will be a problem when they leave.

A woman often feels useless and depressed at this time, and there is pressure upon her husband to satisfy her yearning to feel wanted and loved. How will he respond? Because this is a difficult period for her, she may be understandably less capable of thinking clearly about her marriage and working constructively to strengthen it. Married life is a subject too broad and deep for these few pages. Our purpose here is only to stimulate thought about marital satisfactions.

It is helpful if a man and woman are able to take a fresh look at each other and their relationship. Each has surely grown over these several years of marriage. Both partners need to ask themselves: What is different about me, in what ways do I respond differently now from when we were first married? Does my spouse know this about me? How has he (she) changed? Does our relationship acknowledge this growth, or are we still relating to each other as if we were both those youngsters of years past? Can we relate better to each other's new strengths?

This book has explored communication between parents and child. Many of the same principles (see Chapter 8, for example) hold true for communication between man and wife. Can we, do we, talk to each other, have some constructive way of working out differences? The manner in which people communicate is influenced by past successes or failures. Discouragement and lack of hope affect the way we make our needs and wants known, and thereby influence the outcome. Even if only one person in a marriage becomes more sympathetic, more understanding, more supportive of the other, this can generate hope and positive feelings, which have a chance to grow.

Are we ever—often?—alone together? Are we willing to invest time and energy in finding new things to do together, new ways to share time? Frequently, by the time children depart, a man and his wife are, sadly, doing fewer and fewer things jointly. Decisions tend to be made unilaterally: You handle this and I'll take care of that. Yet a marriage benefits from more shared activity, not less.

Sometimes the problem in a marriage is that a man and a woman have allowed their relationship to become stale, devitalized. They have little enthusiasm for each other any more. Women have complained that they can lose ten pounds or completely change their hair style and their husbands will not even notice. They ache, "Look at me, *see* me." Or a man feels his wife treats him like an old shoe, not a *man*.

When married people derive less satisfaction from their relationship than they had hoped for, than they want and need, their disappointment tends to separate them even more. Each may begin to feel that he (she) has somehow been had. But it is possible to change the direction of a marriage, sometimes with professional help, sometimes on one's own. Over these next years, while our lives are still full with the comings and goings of our young, we need to pay attention, husband and wife, to each other, to what is going on between us. If the birth of children turns a marriage into a family, when they leave, will it still be a family?

Once we have begun to think ahead about our days and our evenings, whatever we decide to do right away will lead to other things. And the fruit of each will bear many seeds. Just as we are determined to give our child's blossoming independence its season, so should we also make time for our own purpose and move along, keeping our new goals in view, when all the while our telephone is still tied up with teen-age gossip.

Self-Evaluation Guide

to

Parents' Magazine's Self-Guidance Program to Successful Parenthood

By Mary B. Hoover

Introduction

THIS SELF-EVALUATION GUIDE is intended for use with *Parents' Magazine's Self-Guidance Program to Successful Parenthood.* The PROGRAM, actually five programs, published in separate "books" in this volume, covers the most crucial years for a child and the most challenging for a parent. It is to help the parent meet this challenge successfully that the PROGRAM was developed. A parent is unlikely to encounter a problem not fully discussed within the PROGRAM.

The first section, BOOK 1, *What Makes a Good Parent?,* is a wide-ranging overview of the factors that influence the making of a successful parent.

BOOK 2, *Your Child's First Three Years,* is concerned with physical and mental development of a child's first three years, a truly decisive period for parent and child.

In BOOK 3, *Guiding Your Preschooler,* are important guidelines for the parent coping with the problems of the three- to five-year-old child's development.

BOOK 4, *The Early School Years,* takes the parent through the child's six- to ten-year age period. The child's future school success may well depend on how the parent responds to the challenges of this period.

BOOK 5, *Growing into Adolescence,* guides the parent from the child's eleventh year to adolescence. At this threshold of adulthood, failure can be critical and not easily reversed. Success, however, will be lifelong.

The *Self-Evaluation Guide* is a device for continuing parental education. A single reading of a book or an occasional reference to it are really not enough—at best a transitory understanding might be gained. The *Guides* are constructed to help stimulate ideas and discussions about the PROGRAM and to gain a deep and long-lasting understanding of the problems of parenthood. The exercises, multiple-choice tests, and suggested topics for discussion, are all designed to achieve the desired goal—a successful parent. The parents' odyssey should be a joyous journey—challenging, yes—harrowing, no. The PROGRAM and *Guide* have charted the way; use them with confidence.

Object of These Guides: Communication

The goal of these *Self-Evaluation Guides* is education. Not the kind that ends up with tests and grades, but an invitation to thinking, for the fun of it—with the expectation that this can lead to learning. Our subject is ourselves. There *will* be implied questions to respond to, by marking a choice or writing a word or two, but they are "questions" to which there are no "right" or "wrong" answers, only *your* answers. There will also be suggestions for pondering those answers, to see what they can communicate about ourselves, or our children, or husband-wife interaction, and how we can use such knowledge to strengthen communication skills. Then there are exercises that involve putting our imaginations, rather than a pencil, to work.

BOOK ONE: *What Makes a Good Parent?*

Rules of the Game

It is suggested that you do not open this *Guide* until you have read *What Makes a Good Parent?* Read carefully all instructions—*printed in italics to catch your eye*—before starting an exercise or turning a page in the *Guide*. For maximum benefit, *do only one exercise at a sitting* and allow a few days to elapse before going on to the next one. You may find it instructive, after a year or so, to go over the material again.

Focus of This Section

Some of you who have just read *What Makes a Good Parent?* may be expecting your first child. Others may already have one or more children, ranging in age from an infant to an adolescent. To stick to common ground, in this guide we will focus primarily on adult functioning. Succeeding *Guides* will tackle the problems of parents with children in a particular age range.

Exercise 1

"Temper . . . Temper"

In this exercise husband and wife are to complete certain statements by checking the one of the choices offered that most nearly applies. Do not go back and change any answers; "second thoughts" will be discussed later.

Each of you is to do your portion of the exercise individually, without consulting each other or looking at each other's answers. The wife's section begins this exercise, and is followed by the husband's section.

When both of you have completed your portions of the exercise, you are to turn to page 448 and talk together about the questions for discussion listed there.

It doesn't matter who goes first. When the wife is ready to start, she should look only at her section. When the husband is ready to start, he should look only at his section. Use a sheet of paper as a cover-up.

Wife starts here: *Check one*

When I am angry I usually . . . .
- level
- explode
- keep cool

When my husband is angry he usually . . . . .
- levels
- explodes
- keeps cool

I get angry . . . .
- very easily
- too easily
- as often as most

My husband gets angry . . . .
very easily
too easily
as often as most

I explode . . . .
very often
too often
from time to time
very rarely

My husband explodes . . . .
very often
too often
from time to time
very rarely

I think of myself as . . . .
controlled
easygoing
very emotional

I think of my husband as . . . .
controlled
easygoing
very emotional

Our disagreements usually end in . . . .
a compromise
a stalemate
one of us giving in

My ability to assert myself is . . . .
good
average
limited

My husband's ability to assert himself is. . . .
good
average
limited

I grew up in a home where disagreements were . . . .
very frequent
too frequent
no big deal
rare

My relationship with my parents was . . . . . .
on the good side
on the poor side

I think disagreements usually. . . . .
clear the air
arouse guilt
cause hurt feelings

Wife stops here.

Husband starts here: *Check one*

When I am angry I usually . . . .
level
explode
keep cool

When my wife is angry she usually . . . .
levels
explodes
keeps cool

I get angry . . . .
very easily
too easily
as often as most

My wife gets angry. . . . .
very easily
too easily
as often as most

Turn to the next page.

I explode ....
- very often
- too often
- from time to time
- very rarely

My wife explodes......................
- very often
- too often
- from time to time
- very rarely

I think of myself as ....
- controlled
- easygoing
- very emotional

I think of my wife as...................
- controlled
- easygoing
- very emotional

Our disagreements usually end in.........
- a compromise
- a stalemate
- one of us giving in

My ability to assert myself is ....
- good
- average
- limited

My wife's ability to assert herself is........
- good
- average
- limited

I grew up in a home where disagreements were ....
- very frequent
- too frequent
- no big deal
- rare

My relationship with my parents was ......
- on the good side
- on the poor side

I think disagreements usually.............
- clear the air
- arouse guilt
- cause hurt feelings

For both husband and wife.

Questions to Discuss

Are there instances in which your description of yourself differs from your partner's assessment of you?

In what ways are the two of you revealed to be alike, and in what ways are you revealed to be different?

Are the differences a matter of how you actually *feel* in certain situations, or how you handle your feelings? (For example, a person may feel very emotional yet behave in a highly controlled fashion—come off as "cool.")

Do you think the differences or similarities may have caused problems in the past?

Can you think of any ways to change this?

Would you say that "exploding" sometimes constitutes an acceptable way of "leveling"?

Do you feel that the information bearing on self-assertion illumines other information brought out by the exercise?

Did you check any phrase beginning with the word "too," and if so, would you now agree that such phrases constitute a *judgment* and that being judgmental is more likely to cause guilt and hostility than to foster acceptance of oneself and of others?

When you were completing the statements bearing on childhood experiences, how did you feel?

About those "second thoughts"—if any—would you say they grew primarily out of the desire to "level" as honestly as possible, or out of other feelings, such as, perhaps, limited confidence in your opinion?

Can you think of ways in which you might be able to help each other feel less guilty about displays of "temper" and about disagreeing?

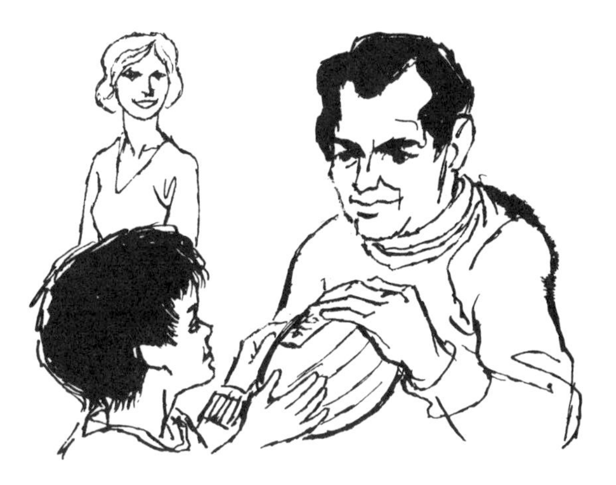

Exercise 2

"How the Shoe Pinches"

Husband and wife are to fabricate a situation in which they disagree with each other. The imagined disagreement should be over some issue that often gives rise to conflict, such

as the family budget, pets, in-laws, choice of recreation, reaction to a particular child, etc., etc. But this is to be an imagined situation, not a re-run of an old quarrel.

Have you settled upon a situation that you know would create dissension between the two of you? Have you got the specifics down to the point where you can talk about this problem as if it were real—as if you were in the process of trying to work it out?

You are going to stage a mock disagreement for 5 minutes. If you have a kitchen timer, use it to time yourselves. Stop as soon as time is up, even if you are in mid-sentence, and proceed immediately to the discussion questions that follow. In your mock disagreement, the wife is to play the role of the husband and the husband is to play the role of the wife. Do your best to get inside the feelings of the person you are supposed to be.

Begin.

Questions to Discuss

What are some of your feelings about your partner at this moment?

What are some of your feelings about yourself at this moment?

Did you hear any familiar words in your partner's mouth?

Did you hear any arguments that surprised you?

Did your mock disagreement take any unexpected turns?

If the situation you have been acting out were to come up in real life, do you think your attitude would be any different as a result of having practiced seeing things through your partner's eyes?

Do you feel that during the mock disagreement your partner showed more respect for your point of view, and for you as a person, than he/she usually shows when you disagree?

Do you feel that during the mock disagreement you showed more respect for your partner's point of view, and for him/her as a person, than you usually show when you disagree?

Can you think of any ways in which two people might fully draw on their capacities for empathy without going through the rigmarole of role-playing?

Would you say that in the past your disagreements with your partner have sometimes been more heated than was justified—that the two of you got caught up in making charges and countercharges that were irrelevant to the issue at hand?

Do you think it is possible to lower the incidence of this kind of unproductive behavior between husband and wife . . . parent and child?

Can you think of a time when you picked an argument with your spouse simply because you were "spoiling for a fight"?

Was there anything your spouse could have done to stop you?

Was there any way you might have stopped yourself?

Have you ever managed to let out powerful feelings of anger or frustration without exploding, picking a fight, etc.?

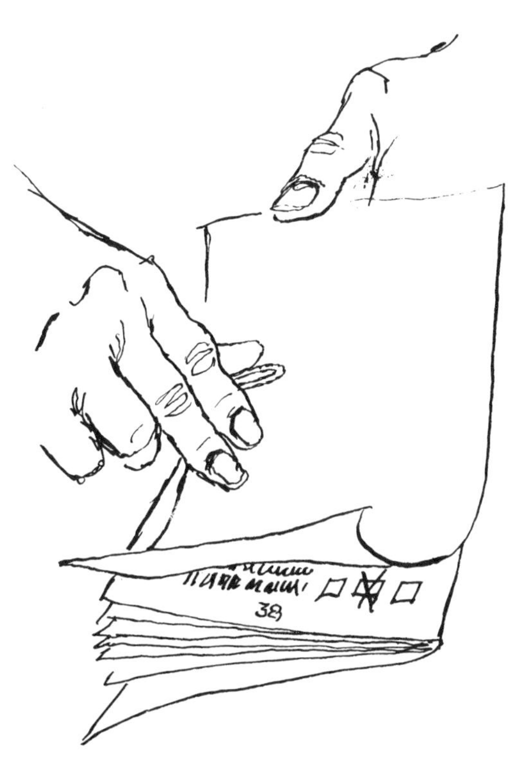

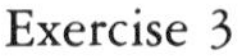

Exercise 3

"Think"

This exercise is a variation on the old True-False test, except that you have a third option:?. Husband and wife take the same test, but without looking at each other's answers. The same test is reprinted, starting near the end of page 452.

Whoever goes first should clip paper over his/her answers to hide them from the other's view.

Express your evaluation of the following statements by placing an X in the appropriate box on the next page.

	True	*False*	*?*
Men make better cooks than women.	☐	☐	☐
Love is more important to a child than good physical care.	☐	☐	☐
Men need sex more than women.	☐	☐	☐

	True	*False*	*?*
Money is the most significant cause of friction in a family.	☐	☐	☐
Birds of a feather flock together.	☐	☐	☐
Genius is 10% talent, 90% sweat.	☐	☐	☐
Everybody has hidden biases.	☐	☐	☐
Boys are better at math than girls.	☐	☐	☐
A little learning is a dangerous thing.	☐	☐	☐
Absence makes the heart grow fonder.	☐	☐	☐
Girls are faster readers than boys.	☐	☐	☐
Power corrupts.	☐	☐	☐
Boys are more active than girls.	☐	☐	☐
A good education is the key to a good life.	☐	☐	☐
Appearances are deceptive.	☐	☐	☐
You can't trust what you read in the newspapers.	☐	☐	☐
Children need respect more than love.	☐	☐	☐

Cover your answers and let partner begin.

	True	*False*	*?*
Men make better cooks than women.	☐	☐	☐
Love is more important to a child than good physical care.	☐	☐	☐
Men need sex more than women.	☐	☐	☐
Money is the most significant cause of friction in a family.	☐	☐	☐
Birds of a feather flock together.	☐	☐	☐

	True	*False*	*?*
Genius is 10% talent, 90% sweat.	☐	☐	☐
Everybody has hidden biases.	☐	☐	☐
Boys are better at math than girls.	☐	☐	☐
A little learning is a dangerous thing.	☐	☐	☐
Absence makes the heart grow fonder.	☐	☐	☐
Girls are faster readers than boys.	☐	☐	☐
Power corrupts.	☐	☐	☐
Boys are more active than girls.	☐	☐	☐
A good education is the key to a good life.	☐	☐	☐
Appearances are deceptive.	☐	☐	☐
You can't trust what you read in the newspapers.	☐	☐	☐
Children need respect more than love.	☐	☐	☐

Now proceed together.

If you feel frustrated, our apologies. The test was designed to dramatize the quicksands that generalizations so often drown us in. With the exception of "Everybody has hidden biases," which is probably true, the sentences are examples of an annoyingly muddled way of thinking about ourselves, our children, and our world. Yes, one might simply dismiss them as false. But what we really need to reject is the cast of mind that breeds such statements. We need to learn to think differently, avoid the either/or attitude and sweeping generalizations, open ourselves to the full range of possibilities that can affect our lives and our relationships with each other.

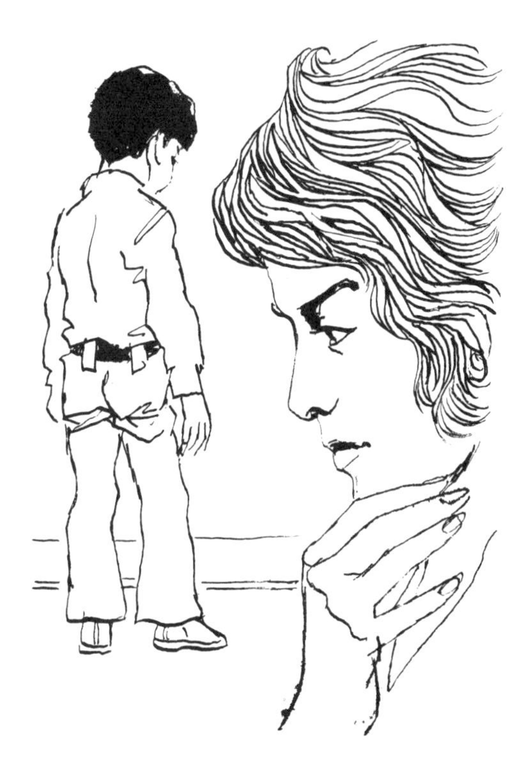

Questions to Discuss

Which statements invidiously compare two important needs of a child, neither of which should be slighted?

Which statements invidiously compare the sexes?

Can you reword them to convey some useful information?

Are there sentences which, if modified by a word or clause, such as "in some cases," would be truly illuminating?

Were there any statements that especially annoyed you, and through exploring your reaction to them can you learn something about yourself?

How do you react to the idea that a "defensive attitude" suggests that a very sensitive nerve is being touched?

BOOK TWO: *Your Child's First Three Years*

Rules of the Game

It is suggested that you do not open this *Guide* until you have read *Your Child's First Three Years.* Read carefully all instructions—*printed in italics to catch your eye*—before starting an exercise or turning a page in the *Guide.* For maximum benefit, *do only one exercise at a sitting* and allow a few days to elapse before going on to the next one. You may find it instructive, after a year or so, to go over the material again.

Focus of this Section

Our focus will be primarily on how we interact with our children during their first three years. The exercises are designed to illumine concepts and a way of thinking, so that they should also interest—perhaps in unexpected ways—parents who have already lived through the period.

Exercise 1

"Baby and I"

In this exercise husband and wife are to arrive at a kind of "profile" of their child during the early months and a profile of each of themselves as parent during the same period. You will select from each group of three phrases the one that in your opinion comes closest to characterizing your baby, yourself, or your partner and put an X in the appropriate box. Each of you is to do the exercise separately, without looking at the other's answers. Whoever goes last should hold a folded sheet of paper over the other's responses to hide them from view. Do not look at the "Questions to Discuss," until both of you have completed the profiles.

Profile of Our Baby:	*Wife's Response*	*Husband's Response*
very active	☐	☐
fairly active	☐	☐
placid	☐	☐
sucks a great deal	☐	☐
sucks some between feedings	☐	☐
never sucks between feedings	☐	☐
eats and sleeps very well	☐	☐
eats and sleeps fairly well	☐	☐
is easily upset or is "colicky"	☐	☐
very sociable	☐	☐
likes to socialize sometimes	☐	☐
quite self-sufficient when awake	☐	☐
often reminds me of someone I know	☐	☐
sometimes reminds me of someone I know	☐	☐
is just a baby	☐	☐

Profile of Myself as Parent:	*Wife's Response*	*Husband's Response*
quick to worry	☐	☐
worry sometimes	☐	☐
quite relaxed	☐	☐
always show when I'm upset	☐	☐
sometimes show when I'm upset	☐	☐
rarely show when I'm upset	☐	☐
feel very tied down by baby	☐	☐
sometimes feel tied down by baby	☐	☐
adjust easily to baby's demands	☐	☐
enjoy infancy stage very much	☐	☐
find infancy stage interesting but trying	☐	☐
very eager for infant to grow up	☐	☐

Profile of My Partner as Parent:	*Wife's Response*	*Husband's Response*
quick to worry	☐	☐
worries sometimes	☐	☐
quite relaxed	☐	☐
always shows when upset	☐	☐
sometimes shows when upset	☐	☐
rarely shows when upset	☐	☐
feels very tied down by baby	☐	☐
sometimes feels tied down by baby	☐	☐
adjusts easily to baby's demands	☐	☐
enjoys infancy stage very much	☐	☐
finds infancy stage interesting but trying	☐	☐
very eager for infant to grow up	☐	☐

When both husband and wife have completed profiles, proceed together.

Questions to Discuss

Since all choices offered fall within the range of normal individual differences, anything that you checked—or considered checking—is perfectly "normal" for a parent or a baby. Were you especially bothered by any of your selections?

By examining which selections bothered you, can you come up with ideas about accepting yourself . . . your child . . . your spouse?

Did the two of you evaluate your baby or yourselves differently in any way, and does this afford any useful insights into your child or yourselves?

In the light of each other's profiles, would you say that there are any ways in which as parents you complement each other . . . and are you making optimum use of each other's different strengths?

If either or both of you indicated that your baby reminded you of some other person, do you feel that you are sufficiently on guard against letting such resemblances influence your reactions to your child or your expectations of him or her?

Do your profiles suggest any situations in which one of you will need to be especially understanding of the other?

Are there areas in which mutual support is called for?

Exercise 2

"The View from Below"

Husband and wife are to talk together about the following questions while lying side by side on their stomachs underneath a table. Place the table and yourselves so that you can look out on as much open space as possible in your home. Make yourselves comfortable, with a rug or blanket to lie on and pillows to rest your elbows on.

Questions to Discuss

After looking around carefully for a few minutes, do you see anything interesting that you do not usually notice?

How might a toddler react to what you just noticed?

What does the furniture look like from where you are?

What can (or might) you see out of a window?

Have your feelings about the height of the room you are in or any of its features undergone any change?

Do you think you have achieved any insight into how a toddler views the world?

How would you describe each of the other rooms of your home, in looks and feeling, from a toddler's viewpoint?

The husband is now to get out from beneath the table, taking the Guide with him. His wife remains as before. The husband stands next to the table, facing his wife, though of course she cannot see the upper portion of his body. The husband reads off to her the questions below. After she answers a question, the two of them can discuss her reply together, especially as it might shed light on relating to their child.

Questions for Wife

Does it make a difference looking at me from your present position?

When I walk casually around a corner of the table and back (*He does this.*), what is your reaction to my movements?

If I stamp my foot (*He does.*), what is your reaction?

Are you ready for the next question? (*When wife indicates she is, husband is to say in a loud voice, "Careful!"*) What was your reaction to that?

If I stoop down so that we can see each other face to face (*He does this briefly.*), do you feel differently?

If I reach my hand down so that you can hold it (*He does this.*), is that an acceptable substitute for face-to-face contact?

Would you like to get out from under the table?

Wife and husband now switch places, with the husband underneath the table and the wife standing up beside it, asking him the questions below. As before, each reply can be discussed in ways the couple considers fruitful.

Questions for Husband

Does it make a difference looking at me from the position you are now in?

When I walk casually around a corner of the table and back (*She does this.*), what is your reaction to my movements?

If I pound the table (*She does.*), what is your reaction?

In your present position are you more inclined to empathize with a child or to be yourself?

Do you think that when I was under the table I was more inclined to empathize with a child or to be myself?

Do you feel that you have ever done anything that might undermine our child's respect for me?

Do you feel that I have ever done anything that might undermine our child's respect for you?

Would you like to come out and discuss this further?

Exercise 3

"Leveling"

Husband and wife are to size up as honestly as possible their feelings about being parents after about three years of experience. (If your child is not that old, postpone this exercise until he or she is.) Each of you, without consulting the other, is to complete certain statements by checking one of the phrases that most nearly applies. The husband works on his section below, the wife on her section which follows. Do not look at each other's portion of the exercise until both of you have finished. Then turn to the discussion questions which start on page 460.

Husband starts here: *Check one*

My confidence in myself as a parent is.....
increasing
good as ever
shaky

My relationship with our child is now .....
very close
average
mixed

It used to be ....
better
less good
the same

Being a parent now seems ....
more rewarding
same as always
more frustrating

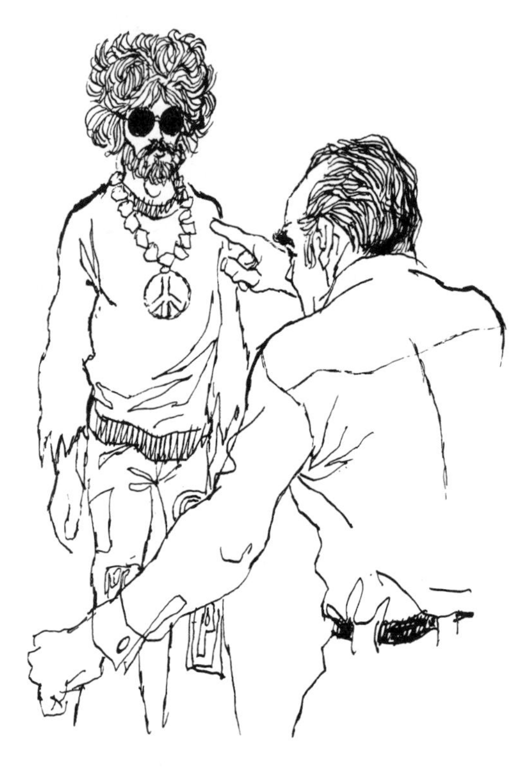

Our child seems ....
very demanding
normally demanding
easier than most

Problems are mostly due to child's ....
age
personality
age and personality

Conflicts with our child are mostly ....
resolved easily
hard on me
hard on my wife
hard on us all

About "no-no's", my wife and I...........
mostly agree
differ sometimes
disagree often

About orderliness, the two of us . . . .
mostly agree
differ sometimes
disagree often

About my helping out, the two of us . . . . . .
mostly agree
differ often

About my helping out, I feel . . . .
okay
somewhat put upon
somewhat guilty

I get my beefs off my chest. . . . .
sufficiently
insufficiently

Husband stops here.

Wife starts here: *Check one*

My confidence in myself as a parent is. . . . .
increasing
good as ever
shaky

My relationship with our child is now. . . . . .
very close
average
mixed

It used to be . . . .
better
less good
the same

Being a parent now seems . . . .
more rewarding
same as always
more frustrating

Our child seems . . . .
very demanding
normally demanding
easier than most

Our child seems . . . .
independent enough
often foolhardy
a bit clinging

Problems are mostly due to child's . . . .
age
personality
age and personality

About "no-no's," my husband and I........
mostly agree
agree sometimes
disagree often

About orderliness, the two of us..........
mostly agree
differ sometimes
disagree often

About his helping out, the two of us.......
mostly agree
differ often

I get my beefs off my chest...............
sufficiently
insufficiently

Wife stops here.

Both turn to the discussion questions below.

Wife continues: *Check one*

Toilet training has been..................
easy
fairly easy
difficult

On this issue my husband has been........
uninvolved
helpful
no help

Sleeping problems are...................
average
very trying

On this issue my husband has been........
helpful
no help

Conflicts with our child are mostly........
resolved easily
hard on me
hard on my husband
hard on us all

Questions to Discuss

Did you both check the same phrase in describing your relationship with your child?

If there is a difference, to what extent do you think the sex of the child might be responsible for it?

What other factors do you think might be involved?

If either your relationship with your child or your feelings about being a parent are revealed as having become more strained, to what would you ascribe this?

Does the exercise reveal any differences of opinion about "no-no's," orderliness, or the husband's helping with parental duties, that need to be aired further?

If you do not always agree on "no-no's," is it more a matter of what limits to set than of how to enforce them?

Did either of you indicate a feeling that it is your child's personality, rather than age alone, that makes for many of the problems in your home currently, and if so, what are your reasons?

Does the husband agree with the wife's evaluation of toilet training, sleeping problems, and your child's degree of independence?

Has your child's activity level shown any significant change since babyhood?

In what ways does your evaluation of your child's personality seem a predictable reflection of activity level?

Are there any "negative correlations" between activity level and personality at the moment (for example, a child with a high activity level is "clinging"), and if so, what do you think this might indicate?

Does your current evaluation of your child's personality suggest that your approach to discipline might need to be revised in any way?

Does it suggest that your child may be going through any of the forms of "separation anxiety" discussed in the book *Your Child's First Three Years?*

Does the concept that "opposite extremes (for example, too much and too little stimulation) tend to produce similar results" make you think of any children you know?

Do you detect any relationship between the attitudes of both of you toward orderliness and your child's degree of independence, especially in dressing, self-feeding, and toileting?

Were you especially bothered when checking any phrases, and if so, what can you learn from this?

Did both of you indicate that you are getting your beefs off your chest satisfactorily?

BOOK THREE: *Guiding Your Preschooler* *(Ages 3-5)*

Rules of the Game

So as not to lose the value of the surprise element in all this, it is suggested that you do not open this *Guide* until you have read *Guiding Your Preschooler.*

Read all instructions—*printed in italics to catch your eye*—before starting an exercise or turning a page in the *Guide.* For maximum benefit, *do only one exercise at a sitting* and allow a few days to elapse before going on to the next one. You may find it instructive, after a year or so, to go over the material again.

Focus of this Section

Our focus in the next group of exercises will be primarily on how we interact with our children of three, four, and five years of age. The exercises are designed to illumine concepts and a way of thinking, so that they should also interest parents who have already lived through the preschool period.

Exercise 1

"Where We're At"

In this exercise husband and wife are to explore some of the typical aspects of living with preschoolers and their own feelings about what is going on. The two of you are to work separately, without looking at each other's responses. Part of the exercise involves completing certain statements by checking the one of the phrases to the right which most nearly applies. Another part involves completing certain statements by filling in the blank spaces with your own word or phrase. The wife's portion of the exercise appears below. The husband's portion begins on the opposite page. When both of you have finished your respective portions, you will turn together to the discussion questions which start on page 465.

Wife or husband turns to indicated page.

Wife starts here: *Check one*

Our child's negativism is now.............
- very high
- average
- low

Our child gets along with other children...
- very well
- fairly well
- poorly

Our child is content to play alone.........
- often
- sometimes
- rarely

Our child's activity level is...............
- very high
- average
- fairly low

Keeping toys picked up in our home is....
- impossible
- difficult
- not that hard

The person who most often picks up is....
myself
our child
my husband

Getting our child to meals is.............
often hard
sometimes hard
usually easy

Our child's appetite is..................
good
poor

Getting our child to wash acceptably is....
very difficult
fairly difficult
not too hard

Getting our child to bed is...............
very difficult
fairly difficult
not too hard

Child waking during the night is..........
very common
fairly common
rare

Conflicts with our child are mostly........
resolved easily
hard to handle

In blanks below write a word or phrase saying how much:

Our child is ______________ aggressive.

Our child is ______________ competitive.

Our child is ______________ whiny.

Our child is ______________ fearful.

The one of the four traits above that most often causes trouble in our household is

__________.

The one of the four traits above that bothers

me most is __________.

Wife stops here.

Husband starts here: *Check one*

Our child's negativism is now.............
very high
average
low

Our child gets along with other children...
very well
fairly well
poorly

Our child is content to play alone.........
often
sometimes
rarely

Check one

Our child's activity level is . . . .
very high
average
fairly low

Keeping toys picked up in our home is . . . .
impossible
difficult
not that hard

The person who most often picks up is . . . .
myself
our child
my wife

Getting our child to meals is . . . .
often hard
sometimes hard
usually easy

Our child's appetite is . . . .
good
poor

Getting our child to wash acceptably is . . . .
very difficult
fairly difficult
not too hard

Getting our child to bed is . . . .
very difficult
fairly difficult
not too hard

Child waking during the night is . . . .
very common
fairly common
rare

Conflicts with our child are mostly . . . .
resolved easily
hard to handle

In blanks below write a word or phrase saying how much:

Our child is ________________ aggressive.

Our child is ________________ competitive.

Our child is ________________ whiny.

Our child is ________________ fearful.

The one of the four traits above that most often causes trouble in our household is

________________.

The one of the four traits above that bothers

me most is ________________.

Both proceed to the opposite page.

Questions to Discuss

Did the two of you disagree significantly in the phrases you checked to describe your child?

Would you say that your opinion of the relative difficulty involved in such activities as keeping toys picked up, getting your child to meals or to bed, etc., reflects not just your child's behavior but also the extent to which each of you finds that behavior a problem? (For example, a parent might consider keep-

ing toys picked up as "not that hard" simply because the parent is not especially bothered by—or even aware of—toys scattered around the home.)

By going back over the phrases each of you checked to describe your child, can you now learn something about how you are similarly or differently exasperated by the problems that parents of preschoolers frequently face?

Can knowing your own and each other's "sore spots" offer any clues as to how you might better support each other?

Is one of you better able to cope with your child under certain circumstances than the other?

Might you use this information to lower the amount of friction in everyday relationships?

Does a difference in the amount of time each of you spends with your child seem to affect the degree to which you are bothered by problems?

What might be done about this?

Does one of you perhaps expect more of your child than the other, and if so, how can you iron out any such differences constructively?

Do your individual approaches to discipline seem to be fairly harmonious, and if not, what can you do about this?

Coming now to how you filled in the blanks, are there any significant differences?

Do you think that the sex of your child, or your own sex, influenced how you filled in the blanks?

Do you believe that girls and boys ought to be different in terms of any of the four traits, and if so, how might your beliefs affect your child's development?

Would you say that whining is simply one way of handling aggression?

What attitude does a whiner seem to have about his chances of getting what he wants?

Have you ever known an adult to whine?

Can you think of some parental attitudes that might cause a child to whine . . . and some other attitudes that might lower the incidence of whining?

Exercise 2 begins on the next page.

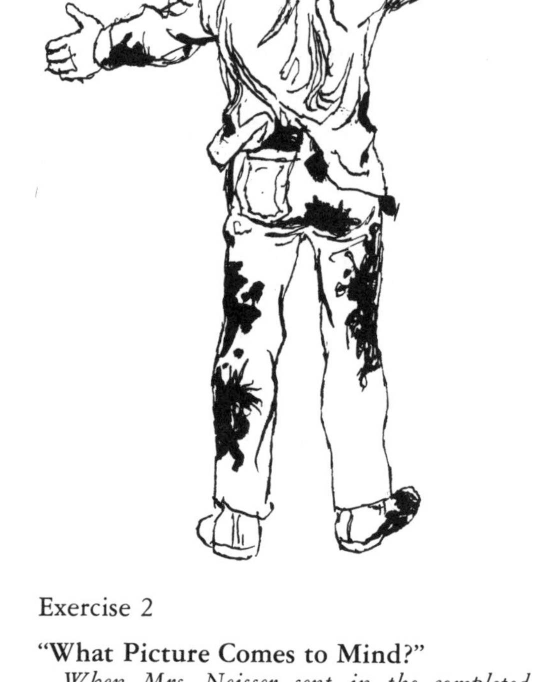

Questions to Discuss

How do you go about sympathizing with your child's obviously hurt feelings and at the same time avoid jumping to the conclusion that the other child is totally to blame for the falling-out that has occurred between the friends?

Did either of you feel secretly that in such situations your child usually asks for trouble by being a patsy—or by being the sly aggressor?

How might you handle such feelings so that they do not become a kind of self-fulfilling prophecy?

As you try to find out exactly what has happened, how do you avoid making your child feel that he (or she) is on trial or that it is silly to get so worked up over a pigeon feather?

How do you phrase your questions so that your child is never tempted to falsify the facts?

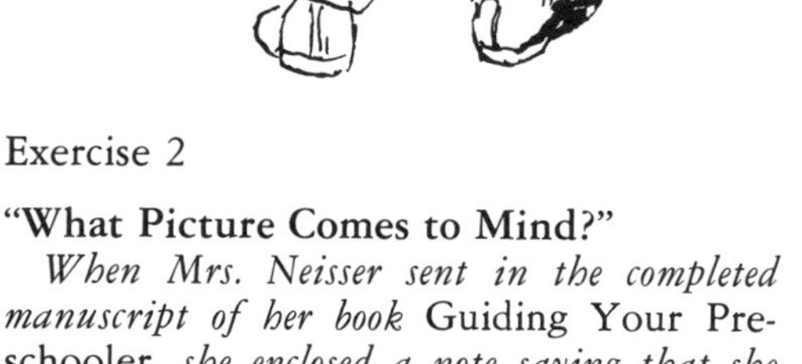

Exercise 2

"What Picture Comes to Mind?"

When Mrs. Neisser sent in the completed manuscript of her book Guiding Your Preschooler, *she enclosed a note saying that she had made no suggestions for illustrations but hoped that if illustrations were used the children in them would appear "appropriately grimy, angry, or otherwise true to life." In this exercise husband and wife will "illustrate" Mrs. Neisser's book. The two of you together are to consider three situations outlined below and visualize yourselves and your child in them. Then you will talk over possible ways of dealing with each situation, using the questions that follow each description to guide your thinking.*

1. Your child has just entered the house with a tear-stained face and a badly torn jacket, saying he (or she) "hates" a certain good friend because that friend "stole my pigeon feather."

How can you handle the matter of the torn jacket so that its importance is not slighted yet it does not take precedence over the crucial issue of the friends' quarrel?

What might you be able to do to help the friends reestablish good relations?

2. Your child returns from playing at a friend's house with an expensive toy which he (or she) says was a gift from the friend.

Questions to Discuss

Can you think of a face-saving way to explore with your child the possibility that the toy may not have been a gift—that it may have been "taken without permission"?

How can you best guard against tempting your child to lie or possibly trapping your child in a falsehood?

In the event you were to discover that the toy was "not exactly a gift," how would you go about helping your child return it without unnecessary loss of face?

Even if you are sure the toy was indeed a gift, would you want your child to return it anyway—or at least want to discuss the matter with the playmate's parents?

If you begin your talk with your child on this note, how can you proceed so as to eliminate any chance of possibly trapping your child in a falsehood—that is, offer ample opportunity for a confession, just in case one is needed?

3. A neighbor calls to tell you that her child has been complaining recently that your child tries to dominate the play of the neighborhood fours and fives. As a result, she has been keeping a careful eye on what goes on, and she feels her child is correct. Her manner is friendly. She says, "I just thought you would want to know."

Questions to Discuss

What do you say to your neighbor?

Would you immediately try to talk to your child about this or first embark on a course of supervising his (or her) play closely for a time?

How could you arrange to supervise your child closely without making him (or her) feel something is wrong?

If the neighbor is right, how do you help your child?

Exercise 3 begins on the next page.

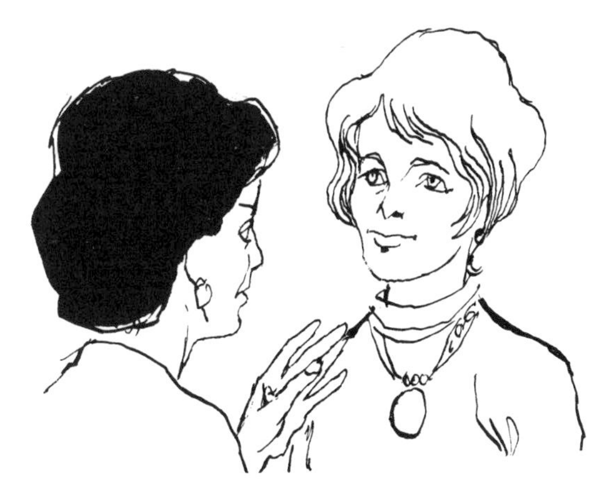

Exercise 3

"Parting is . . . ?"

In this exercise husband and wife are to examine their child's reaction to and their own feelings about the loosening of the apron strings that occurs over the preschool years, climaxing with starting first grade. First, the two of you together will evaluate the statements below as True or False—or, if you can't agree on an evaluation, mark the box labeled "Disagree." Then you will take up the questions on the opposite page.

	True	*False*	*Disagree*
Our child is as independent as most children the same age.	☐	☐	☐
Our child is happy staying overnight with friends or relatives.	☐	☐	☐
Our child has done this often.	☐	☐	☐
This was hard for our child at first.	☐	☐	☐
Our child can now adjust easily to a new sitter.	☐	☐	☐
This was hard for our child at first.	☐	☐	☐
If we are not around, our child asks other adults for help if needed.	☐	☐	☐
Our child now seldom has difficulty leaving us.	☐	☐	☐
Our child may cry when leaving us but will be okay afterwards.	☐	☐	☐

	True	*False*	*Disagree*
We have done what we could to help our child grow up.	☐	☐	☐
We may have pushed our child to grow up faster than necessary.	☐	☐	☐

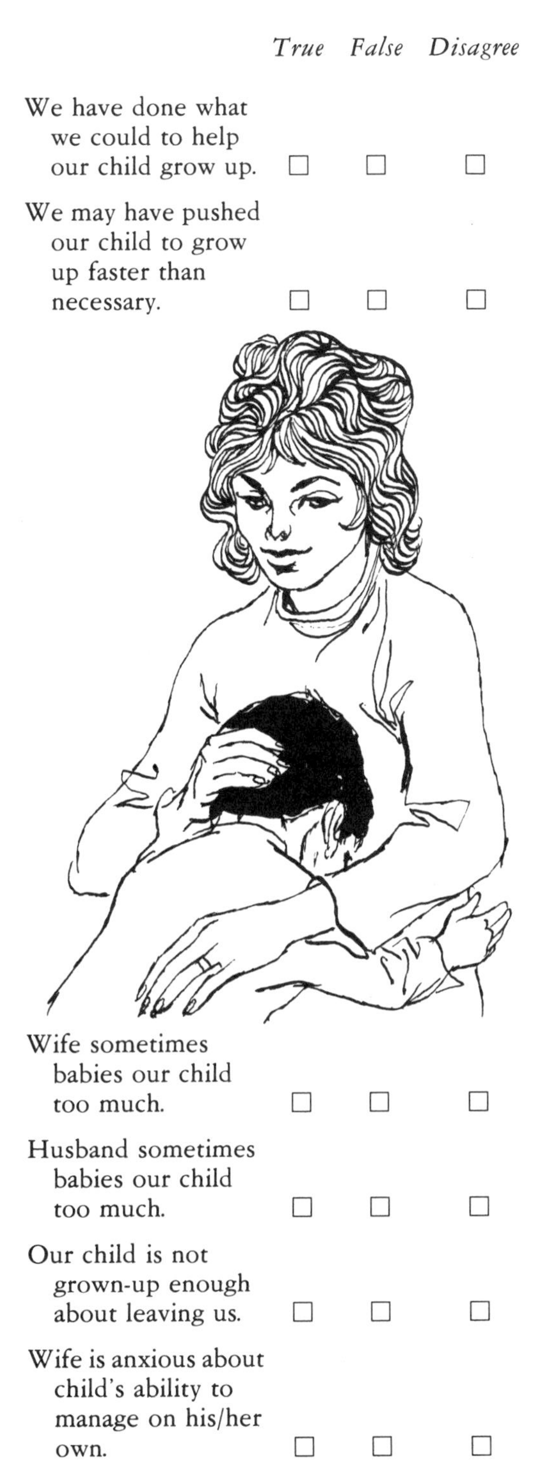

	True	*False*	*Disagree*
Wife sometimes babies our child too much.	☐	☐	☐
Husband sometimes babies our child too much.	☐	☐	☐
Our child is not grown-up enough about leaving us.	☐	☐	☐
Wife is anxious about child's ability to manage on his/her own.	☐	☐	☐
Husband is anxious about child's ability to manage on his/her own.	☐	☐	☐
Shyness is a problem for our child.	☐	☐	☐
Our child has some good friends.	☐	☐	☐

Questions to Discuss

Did the two of you sometimes disagree, and if so, what can you learn from your differences of opinion?

Did the two of you always agree, and if so, were you really equally honest and strong in upholding your opinions?

Is it possible that loosening the apron strings is harder for you as parents than for your child?

Have the two of you ever thought about and talked seriously about what it will be like when your child (or children) is/are grown-up?

Do you think this will hit you both equally hard, or be harder on one of you than the other?

Is there any correlation between your feelings about how you will manage when your child is grown and your anxiety about your child's ability to manage without you?

Would you agree that a child's shyness need not be considered a real problem by parents if the child has one or two good friends?

On balance, do you think your child is adequately prepared to handle the challenge of getting along without you that is posed by first grade?

What might you be doing to prepare your child better for this challenge?

BOOK FOUR: *The Early School Years* *(Ages 6 through 10)*

Rules of the Game

So as not to lose the value of the surprise element in all this, it is suggested that you do not open this *Guide* until you have read *The Early School Years.* Read carefully all instructions—*printed in italics to catch your eye*—before starting an exercise or turning a page in the *Guide.* For maximum benefit, *do only one exercise at a sitting* and allow a few days to elapse before going on to the next one. You may find it instructive, after a year or so, to go over the material again.

Focus of This Section

Our focus in these exercises will be primarily on how we interact with our children during the years from six through ten. The exercises are designed to illumine concepts and a way of thinking, so that they should also interest parents who have already lived through these early school years.

Exercise 1

"Values"

Husband and wife are to examine certain aspects of their child's behavior and consider what values the child seems to be most influenced by on the whole. The two of you are to work separately, completing certain statements by checking the phrase to the right that most nearly applies. The husband's portion of the exercise starts below. The wife's portion is on page 472 through 473. Do not look at each other's responses until after both of you have finished the written portion of the exercise. Then go on together to the discussion questions that begin on page at the bottom of page 473.

Husband Starts Here: *Check one*

Our child likes school . . . .
- a great deal
- fairly well
- only rarely

Our child's friends like school . . . .
- a great deal
- fairly well
- only rarely

I liked school. . . . .
- a great deal
- fairly well
- only rarely

Our child's interest in learning is. . . . .
- very high
- average
- low, at present

His/her friends' interest in learning is mostly . . . . *Check one*
- very high
- average
- low, at present

Our child chooses friends mostly. . . . .
- for compatibility
- to be "in"

Husband continues: *Check one*

Our child is mostly. . . . .
- a leader
- a follower
- independent

Our child's choice of friends is, in my opinion, mostly . . . .
- admirable
- par for the course
- dubious

In economic background our child's friends are mostly. . . . .
- similar
- mixed

In social background our child's friends are mostly. . . . .
- similar
- mixed

In attitudes our child's friends are mostly . . . .
- similar
- different

Our child's loyalty to friends is . . . .
- high
- average
- short-lived

Our child's friends are mostly. . . . .
- loyal
- fairly loyal
- exploitive

Our child is mostly. . . . .
- very honest
- honest enough
- not honest enough

Helping our child admit wrongdoing is mostly. . . . .
- easy
- difficult

Our child's values are mostly . . . .
- excellent
- okay for now
- troubling

Husband stops here.

Wife Starts Here: *Check one*

Our child likes school . . . .
- a great deal
- fairly well
- only rarely

Our child's friends like school . . . .
- a great deal
- fairly well
- only rarely

I liked school. . . . .
- a great deal
- fairly well
- only rarely

Our child's interest in learning is. . . . .
- very high
- average
- low, at present

His/her friends' interest in learning is mostly . . . . *Check one*
- very high
- average
- low, at present

Our child chooses friends mostly . . . .
- for compatibility
- to be "in"

Our child is mostly. . . . .
- a leader
- a follower
- independent

Our child's choice of friends is, in my opinion, mostly . . . .
- admirable
- par for the course
- dubious

In economic background our child's friends are mostly. . . . .
- similar
- mixed

In social background our child's friends are mostly. . . . .
- similar
- mixed

In attitudes our child's friends are mostly . . . .
- similar
- different

Our child's loyalty to friends is . . . .
- high
- average
- short-lived

Our child's friends are mostly . . . .
- loyal
- fairly loyal
- exploitive

Our child is mostly . . . .
- very honest
- honest enough
- not honest enough

Wife continues: *Check one*

Helping our child admit wrongdoing
is mostly ....
easy
difficult

Our child's values are mostly.............
excellent
okay for now
troubling

Now proceed together.

Questions to Discuss

Do you feel that your child is very strongly inclined to "go along with the crowd"?

Do you think this poses a real problem now —or might do so in the future?

Can you see any significant difference between being independent and being "nonconforming"?

Have you ever known a "nonconformist" whose actions in a given situation you could predict just as easily as those of your most conforming friends?

Do you think that difficulty in making or keeping friends might possibly corrupt a child's values?

If you were worried about your child's friends—or lack of friends—do you think you could intervene in a way that wouldn't get your child's back up and might bring about some significant change for the better?

Did your parents ever do anything in this area that you remember as being especially helpful—or the opposite?

Since your child has been old enough to notice, have you ever been involved in any activity that required taking an unpopular stand?

How do you think the economic and social status of a family is likely to affect children's values?

Is your child growing up in significantly different economic or social circumstances from those you grew up in?

If so, how might you guard against a "value gap"?

Does your child's attitude toward school suggest that you should be involved in trying to change conditions there?

If a child is interested in learning, need parents worry if he doesn't like school?

Would you say the answer to the prior question depends in part on how much time and money parents can give to helping their child learn outside school?

Does this leave some children out of luck?

Do you think your child's attitudes toward school—or learning—have been negatively influenced by how you felt when you were your child's age?

Do you think competitiveness significantly affects how your child relates to other children—and they to him?

Do both parents mostly have similar values, or are there differences that could be confusing to a child?

Looking back on your own childhood, were there times when you felt your parents told you to behave one way but deep down wanted you to behave differently?

Exercise 2

"Why Not?"

In this exercise husband and wife are to explore together ways of handling garden-variety confrontations with their child. You are to discuss three everyday situations outlined below, using the questions that follow each to guide your conversation. To insure that your child's point of view is adequately upheld, in the first and third situations the husband will play the role of the child as questions are discussed, while the wife acts as parent; in the second situation, the wife will be the child and the husband be the parent.

1. Your child is invited to a party on Easter Sunday afternoon, which he/she is very eager to attend. You remind your child that the family is visiting Grandma that day, as is the custom every year. Your child says, "But I don't have to go with you to Grandma's. I can spend the day with David. He's going to the party, and his mother said yesterday she'll be glad to have me over while you're away."

Questions to Discuss

How will your child feel and react if you insist that he/she go with you to Grandma's?

If the child were allowed to stay with David, rather than accompany you, would that spoil the occasion for Grandma, or for you?

Are your religious convictions a significant issue in your feelings about this situation, and if so, what does your child think about them?

Are your convictions about the importance of family get-togethers an issue that matters to you, and if so, how does your child feel about this?

How persuasive a case can you make for the idea that your child will in the long run feel better about himself/herself as a person if he/she goes with you?

What does the child say to that?

2. Your child wants to go with a friend to a movie which is rated GP but which, as advertised, seems to contain a lot of violence. You think your child would be upset by the movie. Your child says, "Practically my whole class has been, and they all say it's great and nobody had bad dreams."

Questions to Discuss

How would your child react to the suggestion that you will call around and try to get the opinion of a parent who has seen the movie?

How persuasive a case can you make for the position that you are simply trying to do what is best for your child—not to spoil his/her fun?

Would you consider allowing your child to go to the movie if one of you could arrange to go along?

What does your child say to this?

What interesting alternatives to going to the movies can you suggest, and how does your child react to trying them out on his/her friend?

3. Your child has been pestering you for several months to be allowed to bicycle into the center of town. He/she has just announced that a slightly younger friend who lives nearby has won permission to do this. "Now will you stop treating me like a baby?" your child asks.

Questions to Discuss

Can your child persuade you to reconsider your stand on this issue?

Can you persuade your child that you are not being overprotective about this—or about things in general?

Are there factors other than age that are influencing your feelings about your child's readiness for this step?

How do you think a child can go about gaining experience handling a bicycle in traffic?

Does your child often feel that you treat him or her "like a baby"?

Exercise 3

"Prejudice"

In her book The Early School Years, *Mrs. Mogal points out that any kind of stereotyped thinking is prejudice, and that "without realizing it, all parents sometimes tend to make stereotyped judgments about their own children or their children's friends." In this exercise husband and wife are to examine this proposition together. You are to make certain statements that follow as either "True" or "False"—or, if you cannot agree on the answer, check the box under "Disagree." Do not explore your differences of opinion now; wait until you've finished and are ready for the discussion questions on* *page 477.*

	True	*False*	*Disagree*
Wife always listens respectfully to our child's side of an argument.	☐	☐	☐
Husband always listens respectfully to our child's side of an argument.	☐	☐	☐

	True	*False*	*Disagree*
Wife has never instantly disliked any of our child's friends.	☐	☐	☐
Husband has never instantly disliked any of our child's friends.	☐	☐	☐
Wife has never instantly *liked* any of our child's friends.	☐	☐	☐
Husband has never instantly *liked* any of our child's friends.	☐	☐	☐
Wife never cracks down on our child when she's in a bad mood.	☐	☐	☐
Husband never cracks down on our child when he's in a bad mood.	☐	☐	☐

	True	*False*	*Disagree*
Wife never makes our child feel inferior.	☐	☐	☐
Husband never makes our child feel inferior.	☐	☐	☐
Wife never judges other children by their appearance.	☐	☐	☐
Husband never judges other children by their appearance.	☐	☐	☐
Wife never expects our child to be judged by appearance.	☐	☐	☐
Husband never expects our child to be judged by appearance.	☐	☐	☐
We are never social snobs.	☐	☐	☐
We are never intellectual snobs.	☐	☐	☐

Questions to Discuss

Would you now accept the proposition that all of us are at least occasionally prejudiced —that we wouldn't be human if we weren't?

Would you also agree that, as with other human limitations, it is how we face up to and handle our possible prejudices that really matters?

Have you ever become friends with a person whom you originally "instantly disliked"?

Would you say this indicates an ability to handle prejudice constructively?

Have you ever apologized to your child for something you said or did when you were in a bad mood?

Do you think this indicates an ability to handle prejudice constructively?

How do you think a child feels when told, "You're too young to understand!"?

Would you say that any snap judgment that lumps certain kinds of people together as a group, without allowing for individual differences, constitutes prejudice?

Can you think of any ways, not covered in this exercise, in which you sometimes show prejudice toward your child, other children, each other?

BOOK FIVE: *Growing Into Adolescence* *(Ages 11 through 14)*

Rules of the Game

So as not to lose the value of the surprise element in all this, it is suggested that you do not open this *Guide* until you have read *Growing into Adolescence.* Read carefully all instructions—*printed in italics to catch your eye*—before starting an exercise or turning a page in the *Guide.* For maximum benefit, *do only one exercise at a sitting* and allow a few days to elapse before going on to the next one. You may find it instructive, after a year or so, to go over the material again.

Focus of this Section

Our focus in the next group of exercises will be primarily on how we interact with our children during the challenging years from eleven through fourteen. The exercises are designed to illumine concepts and a way of thinking, so that parents who have already lived through a child's transition into adolescence may find them interesting and instructive.

Exercise 1

"How Much Do We Tell Them?"

The following exercise explores some of the feelings parents have about communicating with their children about sex-related matters. Husband and wife, working separately, are to complete certain sentences by filling in the blank spaces with the word or phrase that first comes to mind. Don't worry about grammar; just try

to get your feelings across. The wife's portion of the exercise begins below; the husband's portion begins on the opposite page. Whoever goes first should clip a sheet of paper over his or her responses to hide them from the view of the other. When both have finished, turn together to the discussion questions that follow.

Wife begins here:

The atmosphere I grew up in made me feel

____________________ about sex.

I want our child to feel __________________.

The information my parents gave me was

____________ true, ____________ complete,

and ____________ reassuring.

I was ____________ prepared for the talk about sex I encountered at school.

I was __________ prepared for menstruation.

I was __________ informed about male development at puberty.

I first heard about contraception from _____.

The information was __________ accurate.

I heard about venereal disease from _____.

The information was __________ accurate.

My information about masturbation was

__________ true, __________ complete,

and ______________ reassuring.

I was __________ in the position of wanting sex information and not knowing where to go for reliable answers.

Husband begins here:

The atmosphere I grew up in made me feel

______________ about sex.

I want our child to feel __________.

The information my parents gave me was

__________ true, __________ complete,

and ______________ reassuring.

I was __________ prepared for the talk about sex I encountered at school.

I was __________ prepared for the physical changes I underwent at puberty.

I was __________ informed about menstruation.

I first heard about contraception from _____.

The information was __________ accurate.

I heard about venereal disease from _____.

The information was __________ accurate.

My information about masturbation was

__________ true, __________ complete,

and ______________ reassuring.

I was __________ in the position of wanting sex information and not knowing where to go for reliable answers.

Both proceed.

Questions to Discuss

Was either of you ever left out of conversations among groups of your peers because of ignorance about sex?

On balance, what effect do you think "locker room" talk about sex had on your development?

Did either of you ever feel tempted to experiment with sex simply to gain information?

Did you ever have any guilt feelings about "bad" thoughts, or masturbation?

Did you look forward to falling passionately in love and having an exciting sex life with your beloved?

Were you as well prepared as possible to do this?

Do you think your child's goals are much different?

Did any novels or stories have an important effect—good or bad—on your attitudes toward sex?

Did you have access to any sex books for young people, and if so, did you find this helpful?

Do you think preadolescents can, on the whole, benefit from having appropriate written material on this subject—even if their parents can talk to them about sex?

Do you think children are likely to fault their parents for feeling embarrassed about explaining sex as long as the parents manage somehow to give their children the facts—if only by handing them a book?

Are we perhaps too hung up on the importance of being able to "talk comfortably with our children about sex"?

Do you hope that your child will be able to talk freely with his/her marriage partner about sex?

How do you think parents can help make this possible?

As a teen-ager could you be scared out of doing anything?

If you would like to give your child a book about sex but can't find one that entirely satisfies you, might giving the child *some* book help you talk with him/her about the subject?

Have you ever found yourself talking honestly with your child about sex during the course of a conversation that opened on an altogether different note?

Have you ever muffed such unexpected opportunities?

Given a second chance, do you feel you might do better?

Did the information about sex that you most value come from your parents, directly or indirectly—or elsewhere?

Do you want to repeat this pattern with your child?

Exercise 2

"Not Again!"

In this exercise parents are to examine the "unreasonableness" of children aged eleven through fourteen. Husband and wife, working independently, will complete certain statements by checking the one of the phrases at the right that most nearly applies. The husband's portion of the exercise begins immediately below. The wife's portion begins on the next page. Do not look at each other's responses until you are ready to turn to the discussion questions on page 483.

Husband begins here: *Check one*

Reminding our child about chores is needed . . . .
constantly
fairly often
rarely

Reminding our child about homework is needed . . . .
constantly
fairly often
rarely

Child's dress is mostly . . . .
attractive
acceptable
sloppy

Child respects our opinion about his/her dress . . . .
usually
sometimes
never

Child's grooming is mostly . . . .
very good
acceptable
sloppy

We remind child about this . . . .
often
sometimes
rarely

Child's views on grooming differ from ours . . . .
radically
in some respects
rarely

Child's care of possessions is mostly . . . .
good
fair
distressing

Conflicts with child are . . . .
very frequent
fairly frequent
rare

Child recovers from run-ins . . . .
quickly
slowly

Child is reprimanded . . . .
very often
fairly often
rarely

Child is criticized . . . .
often
sometimes
rarely

Child takes criticism . . . .
well
fairly well
poorly

Reminding our child about homework is needed . . . .
constantly
fairly often
rarely

Child's dress is mostly . . . .
attractive
acceptable
sloppy

Child respects our opinion about his/her dress . . . .
usually
sometimes
never

Child's grooming is mostly . . . .
very good
acceptable
sloppy

We remind child about this . . . .
often
sometimes
rarely

Check one

Child is praised . . . .
often
fairly often
rarely

Child's self-confidence is mostly . . . .
impressive
average
easily shaken

Husband stops here.

Wife Begins Here: *Check one*

Reminding our child about chores is needed . . . .
constantly
fairly often
rarely

Child's views on grooming differ from ours ....
- radically
- in some respects
- rarely

Child's care of possessions is mostly ....
- good
- fair
- distressing

Conflicts with child are ....
- very frequent
- fairly frequent
- rare

Child recovers from run-ins ....
- quickly
- slowly

Child is reprimanded....................
- very often
- fairly often
- rarely

Child is criticized ....
- often
- sometimes
- rarely

Child takes criticism ....
- well
- fairly well
- poorly

Check one

Child is praised ....
- often
- fairly often
- rarely

Child's self-confidence is mostly ....
- impressive
- average
- easily shaken

Both proceed.

Questions to Discuss

Do you think parental approval matters more to children of this age than they say—or perhaps even realize?

How can parents supply this approval while at the same time giving adequate guidance?

Looking objectively at your responses, do they suggest that home is a morale-boosting place for your child?

Can you think of times when your child has accepted suggestions from you without seeming to feel they were implied criticisms?

Does the timing of suggestions—or the language you use—ever seem to make an important difference?

Would you agree with Dr. Haim Ginott that when disapproving of a child's actions we should focus on the behavior we object to, not attack the child? ("Your bicycle is blocking the driveway," not "Why are you so irresponsible?")

Can you think of any recent conflicts with your child that might have been avoided in this way?

Do you honestly feel you are as tactful with your child as with each other?

To what extent do you think parents need to go along with the "fashions of the times" when it comes to their children's dress and grooming?

Exercise 3

"Romeo? Juliet?"

Husband and wife are to consider together briefly described. Questions follow each of the outlined below. Questions follow each of the situations to guide your discussion. As a means of trying to do justice to your child's feelings, one of you will play the role of your child in each situation, while the other functions as parent. At the end of each sketch of a situation you are told who plays the child.

1. Your child is leaving for a boy-girl party and you want to put the child at ease but also make certain that he/she looks his/her best. (*Parent of the same sex as the child will play the role of the child.*)

Questions to Discuss

How do you respond if your child asks, "Why are you looking at me like that?"

Could you manage to remove a spot from your child's clothes without precipitating a scene?

Could you accomplish other changes without making your child self-conscious, or getting his/her back up?

Do you think any last-minute improvements you might make in your child's looks would really offset the damage you might do to his/her confidence by seeming anxious?

Do you think the children care about each other's looks?

Do you think it would help to say, "Don't be nervous. Remember the others are just as ill at ease as you!"?

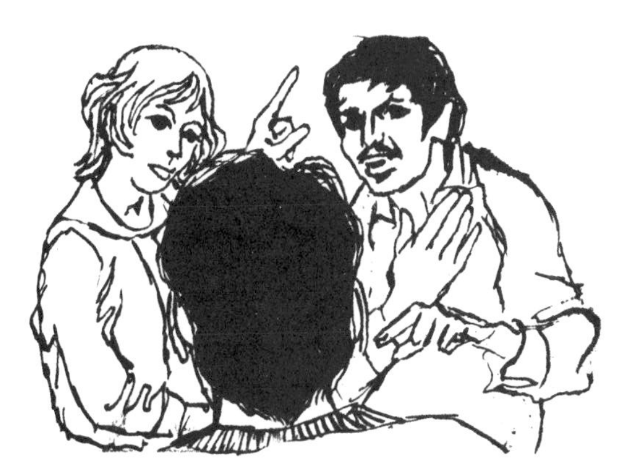

Might it be useful to talk about this with your child at some other, less emotionally charged time?

How can we say to our children this age how much we love them and want them to be happy?

2. Your child walks in on a parental disagreement and says disgustedly, "Why are you two always arguing?" You want to uphold the image of marriage as rewarding, but also feel your child needs to be disabused of the notion that love solves all problems. (*Role of child will be played by parent of opposite sex.*)

Questions to Discuss

Would it help to retort, "We're not always arguing!"?

How might you avoid being drawn into arguing defensively with your child about how good your marriage is?

Can you think of a way to convey persuasively the idea that people can disagree constructively—even if the two of you weren't exactly "disagreeing constructively" when your child walked in?

Do you think humor helps at such times?

How does one summon up humor in a pinch?

If your child's appearance on the scene tempts either of you to encourage the child to take your side in the disagreement, how might your spouse help you cope with this temptation?

When the two of you are angry with each other, do you usually avoid making snide cracks about the opposite sex?

When you have run-ins with your child, do you usually manage to convey the idea that we sometimes temporarily hate the people we love—and it needn't spoil our love?

3. Your child has turned down an invitation to a boy-girl party and you are concerned about the child's reasons. (*Parent of same sex as child will play the role of the child.*)

Questions to Discuss

Why would you want your child to go to the party?

Do you feel your child is cutting his/her throat in some way by turning down the invitation?

Do you think your child really wants to go but refused the invitation from lack of confidence, and if so, how might you encourage him/her to change his/her mind?

Could the problem be yours, not the child's—you want your child to go, but he/she isn't really interested?

In your community are children sometimes pushed into boy-girl relationships before they are ready for this?

A Reminder

Do not consider the use of the *Guides* completed simply because you have answered and discussed all the questions. Return to the specific *Guides* a year after you have completed them, answering and discussing all the questions anew. Compare the replies. Are your responses the same or markedly different? Perhaps a rereading of the specific PROGRAM involved might aid you in understanding the reasons for the changed answers. Use the *Guide* as a "refresher course" by reviewing all the questions and answers every few years.

Bibliography and Suggested Reading

BOOK ONE

What Makes a Good Parent?

1 The Expert in Each of Us

Child Study Association of America, ed., with commentary by Anna W. M. Wolf. *A Reader for Parents: A Selection of Creative Literature About Childhood.* New York: W. W. Norton & Co., 1963.
This out-of-print book is worth looking for in the library.

Mayer, Greta, and Hoover, Mary. *When Children Need Special Help with Emotional Problems* (pamphlet). New York: Child Study Association of America, 1961.
Includes a description of the conventional kinds of special help available and how to go about getting a qualified practitioner.

Perlman, Helen. *Social Role and Personality.* Chicago: University of Chicago Press, 1968.
A gifted social worker discusses the multiple roles of men and women and how the healthy person can continue to grow in adult life.

Rogers, Carl R. *Carl Rogers on Encounter Groups.* New York: Harper & Row, 1970.
A sane description by a prominent therapist of what this approach to self-awareness has to offer.

2 The World We Live In

Bronfenbrenner, Urie. *Two Worlds of Childhood: U.S. and U.S.S.R.* New York: Russell Sage Foundation, 1970.

Ehrlich, Paul R., Ph.D., and Anne H. *Population, Resources, Environment: Issues in Human Ecology.* San Francisco: W. H. Freeman, 1970.

Hoopes, Ned E., ed. *Who Am I? Essays on the Alienated* (paperback). Dell Publishing Co., Inc., 1969.

James, Howard. *Children in Trouble.* New York: David McKay Co., 1970.
Exposé of what goes on in facilities for youthful delinquents, orphans, and neglected and abused children.

Lady Allen of Hurtwood. *Planning for Play.* Cambridge: M.I.T. Press, 1968.
Splendidly illustrated roundup of information on planning playgrounds and play programs and providing opportunities for casual play.

Mead, Margaret. *Cultural Commitment: A Study of the Generation Gap.* New York: Doubleday & Co., Inc., Natural History Press, 1970.
Entertaining and provacative analysis of what the young need from their elders in this era of rapid social change.

Milner, Esther, et al. *Dialogue on Women* (paperback). New York: Bobbs-Merrill Co., Inc., 1967.
Compact, informative, and ahead of its time.

Silberman, Charles E. *Crisis in the Classroom.* New York: Random House, 1970.
Comprehensive discussion of problems and possible solutions.

Skolnick, Arlene S. and Jerome H. *Family in Transition.* New York: Little Brown & Co., 1971.
Wide-ranging source book; raises profound questions.

Thelen, Herbert A. *Dynamics of Groups at Work.* Chicago: University of Chicago Press, 1954.
Excellent introduction to what makes groups function constructively and possible roles of the leader.

Toffler, Alvin. *Future Shock.* New York: Random House, 1970.
Useful exposition of the effects of rapid social and technological change.

3 Preparing for a New Baby

Goodrich, Frederick W., Jr., M.D. *Preparing for Childbirth: A Manual for Expectant Parents.* Rev. ed. Englewood Cliffs, N.J.: Prentice-Hall, Inc., 1966.
Complete and sensible guide to "natural childbirth."

Hoffman, Martin L. and Lois W., eds. *Review of Child Development Research.* vol. 1. New York: Russell Sage Foundation, 1964.
Intended for professionals, but the section on the relative merits of breast- and bottlefeeding will reassure any mother.

LaLeche League International. *The Womanly Art of Breastfeeding.* Rev. ed., 1968.
Overly sentimental and evangelical, but packed with practical tips for women who have decided to breastfeed.

Maternity Center Association. *Guide for Expectant Parents* (paperback), 1969.
Question-and-answer format. Obtainable from the Association, 48 East 92nd Street, New York, N.Y. 10028.

———. *Preparation for Childbearing.* Rev. ed., 1972.
Handbook on preparing for "natural childbirth."

———. *A Baby Is Born: The Picture Story of a Baby from Conception Through Birth.* Rev. ed., 1964.

Spock, Benjamin, M.D. *Baby and Child Care* (paperback). Rev. ed. New York: Pocket Books, 1968.

Twins' Mothers Club of Bergen County, N.J. *And Then There Were Two: A Handbook for Mothers and Fathers of Twins* (pamphlet). Rev. ed. New York: Child Study Association of America, 1971.

4 No Parent Is Perfect

Geist, Harold. *A Child Goes to the Hospital: The Psychological Aspects of a Child Going to the Hospital.* Springfield, Ill.: Charles C. Thomas, 1965.

Hudson, Ian, M.D., and Thomas, Gordon. *What to Do Until the Doctor Comes.* Princeton: Vertex, 1970.

Kubler-Ross, Elisabeth, M.D. *On Death and Dying.* New York: The Macmillan Co., 1969.
Profound analysis of the "stages" through which a dying person passes in coming to terms with death.

Mayer, Greta, and Hoover, Mary. *When Children Need Special Help with Emotional Problems* (pamphlet). New York: Child Study Association of America, 1961.

Ruina, Edith. *Moving: A Common-Sense Guide to Relocating Your Family.* New York: Funk & Wagnalls, Inc., 1970.

Wolf, Anna W. M. *Helping Your Child to Understand Death* (pamphlet). Rev. ed. New York: Child Study Association of America, 1972.

5 What Makes Johnny "Behave"?

Bandura, Albert, and Walters, Richard H. *Adolescent Aggression: A Study of the Influence of Child-Training Practices and Family Interrelationships.* New York: Ronald Press Co., 1959.
Very detailed, technical report of a study comparing a group of delinquent boys with a group of nondelinquents having the same racial and class background.

Helfer, Ray E., M.D., and Kempe, E. Henry, M.D., eds. *The Battered Child.* Chicago: University of Chicago Press, 1968.

6 Parental Example: How It Rubs Off

Easton, David, and Dennis, Jack. *Children in the Political System: Origins of Political Legitimacy.* New York: McGraw-Hill, Inc., 1969.
Detailed study of the political attitudes of 12,000 American schoolchildren of ages 7 to 14.

Lee, Roy S. *Your Growing Child and Religion: A Psychological Account* (paperback). New York: The Macmillan Co., 1963. An English chaplain and psychologist suggests that parents' handling of their young children is the crucial element in their religious education.

8 Tapping a Child's Potential

Bland, Jane Cooper. *Art of the Young Child: Understanding and Encouraging Creative Growth in Children Three to Five.* New York: Museum of Modern Art, distr. by New York Graphic Society, 1968.

Hart, Harold H., ed. *Summerhill: For and Against.* New York: Hart Publishing Co., 1970.
Fifteen essays by educators, psychologists, and sociologists, on the "Summerhill" approach to education.

Kubie, Lawrence, M.D. *Neurotic Distortions of the Creative Process.* Lawrence: University of Kansas Press, 1958.
A psychoanalytical interpretation, not easy reading but lucid, of the roots of what we call creativity.

Sheehy, Emma A. *Children Discover Music and Dance* (paperback). New York: Teachers College, 1968.

Smith, Charles P., ed. *Achievement-Related Motives in Children.* New York: Russell Sage Foundation, 1969.
Research reports by eight psychologists and educators.

Thomas, Alexander, et al. *Temperament and Behavior Disorders in Children.* New York: New York University, 1968.
Report of a longitudinal study (10 years, 141 children) suggesting the range of children's temperamental differences and how an individual child's "fit" with his environment may affect his chances of realizing his potential.

9 The Beautiful Times

Provence, Sally, M.D., and Lipton, Rose, M.D. *Children in Institutions.* New York: International Universities Press, 1962.
Though written for a professional audience, a very clear, readable exposition of the way in which institutionalized babies may lose all capacity for joy and how this is interrelated with the capacity to respond in other ways.

10 Having the Children You Want—and No More

American Friends Service Committee: *Who Shall Live? Man's Control over Birth and Death*

(paperback). New York: Hill & Wang, Inc., 1970.
Superb report on some of the most crucial and sensitive issues of the day, written with unusual clarity and compassion.

Glass, Robert H., M.D., and Kase, Nathan G., M.D. *Woman's Choice: A Guide to Contraception, Fertility, Abortion, and Menopause.* New York: Basic Books, Inc., 1970.

Grover, John W., M.D. *V.D.: the ABC's.* Englewood Cliffs, N.J.: Prentice-Hall, Inc., 1971.
Comprehensive and singularly free of moralizing and scare tactics.

Kadushin, Alfred. *Adopting Older Children.* New York: Columbia University Press, 1970. A research report, but not unreadable and possibly of interest to couples considering this step.

Lader, Lawrence. *A Guide to Abortion Laws in the United States* (pamphlet). New York: Planned Parenthood—World Population, periodically updated. This reprint of an article in *Redbook,* June, 1971, gives a state-by-state rundown of facilities and sources of information for legal abortion. Available for 25c a copy from the organization at 810 Seventh Avenue, New York, N.Y. 10019.

Le Shan, Eda J. *You and Your Adopted Child.* New York: Public Affairs Pamphlets, 1958.
Still fine on attitudes of adopted children and their parents.

11 Our Needs in Perspective

Albrecht, Margaret. *A complete Guide for the Working Mother* (paperback). New York: Award Books, 1967.

Brecher, Ruth and Edward, eds. *An Analysis of Human Sexual Response.* New York: Little Brown & Co., 1966.
A skillful interpretation of the classic Masters-Johnson research on sex.

Buckler, Beatrice. *Living with a Mentally Retarded Child: A Primer for Parents.* New York: Hawthorn Books, Inc., 1971.
Very simple, practical information plus an unusually full and valuable listing of facilities and resources.

Despert, J. Louise, M.D. *Children of Divorce.* Rev. ed. New York: Doubleday & Co., Inc., 1953.
Dated but still may be more valuable than anything else you can find on helping children weather divorce in healthy fashion.

Kirk, Samuel A., et al. *You and Your Retarded Child: A Manual for Parents of Retarded Children.* Rev. ed. Palo Alto: Pacific Books, 1968.
Good on care of child at home and deciding whether residential treatment is needed.

May, Elizabeth Eckhardt, et al. *Homemaking for the Handicapped.* New York: Dodd, Mead & Co., 1966.
Authoritative, helpfully illustrated guide to assist the disabled adult in caring for children and a home.

Robinson, Frank Bennett. *Introduction to Stuttering.* Englewood Cliffs, N.J.: Prentice-Hall, Inc., 1964.

Rubin, Isadore, Ph.D. *Sexual Life After Sixty.* New York: Basic Books, Inc., 1965.

Sherwin, Robert Veit. *Compatible Divorce.* New York: Crown Publishers, Inc., 1969.
Combines psychological insight with legal expertise in suggesting how divorce can be handled to avoid the financial and psychological destruction of a family.

Smith, Bert Kruger. *Your Nonlearning Child: His World of Upside-Down.* Boston: Beacon Press, 1968.
In addition to cluing parents in to the way the world is for children with perceptual and other disabilities, this book offers suggestions for getting appropriate help.

Spock, Benjamin, M.D., and Lerrigo, Marion O. *Caring for Your Disabled Child.* New York: The Macmillan Co., 1965.

Thompson, Helen. *The Successful Step-parent.* New York: Harper & Row, 1966.

Wallis, J. H. *Sexual Harmony in Marriage.* New York: Roy Publishers, Inc., 1966.
Witty and wise discussion of what the author, a British marriage counselor, calls "the sexual conversation" between men and women from adolescence on.

Wright, Beatrice A. *Physical Disability: A Psychological Approach.* New York: Harper & Row, 1960.
A pioneering book, focusing on the ways in which emotional health can be nurtured to make for maximum realization of potential.

BOOK TWO

Your Child's First Three Years

1 Your Baby Will Grow Up

Auerbach, Aline B. *How to Give Your Child a Good Start.* New York: Child Study Association of America, 1961.
The Association is a good source of helpful pamphlets on many areas of child-rearing.

Brazelton, T. Berry, M.D. *Infants and Mothers.* New York: Delacorte, 1969.
A highly readable, nondidactic account of the first years of three babies.

Dodson, Fitzhugh, M.D. *How to Parent.* New York: Signet Books, 1971.

Erikson, Erik H. *Childhood and Society.* New York: W. W. Norton & Co., Inc., 1963.

Fraiberg, Selma. *The Magic Years: Understanding and Handling the Problems of Early Childhood.* New York: Charles Scribner's Sons, 1959.

Fromme, Allan, M.D. *The ABC of Child Care.* New York: Pocket Books, 1969.
Alphabetical arrangement of topics.

Gesell, Arnold, M.D., and Ilg, Frances, M.D. *Infant and Child in the Culture of Today.* New York: Harper & Row, 1943.
An older book, but a pioneering volume on infant and child development.

Gruenberg, Sidonie. *New Illustrated Encyclopedia of Child Care and Guidance.* 4 vol. New York: H. S. Stuttman, Inc., 1968.

Isaacs, Susan. *The Nursery Years.* New York: Schocken Books, Inc., 1968.
Reprint of an old-fashioned classic.

Spock, Benjamin, M.D. *Baby and Child Care.* New York: Pocket Books, 1969.
The standard work most useful for advice on physical care.

Stone, L. Joseph, and Church, Joseph. *Childhood and Adolescence.* New York: Random House, 1968.

Thompson, George G. *Child Psychology.* New York: Houghton Mifflin Co., 1962.

U.S. Children's Bureau. *Infant Care.* Washington, D.C.: Government Printing Office.

———. *Your Baby's First Year.* Washington, D.C.: Government Printing Office.

———. *Your Child from 1 to 6.* Washington, D.C.: Government Printing Office.

Wolf, Katherine M., M.D. *As Your Child Grows: The First 18 Months.* New York: Child Study Association of America, 1971.

2 Getting to Know Your Baby

Duncan Eleanor S., and Whipple, Dorothy V., M.D. *The New Parents' Magazine Baby Care Book.* New York: Parents' Magazine Enterprises, Inc., 1970.

Jones, Eve. *The Intelligent Parents' Guide to Raising Children.* New York: Collier Books, 1961.

Klein, Ted. *The Father's Book.* New York: Ace Books, 1969.

LaLeche League International. *The Womanly Art of Breastfeeding.* Rev. ed., 1968.

U.S. Children's Bureau. *Breastfeeding Your Baby.* Washington, D.C.: Government Printing Office.

Wyden, Barbara W. "The Fat Child Is Father of the Man." *New York Times Magazine,* Sept. 13, 1970, p. 89.

3 You and Your Baby Meet Life As It Is

Beadle, Muriel. *A Child's Mind.* New York: Doubleday & Co., Inc., 1970.

Blyth, Myrna. "Raising a Bright and Happy Child." *Woman's Day,* May, 1971, p. 46.

Gordon, Ira J. *Baby Learning Through Baby Play.* New York: St. Martin's Press, Inc., 1970.

Life. "The Child." December 17, 1971.
An introduction to some current learning and developmental theories.

Pines, Maya. "Why Some 3-Year-Olds Get A's and Some Get B's." *New York Times Magazine,* July 6, 1969, p. 4ff.
A summary of the Harvard University early-learning studies.

Smith, Lendon. *Children's Doctor.* Englewood Cliffs, N.J.: Prentice-Hall, Inc., 1969.

U.S. Children's Bureau. *Safe Toys for Your Child.* Washington, D.C.: Government Printing Office, 1971.

4 Building the Bonds of Love

Bettelheim, Bruno. *Children of the Dream.* New York: The Macmillan Co., 1969.
About the development of children reared in a kibbutz.

Cotton, Dorothy Whyte. *The Case for the Working Mother.* New York: Stein & Day, Inc., 1965.

Mayer, Greta, and Hoover, Mary. *Learning to Love and Let Go.* New York: Child Study Association of America, 1965.

Weingarten, Violet. *The Mother Who Works Outside the Home.* New York: Child Study Association of America, 1965.

5 Your Baby Is Special

Chess, Stella, et al. *Your Child Is a Person.* New York: Viking Press, Inc., 1965.

Scheinfeld, Amram. *Your Heredity and Environment.* New York: J. B. Lippincott Co., 1965.

Thomas, Alexander; Chess, Stella; and Birch, Herbert G. "The Origin of Personality." *Scientific American,* August, 1970, p. 102.

Wyden, Barbara. "The Difficult Baby Is Born That Way." *New York Times Magazine,* March 21, p. 67.

6 Coping with Common Concerns

American National Red Cross. *First Aid.*

Boston Children's Hospital Medical Center. *Accident Handbook.* Dell Publishing Co., Inc., 1966.

Gruenberg, Sidonie. *Parents' Guide to Everyday Problems of Boys and Girls.* New York: Random House, 1958.

Karelitz, Samuel. *When Your Child Is Ill.* New York: Random House, 1969.

McWilliams, Margaret. *Nutrition for the Growing Years.* New York: John Wiley & Sons, 1967.
National Foundation – March of Dimes. *Birth Defects: The Tragedy and the Hope.*
Spock, Benjamin, M.D., and Loewenberg, Miriam E. *Feeding Your Baby and Child.* New York: Hawthorn Books, Inc., 1955.
U.S. Children's Bureau. *Care of Your Children's Teeth.* Washington, D.C.: Government Printing Office.

7 How Your Child's Mind Develops

Alexander, Tom. "Psychologists Are Rediscovering the Mind." *Fortune,* September, 1970, p. 108.
Fremon, Suzanne S. "New Ways to Measure Intelligence in Infants." *Parents' Magazine,* April, 1971, p. 39.
Kramer, Rita and Salk, Lee, M.D. *How to Raise a Human Being.* New York: Random House, 1969.
LeShan, Eda J. *The Conspiracy Against Childhood.* New York: Athencum Publishers, 1967.
Newsweek. "Probing the Brain." June 21, 1971, p. 60ff.
Phillips, John L., Jr. *Origins of Intellect: Piaget's Theory.* San Francisco: W. H. Freeman, 1969. A good breakdown of Piaget's work.
Pines, Maya. *Revolution in Learning: The Years from Birth to Six.* New York: Harper & Row, 1967.
Sharp, Evelyn. *Thinking Is Child's Play.* New York: E. P. Dutton & Co., Inc., 1969.
U.S. Office of Education. *Teaching Young Children to Read.* Washington, D.C.: Government Printing Office, 1966.
U.S. Public Health Service. *Learning to Talk.* Washington, D.C.: Government Printing Office, 1970.

8 It's Your Home – and Your Child's, Too

Consumer Reports. Mt. Vernon, N.Y.
This magazine is a continuing source of information on unsafe toys and other household hazards.
U.S. Children's Bureau. *Accidents and Children.* Washington, D.C.: Government Printing Office, 1970.
———. *Home Play and Play Equipment.* Washington, D.C.: Government Printing Office.

9 When and How Does Discipline Begin?

Briggs, Dorothy Corkville. *Your Child's Self-Esteem.* New York: Doubleday & Co., Inc., 1970.
Ginott, Haim G., M.D. *Between Parent and Child.* New York: Avon Books, 1969.
Gordon, Thomas, M.D. *Parent Effectiveness Training.* New York: Peter H. Wyden, Inc., 1970.

10 Toilet Training and Other Progress

Homan, William E., M.D. *Child Sense.* New York: Bantam Books, Inc., 1970.
Although this book generally advocates taking a pretty tough line with children, the author has a very relaxed approach toward toilet training.

11 Your Baby Becomes a Child

Daniels, Ada, and Hoover, Mary. *When Children Ask About Sex.* New York: Child Study Association of America, 1969.

12 Handling the Hard Times

Bettelheim, Bruno. *Love Is Not Enough: The Treatment of Emotionally Disturbed Children.* New York: The Macmillan Co., 1965.
Blodgett, Harriet E. *Mentally Retarded Children: What Parents and Others Should Know.* Minneapolis: University of Minnesota Press, 1971.
Joint Committee on Mental Health of Children. *Mental Health from Infancy Through Adolescence.* New York: Harper & Row, 1971.
———. *Mental Health of Children: Services, Resources, and Manpower.* New York: Harper & Row, 1971.
Josselyn, Irene M., M.D. *The Happy Child.* New York: Random House, 1955
Kirk, Samuel A., et al. *You and Your Retarded Child.* Palo Alto: Pacific Books, 1968.
Mayer, Greta, and Hoover, Mary. *When Children Need Special Help with Emotional Problems.* New York: Child Study Association of America, 1961.
Spock, Benjamin, M.D., and Lerrigo, Marion O. *Caring for Your Disabled Child.* New York: Fawcett-Crest, 1965.
U.S. Public Health Service. *Mental and Emotional Illness in the Young Child.* Washington, D.C.: Government Printing Office, 1971.

13 Sharing Life

Fremon, Suzanne S. *Children and Their Parents: Toward Maturity.* New York: Harper & Row, 1968.
LeMasters, E. E. *Parents in Modern America: A Sociological Analysis.* Homewood, Ill.: Dorsey, 1970.
Neisser, Edith. *Brothers and Sisters.* New York: Harper Bros., 1951.
Turner, Ralph H. *Family Interaction.* New York: John Wiley & Sons, Inc., 1970.
Winnicott, Donald W. *Family and Individual Development.* New York: Barnes & Noble, 1969.

BOOK THREE

Guiding Your Preschooler

1 The Delightful Age

Almy, Milly. *Young Children's Thinking: Studies of Some Aspects of Piaget's Theory.* New York: Teachers College Press, 1966.

Baldwin, Alfred. *Theories of Child Development.* New York: John Wiley & Sons, Inc., 1967.

Erikson, Erik H. *Childhood and Society.* New York: W. W. Norton & Co., Inc., 1950.

French, Edward L., M.D., and Scott, J. Clifford, M.D. *How You Can Help Your Retarded Child: A Manual for Parents.* Philadelphia: J. B. Lippincott & Co., 1967.
The development, nature, and needs of the mentally retarded child are presented by experienced and compassionate medical men, one of them a psychiatrist, who have directed the famous Devereux School.

Gesell, Arnold, M.D., and Ilg, Frances, M.D. *Infant and Child in the Culture of Today.* New York: Harper, 1943.
"The culture of today" is far different from that of 1943, and some of the features of a child's day as described in this classic volume are so outmoded as to be almost quaint. Yet physical development and patterns of growth have not changed, and the description of these is still valid.

Hoffman, Martin L., and Wladis, Lois. *Child Development Research.* vol. I. New York: Russell Sage Foundation, 1964.

Inhelder, B., and Piaget, J. *The Growth of Logical Thinking from Childhood to Adolescence.* New York: Basic Books, Inc., 1957.

Kagan, J., and Moss, H. A. *Birth to Maturity.* New York: John Wiley & Sons, Inc., 1962.

Landreth, Catherine. *Early Childhood.* Alfred A. Knopf, Inc., 1967.

Linton, Ralph. "Status and Role." In *The Study of Man.* New York: Appleton & Co., 1936.

Murphy, Lois B. *The Widening World of Childhood.* New York: Basic Books, Inc., 1962.

Pearce, Jane, M.D., and Newton, Saul. *The Conditions of Human Growth.* New York: Citadel Press, Inc., 1969.

Spock, Benjamin, M.D., and Lerrigo, Marion O. *Caring for Your Disabled Child.* New York: The Macmillan Co., Inc., 1965.

Stone, L. Joseph, and Church, Joseph. *Childhood and Adolescence.* 2d ed. New York: Random House, 1968.

Stuart, Harold C., and Prugh, Daniel G., ed. *The Healthy Child.* Boston: Harvard University Press, 1960.

Toffler, Alvin. *Future Shock:* New York: Bantam Books, Inc., 1970.

Winnicott, D. W. *The Child, the Family and the Outside World.* New York: Penguin Books, Inc., 1970.

2 When There Are Siblings—and When There Are None

Gehman, Betsy Holland. *Twins: Twice the Trouble, Twice the Fun.* Philadelphia: J. B. Lippincott Co., 1965.

Gilmore, J. B. "Birth Order and Social Reinforcers of Effectiveness in Children." *Child Development* 35:193–200.

LeShan, Eda J. *The Only Child.* New York: Public Affairs Pamphlets, 1960.

Neisser, Edith G. *Brothers and Sisters.* New York: Harper, 1951.

———. *The Eldest Child.* New York: Harper, 1957.

Scheinfeld, Amram. *Twins and Supertwins.* Philadelphia: J. B. Lippincott Co., 1967.
The relationship of twins to each other and to the other children in the family is discussed in helpful, reassuring terms.

Simon, Anne W. *Stepchildren in the Family: A View of Children in Remarriage.* New York: Pocket Books, 1964.

3 Helping Your Child Get Along with Others

Bronfenbrenner, Urie. *Two Worlds of Childhood: U.S. and U.S.S.R.* New York: Russell Sage Foundation, 1970.

Freud, Anna. *Research at the Hampstead Child Therapy Clinic and Other Papers.* London: Hogarth, 1970.

Hoover, Mary, and Mayer, Greta. *Learning to Love and Let Go.* New York: Child Study Association, 1965.

La Crosse, Robert E. *Day Care for America's Children.* New York: Public Affairs Pamphlets, 1971.

Members of the Staff of The Boston Children's Medical Center, and Gregg, Elizabeth M. *What to Do When "There's Nothing to Do."* New York: Delacorte Press, 1967.

Piers, Maria W. *Growing Up with Children.* Chicago: Quadrangle, 1966.
The section on "Animals in the Life of the Child" describes the part live pets can play in the development of sociability and ability to relate oneself to others.

4 Contrariness, and All That

Hartley, Ruth E., and Goldenson, Robert M. *The Complete Book of Children's Play.* Rev. ed. New York: Thomas Y. Crowell, 1963.

Hoover, Mary, and Mayer, Greta. *When Children*

Need Special Help with Emotional Problems. New York: Child Study Association, 1961.
The sections on "Danger Signals" and "When Does a Signal Need Further Attention" are particularly helpful if one is in doubt about a child's development.

Roy, K. "Parents' Attitude Toward Their Children." *Journal of Home Economics,* 1950, 42:652–653.

Sears, R. R.; Maccoby, E. E.; and Levin, H. *Patterns of Child Rearing.* New York: Harper, 1957.

Siegelman, Marvin. "College Students' Personality Correlates of Early Parent-Child Relationships." *Journal of Consulting Psychology,* 1965, 29:558–564.

Spock, Benjamin, M.D. *Problems of Parents.* Boston: Houghton Mifflin Co., 1962.

5 Questions Need Honest Answers

Bruner, Jerome. *On Knowing: Essays for the Left Hand.* New York: Athenaeum, 1969.

Despert, J. Louise, M.D. *Children of Divorce.* New York: Doubleday & Co., Inc., 1953.
You will find help in answering children's questions about divorce in their own family or among the parents of their friends, as well as assistance in meeting this crisis.

Wolf, Anna M. W. *Helping Your Child to Understand Death.* New York: The Child Study Association of America, Inc., 1958.
This sensitive guide, written in question-and-answer form, goes to the heart of the problem of answering children's questions about death.

6 Masculinity . . . Femininity

Benedek, Therese, M.D., and Anthony, James E., M.D. *Parenthood: Its Psychology and Psychopathology.* New York: Little Brown & Co., 1970.

Bennett, G. K., and Cohen, L. R. "Men and Women: Personality Patterns and Contrasts." *Genetic Psychology Monographs,* 1959, 60:101–153.

Fraiberg, Selma. *The Magic Years.* New York: Charles Scribner's Sons, 1959.

Graubart, Stephen, ed. "The Woman in America." *Daedalus,* 1964, 93:2.

Howe, Florence. "Sexual Stereotypes Start Early." *Saturday Review,* October 16, 1971, 76 ff.

Lewis, Harvey Alvin. "The Effect of Shedding the First Deciduous Tooth upon the Passing of the Oedipus Complex." *American Psychoanalytic Journal,* 1958, 6:5–37.

Marmor, Judd, M.D. *Sexual Inversion: The Multiple Roots of Homosexuality.* New York: Basic Books, Inc., 1965.
This book, somewhat scientific in tone and not too easy to read, emphasizes that homosexuality cannot be attributed to any one factor in a child's life.

Rossi, Alice. "Women in Science—Why So Few?" *Science,* 1965, CXLVIII: 1197–1202.

Rothbart, Mary K., and Maccoby, Eleanor. "Parents' Differential Reactions to Sons and Daughters." *Journal of Personality and Social Psychology,* 1966, 4:237–243.

Vidal, Gore. "In Another Country." *New York Review of Books,* 1971, XVII, 1:8–12.

Wyden, Peter and Barbara. *Growing Up Straight: What Every Thoughtful Parent Should Know About Homosexuality.* New York: Stein & Day, Inc., 1968.
This book emphasizes how many different forces go into shaping heterosexuality and homosexuality.

7 Toward a Healthy Conscience

Fraiberg, Selma. *The Magic Years.* New York: Charles Scribner's Sons, 1959.
Although the book does not take up material that is not touched on in this or other chapters, the section on "The Dawn of Conscience" is so outstanding that every parent should be familiar with it. The pages dealing with "Acquisition of Moral Values" are particularly helpful.

8 Fears

Berger, Allan S., M.D. "Anxiety in Young Children." *Young Children,* 1970, XXVII, 1:5–17.

Hirsch, Selma. *The Fears Men Live By.* New York: Harper, 1955.
This book discusses some of the groundless fears that shape our thinking and where they come from.

Overstreet, Bonaro. *Understanding Fear in Ourselves and Others.* New York: Harper, 1951.
The first five chapters of Part I are valuable in understanding and helping a child cope with his fear.

Ross, Helen. *Fears of Children.* New York: Science Research Associates, 1951.

———. *The Shy Child.* New York: Public Affairs Pamphlets, 1953.

9 Encouraging Independence

Boston Children's Hospital Medical Center staff. *Accident Handbook: A New Approach to Children's Safety.* Pamphlet. New York: Dell Publishing Co., Inc., 1966.

Hess, Robert D., and Shipman, Virginia. *Cognitive Elements in Maternal Behavior.* Unpublished report of research. Chicago: University of Chicago, 1967.

Moore, James E. "Antecedents of Dependency

and Autonomy in Young Children." *Dissertation Abstracts,* 1965, 26:1966.

10 Minor Annoyances and Larger Worries

Arnstein, Helene, in cooperation with the Child Study Association of America, Inc. *What to Tell Your Child About Birth, Death, Illness, Divorce, and Other Family Crises.* New York: Pocket Books, 1964.
This extremely helpful book has sections on many of the "larger worries," such as the illness of a parent and the divorce or remarriage of parents.

Brazelton, T. Berry, M.D. Interview. *Chicago Today,* Oct. 19, 1971.

Geist, Harold. *A Child Goes to the Hospital.* Springfield: Chas. Thomas, 1965.
Helpful suggestions to parents for preparing a child for going to the hospital and accommodating himself to hospital routines.

Goldman, R., and Shanes, G. H. "Comparisons of the Goals That Parents of Stutterers and Parents of Non-stutterers Set for Their Children." *Journal of Speech and Hearing Disorders,* 1964, 29:381–389.

Kinster, Donald B. "Covert and Overt Maternal Rejection in Stuttering." *Journal of Speech and Hearing Disorders,* 1961, 26:145–155.

McCord, W.; McCord, J.; and Zola, I. K. *Origins of Crime.* New York: Columbia University Press, 1959.

Randall, Margaret. *The Home Encyclopedia of Moving Your Family.* New York: Berkley Publishing Corp., 1959.

Siegel, A. E. "Film-mediated Fantasy-aggression: Strength of Aggressive Drive." *Child Development,* 1956, 27:365–378.

11 Preparing Your Child for School

Association for Childhood Education. *Feelings and Learning.* New York: International, 1965.
A collection of essays by some of the foremost authorities on early childhood education, among them Lois Barclay Murphy, Dorothy E. M. Gardner, Anna Freud, Merle E. Bonney, and Laura Hopper.

Beyer, Evelyn. *Teaching Young Children.* New York: Pegasus, 1968.
If you have been confused about the methods as well as the strengths and weaknesses of various theories of nursery school education, this book offers clarification. It can be as useful to parents as to nursery school teachers.

Eckstein, Rudolph. "Parents and Teachers: Who Does What?" Address delivered at a seminar, Nov. 3, 1966, of the North Shore Mental Health Association, Winnetka, Ill.

Harvey, O. J.; Hunt, D. E.; and Shroder, H. M. *Conceptual Systems and Personality Organization.* New York: John Wiley & Sons, Inc., 1961.

Hymes, James L., Jr. *Teaching the Child Under Six.* Columbus, Ohio: Merrill, 1968.
Not all the material in this book applies directly to preparing a child for school, but this respected educator's ideas about teaching a child to read before he enters first grade are interesting and convincing.

Mote, Florence B. "The Relationship Between Child Self-concept in School and Parental Attitudes and Behavior in Child Rearing." *Dissertation Abstracts,* 1967, 27:3319.

Pickard, P. M. *The Activity of Children.* New York: Humanities Press, Inc., 1965.
Not entirely easy reading, but worth the effort, because the author makes it clear that children learn best through discovery.

BOOK FOUR

The Early School Years

1 The Special Years

Bruner, Jerome S. *The Process of Education.* New York: Random House, 1960.
A professional book about how and why children learn and at what ages they are "ready" to learn different skills. Chapter 3 is of special interest to parents of children in their early school years.

Menninger, William C., and Leaf, Munro. *You and Psychiatry.* New York: Charles Scribner's Sons, Inc., 1948.
The principles of Freudian psychology explained in readable terms to help us understand why we behave as we do.

Redl, Fritz. *Pre-adolescents—What Makes Them Tick?* pamphlet. New York: Child Study Association of America, 1959.
A description of pre-adolescent behavior during the ages of nine to thirteen; an explanation of "why" together with some "do's and don'ts."

2 Coping with School

Association for Childhood Education International. *Feelings and Learning.* Washington, D.C., 1965.
A sensitive book about how a child's emotions influence his capacity to learn. Articles simply written by experts in child development and illustrated with more than one hundred photographs by Ken Hyman.

Association for Supervision and Curriculum Development. *Life Skills in School and Society.*

1969 Yearbook. Washington, D.C.: National Education Association.
———. *To Nurture Humaneness.* 1970 Yearbook. Washington, D.C.: National Education Association.
———. Robert R. Leeper, ed. *Curricular Concerns in a Revolutionary Era: Readings from Educational Leadership.* Washington, D.C.: National Education Association, 1971.
These three books propose new directions for our schools and give suggestions for bringing curricula and teaching methods up to date. They can be obtained by writing to the Association at 1201 Sixteenth Street, N.W., Washington, D.C.
Coles, Robert. *Dead-End School.* New York: Dell Publishing Co., 1968.
The story of a black youngster from the ghetto whose mother engages in a community action program to help him. The importance of family love and pride shines through every word. For children 9 to 12.
Ets, Marie Hall. *Talking Without Words.* New York: Viking Press, 1968.
A picture book with short texts for children up to 8 years, describing how we show we feel through our everyday gestures and behavior.
Larrick, Nancy. *A Parent's Guide to Children's Education.* New York: Pocket Books, 1963.
All about learning at home and at school. Ways of encouraging a child's creative abilities and helping him *want* to learn are intelligently discussed.
Purkey, William Watson. *Self-concept and School Achievement.* Englewood Cliffs, N.J.: Prentice-Hall, Inc., 1970.
Although intended for teachers, this book is not too technical for parents with a taste for grappling with the concepts behind the teaching-learning process.

3 What Friends Mean

Hoff, Syd. *Who Will Be My Friends?* New York: Harper & Row, Inc., 1960.
A lonely boy in a new neighborhood makes friends when the other boys see how he plays ball when he is by himself. For children up to 8.
Zolotow, Charlotte. *The Hating Book.* New York: Harper & Row, Inc., 1969.
Two little girls straighten out a misunderstanding by talking with each other about how they feel, instead of nursing their grudges in silence. For children up to 8.

4 Coping with Prejudice

Ackerman, Nathan W., M.D. *Prejudice, Mental Health and Family Life.* pamphlet. New York: Institute of Human Relations.
Available for 50¢ from the Institute, 165 East 56th Street, New York, N.Y. 10022.
Burden, Shirley. *I Wonder Why . . .* New York: Doubleday, Inc., 1963.
Described on the book jacket as "a poem of photographs and words," this is a beautiful portrayal of a black child's reaction to prejudice. For children 9 to 12.
Carlson, Natalie Savage. *The Empty Schoolhouse.* New York: Dell Publishing Co., 1965.
Lullah's innocent integrity and her mother's determination to do what is right for her child help to sustain them both in the face of the anger of the white community when Lullah is determined to remain as a student in a newly desegregated school. For children 9 to 12.
Clark, Kenneth B. *Prejudice and Your Child.* Boston: Beacon Press, 1963.
How children's feelings about race, their own and others', are influenced by society and by the home. A plan of action for parents, churches, and schools.
Goldsby, Richard A. *Race and Races.* New York: The Macmillan Co., 1971.
An excellent book, simply written, about the differences between races. Many misconceptions are cleared up against a background of history and current events.
Heilbroner, Robert. *Don't Let Stereotypes Warp Your Judgment.* pamphlet. New York: Institute of Human Relations.
Available for 5¢ from the Institute, 165 East 56th Street, New York, N.Y. 10022.
Jackson, Jesse. *Call Me Charlie.* New York: Dell Publishing Co., 1945.
Charlie's white friends learn that his fight to win recognition from his teacher and admission to the local swimming pool is really their own. For children 9 to 12.
Spock, Benjamin. *Children and Discrimination.* pamphlet. New York: Institute of Human Relations.
Available for 10¢ from the Institute, 165 East 56th Street, New York, N.Y. 10022.
———. *Do Parents Teach Prejudice?* pamphlet. New York: Institute of Human Relations.
Available for 10¢ from the Institute, 165 East 56th Street, New York, N.Y. 10022.
Stevenson, Ian, M.D. *People Aren't Born Prejudiced.* New York: Institute of Human Relations.
Available for 10¢ from the Institute, 165 East 56th Street, New York, N.Y. 10022.

6 Everybody Else Does!

Andersen, Hans Christian. *The Emperor's New*

Clothes. Illustrated by Jack and Irene Delano. New York: Random House, 1970.
The old folk tale has new relevance as we become increasingly aware of the need to see things as they really are and to have the courage of our convictions.

Hoover, Mary B. "Values to Live By." Reprinted from *Parents' Magazine.* New York: Institute of Human Relations, 165 East 56th Street, New York, N.Y. 10022.
An article about the dilemmas parents face when standing up for a principle that involves danger or discomfort for their children.

Johnson, Crockett. *We Wonder What Walter Will Be?* New York: Holt, Rinehart & Winston, 1964.
All the animals in the jungle advise Walter to become just like them when he grows up, but Walter finds that he will have to decide for himself. For children 4 to 10.

Juster, Norman. *The Dot and the Line.* New York: Random House, 1963.
Imaginative cartoons about a "line" who tried to compete with a "squiggle" in making himself interesting, and how he learned the value of self-discipline.

Kennedy, John F. *Profiles in Courage.* New York: Harper & Row, 1961.
Examples from American history of courageous decisions made in the name of integrity and in the face of sacrifice and danger. Available in editions for both adults and children 9 to 12.

Raths, Louise E.; Harmin, Merrill; and Simon, Sidney B. *Values and Teaching.* Columbus, Ohio: Charles E. Merrill Publishing Co., 1965.
The authors clarify the fact that, whether we know it or not, our values determine our behavior. Although the book is intended for teachers, parents can learn a good deal about how children make choices and how to help them make healthy ones.

Stalvey, Lois Mark. *Education of a Wasp.* New York: Bantam Press, 1971.
A true account of a family's awakening to the prejudice around them and of the sacrifices they made in an effort to bring up their children with integrity.

Tillich, Paul. *The Courage to Be.* New Haven: Yale University Press, 1952.
A Christian philosopher discusses the courage of self-affirmation in the face of anxiety and despair as the only way "to become and remain a person."

7 Sex Education in the Early School Years

Cosgrove, Margaret. *Seeds, Embryos, and Sex.* New York: Dodd, Mead Co., 1970.
A book of science describing the biology of reproduction in one-celled organisms, plants, and animals. Excellent drawings. For children 9 to 12.

Gruenberg, Sidonie Matsner. *The Wonderful Story of How You Were Born.* New York: Doubleday, Inc., 1952.
A beautiful and sensitive book, with charming drawings to illustrate well-presented facts. For children 4 to 8.

Lerrigo, Marion O., Ph.D.; Southard, Helen, M.A.; and Senn, Milton J. E., M.D. *A Story About You.* New York: E. P. Dutton Co., 1956.
Beginning with the process of birth and continuing through a description of adolescence. Excellent drawings. Approved by the National Education Association and the American Medical Association. For children 9 to 12.

Levine, Milton I., and Seligmann, Jean H. *A Baby Is Born.* New York: Western Publishing Co., 1966.
An excellent book, easy for a child to read by himself as soon as he can read at all. Down-to-earth, with simple drawings. For children 4 to 8.

8 Communicating About Drugs and Similar Dangers

Coles, Robert. *The Grass Pipe.* Atlantic Monthly Press. Boston: Little Brown Co., 1969.
A story about a boy who confronts the temptations of smoking marijuana, and how he makes his decision. Helpful to parents in its realistic portrayal of peer pressure. For children 10 and up.

Greenberg, Harvey R., M.D. *What You Must Know About Drugs.* New York: Scholastic Book Services, 1971.
All about drugs, with a chapter on inhalants that is especially pertinent for this age group. Includes a "drug dictionary" and a list of treatment centers throughout the United States.

Hyde, Margaret O., ed. *Mind Drugs.* New York: Pocket Books, 1971.
The "who" and "why" of drug use and dependency discussed by experts in brief and readable text. Includes descriptions of all drugs currently "on the scene," including alcohol, which is now recognized as the most widely abused drug.

Stamford Curriculum, The. A Study Guide to Help Schools and Teachers Combat the Drug Epidemic. Grades 4–12.
For possible use as a model in your child's school. Available from WTIC-TV, 3 Broadcast Plaza, Hartford, Connecticut 06115.

9 Teaching About Money

Weiss, Richard. *The American Myth of Success.* New York: Basic Books, 1969
Historical survey of how the American concept of success was influenced by the early demands of geography, religious beliefs, and industrial development.

10 A Sensible Approach to TV and Movies

Morris, Norman S. *Television's Child.* Boston: Little Brown Co., 1971.
An examination of television as one of the most important influences on family values. Includes extensive discussion about the industry and the effect of commercial requirements on programming.

12 Health: Your Concern and Your Child's

Accas, Gene, and Eckstein, John H. *How to Protect Your Child.* New York: Simon & Schuster, 1968.
Intelligent descriptions of everyday dangers facing children and suggestions for protecting your child. Topics include child molesters, pornographic material, accidents, baby-sitters, cars, family outings, toys, games and pastimes.

Bibby, Dr. Cyril, and Morrison, Ian T. *Your Body and How It Works.* New York: American Heritage Press, 1969.
A simple and direct description of how cells, bones, tissues, glands, and internal organs grow and change from birth to maturity and are all directed by the brain. Excellent illustrations. For Children 8 to 12.

Collier, James Lincoln. *Danny Goes to the Hospital.* Photographs by Yale Joel. New York: W. W. Norton Co., 1971.
Excellent for preparing a child realistically for a hospital experience. For children 4 to 9.

Colt, Bryson, R., and Bass, Ralph. *The Mother's Guide to Child Safety.* New York: Tempo Books, 1971.
Concise paperback with all the essentials. Very sensible.

Fassler, Joan. *The Boy with a Problem.* New York: Behavioral Publications, 1971.
Lots of grown-ups had answers to Johnny's problem, but none of them was the right one until he met a friend who just listened to him talk about it. Helping a child to talk about how he really feels. For children 5 to 8.

———. *Don't Worry, Dear.* New York: Behavioral Publications, Inc., 1971.
A picture book with short text about a little girl who outgrows her babyish habits of stuttering and thumbsucking as she grows bigger and begins to *feel* more grown-up. For children 4 to 6.

Hudson, Ian, M.D., and Thomas, Gordon. *What to Do Until the Doctor Comes.* Princeton, N.J.: Auerbach Publishers, 1970.
A complete and trustworthy medical guide to all emergencies, as well as the care of chronic and less urgent ailments.

Spock, Benjamin, M.D., and Lerrigo, Marion O., Ph.D. *Caring for Your Disabled Child.* New York: Collier Books, 1965.
An authoritative presentation of the needs of handicapped children and their families. Detailed suggestions for coping with physical, mental, and emotional problems can prepare parents and children for a healthier adjustment.

BOOK FIVE

Growing Into Adolescence

1 Suddenly: Adolescence

Beauvoir, Simone de. *Memoirs of a Dutiful Daughter.* New York: World Publishing Co., 1959.

Blos, Peter. *On Adolescence: A Psychoanaltyic Interpretation.* New York: The Macmillan Company, Free Press Paperback, 1962.

Carroll, Lewis. *Alice's Adventures in Wonderland.* New York: Penguin Books (first published in 1865).

Committee on Adolescence of the Group for the Advancement of Psychiatry. *Normal Adolescence: Its Dynamics and Impact.* New York: Charles Scribner's Sons, 1968.

Erikson, Erik H. *Childhood and Society.* 2d ed. New York: W. W. Norton & Company, Inc., 1963.

———. *Identity: Youth and Crisis.* New York: W. W. Norton & Company, Inc., 1968.

Kiell, Norman. *The Universal Experience of Adolescence.* New York: International Universities Press, Inc., 1964.

Lidz, Theodore. *The Person: His Development Throughout the Life Cycle.* New York: Basic Books, Inc., 1968.

Stone, L. Joseph, and Church, Joseph. *Childhood and Adolescence: A Psychology of the Growing Person.* 2d ed. New York: Random House, 1968.

2 Communicating About Puberty

Arnstein, Helene S. *Your Growing Child and Sex.* In consultation with the Child Study Association of America. New York: Bobbs-Merrill Co., Inc., 1967.

Breasted, Mary. *Oh! Sex Education.* New York: Praeger Publishers, 1970.

Child Study Association of America. *When Children Ask About Sex.* Revised by Ada Daniels and Mary Hoover. New York, 1969.

Davis, Maxine. *Sex and the Adolescent: A Guide for Young People and Their Parents.* New York: The Dial Press, 1958.

Freud, Martin. *Sigmund Freud: Man and Father.* New York: Vanguard Press, 1958.

Johnson, Eric W. *How to Live Through Junior High School.* New York: J. B. Lippincott Co., 1959.

———. *Love and Sex in Plain Language.* Rev. ed. New York: J. B. Lippincott Co., 1967.

———. *Telling It Straight.* New York: J. B. Lippincott Co., 1970.

LeShan, Eda J. *Sex and Your Teenager: A Guide for Parents.* New York: David McKay Co., Inc., 1969.

Pomeroy, Wardell B., Ph.D. *Boys and Sex: A Long-needed Modern Sexual Guide for Boys.* New York: Delacorte Press, 1968.

———. *Girls and Sex: A Long-needed Modern Sexual Guide for Girls.* New York: Delacorte Press, 1969.

Rabinowitz, Oscar, with Brenton, Myron. "How to Talk to Your Parents About Sex." *Seventeen,* March, 1971.

3 Boy-Girl Relationships

Drury, Michael. *How to Get Along with People.* New York: Doubleday & Co., Inc., 1965.

Duvall, Evelyn Millis, Ph.D. *Today's Teenagers.* New York: Association Press, 1966.

Hechinger, Grace and Fred M. *Teenage Tyranny.* New York: William Morrow & Co., Inc., 1963.

Holt, John. *What Do I Do Monday?* New York: E. P. Dutton & Co., Inc., 1970.

Paradis, Grace D. and Adrian A. *Your Life: Make It Count.* New York: Funk & Wagnalls, Inc., 1968.

Purtell, Thelma C. *The Intelligent Parents' Guide to Teenagers.* New York: Paul S. Eriksson, Inc., 1961.

Spock, Dr. Benjamin. *A Teenager's Guide to Life and Love.* New York: Simon & Schuster, Inc., 1970.

4 The Struggle Over Limits

Fremon, Suzanne Strait. *Children and Their Parents Toward Maturity.* New York: Harper & Row, 1968.

Redl, Dr. Fritz. *Pre-Adolescents: What Makes Them Tick.* New York: The Child Study Association of America, Inc., 1959.

5 Values

Black, Algernon D. *The First Book of Ethics.* New York: Franklin Watts, Inc.

Bronfenbrenner, Urie. *Two Worlds of Childhood: U.S. and U.S.S.R.* New York: Russell Sage Foundation, 1970.

Hunt, Morton. "The Gentle Art of Understanding Your Parents." *Seventeen,* May 1970.

Keniston, Kenneth. "Youth and Violence: The Contexts of Moral Crisis." In *Moral Education.* Cambridge, Mass.: Harvard University Press, 1970.

Kohlberg, Lawrence. "Education for Justice: A Modern Statement of the Platonic View." In *Moral Education.* Cambridge, Mass.: Harvard University Press, 1970.

Lukas, J. Anthony. *Don't Shoot—We Are Your Children!* New York: Random House, 1971.

Marin, Peter, and Cohen, Allan Y. *Understanding Drug Use: An Adult's Guide to Drugs and the Young.* New York: Harper & Row, 1971.

Reich, Charles A. "The Limits of Duty." *The New Yorker,* June 19, 1971.

Roiphe, Ann Richardson. "The Family Is Out of Fashion." *The New York Times Magazine.* August 15, 1971.

6 Changing Attitudes Toward School

Gesell, Arnold, M.D.; Ilg, Frances L., M.D.; and Ames, Louise B., Ph.D. *Youth: The Years from Ten to Sixteen.* New York: Harper & Row, 1956.

Holt, John. *What Do I Do Monday?* New York: E. P. Dutton & Co., Inc., 1970.

Kagan, Jerome. "A Conception of Early Adolescence." *Daedalus* 100 no. 4, Fall 1971.

Lurie, Ellen. *How to Change the Schools: A Parents' Action Handbook on How to Fight the System.* New York: Random House, 1970.

Martin, Edward C. "Reflections on the Early Adolescent in School." *Daedalus* 100 no. 4, Fall 1971.

Silberman, Charles E. *Crisis in the Classroom: The Remaking of American Education.* New York: Random House, 1970.

7 Everyday Health Guide

Burton, Benjamin T., Ph.D. *Heinz Handbook of Nutrition: A Comprehensive Treatise on Nutrition in Health and Disease.* New York: McGraw-Hill Book Co., 1959.

Englebardt, Stanley L. "If Your Child Has Acne." *Parents' Magazine.* October 1970.

Fisher, Patty, and Bender, Arnold. *The Value of Food.* London: Oxford University Press, 1970.

Gersh, Marvin J., M.D., and Litt, Iris M., M.D. *The Handbook of Adolescence: A Medical Guide for Parents and Teen-agers.* New York: Stein and Day, Inc., 1971.

Katz, Marcella. *Vitamins, Food and Your Health.* Public Affairs Pamphlet no. 465, 1971.

King, Charles Glen, and Lam, Gwen. *Personality "Plus" Through Diet: Foodlore for Teen-agers.* Public Affairs Pamphlet no. 299, 1960.

Levine, Milton I., M.D., and Seligmann, Jean H. *Your Overweight Child.* New York: World Publishing Co., 1970.

Mason, Gussie, with Wilson, Jean Sprain. *Help Your Child Lose Weight.* New York: Hawthorn Books, Inc., 1969.

McKay, Stella. *Your Child's Health from Birth to Adolescence.* New York: Doubleday and Co., Inc., 1965.

President's Council on Physical Fitness. *Vigor: A Complete Exercise Plan for Boys 12 to 18.* Washington, D.C.: U.S. Government Printing Office.

———. *Vim: A Complete Exercise Plan for Girls 12 to 18.* Washington, D.C.: U.S. Government Printing Office.

Rossman, Isadore, M.D. *Nutrition for Your Family's Health.* New York: The Emily Post Institute, Inc., 1963.

Seely, Janet E.; Zuskin, Eugenija; and Bouhuys, Arend. "Cigarette Smoking: Objective Evidence for Lung Damage in Teenagers." John B. Pierce Foundation and Department of Medicine, Yale University School of Medicine. *Science.* May 14, 1971.

Shultz, Gladys Denny. *The Successful Teen-Age Girl.* New York: J. B. Lippincott Co., 1968.

Van Atta, Winifred. "A Program for Overweight Teenagers." *Parents' Magazine.* November, 1968.

Watt, Bernice K., and Merrill, Annabel L. *Composition of Foods: Raw. processed. prepared.* Washington, D.C.: United States Department of Agriculture. Revised, 1963.

Wilkes, Edward T., M.D. *The Family Guide to Teenage Health.* New York: Ronald Press Co., 1958.

8 Adolescent Misery

Baruch, Dorothy. *How to Live with Your Teenager.* New York: McGraw-Hill Book Co., 1953.

Bashkirtseff, Marie. *The Journal of a Young Artist.* New York: E. P. Dutton & Co., 1926.

Benedict, Ruth. *Patterns of Culture.* New York: The New American Library, Inc., 1934.

Bienvenue, Millard J., Sr. "Why They Can't Talk to Us." *The New York Times Magazine.* September 14, 1969.

Frank, Anne. *The Diary of a Young Girl.* New York: Doubleday & Co., Inc., 1952.

Ginott, Dr. Haim G. *Between Parent and Child: New Solutions to Old Problems.* New York: The Macmillan Company, 1969.

———. *Between Parent and Teenager.* New York: The Macmillan Company, 1965.

Mill, John Stuart. *Autobiography.* Library of Liberal Arts, 1957.

Rice, John A. *I Came Out of the Eighteenth Century.* New York: Harper & Bros., 1942.

Senn, Milton J. E., M.D., and Solnit, Albert J., M.D. *Problems in Child Behavior and Development.* Philadelphia: Lea and Febiger, 1968.

9 Money: Earning It and Having It

Frank, Lawrence K. and Mary. *Your Adolescent at Home and in School.* New York: The Viking Press, 1956.

10 Drugs and Other Escape Mechanisms

Child Study Association of America. *You, Your Child and Drugs.* New York: The Child Study Press, 1971.

Coles, Robert, M.D.; Brenner, Joseph H., M.D.; and Meagher, Dermet. *Drugs and Youth—Medical. Psychiatric and Legal Facts.* New York: Liveright Publishing Corp., 1970.

Gallagher, Dorothy. "Johnny Cash: 'I'm Growing, I'm Changing, I'm Becoming.'" *Redbook.* August 1971.

Gersh, Marvin J., M.D., and Litt, Iris J., M.D. *The Handbook of Adolescence: A Medical Guide for Parents and Teenagers.* New York: Stein and Day, Inc., 1971.

Goode, Erich. *The Marijuana Smokers.* New York: Basic Books, Inc., 1970.

Greenberg, Harvey R., M.D. *What You Must Know About Drugs.* New York: Scholastic Book Services, 1970.

Grinspoon, Lester, M.D. *Marihuana Reconsidered.* Cambridge, Mass.: Harvard University Press, 1971.

Land, Herman V. *What You Can Do About Drugs and Your Child.* New York: Pocket Books, 1971.

Marin, Peter, and Cohen, Allan Y. *Understanding Drug Use: An Adult's Guide to Drugs and the Young.* New York: Harper & Row, 1971.

National Clearing House for Drug Abuse Information. *A Federal Source Book: Answers to the Most Frequently Asked Questions About Drug Abuse.*

National Institute of Mental Health. *Alcohol and Alcoholism.*

11 Planning for When the Children Leave Home

Benjamin, Lois. *So You Want to Be a Working Mother!* New York: McGraw-Hill Book Co., 1966.

Catalyst. *Westchester Project Vocational Kit: Designed for Family Women Who Wish to Begin or Resume Work.* New York: Catalyst, 1971.

Friedan, Betty. *The Feminine Mystique.* New York: W. W. Norton & Company, Inc., 1963.

Gould, Jane Schwartz. "Our Changing Careers." *Barnard Alumnae Magazine.* Winter, 1971.

Lindbergh, Anne Morrow. *Gift from the Sea.* New York: Pantheon Books, 1955.

Peterson, James A. *Married Love in the Middle Years.* New York: Association Press, 1968.

Schwartz, Felice N.; Shifter, Margaret H.; and Gillotti, Susan. *How to Go to Work When Your Husband Is Against It, Your Children Aren't Old Enough and There's Nothing You Can Do Anyhow.* New York: Simon & Schuster, Inc., 1972.

Schwartz, Jane. *Part-Time Employment: Employer Attitudes on Opportunities for the College-Trained Woman. Report of a Pilot Project.* New York: Alumnae Advisory Center, Inc., 1964.

Scobey, Joan, and McGrath, Lee Parr. *Creative Careers for Women: A Handbook of Sources and Ideas for Part-Time Jobs.* New York: Essandess Special Editions, 1968.

Women's Bureau. *Continuing Education Programs and Services for Women.* Rev. ed. Washington, D.C.: U.S. Department of Labor, 1971.

———. *Handbook on Women Workers.* Washington, D.C.: U.S. Department of Labor, 1969.

———. *Jobfinding Techniques for Mature Women.* Washington, D.C.: U.S. Department of Labor, 1970.

———. *Job Training Suggestions for Women and Girls.* Washington, D.C.: U.S. Department of Labor, 1970.

Index

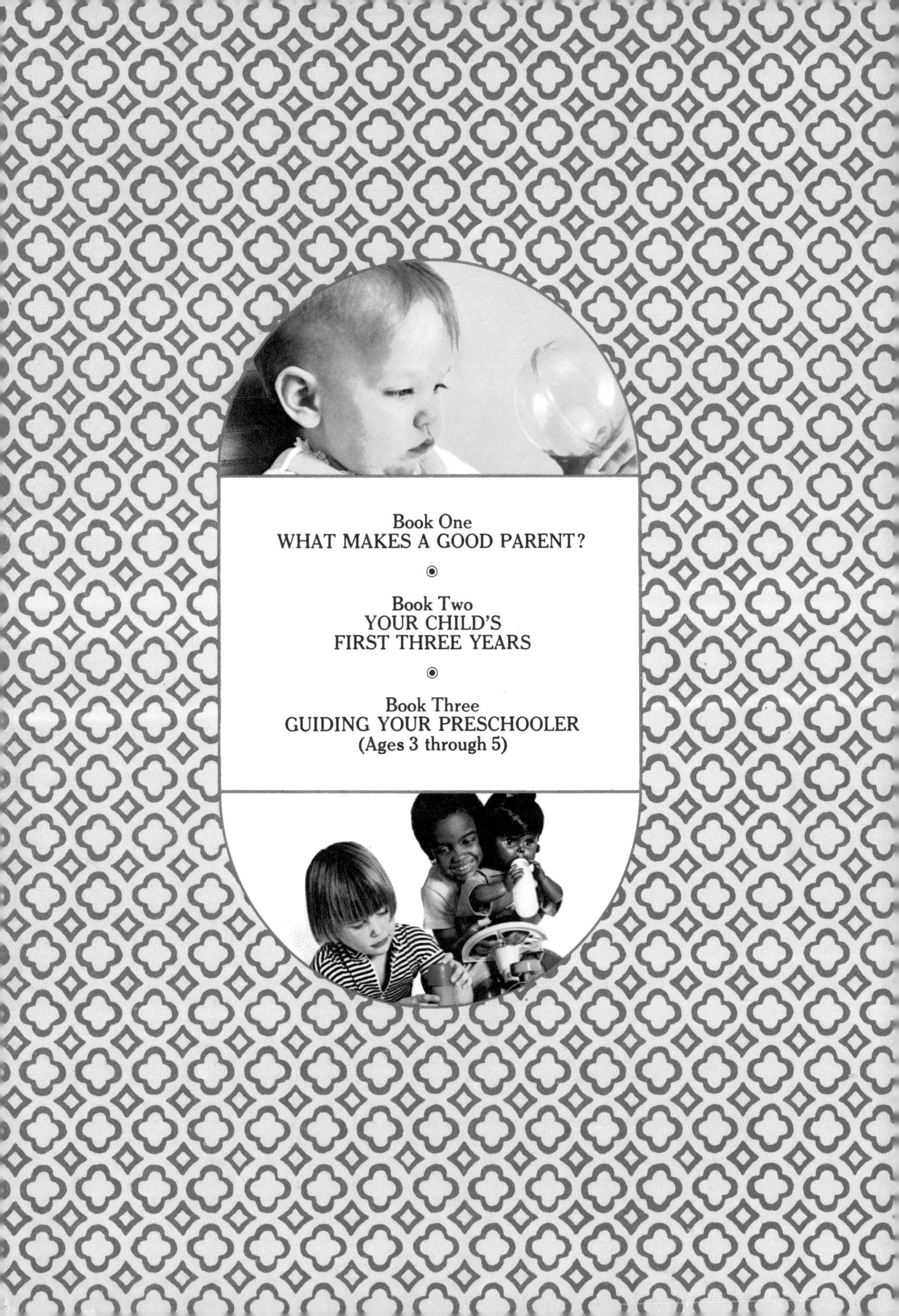
Book One
WHAT MAKES A GOOD PARENT?
Book Two
YOUR CHILD'S
FIRST THREE YEARS
Book Three
GUIDING YOUR PRESCHOOLER
(Ages 3 through 5)